T0329455

CITY OF THE SUN

CITY OF THE SUN

DEVELOPMENT AND POPULAR RESISTANCE IN THE PRE-MODERN WEST

MICHAEL MARTIN

Algora Publishing
New York

Library of Congress Cataloging-in-Publication Data —

Names: Martin, Michael (Michel), author.
Title: City of the sun: development and popular resistance in the pre-modern
    West / Michael Martin.
Description: New York: Algora Publishing, 2017. | Includes bibliographical
    references.
Identifiers: LCCN 2017005098 (print) | LCCN 2017007903 (ebook) | ISBN
    9781628942798 (soft cover: alkaline paper) | ISBN 9781628942804 (hard
    cover: alkaline paper) | ISBN 9781628942811 (pdf)
Subjects: LCSH: Social classes—Europe—History—To 1500. | Social
    classes—Mediterranean Region—History—To 1500. | Social
    control—Europe—History—To 1500. | Social control—Mediterranean
    Region—History—To 1500. | Government, Resistance to—Europe—History—To
    1500. | Government, Resistance to—Mediterranean Region—History—To 1500.
    | Social change—Europe—History—To 1500. | Social change—Mediterranean
    Region—History—To 1500. | Europe—Social conditions—To 1492. |
    Mediterranean Region—Social conditions.
Classification: LCC HN373 .M37 2017 (print) | LCC HN373 (ebook) | DDC
    306.094—dc23
LC record available at https://lccn.loc.gov/2017005098

Printed in the United States

Acknowledgements

This book has been improved immeasurably by the comments and suggested revisions brought to my attention by my brother, the management consultant Richard Martin, and by two longtime friends, Carmine Fabiili and Sylvain Topping. The former served as a sounding board while I was researching and writing the book. The latter helped me with computer issues in the presentation of this book. American labor educator Charles Micallef was good enough to provide me with a copy of his 2005 doctoral dissertation at the University of Michigan, entitled "Ancient Labor's Untold Story: Evidence of Workers' Organizations from 3000 BCE to 550 CE," as well as discussions related thereto. I also thank Lise Lafond and her co-workers at the municipal library in Gatineau, Quebec. During several years of research, they were able to supply me with relevant publications from all parts of Canada. None of the above, however, are responsible for any errors contained herein.

TABLE OF CONTENTS

PREFACE

This book is an attempt at writing macro-history, whereby we look for secular trends in the long run of history. Starting with a premise that workers have resisted domination by other classes since the onset of industrial capitalism in the 19th century, we address the questions of if, when, where, why, and how did working people resist social domination in the eras before the modern era. Historians usually agree modernity began in 1492, the year that marked the first regular contacts between Europe and the Americas as initiated by the voyages and activities of Christopher Columbus.

During the last two centuries of modernity, in response to industrial capitalism, workers have developed tools of defense and promotion of their class interests that were, in large part, the expression of working class culture. These workers' organizations have included unions, political parties, co-operatives, credit unions, mutual aid societies, clubs, charities, religious, community and popular organizations. Even the organizing and pursuit of certain educational, sporting, artistic, and religious activities have been marshalled to help workers resist the social domination of other classes. In addition, the major political movements of the modern era—anarchism, communism, socialism, feminism, social democracy, and radical democracy—also have given voice to the perspectives and resistance by working people. So, the questions we ask in this book relate to if, when, where, and how popular classes resisted domination in pre-modern times before the advent of industrial capitalism and modern tools of workers' defense and promotion of their interests.

These questions are important today since contemporary workers are besieged by attacks on their tools of defense and promotion of their interests they have developed during the last two centuries of modernity. These aspects of workers' culture have been under assault for more than two generations by globalization, free trade arrangements, multinational corporations, neo-liberal ideologies and governments, rollbacks of public services and social democracy, and a general attempt to discredit socialism, trade unionism, and social democracy and workers' political movements as *dépassés*, no longer relevant to our times. If we can indeed uncover evidence that laboring people did resist domination before modern tools of resistance, this might offer some faith and hope for working people. Workers might be further encouraged to continue to resist social domination by ruling classes, even if some workers and working class activists might be dispirited by recent political offensives against their interests, culture, and means of resistance.

In terms of form, my previous books contained the usual accoutrements of academic literature, footnotes or end-notes, and extensive, complete bibliographies covering the entire subject matter of my inquiries, including primary sources. Owing to the broad sweep of this book, my scholarly aims are more limited in terms of references and bibliography. As well, while this book may be useful for academic purposes, the intent has been to produce a work that is accessible to the intelligent lay person and, therefore, is not too imposing, or at least so we hope. Still, I have made clear the sources for citations and for novel and important ideas from others that I have pursued and developed further within the text, using references in parentheses to the publications listed in the reading list at the end of the book. It is hoped that this will make the text less formidable and more accessible. Moreover, for the most part, I conducted no primary research in writing this book, rather only a review and analysis of secondary sources. The exceptions are references to a few primary sources from ancient times, mostly Roman writers. Readers who want to pursue specific subjects mentioned in the book in depth can consult the reading list that accompanies this book to undertake a beginning. By no means, however, do I claim completeness for this reading list.

A word about the title of this book. From time to time, ancients imagined a city-state where social justice and equality would reign supreme among the social classes and between women and men. This utopian vision referred to a 'city of the sun', *heliopolis* in ancient Greek, as just such a place. A famed evocation of this utopia was even co-opted by Saint Paul in an epistle to the Galatian Christians: "There is neither Jew nor Gentile, nor is there slave nor free, nor is there male and female, for you are all one in Christ Jesus." (3: 26-28)

Michael Martin
May 2017

CHAPTER 1. SOCIAL COMPLEXITY

Introduction

Contemporary working class militants face a dilemma in this post-industrial, post-modern world. During this fourth wave of industrialization, ruling classes and the governments that represent them have taken to attacking the legitimacy and credibility of the principal means of defense that workers employ in response to capitalism: unions, political parties, social democracy, and other tools of workers' self-protection. Moreover, other classes even try to define workers and the working class out of existence. How can we continue to call ourselves working class when propaganda by others tells us we're middle class alongside the traditional petite bourgeoisie of small business people and independent professionals, or when we're categorized by 'lifestyle' choices based upon trivial choices in individual consumption, or when other means of categorizing people mute the self-awareness of workers as a class? What is the working class when working class awareness sometimes seems to be a shadow of what it used to be; or when current expressions of working class culture are reduced to triviality or marketing sloganeering by corporations, or are presented as evidence that most workers are right-wing, as opposed to the well-intentioned, progressive people from other classes?

On the other hand, if we take our pulse, we find that workers are still laboring away, selling their labor to corporate, public, petits-bourgeois, or bourgeois employers in order to survive. We find business and governmental leaders persistently acting against workers' interests, chipping away at hard-earned pensions, public services, social programs, wages, employment, educational opportunities, and social benefits. Our working class parents and grandparents strove mightily to achieve these improved social conditions in order to make better lives for their children and grandchildren. Moreover, we look around the world to see workers active in working for improved socio-economic conditions: for peace, human rights, women's rights, and too many progressive causes to be listed. Militants of these causes sometimes might not even seem to recognize themselves as being working class. Nonetheless, we take our pulse as workers to find that it is still beating after all.

What this book offers, it is hoped, will be a measure of faith and hope to contemporary workers and working class activists in light of contemporary attacks on workers. In order to do so, this book addresses the questions of whether laboring people resisted domination by other classes in the pre-modern eras before capitalism and modern tools of workers' defense and workers' culture and, if so, how, where, and when did they do so, and what were the consequences of this resistance. Readers then might take succor knowing that their own strivings are part of a *longue démarche*, a long struggle of laboring people, marked by failures, it is true, but also by successes. Readers will learn herein that pre-modern, laboring people long before the advent of modern tools of workers' defense persistently resisted domination by other classes, even if and when they were not fully aware of the class nature of this resistance. The idea that there were eras when laboring people quietly accepted their fate to be dominated is simply not true, as we shall see. Moreover, social domination has been usually initiated and maintained by force by use of armies, police, law, ideologies, religion, and other tools of ruling classes. This book inventories and describes the diverse forms of resistance used by pre-modern popular classes over the centuries so that we might attempt to develop a model of the phenomenon.

Obviously, the subject of this book could be a vast undertaking since each form of resistance and the periods covered are subjects of intensive study by specialists. Nevertheless, this book will demonstrate that it is possible to provide a generalist overview in response to the questions of our inquiry without getting lost in the minutiae of the various, specialized fields of inquiry, tempting and interesting though they might be.

Periodization

This book uses a development approach, that is, the study of social transformations during various periods of human history. During these periods, the nature of work changed, as did the methods by which non-producers extracted economic surplus from the labor of working people. Likewise for the methods of resistance employed by the popular classes to the extraction of economic surplus and the tools used to initiate, facilitate, and continue these processes. The actual periods we employ, as per the chapter titles in the table of contents, are well-known, and are used often in history, the social sciences, and archaeology. There might be other valid schemes of periodization in circulation, but this one is as practical as any other. History deals with the written record, which first appeared in Mesopotamia about

5,500 years ago. Thus, we must refer to other disciplines—archaeology, philology, theology, mythology, and anthropology—when we consider prehistory.

Definitions

Some basic definitions are in order. Domination of laboring classes refers to the oppression or exploitation of laboring people based upon the extraction by non-producers of the economic surplus produced by slaves, peasants, artisans, or other workers, as well as the methods of initiating, facilitating, and maintaining this domination. Economic surplus is the wealth created by laboring people greater than the production needed for them to survive and to reproduce. Non-producers who extract the economic surplus produced by others and otherwise dominate form part of the ruling class. Sometimes, those who serve the rulers and their processes of extracting surplus can be included among the ruling class. Such people include scribes, priests, and bureaucrats. On the other hand, these people can also display an ambiguous relationship to ruling powers, sometimes supportive, at other times getting closer by choice to laboring people and their interests, including even leading the popular classes in resistance. The terms 'laboring people', 'laboring classes', or the 'ruled' cover the various classes of working people: peasants, laborers, independent or salaried craftsmen, slaves, servants, serfs, what we label in general as the popular classes.

The pre-modern West refers to the eras before the first contacts between Europeans and Americans, which began in 1492 with the voyages of Christopher Columbus. The West, or the Occident, refers to the lands with coasts on the Mediterranean Sea including southern Europe, North Africa, the Middle East, and the Mediterranean islands, and the rest of Europe as far east as the Urals in Russia, including the Pontic-Caspian Steppe. Since this book is limited to the pre-modern West, the Americas *prima facie* are excluded from our definition of the West.

Resistance includes all forms of resistance by laboring people, individual or collective, overt or covert, explicit or implicit, ranging from seemingly minor things such as an individual slowing down the rhythm of his work to outright rebellion, revolt or revolution, and all gradations thereof. Even so, this book concentrates on overt, explicit forms of resistance such as outright rebellion, revolt or revolution, and the gradations thereof.

Cultural Universals

This book touches on prehistory: both the late Paleolithic era, or the Stone Age, and the Neolithic era, when horticulture and animal husbandry were first developed by humankind. This requires that we make use of findings from archaeology, and from anthropology with respect to peoples who during modern times have continued to live somewhat as prehistoric peoples. Recourse to these disciplines allows us to trace how social classes might have first emerged. By studying prehistoric people, we learn that class and domination are not human universals but rather phenomena that emerged at specific points in history.

Nevertheless, there are a few characteristics of humankind that are universals. Modern humankind in scientific discourse is known by the Latin term, *Homo sapiens sapiens*, or wise man. Still other terms characterize humans based upon universals that apply to all humans. For example, *homo loquens* refers to the capacity for language; without language imparted to children by their elders, children do not develop fully as human beings. *Homo socius* or *politicus*, as described by Aristotle, is the capacity for social organization and social life. In fact, without society, a child cannot survive or become fully human; therefore, man is of necessity a social animal. Another important universal describing human beings is the term, *homo faber*, or man the worker or maker and user of tools. Man needs to work in order to meet his basic requirements of food, clothing, and shelter. The second basic need if humankind is to survive is the need to reproduce. This fundamental need includes the rearing, education, and care of the young, including the transmission of language, knowledge, and work skills from one generation to the next. In fact, social organization is essential for ensuring that these two fundamental needs are satisfied. The wonder is that the two fundamental needs of production and reproduction are met by employing the resources in such extremes of physical environments—from the Arctic to the Sahara, and everything in between—in such a dazzling variety of social, economic, and cultural arrangements.

Development

By no means do societies meet these universal needs the same way or in an unchanging manner. To test the truth of this assertion, all one has to do is compare the 21st century with our knowledge of the 19th century. We are struck with the differences, let alone imagining the differences between modern times and those of ancient Romans or prehistoric peoples. These secular or long-term processes of change within human societies through the course of time comprise development. To explicate this, consider a Cartesian graph with time on the horizontal or X axis, in effect, an independent variable, whose arrow of direction is inevitable and constant. On the vertical or Y axis is the dependent variable, development, the direction of which is contingent, uneven, ever-changing. Not only is there not a requirement that the development arrow proceed evenly and predictably, but neither are there inevitable stages through which development must proceed. Instead, human social evolution is completely contingent and particular to what actually has occurred or, at least, according to what has occurred according to the theories and evidence of historians, social scientists, archaeologists, and others.

Even within a given society, development can be uneven. Moreover, any given society interacts and combines with other societies in particular ways. At the same time, other societies also experience different patterns of development and interacting and combining with other societies. Thus, patterns of class domination and forms of resistance thereto can vary among societies or even within parts of the same society. These uneven patterns were observed and described by the future Russian revolutionary, Leon Trotsky, at the beginning of the 20th century. Thus, different societies, indeed parts of societies, develop independently of each other, and in combination with other societies or parts thereof in ways that are quantitatively unequal and qualitatively distinctive. On the other hand, societies are still joined by economics, warfare, culture, migration, exogamy, communications, and still other means of social interaction. This is called uneven and combined development. Its initial application was for understanding the evolution of history and politics. This concept is also commonly used today in the disciplines of archaeology and anthropology. It is this concept of development that we employ.

Power

Domination implies the exercise of power in order to organize and control social life, at least partly to benefit those who do the organizing and controlling. Where there is power, there is also resistance to that power. This is comparable to physics where an action produces an equal and opposite reaction. Owing to this resistance, power requires, in order to be both installed and maintained, ideologies that ease the exercise of power, that grease the wheels of domination, as it were. These ideologies "tend to represent as universal what is partial...as permanent what is in flux...as natural what is cultural...as coherent what is in conflict." (Miller and Tilley). These ideologies are part of the culture of dominant classes that help facilitate and smooth their exercise of power. This is countered by the culture of the dominated classes, the laboring classes, that informs their resistance to domination. Thus, we can summarize the relationship between the human universals, between domination and resistance, and the conflict among the social classes in the following manner, going from left to right and down the page.

Universal needs for production and reproduction—labor—laboring people—production of economic surplus—extraction of surplus by dominant classes, or non-producers—power to determine social life and exercise social control in support of the extraction of surplus—dominant classes' ideologies and culture—culture of the dominated—resistance by the dominated—class conflict.

Tools, Language, Society

In an originally unpublished essay, Karl Marx's long-time collaborator Friedrich Engels speculated about the transition of our ancestors from ape to man. For Engels, what distinguished man from ape was labor. Deriving from bipedalism whereby humankind's ancestors stood upright on two legs on the African savannah rather than four legs, the better to see and escape predators, evolution pushed humans in the direction of using their hands to make things; thus, the emergence of humankind as *homo faber*. The species where this capacity first appeared was *homo habilis*, or handy man, which appeared about 2,500,000 years ago. The telltale signs of this ancestor are the remains of simple tools whereby humans increased their physical capacities by using objects, either found or constructed, as extensions of the human body. Writing at the end of the 19th century, Engels proved to be prescient since evidence collected since then seemed to support this notion, such that even non-Marxists have embraced Engel's idea as central to the definition of humanity.

In more recent times, however, evidence has been gathered that demonstrates that many animals also use tools. This implies that tool use is no longer taken as the ultimate sign of humanity, distinguishing us from other animals. Marine mammals such as dolphins and sea otters; primates such as chimpanzees and gorillas; and birds such as crows, ravens, gulls, and parrots have all been found to use tools and, perhaps, to impart knowledge of these tools to their young. There is even a species called the veined octopus, found in Australian waters, that has been observed using coconut shells to lodge itself underwater. This now requires a qualification to be added to the old designation; it is now man the user of complex tools.

Moreover, while Engels and others may be right about the importance of the idea of man the tool maker as a spur long ago to human evolution, in our day, we are more likely to consider the importance of language as a human definer, indeed the spur to recent human evolution. While not a view without its detractors, many academics now consider that language evolved over a long period of time rather than appearing suddenly with the arrival of modern humans. As part of this view, the existence of proto-language is now postulated. Proto-language would have slowly evolved into our present language capacities. Proto-language is comparable to a pidgin, which emerges when people with mutually unintelligible languages are drawn together in close quarters with a need to communicate. Pidgin draws on the originating languages by selecting words or signs or symbols which are then formed into strings of the same. Pidgin eventually evolves, often among the children of the original pidgin-speakers, into a complex language with syntax and grammar, part of a process called creolization. For instance, slaves brought to the Americas from Africa evolved a pidgin to communicate among themselves even while they were being transported to the New World. Once in the Americas, these pidgins developed into creole languages. Thus, not only is man *homo faber*, he is also at the same time and just as importantly *homo loquens*, the speaker of language. In fact, without language, it is difficult to imagine modern humans.

Moreover, and just as fundamentally, language cannot be acquired in the absence of society. So, just as central to defining humankind is the designation of humankind as *homo socius* or *homo politicus*, or man as a social being. It might be pointed out correctly that many animals are also social in nature. Ultimately, what distinguishes humankind is that all three capacities are essential for the emergence of humankind: man the maker, man the speaker of languages, and man the social creature. Human sociability permits learning by the young of tool making and use in labor as well as language and social mores and behavior. I call this in short form the LLL phenomenon. Humans are creatures of labor, language, and love, combined in a trinity of co-equals, to borrow a metaphor, in which all three are necessary and essential, and whereby the three evolved simultaneously.

The Egalitarian Impulse

One finds that generally in human society there is evidence of hierarchy and patriarchy, exploitation and oppression. Some political philosophies argue that this a biological imperative of human nature. In actual fact, the evidence about earliest humankind points to the exact opposite, that there is nothing natural or imperative about this state of affairs. Anthropologist Christopher Boehm studied 48 societies, from small, nomadic hunter-gatherer bands to sedentary chiefdoms. The evidence demonstrates a universal egalitarian impulse among all of these societies, such that with the advent of anatomically modern humans who continued to live in small groups, and had not domesticated plants and animals, it is very likely that all human societies practiced egalitarianism and that, most of the time, they did so successfully. In fact, Boehm writes that "...deliberate control of leaders may remain for the most part highly routinized" and not even immediately obvious to the outside observer. In fact, the members of the band employ several tools to enforce egalitarianism such as public opinion within the community, ridicule, criticism, disobedience, extreme sanctions towards offenders of egalitarian mores such as murder by expulsion of offenders, or temporary escape or permanent departure of victims of offences by members of the group.

Simple Hunter-gatherers

In simple hunter-gatherer societies our long-ago ancestors survived by foraging, fishing, and hunting. They lived in small bands of fifty or so related people. Anthropologists know quite a bit about them by studying similar peoples that continue to exist today. These bands are intensely egalitarian with no formal leaders such as chiefs or big men, that is, men who display importance and influence. Furthermore, they display mechanisms for ensuring that individuals don't breach this equality. As well, there is no division of labor other than for a few tasks based on age or sex. For instance, women obviously work harder in childbirth and in feeding the very young than do men, while the aged perform such specialized tasks as teaching the young, story-telling, communicating memory, and food preparation. It was long thought that most of the gathering of food was the province of women, while men engaged in the hunt. This has proven to be doubtful as further research demonstrates that all, including children and both women and men, would have been involved in all food-seeking ventures including foraging, fishing, and hunting. A supposed sexual division of labor with respect to the labor involved in producing food is now mostly held to be a retrojection of current patterns. Descent lineages were ambivalent, with some societies being patrilineal, while other societies were matrilineal. For example, Iroquoian peoples in North America identify children as belonging to their mother's clan, complete with titles, privileges, and responsibilities that accrue to membership in that clan.

The Development of Agriculture

Scholars refer to the period when agriculture, both horticulture and animal husbandry, emerged in the Middle East as the Neolithic era. It appears to have started first among certain peoples about 12,500-9,500 years ago, and then later among other peoples. During this period, some populations appear to have become semi-sedentary. While continuing to wander in search of food, these people also started to harvest wild cereals, returning regularly to the same places. From this initial step, the next step was for people to plant seeds of these wild cereals in the expectation that they would return to harvest the product of their labor. In actual fact, however, even with normal human elimination and production of food waste, cereals would have reproduced in these places of human habitation without intentional planting.

What appears to be the first, major urban agglomeration, Jericho, emerged on the west bank of the Jordan River. Jericho appears to have included a population of 2,000–3,000 people. Elsewhere, people were now associated in small tribes of somewhere between 150 and 3,000 people, with component clans organized around descent lineages, and the still smaller bands of about 50 in which people actually lived. These societies were still egalitarian. By about 8000 BC, they started practicing animal husbandry, breeding and herding animals they previously had hunted or culled. Thus, another step was taken on the path to sedentarization. Another early, Neolithic town was the settlement at Catalhoyuk in eastern Anatolia, the Asian portion of modern Turkey, one of several such settlements in the region. Catalhoyuk appears to have been occupied from 7500 to 5700 years BC by populations of about 5,000–8,000 people who grew wheat and barley that they stored in bins, while also collecting almonds, pistachios, and berries. They also domesticated cattle, goats, and sheep. There do not appear to be, however, signs of class distinction, sexual differentiation, nor of slavery in Catalhoyuk. All housing units were the same. Diet seems to have been the same for women as for men. No religious nor royal hierarchies appeared, nor are their signs of control of labor, nor of inter-group conflict and warfare.

Well before these cultures, however, about 20,000–25,000 years ago, there had existed a populous settlement at Sunghir, near the Russian city of Vladimir, about 180 kilometers east of Moscow. Judging by the complexity of burial rites and accoutrements, it appears that some people including children appear to have been considered royal, displaying the associated wealth of royalty. This was an example of a forager society in which some   became wealthy, owing to the proximity of crossroads of mammoth migration that provided a ready supply of ample food and building and clothing materials. (Hitchcock) There is no evidence, however, of the existence of slaves in this society. Elsewhere in Europe, forager societies appear to have been the norm until about 5000 BC. During the fifth millennium BC, forager societies appear to have become somewhat more complex. From burial sites, it appears that these societies displayed social differentiation including inheritance of wealth and power. Their economies even included importations from other societies. (Noyer) These societies, labelled by scholars 'Old Europe', were located in the lower Danube Valley and the Balkans. In spite of their complexity, some urbanization, and farming, it has been suggested that they were still, nonetheless, peaceful, matrilineal, and egalitarian societies. (Coppens). They also may have been the ancestors of such peoples as the Minoans of Crete, the Etruscans of Italy, the Basques of southwest France and northern Spain, and the Iberians of Spain and Portugal.

Complex Hunter-gatherer Societies

It had been long held that the advent of agriculture led to hierarchical distinctions, social class, and subjection of women to men. According to this account, mankind initiated horticulture and animal husbandry in the Fertile Crescent, the arc of land that runs from northern Egypt northeast through the Levant to southeastern Anatolia, then southeast to Mesopotamia and southwest Iran. By the time of the Bronze Age about 3500 BC, Mesopotamian civilization emerged. It was based upon agricultural surplus, and was rife with class and distinctions between men and women. According to this narrative, mankind had made a Faustian bargain. With agriculture, there would normally be food for all. Only normally, however, since periodic famine owing to changing weather conditions and crop and animal disease was a regular occurrence. This bargain was also struck at the price of inequality since humans had survived previously in relative affluence working just a bit with no social hierarchies nor substantial differentiation in the conditions of men and women.

As with many narratives, however, the reality was more complex. As we've seen above, the earliest urban settlements in Anatolia and the Levant whose economies included agriculture did not show signs of class nor of important differentiation based on sex. These seem to have appeared only in Mesopotamia and Egypt about 3500–3000 years BC. In fact, the emergence of both social class and men's control of women and children only appeared as part of a constellation of inter-related developments. These included the development of hydraulic techniques such as irrigation and drainage, and of technologies such as the wheel, cart, sail, and metallurgy in copper and bronze; the development of inter-urban trade of economic surplus, natural resources, and luxury products; increasing frequency and profitability of military conquest; and the emergence of bureaucracies of scribes, managers, and priests who developed arithmetic and writing to control and record the contributions of economic surplus from working people to the ruling classes. (de Laet, p. 647)

Contemporary research, however, has established that there was another route to class and sex divisions other than civilization based on agricultural surplus and related phenomena. Class also developed among complex hunter-gatherer societies often led by hereditary chiefs or 'big men' who enjoyed important social status. Sometimes, semi-nomadic peoples would return at regular intervals to certain locations, for example, at salmon runs or animal herding points, where there was a wealth of food to be had with relative ease. This wealth of food seemed to spur the emergence of class and hierarchy. In other words, the key element that activated social class as a noticeable phenomenon among complex hunter-gatherer societies was the presence of ample food leading to surpluses that went beyond the needs of producers, permitting greater sedentarization. The production, storage, distribution, and use of food then became the object of control by a ruling class. This brought the beginnings of the social power of some people over other people.

What exactly were complex hunter-gatherer societies? Anthropologist Robert Kelly elucidates the question with his taxonomy for distinguishing simple from complex hunter-gatherer societies. Here are distinctions between the two types of social organization, the left side listing the characteristics of simple societies, while the right side describes those of complex societies:

- variable vs predictable environment;
- diet of land game vs marine or plant food;
- small settlements vs large settlements;
- nomadic or semi-nomadic vs sedentary existence;
- little investment in food storage vs dependence on food storage;
- egalitarian society vs hierarchies based on class, descent, and sex;
- warfare being rare vs warfare being commonplace;
- generalized reciprocity vs individual accumulation and displays of wealth.

The most startling difference between the two types of societies, however, was the absence of slavery among simple societies, while it was commonplace among complex hunter-gatherer societies. This last difference represents the most compelling evidence with respect to complex hunter-gatherer societies and the emergence of class domination.

In North America, examples of these complex societies were found among the native peoples of British Columbia, where slavery emerged between 500 BC and AD 500, the Chumash of California, and the extinct Calusa people of southern Florida. There were other societies among North American native peoples who practiced slavery. For example, Great Plains Indians in the U.S. enslaved war captives. Iroquoians used to enslave men among captured enemies, while adopting captured women and children to replenish their populations thinned by warfare or illnesses. Crees in western Canada used to organize frequent war parties in order to enslave peaceful Athapaskan Indians in northern Alberta. 'Slave' was the term the Cree gave to these people in their language, thus, Great Slave Lake and Slave River. Around 1150 BC in modern-day Illinois near the confluence of the Illinois, Missouri, and Mississippi rivers, the Cahoki people built burial mounds to house dead rulers nearer to the sun they worshipped. They also killed slaves in ritual sacrifice to be buried with their rulers, and even buried some slaves alive while they were struggling to escape. Finally, Indians of the American Southeast owned African American slaves in the early days of the U.S. republic.

These examples from North America compare with others from the Old World. It appears that Celtic peoples of about 1000 BC practiced slavery in societies that were clearly hierarchical with several social classes: nobility, free property owners, propertyless freemen, tenant farmers, who were treated almost like medieval serfs, and slaves. During the 7th and 8th centuries BC, the Celts of France, known as Gauls, engaged in a slave trade with the Etruscans. During the Roman era, the Germanic peoples kept slaves, usually captured warriors. Germanic slaves had their own housing, however, and were treated with some autonomy, in fact, more or less similar to tenant farmers who owed regular tribute to their masters. (Hackney Blackwell)

These complex forager societies emerged because of an abundance of regularly-occurring natural resources, especially available foods. The increased work necessary to harvest and store these abundant foods induced nomads to settle, at least seasonally, if not permanently. There are two rival ideas as to why chiefdoms with their warrior, priest, and chief classes emerged in these societies. One is the functional idea whereby leaders emerged to resolve issues of competition and distribution of food and related social problems as population grew and concentrated in fewer locations. The second idea is based on conflict, that these societies became hierarchical owing to the exploitation of labor they displayed, for example, in the organization of the production and storage of food, or other collective endeavors such as digging canals or building other hydraulic works to control rivers. A variant of the conflict principle is that it was warfare between peoples that led to slavery and subjugation of whole peoples and defeated warriors to conquerors. In fact, there is no reason why both the functional and each of the conflict explanations cannot all be relevant, depending upon the mix of evidence available under varying conditions in different societies.

Summary

In the 19th century, mankind was defined by the essential capacity to labor. In contemporary times, however, we are more likely to consider language to be the essential, defining element of humankind. In fact, both the capacity to labor and to use tools as well as the language capacity are dependent on the social nature of human beings, who transmit to their young language and the use of tools and methods of work as well as social mores and behaviors.

While direct ancestors to modern humans probably emerged about 200,000 years ago, there are considerable differences of opinion about when our ancestors first emerged from Africa. Simple hunter-gatherer societies and the first, semi-sedentary culture in the Middle East were egalitarian societies. It is with complex hunter-gatherer societies that class and social differentiation emerged, important evidence of which was the existence of slavery. With respect to this study we posit a few important points. Firstly, inequality is not endemic to humankind owing to biology; in fact, it is relatively recent if we consider the whole march of human development. Secondly, social class, patriarchy, and social complexity emerged at specific moments in time among complex hunter-gatherers, with a key indicator of social complexity being the existence of slavery. Thirdly, a catalyzing factor for social complexity appears to be a comparatively ready supply of food easily and regularly obtained in the same locations.

We should disabuse ourselves of the idea that class and inequality between men and women reflect obligatory biological imperatives. They result from human culture. Knowing this helps us imagine the undoing of social inequalities and unnecessary, oppressive sexism. This tentative sally into prehistory via some basic anthropology has permitted us to gain some understanding of the prehistoric origins of social domination. This book deals with how the dominated resisted domination in the pre-1492 West. To do so, we now turn to the surer footing of the history of the ancients of the West.

CHAPTER 2. CIVILIZATION AND THE STATE

The Advent of Civilization

What is most striking about the emergence of civilization and the state, according to Stephen Sanderson, is how they seem to have appeared in the same manner following similar patterns throughout the world, regardless of the time period during which they actually emerged, whether in China or India or the Americas, or more relevant to our study, in the Middle East, North Africa, and Europe. Civilization and states first appeared in the Fertile Crescent about 5,500 years ago in two places: firstly, among the city-states in the southernmost valleys of the Tigris and Euphrates rivers in Mesopotamia, modern-day Iraq, and secondly, about 400 years later, along the Nile River in Egypt.

After several thousand years of gradual evolution, nomadic forager peoples eventually had become semi-sedentary then sedentary. The first step was the use of wild cereals repeatedly at the same times of year and in the same places. People began to plant and preserve these wild cereals, in the process domesticating them and initiating horticulture. About a thousand years later, animal husbandry developed whereby people began to domesticate and herd some of the animals they had previously hunted or culled. Reliance upon agriculture increased the ease of food procurement, but subjected people's fate to the elements. Sedentary mankind was introduced to the reality of recurring famine as crops would fail periodically. The idea appeared of preserving some agricultural surplus for use in the future in difficult times. This meant building bins and other granaries for food storage. Some of the people who managed these storage dépôts grew in importance, becoming priests or even god-kings who supervised agricultural ventures and distributed agricultural production. Granaries eventually evolved to become temples since the gods were held to be responsible for agricultural fertility, while granary/temple managers became religious, socio-economic, and political leaders. Thus, social class had appeared.

The emergence of social class was also encouraged by the proximity of human settlements to water. Rivers flooded annually, in the process fertilizing what otherwise would have been dry land as in the surrounding deserts of the Middle East. Irrigation was first practiced by making breeches in the riverbanks so that water could spread into cultivated areas. The apparent advantages and need for irrigation works, canals, and levies emerged, a need that also helped increase the power of granary managers/priests/kings. Another important technical development was the plow, a large hoe made of wood with a stone tip powered by oxen and, eventually, by horses. Whereas the hoe could be manipulated by either women or men, the plow demanded more strength. As such, this work became the preserve of men, thus helping create sexual differentiation in work. In the process of specialization of work this meant that other tasks fell to women.

A Taxonomy of Social Transformation

In the transformation from simple hunter-gatherers to complex forager societies to agriculture-based societies and to pastoral nomadism whereby people followed their herds and flocks, there were five stages of social and political organization. According to Stephen Sanderson and Elman Service, these stages included bands, tribes, chiefdoms, states, and empires. Bands were the smallest social formations of up to about 50 or so related nomads. Tribes comprised several bands and clans of families that joined in one or more settlements. There might have been ancestral links among the clans such as a common great-grandparent or other ancestor. This person or entity could have been real or imagined, in the latter case sometimes even an animal, a spirit, or even a god or goddess. Tribes survived by horticulture and animal husbandry or by pastoral nomadism. These societies were egalitarian and democratic, although respected people such as elders, shamans, or skilled hunters might have exercised influence. Chiefdoms featured hereditary leaders and an aristocracy, and might have comprised several tribes. Even if they exercised some form of government or councils, chiefdoms possessed few means of enforcing social discipline. Examples of such societies could be found among the Great Plains Indians where chiefs might have been influential and respected, but had no real power to compel obedience. In these societies, groups of young braves often undertook warfare without the support of elders and chiefs and, sometimes, despite the explicit opposition of the latter.

Chiefdoms first appeared about 5,000 years ago. They might have numbered populations of an approximate range of 10,000–100,000. States exercised normally a monopoly of force, or at least attempted to do so even if not always successful. They first appeared in Mesopotamia around 3500 BC and in Egypt about 3100 BC. States normally numbered at least

100,000 people. The first empires appeared in Mesopotamia about 2300 BC. Populations of empires could number from the hundreds of thousands to the millions. In the empire, the people of several or many states owed tribute to an emperor who had subjected peoples militarily, politically, and economically.

Characteristics of States and Empires

States and empires are ruled by classes that extract economic surplus from the producing and trading classes. Anthropologists identify other common characteristics that ancient states and empires display:
- attempted or actual monopoly of the use of force;
- agricultural or pastoral economies;
- economic specialization of trades and occupations;
- systems of laws to mediate disputes and enforce central powers;
- trade with other peoples;
- bureaucracies to administer the state or empire;
- armies to wage war, including against inhabitants of the state or empire themselves if deemed necessary by authorities;
- religion and other ideologies that served to explain and justify existing social organization.

Mesopotamia

Thirteen city-states and their rural hinterlands in the southern part of the Tigris and Euphrates Valley system produced Sumerian civilization. These city-states were usually politically independent. Occasionally, they squabbled over resources and wealth; however, they united at other times to resist the aggressions of the Semitic people to the west or the Elamite peoples to the east in southwest Iran. The first of these Sumerian cities was Uruk, with a population of greater than 10,000 people. Other notable city-states were Lagash, Eshnunnu, and Ur, the supposed birthplace of the Hebrew patriarch, Abraham. Techniques displayed in these city-states included the building of structures such as ziggurats, or stepped towers, granaries, and temples, and technologies such as brick making, the potter's wheel, wheeled carts, metalworking in copper and bronze, sailing, and writing and arithmetic. The Persian Gulf extended considerably more inland than it does today, such that some of the Sumerian city-states were actually maritime states. These states traded significantly in order to obtain raw products such as wood and metals. Thus, these states also included important, even wealthy merchant classes.

Sumerian civilization was marked by the existence of social classes. Under a god-king was an aristocratic class of leading warriors. Next came merchants, and then came skilled artisans; both of the latter two classes were probably organized by guilds in order to transmit skills and techniques from old to young. Members of these guilds worshipped the gods whose mythology best-suited or resembled these workers. Finally, there were the peasants, laborers, servants, and slaves. R.J. Forbes writes:

> As specialization increased, most of the craftsmen of antiquity began to be organized into guilds. The greater part of these guilds were closely associated with the temples, or were in some way organized by the state. The overseers of the guilds were often of priestly rank. They were scribes who had mastered the mysteries of language and writing...They might have been educated in the temple schools which were then...the centers of education. (p. 40)

American anthropologists Kent Flannery and Joyce Marcus offer more information about the organization of Sumerian guilds. (P.478-479) Many free commoners belonged to corporate social units called *im-ru a'*, or clans. Families might have been grouped into larger units called *dumu-dumu*, extended families or lineages which, in turn, were grouped into the clans. One text mentions 539 dumu-dumu grouped into seven im-ru-a, some of which were named for deities, animals, or professions. It appears that, over time, these traditional, clan-like segments gave way to politically organized units based on residence or occupation; a similar transformation took place among ancient Greeks and Romans.

Some workers organized in guilds including masons, potters, weavers and other textile workers, leather workers, smiths, quarrymen, millers, brewers, sailors, fishermen, scribes, glass makers, and sculptors. Palace and temple workers included cooks, stewards, concubines, and messengers. In 1900 BC, evidence seems to indicate, according to the doctoral thesis of American labor educator Charles Micallef, that weavers bargained as a group for better wages. The civilization ruled by Hammurabi in Babylon circa 1800 BC featured a legal code that set basic wages for workers in one of the early legal codes. According to Mark Wischnitzer, sometime during the second Babylonian empire, circa 626–539 BC, stone-cutters struck for payment of wages that were two months late, providing further evidence of workers' organization in guilds.

At the bottom of Sumerian societies, in addition to war captives, prisoners, and children, there were at least three other classes of workers: free peasants, *shub-lugals*, and slaves. The second class were formerly free peasants who were obliged to work on the land held by temples, palaces, and the ruling classes, or who worked digging canals, or who served as soldiers. In return for this work, they received rations and small plots of land to work when they were not laboring for others. As for slaves, Chris Harman writes that a tablet with the sign for slave girl has been dated to about 3000 BC; a little later appears evidence of the sign for male slave. One tablet lists 205 slave girls and women by name who were employed in a weaving establishment. Still other women slaves worked at milling, brewing, and cooking.

An edict in Lagash in about 2400 years BC revealed that priests extorted by overcharging for burials. Priests treated the slaves, ostensibly the property of the gods or the community, as essentially their own. They also stole from the poor with impunity. In the same state, a dozen temples were responsible for the cultivation of almost all the arable land. Half of the crop went to workers and their animals, a quarter went to the ruler, and the remainder went to the priests. It was to address such inequities and injustices that a popular movement led to the advent of a reforming king named Urukagina. Under his leadership, a number of measures were adopted:

- tax exemptions for widows and orphans;
- city-paid funerals;
- preventing the rich from demanding that the poor sell to the rich even when the poor did not want to do so;
- limits on the powers of priests and large property-owners;
- controls on usury and seizure of property and persons;
- controls on corruption of officials who demanded private payments for services rendered on behalf of the state;
- cancellation of debts owed by debtor families based on grain taxes and the like.

Urukagina's reform edict now is considered to be among the first legal codes in recorded history, preceding even that of Hammurabi, long thought to be the first.

Sumerian states warred amongst themselves over water and land rights. Eventually, some states began subjecting others. About 2300 BC, an aggressive empire emerged in the area north of Sumer where the distance between the two Mesopotamian rivers is at its narrowest, a land known as Akkad, whose people may have been originally Semitic nomads from the west. Led by Sargon, these people subjected the Sumerian cities, even those who adopted Sumerian writing and language, among other techniques. This was still not the first empire, however, as King Lugal-zage-si of the Sumerian city-state of Umma appears to have organized an empire of Sumerian city-states and their hinterlands even before Sargon of Akkad. Lugal-zage-si is reputed to have conducted successful raids west right to the Mediterranean shore, which might have seemed to Sumerians to have been the western edge of the known world.

Egypt

In prehistoric times, Egypt was lush with vegetation, animals to hunt, and arable land. Climactic conditions changed, however, such that deserts grew in the region. In response, proto-Egyptians began settling around the Nile River, which flooded annually, leaving fertile land, much as the Tigris and Euphrates rivers did in Mesopotamia. The Nile settlements began to coalesce into a distinct civilization about 3100 BC, approximately 400 years after states and civilization had first appeared in Mesopotamia. Around 2700 BC, the first pyramid was constructed for a king named Djoser.

Similar to Mesopotamia, Egyptian society was organized by class. Unlike Mesopotamia, however, Egypt originally was not a slave society, at least not until Egypt became an empire about 1550 BC when Egyptians began to enslave war captives and other foreigners. As per Mesopotamia, nonetheless, ancient Egypt was a theocracy. Its rulers were drawn from the class of aristocrats called *nomarchs*, who were rulers of the small, previously independent kingdoms that had united in the Egyptian state to be then constituted as provinces called *nomes*. Early Egypt was a geographically isolated, inward-looking society that considered other peoples to be scarcely human. Egyptian isolation was reinforced by the fact that it did not trade with other societies until about 2500 BC. Thus, there was no merchant class in early Egypt, as there had been in Mesopotamia. Egypt was a hierarchical, centralized society with a god-king, the pharaoh at the top. Priests and scribes and other officials of pharaohs organized mortuary cults and temples to honor the rulers and to ensure their happiness in the next world. With time, some royal officials serving as regional governors of nomes became as important as the original nomarchs. They became so powerful that they eventually were able to contest the central authority in order to become pharaohs themselves. Next in the social hierarchy after the royals, nomarchs, and royal governors of nomes came their priests and scribes, then wealthy farmers, craftsmen, soldiers, and peasants. The pyramids and other monuments are obvious signs of the hierarchical, class nature of ancient Egypt. These structures were built by peasants as religious and civic obligations as part of corvées during periods when farming duties were light, such as when the Nile was flooding. This is contrary to a long-existing, popular view that they were built by slaves, an impression vividly enforced by the likes of Cecil B. de Mille and other Hollywood producers.

The French Egyptologist Alexandre Moret, writing in the 1920s, provided valuable information about Egyptian society. In addition to temples and pyramids built by peasants as part of corvées, obligations upon peasants also extended to farm work on lands held by pharaohs and nobility, and to working on the canals and other hydraulic works related to the Nile. All this building work plus demand for luxuries for the consumption of the ruling class and, eventually, foreign trade after imperial conquests meant that there came to be considerable demand for the work of skilled craftsmen. Over 170 confraternities of craftsmen were inventoried by Moret. These were hierarchical, religious organizations with their own gods and temples wherein were defined the rights and responsibilities of member craftsmen.

The work day in ancient Egypt was normally eight hours long with two shifts of four hours separated by lunch breaks, while the work month was divided into three parts of eight work days with two days off between each work period, in addition to religious holidays. Workers were paid in rations, primarily wheat and barley but also berries, fruits, fish, and game since no currency existed in ancient Egypt. During imperial times, gold was mined by Nubians to the south of Egypt in what is the modern-day Sudan. Nubians were subjects of the empire who eventually produced pharaohs themselves. Nubian gold was used for luxuries of the ruling classes and as decorations in temples and palaces rather than as currency.

There is some evidence that workers sometimes fled their corvée and work responsibilities. Punishment was severe for such flights; families of these workers were imprisoned and held until the fleeing worker returned. If he did not return, the family was then assigned to new masters. Hypothetically, workers could appeal to the justice system for redress, including going directly to the vizier, the leading minister of government, in the event of abuses by masters. In practice, abuses were legion. Foremen, scribes, and royal officials sometimes obliged workers to perform unpaid work. Payment of workers' bills by wealthy buyers for work done was slow. There is evidence of foremen sexually abusing the wives and daughters of workers. The wheels of justice ground slowly, if at all, on behalf of workers who sought legal redress to correct such abuses.

Social Revolution

Around 2200–2150 BC, a severe cooling of the earth reduced rainfall upriver south of Egypt. The result was two or three decades of low Nile floods, which induced general famine and immense social strife. Local nomarchs and nome governors revolted against central authorities. Social revolution followed, and class conflict was the rule of the day. This period was described in a literary work called *The Admonitions of Ipuwer* or *The Dialogue of Ipuwer and the Lord of All*. Stored in the Dutch National Museum of Antiquities, the original document was probably written well after the turmoil, likely hundreds of years later. It is a poem, a series of laments about the period, addressed to the then-current king by the sage Ipuwer. Here are some examples of the laments as assembled by the Israeli Egyptologist, André Dollinger, rewritten rather prosaically by this author:

- the king has been removed from power by the poor;
- pyramids and temples have been emptied of their contents;
- the poor have become rich, and the rich have become poor;
- people who couldn't afford a single room now own large domains;
- those who slept on the ground previously now have beds;
- those without shade now have shade, while the formerly rich are unprotected from the elements;
- those who couldn't afford a pair of oxen now own herds of cattle;
- formerly grand ladies now sleep on hides rather than on beds;
- former servants address their ex-masters with no respect;
- ex-slaves now own luxuries such as gold, silver, bronze, and marble.

On and on goes the lament. This is indeed revolution being described. In the province of Herakliopolis, in central Egypt, local rulers came to rule

Egypt during this same period. They left a legacy that changed the nature of kingship in Egypt. Henceforth, kings now had a responsibility to treat the people they ruled with mercy and equity. The idea of social justice had been introduced to rulers. Theban rulers eventually restored the Egyptian kingdom by defeating Herakliopolis in war, once again reuniting Egypt by a counter-revolution. Nonetheless, it does appear that a vision of social justice among the ruling class had emerged in ancient Egypt.

Labor Strife

There is evidence that individual workers often appealed to the justice system and to local or central officials for redress even if justice was difficult to obtain. In fact, workers were quite feisty, although haughty behavior by kings, officials, and employers was also common. Food riots by the lower orders appear to have been frequent during the seemingly common periods of famine, especially when food rations, the payment method, were late or smaller than promised or were absconded with by corrupt officials. The poor and disaffected also engaged in robbery of pyramids and temples during hard times and periods of social turmoil. The first recorded strike in historical times occurred during the rule of the emperor Ramses III, who ruled from 1187 to 1156 BC. Craftsmen working on the building of royal tombs living in Deir El Medina struck successfully for their rations when they were inadequate and late. Led by a worker named Mesou, workers even broke into government stores with the support of the local chief of police, Mentmose, and the worker's foreman, Khons, as well as the scribe, Amennakhte, who witnessed and took part in the events, then recorded them for posterity.

The Amarna Revolution

The isolationist culture of ancient Egypt underwent important change owing to immigration of Asians into Egypt during a period of foreign rule by a Semitic people the Egyptians called the *Hyksos*. A second period of important social change occurred with the advent of the Egyptian empire that included the Levant as far north as Syria, extending south to include the Sudan. Egyptian beliefs originally held that only Egyptians were created by the plethora of the 300-plus Egyptian gods. This changed abruptly during the period of 1379–1362 BC when the emperor Amenhetop IV changed his name to Akhenaten to honor the sun-god Aten. With his wife Nefertiti, he instituted the world's first, attempted monotheism. Worship of most Egyptian gods was banned while temples and monuments were closed. The priests lost their *raison d'être* and source of power; in fact, the political motive of controlling the priests might have been what drove the imperial couple to take such measures. Monotheism greatly increased the pharaoh's power, further centralizing Egypt since only the pharaoh was allowed to worship Aten directly, while all others had to worship the pharaoh. Akhenaten built temples to the sun-god at Karnak and at his capital at Tel El-Amarna. Aten was the god of love and light who gave life itself, which, in fact, is the actual reality of the essential nature of the sun for life on earth. Aten was also held to have been responsible for the creation of all, including foreigners, which was recognition of non-Egyptians for their humanity. The new humanism was also reflected in arts and crafts, which now included human concerns and not just those of the gods or the pharaoh. As well, the obsession with the afterlife of the pharaoh was curtailed somewhat.

The loss of power by the priestly class was reversed after the death of the emperor Akhenaten. His successor, Smenkhare, died within a year, and the priesthood reclaimed its powers during the subsequent reigns of Tutankhamun, Ay, and Horemheb. Egyptologists call this reversal of fortunes the Theban counter-revolution since it was based at the old capital at Thebes. The temple at Karnak and the capital at Tel El-Amarna were destroyed, and the official memory of Akhenaten was obliterated for subsequent generations. Nonetheless, this first attempt at monotheism demonstrated that it was a powerful force that was going to change societies dramatically in the future.

Glimmers of Humanity and Justice

At the same time, Egyptian civilization eventually did evolve socially. Particularly during the first intermediate period between 2200 and 2050 BC, there appears to have occurred a marked change in social mores and organization, such that some in society might propose an agenda of social justice and human concerns beyond the first millennium's obsessions with the sanctity and the afterlife of god-kings. This appears as a glimmer, a hint of changes to come in social development. In fact, the first glimmers of social justice in the Bronze Age have been left to us by scribes who produced the world's first great literature in Mesopotamia and Egypt around 2000 BC.

In Mesopotamia, poems about the fifth king of Uruk, Gilgamesh, were assembled in an epic format sometime during the period of 1300–1000 BC, having been composed possibly about 2100 BC. According to the epic, Gilgamesh is a man blessed with great beauty and strength who has built a great city by using forced labor. His behavior is that of a cruel despot. The gods are displeased with Gilgamesh so they send Enkidu, a wild, untamed man who lives with animals, to make the king change his ways. After initially fighting, however, the two men become best of friends, and go off into the world in search of adventure. This displeases the gods whose intentions have been foiled, so they destroy Enkidu in order to punish Gilgamesh. After his friend's death, stricken with profound grief, Gilgamesh goes on a search for immortality. After many adventures and misadventures, he returns to Uruk a chastened man. He has learned that people must die if humankind is to survive. He has learned how to live a good life, how to worship the gods, and how to be a good ruler. Finally, he now also appreciates the magnificence of

Uruk, and recognizes that Uruk will be his legacy that will allow him to live in the memory of future generations. This is the nearest humans can come to immortality other than though the memory of their progeny. The reader will appreciate that this author's prose summary unfortunately doesn't do justice to the poetry of the epic.

In ancient Egypt, there was a kind of literature called 'wisdom literature'. According to K. M. Jonsson, wisdom literature "...usually takes the form of an elder teaching a young son or future king how to behave and conduct himself..." Here are two examples of these writings. In one example, Duauf, a scribe of humble birth, teaches his son Pepi about the importance of behaving ethically and of demonstrating kindness to those of lower social ranking. In the second example, Khety III was the king of Herakliopolis, which was, as we saw earlier, the region that rose to prominence in Egypt during the first intermediate period. In his instructions to his son Merikare, King Khety IV, in addition to offering a long exposition of practical, political advice, advises Merikare to "Do justice...calm the weeper, do not oppress the widow, do not expel a man from his father's property...he who is merciful will (increase his) lifetime... do not prefer the well-born to the commoner, but choose a man on account of his skills, then every work and craft will be done..." (Wim Van den Dungen)

The Tale of the Eloquent Peasant is a poem written somewhere in the period 2000–1700 BC. It is still studied by some students of law. The story is about a peasant who has been wronged by a social superior, an overseer working for a nobleman. The peasant appeals for justice from the nobleman. The peasant argues passionately and eloquently about the nature of justice, especially how a judge must be a protector of the poor and be...

a father to the orphan
and a husband to the widow,
a brother to the divorced,
an apron to the motherless.

The peasant further pleads with the nobleman:

Let me make your name
in this land
according to every good rule:
a leader free of greed,
a great one free of arrogance,
a destroyer of falsehood,
a creator of truth. (Nederhof)

The lord and the king are so impressed that the eloquent peasant receives justice and generous compensation, while the cruel overseer is punished.

These few, brief examples of ancient literature demonstrate awareness among Bronze Age ruling classes that they should behave justly towards the ruled. This intellectual thread is one that is developed and amplified throughout Western history. The realization of the ruler's responsibility towards his subjects was neither a simple top-down affair nor one of *noblesse oblige*. It was also a reaction to pressures from social inferiors resisting domination, as we shall see throughout this book.

Other Ancient Empires

As we saw earlier, the first empires were those of Lugal-zage-si in the Sumerian city of Umma and the Akkadian empire founded by Sargon around 2300 BC in central Mesopotamia. The latter had first subjected Sumer, then adopted the culture of the Sumerian city-states of southern Mesopotamia. These empires were followed by the succession of empires that marked ancient history: the Babylonian empires of central Mesopotamia; the Mitanni-Hurrian empire of northern Mesopotamia that was created when the indigenous Hurrian culture was conquered by invaders from the north, the Mitanni people; the latter hailed possibly from the Caucasus region; the Hittite empire of eastern Anatolia; the Egyptian empire; and the successive Assyrian empires, whose capital was the city of Assur in northern Mesopotamia. The commonly-held assumption of constant warfare among these empires is likely true. These empires were slave societies that enslaved captured prisoners of war. They were highly stratified socially, ruled by powerful kings supported by nobility and priestly classes; they also included wealthy merchant classes engaged in important trade. The aim of the imperial wars appears to have been securing valuable natural resources, luxury products for the use of the wealthy and powerful, slaves, and trade advantages. Peasants' roles in these empires, beyond supporting themselves and their families, were limited to feeding the ruling classes and the soldiery as well as serving as soldiers themselves. The social hierarchy was completed by the skilled craftsmen needed to build religious monuments, cities, weapons, and luxury products as well as the priests, scribes, generals, and officials who supported royal power and the ruling classes.

Ancient Crafts and Guilds

Craftsmen of these societies were grouped into guild-like assemblies to worship gods appropriate to their crafts, to provide solidarity and sometimes justice vis-à-vis the state and the powerful and wealthy, and to train the young for trades and crafts. This last point was made earlier with respect to Sumer. It is a reasonable assertion that guilds were the institutions that provided the framework and organization for training young people. In fact, labor unionist Charles Micallef and scholars have uncovered evidence that indicates the existence of such craft associations representing the interests of laboring people, often in opposition to other classes. The existence of craft guilds is thus evidence of an important tool of popular resistance in ancient times. In a perfect example of silo thinking, however, it is clear to medievalists that guilds only started in the Middle Ages, even if most do recognize the existence of Roman *collegia* of craftsmen.

The existence of guilds in ancient times deserves some further analysis. In our times, since the advent of industrialization, families have evolved into social units organized around the functions of consumption in the nuclear family. In pre-industrial eras, however, the extended family was the basic unit of production, whether among laborers, crafts people, or peasants. In agricultural production, work was done by slaves or by subordinate peasants in the case of land owned by the wealthy, or farmed in commons when farming was done by peasants on their own lands. Commons land was worked by parents and their children, siblings, cousins, aunts and uncles, and by slaves, servants, and associated retinues of these extended families. Patriarchs and matriarchs of extended families worked themselves, and were ultimately responsible for production. Living and working in close quarters, a craftsman or peasant would also impart his skills to his son or son-in-law or grandson or to his younger brother, cousin, or nephew, while he worked alongside his relatives. A similar situation probably existed for women including for the domestic and farming work or the craft work performed by girls and women.

Some have posited a clear distinction between the family and the guild as the unit and organizing base for production. In actuality, there was no such distinction. Guilds were formed of linked, extended family units. Perhaps, this distinction grew because historians who studied workers during the 19th century industrialization in North America observed that work was performed less in extended family units and more in atomized, nuclear units. This loss of relevant, extended families in North America was replaced by pubs and taverns, voluntary associations, religious organizations such as parishes or confraternities, charitable organizations, fraternities, lodges, and masonic societies. Prior to 19th century North America, work was done by extended families organized into commons or craft associations. Perhaps, the exception to the existence of guilds might have been earliest Egypt of the first millennium. Theocratic and centralized, where all served the god-kings, early Egypt was isolated, with no substantial trade or contact with foreigners. After Egyptian isolation was broken down by warfare, invasions, immigration, and imperial conquest, however, traders and craftsmen became more plentiful as demand increased for their skills and knowledge. Let's examine three other cases for evidence of the essential nature of trader and crafts associations in three more societies of the ancient Middle East: Phoenicia, Palestine, and Anatolia.

Phoenicia

Phoenicia was the land north of Palestine and south of Syria alongside the eastern shore of the Mediterranean, which corresponds more or less to modern-day Lebanon. Hemmed onto the shore by empires blocking their access to hinterlands to the east, Phoenicians solved their problem of economic survival by becoming a crafts and trading center. Glenn Markoe has described their social organization. Around 1200 BC, Phoenicia was a collection of city-states such as Sidon, Meggido, and Byblos, with a capital located at Tyre. The goods made in Phoenicia or imported to Phoenicia were exported throughout the ancient world in return for metals and agricultural produce. Phoenician traders and craftsmen established trading outlets in Sardinia, Greece, Sicily, Spain and, most importantly, at Carthage, in modern-day Tunisia in North Africa. At the social top of these city-states were wealthy trading oligarchies organized into guilds. In the middle were craftsmen and their guilds, free wage laborers, and peasants. There were many foreigners permanently resident in Phoenician cities doing work as craftsmen and laborers, especially in the port towns and cities. Below foreigners socially came the slaves who worked in mines and shipyards, as soldiers in the army, or as farm workers and servants on wealthy estates.

Phoenicians and Carthaginians were ingenious shipbuilders, navigators, and sailors. They travelled throughout the Mediterranean and even into the Atlantic to the Canary and Azores Islands. They sailed as far north as Cornwall in England and Brittany in France in search of the tin used to make bronze when alloyed with copper. They also searched far and wide for other metals such as copper, gold, silver, and iron. Cities served as warehouses and clearinghouses for their goods including for the foreign goods they exported. They were also among the most important slave merchants of their times. Phoenicians developed the first phonetic alphabet, a variation of which we still use today, and ingenious systems of mathematics, which we still use, as well. Politically, they governed themselves with councils of elders and people's assemblies with a measure of what we might recognize as democracy. Their travels and trade meant that they were continually influencing foreign peoples such as the Greeks and the Berbers of the Maghreb with their culture, probably including spreading their organizations of craftsmen.

Palestine

Phoenicians, Assyrians, Babylonians, Hittites, and Egyptians introduced the ancient Hebrews, who originally were mostly herders and peasants, to crafts and trade. In the Hebrew Tanakh, which constitutes part of the Christian Old Testament, one can read references to brick and glass makers, goldsmiths, carpenters, engravers, stone-cutters and masons, potters, dyers, weavers, embroiderers, painters, apothecaries, and merchants as well as paper, tent, leather, and wine makers. The book of Nehemiah (3:8,31,32) refers to the guilds of goldsmiths, apothecaries, priests, perfume-makers and vendors, masons, carpenters, smiths, and merchants each working as separate groups on the rebuilding of the walls of Jerusalem around the mid-fifth century BC after the return of Jews from the Babylonian exile. In fact, even the Hebrew prophets had originally been holy men who isolated themselves from the rest of society in guilds in the wilds in order to get closer to God before they began their prophecy to their contemporaries. The

Jews brought their guilds to Europe, North Africa, Egypt, and elsewhere in the Middle East and the Mediterranean region as part of the Jewish diaspora.

Anatolia

In the 8th and 7th centuries BC, Greeks migrated from the Greek islands and mainland to a land they called Ionia in western Anatolia. The indigenous peoples of that part of the world had long been organized by guilds and trades owing to Mesopotamian, Syrian, and Phoenician influences. The work organization was their basic unit of local life, whereas the Greeks' basic unit of social life was the polis, the city-state. There is evidence of the traditional, local guild organization in the seven Anatolian cities of Smyrna, Sardis, Pergamum, Thyatira, Miletus, Philadelphia, and Ephesus, where St. Paul first formed the early Christian communities.

Summary

The emergence of civilization and states followed the same pattern of development after the initial appearance of social complexity, regardless of the time period or the particular region of the world. The first states appeared in the Fertile Crescent of the Middle East in Mesopotamia and Egypt, along the banks of the Tigris and Euphrates rivers in the former and the Nile in the latter.

Reliance upon agriculture brought with it a certain problem: regular famine in times of crop failure owing to disease, floods, drought, warfare, or poor weather conditions. Complex societies developed the solution of storing crop surpluses in good times. The people who managed these surpluses came to be priests and god-kings, while storage facilities developed into temples for the gods who would ensure adequate supply of food if the proper sacrifices, prayers, and rituals led by priests and kings were performed. The authority and power of these storage facilities' managers increased further owing to the development of irrigation to help ensure the production of food surpluses.

The first empires, where thousands of people in distinct communities came to be subjected to a state and its leaders, appeared about 2300 BC in Mesopotamia in the city-state of Umma and among the Akkadians, a Semitic people who conquered the Sumerian city-states. These empires were followed by a succession of other empires in the Middle East.

In ancient civilizations, artisans were organized into guilds of extended family members for religious observances dedicated to particular gods. These guilds also performed practical duties of imparting skills to the young and protecting members. The first civilizations were organized by social class, and included slavery and class conflict. In response to social pressures from below, however, the idea of social justice took root among rulers, who came to be influenced by the ideas of social justice that should guide the actions of rulers.

Chapter 3. Of Metals and Morality

Introduction

We have seen how the ancient civilizations and states of the Bronze Age emerged in Mesopotamia, Egypt, and elsewhere in the Middle East. Originally theocratic, the Mesopotamian and Egyptian states developed into empires that conquered other peoples and, in turn, were succeeded by the hegemony of other empires.

We've also argued that it's a reasonable assertion that in ancient societies, extended families of working people organized themselves into guilds, while peasants would have organized themselves similarly in their agricultural commons, if only to impart work skills and other elements of culture to the young. In fact, there does appear to be sufficient evidence to verify the existence of guilds in ancient societies. We've also seen from examples of ancient literature that some members of the ruling classes came to understand that they owed justice and social equity to their social inferiors, at least partly in response to social pressure from the lower classes.

The Iron Age

The metallurgical technology of ancient Mesopotamia and Egypt involved the use, first of copper, then of bronze, an alloy of copper and tin. Bronze was a malleable substance that could be used for many purposes including luxuries and weapons. The next metals technology to be discovered involved the use of iron, which brought in its wake important social changes. Perhaps first discovered in Armenia about 2000 BC, iron was used in eastern Anatolia around 1400 BC. Use of iron spread to the Middle East around 1200, then to Greece around 1000 BC.

R.J. Forbes describes the development of iron-making among the chalybus, ironsmiths from the southeast shores of the Black Sea.

> They had discovered that wrought iron, reheated frequently in a charcoal fire and then hammered, would thereby become harder than any bronze, and would keep its hardness after long use. We now know that the reason for this change is that the iron absorbs charcoal particles on its surface, causing the latter to develop a steel structure. The new metal thus consists of a core of wrought iron enclosed in a shell of steel. (p.54)

The use of iron by peasants increased their prosperity since iron tools such as plows could break heavy soils more readily than wooden or stone tools, thus adding arable land and, eventually, increasing population owing to the availability of more food. It also democratized warfare since iron weapons operated by commoners were superior and more lethal in warfare compared to bronze weapons and chariots operated by small groups of elite warriors. The Iron Age also wrought perennial warfare among empires and the smaller states that developed in the spaces between empires, states such as ancient Israel, Judah, Phoenicia, and the city-states of western Anatolia as well as the civilizations of the Mediterranean such as the Minoan civilization of Crete and the Mycenaean civilization of southern Greece. In addition to engaging in constant warfare with other states over trade and natural resources, the ruling classes of these small societies also learned and refined, as had done the first states and empires, the art of extracting economic surplus from the labor of the common people.

Extraction of Economic Surplus

As with the powerful empires that swept over the Middle East, ancient small states were stratified societies led by kings allegedly descended from ancient, common ancestors or gods, if they were not deemed to be gods themselves. These states included aristocracies composed of leading warriors; wealthy merchants profiting from trade and the persistent warfare over trade and resources; peasants who fed all and also served as warriors; craftsmen of extended families of artisans united in guilds; and poor laborers. There was another category of persons legally excluded from society even if numerous. These were the slaves, who emanated from several categories of people: war captives who owed their lives to victors in war; persons for whom slavery was a voluntary respite from death by starvation or other calamity; persons bred for slavery; persons delivered by families as payment for debt, or who offered their liberty as payment for debts they could not repay; or persons preserved from murder when captured by pirates, thieves, or kidnappers then sold into slavery for a profit. Slaves were provided with enough to survive and, in some cases, to breed other slaves. The labor from these slaves provided much of the wealth of the ruling classes. In the ancient world the very real possibility of slipping into slavery terrorized and haunted commoners. Debt servitude often was contracted by previously free people during the frequent periods of famine or natural calamity. As we shall see later, debt servitude and curbing and controlling it were prime, motivating, political forces in ancient times.

Beyond slave labor, the ruling classes grew wealthy from the labor of peasants on the domains of the wealthy and powerful and on the domains of temples and royal palaces; by rents, that is, a portion of the peasants' produce handed over to landowners; or by advancing credit to social inferiors forced to delay their payment of rents or other obligations to their social superiors. The state itself was another source of wealth extraction for rulers, whether from use of resources or from royalties thereupon; from tolls on roads and bridges and trade routes; from taxes and tribute paid by conquered peoples; from corvée labor provided by commoners on public works, religious structures, and the like; from fees paid for using temple and state services; or from interest on credit advanced to merchants engaged in foreign trade. Being a member of the ruling class in ancient times was a sweet business indeed, well before modern capitalism.

For commoners, life was one long set of fears during the persistent warfare between states and class exploitation within states, where the descent to the hell of slavery was an ever-present possibility if one could survive the warfare and internal social conflict. This negative situation caused by the advent of the Iron Age demanded responses from and on behalf of the socially inferior. These came from two principal sources: the religious and philosophical advances of the so-called Axial Age, and the resistance offered by the downtrodden themselves.

The Axial Age

In response to the violence and travails of the Iron Age, some men withdrew to the wilds to isolate themselves physically and socially. Via contemplation, meditation, prayer, and reason, they confronted the great questions of human existence. They gained the wisdom that being fully human and living the good life required that people transcend their current base behaviors towards one another. They then began to preach to their fellows about their new insights. From China to Greece, they all arrived at variations of the Golden Rule as enunciated by Confucius: *Do not do unto others what you would not have them do unto you.* The religions that emerged in this period also displayed a concern for social justice towards the socially inferior as a prime element of the new beliefs, as we shall see in greater detail when we study the three Western monotheisms.

The German philosopher, Karl Jaspers, noted in his book first published in English in 1953, *The Origin and Goal of History*, that the great religions and the philosophies emerged during the Iron Age, more specifically, in the period from 800 BC to AD 200. Jaspers called this period the Axial Age. Consider the religious and philosophical advances of the Axial Age: Zoroastrianism in Persia; prophetic Judaism and the redaction of the Hebrew Bible in the 6th and 5th centuries BC during and after the Jewish exile in Babylon; Buddhism, Jainism, and Hinduism in India; Confucianism and Taoism in China; the Greek philosophers; and the monotheisms that followed the Jewish example, that is, Christianity and Islam. So, we ultimately might speak of an extended axial period as actually lasting about a millennium and a half from about 800 BC to about AD 650.

At first, the ruling classes of these societies scoffed at the ideas of the wise men. Not so certain literate people and members of the lower social classes who perceived that these ideas might improve society in order to benefit all. Some rulers understood and absorbed these ideas, then adopted and promoted them for the societies they ruled, even if there was always a tension between the noble ideas of the wise men on one hand, and the brutal and cynical *realpolitik* of the day on the other hand. In an important way, however, the religious and philosophical advances of the Iron Age presented solutions to societies grown weary of perpetual violence, social conflict, and the social change wrought by the primacy of the marketplace that was replacing the traditional ways of organizing society as seen in the Bronze Age.

Debt Crises

A second Iron Age phenomenon was the resistance by popular classes to domination by the ruling classes. American anthropologist David Graeber describes some of this phenomenon in his book, *Debt: The First 5,000 Years*. Before the introduction of currency and markets, economies functioned by a system of credit and debit whereby tallies were kept, both written and unwritten, of receivables and debts using units of measure such as units of barley or wheat, or units of the gold and silver maintained in temples and palaces. In fact, this was the origin of writing in ancient Sumer where the amounts due to temples or palaces from commoners were scratched on clay tablets by administering scribes. Ancient Mesopotamia was originally composed of independent city-states whose economies might be described as state communism whereby peasants delivered their produce to granaries/ temples and palaces from which it was distributed to all in the community. The agricultural products were the property of the community as represented by the gods and mediated by the priests and kings who directed and administered the common produce with the help of scribes and officials. On the other hand, within the popular classes, among craftsmen, laborers, and peasants, dealings were transacted by unwritten credits and debits. All could easily remember amounts due or receivable owing to the small size of communities comprised of people often related by family, or at least well-known to individual families.

As mentioned earlier, dependence on agriculture meant inevitably the unfortunate reality of periodic famine. In such conditions, amounts due could become permanent debts which might accumulate on the backs of peasants, and in the tallies and on the ledgers of the ruling classes. When these debts became so onerous that peasants could not survive by remaining in the city-states, some took one of the most important actions of self-defense the poor have taken throughout history: they migrated to seek their fortunes elsewhere. In the Middle East, this often meant joining or rejoining Semitic nomads who lived west of Mesopotamia, where they would return to the ancient, nomadic means of survival by tending herds and flocks, and by hunting and gathering. The rulers of the city-states were left with fewer people to rule and fewer still to produce the food necessary for their own survival, or to fight their wars with other states. Furthermore, ex-city dwellers who had returned to nomadism, in fact, or did themselves periodically invade the city-states from which they had hailed originally in order to establish new régimes. There, the erstwhile nomads might even become the new rulers in sort of a political revolution.

In response to these very real possibilities, one ruler, King Enmetena of Lagash in Sumer instituted a political measure in 2400 BC that was to echo a recurring theme throughout Western history. He instituted a debt amnesty by which all debts, excepting commercial loans contracted by traders, were abolished. Land redistribution followed so that peasants could return to their lands to resume feeding themselves and the rest of the state including, of course, its ruling class and kings. Graeber writes that the ruler of Lagash had introduced *amargi*, or freedom from debt, the first recorded use of the word 'freedom' in a political document. This same measure was repeated fifty years later by a successor in Lagash, Uruinimgina, who once again cancelled debts and debt servitude. This pattern repeated throughout the history of Sumer, Babylon, and Assyria. In 1761 BC, Hammurabi abolished debts in Babylon in order to protect the weak from the strong, and to restore social justice and equity.

The situation in Egypt was different since empires appeared later than in Mesopotamia, so that ancient, informal credit and debit systems applied longer. Nevertheless, there is record, however, of the pharaoh Bakeranef, who reigned from 722–715 BC, granting debt amnesties. In fact, the Rosetta Stone, the famous document that permitted the decoding of ancient Egyptian by virtue of the ancient Greek translation which it included, contained records of debt amnesties granted by the Egyptian ruler Ptolemy V around 200 BC.

The pattern had been established. Inevitably, agricultural reliance produced famine which produced debt crises during which popular parties and factions demanded debt relief and redistribution of farmlands. This pattern also obtained, as we shall see later, in the ancient Levant, Greece, and Rome. In fact, for the latter two, recorded history almost begins with the social turmoil wrought by debt crises. Prior to the debt crises in Greece and Rome, history is mostly a foggy story of myth and epic poetry, the real historical details of which are murky.

Perennial debt crises relented temporarily when coinage was introduced. First used in the Anatolian kingdom of Lydia around 625 BC, coins of silver and gold were paid to Greek mercenaries as a practical replacement for the ancient method of paying soldiers by permitting them to pillage and loot the territory of their defeated enemy. The use of coinage spread throughout Greek Ionia, then to the mainland and islands of Greece. Paid to peasant-soldiers, these coins helped create recognizable markets where supply and demand operated. The first, principal market was for slaves, mainly war captives, who were then set to working mines in search of gold and silver that, when centrally located by the state in temples and palaces, served as a basis for issuing still more coins.

During his conquests during the fourth century BC, Alexander the Great issued 180,000 talents (an ancient measure of currency) in coins, the current-day equivalent of about $300 billion U.S. suddenly introduced into the Mediterranean region and the Middle East. The surplus of coins caused considerable social turmoil and price inflation as coins quickly were devalued vis-à-vis the commodities they could buy. Coinage and the chances to earn it had provided, however, some temporary respite from the perennial debt crises. Governments imagined many reasons to issue coins to the populace, who then paid taxes using the same coins. In ancient Rome, coins were first introduced in 338 BC, while debt servitude was abolished about the same time in 326 BC. The respite for the popular classes, however, was only temporary. What had been created was an economic system of warfare/slavery/markets, all lubricated by the innovation of coinage, first privately issued, then quickly taken over by states. The poor continued to find themselves in debt and servitude to the wealthy from which they demanded relief, while these phenomena continued to fuel social relations. Nevertheless, one of the first effective, popular methods of resistance to domination had been recorded for history, that is, demanding and obtaining cancellation of debt. This combined with the religious advances of the Axial Age will now be analyzed as far as they concerned the ancient Hebrews.

The Ancient Hebrews

The ancient Hebrews were a nomadic, herding people from Mesopotamia and the land west of Mesopotamia. They traced their mythic and legendary ancestry to a common person, the patriarch Abraham, a Semite from Haran in northern Mesopotamia, whose father hailed from the Sumerian city of Ur. During one of the frequent periods of warfare and social conflict in Mesopotamia, Abraham and his clan left to seek a better life. They took up the nomadic life, moving across the deserts west of Mesopotamia leading eventually to Anatolia, Syria, Egypt, and finally, to Palestine. As per other tribal peoples, their society was organized around kinship and their gods. Peoples who did not worship their gods could not be considered Hebrew.

Later Hebrew history in prophetic times was marked by a perpetual conflict between those who insisted that Hebrews worship only their tribal god, Yahweh, and those who also wished to worship the ancestral gods of fertility of Canaan in Palestine, where Hebrews settled for the most part around 1300 BC, or indeed even the moon and sun cults of desert nomads and Mesopotamia. This religious conflict might have been the tip of the iceberg of social conflict among the Hebrews, affecting ideas about where and how they should live. Were the Hebrews divided between those who wished to integrate into the agricultural life and the population of indigenous inhabitants of Canaan, and those who wished to resume their nomadic life in the desert west of Mesopotamia, or even those who wished to return to Mesopotamia?

The Hebrews' lack of knowledge of such skills as iron-smithing and armoring put them in an unfortunate position during the Iron Age warfare in the area. They, however, did eventually learn these iron-related crafts and many others through contact with peoples such as the Phoenicians and Mesopotamians, and a people known as the Kenites of Midian. This last people were nomadic ironsmiths descended from the ironsmiths of the Hittite Empire, which had been overthrown by invaders from a subject people from the Balkans called the Phrygians, who overthrew their imperial masters to settle in central Anatolia. The erstwhile Hittite ironsmiths then wandered about the Middle East. A woman from this people is reputed to have married the Hebrew leader, Moses. (Forbes, p. 55, 56) Extended families of these craftsmen grouped themselves into guilds, as did merchants, craftsmen, and priests among the ancient Hebrews. These guilds eventually spread throughout the Jewish diaspora in the Mediterranean region, the Middle East, and Europe. According to Mark Wischnitzer, an American student of the phenomenon, "Despite all the questions still to be solved, modern research has established the existence of certain forms of social organization among Jewish craftsmen in Biblical times." (p. 12) In fact, many of the sages and prophets who appear throughout the Bible were actually craftsmen themselves.

Jewish Prophecy

Edward Searl, an American Unitarian minister, divides the tradition of Jewish prophecy into three parts. Firstly, around 1000 BC, groups of men organized in guilds withdrew from the violence and social conflict of the Iron Age to the wilds in order to contemplate and attempt to know God, then called 'Elohim' or 'Adonai', via ecstatic practices, fasting, prayer, reason, and reflection. Secondly, during the ninth century BC, prophets emerged from their isolation with a mission of confronting rulers with a higher law, God's law, to which all, ordinary people and rulers both, were subject to the prophetic call for social justice. Writes Searl, "This challenging of authority in the name of justice was a radical departure in the course of civilization." We know the stories of Elijah, Elisha, and Nathan even if there are no writings in their name. This was not the case, however, of the writing prophets, who defined Judaism in the period of 800–400 BC during part three of the tradition of Jewish prophecy. We recognize the names of some of these prophets: Amos, the first Isaiah, Micah, Jeremiah, Ezekiel, the second Isaiah, Ezra, and still others. These prophets lived in periods of social conflict in which the ruling classes exploited and oppressed ordinary Jews. The ruling classes also reconciled themselves with surrounding states and empires, the better to ensure their continued power and wealth. Many gods were worshipped as part of official policy, including fertility gods such as Ba'al and other ancient gods of pre-Hebraic Canaan, Mesopotamia, Egypt, and the deserts. The prophets were outraged at this unfair treatment of God's chosen people by Jews themselves. Under the monotheism the prophets preached, all were equal before the eyes of the one, true God, YHWH, while they were not equal before the other gods. In the eyes and words of the prophets, according to Benjamin Scolnic:

> Those who live in luxury do not worry about the destitute at their doors, landowners are greedy, creditors are heartless, the vain are rich and irresponsible. Hosea speaks of murder; Jeremiah talks of trapping men like birds; and Micah speaks of the ruling classes as cannibals who eat the flesh of those who are under-nourished....Amos talks about robbery with violence and commerce in human life. (p. 22)

So, the prophets exhorted the people,

> to be charitable and merciful to the poor, and to help those who are defenseless and needy, widows and orphans, oppressed people, strangers, and those without legal rights. They stipulated impartiality in justice and fairness...respecting the property of others...respect for every human life. (Scolnic, p. 23)

Thus, the demand and promotion of monotheism was combined with a moral imperative in favor of social justice, once again as Searl writes, for "... an equitable and fair society kept through laws that reflected transcendental or divine ideals, not special interests."

Social Justice

The Jewish ideal as espoused by the prophets was a society united in worship of the one true God, YWHW, based upon equality of its members, the dignity of all, and the solidarity of Jews of all classes. What did this mean in practice? A story from the Book of Nehemiah (5.1-13) is useful. Nehemiah was a Jew who had been an office-holder in Babylon. The Persian emperor appointed him as royal governor of the state of Judah in the middle of the 5th century BC. After Nehemiah arrived, poor Jews staged a protest about the conditions to which the powerful had subjected them. Nehemiah summoned the powerful and wealthy, and castigated them for their behavior. He called a great assembly of Jews at which Nehemiah demanded that the wealthy restore what had been taken from the commoners, to which the wealthy voluntarily complied. This story demonstrates that there was a basic presumption among ancient Jews that the poor had a right to demand fair treatment from the rich and powerful, and did not have to seek leave to appeal for justice, nor battle to obtain a hearing. This was a radical advance quite different, as we shall see later, from the rest of the ancient world. The rights of the poor and the prophets to demand social justice on behalf of the poor was a theme that repeated throughout the history of the ancient Hebrews. So did, however, the oppression by the wealthy and powerful. In response, the poor and their prophetic champions campaigned for social justice on three fronts during five centuries of class conflict between 900 and 400 BC.

The first front was the struggle for debt relief and land distribution. As elements of regular social and religious practice, the poor obtained the rights to cancellation of debts in the Sabbath year, every seventh year, as well as free access to fallow lands to grow their own food, and to liberation of indentured servants and slaves. In the Jubilee year, the 50th year following seven cycles of Sabbath years, slaves and indentured servants were freed; debts were abolished; free access to fallow land was granted so that the poor could farm and feed themselves; while all lands were returned to the descendants of the original owners who had lost them in payment of debts.

The second front was the violent resistance during revolts and rebellions of the poor, and even during successful revolutions whereby the wealthy and powerful and their representative rulers were overthrown. These instances of violent resistance began as soon as kings began to rule ancient Israel. Around 1000 BC, Absalom, a son of a tribal leader named David, led a revolt against his father's exactions upon the lowly. David killed his son, but soon after another son, Solomon, came to power by killing another of his brothers. During the next generation, David's grandson, Rehoboam, continued the oppressive ways of his grandfather. Around 920 BC, Jeroboam led a successful revolution against Rehoboam to become ruler of a new northern state called Israel, while a southern state, traditionally considered by ancient Hebrews to have been the home of the ancient tribe of Benjamin, descendants of one of the twelve sons of the Hebrew patriarch, Joseph, called itself Judah. In 842 BC, Jehu, a general supported by the prophet Elisha and the poor, rural folk, revolted in the northern kingdom of Israel. Kings 9 of the Bible relates the story of how Jehu overthrew King Joram, the son of King Ahab and Queen Jezebel, who continued the policy of his parents of worshipping pagan gods. Writes an American Protestant pastor, James Newsome: "The bloody uprising and the violent overthrow of Joram not only signaled the violent suppression of Ba'alism in Israel, but it also took the form of a peasants' rebellion in that it marked the overthrow of the rich and powerful by the poor people of the land." (p. 15)

The small, independent states of Israel in the north and Judah in the south eventually succumbed to the empires that surrounded them: Assyrian, Seleucid, Roman, and Byzantine. In order to ensure their survival in power and wealth, the Jewish ruling classes made arrangements to collaborate with their imperial masters, collaboration that was often violently resisted by poor Jews. In 701 BC, Jews revolted against the Assyrian empire. There was later a lengthy and continuing revolt against the Seleucid empire, one of the descendant Greek empires that followed the conquests of the late Alexander the Great. This revolt lasted from about 193 BC to 160 BC. This was the so-called Maccabean or Hasmonean revolution, which created an independent, Jewish theocratic state that lasted about a hundred years until the Roman conquest, when the Romans then created the state of Judea comprising both the northern and southern Jewish states. Then followed the famous, unsuccessful revolts against Rome during the Great Jewish War from AD 66 to 73, and the Bar-Kochba revolt of 135. These are well-known, but lesser-known is the Kitos War of AD 117. Kitos is a corruption of the name of the Roman general Quietus, who pacified the Jews after their outbreak of violence in AD 117. The rebellions were started by a name named Andreas, who led a revolt by the Jews of Cyraenica, in modern-day, eastern Libya. During the revolt Jews destroyed Roman temples and civil structures, and wiped out the entire Roman population of the region. They then entered Alexandria in Egypt, and burnt it to rubble. Then, Jews in Cyprus under the leadership of Artemion killed most of the Greeks in Cyprus.

After Rome re-conquered the island, a law was passed that forbade Jews from living in Cyprus. There followed important Jewish revolts in cities of Anatolia and northern Mesopotamia, which were put down by the Roman emperor, Trajan himself. While Trajan was successful against these Jewish revolts, he got a case of heatstroke from which he died. Jews revolted again against the eastern Roman empire in 351-352 AD. During the sixth century AD, the Samaritans from northern Israel near Galilee revolted four times against Byzantium, the last of which lasted from about 554 to 572. Finally, Jews revolted again against the Byzantine emperor, Heraclius, during the period from 610 to 628. All this violent resistance superficially resembles the other proto-nationalist revolts which the Roman empire perennially faced. Among the Jews, however, the violent revolts involved religious disputes combined with internal class conflict, both in ancient Palestine and in the Jewish diaspora.

Jewish Labor Rights

The third social front of the prophets' message on behalf of the poor involved the struggle for labor rights for Jewish workers. Towards the end of the sixth century BC, the prophet Zechariah wrote:

> This is what the Lord Almighty says: administer true justice; show mercy and compassion to one another. Do not oppress the widow or the fatherless, the alien or the poor. In your hearts, do not think evil of each other. (7:9–10)

In spite of the power and wealth of businessmen in the Jewish diaspora, the message of the Yahweh prophets as well as the Hebrews' roots in nomadic equality ensured that working people benefited from more rights than did commoners among other peoples in the ancient world. Michael Perry of the Jewish Labor Committee in New York City has described the labor rights of Jewish workers that follow upon religious sources, the Tanakh and Talmudic and oral traditions. Of prime importance is the fundamental dignity of work and of those who work. Personal ownership of land is permitted, provided that it is not in conflict with the welfare of society or religious norms. Landowners are enjoined to leave the harvests from the corners of their fields for the poor to feed themselves. Jewish law holds that workers have the advantage in their relationship with employers, thus workers have the right to prompt payment in cash, not in kind. Perry writes:

> The Talmud warns that employers who withhold wages are guilty of violations: oppressing a neighbor, stealing, oppressing the poor, delaying payment of wages, failing to pay wages at the due date...before sunset... as though he (the employer) deprived him (the worker) of his life. (p. 5)

Jewish law set limits on hours of work, the most famous being the right to rest on the Sabbath, a right later retained in Christianity and Islam. Elsewhere, farm workers were allowed to partake of the food they were harvesting; the same right applied to servers of food. Jewish law also allowed sick and disability pay during which time workers did not lose accumulated rights from their service to their employers. Workers could not be required to put themselves in physical danger while working. They were allowed to associate in guilds, associations, or unions, and had the rights to engage in collective bargaining and to withdraw their services during strikes.

Perry notes that many of the prophetic and other originators of Jewish traditions vis-à-vis workers were themselves craftsmen. Jewish labor rights have been a beacon to the western world. During the industrial revolutions of the 19th century, Jewish law and traditions inspired various stripes of socialists, trade unionists, and Christian reformers. At the end of the 19th century, the pope issued an encyclical, *Rerum novarum*, which incorporated many of the longstanding Jewish traditions with respect to workers into Catholic social policy, a policy reconfirmed by Pope John Paul II. More generally, the Jewish notion of social justice has inspired all manner of workers and social reformers; so much so that it is part of the broad fabric of western culture.

Summary

The first metals that civilizations used to make tools, weapons, and luxuries were made of copper, followed by bronze, an alloy of copper and tin. By the end of the first millennium BC, the fabrication and use of iron had spread throughout Anatolia and the Middle East and into Greece. While iron brought with it certain benefits such as iron plows that permitted an expansion of arable land, it also bought with it more deadly, frequent, thoroughgoing, and widespread warfare. This chapter has also explained how the same period produced a greater extraction by ruling classes of the economic surplus produced by laboring people as evidenced by the spread of slavery and debt servitude of the poor.

The Iron Age created two broad reactions to the problems raised by the use of iron: the Axial Age, during which the great world religions appeared, and resistance in various forms by the popular classes to the violence and oppression of the era. Within the former category there emerged religious and philosophical systems based on the Golden Rule of treating others as you would wish to be treated. In this period also appeared the monotheisms under which all were deemed equal before the eyes of God, under which there was an abiding concern for social justice and the plight of the poor. Within the category of popular resistance, there were various means of struggle such as revolution, revolts, and rebellions as well as schemes of land redistribution and resolutions to the periodic debt crises that befell ancient agricultural societies. In the Middle East, the society that addressed these problems most lucidly was that of the ancient Hebrews, so much so that their solutions have remained part of the cultural legacy of Western societies even today.

CHAPTER 4. THE ANCIENT GREEKS

Introduction

We now turn our attention to another pillar of western history and culture, the ancient Greeks. Our concerns remain the patterns of development and social domination, and the resistance of working people to this domination. Compared to the ancient Hebrews and other ancient peoples, historians have many more useful historical sources for studying the Greeks. The Greeks were a literate people who played an important role in defining the pursuit of knowledge in the West, including initiating what can be reasonably defined as the discipline of history. This supplements the study of mythology, theology, archaeology, philology, and the social sciences with respect to the ancient Greeks. Owing to the quantity and quality of historical evidence, the story of the ancient Greeks is complex and detailed. In the interests of situating the events and arguments to be presented in this chapter, here is an approximate timeline of major events in the prehistory and history of ancient Greece.

Timeline for Ancient Greece

All dates are BC. Dates are approximate and in the case of earliest dates, subject to conjecture and debate.

6800–3000: Neolithic period in Greece when indigenous nomadic peoples developed horticulture and animal husbandry, in the process becoming semi-sedentary and sedentary.

6500–4000: Hundreds of archaeological sites of villages in Greece of about 100 people or so are established; one of the most studied sites today is at Sesklo, near the city of Volos in Thessaly. These communities form part of what is called Old Europe in the Balkans and the lower Danube Valley.

3000: Bronze Age migrants arrive in Greece from Anatolia and the Pontic–Caspian Steppe north of the Black Sea. This latter region, most likely, is the source of the proto-Indo-European (PIE) language, the ancestor language for the languages of Europe, Iran, and India; among the descendant languages of PIE is ancient Greek.

1700: Minoan civilization flourishes on the island of Crete.

1600: Mycenaean migration to southern Greece, possibly originating from northern Greece and elsewhere in the Balkans.

1500: Egyptian settlements and trading posts established among Greeks.

1450: Collapse of Minoan culture on Crete owing to volcanic disasters and to Mycenaean invasions or migrations from mainland Greece.

1400: Mycenaean civilization of southern Greece flourishes.

1250: War between Troy in northwestern Anatolia at the Dardanelles Strait that joins the Black and Mediterranean seas and the Mycenaean Greeks of southern Greece, ostensibly and lyrically over the kidnapping of Helen of Troy, more prosaically possibly about control of trade through the Dardanelles.

1200–800: Greek Dark Ages with reversion from Mycenaean civilization to previous nomadic and semi-nomadic ways.

1000: The Iron Age begins in Greece, replacing the Bronze Age technique of the Minoan and Mycenaean civilizations; iron technique is brought to Greece from Anatolia.

776: Signs of the return of civilization to Greece, including the first Olympiad held in northeast Greece.

750: Creation of *poleis*, regional city-states, throughout the Greek mainland; the *polis* combines villages, farmland, and a central town to become the prime political community in Greece and the object of Greek attachment and allegiance.

750: Monarchs descended from traditional, tribal chiefs are replaced as rulers of poleis by councils of elders, in effect, clan leaders who advised the kings; among these clan leaders are leading landowners and warriors.

750: Greeks from the mainland colonize islands in the Aegean as well as Sicily, Sardinia, Corsica, Cyprus, western Anatolia, southern France and Italy, and the southern coastlines of the Black Sea.

750: Greeks trade with seafaring Phoenicians, resulting in the latter's cultural and economic influence on the Greeks, so much so that the Greeks adopt the Phoenician alphabet, adapting it by adding letters to represent vowel sounds.

750: Resuscitating ancient oral tales, Homeric bards sing and redact the *Iliad* and the *Odyssey*, the former about the Mycenaean–Trojan War, the latter about one man's wanderings returning from that war. They serve as founding myths for the Greeks, and are considered to be among the world's greatest poems.

700: Hesiod, poet and successful farmer, writes *Works and Days*.

680: In Argos the Hoplite Revolution occurs, which sets the standard for citizen participation in Greek warfare. In return for their participation in wars, hoplite soldiers demand and receive additional political power, granted to all who can afford the equipment of a hoplite, or a heavily-armed infantryman.

650: Sparta adopts the hoplite form of military organization.

620: Lykurgus develops and installs the typically Spartan form of military, political, and social organization.

594: In Athens, the aristocrat Solon institutes laws that eliminate debt servitude, and provides other measures to assist the common people.

6th century: Popular tyrants often rule Greek cities in the name of the peasantry and the middling types, uniting against the increasingly self-serving, oligarchical rule of powerful landowners and merchants made wealthy by trade.

520: Philosopher-poet, Xenophanes, writes a critique of the Greek anthropomorphic gods in the Homeric poems as being silliness, then describes a monotheistic God similar to the views of God held by some modern people.

509: Aristocrat Kleisthenes establishes democracy in Athens which endures until the death of Alexander the Great in 322; democracy overcomes and survives temporary oligarchic rule in 411 and 404. The example of Athenian democracy spreads to other Greek cities, not in small measure owing to Athenian imperialism.

490–468: The Greek–Persian War is provoked by a revolt of Greek cities in Ionia in western Anatolia, supported by Athens and other mainland Greek cities in the Ionian conflict with the Persian suzerain.

462: Ephialtes further refines democracy in Athens.

458–429: Flowering of Athenian democracy, culture, architecture, and public works under the leadership of Pericles.

431–404: Peloponnesian War between Sparta and Athens and their respective allies among the Greek cities.

411: Oligarchs rule Athens.

404: Sparta establishes another oligarchy in Athens after Sparta defeats Athens; the oligarchy is known as the rule of the Thirty Tyrants.

403: Democratic revolution in Athens, under the leadership of General Thrasybulus and the archon Eucleides, re-establishes Athenian democracy, which endures three more generations.

400: Influenced by Socrates, philosopher Antithenes founds a school of philosophy called cynicism, the most notable proponent of which is Diogenes, who lives from 412–323.

387: Plato establishes the *Academy* in Athens.

338: Philip II of Macedon subjugates all of Greece with the help of local oligarchies normally divided one against the other but united in their opposition to democracy.

338–326: Philip's son, Alexander the Great, conquers the known world east of Greece including Egypt (but excluding Palestine) all the way to Persia, even trying unsuccessfully to conquer Afghanistan and India.

325: Alexander's teacher, Aristotle, founds the *Lyceum* in Athens.

322–312: The Hellenistic period begins with the death of Alexander; his Greek successor, Antipater, suppresses the political power of Greek cities in 322. The Hellenistic period is considered ended when the Roman emperor adopts Christianity as the state religion towards the end of the fourth century AD.

300: Zeno from Cyprus founds the philosophy known as stoicism.

168: Rome conquers Macedon.

146: Greece is subjugated by Rome.

Early Greece

Much ink has been spilt about the racial origins of the Greek people. In his once-controversial book, *Black Athena*, Martin Bernal argued that it was European racism, chauvinism, and imperialism during the 19th century that led scholars until only recently to argue that the Greeks were direct descendants of Aryan, PIE-speaking invaders from the north. This pastoral horse culture from the Pontic-Caspian Steppe allegedly swept down on Greece, conquering and eliminating the natives indigenous to that part of the world, descendants of the original, Old European cultures of the Balkans and the lower Danube Valley. Bernal argued that Europeans, in the fullness of their imperialism, could not accept the ancient Greek idea of settlements and influence from ancient Africa, Phoenicia, and Anatolia as being instrumental in forming the Greek people who were, after all, the fount of European culture.

Beyond the obvious problem that most anthropologists and other social scientists today argue that race does not even exist as a substantive reality, it is a mug's game trying to identify precise ethnic origins. Writes Oral Sander, it is not possible "...to find the exact origins of man's material and spiritual products in the depths of history." (p. 1) Furthermore, Sander continues: "...in the case of geographic regions where contact between numerous peoples has been shown to have occurred...to attempt a clarification of every individual thread of development is a meaningless and absurd endeavor." (p. 1, 2)

One look at a map of that part of the world allows us to observe the proximity of other civilizations to Greece. It appears to be indeed quite plausible that peoples did migrate to Greece from Asia (Anatolia, Syria, Phoenicia); from the Black Sea region (the Pontic-Caspian Steppe and the Caucasus); and from Africa (Egypt, Nubia, Libya, Ethiopia, and Carthage) to unite with the indigenous, neolithic peoples of Greece. Consider the example of how people spread in the South Pacific, sailing and rowing from island to island in the South Seas, eventually crossing the immense Pacific Ocean to settle Easter Island only 3,500 kilometers from Chile. In fact, recent evidence suggests that Polynesians might have even made it to the Americas. (CBC-TV) In light of this example, the probability of ancient peoples engaging in island-hopping in the relatively small Aegean Sea is high.

Moreover, historians used to speak of invasions and military conquests in this part of the world, with one civilization succeeding the other by destroying it in warfare. Just as plausible, if not more so, might have been migrations wherein peoples would mix via trade, exchange of marriage partners, and other collaborations. This might also have applied to the original PIE-speakers from the Pontic-Caspian Steppe. Since people in the neolithic era were still semi-sedentary or had only recently become sedentary, migrating might have been a plausible solution for peoples looking for better livelihoods and land. Furthermore, consider the possibilities of Egyptian influence and settlements in Greece. The Egyptian empire of the Middle Kingdom extended north into the Levant and Anatolia, then southeast to Mesopotamia. Why couldn't Egyptians have sailed or rowed onto the nearby Greek islands? Same for the Phoenicians who were great shipbuilders and sailors. If they colonized much of southern Europe and North Africa, why could they not have done the same in Greece and the Aegean islands?

Within Greek culture itself, there were many signs of influence from abroad. Greek religion showed influence from many sources including the Egyptian pantheon of gods and goddesses, the Great Mother goddess from Anatolia, and fertility deities from the Middle East. The philosopher Plato studied in Egypt, which he said was a constant influence in his reflections. The Greeks adapted the Phoenician alphabet to make it their own by adding letters to represent vowel sounds. Bronze Age arts and crafts and knowledge would have moved to Greece from Africa and Asia along with migrants from these areas. When the Bronze Age collapsed, other migrants introduced Iron Age technique from Anatolia and possibly the Middle East.

Greek Identity

From this amalgam of foreign influences upon the indigenous culture of native, neolithic Greeks emerged a pan-Greek identity. After the Greek Dark Ages during which the Bronze Age, Mycenaean civilization ended, an Iron Age culture emerged in Greece around 1000 BC. It crystallized during the 8th century BC, uniting Greeks based on several factors: iron technique, a common language and alphabet, religion, trade, patterns of warfare, and the devotion of Greeks to their cherished poleis. Regardless of origins, there was now a common Greek identity, which grew stronger during the Persian War.

Formation of the Poleis

Much of what we know about the Greeks comes from our knowledge of the Athenians, usually written by writers who supported Athens in the perennial, inter-city competition among ancient Greeks. While at first blush this might appear to introduce an unfortunate bias in our knowledge, in actual fact, the problem is less important than it might appear. Firstly, Athens was by far the biggest of the Greek city-states. At the height of its power in the middle of the fifth century BC, there were about 40,000 free citizens in Athens. The nearest competitor city in terms of population, Corinth, only had about 15,000 citizens, while the entire Spartan territory of Messenia and Lakonia only held about 16,000 citizens. Secondly, Athens did provide leadership to the Greek states politically, economically, militarily, and culturally. Thirdly, Athens' democratic politics was exported throughout Greece and the Mediterranean, at least in part owing to Athenian imperialism. In fact, the pattern of how the Athenian polis emerged serves as a useful model for other Greek states and, in fact, for ancient civilizations generally, including that of Rome. In the founding mythology of Athens, a king named Theseus was reputed to have unified the peninsula of Attica under the rule of Athens. As part of this narrative, four tribes were united in the Athenian polis: the *Gedeontes, Aigikoreis, Ergadeis,* and *Hopletes.* The four tribes lived in Athens itself and on the nearby mountains, plain, and seacoast. Each of these tribes had a different economy, thus different political interests and resources, which could come into conflict. Politics provided the means of combining this diversity peacefully since each tribe had representatives in the political structures of Attica.

The four tribes united clans and families whereby leaders and followers owed responsibilities to each other in a mostly agricultural society much celebrated in the literature of the ancient Greeks. Agriculture was the subject of literary paeans in which independent farmers purportedly made ideal citizens. Nonetheless, the reality of agriculture was quite different, accompanied as it was by recurrent famines and by diseases introduced to humankind from animal husbandry. Typically, some farmers became large landowners who could support less successful farmers by means of extending credit. So, well before coinage was developed by the Greeks in the seventh century BC, commoner Greeks often were in hock via taxes, rents, and debt to wealthy landowners, as indeed also occurred in the ancient Middle East. With the development of coinage, markets developed which led to some citizens being made wealthy from trade, in addition to the wealth created by holding concentrations of land. These traders demanded their fair share of political power, as did the tenants and debtors of the great landowners. Four distinct groups emerged depending upon different means of livelihood. No sooner had the nobles, the great landowning families, wrested power from the traditional kings than the oligarchs, made wealthy from trade, demanded power from the aristocrats. Both groups needed labor to ensure their source of wealth, which they obtained from the *thetes,* the poor free citizens, who themselves would soon demand their own share of political power through democracy. A fourth group made its living by supplying the products of their crafts. Whereas Greeks were once united by families, clans, and tribes, they now came to be divided by class. Gustave Glotz writes:

Thus, the individuals who were once united in the same group and dedicated to a common task were separated from each other by an increasing divergence of interests and, on the other hand, they felt that they were at one with other individuals who had once belonged to other groups, and had left them for the same reasons. Everything was ready for a class struggle. (p. 71)

The Pursuit of Prosperity

No sooner had Greeks embarked on a pursuit of prosperity with the return of civilization to Greece than a major agricultural crisis struck the Greeks owing to over-population. As part of the solution, wealthy landowners organized colonization programs to Ionia, the Mediterranean islands, and elsewhere in the region. These proved to be particularly profitable for the wealthy. Furthermore, new markets were created for the export of fabricated goods from the Greek mainland. The development of coinage did much to create internal markets satisfied by craftsmen working at producing arms and textiles, leather, pottery and other goods needed by Greeks for everyday and for military use, and luxuries for the wealthy or for export. Crafts such as metal working and armory were organized in large shops rather than shops of individual craftsmen. The actual work in these shops was done by thetes, slaves, freedmen (ex-slaves), and *metics*, foreigners from other Greek cities or even non-Greeks. Other important industries that were centered on the ports included shipbuilding and the import-export trade. Most building craftsmen worked on public works projects organized by the cities. Mines such as the silver mines at Laurium in Attica were public projects worked by slaves. Women workers worked at crafts such as weaving and wool working, pottery production, food production and preparation, midwifery, doctoring, and wet nursing. It should be noted, however, that the first and most important market to be facilitated, indeed lubricated by the development of coinage, was the slave trade. All this economic activity meant that some Greeks were made wealthy by trade rather than by the lands held by traditional aristocrats.

As part of his lawmaking in 594 BC, the aristocrat Solon formally divided Athenians according to their wealth, with political authority and military obligations increasing the higher a man sat in the social hierarchy. The *pentacosiomedimni* generated annual wealth of at least 500 measures of agricultural produce. Among these men were the officials, politicians, and generals who led Athenian society. The *hippeis* held 300 measures or more, and were required to provide a horse to serve as cavalrymen during warfare. This class produced many of the traders made wealthy by internal and foreign trade facilitated by horsecraft. The *zeugitae* produced 200 measures; they were free peasants who might own a pair of oxen. They were required to buy the arms and equipment necessary to serve as the heavy infantry, the hoplites. The thetes were the poor, free men who sold their labor to survive.

They served in warfare as mobile, light infantrymen, or as rowers and sailors in the Athenian navy.

Ever-increasing, general prosperity produced an elevator effect within Athenian society. Ample coinage based on gold and silver meant inflation with respect to the relationship between coins and commodities, such that Solon's legally endorsed social divisions became increasingly alienated from social realities. People moved up in social categories, and demanded an increasing share of political power to correspond to their new wealth. As well, they bridled at the public authority and privileges that accrued traditionally to people of the highest social level. This dynamic produced three social changes: firstly, oligarchs made wealthy from trade and crafts sought the political power held traditionally by large landowners; secondly, lower social orders pursued democracy as a strategy to improve their lot; thirdly, thetes who did not move up socially formed an ever-growing proletariat composed of wage-earning laborers, slaves, freedmen, and metics. Within this proletariat, actual work itself was performed increasingly by slaves and metics, so that to be free often came to mean one did not have to work. Instead, one could spend one's time at politics and public matters, for which free men even came to be paid.

Numbers

It is not easy to estimate the population of ancient Greece. We do know that population increased considerably in the period from the eighth century to the fifth century BC owing to increased prosperity brought by economic and agricultural development. In fact, the population of ancient Greece may have increased by as much as a factor of twelve from about 700,000 around 800 BC to about 8–10,000,000 by the mid-fourth century BC, according to the Danish demographer, Mogens Hansen. Estimates vary considerably for each polis, however, one might suggest that the population of the peninsula of Attica, where Athens was located, numbered about 350,000 at the middle of the fifth century BC. Of this figure, there were about 40,000 free, male citizens, of which about 18,000 were the lowest-ranking thetes. There were about 30,000 freedmen and metics, including women and children, about 115,000 slaves, including women and children, and another 130,000 women and children of free men. This large population made Athens the metropolis of ancient Greece.

The principal rival of Athens, Sparta, possibly had a population of about 300,000 in the Peloponnese peninsula, but with fewer citizen-soldiers. At about the same period during the mid-fifth century, there were about 16,000 spartiates, the male citizen-soldiers of Sparta, with roughly an equivalent number of spartiate boys in training. The largest population was that of the helots (more about them below), about 170,000 in all of Lakonia, the homeland of the spartiates, and in conquered Messenia, west of Lakonia. There were about 50,000 *perioikoi*, Lakonians like the helots who, instead of farming, worked as craftsmen, traders, and merchants. Much of their work involved the production of arms, without which the perpetual warfare and military preparation by spartiates would have been impossible. Spartiates were not permitted to do this craft work since the only fit employ for them was soldiering. A reasonable estimate might be another 50,000 women and children of the spartiates. Corinth had a comparable number of free, male citizens to that of Sparta, but probably not nearly the same number of helots.

The Greek response as populations grew in a polis and agricultural pressures increased was colonization or other forms of migration, such that the largest number of Greek city-states remained about 20–30,000 in population. The might have been as many as 1,500 city-states, although many were quite small indeed. In truth, the real value of estimating population size is to demonstrate the effects of long-term economic development upon the Greeks and the social composition of the poleis, and to provide comparative perspectives, rather than establishing actual figures with statistical veracity, a difficult task indeed.

Helotry

There was a special form of control of labor that permitted ruling classes to engage in the pursuit of wealth. Helotry refers to a form of servitude found throughout ancient Greece. Helots, as they were called originally in Sparta, comprised the majority of the Spartan population. They were the original inhabitants of the region of Lakonia in the southeast of the Peloponnese who were conquered by the spartiates. The latter hailed originally from only a few villages. Spartiates were granted equal portions of land upon their birth, which helots farmed for their Spartan masters. As well, helots farmed their own land, from which as much as one-half of their produce was paid as tribute to spartiates. Helots belonged in theory to the entire Spartan community rather than to individual masters. Since there seemed to have been significant gradations in wealth among the spartiates, there must have been breaching of this rule since some wealthy, powerful spartiates controlled a disproportionate number of helots.

There were several nuances within Spartan helotry. Firstly, *mothakes* were bastard sons of spartiates and helot women who were free, even if not citizens. They received a military education like their legitimate half-brothers, and might even serve in battle. Secondly, *mothones* were children of the relatively small slave population who served as personal slaves to spartiates, even carrying the armor and weapons of their masters in battle. The treatment of helots by spartiates was so cruel as to be legendary. Every fall, spartiate boys about to graduate from their military education set out on a manhunt of sturdy, young helot men, whom they murdered with impunity. In 425 BC, after battles in which helots distinguished themselves, the Spartans announced that 2,000 men, selected by the helots themselves, would be awarded laurels for their service, and even might be set free. Instead, once these helots were identified, Spartans figured they might be independent spirits and leaders who might lead a revolt, so they were 'disappeared' one by one by unknown means. Spartans ruled helots through a form of state terror that would have done proud to the Stalinists and fascists of the 20th century.

Helotry was a common form of servitude for the extraction of economic surplus from labor throughout ancient Greece. For instance, this same type of servitude was applied to people of northern Greece known as *penestae*. These people were the original inhabitants of a region of Greece called Boeotia; they were forced to pay rents to their Thessalian masters who had conquered them. There were also penestae in Macedon, northeast of Greece, and in Illyria, northwest of Greece, which might suggest that they may have been the same people, ethnically speaking. On Crete, the subjected, native farmers were called *klerotai*, while there were also slaves called *mnoitai*. There were similarly subjected, indigenous peoples around Byzantium called *bithynii*; *mariandynoi* around Heraclea Pontia; *kyllyrioi* near Syracuse in Sicily; *korynephoroi* in Sicyon; and *gymnetai* in Argos. There were also helot-like peoples attached to Corinth and to Epidaurus, and possibly to still other cities. Finally, in Athens, the *hectemoroi* were not technically helots, but were nominally free citizens who, owing unpaid debts, were required to turn over 5/6 of their production until their debts were paid in full. Under such terms of debt repayment, it is easy to see how these unfortunates and their descendants might be in permanent hock to their creditors, living a form of debt-peonage.

Slavery

As per elsewhere in the ancient world, Greek slaves originally were war captives who were spared their lives, which they then owed to their captors. Rather than keeping a large number of slaves, however, a victorious soldier would keep only a few for domestic service, farm work, or concubinage. The rest he would quickly sell as surplus to his immediate needs, in fact, avoiding obligations in the process since he would have to feed, clothe, and house his new slaves. This resale market for slaves was supplemented with the development and spread of coinage. There was good money to be made in the buying and selling of slaves. Foreign piracy of slaves and even enslavement of inconvenient, poor citizens also grew to fill market demand. Eventually, slaves were bred from the union of masters and slaves, or by the unions of slaves themselves. On the Aegean island of Delos, there was a vast emporium of foreign slaves for sale, where as many as 20,000 slaves might be available at times for sale.

The size of the slave populations varied from city to city. For instance, while Athens' population is estimated to have been about a third slave, there were fewer slaves in Sparta owing to Spartans' recourse to helotry to control labor. Greek slaves did every manner of work as farm workers, craftsmen, domestic servants, teachers and tutors, traders, minor public service workers such as policemen, miners, and laborers on public works projects. It was this labor that freed Greek citizens for higher cultural pursuits. In fact, both Plato and Aristotle wrote as much, arguing that a requirement to labor was incompatible with these higher pursuits. The disdain with which they wrote of workers was flagrant. It is thus that we can say that ancient Greece was indeed a slave society, a judgement we shall see later also applies to ancient Rome. Slavery and helotry were essential to the economy of ancient Greece. By no means, however, was the extraction of the economic surplus from labor not contested by the lowly. It is to this resistance that we now turn.

Iron Age Greece

After the collapse of Bronze Age, Mycenaean civilization, there were 400 years about which we have little knowledge since writing was absent from this period in Greece. It is suspected that Greeks retreated to earlier forms of semi-nomadic and nomadic existence during these 'dark ages'. Iron technique was introduced perhaps around 1000 BC, possibly by migrants from Anatolia or the Levant. The technique was present in Greece when the Dark Ages ended. In fact, iron was an important part of Greek civilization in the eighth century BC when literacy and civilization returned to Greece. Iron technique brought with it weaponry superior to that of the Bronze Age. In addition, the advent of hundreds of statelets in Iron Age Greece meant that warfare that used to be characterized by low-grade, frequent, and persistent skirmishing among small groups of warriors graduated to become state-sponsored warfare between larger armies of citizen-soldiers, whereby wars were settled by fewer but distinct, decisive, and bloody battles. Greeks were geographically isolated one from another by mountain ranges, valleys, peninsulas, bays, and the sea; the different economies and political interests of these regions clashed in spite of a common Greek culture. The existing geographic isolation and inter-city economic and political competition were now amplified by the increased severity of inter-city warfare during the Iron Age.

Elsewhere in the ancient world, the violence and brutality of the Iron Age led wise men to withdraw from society in small groups to contemplate God in order to develop wisdom about their violent, brutal world. They then returned to their societies with new moral claims in favor of social justice reinforced by new visions of religion, for example, Zoroaster in Persia, the Hebrew prophets, and the Buddha in India. The Greek responses to the violence and brutality of the Iron Age rather than being religious instead included democracy and the development over several centuries of philosophy, broadly defined as the pursuit of knowledge and the search for an ethically good life.

Homer

The first, historical inklings that someone recognized the brutality of the Iron Age in Greece came in a backhanded way in the epic poems credited to Homer, the *Iliad* and the *Odyssey*. In actual fact, these epics were not so much composed and written as they were probably redacted based on existing oral traditions. The Homeric guild of bards went about Greece singing of the heroic exploits of the Trojan War. It was a feat of oral memory recalling the exploits from the Bronze Age from over four centuries earlier. The feat was facilitated by the rhythm of poetry set to music. In the eighth century BC while Greece was emerging from its Dark Ages and literacy was growing among the Greeks, the poems were credited to a bard, real or legendary, named Homer.

The *Iliad* is a tale of the bloody battles and personal disputes that took place during a few months of a relentless, ten-year war between the Greeks and the Trojans. The senseless and pointless killings and tragedy persisted unabated. The men were driven by feuding goddesses who manipulated them like puppet-masters such that the men continued in their folly in order to slake their thirst for honor, glory, and revenge. They pursued their fate relently in the face of possible mortality. It was a relentless juggernaut irresistible to mortal men.

In the second book of the epic, however, a common soldier named Thersites does raise the whole folly of the enterprise. Thersites challenges the leaders of the Greeks including the lord, Agamemnon, son of Atreus:

> Son of Atreus, what's your problem, now?
> What do you lack?
> Your huts are stuffed with bronze,
> plenty of choice women too,
> all presents we Achaeans (Greeks) give you as our leader
> whenever we ransack some city.
> Or are you in need of still more gold,
> a ransom fetched from some horse-taming Trojan
> for his son tied up and delivered here
> by me or some other Achaean?
> Or do you want a young girl to stash away
> so you're the only one who gets to screw her?
> It's just not fair that you, our leader,
> have botched things up so badly for us,
> Achaea's sons. But you men, you soldiers,
> cowardly comrades, disgraceful people,
> you're Achaean women, not warriors.
> Let us sail home in our ships, leave this man,
> our king, here in Troy to enjoy his loot...

So we are clear which side is the right one in Thersites' challenge, Homer paints this portrait of Thersites, as clear as a lower class caricature can be:

> He was the ugliest:
> bow-legged, one crippled foot,
> rounded shoulders curving in
> toward his chest.
> On top, his pointed head
> sprouted thin, scraggly tufts of hair.
> (See Johnston for both quotations.)

In response to this effrontery, Odysseus cows and bullies Thersites, beating him to a pulp. The men laugh at Thersites' fate, but we readers do not. It is clear that the *Iliad* has been written from the perspective of members of the ruling class, too stupid to notice that they could stop the folly of war if only they could overcome their code of manly honor that sweeps them along as if they were unconscious.

Nevertheless, the second epic poem attributed to Homer, the *Odyssey*, redacted a generation or two later, does demonstrate social evolution, even if it is still a document of the ruling class. Women are full agents in the story of Odysseus' wanderings, and not just objects of desire over which men wage pointless wars, nor are women childishly feuding goddesses. In fact, the *Odyssey* is not so much a war story but a tale of Odysseus' adventures as he strives to reach homeland, hearth, wife, and family. With these elements, the poem thus does demonstrate social progress.

Hesiod

There is another bard, Hesiod, who clearly understands the impact of the Iron Age on Greece. It is thought by most scholars that the *Iliad* was redacted about 750 BC, while the *Odyssey* was assembled about 720 BC. Hesiod wrote his classic, *Works and Days*, possibly about 700 BC, although ancient Greeks thought that Hesiod lived and wrote before Homer. The poem is addressed to his brother, Perseus, who has sued Hesiod for a share of the legacy Hesiod has inherited from his father under circumstances and for reasons we don't fully understand. In the poem, Hesiod castigates his brother and instructs him about the best ways of farming to avoid the hunger and destitution facing Perseus. Hesiod's poem is sort of a farmer's almanac, providing a calendar of things that a farmer must do according to the time of year. Students of agriculture have been taken with Hesiod's homey farm advice, however, the social context of the poem is more consequential for us. Despite being a bard like Homer, Hesiod is decidedly not from the ruling class. He is a peasant, although perhaps a prosperous one who owns slaves and has plenty of food. *Works and Days*, however, in its less pedestrian moments, outlines a myth of five races of men that the gods have created, of men who have lived on this earth in five different eras: men who were like gold who lived with the gods; men who, being made of silver, were not so blessed; men of bronze; men who were like the demigods who had fought in the Trojan War; and finally, the current race of men of iron, of whose times Hesiod writes:

For now, the race is indeed of iron.
Not ever during the day will men cease from labor and grief;
not even at night will they cease from being oppressed...
They will be men for whom justice comes from the
strength of their hands.
One man will sack another's polis.
There will be no goodwill for him who keeps his oath,
not for the just, not for the good man,
but men will sooner honor the violence
of the man who is a doer of evils...
Shame will not exist.
The evil man will hurt the superior man
by speaking with crooked words,
and will swear an oath on them.
Envy, foul-mouthed, evil-rejoicing and ugly-faced,
will occupy all pitiful people....
Pernicious pains will be left behind for mortal people.
There will be no defense against evil. (Tandy and Neale, p. 73, 74)

Hesiod's crankiness is fueled by more than the particulars of his brother's legal case against him. His poem sounds like a social lament that represents the views of more than one person, perhaps of many peasants in Hesiod's times who were not happy with the state of society in the Iron Age. Tandy and Neale provide a credible, useful explanation of the social context in Hesiod's time for peasants like Hesiod. (p. 14–18) In Mycenaean civilization, villages were ruled by men called *basileis* (singular, *basileos*). The basileis, in turn, were ruled by the *wanax*, who was a sort of overlord such as Agammenon had been. Men such as Agammenon received produce from peasants from the villages to redistribute in times of need. This social organization was similar to the ancient societies of the Middle East. The village basileis resolved disputes, and served as the local voice of the overlord.

When the central Mycenaean authority was no longer there, the power of the basileis increased such that it was they who performed the central redistributive role. When trade with Asia increased in the eighth century after civilization returned to Greece, the basileis increased their wealth and power since they commanded the resources to benefit from the new economic activity. The basileis came to rely less on subordinate peasants, while they developed other sources of wealth. They were less interested in helping subordinates in times of need even if they did maintain their original political authority. This meant that peasants had to rely on each other or on kinfolk in times of need, in other words, particular and uncertain sources rather than the general, mutual obligations of previous generations and societies. Obviously, a man such as Hesiod being sued by his brother would have not been terribly impressed by the utility of kinfolk for relieving needs in times of stress. Thus, the reality of debts increased because of credit offered by the basileis and other newly wealthy. Since there was much variability in rainfall and diseases of crops, farm animals, and humans as well as other changing conditions from year to year, a peasant might very likely face the need to borrow in his lifetime, or to delay the delivery of produce owed to the basileis. This situation was temporarily relieved by the use of coinage which began among the Greeks around 600 BC, and which created cash markets for agricultural products that would have provided at least some relief from credit problems.

Agrarian Crisis

The debt situation among peasants was aggravated by a general, agrarian crisis that occurred as Greek civilization was returning after the Dark Ages. This crisis was in part the result of over-population, which was solved in typical, Greek fashion by migration. Wealthy Greeks increased their wealth by organizing colonies of Greeks throughout the Mediterranean world and on the coasts of the Black Sea. Peasants and other poor people would have been among the migrants to these colonies, which then provided ready markets for manufactured and luxury exports from the Greek mainland. Thus, colonizing Greeks used a strategy forever employed by people to improve their prospects and those of their children and grandchildren; they migrated.

The Hoplite Revolution

Another strategy for improving the welfare of the peasant class involved a frequent activity of the Greeks, warfare among the various poleis. First appearing in the city-state of Argos around 680 BC, the hoplite revolution greatly increased the power of peasants such as Hesiod. The hoplite was a citizen-soldier, often a peasant, who had sufficient wealth to pay for heavy armor and weapons. In battle, the hoplites stood in close order, protected by a wall of their shields, with their long spears protruding. Behind his shield, the hoplite carried a small sword and a knife for close combat. This method of warfare was adopted by Spartan citizen-soldiers around 650 BC, and then by other poleis thereafter. Hoplites would unite for a few, short days under the leadership of a *strategos*, a general the hoplites might have had a role in naming, in order to fight a short, decisive battle, it was hoped, to be followed by an immediate return to fields and homes. Since their military participation was vital and decisive to the outcome of inter-city political or trade disputes that often degenerated into warfare, the political power of the hoplites increased vis-à-vis the basileis and the wealthy and powerful. Serving as a hoplite allowed a man to participate as a full citizen in the public deliberations and offices of the poleis. In effect, this was an important causal element in the beginning of democracy.

Tyranny

Over a period of about 300 years, the Greek political system evolved from rule by the basileis to rule by a council of elders of the poleis, in effect, the local nobility, to rule by the oligarchs, the wealthy and powerful people made thus by the increase of economic activity in the Greek world. As stated above, these *nouveaux-riches* often ruled in their own interests without respecting traditional obligations to the whole community. So, individuals known as tyrants frequently came to power by means illegitimate or violent, with the support of peasants and other commoners. The Greek *tyrannos* did not carry the same, nasty implications as today, even if some tyrants did employ oppressive methods. Instead, the Greek word implied rule by an individual rather than the group rule of members of the ruling class favored by the latter. Thus, another strategy emerged for peasants such as Hesiod to increase their power, and to modify social conditions, that is, supporting the rule of tyrants.

The Great Law-givers

During the seventh century BC, certain wise men emerged among the Greeks. These were the original law-givers who established basic legal and political precepts that allowed the Greeks to make important social advances. In order to better understand this phenomenon, we consider an example that might be familiar to readers in North America, the case of the Iroquois. The Iroquois are the People of the Longhouse, or the *Haudenosaunee*. They tell an important legend about the Great Peacemaker, the prophet Deganawidah who, along with the warrior Hiawatha, sometime between 1450 and 1600 AD established a general peace and constitution to govern the peoples native to western New York and the northern Ohio valley. The peoples of the Iroquois had been constantly at war. Mohawks, Senecas, Onondagas, Oneidas, and Cayugas engaged in vengeful blood feuds, black magic, and cannibalism. Deganawidah and Hiawatha convinced the Iroquois to swear off these practices. These destructive behaviors were replaced with rituals of condolence that permitted the wronged to reach inner peace through consolation and grief. The wronged then had access to peaceful methods of obtaining justice, rather than producing endless cycles of blood revenge.

Furthermore, the five Iroquois peoples swore peace amongst themselves, then derived a just and equitable form of government to regulate disputes, and to reach consensus about community decisions. In addition, they allied themselves against their common enemies among other Iroquoian peoples: the Wendate, or Huron, the Eries, and the Neutrals, also known as the Pétun or Tobacco; and their enemies among the Algonkian-speaking peoples of the Canadian Shield and eastern North America. This gave the Iroquois League, at the time of first contact with Europeans, a formidable military force and a complex, practical, and relatively just system of government.

In a similar manner, the cities of ancient Greece benefited from the innovations of early lawgivers and peacemakers who established basic laws, usually written, that permitted social advances despite the brutality of the Iron Age. Two characters, Minos and Rhadamanthys, were legendary law-givers among the Cretans. During the Greek, archaic period, the phenomenon occurred firstly among the Greek colonies in the Mediterranean: Zaleucus in Italy; Charondas in Sicily; Demonax in Cyraenica, in eastern Libya; Aristarchus in Ephesus in Anatolia. For these peoples, basic constitutions had to be formally established by these law-givers since they had neither the benefit nor the encumbrance of the oral tradition of their homeland cities whence they hailed originally. This example then was repeated in cities on the Greek mainland beset with conflict among the social classes. Law-givers such as Philolaus of Corinth established laws at Thebes; Pittacus did the same at Mytilene; Andromadas at Chalcidice; Aritides at Kea; Pheidon at Corinth; and Phaleas at Chalcedon. In these cases, the original law-givers' task was to establish social peace among the warring classes of these poleis. These early law-givers also wrought basic social advances, among them the following:

- laws written for the first time in Greece, rather than being subjected to the whims of aristocrats or the vagaries of oral law and tradition;
- legal development with respect to certain matters such as commercial transactions, land holdings, and citizen participation in judicial bodies;
- methods of judicial dispute resolution to replace endless cycles of blood revenge, violence, and feuding; beginnings of social justice for the under-classes.

Readers might be familiar with three of the most important law-givers among the Greeks, whom we next consider: Lykurgus of Sparta, and Drako and Solon of Athens. Lykurgus was the son of one of the two basileis who jointly ruled ancient Sparta. It was he who developed the laws for the austere family and community life, and perpetual military training and preparation commonly associated with Sparta. Around 620 BC, when the people of Sparta asked Lykurgus to come to their aid, Sparta was riven by class divisions between wealthy creditors and poor debtors. Lykurgus divided land equally among the free members of the community. He instituted common meals for all Spartan citizens. All men were equal, so much so that spartiate men came to be known as the Equals. To limit personal property, Lykurgus issued to Spartans coins made of iron dipped in vinegar so as to make them brittle and worthless outside of Sparta. Gold and silver were banned in Sparta, thus the effect that coinage had elsewhere of increasing distinctions of wealth was limited somewhat by these measures. Of course, this was the Spartan ideal which was often observed only in its breach. As we shall see later, post-Lykurgus Sparta was not immune to the class divisions that plagued other Greek cities.

About the same time in Athens, Drako was an aristocrat who was called to address social problems in his city caused by perpetual blood feuding. This he did by installing a system of dispute resolution of appeal to the *aeropagos*, a body that included all current and former *archons*, the magistrates of Athens. In his written laws, Drako distinguished between murder and involuntary homicide or manslaughter, the penalty for the latter being exile. Unfortunately, his laws were otherwise excessively harsh, with the death penalty imposed even for petty offences, hence, the term draconian. Moreover, debtors were forced legally into slavery unless the debt was owed by a social superior to a social inferior.

It was another aristocrat, Solon, who produced a constitution for Athens that was less draconian, as it were. By then, the effects of Drako's provisions for debt had been growing for a generation. As well, in the absence of primogeniture among farmers whereby only one son, usually the eldest, inherited his father's land, land lots became too small to permit survival, making debts even more frequent. Increasingly, the two, lower social orders were in hock to the two, upper social orders. Solon introduced reforms that improved the lot of lower classes, the *zeugitae* and the *thetes*. All debts for which the person himself was pledged as security were cancelled and, henceforth, made illegal. Lands that had been lost by being pledged as security on debts were returned to their original owners. Interest on debts was lowered, and exports of all farm produce save olives were banned, thus ensuring a ready supply of food in Athens, which helped keep prices low for basic necessities. Being an aristocrat himself and a conservative, however, Solon resisted calls for a general land redistribution, and maintained the political authority of archons and the *aeropagos*. Furthermore, it was Solon who made the fourfold division of Athenian society we saw earlier formal and legal.

Craft Associations

We have already argued that is a reasonable assertion that craft associations in the ancient Middle East were necessary for transmitting craft skills and knowledge to the young of extended families of artisans. Moreover, there is also evidence to this effect in ancient Mesopotamia, the Levant, and Anatolia. In pre-Greek times, the region the Greeks called Ionia contained many cities organized by trade and craft associations, since this was the traditional way of organizing Anatolian cities. This was also the case in Hellenistic times in Ionia, according to the Russian scholar, Mikhail Rostovtzeff. (1957, p. 1066) There, the Greeks mixed their basic form of organization, the polis, with craft organizations. According to S. G. Wilson, there is some evidence of religious associations among aristocrats such as the *iobacchoi* in Athens and the cult of Asclepius at Pergamum in Anatolia. (p. 110) For the most part, however, once again according to Wilson, "...membership in associations was confined largely to the lower classes, typically, the urban poor, slaves, and freedmen." (p.10) Members of the ruling class generally did not need such associations since they met and associated regularly in the organs of the state in their capacities as magistrates and public officials.

In addition to their function of imparting skills to the young, associations met religious, funeral, social, recreational, and mutual assistance needs among commoners, including among metics and slaves. In the archaic and classical periods after the Dark Ages, Greeks organized themselves around their poleis, but when the central role of the polis was greatly reduced during the Hellenistic period after the death of Alexander the Great, associations increased in political and economic importance for the non-elite of Greek society. Charles Micallef presents evidence of associations acting as unions among Greek dancers, actors, musicians, artists, builders, masons, and sawyers. (p. 10) Rostovtzeff found similar evidence among Greek millers, cooks, and ditch-diggers (p. 323-324). Among the most active of these associations were those of theatre artists in regions such as Athens, Syracuse, Ionia, the Dardanelles, Pergamum, and Rhegion. In Greek Egypt, there were even federations of theatre artists grouped by district branch. We know that these *collegia*, as the Romans called the Greek associations, disturbed the ruling class since, from time to time during the Hellenistic era, the state banned these associations and, ultimately, organized them in official capacities as organs of the state. This allowed imperial and municipal authorities to control them better in order to ensure the fidelity of their services and to keep them apolitical.

Emancipation and Manumission

In ancient Greece, slaves worked alongside metics, freedmen, and thetes. Combined, they formed a proletariat who were usually paid the same low wages, although the slave also owed part of his earnings to his master. Even so, Greek slaves did not have the same, abjectly low, legal status of slaves in other societies. They did have some legal rights: they could marry, have families, and even own slaves themselves. Most importantly, they could earn sufficient money, credit, or other favor to buy their freedom from their master, even if the child of a slave woman usually remained slave. During the Hellenistic period under Roman rule, 'manumission', the Roman legal term, was quite common. It eased the general oppression within the slave society that was the ancient Greco-Roman world. Freedmen could rise high in society, even becoming wealthier than many citizens. Freedmen occupied important mercantile and public administration positions under Roman rule. Freedmen, however, could not become citizens with full political rights in the Greek cities, although their children and grandchildren could do so. At one point during the rule of Pericles, Athenians thought there were so many of these new citizens that they were disturbing the social and political order, so legislation was adopted that limited citizenry to men born of parents who were both free citizens.

In Sparta, there were several occasions when hundreds of helots volunteering for military service or logistical work on the battlefield were emancipated, as had been promised during periods of military crisis facing Sparta. They would then join the social order of the *perioeki*, the Lakonians who worked as merchants or crafts people in Sparta, to be then called *neodamodeis*. It was also possible for helots to purchase their freedom or to become free if they submitted themselves or were volunteered as boys for Spartan military education.

Popular Revolts

One of the obvious ways that the downtrodden historically have tried to improve their lot and resist the powers that be have been popular uprisings. To many classicists and ancient historians, a putative absence or, at least, paucity of such revolts is a sign that the lower classes accepted the rule and domination by others over them. Hardly surprisingly, this is not a view this author shares. Firstly, social domination is a phenomenon supported by ideology and the brute force of armies, the law, prisons, and the rest of the state apparatus, so that the notion of acceptance by the dominated is quite overstated. Secondly, even with shortfalls in evidence, we do know of many popular revolts in ancient Greece, and we list some of them below. Thirdly, in many provincial or tribal revolts against Rome, the popular classes were participants, taking sides, fighting and influencing the course of events even if the revolts might be proto-national revolts. Similarly for factional fighting within ruling classes in which the common people were vital players who influenced the course of events, and whose support the factions deliberately sought, even if the issues at play and the struggles seemed *prima facie* irrelevant to the lower classes.

Proceeding chronologically then with popular revolts among commoner Greeks, around 657 BC, the ruling oligarchy of Corinth was overthrown by a popular tyrant, Kypselos. At some unknown date, perhaps in the 7th century BC in the Ionian city of Miletus, wealthy landowners and the poor waged a bloody class war. Andrew Lintott describes the brutality of the conflict as recounted by the first Greek historian, Herodotus:

> The working people were for a time victorious, and had the children of the wealthy exiles trodden to death by oxen on threshing floors. In return, the rich burned everything they could get hold of belonging to the poor, including their children, and eventually prevailed in the war (p. 55).

Greek poleis were comprised of tribes joining forces, tribes that were composed of families and clans that had inter-married and co-mingled. So, vicious class warfare occurred among people who might have grown up in proximity or even have been related, even if it was as distant cousins. About 600 BC, ruling oligarchies on the islands of Lesbos and Samos were overthrown by popular tyrants. Sometime after the start of the fifth century BC, a popular, democratic revolt in Syracuse took place in which the class of large landowners and aristocrats known as *gamorai* were expelled from the Greek colony. Later in the same century, in the Greek colony city of Croton in southern Italy, the ruling oligarchy was expelled in a similar manner. There were popular revolts during the Peloponnesian War in 427 BC in Korkyra and Mytilene. In 415 BC at Leontini, the rural proletariat revolted against the local aristocracy, once again according to Lintott (p. 258-261).

During the Hellenistic period, popular rebellions were commonplace. Free laborers were becoming ever poorer owing to unemployment and under-employment, competition from slave labor, and diminishing wages. Of these popular rebellions, Michael Grant writes:

> When internal rebellions occurred, as frequently happened, it is often unclear if and to what extent social protest was involved. Certainly, such uprisings were political, against the Hellenistic governments which, between them, had organized the destruction and abolition of Greek democracy. Yet, these movements did contain a social element, as well. For the situation of the Hellenistic poor was bad. Mass starvation was an ever-present threat, and every Hellenistic state...stood in fear of revolution; understandably, since we know of no fewer than sixty such uprisings, and there must have been others. (p. 68)

Agathokles and Aristonikos

There are two personalities in Greek colonies who led popular rebellions, and merit special consideration, Agathokles of Syracuse and Aristonikos of Pergamum. Agathokles was a potter from Syracuse who became a soldier. In 333 BC, he married the widow of his wealthy patron, which greatly increased his own personal power and wealth. He twice tried to overthrow the oligarchy that ruled Syracuse and twice failed; each time he was banished from the city. In 317 BC, he returned to Syracuse with a mercenary army, and defeated the oligarchy in a bloody campaign in which about 10,000 were killed or banished, after which he established a democratic constitution. He then conquered most of Sicily, which he ruled as a popular tyrant, even deigning to call himself king of Sicily. His power brought him into conflict with Carthage which also ruled a part of Sicily. Carthage eventually defeated him, but only after Agathokles had won several military victories. In 306, he concluded a peace with Carthage, which allowed him to continue ruling the Greek part of Sicily. On his death bed, he restored democracy to Syracuse because he knew his sons did not share his views, and he did not want them to succeed him. Agathokles is presumed to have died sadly, giving up his ultimate dream of bringing a voice to the people of the world.

In Pergamum in Asia Minor when the basileus Attalus III died, the city became Roman territory as per its late leader's last will, written in response to Roman pressure. Nevertheless, a local philosopher, Aristonikos, an uncle of Attalus III, claimed the throne for himself and the citizens of Pergamum. He promised to establish a city of the sun called *Heliopolis*, where all including slave and poor might live in freedom and equality. When the stoic philosopher, Gaius Blossius of Cumae in southern Italy, heard of Aristonikos' venture the former teacher and advisor to the Roman popular hero, Tiberius Gracchus, joined Aristonikos. Of course, the Romans had other ideas, and twice sent military forces to subdue Aristonikos, the second time successfully in 129 BC. The rebel was executed in Rome. When he heard of this, Blossius committed suicide.

In spite of the ultimate failures of each of these men, they might be characterized as revolutionaries who were centuries ahead of their times. Just as importantly, in the name of the downtrodden, they were popular leaders who tried to represent politically the poor and the enslaved of the Greek world. The lowly thus were able to claim another means of trying to improve their lot, that is, bloody revolt.

Rebellion in Sparta

The facts that Sparta was a military society through and through, and that it maintained its control over the helots of its native Lakonia and neighboring and conquered Messenia with a legendary program of terror, might lead one to believe that Sparta's social régime was unassailable. In fact, Spartan society as organized by Lykurgus was as fragile as that of any city-state in ancient Greece. Lykurgus had established a society of equals among spartiates with equal land plots assigned to each spartiate from birth, lands that were inalienable. We let Claude Mossé describe, however, what actually happened.

> In actual fact, Spartan communism was theoretical rather than real. The city would have had to have cut itself off from the rest of the Greek world in order to maintain it. This was hardly possible, and from the 4th century BC onwards, Sparta was the scene of disturbances caused by an increasingly unequal distribution of land; in the third century, attempts at revolution even involved the helots. (p. 10)

Thus, owing to trade, warfare, and alliances with other Greek cities during the Peloponnesian and Persian wars, Sparta was not an island, and was subject to foreign influences upon its utopian society of equals. The case of Cinadon and his conspiracy in 397 BC provides an example of one mechanism that made Sparta as socially divided and restless as any other ancient Greek community. Cinadon was a successful soldier from a poor background who led an unsuccessful conspiracy to overthrow the oligarchy that ruled Sparta, a conspiracy that even included helots. In spite of being an educated spartiate, Cinadon had slipped into poverty as did many others from his class in Sparta. The immediate cause was his inability to pay the monthly *syssitia*, the fee required to support participation at the common meals of the spartiates. This fee, even to a modern, appears significant: 77

litres of barley, 39 litres of wine, three kilograms of cheese, 1.5 kilograms of figs, and money for the purchase of meat. Failure to make this payment put one into the category of the *hypomeiones*, inferiors who lost their rights as citizens, even if they did remain nominally free. This Cinadon could not accept. One time in the agora, Cinadon pointed out to a co-conspirator that of the 4,000 citizens present, only forty were equals, the rest being social inferiors like Cinadon. According to this co-conspirator, who, in fact, denounced Cinadon to the authorities, Cinadon nursed a profound and passionate hatred of the equals. Cinadon and his associates in potential revolution were executed in a most horrible fashion, thus ending abruptly both the career of this would-be revolutionary and the revolution he had planned.

In actual fact, the Spartan régime was unstable, even from the point of view of its control of the helots. The initial spartiates had come from two small tribes in Lakonia, each of which occupied two villages. The initial constitution had required two basileis, one from each tribe. The two tribes then submitted all of Lakonia to their military control, but left the Lakonians in control of their farms if they paid one-half of their produce to the spartiates in return for peace, an extortion racket if ever there was one. The Spartans then turned to their western neighbors on the Peloponnese peninsula, and submitted them during the first Messenian war between 740 and 720 BC, as a result of which Messenians also came to serve the Spartans as helots. The Messenians revolted in 650 BC during what is qualified as the second Messenian war. As a result of this war, Lykurgus installed his reforms in Sparta to create a society of equals among spartiates and to turn the aristocratic body, the ephors or elders, originally advisors to the two basileis, into a senate elected by a citizen assembly of all Spartans. These measures were organized in return for the military services of the common people of Sparta to help defeat the Messenians. After an earthquake in 464 BC, the Messenians revolted once again, this time with the support of the Lakonian helots as well. This third Messenian war was ultimately unsuccessful after 11 years of conflict. It was after this revolt that the Spartans introduced their infamous methods of terror to maintain social order among the helots, including the annual hunt and murder by young spartiates of young helot men. In 372 BC, Messenians finally gained their liberty with the military aid of a victorious army from Thebes, at the time the leading rival city to Sparta. The blow to Sparta by the Thebans was significant as Sparta lost a third of its territory and half of its helots.

In the latter half of the third century BC, the free poor citizens of Lakonia finally gained their freedom with the help of two reformers, the basileis, Aegius IV and Cleomenes III, and the tyrant, Nabis. Aegis IV was one of the two traditional basileis who ruled Sparta between 245 and 241 BC. When he came to power, there were only 700 families of remaining descendants of the original spartiates whose men were still free citizens. The original law that granted equal allotments of land to each spartiate at birth had been repealed. There were now fewer than 100 families that owned land estates, while the remaining citizens were poor debtors. With the support of the poor, Aegis IV proposed the abolition of all debts, a new partition of lands among citizens, and the provision of land estates to a number of the perioiki, Lakonian merchants and craftsmen. While debts were indeed abolished, the wealthy successfully resisted the land redistribution scheme, and eventually obtained the execution of Aegis IV, the first time the Spartans had ever killed a basileus.

Cleomenes III ruled Sparta from 235 to 222 BC. He managed to put into effect Aegis IV's land redistribution scheme. He also trained as spartiates 4,000 helots, which greatly increased the military power of Sparta. Unfortunately, Cleomenes suffered a resounding military defeat in 222, whereupon he fled to safety in Alexandria. A new pharaoh placed Cleomenes under house arrest, from which he managed to escape. He then fomented revolution unsuccessfully in Greek Egypt, which led him to commit suicide in 219 BC.

In our third example, the tyrant Nabis usurped power from the traditional, dual basileis of Sparta, then had them executed. These two men were the last in their lines of rulers. Nabis ruled as a popular tyrant from 207 to 195 BC, while continuing the land policies of Aegis IV and Cleomenes III. He even went further in this regard by exiling the remaining wealthy landlords, and redistributing their lands to poor citizens. He freed slaves to make them citizens although he maintained helotry. Nabis' policies led him afoul of Rome, which led to his demise. Nonetheless, according to the Roman historian, Livy, Nabis remained defiant. Livy quoted him commenting about the Romans:

> Do not demand that Sparta conform to your own laws and institutions. You select your cavalry and infantry by their property qualifications, and desire that a few should excel in wealth, and the common people be subject to them. Our lawgiver did not want the state to be in the hands of a few, whom you call the senate, nor that any one class should have supremacy in the state. (Ali et al., p. VIII)

Nabis was the last leader of an independent, powerful Sparta, even if he had a bad press among contemporary Greeks from the ruling class. The historian Polybius referred to him and his followers as a "crowd of murderers, burglars, cutpurses, and highwaymen."

Slave Revolts

Given the ubiquity of the institution of slavery in ancient Greece, it is perhaps surprising that there were not more slave revolts than there were. It was a policy of slaveholders to try not to put slaves together who spoke the same language the better to prevent revolt. This might have had a temporary damping effect on rebellion, however, since slaves would have to learn the language of their masters anyway, it would not have taken long for slaves to start talking, conspiring, and planning amongst themselves, even if in Greek and not in their native tongues. Conservatives put the lack of slave revolts as a sign of acceptance of the institution of slavery as normal even by slaves themselves, and by a refusal of free, poor citizens to come to the aid of their slave brethren. In actual fact, slaves and free poor often worked together and participated together in craft and other associations, wherein they developed solidarity. There were indeed some revolts of free, poor citizens, who had more latitude for political and social protest in which slaves and helots might take part.

Perhaps the real reason there were not more slave revolts than actually took place is that maintaining the system was a primary occupation of the polis. Armies, legal systems, prisons, and other elements of the state worked to maintain social order among the lowly including slaves, especially since slave labor was so vital to Greek culture and the Greek economy. Furthermore, since the Greeks were almost constantly at war, there was a constant renewal of the slave population from war captives. As well, slaves also came regularly from other sources: piracy, kidnapping of poor people, debt servitude, and slave breeding.

For their part, slaves had implicit, covert tools at their disposal short of armed revolt in order to struggle against their situation such as working slowly and using other informal means in the workplace. Most importantly, slaves could always flee, one of the oldest methods of avoiding danger and stress, while attempting to improve one's lot in life. Slaves were constantly escaping, melting into the populace since they usually were indistinguishable from Greeks or were, in fact, Greeks themselves. Runaway slaves might leave for other cities or countries, sometimes whence they hailed. Slaveholders and states spent considerable resources preventing flight, and returning slaves to their rightful masters. For conservatives, the fact of few armed revolts means that the institution of slavery was never really challenged politically, militarily, morally, or philosophically, although we shall see later that this was simply not true. The fact that slaves were trying to avoid the effects of slavery by their own actions was their argument against the system, even if they might be illiterate or uneducated and, thus, usually did not write about their opposition to slavery. Even so, the stoic philosophical movement among Greeks, nevertheless, did include renowned educated and literate freedmen such as Epictetus who did write about the brutality of slavery and their opposition towards it.

We do know, however, about a handful of slave revolts among the ancient Greeks. In 414 BC during the Peloponnesian war while an Athenian army was besieging Syracuse, the poor people of Syracuse including slaves revolted, while 300 slaves from Syracuse actually joined the Athenian enemy in order to gain their freedom. During the same war the next year 20,000 slaves from the silver mines in Laurium, south of Athens, escaped Athenian control to join the Spartans. In 388 BC, Iphrakates led a failed revolt among slaves on the Aegean island of Chios. During the next century, a slave named

Drimakos led a successful slave rebellion among slaves on Chios, who fled to the mountains to set up their own free communities. These are known as maroon communities, and they appeared continually throughout the history of slavery. In the Hellenistic period, according to Graham Stevenson, there were more slave revolts in Attica in 198 BC, again two years later in Macedon, and on the Aegean island of Delos in 185 BC. The last was especially significant since Delos was the site of a giant emporium for the sale and purchase of slaves brought there from all over the Mediterranean world. There was another revolt of mining slaves at Laurium in 134 BC, and yet again around the beginning of the first century BC. Finally, Rome suffered a major setback during the revolt of 134–132 BC in Greek Sicily when a slave from Syria named Eunus set up a maroon community composed of rebel slaves. This led to a major war that was well-documented by Roman historians; it will be examined in more detail in the chapter about ancient Rome.

War and Social Advances

For all the pain and suffering that war entailed for the ancient Greeks, it was also a motor of social advance for the lower classes. An analogy from our own times might be useful. Despite the horrors of WWII, the radicalism of Allied soldiers and of workers on the home front brought important social change that workers had been seeking for generations: recognition of labor rights including the rights to organize and to strike as well as many social policies and programs that provide a social wage to workers under capitalism. In a comparable fashion, Andrew Lintott writes:

> War was indeed the main cause of political change in the ancient world at this period, especially for the smaller cities. Their inward-looking exclusiveness and solidarity tended to be conservative, and (they) only underwent change through convulsions. (p. 262)

The social stress of war brought internal divisions based on social class to a head. Furthermore, it increased the bargaining power of the lower orders. The previous, low-scale warfare during the Dark Ages conducted by bands of warriors had been transformed under Greek civilization into wars between competing armies composed of citizen-soldiers. Witness the hoplite revolution in the mid-seventh century which ensured political rights for citizens who could afford the equipment used by heavily-armed infantrymen. Popular tyrants who served the needs of the lower classes often came to power by using mercenary soldiers who had been exiled from other Greek cities during social convulsions often caused by warfare. Finally, the recourse to poor, free citizens to man the ships of Athens turned Athens into a major naval power that greatly increased the political store of the common man. This was an important, contributing element in the development of Athenian democracy, which indeed spread throughout ancient Greece partly owing to the imperial, naval power of Athens.

Athenian Democracy

A major part of the social legacy of the ancient Greeks to the Western world is democracy. Greek democracy, however, was not electoral, representative democracy. Rather, it was direct democracy whereby the citizenry was directly involved in ruling and in all manner of public decisions in the assemblies and the decision-making bodies of the city-states. The advent of Greek democracy was the result of a *longue démarche* over generations of social conflict between oligarchies of wealthy and powerful people and the rest of the free citizenry of craftsmen, poor laborers, and the peasantry. The first achievement in the secular development of democracy was balancing power among classes somewhat; the second involved the development of direct rule by the *demos*, the people. Of course, modern-day commentators about Greek democracy are right to point out that even if free women enjoyed the legal rights of citizens, they had no political rights nor power. The same can be said of children and adolescents, slaves and metics, even if, as with women, legal rights slowly developed, offering some legal and political recognition, status, and protection to these people.

In Greek democracy, most officials were randomly selected, rather than being elected. This was so that wealth and renown could not increase the power of some vis-à-vis the lower classes or, at least, this was the ideal. The main skill that swayed people in political debate was oratory, a skill that Greeks valued highly, a skill for which some trained rigorously. It was also, hypothetically at least, accessible to all. Over the course of a man's life, he might serve several times in different offices, and would take part in all the major decisions of the polis—to declare war, conclude peace, set taxation levels, supervise public works and finances—indeed the entire public administration of the city-state. As such, the legacy of Greek democracy has inspired modern-day liberals, radicals, anarchists, and socialists, all of whom can claim political ancestry in Greek democracy.

We know most about Athenian democracy for several reasons. Firstly, many of the literate observers who described Greek democracy were Athenians and / or supporters of Athens in the endless political, economic, and military conflicts among the Greek poleis. Secondly, Athens had the largest population of any Greek city; it was, in fact, the Greek metropolis. Thirdly, many city-states established their constitutions in imitation of the Athenian model, or borrowed from its features when writing constitutions. Athens united many poleis under its leadership in the Delian League during the war with the Persians. This organization was called so because its treasury was located on the island of Delos before being relocated to Athens. The Delian League eventually became a tool of Athenian imperialism, threatening Sparta with control of the Peloponnese, which led to bitter resentment from other cities and war between Athens and Sparta and their respective, allied factions and poleis. In actual fact, in some cases, democracy spread throughout Greece because Athens installed it in many cities over the objections of local oligarchies. For Athenians, democracy offered rule and power (the Greek term was *kratos*) to the *demos*. This last term, according to Christopher Blackwell, had several meanings: village, the smallest administrative unit of the polis, and the people generally, the body of citizens. A young man who reached twenty years of age enrolled in his deme's assembly list, which permitted him to serve in the offices and in the central institution of Athenian democracy, the *ekklesia*, or assembly.

Development of Athenian Democracy

We saw earlier that towards the end of the 7th century BC, Drako established the first penal and civil law codes. As harsh as the codes were, they did establish a difference between murder and involuntary homicide, the punishment for the latter being exile. Thus, Drako's laws did help arrest the endless cycles of blood feuds and violence in response to the original violence, even if the state still could not prosecute nor apply mercy in application of laws where punishments were specified in law. In 594 BC, an aristocrat named Solon, whom we met earlier in the discussion about debt relief, was elected archon, an annual position in which were vested military, executive, judicial, and religious powers. As part of a constitutional reform, Solon increased the power of the assembly, established a council of 400 to represent hoplites, and set up jury courts to hear legal cases. Solon extended political rights to the metic *demiourgoi* who worked as craftsmen working as armorers, smiths, carpenters, and potters. A further agreement reached in 580 BC set up a council of archons with one member from each of the original, four tribes who would then select the chief archon. This council also included three representatives from the peasantry and two from the *demiourgoi*. The ultimate result of Solon's reforms was to balance somewhat the power of the traditional, patriarchal tribes with powers for the lower social orders.

A further improvement in the political status of the lower orders occurred in the mid-sixth century BC when a popular tyrant named Pisistratos came to power in Athens with the support of peasants and craftsmen. According to the French scholar, Claude Mossé, Pisistratos helped peasants by arranging for the state to lend seed and tools, by offering grants to plant olive trees, and by redistributing lands Pisistratos had expropriated from his political enemies. (p. 12) His program of public building projects provided employment to Athenian craftsmen, and attracted skilled metic artisans to the city. Pisistratos was succeeded by his sons, but they did not have the common touch nor the support that Pisistratos enjoyed. His son, Hippias, was overthrown by an aristocrat named Kleisthenes with the help of the latter's tribe and the Spartans. Once in power, Kleisthenes proclaimed that all citizens henceforth would be part

The *hetairia* were political associations which grouped the *hetairioi*, or the associates, around a politician whom they supported and whose clients they became. Thus, the entire demos became supporters of Kleisthenes and, in exchange, obtained from him the means of...exercising political power (p. 8, 9).

Another archon named Isagoras, however, opposed Kelisthenes' program, and appealed to a basileus of Sparta, Cleomenes. Together they were able to effect the exile of Kleisthenes and his clan, but the latter's popular supporters rebelled and obtained, in turn, the exile of Isagoras and the return of Kleisthenes to power. After this civil commotion, Kleisthenes began to reform Athens' government in order to avoid repetitions of recent events. He eliminated the four, original tribes based on clan and family, and organized citizens into ten civic divisions based upon their demes, that is, their village or place of residence, each of which comprised 150-300 citizens. The demes were then organized into thirty groups called *trittyes*, of which ten were assigned to each of three geographic regions in Attica: Athens itself, the coastal region, and an inland region comprising the rest of Attica. The trittyes thus included demes from each of the geographic regions. The point of these changes was to break the power of the wealthy families of each geographic sector in order to reorganize social solidarity around demes and around new groupings called *phylai*, rather than around the four traditional tribes. Thus, a citizen at one and the same time was part of his deme, a regional grouping, and the tenfold division of the polis. In view of such complexity, rather than being a tribesman, the citizen came to be and think of himself, above all, as an Athenian. Kleisthenes also reorganized the council of 400 to become a council of 500 called the *boulé*, comprised of fifty members from each of the ten civic divisions. He also reorganized the legal system such that 5,000 jurors were selected for each day of court hearings, 500 from each division. Finally, Kleisthenes introduced ostracism, by which citizens could vote to exile a man from the city for ten years in order to ensure that a politician with too much political power might be defanged politically. Kleisthenes characterized his reforms as being productive of the quality of *isonomia*, or equality of political rights.

The next great reformer in Athens was Ephialtes, a general in Athens' Aegean navy. In 463 BC, after an earthquake had enticed Sparta's helots to rebel, Sparta asked for the aid of Athens to put down the revolt, a request that received the support of the leading oligarch in Athens, Cimon. Ephialtes led, originally in vain, the opposition to the Spartan request. Ephialtes then began attacking the *areopagos*, the conservative body of ex-archons that, in effect, ruled Athens under Cimon's leadership. He obtained the prosecution of leading members of this body for maladministration. He then got adopted reforms that divided the jurisdictions of the *areopagos* among the ekklesia, the boulé, and the popular courts. Cimon was ostracized, after which Ephialtes' faction now was firmly in control of Athens. Lest one delude oneself into thinking that democracy had been obtained relatively peacefully after all, it should be noted that Ephialtes was soon assassinated in 461 by a plot of the oligarchs. Thus, the march to democracy continued, but only with violence and struggles of the commoners against the oligarchs.

Ephialtes was succeeded by one of his allies, the famed Pericles, under whom democracy flourished at the same time as did Athens' culture and imperialism. Over the course of his life, as was common in Athenian democracy, Pericles occupied many positions including general. It was, however, mostly with his skill as an erudite, intelligent orator that he was able to influence the course of events over the thirty years of his public life from 462 to his death in 429 BC. Pericles' politics could be summed up as Athenian democracy, public works in Athens including works of great art and craftmanship, and Athenian imperialism vis-à-vis other Greek cities. After Ephialtes was assassinated, Pericles became the democratic leader. One of his first actions was to obtain legislation that permitted anyone to serve as one of the leading magistrates of the polis, that is, one of the nine archons regardless of wealth or family. Next, Pericles made the assembly the central decision-making body of the state, with sole approval or veto power over all public decisions. Before the time of Pericles, anyone born of at least one Athenian parent was a citizen. This went back to the time of Solon, who had admitted many metics and half-Athenians to the citizenry. Pericles closed this provision, thus limiting citizenship to only the 40,000 people born of two Athenian citizens, rather than the figure of 60,000 citizens it had become before Pericles' rule. The reformer gave the assembly ultimate power over all 1,100 officials of the state, 100 of whom were elected and 1,000 of whom were chosen by lot. Finally, Pericles instituted the practice of paying citizens for participation in the assembly and for occupying public offices. This permitted the poor as well as peasants and craftsmen to participate in public affairs since they could then leave their farms and workplaces without financial penalty in order to participate in public life and democracy.

After three decades, the Peloponnesian War ended with Sparta victorious over Athens. In 404 BC, Sparta installed in Athens an oligarchic government known as the régime of the Thirty Tyrants. It lasted only until the next year when Athenians led by the general Thrasylubus, the archon Eucleides, and the democratic forces chased away the pro-Spartan oligarchs to reinstate democracy. Eucleides instituted an amnesty by which anyone who had committed a crime either during or before the rule of the Thirty Tyrants could not be prosecuted, thus undoing the legislation of the short-lived oligarchy. Eucleides then installed some minor changes to the democratic constitution of Pericles. This democracy is the constitution of Athens that has come down in history to us. It is the ultimate Athenian democracy, the workings of which we now consider.

The Workings of Eucleides' Democracy

The heart of the Athenian system of democracy was the assembly of citizens, for which quorum was 6,000. The assembly had originally been an appeal body with respect to decisions of the archons. It was now the prime democratic body that voted on laws, decrees, and treaties. Any participant in the assembly could initiate a debate. The assembly voted in the occupants of the hundred positions for which election was required. The occupants of the other thousand public positions were chosen randomly using a special machine, a kleroterion, that apparently would have done proud to any modern-day casino. The council, the boulé, was composed of 500 citizens, fifty selected by lot from each of the ten civic divisions, each to serve for a year. The council served as the administrative body of the city, and included a randomly selected executive that set agendas for discussions of the council and the assembly. On a day when there were criminal or civil court cases to hear, 6,000 citizens from the assembly were chosen by lot to serve on a popular tribunal called the heliala, from which jurors were selected to serve for the day. These jurors also served as examiners of magistrates and their performances, including those of archons, generals, and all other magistrates, whether randomly selected or elected. The *heliala* also selected members by lot to vote about proposed laws or decrees before they went to the popular assembly. The ancient body known as the *areopagos*, composed of current and former archons, which effectively had ruled Athens in early times, was reduced to the role of judging homicide cases. The democratic system of Athens was a marvel to behold for many reasons:

- its complexity, detail, consistency, and logic;
- its ultimate reliance on the assembly of all citizens who wished to participate as the ultimate arbiter of public matters;
- the division of tasks among democratic bodies, each of which was left to do its own job while, at the same time, being subjected ultimately to review by the general citizenry;
- the attention to ensuring the random selection of people to perform most public functions;
- the attention to ensuring that no one man or faction could develop overwhelming power owing to term limits and restrictions about occupying most posts twice or for consecutive terms;
- the protections against the temptations of bribery or corruption;
- the separation of administrative, executive, legislative, court, ceremonial, and religious functions;
- the popular education occasions offered by political and intellectual participation of the general citizenry, such that democracy served as a continuing school of adult education for ordinary Greeks;
- the ultimate control by the common man the system provided, especially when compared to the self-serving rule of wealthy and powerful aristocracies and oligarchies that had marked earlier political development, and which Athenian democracy was designed to counter.

This description of the workings of Eucleides' democracy might be missing certain details, but readers who want to know more can consult the Wikipedia essay about Athenian democracy, including its excellent flow chart entitled "Constitution of the Athenians in the 4th century BC." In conclusion, when one studies the workings of democracy in ancient Athens, one can see why it has been viewed as a marvel by students of history, public administration, political science, and law as well as offering useful historical models for political parties and activists, working-class militants, and exponents of local and direct, participative democracy.

Unfortunately, the edifice of Athenian and Greek democracy all came crashing down with the conquest of Greece by Philip of Macedon who had the active support of local oligarchic factions in the Greek cities. After the death of Philip's son, Alexander the Great, political rule in Greece devolved to a Greek named Antipater, who greatly reduced the political saliency of the Greek cities. For Athens, the cradle of Greek democracy, Antipater established a constitution whereby political participation required wealth of at least 2,000 drachmas, a considerable sum that limited political participation to only about 5,000 people. Oligarchy was thus legally formalized as the political system in Greece. During the Hellenistic period, Rome preferred to deal with these local oligarchies to help ensure its dominion over the Greeks. The fortunate western world, however, still benefits from the legacy of Athenian democracy.

Greek Philosophy

The Greeks developed philosophy as means of defining and living the good and ethical life as a counter to the violence and brutality of the Iron Age. In fact, ancient Greeks' inquiry and thought were central to the development of philosophy in the Western world, and to the pursuit of knowledge, in general. One of the fathers of Western philosophy was Socrates, who lived in Athens about the time of its zenith of power. A masterful teacher, his methods have descended to us as valid techniques of logic and inquiry still in use today. This despite none of his writings having survived if Socrates indeed wrote, other than being a paragon of oral methods of inquiry. We only know of him from the writings of others including his students, Plato and Xenophon. Hailing from the artisan class, Socrates was the son of a stonecutter and a midwife. He himself was a master stonecutter, and also acquitted himself as a valiant and successful soldier and occupant of public office before deciding to devote himself entirely to philosophy and teaching. Socrates is famous for having been a gadfly in the side of Athenians, perpetually questioning conventional wisdom and the powerful about ideas of justice. One of his targets was the-then prominent notion among Greeks that might makes right. He also reputedly argued that slavery was an outrageous theft since it stole a man's life and liberty. (Langston, p. 1) Socrates is famous for arguing that the wise man knows little and admits it, rather than pumping himself up with ideas that do not stand up to logic and inquiry. That Socrates was among the fathers of Greek philosophy might be surmised by the fact that Greek philosophers are characterized as being either pre-Socratic or post-Socratic.

There were several philosophical strands that demonstrate the legacy of Socrates. It might be argued that these strands provided some succor to the common people, or were at least relevant to the common people and their pursuit of their interests, even if indirectly since the latter usually did not participate in the philosophical enterprise themselves. The first strand is the practical and scientific bent to Greek philosophy, as demonstrated by Archimedes and others who addressed practical problems that craftsmen might face in their work. For the two great philosophers, however, Plato and Aristotle, the manual labor that was the lot of craftsmen, laborers, and peasants was an object of disdain. As for slavery, for the great duo, it was an essential institution that permitted the progress of human culture, even if Plato's master, Socrates, had questioned the validity of the institution. In the Greek context, the assertions of Plato and Aristotle were certainly true since Greek cities including Athens to varying degrees were slave societies. Moreover, in poleis where there were fewer slaves such as Sparta, manual work was the lot of helots or their equivalents elsewhere.

Two philosophical movements owe much to Socrates, and are of some interest with respect to the concerns of popular classes. The first of these was the movement known as cynicism. The founder of cynicism was an Athenian named Antisthenes, who lived from 445-365 BC. His father was a citizen, and his mother was a slave from Thrace. In the opinion of Antisthenes, Socrates was wiser than he, so he asked him to become his master. Nonetheless, Antisthenes did teach at the Cynosarges gymnasium, established to serve the bastards of Athens. The basic tenets of cynicism were simplicity, non-materialism, and life lived in nature and poverty since the material was irrelevant to the search for truth and the ethical way to live. Socially speaking, cynics believed that all men were brothers, while they also were opposed to war and slavery. While they were not really combatants on behalf of the poor and lowly, they did live as did the poor and lowly. They offered a counter-culture to Greek society as it was organized. There is a tale, perhaps apocryphal, about the most famous student of Antisthenes, Diogenes, who lived from 412 to 323 BC. The Macedonian emperor, Alexander the Great, who knew of the philosopher's renown, once asked Diogenes if there was anything he could do for him, upon which Diogenes asked him to move to stop blocking the sun. Social hierarchy was of no importance to cynics such as Diogenes, who reputedly once searched Athens in broad daylight with a lamp lit searching for an honest man.

A second movement, stoicism, was founded about 300 BC by a man named Zeno, who hailed from Cyprus. He was perhaps a Phoenician who lived between 333 and 262 BC. Socially speaking, stoicism held that all men were brothers who ought to develop a universal state in order to further the brotherhood. Stoics believed in the natural rights of human beings, and either monotheism or pantheism in nature, pooh-poohing the anthropomorphism of the Greek pantheon. They also admitted that a woman could be strong, wise, and virtuous despite her sex, even if they did not go so far as to admit that women generally were the equal of men. One Greek slave named Epictetus eventually became a freedman, and lived from 50 to 138 AD. He wrote eloquently about the basic tenets of stoicism: the concept of self-control, and controlling what one could while leaving aside what one could not, and having the wisdom to know the difference between the two. He was a major influence on the stoic emperor who lived late in the second century AD, Marcus Aurelius.

Beyond stoic ideas about the behavior of individuals, there were, at least, two stoic philosophers who advised social revolutionaries and reformers: Blossius of Cumae, whom we have already met, advisor to Tiberius Gracchus of Rome and to Aristonikos of Pergamum; and Sphaerus, who served the Spartan reformer, Cleomenes III, helping him reform Spartan education. Even so, stoics themselves were no social revolutionaries leading the poor to dismantle Greek social hierarchy, mostly because they were theoreticians of individual ethics.

Of more direct interest for his social views was the cynic philosopher, Kerkidas of Megalopolis. It is known that he lived late in the third century BC since he was an infantry general for his city in a battle that took place in 222 BC. Kerkidas was profoundly opposed to the concentration of wealth in his city and to his city's social organization. Here is part of a poem he wrote about a wealthy man named Xenon. Known as fragment 2, it is available on p. 184 of a book by Graham Shipley. The translated poem has been revised slightly by this author.

> Why did God not choose
> that greedy, cormorant wealthpurse,
> that sweet-scented, out-of-control Xenon,
> make him a pathetic poor man,
> and transfer to us who deserve it
> the silver that now is flowing away uselessly?
> What can there be to prevent God—
> suppose you ask him the question
> since a god, whatever comes into his mind,
> can easily get it all done—
> if a man is a turd of a loan shark,
> a real old die-for-a-penny
> who squanders it all out again,
> one who's the death of his fortune,
> why can't God just empty this man of his swine wealth,
> and give to a thin feeding, common cup-dipper
> all the man's damned expenditure?
> Has the eye of justice been blinded like that of a mole?

A philosopher of such views, teaching the young, might he not have had some social influence, asks this author?

In actual fact, we know of few philosophers whose tongue so stung the wealthy and powerful in Greece, perhaps since Greek philosophy was all about how a man could live the ethical, good life as an individual. Even if philosophers posing political acts were few, according to Mikhail Rostovtzeff, there was, nevertheless, a general mood in the air during the Hellenistic period of broad support for the idea of brotherhood among Greeks.

> Greek public opinion in the third and second centuries BC vehemently resented the brutal treatment of Greeks in the frequent wars between Greek states: the wholesale massacre and enslavement of the population of captured cities, the violation of sanctuaries, the savage and purposeless devastation of the countryside by belligerents. It never accepted, but took strong exception to the enslavement of individual Greeks by pirates. (1957, p.1110)

This feeling of brotherhood among the Greeks was accompanied by an even more radical concept:

> that of the brotherhood of man, of human beings in general. The idea was in the air. It was formulated and advocated in logical discussions by... cynics and stoics, who endeavored to show...how artificial, conventional, and irrelevant from a philosophical standpoint were the distinctions between man and woman, barbarian and Greek, slave and free. The new idea appealed to many in the Greek world. (reference as per above)

The new attitude showed itself in the treatment of slaves, which gradually came to be less malicious and more humanitarian, even while stopping short of advocating the end of slavery as an institution. This attitude greatly influenced early Christians such as Saint Paul. Once again, we refer to Rostovtzeff for examples of the gradually improving treatment of Greek slaves during the Hellenistic period, such as: extending legal holidays to slaves; offering educational opportunities; making charitable donations to slaves on the same terms as free men; admitting slaves to religious associations hitherto limited to free men; granting permission for slaves to form their own associations; offering greater economic freedom to them; and increasing the quantity of manumissions of slaves. According to stoics and cynics, slaves had a potential for virtue and humanity irrespective of their social status. (Rostovtzeff, 1957, p. 1111)

Summary

The ancient Greeks, as do the ancient Hebrews, represent founding pillars of Western culture. Even before the classical period of Greek culture and society, there had developed a pan-Greek identity based on iron technique, a common language and alphabet, religion, trade, warfare, and the poleis. Athens and Attica, the Greek city and region with the largest populations, emerged as a confederation of four tribes from the city, mountains, plains, and seacoast in a mostly agricultural society where politics permitted leaders and followers to resolve their many differences based on their varying interests. Colonization abroad was a favored solution when the population of city-states exceeded 20-30,000. Greek colonies were established on the shores of the Mediterranean from southern Spain to western Anatolia and the southern coast of the Black Sea.

Coinage was introduced to the Greeks by the Lydians of Anatolia. It spread throughout the Greek world, and made some wealthy via commerce and markets, the most important market being the slave market. It also provided a short respite to the problems of large-scale debt that plagued Greek society as elsewhere in the ancient world since peasants could now sell their surplus farm produce for their own benefit. Solon divided Athenians into classes according to wealth which, coincidentally, defined the political powers of each class and the military obligations upon them. Economic growth and societal change, however, eventually made Solon's categories irrelevant. Non-elites demanded more political power, while a proletariat of poor, free citizens and slaves emerged.

Non-elites used many means to increase their political store and general welfare in their resistance to the aggregation of wealth and concentration of political power by oligarchies. Among the tools of the popular classes were the law codes developed by men such as Solon in Athens and Lykurgus in Sparta; the gradual but inevitable extension of certain legal rights to slaves, women, and the poor; the extension of political participation to commoners via military service in the perpetual, inter-Greek warfare; land redistribution; debt relief; craft associations that sometimes acted as labor unions; slave revolts; increased emancipation and improved treatment of slaves, especially under Roman rule following the Servile Wars; popular revolts and rebellions; political revolutions; the philosophies of cynicism and stoicism, including utopian visions and general ideas of brotherhood among Greeks and humanity, in general; and, finally, Greek democracy. Whereas the solution to the violence, warfare, and class conflict of the Iron Age was religion among Persians in the form of Zoroastrianism and in the form of prophetic Judaism among the Hebrews, the solutions of the Greeks to the social injustice and violence of the Iron Age lay in the development of philosophy about how people could live the ethically good life, and political democracy that increased the political power of the common people.

CHAPTER 5. THE ANCIENT ROMANS

Introduction

It is a useful starting-point when writing about ancient Rome to draw comparisons with ancient Athens. Both were city-states that started as tribal confederacies with an economic base of agriculture and animal husbandry during the Iron Age; in both, religion served as an organizing social and cultural glue. In fact, many parts of Italy that fell to Roman rule in the mid-second century BC were actually Greek in culture: southern Italy, Sicily, Corsica, and Sardinia. Furthermore, the Roman republic of the second century BC included Macedon and mainland Greece, legacies of Alexander the Great and classical Greece respectively. Both Greece and Rome were societies almost always at war. The economies of both were based largely on slave labor. Roman philosophy and religion, including its pantheon, were largely derivative of Greek discourse, both in form and substance. Thus, many historians, classicists, and social scientists tend to speak and write of the Greco-Roman world as if it were a unity.

On the other hand, ancient Roman history, at the same time, is different from ancient Greek history in many respects. The appellation 'Greco-Roman' is somewhat misleading if our purpose is to elucidate the patterns of development and domination enabling the extraction of economic surplus and the resistance to this domination as they appeared in ancient Rome. For these purposes, the notion of Greco-Roman unity belies the patterns distinctive to each of ancient Greece and ancient Rome, so that it is valuable to treat each on its own terms.

Rome lived through the Bronze Age only peripherally since there was no tin in Italy to alloy with copper. The use of bronze in early Rome owed principally to its use by the wealthy in imported luxury products. Ancient Rome enters history during the Iron Age, and remains defined by it, locked in the era with its attendant violence, brutality, and warfare. Ancient Rome never produced a broad counter-culture that questioned basic Roman principles until Christianity issued from Judaism, itself a counter-culture in reaction to the brutality of the Iron Age. The ancient Chinese, Indians, Persians, and Hebrews produced religious or ethical movements to respond to the violence of the Iron Age. The Greek response to the brutality of the Iron Age involved the development of the fundamentals of Western philosophy and political democracy, legacies that remain today. There is no such legacy from ancient Rome. The Roman legacy to the Occident involves imperial, autocratic government, Roman law, and the military organization of empire, including its systems of transportation and communications. The republican form of government, which lasted between 509 and 31 BC, resembled only somewhat the forms that led to democracy in Athens and other Greek cities. In fact, the Roman term for republic, in Latin *res publica*, sometimes even written as one word, only referred to public matters as distinguished from private matters.

The political, constitutional, and legal development of the Roman republic in large part was motivated by a process whereby the *plebs*, the people of Rome who were not descended from its founding families and clans, fought to gain inclusion to the discussion and administration of public matters in Rome. Participation in Roman public matters was originally limited to the *patres*, the patriarchs of the founding families, clans, and tribes, and their descendants and clients. The republican balance between the two social groups was worked out in the development of Roman constitutional and civil law, even as Roman criminal law remained brutal, mired in the violence and cruelty of the Iron Age. Witness the practice of crucifixion as one means of state terror, to cite just one example of the latter. On the other hand, much of the Western world's constitutional and civil law is based on tenets of Roman law. This applies to continental Europe, the United States, and Latin America. Roman law, however, with the exception of manumission by which slaves were granted their freedom, only begrudgingly advanced the cause of the socially lowly. Only with the development of Christianity in the first century AD, was there a counter-culture devoted to social justice on behalf of poor, common people. After the emperor Constantine converted to Christianity, which in the fourth century became the official religion of the Roman empire, the history of Christian development was one of endless conflict between the requirements of social justice on behalf of the lowly on one hand, and hierarchical Christianity as a social pillar of secular power on the other hand, a conflict that arguably continues even today.

In spite of this, many historians of ancient Rome have served as cheerleaders for ancient Rome, evoking nostalgia for what is seen as the pinnacle of Western civilization, from which heights we have ever descended, this in spite of the brutal inhumanity of ancient Rome. The reader should be forewarned that the opinions expressed in this chapter definitely do not serve as arguments in support of a supposed greatness of Rome.

Timelines

To write about ancient Rome is to cover two millennia of history, starting from the legendary founding of the village of Rome by Romulus, allegedly a descendant of the Trojan warrior, Aeneas, to the final disappearance of the Byzantine empire with its capital at Constantinople, present-day Istanbul, Turkey, in the 15th century. Obviously, such a vast period of time means that the realities and meaning of Rome changed dramatically through the centuries, so that one has to specify the periods being considered when making generalizations about ancient Rome. For the most part, the eras beyond the fall of the Western Roman empire will be covered in subsequent chapters. In this chapter, we explore in greater detail these important events of Roman history, among others.

753 BC—The mythic figure, Romulus, supposedly founds Rome on the southern bank of the Tiber River.

715–673 BC—The legendary second king of Rome, Numa Pompilius, allegedly establishes the traditional guilds for Roman craftsmen: musicians, goldsmiths, carpenters, dyers, shoemakers, skinners (leather workers), braziers (bronze workers), and potters with an additional guild to include all other craftsmen; Numa grants these guilds the rights to establish their own courts, councils, and religious observances.

578–535 BC—The sixth king of Rome, the Etruscan Servius Tullus, rules Rome, enacting popular reforms supported by plebs and offending patricians.

510 BC—The Romans expel the last Etruscan king, Tarquinius Superbus, allegedly for moral violations; more likely because the increasing power of kings allied with plebeians increased both royal and plebeian power at the expense of patrician power, greatly displeasing patricians.

509 BC— Creation of the Roman republic.

494 BC—Plebeians leave Rome en masse while Rome is at war as a pressure tactic against the patricians; known as the plebeian secession, it results in the recognition of two officials called tribunes whose mission is to defend the plebs; furthermore, plebeians swear an oath known as *lex sacrata*, which commits them to protect the tribunes if ever the latter are menaced.

471 BC—The *concilium plebis*, a popular assembly, is created. Its members are elected by the tribal councils of the plebs; as well, the number of tribunes is doubled.

450 BC—At plebeian insistence, the basic laws of Rome, previously unwritten and known only to patricians, are inscribed on twelve tablets in easy-to-understand format.

367–366 BC—Important reforms allow plebeians to sit in the highest offices previously occupied only by patricians, while land conquered by Rome is limited in the amount any one person can own, a measure that attempts to limit the concentration of wealth in order to give the common people access to newly conquered lands.

357 BC—A first plebeian is named dictator, a special position of absolute power to which a man is named for six months during crises and emergencies; the plebeian, Gaius Marcius Rutilus, leads a successful defense of Rome against invading Etruscans, for which plebeians grant him a special ceremony known as a triumph over the objections of the patricians.

345 BC— *Lex canuleia* permits inter-marriage between plebeians and patricians, previously prohibited.

342 BC—*Lex genucia* requires that at least one of the two consuls be a plebeian; the consuls rule for a year, and are the chief magistrates of Roman government, including its military; this advance for plebeians occurs because of another secession of plebeian soldiers.

339 BC—*Lex publilia* effects an important constitutional change; previously, the patrician senate had the right to veto adopted plebeian laws on religious or traditional grounds; now, they have a right of regard only before the law is passed, which reduces the importance of their veto to symbolic approval.

326 BC—*Lex poetelia papiria* abolishes the condition called *nexum*, debt bondage by which debtors become effectively slaves to their creditors.

300 BC—Plebeians are now permitted to hold the traditional, religious offices previously held only by patricians.

293 BC—*Lex maenia* removes the requirement of senate approval of election results.

287 BC—The plebs secede again from Rome during a period of war, and obtain a reform such that laws and decrees of the plebeian assembly now apply to all Romans.

146 BC—A Greek insurrection against Roman rule is defeated, after which Greece becomes a Roman province.

139 BC—*Lex gabinia tabellaria* provides for secret votes for elected political positions.

135–132 BC—The first slave revolt in Sicily is defeated by Rome, which slaughters 20,000 slaves in revenge.

133 BC—The popular agrarian reformer, Tiberius Gracchus, is murdered when he seeks re-election as a tribune.

123 BC—Gaius Gracchus, younger brother of Tiberius, espouses popular agrarian policies similar to those of his brother, but is murdered during riots in Rome.

104–101 BC—Second slave revolt in Sicily proves to be unsuccessful.

100 BC—The tribune Saturninius unsuccessfully proposes agrarian reforms that would have settled military veterans on conquered land.

9180 BC—The Social War between Rome and the other Italian cities results in the defeat of the other Italians, but half a million Italians do gain the right to Roman citizenship owing to the war.

73–71 BC—A Thracian gladiator, Spartacus, leads an ultimately unsuccessful rebellion of slaves from several countries that traverses and occupies much of Italy; in punishment, 6,000 slaves are crucified.

63 BC—A popular insurrection with the aim of overthrowing the senate is led by a wealthy politician, Cataline, but the rebellion is suppressed.

58 BC—*Leges clodiae* are a series of popular political reforms passed under the leadership of the tribune, Publius Clodius Pulcher.

46-44 BC—Popular dictatorship of Julius Caesar until his assassination by wealthy conspirators in 44.

31 BC—Octavian, Caesar's chosen successor, achieves sole power in Rome after defeating his erstwhile allies Pompey and Anthony.

27 BC—Octavian renames himself Augustus, and becomes the first emperor of the Roman empire, which replaces the republican constitution even if some republican forms are retained.

14 AD—Augustus dies.

212—The emperor Caracalla extends Roman citizenship to all free citizens of the empire, not so much as a progressive measure but in order to expand the tax base to help relieve the perennial fiscal problems of the Roman state.

235–238, 249-251, 257, 303-311—Persecutions of Christians.

235–285—The empire is in crisis owing to epidemics, runaway inflation, barbarian invasions, and underlying economic weaknesses.

312—Emperor Constantine converts to Christianity.

313—The edict of Milan ends persecutions of Christians in favor of tolerance of Christianity, which significantly improves the lot of Christians by making it acceptable, especially for members of the ruling class, to profess Christianity openly.

330—Constantine establishes his new capital at the site of the Greek city of Byzantium at the straits that divide Europe from Asia; it will become eventually the capital of the eastern empire named Constantinople.

370-453—Hunnic peoples from the steppes north of the Black and Caspian seas migrate west, perhaps in response to pressure from other peoples to the east, in the process the Huns invade the Roman empire.

380—Christianity becomes the official state religion of the Roman empire.

395—The empire is divided into eastern and western empires with sons of the late emperor, Theodosius, each taking leadership of half of the empire.

410—Originally from Scandinavia and northern Germany or Poland, Visigoths sack the city of Rome.

439—The western empire is overrun by barbarians.

476—Odoacer, a German general in the imperial army, deposes the Roman emperor of the western empire, Romulus Augustulus, and proclaims himself king of Italy.

711—Muslim Arabs control all of previously Roman North Africa and Egypt, as well as much of modern-day Spain and Portugal.

1453—The Byzantine empire collapses under attacks by the Muslim Ottoman Turks.

Early Rome

In Neolithic times, the Italian peninsula was subjected to migrations and colonizations by people from elsewhere in Europe, North Africa, and Anatolia. The indigenous, Italic peoples mixed with these new arrivals to form the cultures of the tribes of Italy. The culture of 1000 BC around the collection of small huts that was then Rome is known to archaeologists as the Villanovan culture. An Iron Age culture, the Villanovans cremated their dead, and stored the ashes in religious shrines above the earth. Usually, a tribe included a collection of villages that shared these religious shrines. The tribe was composed of clans descended from common ancestors, real or imagined. Around the village of Rome lived several tribes, chief among them, the Latins and the Sabines. The original village of Rome was placed fortuitously at the last crossing of the Tiber River before it emptied into the Mediterranean Sea. Thus, Rome sat on trade routes running north-south and east-west, possibly allowing Romans to benefit from tolls charged on traders passing by and through Rome. The original inhabitants of Rome farmed and practiced animal husbandry. One incentive to form the polity of Rome might have been the need to protect farm produce, herds of cattle, and flocks of sheep and goats from traders and migrants passing through Rome.

To the north of the Tiber was a people whose origins are the object of considerable differences of historical opinion, the Etruscans, whose lands stretched north from Rome into northern Italy. The Etruscans may have descended from the Old Europeans who had occupied the Balkans and the Danube Valley in the years of 6500–4000 BC. They were considerably advanced, technologically speaking, when compared to the tribes to the south of the Tiber. The Etruscans were skilled craftsmen in ceramics and metallurgy. They also introduced innovations of the Greeks to Rome, such as bronze products not native to Italy; certain engineering structures such as arches and drainage and sewage systems; the Greek alphabet, adapted to become the Latin alphabet; urban social organization; and the Greek pantheon of gods and goddesses, and other elements of Greek religion.

Of the tribes in the vicinity of Rome, three coalesced with the original population of the village of Rome itself: the Ramnes, or the Latins; the Tities, or the Sabines; and the Luceres, or the Etruscans. Heads of clans, known as *patres*, *sat on a* body that came to form the basis of the patrician senate. The people known in history as the *plebs* were relative newcomers to Rome, attracted by Rome's wealth and prosperity. Conflict between patricians and plebeians animated the political, constitutional, and legal development of the Roman republic.

The Roman Kings

According to Roman writers and legend, between the fabled founding of Rome by Romulus in 753 BC and the initiation of the Roman republic in 509

BC, Rome supposedly was ruled by seven kings: one Sabine, three Latins, and three Etruscans. Two of the seven can be compared to the great law-givers of other city-states in the ancient world such as Drako and Solon in Athens or Lykurgus in Sparta. The first, great law-giver of Rome was Numa Pompilius, who reigned from 715 to 673 BC. Numa Pompilius did much to establish the religious practices of Rome. He also set boundaries in order to diminish conflicts over territories. Of most significance for our study, however, was that he reputedly established the craft guilds of ancient Rome. These crafts then held a certain historical cachet owing to their traditional legitimacy and religious standing. This also provided some protection for crafts when the ruling class tried to limit the authority of guilds, which occurred several times in both republican and imperial times.

In the sixth century BC, Rome was ruled by Etruscan kings who had followed the Latin kings. The Etruscan kings were the last to rule Rome before the third, Tarquinius Superbus, was expelled from Rome as the republican form of government was established. The first Etruscan king was Tarquinius Priscus, the grandfather of Superbus. Tarquinius Priscus was succeeded by his son-in-law, Servius Tullius, the second of the great law-giver figures. Servius was of humble origins, being either a freedman and/or a successful mercenary who rose through the military ranks, then married the daughter of Priscus. Servius acceded to the monarchy owing to popular support, even if the *patres* of the Senate did not approve of him. Servius appears to resemble the Greek tyrants in behavior, and he may have come to power by force. Once in power, Servius produced important, lasting constitutional innovations that formed part of the foundations of republic in Rome. Among his early actions, Servius extended Roman citizenship to include commoner plebeians and freedmen. As well, in a manner similar to what Kleisthenes did late in the sixth century BC in Athens, Servius dramatically changed the tribal system of Rome in order to diminish the power of the traditional, patrician leaders who had opposed his accession to power. He thus ended the threefold, tribal divisions of the Ramnes, Tities, and Luceres representing respectively the Latin, Sabine, and Etruscan elements. In their stead, he set up four urban tribes according to geography: the Palatina, Collatina, Esquilina, and the Suburbana. To these, he added sixteen more from the *ager romanus*, the countryside around Rome. He also set up the rural, administrative divisions called *pagi*, which often coincided with regional or local marketplaces.

Over the years, tribes were added as Roman territory continued to expand such that in 241 BC, when two more tribes were added, the number of tribes was set finally at 35. From the mid-2nd century onwards, these tribal appellations were even included in a person's name, for instance, Gaius Martinius Claudia, where the last name referred to the person's tribe. Each tribe was headed by a tribune who represented the tribe in religious, civil, and military matters. The tribes were further divided into ten voting wards called *curiae*, which assembled in the *comitia curiata*. Tribunes assembled in an assembly called the *comitia tributa*, which acted as a legislative body and a court of appeal in criminal cases where no death penalty was involved. All this appears to have produced a decentralized form of government and public administration that, even if not democratic, was at least familiar and physically close to the members of the tribes. As well, it reduced the senate to an advisory and religious role, sort of a council of elders to advise the king.

His constitutional reforms, which seemed to favor popular forces, made Servius popular with the common people, but considerably less so with wealthy patricians. Perhaps in response to pressures from the latter, constitutional developments later in the régime of Servius favored the wealthy. A new legislative body was established called the *comitia centuriata*, the assembly of soldiers, which dealt with military and foreign policy matters, and which elected the most important magistrates. The assembly was organized into the basic, military divisions of 100 soldiers, or centuries. It also defined the military contribution that was expected from people according to their wealth. In recompense, the number of legislative votes reflected this military contribution. The more one contributed militarily, the greater was the number of votes held. Since Rome was perpetually at war, this principle was not insignificant. Servius divided the composition of the *comitia centuriata* thus: those whose estates were worth at least 100,000 sesterces—85 centuries. The next gradations were 75,000, 50,000, and 25,000 sesterces, each level set at 20 centuries higher than the lower gradation. Then followed the next level at 11,000 sesterces of estate wealth, which was reserved to ten of the traditional guilds at three centuries apiece, for a total contribution of thirty centuries from the craft guilds. The lowest level was the *proletarii* who had no estate or wealth, and who were accorded only one century in total. Simple arithmetic yields 85 centuries or votes for the wealthiest, and 91 votes for all other categories combined. In actual fact, however, voting was done in blocks according to wealth categories. Only if there were deadlocks within the wealthiest category would voting be done at the next wealth level and so on until a decision was reached. All the wealthy had to do was to reach a mutually acceptable decision, which then would hold sway in the assembly. This cynical system favored the wealthy, directly contradicting the earlier popular measures established during the reign of Servius. It also presaged a social evolution away from the close-knit agricultural communities that constituted Rome's initial makeup to that of Rome becoming a militarized power constantly at war and expanding in territory, becoming wealthier with ever greater social inequalities. We now consider this social evolution.

Socio-economic Development

In its beginnings Rome was a small agricultural community where most people produced the food they consumed. There was little economic surplus, while most people farmed at least some land. As much as 80% of agricultural produce was consumed by farmers themselves, while the small surplus went to feed urban dwellers such as craftsmen, traders, public office-holders, and urban patricians. Early Rome was a thoroughly religious society, in fact, profoundly superstitious. Spirits of the ancestors, of the legendary founders of Rome, and of the gods of families, clans, tribes, and associations were ubiquitous. The head of a family, the *paterfamilias*, served as its priest, while patricians occupied religious offices on behalf of the entire community. The spirits, ancestors, and gods were honored with regular prayer and animal sacrifice. This reality of a profoundly religious and superstitious society continued through the generations and among all classes, in a society where ghosts were everywhere influencing events. It was one of the reasons why the patrician class could hold on so long to its power. Patricians justified their power as a means of maintaining proper religious observance that only they fully understood, as opposed to uncultivated and irreligious plebeians. Patricians regularly consulted with augurs before battles and other important events to determine the chances of success. In fact, battles or important debates or adoption of legislation could be called off if the augurs determined the omens were not propitious when they examined the entrails of a chicken, or a crow flew by, or some other silliness.

Early Rome and its patricians were devoted to public service, especially military service. The highest form of service among patricians was service to Rome in military command of the armies of free peasants, or occupation of public or religious offices. Business, crafts, and trade were viewed by the patricians as being unworthy pursuits that were beneath them. The small numbers of traders and craftsmen that did exist worked in the traditional guilds recognized by Numa Pompilius, or worked as smiths, armorers, and textile workers fabricating the iron weapons, armor, equipment, and clothes soldiers needed. In the countryside, small farmers might work for wealthier farmers in their free time. They might also borrow from their wealthier neighbors when hard times struck, thus eventually creating the problems of popular debt familiar to all ancient societies. Nevertheless, the small agricultural surplus, the small plots of land, the early absence of coinage, the small scale of trade, and military obligations tied to land ownership all meant that a majority class of peasants farmed land they owned, and served as short-term soldiers when the need arose. This was the class that was celebrated in Roman literature, even for years after yeoman farmers were no longer the majority. The mythic model of Cincinnatus, the patrician-farmer who left his land to serve as dictator at public demand during a military crisis, then promptly returned to his humble abode to farm his land after his public service, was celebrated as the most heroic form of Roman citizenship, long after the actual phenomenon of yeoman farmers had disappeared. This agricultural hero, the Roman yeoman, served as the ideology for generations of the ruling class, even if the ideology bore less and less relation to actual social organization.

There was another, important social phenomenon in early Rome, one that continued throughout ancient Roman times. This was the social institution of patronage and clienteles. Common people regularly turned to wealthier patrons for such services as interpreting laws and providing legal protection, while clients owed services to patrons such as political support for election to public offices. Thus, a man who owed money to someone wealthier might be expected to extend political support to the wealthier man. As innocuous as the relationship between patron and client might sound to modern ears, it was a powerful social force throughout Roman history. The institution led to foreign wars of conquest, civil wars, riots, revolutions, and rebellions as patrons could command armies of faithful clients if the patron did indeed deliver on his promises of help for his clients.

Another important social phenomenon was the oligarchic nature of Rome's politics even if, socially speaking, most people had been yeoman farmers in early Roman times. All important political and religious offices were occupied by the patrician members of this oligarchy. A second wealthy class was comprised of the *equites*, knights who originally served in the cavalry since they could afford horses, even if this class originally held no political or religious offices. This group transformed itself over time to become traders and businessmen, many of whom eventually became wealthy. Membership in the two upper classes required a minimum amount of income, as well as the service in public office or in military commands in the case of patricians. Ex-magistrates who had served in the military or public offices afterward became senators.

Military Expansion

Republican Rome was constantly at war with its neighbors, wars that wrought grand social changes to Rome. Roman territory continued to grow as neighboring tribes in peninsular Italy, and then as the Carthaginians and the Greeks of Sicily, Sardinia, Corsica, and southern Italy were defeated by Roman armies. After all of Italy fell to Rome, eventually the entire Mediterranean world fell including the rest of the Greek-speaking world in the Levant, Anatolia, Syria, Egypt, Greece, Macedon, Thrace, and the Balkans, to be then followed by North Africa, Gaul, Spain, and Britain. Generally speaking, the borders of Rome stretched, even before Rome formally became an empire ruled by the emperor Augustus, from the Euphrates River and the shores of the Black Sea in the east, to the Atlantic Ocean in the west, including all of Europe west of the Rhine and south of the Danube, and southward to the natural borders presented by the Sahara and Arabian deserts. Even by the third century BC, there were Roman citizens living hundreds of miles from Rome. Political participation in the republic became indeed difficult so voting assemblies became less important than they had once been. On the other hand, the Senate grew in importance. Although Rome was never a democracy like Athens and other Greek cities, even Roman republican forms became hollow as the real rulers became the senators and other wealthy men, while others struggled to earn political influence and power. It was against this background that the conflict between the plebeians and patricians grew in importance to become the motivating force of Roman legal, constitutional, political, and social development.

Nonetheless, contrary to Athens and the other Greek cities where citizenship and accompanying political rights often were jealously guarded privileges, both republican and imperial Rome were liberal in extending Roman citizenship. P.A. Brunt suggests an important point about the political impact of this liberal citizenship. It served to integrate local noblemen to Rome rather quickly, as with the example of the Italian town, Tusculum. Only a generation after its citizens became Roman citizens, Tusculum sent its leading nobleman, Lucius Fulvius, to Rome to serve as consul in 322 BC. (p. 9) As for the internal politics of these communities of Roman citizens, Brunt continues.

> The municipalities of Roman citizens...were governed in much the same way as the Romans. They had their own popular assemblies, their own elected magistrates, their councils of men of birth and wealth sitting for life. No doubt in these small communities...there were lively internal struggles and feuds between families that could result in bloodshed when the Roman state was itself torn by civil wars and political disputes dividing classes...

Generating Wealth

In addition to the political impacts of continuing Roman expansion, there were other dramatic socio-economic effects of Roman expansion. Ramsay MacMullen summarizes them this way: continuous war brought an influx of booty of treasuries of conquered cities, luxuries, gold and silver, minerals, taxes, tribute in the form of agricultural produce especially grain, slaves in the form of war captives, and new soldiers. The increasingly wealthy magistrates and patricians of Rome bought land near the capital, in the process expelling the original yeoman farmers whether by means fair or foul. This impoverished peasants, forcing them into the cities, especially Rome. Others were forced to emigrate to the provinces where new urban markets developed for the food the wealthy produced on large estates by the labor of slaves and tenant farmers in Italy, or on Roman land in the conquered provinces. Once in the city, these now-poor but still free citizen-peasants might find employment on public works projects funded by the wealthy, or might become under-employed or unemployed, dependent upon the dole of cheap or free food imported from the provinces. Roman methods of extracting surplus from the empire formed a recognizable system where the wealthy and powerful became richer through their plunder of the provinces and their exploitation of the work of provincial peasants and slaves.

With Rome perpetually at war, yeoman peasants were conscripted regularly to military service. At the beginning of the second century BC, the Roman military absorbed about 140,000 young men from a total of about a million men in Italy. In addition, Roman wars of conquest, wars with invading Celtic tribes and the Carthaginians, slave rebellions in Italy, and civil wars contributed to devastating the Italian countryside, environmentally speaking, as well as displacing peasants. If the Roman military campaigns were successful, the private soldier cum free peasant might receive a share of the booty, however, the time away from his farm usually meant poverty for the soldier's family back home. He might return from military service to find that a wealthy urban-dweller had absconded, legally or not, title to his land in order to place slaves on it or to strike tenant arrangements with remaining peasants in his locality. So, he and his family then might head for the city to be fed on the public dole. By the second century BC, there was an insufficient number of free yeoman farmers to serve in the army, so the army became professional with soldiers spending their whole productive life in the army, regularly at war.

Defiance of the law and traditions by the *nouveaux-riches* led to eviction of poor free peasants, the supposed heart of the Roman republic. This was contrary to the ruling ideology of the day about the Roman yeoman farmer. This conflict also showed up over the issue of the rich absconding public lands from conquered territories, land that was to be available supposedly for all. This conflict inspired the Gracchi brothers who tried to reallocate conquered, public land for the use of the poor. The conflict was the source of the civil wars of the first century BC, which eventually ended the republic when Rome became an empire. It is estimated that during the last century BC, as many as a million and half free peasants were extricated from their land in Italy. Michael Grant points out that to protect themselves from the exactions of the state and the wealthy, the poor then threw themselves ever more into becoming clients of wealthy patrons, losing their freedom while gaining some protection in return. (p. 80) Those who remained in the countryside eventually became so attached to the land owned by the wealthy that the poor almost became serfs in what was, in fact, a precursor of their descendants' social position during the Middle Ages. Writes Julian Fenner, an English scholar:

> the condition of the tenant farmer had become one of semi-servile dependence. His legal freedom became very limited, and his economic position increasingly depended on the preservation of a holding often blighted by encroachments....to be a *colonus* (the term for a tenant farmer who was often a military veteran from Italy, from the provinces, or from Italy before being resettled in the provinces) was to be attached to a specific plot of ground with which he himself was transferable.

Slaves and Freedmen

At the same time as free peasants were being evicted by the powerful by means legitimate or otherwise, they essentially were replaced on Italian farmlands by the slaves that had been captured by the armies of free Roman peasants. These armies were led by the same wealthy people who were absconding the land of free Roman peasants. In the last century BC, as much as a third of the six million people living in Italy were slaves. For the free Roman to work for others meant becoming dependent upon an employer, a concept scarcely tolerable to a free Roman. Nevertheless, the importing of massive numbers of slaves created a labor market for workers on farms and *latifundia* in the countryside, or for workers employed by the state, or businessmen and traders in the cities. This labor market helped push free men whether they wanted or not into situations where they too were now working as tenant farmers or part-time laborers on the estates of the wealthy or as free urban workers, all of whom had to face the competition of slaves.

Slave labor was an important cog in the extraction of economic surplus by the powerful. Roman slavery also could be vicious and cruel. For instance, in AD 61, a magistrate in Rome named Pedanius Secundus was killed by one of his slaves, perhaps a slave who had been promised freedom only to see the promised unfulfilled. Most senators supported the traditional retribution for such a case, which had that all 400 slaves working for the slave owner be executed as punishment to ensure social discipline and loyalty. The reasoning was that on property where slaves lived and worked, potentially all slaves could have some knowledge of the intentions of the murderous slave, hence, they were complicit. Through mass terror, slaveholders and the state ensured that slaves did not try to kill their masters, although murder was still a frequent occurrence in the case of cruel masters. Roman slavery was preserved by a system of terror that maintained public order and the continuing extraction of economic surplus by non-producers. In this particular case, execution of the 400 slaves was blocked initially by a riot of common people scandalized by the brutality of the proposed mass punishment, however, the emperor Nero intervened with a deployment of soldiers to ensure that the 400 executions indeed took place.

Even as Roman slavery was violent and brutal, there was also a paradoxical aspect to it, especially after the mass rebellions of slaves in the last century of the republic. Many Roman slaves were manumitted, so there was a chance that slaves could hope to gain their freedom. Slaves were paid a *peculium*, an amount for their labor, which they could save to buy their freedom. Slaves often worked alongside free men and freedmen, and were paid salaries like their co-workers, even if the slaveholder then would take his or her share of the slave's earnings. In the case of imperial slaves who held administrative jobs, earnings could amount to significant money depending on the skills and education they had to offer. Well-paid slaves included public servants, pedagogues who taught the children of the wealthy, doctors, bailiffs of estates, supervisors and foremen, traders and business people, and craftsmen. Slaves could hope to win their freedom by saving their money, then buying their freedom from their master. Why did masters acquiesce? The incentives that allowed slaves to gain their freedom might have helped increase productivity, assiduousness, and loyalty of service. Most probably, the price of freedom for a slave was probably close to his or her market value. A slave who bought his freedom might permit his owner to use the money then to buy a younger slave to replace the older freedman. All the while, the owner continued to benefit from the hoped-for increased productive labor of his or her slave. Furthermore, even after slavery, indeed as part of the process of granting freedom, the ex-slaveholder could set terms of services the slave might continue to owe him or her similar to the relationship between clients and patrons. Not to be dismissed were bonds of affection and sometimes even love and marriage between slaveholder and slave which might encourage manumission, and which became more commonplace as Christianity and stoic ideas took hold in Roman society. Cicero wrote that slaves realistically could hope for liberation after seven years of service, which sounds like arrangements for the employment of indentured servants that prevailed in later periods in the West. In one sample of tombstones in the western empire, Keith Bradley reports that over 60% of freedmen and freedwomen were liberated before they reached thirty years of age. Imperial slaves typically were released before the age of forty, again according to Bradley. (p. 127) Freedmen often received Roman citizenship, even if they might still have to deal thereafter with some restrictions on their political rights. These restrictions did not prevent, however, some freedmen from occupying important public administration or business positions. Many freedmen became wealthy from trade and crafts. Others became writers, poets, and philosophers, or occupied themselves with other intellectual employment. Children and grandchildren of freedmen knew few restrictions, even if the wealthy might sneer at them since Romans were profoundly snobbish. Nonetheless, one son of a freedman, Pertinax, became emperor in AD 193.

As the same time as slave labor was essential to the production of wealth, paradoxically slave labor was also undermining the empire. Chris Harman provides a fascinating description of the processes of imperial disaggregation at work owing to Roman reliance upon slave labor. (p. 84-6). The years of Roman conquest, for the most part, came to an end during the first 200 years AD. Emperors consolidated territorial gains from the military expansion, while the supply of new slaves diminished. This increased the price of slaves, so some slave owners let their land to tenants called *coloni*, often ex-soldiers who would bear the expenses of their families themselves. This was an alternative to having lands worked by slave labor with the master being responsible for feeding and supporting slaves' families. This change was a factor eventually leading to the institution of serfdom as a replacement of slavery. The taxation that had helped ruin the Italian peasantry rose from about 10% of the produce of a farm to a third during the 6th century AD as Byzantine landowners squeezed harder on their tenants for payment of taxation and rents, while the eastern Roman state squeezed harder on the provinces for tribute such as grain for the cities. Starting in the second century AD, peasants rose up against this unbearable tax burden. Many simply left the land, with the result that the empire adopted laws trying to tie peasants to their land and workers to their crafts, especially in essential trades such as shipping and transformation of food.

The endless civil wars and military usurpings by generals seeking the imperial crown further devastated the land and added to the burden of farmers. According to Julian Fenner, in the century between 180 and 285 AD, all but two of the 27 emperors or pretenders to the imperial purple met violent deaths during civil wars. Roman cities and countryside were always dangerous places. Now traders, craftsmen, and businessmen stopped travelling, further diminishing economic activity. Thus, reliance on slave labor carried the seeds within itself of transformation to new forms of extracting economic surplus from producers who, for their part now sometimes sought the direct protection of the powerful in the regions. The empire was evolving to becoming a series of small local states where local strongmen ruled serf peasantries, sometimes even using military means to protect their clients from imperial tax-collectors. The seeds of the Middle Ages were being planted.

Crafts and Collegia

Earlier, we described how Roman society and its patricians were profoundly religious and superstitious. The same thing applied to urban workers, who were organized into street associations known as *vici* and craft guilds known as *collegia*. At crossroads known as *compitalia* were placed statuettes called *lares* which represented the guardian spirits of local neighborhoods. Vici served religious, social, and fraternal purposes. As many as 500 men might be members of the local street association. Roman streets and neighborhoods were divided by trades where craftsmen plied their trades, and customers came to purchase their wares. Cobblers, smiths, wrights, carpenters, and other craftsmen lived in their own neighborhoods, protected by their deities and guardian spirits. Thus, the craft association often coincided with the street association. During the early republican period, and again after Augustus revived them, there were regular festivals and games held at the compitalia, sort of neighborhood fairs. Shrines at compitalia were funded by local, free workers, freedmen, and slaves who were members of the street associations. Compitalician games included popular theatrical performances of a bawdy and subversive nature that provided commoners with religiously sanctioned outlets for free speech, including expressing subversive ideas. Thus, workers were represented by both their street association and their neighborhood craft guild. These became foci of political mobilization during food riots, civil commotions and wars, strikes, and election campaigns, and for extending political support to favored politicians and patrons. In this way, the common people affected the politics of the upper classes.

Nonetheless, these organizations of popular control were frequently repressed by the state during both republican and imperial times. However, Augustus re-installed the *vici* and *compitalia*, under the specific control of freedmen assisted by slaves, to serve as places for worship of the emperor as a god, joined with the culture of local deities. When the empire faced a chronic shortage of labor owing to the limits of conquest and the diminished supply of slaves, the once-free colleges were turned into state institutions for ensuring the supply and distribution of free or cheap bread and for other essential economic purposes. The guilds then became traps from which it was next to impossible for workers to escape. State-organized colleges thus became another means of extracting economic surplus from the work of craftsmen where once they had been manifestations of popular culture, politics, and resistance.

Throughout Roman history, the wealthy, powerful, literate Romans held workers in disdain. This was not the case, however, for workers themselves. Even when the colleges had become instruments of state control later in the empire, workers derived satisfaction and self-worth from their labor and from membership in their craft guilds. This applied to all workers, whether free, freed, or slave. Tombstones and other epigraphical evidence point to the pride and self-esteem that working people gained from their labor despite the disdain that their work earned from their social superiors.

The Army

The Roman army was another important cog for extracting economic surplus as part of the Roman social and economic system. It was the army composed of free peasants that, well into the second century BC, conquered peoples of the Mediterranean and western Europe. One result of these Roman conquests was that young people among the conquered were turned into slaves to work the estates of the Roman ruling class. In turn, this facilitated the expulsion of previously free peasants cum soldiers from their lands. Moreover, it was the army that allowed public coffers in Rome to be filled with taxes collected from the provinces.

By the second century BC there was an insufficient number of free citizens to man the army, so it was professionalized, composed of Italians and people from conquered territories who had not been turned into slaves. The army became a force for social and political mobility of its soldiers. Support of the army was vital for those who strove for the imperial crown. Armies made and unmade imperial candidates and emperors, and fought civil wars to determine imperial victors and successors. Beginning in the third century AD, just as Greeks, Jews, Egyptians, and other conquered peoples had done before them, Germanic peoples joined the Roman army, eventually becoming generals and even eventually emperors.

Social Conditions

The 17th century, English philosopher, Thomas Hobbes, wrote of life without civilization and government as being naturally nasty, brutish, and short. The same description, however, might apply to ancient Rome, offered by many as the pinnacle of ancient civilization and government from which heights of glory some have purported the West has descended ever since. In actual fact, life expectancy was only 19-20 years in ancient Rome as both republic and empire were beset by wave after wave of contagious diseases from the conquered peoples in the east, including small pox, malaria, and measles. There were, at least, 14 epidemics during the years of the republic, one every 27.5 years, roughly one for each generation. In imperial times, there were important, long-lasting epidemics between 165 and 180, and again between 251 and 256. A short-lived but catastrophic epidemic swept the eastern empire in 541-542 during which the first, known instance of bubonic plague killed about 40% of the population of Constantinople at a rate of 5,000 people per day, as well as 25% of the population of the eastern Mediterranean and about 25 million world-wide. Furthermore, the Plague of Justinian, as it is called, returned once each generation well into the 8th century throughout the Mediterranean basin.

In terms of other health issues, according to Jerry Toner, poor Romans also knew poor mental health, hardly surprising what with all the social stress they faced. Toner argues that the common people in the Roman empire were more directly exposed to death on a regular, daily basis than even the most afflicted, under-developed country in the modern world. (p. 62) Furthermore, as many as a third of the Roman population lived in perpetual poverty, devoting most of the day's earnings to immediate wants, while accumulating neither property nor possessions but plenty of debts, according to Ramsay MacMullen. (p. 93) During the 482 years of the existence of the Roman republic over approximately twenty generations, there were 28 economic crises, almost 1.5 crises per generation. Furthermore, economic problems were among the factors that contributed to the gradual deterioration of the western Roman empire during the crises of the third century, as they are known to historians.

As well, life was physically dangerous in cities and towns where few ventured out at night. In the countryside, MacMullen cites evidence of farmhouses with walls and towers and strong gates, and describes a state of "endemic warfare" where banditry and outlaws prevailed. (p. 4)These physical dangers were among the factors that forced poor people to throw themselves into the arms of local strongmen for protection from criminality, marauding armies, civil wars, political conflict, and economic exploitation.

Then, there were the direct and indirect social effects of persistent warfare. Warfare brought home the realities of injury, capture, and death of soldiers. Widowhood with orphaned children meant dire social and economic consequences for survivors of soldiers. During the years of the republic, there was an average of one foreign war every six years, such that a person who lived to the ripe, old age of fifty would have experienced about eight wars in his lifetime. Nevertheless, there were indeed salutary effects on the lower classes from constant warfare in the early days of Roman military expansion. According to 'Pertinax', the *nom de plume* of a contributor to the UNRV-Roman Empire website, whose logic appears right to this author:

> The acquisition of the neighboring territory aided the plight of the urban poor. [It] became the motif of Roman strategy, extension of food production as a palliative to domestic shortfall...The assimilation of provinces is, in essence, the monopolization of existing grain production. Still, the frequency of civil wars must have had devastating economic and environmental effects. In the last century of the republic, filled with social turmoil as Rome evolved into the empire, there were thirteen civil wars. During the time of the western empire, there were another nine civil wars, several of which lasted many years.

Population growth of Rome was often stagnant for years at a time, or might demonstrate precipitous decline in other periods; most likely, social conditions were a factor in population loss. Here are figures for approximate, average population size in republican Rome, with all years indicated being BC.

509–498: 135,000

493–459: 110,000

392–323: 150,000

294–234: 260,000

209: 137,000

204: 214,000

179–174: 262,000

169–131: 320,000

125–115: 394,000

86: 463,000

70: 910,000, which includes Italian allies in central Italy as citizens after the Social Wars

27: 7,000,000, which includes all Italians.

At the height of the empire's extent during the first two centuries AD, the population of the empire probably numbered between 50 and 60 million; at least, this is the consensus among scholars. Of this, about 200,000 wealthy men in Rome, Italy, and the provinces actually ruled the empire, according to Jerry Toner. (p. 2)

Popular Resistance

From the earliest times, Romans were presented with opportunities to exercise their civic, martial values. Lying in a river valley, the Romans had to defend themselves from invasions by neighboring, hill-dwelling tribes. Very early a pattern emerged whereby a defensive military action was followed by successful counter-attacks by the Romans that netted new territory, wealth, slaves, and soldiers for the Roman state. This pattern repeated in the Mediterranean region during the last three centuries of the republic when the greatest territorial expansion took place. When Augustus came to power in the early days of the empire, a new agenda faced rulers. The needs for consolidation, defense of territories and borders, and putting down rebellions by conquered peoples added military demands beyond those of territorial expansion. In fact, limits to territorial expansion were being reached, with attendant socio-economic consequences. Vicious circles were starting to appear. New sources of slaves dried up so the Roman ruling class had to turn to breeding slaves, which brought new costs of maintaining less productive slave women and children, not all of whom could be employed. This provided incentives for the wealthy to strike tenant arrangements with free peasants, presaging feudalism and serfdom. The free, Italian peasant class that had been diminished by constant warfare and the land hunger of urban landlords was further diminished in status, providing still more incentive for farmers to desert their lands and move to the cities.

The army of free peasants had enabled Rome to gain all its territory and wealth, however, by the second century BC the army was professionalized and manned by urban-dwellers, who no longer could live off Italian lands, and by young men from conquered territories, who had not been enslaved. Policing, administering, and defending the conquered lands required a massive army that grew eventually during imperial times to a size of about 400,000-500,000 soldiers. Supporting this immense army meant increasingly taxing provincial populations. Vicious circles now limiting economic growth were also fueled by the resistance that common people put forward to domination, resistance that was displayed in several forms: in the proto-national or tribal popular revolts by conquered peoples; in the criminality that plagued Rome and the empire; in the problematic social and political evolution of the army, including the frequent civil struggles for the imperial crown; in debt crises, tax revolts, and peasant revolts; in class conflict as it evolved through the years, starting with the king-patrician conflicts of the years of monarchy leading to the civil wars of the last century of the republic prior to the empire under Augustus; in the craft guilds known as *collegia*; and in slave rebellions. We next explore these different forms of popular resistance to Roman rule.

Proto-National and Tribal Rebellions and Revolts

The first form of resistance to the Roman conquerors we consider involved the rebellions and revolts of conquered peoples, or of peoples who ventured near the borders of the empire, or of peoples the Romans were still trying to conquer. The term national is an anachronistic qualifier when used to describe these actions since nations did not appear for another millennium and more. Moreover, Romans themselves organized conquered territories into provinces under imperial administration. So, the tribes and regions that rebelled in some cases were defined into existence in some sense by the Romans themselves since peoples were grouped and labelled according to Roman convenience. Rebelling peoples might be tribes or chiefdoms or city-states that might be more or less Romanized depending upon local history and circumstances.

The Roman historian, Tacitus, puts words into the mouth of Calgacus, a first-century leader of the Picts, the indigenous people of Scotland, that express the spirit of peoples rebelling and defending themselves from the Roman empire. Calgacus described the Romans thus:

> For in them is an arrogance which no submission or good behavior can escape. Pillagers of the world, they have exhausted the land by their indiscriminate plunder...A rich enemy excites their cupidity; a poor one, their lust for power. East and west alike have failed to satisfy them. They are the only people whose covetousness for both riches and poverty are equally tempting. To robbery, butchery, and rapine, they give the lying name of 'government'; they create a desolation and call it peace.

According to Eric Adler, Roman historians frequently invented speeches of Roman enemies in their accounts that actually reveal criticisms by Roman intellectuals of Roman imperialism. For example, the enemy Mithridates VI, king of Pontus, according to the historian and popular politician, Sallust, described the Roman motivation for imperialism: "For the Romans, there is a single, age-old cause for instigating war on all nations, peoples, and kings, a deep-seated lust for empire and riches." (Adler, p. 20) Similarly, the Gallic historian, Pompeius Trogus, put these words into the mouth of Mithridates, who described the Romans thus: "Their whole population has the spirit of wolves, insatiably bloodthirsty and sordidly greedy for power and riches." (Adler, p. 49)

There is evidence of many of the rebelling peoples federating with allies or even with their traditional enemies to make war with the Romans. This was the case of the Lusitanians in modern-day Portugal and of the Celtiberians in modern-day Spain as well as the many tribes of Gaul and the Germanic peoples, to cite a few examples. While many of these revolts were crushed ruthlessly by Roman armies with disastrous effects for the peoples offending Rome, witness the Jews of Judea, others were successful. For instance, a warrior named Viriathus organized an army of 10,000 regular troops and a guerrilla force among Lusitanians in 147–139 BC that defeated the Romans, forcing the latter to recognize Viriathus' territorial gains. Arminius led a confederacy of Germanic tribes successfully resisting conquest in northwestern Germany in 9 AD. Gaius Julius Civilis led a successful revolt in Batavia in the southern Netherlands, what was the Roman province of Germania Inferior in 69-70 AD. These rebellions were constant; a millennium later under the Byzantine empire, Serbs gained their independence in 1035, while Bulgarians did likewise in 1185–1186.

These revolts were not imperial adventures by peoples seeking territorial aggrandizement. Even if led by generals or princes, they were very much popular rebellions against Roman taxes and tributes paid to Rome of grain, minerals, gold and silver, treasuries from cities and towns, and excessive debts or usurious interest on loans owed to Romans. Ramsay MacMullen describes the process that led to provincial rebellions:

> First, initial conquest by the Romans; next, the rapid confiscation of all hidden weapons; then, the assessment by the conquerors of what they had gained, so as to exploit riches methodically; the consternation of the censused; and, thereafter, recurrent spasms of protest against the weight of tribute harshly calculated, and still more harshly exacted. (p. 35)

Local subject populations sometimes even joined in invasions from outside the empire. For instance, in 367 AD, when Goths were penetrating the empire, enslaved gold miners in Thrace escaped to join the Goth campaign against Rome. So while redoubtable, the Roman empire was not a monolith nor a leviathan, even from early republican times. In fact, the Roman state was a fragile thing, of which the provincial and tribal revolts were but the tip of the iceberg. It was an organization structured to enrich a certain class, "the *possessores*, the landowning class by whom and for whom the empire was run." (Heather, 2006, p. 492) The Roman state had many weaknesses, making it permeable and fragile. These structural weaknesses, in fact, were aggravated by popular resistance, sometimes reflected in a mirror-image of the Roman wealth-making system.

First among these fundamental weaknesses was that the empire never had an agreed system for the orderly transfer of power from a dead emperor to a successor. Sometimes, the imperial purple went to an imperial son. In other cases, it went to an 'adopted' son whom the previous emperor had chosen. This was the case when Julius Caesar chose Octavian but, even in that case, years of civil war were required before Octavian became Caesar Augustus, recognized by all. Mostly, emperors came from military ranks with little claim to power other than that their army had defeated other pretenders.

Secondly, the empire very much was the creature of the landowning class, the wealthy who normally numbered only about 5% of the population, and who developed law and government to protect their wealth. (Heather, 2006, p. 139) Hardly a broad base of support in times of crisis. In fact, even the Church, originally a counter-weight of opposition to Roman society, became the province of the rich and powerful of the empire. "From the 370s onwards, bishops were drawn increasingly from the landowning classes, and controlled episcopal successions by discussions among themselves." (Heather, 2006, p. 126) Even the transportation and communications systems developed by the empire ultimately were primitive, and could hardly have been otherwise when one considers the extent of the empire and the state of technological development. The state's capacity was limited to collecting taxes in order to pay for the army and the dole in the cities, and little else of public expenditure that might have been invested to increase the solidity of the empire. Edward Gibbon and others of his school of thought perhaps misunderstood the nature of the Roman empire, especially if their views were based on the example of the monarchies that had established themselves in Europe, and that evolved into nation-states in modern times. Whether from its earliest days as a monarchy, through the early or later republic, or during the early or later empire, western or eastern, Rome was never a leviathan. The state's character as a solid, impermeable organization was always limited.

Moreover, long gone were the early days of early Rome when public and military service to Rome by its patrician class was a religious obligation in honor of ancestral gods or spirits. The spirit of service had been replaced by the workings of imperial Rome as a wealth-creating racket for the benefit of a privileged class of a few rich and powerful. Moreover, resistance to this racket was so much a part of popular culture, that as the French writer Yves Fremion comments, "The Roman empire melted away and vanished to widespread indifference" of the common people. (p. 14)To many among the common people, the demise of the western empire was anything but a catastrophe and more of a relief, an improvement upon existing conditions. Moreover, according to Julian Fenner:

> The attitude of the lower classes towards the barbarians was, by no means, one of fear and hostility. They (the barbarians) often were met with feelings of relief and the desire to co-operate, especially among the poorer men...Evidence shows us examples of people deserting to the barbarians, or appealing for help from them.

Popular Criminality

When we consider the solidity of the Roman state, we need to consider two worlds. The first world included the city of Rome which, at its peak, might have contained as many as a million people, the Italian and provincial cities, and the Italian countryside near Rome. The second world was the Italian countryside distant from Rome and the rural hinterlands of the provincial cities. Each world presented its own dangers. For working people, life in a Roman city was spent outside during the day. Living quarters were small, ill-furnished rooms in buildings five or six storeys high where risks of fire and defective, dangerous construction were considerable. Outside, workers practiced their trades or hawked their wares in public view. Roman cities teemed with people during the days, but at night few ventured outside since cities were dangerous places where theft and violence were regular occurrences. Protection was a private matter. Wealthy patrons could move about at night protected by their slaves, servants, or clients, but there were no police to protect the common people who could only move about in gangs for safety. In fact, policing in cities only came into existence when Augustus set up special army units to keep urban order. The possibility of being a victim of crime was indeed real in urban areas.

Socially speaking, civil commotions in Roman cities occurred frequently, caused by political manifestations by politician-patrons with their client gangs, or even with their virtual or real armies. There were also the public disturbances associated with civil wars. In the last century of the republic, there were thirteen civil wars and three, major slave revolts. This lack of public order was another sign of the weakness of the state. Instead, security such as it existed was imposed from on high by powerful patrons. For the lowly, criminality such as theft might one be a way of improving one's lot, just as was performing services for wealthy patrons by taking part in public disturbances in support of their patrons' interests. Common occurrences were the urban riots when the populace was politically dissatisfied or hungry. Ramsay MacMullen colorfully describes the phenomenon:

> Someone who hoarded grain in time of shortage, or brought defilement in the eyes of the gods, or in any way attacked the whole community, risked mob violence. People would pick up anything that lay in the street—cobbles, broken tiles, rocks—and let fly. Stoning, actual or threatened, stains the history of all the chief cities of the empire, and a chance scattering of the minor ones. It was a common form of group vengeance... If it availed nothing against a powerful citizen in a strong house, the mob tried arson. (p. 66)

One infamous riot was the Nika riot of 532, which started as an exhibition of chariot racing and degenerated into the most violent riot in the history of Constantinople. Half the city was destroyed, while 30,000 people were killed. Riots were serious affairs. The Nika riot started because of tensions between the competing teams of racers, the blues and the greens, and their supporters, who also wore their team colors. As well, blues and greens held different theological positions during the seemingly endless theological debates of early Christianity. In actual fact, chariot races regularly were followed by riots. The Nika riot was inflamed, as well, by the rival teams' supporting the emperor Justinian and a pretender candidate to the throne named Hypatius, each of whom held to different taxing and legal policies as well as theological positions. The Nika riot lasted almost a week, only ending when Justininian was able to wipe out his opposition's supporters. Justinian then rebuilt the city, including the famous church, Hagia Sophia, which had also been destroyed during the festivities.

Tax policies also could provoke riots. For instance, in 370 AD, a riot occurred in Antioch when a special tax was imposed. The emperor had to impose peace by means of conciliation that took into account the needs of the rioters. It is, admittedly, from a completely different context, but the way Orlando Figes describes the social ferment during the period of 1905–1917 in pre-revolutionary Russia might have applied somewhat to the popular criminality of Roman times.

> The closer one looks at the crowds on the streets, the harder it is to distinguish clearly between organized forms of protest...and criminal acts of looting and violence. It was not just a question of hooligans or criminals joining in labor protests, or taking advantage of the chaos they created to vandalize, loot, and assault. Such acts seem to have been an integral element of labor militancy, a means of asserting the power of the plebeian crowd, and of despoiling and destroying symbols of wealth and privilege. (p. 188)

In the Italian countryside far from Rome, or in the provincial hinterlands, or in recently-conquered territories, thieves, brigands and highwaymen wreaked havoc such that they presented a constant danger to travelling businessmen and craftsmen, public officials conducting state business, or wealthy urban-dwellers travelling to and from their country villas and estates. The term *latrones*, or bandits, as they were called, applied to more than common thieves trying to survive. Latrones were enemies of the state who stole and killed, often with local popular support, or even with the support of local elites planning rebellions against Rome. One well-known example of such brigands was the outlaw, Felix Bulla, who terrorized Romans around 200 AD. Bulla was an ex-slave, possibly an animal herder, who drew together an army of 600 ex-slaves and herders as well as disenchanted state workers. Bulla's terror endured for two years in the hills east of Rome. As was the case with Bulla, shepherds, goatherds, and cowherds, many of whom were slave, often became rural brigands. This occurred even with the knowledge of slave-owners, who reasoned that as long as slaves maintained slave owners' flocks and herds, slaves were free to moonlight as brigands. Slave owners' passive support of brigands and outlaws even became a public issue, an object of political debate. In the case of Bulla, the emperor assigned troops to the capture of Bulla and his followers. Finally, Bulla was entrapped by intimates who had been bribed. Bulla was killed publicly and gruesomely as a means of discouraging other would-be latrones.

On the Mediterranean, piracy was ever a problem. Among other incentives to piracy was the possibility of capturing people for sale in the lucrative slave trade. There were certain states, however, who had fought piracy successfully in order to protect their foreign trade. In the first century BC, however, Rome had conquered the Mediterranean states without assuming responsibility for controlling piracy. Rome was a land power, not a naval power. Nevertheless, Rome was forced to take naval military action to stop the pirate activity. The piracy issue was another example of the weakness of the Roman state. Rather than being able to control and to monitor foreign trade peaceably by administrative and economic means, the Roman state needed a major military effort in order to control piracy.

Peasants suffered the most from the imperial tax burden in the provinces. Rome delegated to cities the collection of taxes, who shifted the tax burden to the peasants as collected by equestrian tax-farmers and publicans. One apparently passive means of resistance, however, was indeed effective. In spite of Roman legislation, peasants threatened to leave the land unless tax relief was extended. If the relief was not forthcoming, they made the threat come true. In Egypt, this came to be a well-documented phenomenon known by its Greek name, *anachoresis*, flight from one's farms and villages or from one's debts and creditors. In response to this problem, the Roman state used a stick approach, enforcing laws that attempted to keep peasants on their lands as food shortages became a continuing problem in the empire since the profitability of farming was greatly diminished owing partly to the tax régime. In a more carrot or positive sense, the state was continually settling military veterans on conquered farmland, both as a social justice measure and as an economic policy. Still within the carrot approach, there was another phenomenon that occurred periodically, as described by Ramsay MacMullen:

> the remission of back-dues accompanied by the burning of government records, not so much from the rulers' beneficence as from the sheer inability of their subjects, over repeated years of failure, to keep up their payments. Making the best of a bad job, the government wiped its books clean, advertised the ceremony as an act of bounty through pictures on the coinage, bas-reliefs on public buildings, or proclamations posted in the marketplaces, then began again from scratch. (p. 35)

Provincial and tribal revolts often contained a significant element of peasant unrest. In Cilicia in southwest Anatolia, a region famous for producing maritime pirates, the fourth century AD saw another type of protest against taxes on peasants. A group of bandits called the *maratacupreni* became famous for roaming the land in the guise of tax collectors absconding both money and possessions of the wealthy for themselves. (Heather, 2006, p. 134) Yet another example of peasant protest can be seen in the bandit revolts called the *bagaudae*, which were well documented in Gaul and Spain, although they also appeared in other parts of the empire as well. In 186 and 187 AD, a private Roman soldier named Maternus deserted in Gaul. No ordinary private, Maternus soon organized an army of deserters and mutineers into an army that came to represent the downtrodden of Gaul. Maternus and his force attacked the rich, Roman cities to make away with riches and to free prisoners, inviting the latter to join his merry little band. Soon, runaway slaves, urban paupers, landless peasants, poor tenant farmers, and rural workers joined his force. Maternus took over great estates from the wealthy. The governor of the region where Maternus operated was a brutal African, Septimius Severus, who eventually became emperor. Even this future emperor could not put down the Maternus revolt, however, so an army from Italy had to be sent to try to subdue Maternus. This was still unsuccessful. Maternus met his undoing when he crossed into Italy with the intention of becoming emperor himself. This was too much for his men, however, who betrayed him to the authorities for money.

Two decades later, however, the phenomenon recurred briefly under new leadership. There were several episodes of bagaudae rebellions in Gaul and Spain. Yves Fremion writes that after Julius Caesar's campaigns against the Gauls, which cost a million or so Gallic lives and a million war captives,

> *pax romana* prevailed...throughout her colonies, of which Gaul was one. This Roman peace was one of history's most protracted wars, dragging on for four centuries. Whilst the Gallic nobility and wealthy merchants collaborated with the occupation, a habit they never were to lose, the serfs and peasants fought on, rebelling regularly against the invader, region by region. (P.12)

About AD 283, the bagaudae resumed activities in Gaul, this time under the leadership of two Roman officers who had deserted, Amandus and Aelienus. They organized an army headquartered at the junction of the Marne and Seine rivers. As per bagaudae methods, they raided wealthy estates and cities, inviting the poor and downtrodden to join them. Small-scale bagaudae continued throughout the next two centuries. In the 5th century, there were several, well-organized movements. Between 404 and 417, bagaudae in western France from Normandy in the north to Gascony in the south fought against Rome, sometimes in conjunction with Germanic invaders. The movements developed into full-fledged separatist movements in Roman Gaul. The region of Armorica, which included modern-day Brittany, under the leadership of the bagaudae leader, Tibattus, became independent of Rome for about a generation. Shortly after the revolt led by Tibattus, a similar revolt took place in Spain. In 448, a doctor named Eudoxius led another, short-lived bagaudae in Gaul. Fremion describes the impact of the bagaudae:

> A severe blow had been dealt to the decomposing Roman system, more assuredly perhaps than by the incessant invasions from without. Even

more effectively, the internal erosion caused by the empire's moral, social, and political decadence undermined its remaining crutches. (p. 14)

Perennial Plebeian-Patrician Conflict

In order to analyze further the nature of class conflict and popular resistance in Rome, we need to return to monarchical times in early Rome during the conflict between the kings and the patrician class, and to the conflict between the patricians and the plebeians during republican times. For almost 300 years, first the kingdom, then the republic were rent with social and political conflict between the plebs and the patres. The latter were represented in the senate, which was composed of a hundred patricians from each of the original, three tribes of Rome. They were the patriarchs of Roman society. They were also the priests of a very religious, superstitious society. They performed vital social and religious functions, ensuring that traditional, customary ways were followed in Roman politics and law. The senate supposedly had an advisory role under the monarchs even if it was also in fairly permanent conflict with the kings, especially the last king, Servius Tullius. In order to increase their power, kings often sided with plebeians against patricians.

After the republican revolution of 510 BC, the senate assumed more of a public role beyond its religious functions and advisory role. In effect, it became the most powerful political body, this in spite of there being another powerful assembly, the century assembly of Roman soldiers. The latter assembly annually elected public magistrates who served for a year. The chief magistrates of Rome were two consuls who commanded the military, supervised civil affairs, and acted as judges. Each consul could veto the decisions of the other. Upon leaving their positions, they sat ex officio in the senate.

Roman historians wrote that for years plebeians were shut out from public offices reserved for the patrician class. Over a period of about 15 generations, public offices in Rome were opened gradually to plebeians. While many historians have held that the plebeians were poor commoners, this is not so certain according to current-day historians such as Richard Mitchell. Mitchell claims that the plebeians simply did not occupy the original religious offices reserved to patricians, even if some plebeians were actually wealthy. Furthermore, some patricians were not wealthy.

From a historiographical point of view, there were no historians writing during the period of the political conflict between the two orders. The sources wrote about this conflict well after the fact. Some even have argued that Roman writers in the periods of the end of the republic and the beginning of the empire had no first-person reports. Furthermore, Roman writers might have retrojected the intense class conflict of the period in which they were writing, assuming it was ever thus. As well, legend also played an important role as an historical source for these writers. Determining exactly who were the original plebeians and patricians is still a subject of conjecture and debate, however, a few points can be made fairly safely. Firstly, there was indeed a longstanding conflict between the two orders as they were called, even if they might not be social classes in a Marxist sense. The proof is the long list of legislation adopted over the decades that specified that plebeians, henceforth, could serve in this or that function, and that they could occupy this or that public office. If the plebeians were not originally excluded from the political process, why was all the legislation necessary? This legislation represents a large part of the political, legal, and constitutional development of the Roman republic. Why else were the minority patricians and the majority plebeians in perpetual conflict if it was not about political power? Secondly, it seems safe to say that there may have been plebeians that issued from the original Romans. It is probably not likely that all original Romans would have served as priests on behalf of Rome. Since Rome liberally granted Roman citizenship to newly conquered peoples regardless of their wealth or whether they were poor or yeoman farmers or free craftsmen, it seems most probable that plebeians were those who came later to Roman citizenship than the original patres or descendants of the patres. According to the Dutch historian, Jona Lendering, "the word *plebs* is said to be derived from the verb *plere*, meaning 'to fill up'. Plebeians were, therefore, people who were considered additional to the first, real Roman population."

There was not always disunity between old Romans and newcomers. In 510, the two groups collaborated to terminate the Etruscan monarchy, then establish the republic wherein some collaboration did continue. A patrician named Publius Varelius served several terms in the first decade of the sixth century BC as consul. He installed several measures that favored the plebeians: permitting appeal against consul decisions about judicial matters; exempting needy plebeians from taxes; and removing control of the treasury from the hands of the consuls, and transferring it to the temple of Saturn, site of a popular cult under the control of quaestors, treasurers who dated from the time of the monarchies. For these and similar measures that pleased the plebeians, Varelius was given the moniker of *Publicola* or *Poplicola*, meaning friend of the people. Still, it was the stubborn refusal of most patricians to concede total and perpetual control of public offices as well as patricians' refusal to grant the right to plebeians to sit in these positions that divided the two groups. Just as stubbornly, plebeians sought the right to these public offices, especially since they had to serve in the military in the all-too-frequent wars that were often the object of the public debate that the patricians controlled.

Plebeians had several factors on their side: their numbers, since they were by far the majority, while patricians represented the minority; the unity of the plebeians comprised of poor commoners, middling peasants and craftsmen, and wealthy businessmen and traders; and the brilliance of plebeian tactics. Roman historians report that at least five times, the plebeians left Rome during military crises in support of their demands, leaving patricians to fight their wars alone or, at least, leave them with that impression. This created disunity among patricians, some of whom stepped forward to negotiate by offering compromises to the striking plebeians. In 494 BC, fleeing the autocratic rule of Appius Claudius Sabinus Inregillensis, the plebeians repaired en masse to *Mons Sacer*, a sacred Roman mountain, in order to found a new town. In response, the patricians freed certain poor plebeians from their debts and recognized that two plebeian officers known as tribunes had the authority to veto actions of patrician magistrates and the senate when they violated plebeian rights. It should be noted that the plebeians already had recognized magistrates known as aediles who supervised the temples on Aventine Hill dedicated to the goddesses, Ceres and Libera, and the god Liber, who were deities of grain, wine, fertility, and freedom. To celebrate the 494 accord between patricians and plebeians, Romans built the Temple of Concord. Moreover, there were four more plebeian secessions in the years 449, 445, 342, and 287 BC, all of them successful in terms of achieving their political aims

On their side, the patricians could count on custom and tradition, and the veneration of the ancient, which held all Romans in their sway. There was also the influence of religion in a society that was profoundly religious and superstitious. As well, the patricians negotiated skillfully, even cynically, offering concessions to the plebeians, while maintaining their fundamental patrician authority. When they did concede real power to the plebeians, they were able to continue holding on to positions legally open to plebeians owing to their political prowess and control of the century assembly. For instance, plebeians long had demanded access to the chief magistrate position of consul, which patricians stubbornly resisted. In 445 BC, plebeians were granted the right to the new position of military tribunes with consular powers, which recognized plebeian military authority outside Rome. Nevertheless, patricians continued to hold on to these new positions, putatively created for plebeians, for another 45 years. Similarly for quaestor positions opened some years earlier to plebeians, but which patricians continued to dominate until 421 BC, when half of the quaestor positions finally were guaranteed to plebeians. (Mitchell, p. 14) When positions were finally opened to plebeians, such as the consulship in 366, then the patricians created other positions open only to them such as the office of praetor responsible for justice in Rome and the office of censor, whose occupant conducted the census that determined class membership in the century assembly as well as carrying the momentous responsibility of ensuring morals in the conduct of citizens. Full equality between the two groups was achieved only in 287 BC but, by then, the small number of plebeians who had gained access to political office now had little in common with lower-class plebeians, and much more in common with wealthy patricians. Together, they came to form a new class of wealthy, landowning aristocrats called *nobiles* that now dominated Roman society and politics. Wealthy plebeians whose sons had not yet acceded to public office now formed most of the membership of the class of the *equites.*

Economic Rights for Plebeians

We saw earlier that the legendary second king of Rome, Numa Pompilius, is alleged to have established the traditional guilds of craftsmen in early Rome, allowing them to set up their own councils, courts, and religious observances. The common people of ancient Rome eventually also included yeoman peasants, tenant farmers, landless farm laborers, urban laborers, and other lowly people such as porters, carters, messengers, food vendors, prostitutes, criminals, bandits, and slaves. Whereas Ramsay MacMullen estimates that a third of the Roman population lived in dire poverty, Robert Knapp's figure has it that twice that proportion was poor. These people typically faced the possibility of death if their personal circumstances deteriorated owing to famine, economic crisis, unemployment, or warfare. (Knapp, p. 103) Whosoever is right between MacMullen and Knapp, it is true that the prosperous people who formed the ruling class and the equestrian class were, by far, the minority in Rome.

As per elsewhere in the ancient world, problems of debt plagued ordinary people. Roman laws were indeed pernicious, permitting creditors to imprison debtors or to turn them into slaves, a legal status called *nexum*. This was often the lot of debt-ridden peasants. In the late republic, then again during the empire, free peasants might be turned legally into the tenant farmers called coloni, whose condition evolved later in the Middle Ages into serfdom. Debt was always a concern of plebeians and their political representatives. As a result of the plebeian secession of 494 BC, patricians absolved debts of insolvent plebeians, and released debt prisoners. In 367 BC, under the leadership of the tribunes, Licinius Stolo and Lucius Sextius, measures were adopted that eased debts by subtracting interest on debts already paid from remaining principle, and by providing three additional years to clear debts. In 357 BC, *lex manlia* set limits for interest rates, but the limits were observed only in their breach. In 352 BC, a novel approach was introduced. *Quinqueviri mensarii* were public bankers working for the state who were authorized to make low-interest loans to people facing debt problems, who could offer cattle or other animals or other forms of property as security, while being fairly evaluated for this property. In 326, *nexum* finally was abolished, but creditors could always lean on debtors informally, turning them into clients or tenant farmers.

A more fruitful avenue for public dissent and the demands by the common people involved redistributing land. Between the early fifth century and 367 BC, according to Richard Mitchell, two dozen agrarian bills addressed the problem. (Irani and Silver) In the fifth century, the first agrarian bill was sponsored by a patrician consul named Spurius Cassius Viscellenus. The measure was foiled by the patricians. For his trouble, the state executed the popular Spurius, using the excuse that he had been currying public favor with a view to becoming a king, the Roman crime of *regnum*. Patricians used the same reasoning in the middle of the fifth century BC when a wealthy plebeian named Spurius Maelius bought wheat during a famine and resold it at low prices to the needy. At the beginning of the fourth century BC after an invasion by Gauls was repelled, a wealthy man named Marcus Manlius sold his estate and used the proceeds to assist poor debtors whose lands had been ruined during the invasion. These civic-minded and charitable public figures were put to death under the accusation of *regnum*.

In 367 BC, Licinian laws limited the amount of conquered public lands one man could own to a maximum of 300 acres. In 356 BC, *lex icilia aventino publicando* made available to plebeians the public lands of the Aventine Hill, already sacred to plebeians as they were the location of temples to the god Liber and the goddesses, Ceres and Libera. Plebeians were suffering at the time from a famine caused by excessive rains. Over time, the Aventine Hill became an important mercantile and popular quarter.

A more typical law aimed at making land conquered during war available to plebeians. Often, *ager publicus* was rented at low prices to wealthy landowners, a privilege they defended arduously, thus preventing the common people cum soldiers from access to the lands the latter had conquered. So, laws were adopted for these public lands to be distributed to peasant-soldiers as part of the booty for their role in conquests. One such law was sponsored successfully by a tribune named Gaius Flaminius Nepos who, in 232 BC, transferred land conquered from the Gauls in northern Italy to peasants whose lands had been ruined during the warfare with the Gauls. In the early days of the republic, this policy helped eased social tensions in Rome. As Roman territory spread further abroad, Roman soldiers were granted conquered lands in the provinces, which compensated somewhat for the ruination of their lands in Italy by warfare, absence, environmental destruction, and theft by the wealthy. In 396 BC, soldiers came to be paid *stipendaria* from public money raised through land taxes, the *tributum*, from which serving soldiers were absolved.

Equal Treatment before the Law

The story of how plebeians acquired equal treatment before Roman law was told in 1901 by an American historian, William Morey, and it still remains a useful treatment of the subject. In 462 BC, a tribune named Gaius Terentilius Harsa proposed that basic Roman laws be written for all to know, including plebeians. Up to that point, patricians had resisted writing the laws that they administered. Morey wrote about the law and patricians "...who kept the knowledge of it to themselves, and who regarded it as a precious legacy from their ancestors, too sacred to be shared with low-born plebeians." Terentilius proposed that a commission be appointed to gather the laws and publish them so that plebeians might know of what they were being charged. Patricians resisted this simple recommendation for a decade during which dissension reigned. Instead, they offered concessions to the plebeians, among them, limiting the amount of fines for illegal acts and increasing the number of tribunes to ten. Still, Terentilius pursued the matter. It was agreed finally that a commission of ten men called *decemvirs*, all patricians, would publish the laws. It is possible that the commissioners consulted Greek law in southern Italy, which was then still Greek territory. As part of the commission agreement, patricians gave up their consul and quaestor positions, while the plebeians did likewise with their tribune and aedile positions so that the commission might govern. At the conclusion of the commission's work, ten tables of brass were erected in the Forum with the laws inscribed in a language easy for all to know and follow. The next year, a second commission was appointed to complete the work, and it produced two more tables. The rule of the second commission, however, was brutal and unjust, so the plebeians seceded for the second time. In response, the old form of government was then restored, led by two consuls supportive of the plebeians, Valerius and Horatius. Among their reforms was the legal recognition of a popular assembly of plebeians known as *concilium plebis*, and a tribal assembly composed of citizens from both orders known as *comitia curiata*, whose laws in time became binding upon all Romans. When, in 445 BC, *lex canuleia* permitted inter-marriage between members of the two orders, at least nominally all Romans were now equal before Roman law.

The Plebeian Ascendancy

The plebeian rise to power and legal status equal to those of the patricians took over three centuries to achieve. Moreover, further improvements in the legal situation of plebeian commoners continued after this period. After formal equality was achieved, wealthy plebeians and patricians now combined to form a new ruling class of wealthy aristocrats known as *nobiles*. Newer arrivals to this class were known as *homines novi*, new men. While patricians and old wealth might have sneered at these men, the typical Roman snobbishness usually did these new men no specific harm in their exercise of power. The accession to formal, legal equality was an arduous process whereby plebeians demonstrated their resolve, and patricians their stubbornness in attempting to retain their exclusive power and legal status. Both sides demonstrated cleverness in their tactics. Unity and solidarity within each order usually meant victory in obtaining or resisting specific gains for the plebeians. It was, despite what some historians argue, somewhat of a form of class conflict within which commoners resisted the ruling class, thus improving their lot and social position, while directly influencing the course of Roman social development.

By way of clarification of what was a complex and complicated process, we provide a summary of particular plebeian gains over the centuries in economic, legal, and political matters. This author makes no claim of completeness. It also should be noted that both historians and Roman sources sometimes disagree both about dates, and the exact nature of some of the laws and measures that were adopted. The main source for this chronology is H.H. Scullard. All dates are approximate and BC, except for the last line of this chronology.

510–509—Patricians and plebeians unite to overthrow the Etruscan monarchy, while installing the republic.

494—Plebeians appoint two tribunes, whose physical integrity will be protected by plebeians.

471—The number of tribunes is doubled; they are now elected by an assembly of the plebeians.

459—The number of tribunes increases to ten.

456—The public lands of the Aventine Hill are made the exclusive domain of the plebeians.

451–450—The XII Tables of basic laws are collected and published for all to know and observe.

449—Plebeian plebiscites adopted by the assembly of the plebeians are given the force of law.

447—Quaestors, financial officials, are elected by a joint, plebeian-patrician assembly.

445—The consul position is replaced by military tribunes with consular power, positions to which plebeians can aspire.

443—The position of censor, limited to patricians, is created to do important tasks formerly performed by the no-longer existing consuls.

421—The number of quaestors is raised from two to four; the position is now open to plebeians. In 267, the number of quaestors is increased to ten, half of whom must be plebeians.

396—Plebeian soldiers start receiving stipends.

367—The consul position is reintroduced, while the patricians create the judicial position of praetors, in effect, judges who take over judicial power from the consuls, and who are answerable only to patricians.

366—The first plebeian consul is elected, while a newly-created aedile position is now alternated annually between the two orders, thus replacing plebeian aedile positions. Limits are created for the amount of public land any one individual can own, and for the number of animals owned by an individual that can graze on public land.

357—Interest rates are fixed.

356—A first plebeian dictator is named to rule during a foreign invasion.

352—Public bankers are created to make low-interest loans to debtors.

351—The first plebeian censor is elected.

345—Inter-marriage between plebeians and patricians receives state sanction.

342—At least one consul must now be plebeian; moreover, both consuls can be plebeians.

337—The first plebeian praetor, or judge, is elected.

326—Debt bondage is abolished.

312—Sons of ex-slaves can now be named to the senate; as well, landless, rural tribesmen living near Rome receive the right to vote.

304—One jurist, son of a freedman, publishes an account of legal procedures, helping make knowledge of the law accessible to all.

300—Religious positions formerly reserved to patricians are opened legally to plebeians.

293—The requirement for senate approval of elections is terminated.

287—Plebeian laws now became binding on all assemblies and all citizens, patrician or plebeian.

221—The century assembly of soldiers is reformed to make it more equitable for the poor.

139—Elections for public office are now conducted by secret ballot.

AD 91–80—As a result of the Social War, Italians become Roman citizens.

AD 58—A number of measures favorable to commoners are adopted under the leadership of Publius Clodius Pulcher, among them: preventing magistrates from dissolving assemblies by using bad omens as a rationale; restricting the authority of censors to censure the morals of citizens; providing for exile for the crime of executing citizens without trial; making political associations and collegia once again legal after the consul Sulla had made them illegal thirty years earlier; providing free grain to poor citizens where it had been offered previously at low prices; and extending voting rights to freedmen.

AD 212—Roman citizenship is extended to all free people in the empire.

The Populares-Optimates Conflict

By the latter half of the second century BC, Rome had evolved considerably from its origins as a small farming community. Massive social changes had been wrought by Rome's military expansion, by the influx of slaves and wealth, and by negative impacts upon the yeoman peasantry that had fed Rome previously, and fought its battles of conquest that had permitted its expansion. In the words of Michael Grant:

> Greed unbounded in its appetite, unchecked by any scruple, and now allied with power, spread throughout the life of the community, corrupting or devouring everything in its path; it respected nothing, and held nothing sacred until, finally, it worked its own destruction...then the foundations of the state were shaken, and civil strife made itself felt like some convulsion of the earth. (p. 52)

The Roman historian and *popularis* politician, Sallust, wrote of his era:

> As soon as riches came to be held in honor, and brought glory, imperium and power, virtue began to grow dull; poverty was seen as disgraceful, innocence as malevolence. Therefore, because of wealth, youths were seized by luxury, greed, and pride; they stole and squandered; reckoning their own property of little worth, they coveted other peoples'. Contemptuous of modesty and chastity, of everything, divine or human, they were without thought or restraint. (Ali, p.8)

Moreover, beyond the cultural changes, there was a chronic food shortage in Rome caused by the decrease in grain and other food hitherto produced by Italian peasants, which itself was caused by a shortage of agricultural manpower. Just as ominously, some worried where the next generation of soldiers was to come given that social change was forcing the yeoman peasants off their lands and into the cities. The social conflict between the patrician and plebeian orders had become a class conflict between the rich nobility, Rome's ruling class, and the common people. Wealthy plebeians joined with the traditional, patrician families to form this new ruling class. These wealthy plebeians now occupied the formerly popular tribune positions from which they united with the senators, even joining the august body themselves. In fact, the actual number of patrician families was diminishing. Some families even had died out owing to a low rate of reproduction, while others had become relatively poor in spite of high social status. Some patricians had to marry into wealthy plebeian families in order to maintain their membership in the ruling class. Such was the case of the Gracchi brothers, whose mother was of patrician lineage, while their father was a wealthy plebeian.

The Gracchi

It was under such social circumstances that Tiberius Gracchus fired the first volley in 133 BC of a political campaign that degenerated eventually into a series of thirteen, full-fledged civil wars during the next hundred years. These wars destroyed the republic and gave birth to the empire of Caesar Augustus. Tiberius Gracchus and his younger brother, Gaius, were among the aristocratic and wealthy politicians who strove to address the social problems of the republic and its common people. They were called *populares* (*popularis*, singular). While they did not form a political party as we would know it in modern-day terms, and while there were important differences among them, populares, nevertheless, formed a distinct strain in the factional politics of the last century of the republic. The ultimate popularis, in terms of fame and the nature of his politics, was Julius Caesar. Just as ardently were the populares opposed by wealthy conservatives called Rome's best people, or the *optimates*. There always had been politicians from the ruling class of patricians and wealthy plebeians who had tried to represent the interests of commoners who, for their part, pressured these politicians to promote popular policies, men such as Terentilius, Spurius Cassius, Marcus Manlius, and Flaminius Nepo, just to name a few. The last century of the republic produced many politicians who tried to respond to the pressures and needs of the common people.

During a trip through the countryside, Tiberius Gracchus was struck by its degeneration, and by the way slave labor on large farms had replaced the yeoman peasantry. While this inspired him to take political action, Gracchus was also pushed towards it by the common people who inscribed "slogans and appeals on porticoes, monuments, and the walls of houses, calling upon him to recover the public land for the poor." (Grant, p. 72) Gracchus must have been very moved to have spoken these words in a supposed speech to the people, as recorded by the Roman historian, Plutarch.

> The beasts that roam over Italy have every one of them a cave or a lair to lurk in; but the men who fight and die for Italy enjoy the common air and light indeed but nothing else; houseless and homeless, they wander about with their wives and children. It is with lying lips that their imperators exhort the soldiers in their battles to defend sepulchers and shrines from the enemy, for not a man of them has a hereditary altar, not one of these many Romans an ancestral tomb, but they fight and die to support others in wealth and luxury, and though they are styled masters of the world, they have not a single clod of earth that is their own. (Irani and Silver, p. 211)

In addition to providing subsidized grain to the needy, and arranging for the state to pay for the clothing of its poorest soldiers, Gracchus, who was elected tribune for the plebeians in 133 BC, set about to reclaim public lands now in the hands of speculators or large landholders in order to redistribute them to military veterans and to poor, displaced peasants. In order to do so, he revived the Licinian law that limited use of public lands by one person to a maximum of 300 acres, while also limiting the number of animals that one person could graze on public lands. He set up a land redistribution commission composed of his patrician father-in-law, his younger brother, Gaius, and Tiberius Gracchus himself. The senators promised to prosecute Gracchus at the end of his annual tribune term, possibly for the crime of *regnum*, so Gracchus decided to run again for tribune in order to continue his work. His senatorial opponents, however, obstructed his re-election, and had him and 300 of his supporters clubbed to death in the Roman forum. The commission continued its work but senators now were able to use legal means to slow the rate of land redistribution.

In 123 BC, Gaius Gracchus ran for tribune with a similar land redistribution scheme. Gaius was a skilled politician who was able to draw together a program that appealed to peasants, soldiers, the urban poor, and equestrians interested in limiting senatorial power. His program had broad public appeal. Nevertheless, while land was redistributed more successfully than under the leadership of his older brother, Gaius too suffered the same fate as Tiberius, and was murdered eventually by wealthy landowners.

Other Populares

The example of the Gracchi inspired other populares despite the apparent dangers that awaited those who contested the conservative, landowning class. Many populares met violent deaths, while others became embroiled in the civil wars of the final century of the republic. Men such as Sulpicius, Marius, Saturninus, Drusus, Cinna, Lepidus, Cataline, and Clodius presented measures, sometimes successfully in spite of the opposition of senators and the wealthy, that offered debt relief, extended voting rights, and provided cheap grain to the urban poor as well as land to ex-soldiers in Italy and in the provinces.

One of these populares, Gaius Marius, implemented important changes to the Roman army that dramatically changed both military and politics in the long term. Facing invasions with a chronic shortage of soldiers, Marius recruited soldiers from all Roman citizens, including from the landless and the poor. The disenfranchised then had access to paid, permanent employ as soldiers, along with the chance to retire from the army after 20 or 25 years of service with the prospect of gaining farmland. Roman soldiers had had to equip themselves previously, a legacy of the times when yeoman peasants were the backbone of the army. Marius instituted reforms to allow soldiers to be armed, equipped, and clothed from the public treasury.

The populares were not just proposing and implementing these measures out of charitable impulses nor as part of their pursuit of power. They were responding to popular pressures, and the common people knew where their interests lay. Writes American political scientist, Michael Parenti:

> The proletariat played a crucial but much ignored role in the struggle for democratic policies. They showed themselves to be neither a mindless mob nor a shiftless rabble, but a politically aware force capable of registering preferences in accordance with its needs, able to distinguish friend from foe. That their political efforts have been deemed worthy of little more than passing condemnation is but a further reflection of the class biases shared by both ancient and modern historians. (p. 220)

Julius Caesar

The final republican-era popularis to be considered is Julius Caesar. Much maligned in both ancient and modern times, Caesar was, in fact, a social and political reformer whose reputation has been sullied unnecessarily as being a megalomaniac. While Caesar was a ruthless conqueror in Gaul on behalf of Rome, his attitude towards the common people of Rome shows up in the many progressive measures he adopted on behalf of the poor during his occupation of various public offices. These measures have been catalogued by Michael Parenti. (p. 149–165) Among them are the following:
- distributing land to army veterans and to 80,000 commoners, including to 20,000 poor families who had three or more children;
- employing the unemployed to repair ancient cities in the provinces, and to work on public works projects in Rome;
- mandating that large landowners employ freemen rather than slaves for at least a third of their workforce;
- remitting a year of rent to poor renters;
- donating substantial amounts of money to soldiers and commoners;
- prohibiting hoarding of huge amounts of cash;

- introducing duties on luxury imports in order to encourage domestic production;
- introducing sumptuary laws to limit the ostentatious attire, funerals, and banquets of the wealthy;
- improving provincial administration, including lowering taxes on the provinces;
- addressing debt problems by imposing limits on creditors' interest rates; by forbidding fines on debtors and confiscation of debtors' property; by erasing a quarter of outstanding debts by restricting interest that could be collected; and by allowing debtors to cede their property in payment of debts, regardless of whether it sufficed or not as repayment for the debt
- granting the right to Jews to practice their faith in Rome and throughout the Jewish diaspora;
- adopting a number of measures to make political bodies more accountable to the citizenry including divesting the senate of its illegal control over the treasury, and ensuring that tribunes could initiate legislation;
- appointing freedmen, soldiers, and scribes to the senate as well as equestrians and provincial representatives;
- allowing Athenians to re-institute democracy after the city had been conquered by Rome.

This partial list should suggest to readers the progressive and reforming proclivities of Caesar. They also suggest the real reason why Caesar was assassinated by wealthy senators, and why his name was besmirched in ancient times by his contemporaries from the ruling class including by ancient historians. Caesar and other populares behaved as they did not just because they were seeking absolute personal power, nor because they were doing the just and necessary thing according to their views of Rome's needs. They did so in response to popular pressures from the poor, soldiers, craftsmen, and peasants, who could distinguish which politicians were on their side and which ones were not. Sometimes, when we find ourselves being repulsed by the ugly and pernicious behavior of rulers from ancient times, modern-day historians tell us that we shouldn't impose our values upon people from the past. Parenti responds to this putative maxim:

> We hear that we must avoid imposing present values upon past experience, and we must immerse ourselves in the historic context under study, but few historians immerse themselves in the grim and embattled social experience of the Roman proletariat...They see the poor, especially the rebellious poor, through the prism of their own class bias...It has been a longstanding practice to damn popular agitation as the work of riffraff and demagogues. As far as the gentleman historians can see, insurgency is not inspired by legitimate grievances, but by the misplaced and manipulated impulses of the insurgents. (p. 221)

The Collegia

We have seen above that in imperial times, collegia became cogs in imperial administration and a source of wealth creation for the state, allowing the state to feed urban-dwellers. This state control applied to butchers, bakers, ship owners, transportation workers, and all workers who were essential to food preparation and supply. Throughout most of the republican era, however, this was not the case since collegia were free organizations of workers. The collegia provided vital means of identity to workers, whether they were free, freed, or slave. Work was a source of immense pride, as seen in funeral epigraphs of the common people that almost always identified the work the deceased had done in their lives. This is exactly the contrary of the elite who, in the words of Robert Knapp,

> do not mention work as for them it is not something to be proud of; all others—free, freed, or slave—do mention it prominently. Here is clear evidence that one of the marks of the ordinary man's mind...is the value of work.... Indeed, the elite prejudice that looks down on labor and business helps to explain ordinary man's invisibility...the elite's devaluation of labor does not extend, (however) to the vast majority... (P. 11)

In spite of the constraints of the official roles that collegia played, combined with the street associations, the collegia were democratic and still egalitarian organizations of workers. Women and men, slave, freed or free, Christian or non-Christian, young and old; all could participate in the deliberations, ceremonies, religious observances, training opportunities, and banquets of the collegia. They made life tolerable for poor workers, providing identity, chances for socializing and recreation, dignified funerals, structure and organization, and quality to plebeian life. This, in itself, was a form of resistance to the social domination and disdain by the ruling class to which working people were perpetually subjected.

Conservative historians generally deny that collegia provided a source of political and economic power to workers, insisting on the apolitical nature of these organizations. This only makes one wonder why collegia were outlawed in late republican and early imperial times, or subjected to strict state controls during the later empire. These same conservative historians insist that collegia were not like medieval guilds controlling quality of work and access to raw materials and the like, nor they were like modern trade unions that strike to improve their social and economic situation. This is indeed puzzling since there is clear evidence to the contrary, at least with respect to the latter. Furthermore, our knowledge of ancient collegia is quite incomplete, limited to the tip of the iceberg. The evidence that does exist suggests that collegia were important actors in, at least, four means of resistance by the common people: taking part in riots about food or similar matters; demanding certain policies in the programs of the populares; operating soldiers' associations in spite of prohibitions; conducting strikes and similar labor actions. When riots occurred, indeed a frequent form of protest by the common people, they were usually organized by the street associations where the various trades people lived. According to Ramsay MacMullen:

> When Cicero describes how agitators set about collecting a mob, it is street by street...when Augustus tries to infuse some order and support for his régime into the population, he does so through the formal recognition of 265 vici... five hundred males to each vici, whom he banqueted at state expense, and encouraged in the offering of prayer to the capital's divine protectors through crossroads cults... (p. 68)

Furthermore, according to P.A. Brunt,

> These collegia all had elected officers and, by their agency, it was easy to raise them for a demonstration or riot, just as the *menu peuple* of the French Revolution were raised through the *sections*. (p. 128)

We have discussed the role of collegia in the political campaigns of the populares in terms of rousing plebeians' support or disapproval for specific politicians and their policies in Rome. In the volcanic remains at Pompeii, according to Charles Micallef, whitewashed and stucco walls bear graffiti in favor of political candidates, graffiti inscribed by representatives of goldsmiths, carters, farm workers, builders, fruit vendors, and skinners. (p.196-200) Collegia that emerged among soldiers in spite of their prohibition might have been the organizations that allowed soldiers to extend their support to specific generals and emperors, or to withdraw their support from the same men. In addition, contrary to much received historical opinion, there does exist evidence for strikes and labor action, particularly in Anatolia, a society whose cities had been organized traditionally by trades before the arrival of the Greeks. John Kloppenborg inventories builders' job actions at Pergamum and Miletus in the 2nd century AD, as well as a bakers' strike in Ephesus in 200 AD. (p. 19). Micallef inventories strikes among builders in Sardis in 459 AD and again in Ephesus. (p. 292-293). He also writes about ship operators working in the wine trade in Provence threatening to strike in the second century AD. (p. 211-212) In AD 271, a magistrate named Felicissimus led a revolt of mint workers against the emperor in which 7,000 soldiers were killed. The mint of Rome, in fact, was inactive for three years, probably owing to this revolt. Since the literary, ruling classes held labor and workers in such disdain, the number of job actions probably was under-reported. As well, such actions might have been described by the literate as pointless rioting or some other criminal activity. To describe a disturbance as being supportive of better wages would have required a basic empathy with workers and knowledge of their demands, which was not at all in the DNA of the ruling class.

Slave Resistance

Conservative historians suggest that slaves seldom resisted the ruling classes of republican and imperial Rome. Some even go as far to suggest that one of the reasons for this was that slaves accepted the discourse of the ruling class about their innate inferiority. In fact, slave resistance showed up in several forms: in the informal resistance of individual slaves; in small-scale, local rebellions; and in the three major revolts that took place during the last century of the republic, two in Sicily and, most famously, the Spartacus-led revolt in Italy.

Robert Knapp describes several manifestations of informal resistance by individual slaves. (p.154–159) Slaves might whine and complain; they might work poorly, or engage in work slowdowns; they might feign ignorance or illness on the job; they might damage or steal the property of slaveholders; and they might intimidate or even assault their masters, especially during riots or demonstrations. Slaves even murdered particularly malicious slave owners. Although this was not a frequent occurrence, masters lived in perpetual fear of this eventuality. Finally, slaves might maim themselves in order to cease working, or even commit the ultimate act of suicide if they could not tolerate any further their servitude, a most drastic way of depriving slave owners of their property. The most common form of individual resistance by slaves, however, was flight. We know this occurred frequently since the state continually undertook measures to help return runaway slaves. For example, Augustus boasted of having recaptured 30,000 runaway slaves, an indicator of the frequency of slave flight. According to Knapp, the runaway slave...

> might have a very hard life, and he might eventually be recaptured, but the harping of the elite literature on runaways...and the ease with which a runaway could melt into the population combine to show that running away was a very live choice for a slave...

The runaway slave also might join roving bands of brigands such as the 600 men led by Felix Bulla in 200 AD, whom we met earlier. By such action, the individual slave joined in collective slave rebellion, even if on a small scale.

There were many small-scale, collective rebellions of slaves, even if evidence about them is sparse and perfunctory. As well, we know virtually nothing about the slave revolts that took place in 501-500, 460, 419, 259, and 217 BC, other than to say that Roman writers and historians did mention them. There was one odd revolt, to say the least, in 258 BC. A young wealthy nobleman named Titus Minucius Vettius, from Capua in Italy, was lovesick for the slave girl of a neighboring landowner. He bought her for an outrageous sum, which he could not actually pay in spite of negotiating several delays, even though the deal indeed was consummated between new master and slave girl. He seemed to be able to buy arms and shields, however, with which he armed his slaves. Titus and his slaves started invading neighboring farmsteads, and adding further numbers of slaves to his army, such that it reached the figure of 3,500 slaves. A Roman army of 4,000 men finally put down the rebellion, but only owing to betrayal by Titus's general, Apollonius. Of the rebelling army, 700 slaves were put to death. While this is a very colorful narrative by the Roman writer Diodorus Siculus, it does seem implausible without some social context to help explain it, such as a regional rebellion or a pre-existing slave revolt against Rome, or something of the ilk.

In addition, there were also well-documented, small-scale slave revolts in 198 BC among Carthaginian slaves captured during the Punic wars, in 196 in Etruria and in 185 BC in Apulia, in Italy. In 134 BC, enslaved silver miners in Laurion in Attica revolted, only one of many such revolts among the miners, even if it was the first under Roman rule of Greece. At the same time as the first great slave rebellion in Sicily in 133 BC, Diodorus writes of sympathy revolts of 150 slaves in Rome, of 1,000 in Attica, of 30 in Nuceria, of 200 in Capua, and of still more slave revolts on the Greek island of Delos, home to the largest Mediterranean slave emporium. We already have met the rebel leader of slaves in 133 BC in Anatolia, Aristonikus, in our chapter about the ancient Greeks. It is perhaps not coincidental that all these slave revolts occurred in the same years that Tiberius Gracchus was trying to improve the lot of poor plebeians in the republic. In 60 BC, the father of Caesar Augustus, Gaius Octavius, wiped out a band of runaway slaves in the mountains of Thurii in southern Italy. The slaves were fugitives from the rebel armies of Spartacus and Cataline, and seem to have operated for several years in the mountains. During the first century AD, there were threatening, rebellious movements of slaves under the reigns of the emperors Tiberius, Caligula, and Nero. In AD 399, slaves in Thrace joined with invading Ostrogoths. In 408-409 AD, 40,000 Romans including many slaves joined the invading Visigoths led by Alaric. Michael Grant also reports that slaves in a Gallic town turned the town over to invading barbarians in 417. (p. 111)

Slave Revolts in Sicily

The two major revolts in Sicily involved thousands of slaves who seriously threatened Roman security. Sicily was the home to large latifundia owned by Romans, with large flocks and herds tended by slaves. By the year 132 BC, furthermore, Sicily was one of the prime sources of grain for Rome. The rebellion appears to have been sparked on one of these immense farms owned by a particularly cruel Greek named Damophilius. The rebellion started among slaves from Syria and Anatolia. It was led by a Syrian named Eunus, who was a *magus* highly regarded by others, a magus being a sorcerer cum magician who were commonplace in the Middle East. His general was a man named Kleon, who hailed from Cilicia in southern Anatolia. Eunus styled himself a king, a title that would have been quite comprehensible to his slave compatriots since there were many kingdoms in Asia Minor. Eunus renamed himself Antiochus, the name of some respected rulers in Anatolian history.

The army he and Kleon led won several victories against Roman forces sent to quell the revolt that lasted three years. During the revolt, the rebels captured the important Sicilian towns of Agrigentum, Enna, Tauromenium, and Morgantina. As well, they controlled most of rural Sicily. It is estimated that the number of slave followers of Eunus and Kleon reached 200,000 at its peak.

The second slave revolt was occasioned unwittingly by the popularis Gaius Marius in 104. As consul, Marius led the fight against invading tribes who hailed originally from Denmark, the Cimbri and the Teutones. Recall the acute shortage of soldiers in Rome and Italy owing to the social changes that had been wrought when the republic gained so much new territory. So, slaves were then employed on agricultural estates in Italy, thus displacing the free peasants who had formed the republican army in past times. In his search for soldiers, Marius appealed to the senate to allow him to search for soldiers abroad. This is how the Roman historian, Diodorus Siculus, described what happened next, in part 36.3 of his chronicles.

> In the course of Marius' campaign against the Cimbri, the senate granted permission to summon military aid from the nations situated beyond the seas. Accordingly, Marius sent to Nicomedes, the king of Bithynia, requesting assistance. The king replied that the majority of the Bithynians had been seized by tax farmers, and were now held in slavery in the Roman provinces. The senate then issued a decree that no citizen of an allied state should be held in slavery in a Roman province, and that the praetors should provide for their liberation. In compliance with the decree, Licinius Nerva, who was at that time governor of Sicily, appointed hearings to set free a number of slaves, with the result that in a few days more than 800 persons obtained their freedom. All the slaves throughout the island were agog with hopes of freedom. The notables, however, assembled in haste, and entreated the praetors to desist from this course.

Marius was forced to concede, thus allowing masters to force freed slaves to return to their owners. The genie of liberty, however, was out of the bottle. The freed slaves banded together near Syracuse, where a slave named Varrus killed his masters. Varrus then led other slaves from his masters' property in raiding other farms, in the process collecting more rebel slaves. The second slave revolt in Sicily had begun. Six thousand slaves elected as their leader a man named Salvius, who set up his capital in the captured town of Triocola in southeastern Sicily. In the west of the island, a Cilician slave named Athenion assembled 10,000 escaped slaves. The two slave leaders met, and agreed that Salvius would be their leader, while Athenion would serve as his general. The latter assembled a slave army of 2,000 cavalry and 20,000 infantrymen that won several victories against Roman armies. When the slave rebellion was crushed finally in the year 100 BC, the leadership of the last 1,000 captured slaves fell to a man named Satyrus. Rather than submitting to the distinct possibility of being torn to bits by wild animals in the Roman forum, the captured slaves chose mass suicide, at the end of which Satyrus killed his last companion before killing himself.

Spartacus

The name of Spartacus sent chills among Roman matrons and their children for centuries, while Spartacus has been a symbol of the downtrodden rising up for even longer. German communists in the wake of WWI called themselves Spartakists. Spartacus possibly had been a humble shepherd in his native Thrace before being captured, then turned into an unwilling Roman gladiator. In 73 BC, three such gladiators, Spartacus, a Gaul named Crixus, and a German named Oenomaus, led 78 gladiators in an escape from servitude. The men were mostly Thracians, Gauls, and Germans. They continued to draw escaped slaves and even poor freemen to their cause, eventually forming an army of about 150,000 soldiers, craftsmen, women, and children that controlled the regions of Lucania and Bruttium in southern Italy.

For eighteen months, they moved north then south on the Italian peninsula, following their flocks and herds that were their means of subsistence. It took seven legions to defeat Spartacus after the latter had won at least four major victories. At some point, it appears there were differences of opinion among the rebels about next steps, with some wanting to invade Rome, while the majority seemed to prefer trying to escape to the north from the Italian peninsula. Crixus already had led a force of Gauls and Germans toward the Adriatic in southeastern Italy, where it quickly met defeat at the hands of the Romans. Spartacus attempted a breakout through northern Italy with the probable aim of escaping from the empire, but the path of his forces northwards was blocked by Roman armies. While the forces led by Spartacus fought with skill and guile, they were forced to retreat south planning to escape to Sicily. They paid Cilician pirates for this purpose, but the pirates absconded with their money under Roman pressure and possibly Roman money, without sailing the rebels to Sicily. An immense army led by Crassus finally was able to corner and beat Spartacus and his army in southern Italy in Bruttium. Spartacus was killed in battle. To set an example in what provides further evidence that Romans depended upon state terror, Crassus, one of the wealthiest men in Rome, had crucified 6,000 of the rebel slaves along the Appian Way between Capua and Rome.

Manumission

All three of the major slave revolts ended in failure. Nonetheless, they did have the effect of making terrified Romans change their practices towards slaves. Treatment of slaves was humanized somewhat, with manumission becoming more frequent as one way to prevent rebellions. A new culture emerged whereby it was considered wise to treat slaves better. In imperial times, eventually, slaves received legal recognition that protected them somewhat from abuse by masters, thus improving their social status. So, while an argument that slaves accepted their condition is not true, it is, nevertheless, true that there were never any slave revolts that were ultimately successful, dealing serious blows to Roman hegemony. Robert Knapp explains that

> the usually overwhelming ability of the powerful to direct effective force against the recalcitrant poor explains in large measure why such revolts were few and far between, and why they were never successful in replacing the powerful with a hegemony of the poor. (p. 117)

Soldiers' Resistance

There is evidence of desertion among both the ranks and officers of soldiers, as happened with the *bagaudae* in Gaul and Hispania. Furthermore, soldiers sometimes defected to the enemy as happened in the Batavian revolt in the Netherlands, or when barbarian forces were invading or threatening the empire. Disciplinary treatment of Roman soldiers was harsh, leading sometimes to mutinies. Robert Knapp cites the Roman historian, Tacitus, who writes about a mutiny in Pannonia, in territories that form part of modern-day Hungary, Austria, and the former Yugoslavia.

> Their issues include abusive centurions and officers, low pay...frequent and vicious corporal punishment, many and dangerous military expeditions, compulsory extension of their legal tours of duty, and officers reneging on promises of land as a reward after service was ended. (p. 231)

Collegia of soldiers, in spite of their supposed illegality, might have participated in organizing defections, desertions, and mutinies since they would have provided a source of leaders and organization for the men.

One source of the power of soldiers was the sheer number of poor men who served in the Roman army. After Gaius Marius began the recruitment of full-time, long-term soldiers among the urban poor, enormous numbers of men served in the army that numbered up to half a million in imperial times. In fact, early in the second century BC, Keith Hopkins estimates that half of the male citizenry served in the army an average of at least seven years. Under Augustus, a sixth of Italian citizens performed military duty for twenty years. (p. 30) Often posted far from Italy, armies took on lives of their own separate from surrounding communities, in which generals played an inordinate role in the lives and opinions of the men. The reverse was also true. Soldiers could both make and unmake their leaders both in terms of military success and their political ambitions. Both in the late republic and then in the empire, most emperors were generals who were favorites of their men, and often wore the imperial clothes owing to the essential support of their men. Armies also provided a source of upward social mobility for the common people, both in terms of common soldiers rising in the ranks as well as in their political power as a group. Thus, just as the armies formed of the common people provided a means of wealth creation for the ruling class, armies also came to comprise part of the power and capability for resistance by the lower classes of the Roman empire to the Roman state and its ruling class.

Summary

We have seen in this chapter that ancient Rome produced wealth for its leading citizens under a system of military conquest, slavery, and oppression and exploitation of free commoners among its methods of social domination. Just as true, however, is that fact that the same methods of wealth creation and the social and state controls needed to ensure social domination by the wealthy also provided occasions for the socially dominated to rebel and to resist, many times successfully. To the same methods of resistance found elsewhere in Greece and the rest of the ancient world must be added the long-term patricians-plebeians conflict that eventually diminished the exclusive political power of the patricians.

Japanese scholar Hidemichi Ota summarizes the relationship between wealth creation and the resistance of the lowly in ancient Rome.

> The structure of resistance movements...was thus conditioned by the socioeconomic formation of the society and by the system and apparatus of the state-force itself. The form and mind of resistance movements was determined by the existing form or the collectivity of resistants themselves, the kinds of pains and severity they suffered, and their understanding or interpretation of their sufferings in this world, or in relation to future life. (Yuge and Doi, p. 13)

Appendix to Chapter 5. A Roman Holocaust

Keith Hopkins writes about ancient Rome in *History Today*:

> Rome was a cruel society. Brutality was built into its culture in private life, as well as in public shows. The tone was set by military discipline and by slavery. The state had no monopoly of capital punishment until the second century AD. Before then, a master could crucify his slaves publicly if he wished... Roman commitment to cruelty presents us with a cultural gap which is difficult to cross.

If this is indeed the case, therefore, it is difficult to imagine how conservative historians for years have adopted willy-nilly the conservative positions of the literate Romans who are our sources of primary documents about ancient Rome. While it is admittedly anachronistic to say so, Rome was a proto-fascist state and society, in fact, an excellent model of such a state and society. Peter Heather's equally anachronistic metaphor compares ancient Rome to that of a modern-day, one-party state. Pick your choice of metaphor.

Let us consider figures for two types of evidence of Roman cruelty: the violent games in the Roman Coliseum and like arenas and fora elsewhere, and the numbers of victims of Roman wars. According to the German scholar, Georg Oesterdiekhoff, the first gladiatorial combats in arenas took place in 231 BC. The Roman Coliseum was built in 80 AD, and was in use for about 500 years, during which 700,000 people died in public spectacles meant to entertain Romans. (p. 174) These included gladiators, criminals, latrones, Christians, and political criminals. At the same time, the wealthy were allowed to die on their swords privately in seclusion for their transgressions, thus avoiding the humiliation of the public arena. Millions of wild animals also were killed in the Roman arenas.

For almost 700 years, these spectacles provided a principal form of entertainment for Romans. Augustus set aside 66 days per year for these festivities; the emperor Marcus Aurelius in the late second century AD set aside 135 days per year. (Oesterdiekhoff, p. 321) Matthew White provides an estimate of a million human deaths in the near-700 years of existence of these games. For the most part, there is little written evidence of sympathy or empathy among Romans with the victims of this sport, other than in the writings of the stoic philosopher, Seneca, or the Christian theologian, Tertullian of North Africa. In fact, such reactions were considered among Romans to be signs of cowardice and weakness. Only in 404, then again in 438 under the influence of the Church did western emperors forbid pagan entertainment in the arenas, including the mortal gladiatorial combats. (*Historia*, p. 10)

As for warfare, Matthew White provides estimates for the numbers of enemies killed in the Roman wars in addition to the near 900,000 Roman soldiers who died in the same wars. With an estimate of 50 or 60 million people in the empire at its peak, consider these estimates for numbers of deaths for these Roman enemies of war (years are BC):

- 8,000 Lusitanians in Hispania in 150;
- 500,000 Carthaginians in the third Punic war of 147;
- 500,000 Carthaginians in the first two Punic wars during the third century BC;
- 300,000 in Marius' war against the Cimbri and Teutones during the period 105–101;
- 300,000 in the so-called Social Wars between Romans and other Italians in 9180;
- 300,000 Pontics and 100,000 Armenians in the wars with Mithridates in the last century BC;
- One million-plus slaves during the three, major slave revolts and related wars, including 40,000 slaves who were crucified;
- One million Gauls killed, with another million captured and enslaved in Caesar's Gallic campaigns during the sixth decade BC;

- 500,000 Jews during the three Jewish rebellions cum wars;
- 3 million in the wars during the years of the demise of the western empire.

These figures are incomplete and only estimates. There were still other military campaigns and deaths. Thus are we justified in calling these deaths part of a Roman holocaust.

CHAPTER 6. CHRISTIANITY IN THE ROMAN EMPIRE

Introduction

The story of the Roman empire is incomplete without considering the development of early Christianity. Christianity was not part of the ideology of social domination until it became the state religion in the fourth century. Until that time, Christianity was a counter-culture to the Roman empire. It helped inspire the resistance of the poor to the power of the empire, locked as it was in the logic of the Iron Age where little critical difference of opinion apart from that of a few Roman intellectuals and rebelling peoples existed with respect to Roman imperialism. After Christianity became the established religion of the empire, the Christian dialectic became one of conflict between the Church hierarchy's basis in and support of secular, temporal power on the one hand, and Christian beginnings in rebellion and resistance on the other hand.

Christianization of the empire helped support the extraction by the ruling class of the economic surplus produced by the popular classes. By providing a common religion and ideology for the empire Christianity lent support to social domination by the ruling class. Moreover, we shall see later that Christianity provided a framework and an organizing element throughout the Middle Ages for the extraction of economic surplus, indeed for social and economic development generally.... However, we run ahead of ourselves... Nonetheless, it is also true that even after its acceptance as the state religion of the empire Christianity did serve to mollify some of the harshest effects of slavery, and to improve the position of women as well as serving as the main charitable organization for providing social services.

Until Christianity became the state religion in the 4th century, there were several facets to the original Christian counter-culture that contributed to popular resistance: its birth in the cauldron of Jewish rebellion during the first two centuries of the common era; early Christian practice of communalism whereby wealth was shared within Christian communities; support for Christianity among the popular classes of the Roman empire; and even the popular heresies amidst the many competing versions of Christianity from which orthodoxy was developed. With respect to the last facet, the study of heresies provides a useful prism through which one can study social and class conflicts of which theological controversies often were but the tip of the iceberg.

Christian Beginnings

Not much is known with historical certainty about the original object of Christianity and Christian devotion, Yeshua bar Yosev, of Nazareth. Since the letter 'J' only came into use in the 17th century BC, Yeshua is a more plausible name for a first-century Jew whose name was rendered *Iesous* in Greek and *Iesus* in Latin. The sources about Yeshua, the Galilean carpenter-teacher, are the documents of the New Testament and the apocryphal gospels, epistles, sayings, and didactic documents that are not part of the recognized Christian canon. None of these are historical documents but rather theological documents written after Yeshua's existence that are, in fact, replete with contradictions in content. They were written after the Christian sect emerged, in response to changing, contemporary conditions and the developing needs of the new religion and its practitioners.

The Judea in which Yeshua preached, built a movement of followers, then died a horrible death by crucifixion, was a cauldron of social and class ferment. Yeshua was only one of many Jewish rebels that the Romans put to death in that period. In fact, during the first century AD, according to Joseph Telushkin, between 50,000 and 100,000 Jews were crucified by the Romans in their attempt to control social ferment among Jews.

Earlier, around 150 BC, under the Hasmonean dynasty of kings Israel had become an independent, theocratic state. The Maccabees had led a successful rebellion against the Hellenizing empire of the Syrians that ruled over the Jewish homelands. The Seleucid empire, centered at Antioch, was a successor régime to that of Alexander the Great. It perennially competed with another successor régime, the Ptolemaic empire in Egypt, for control of Israel. The Seleucids were ultimately successful, proceeding to Hellenize Israel with the co-operation of the ruling class of Israel. They instituted measures considered blasphemous and offensive to many Jews. In response, during the middle of the second century BC the Maccabee family led a successful military campaign that was both a religious campaign and a social campaign of rural protest against the urban, collaborationist ruling class of Jerusalem. Towards the end of the last century BC, however, Israel came under Roman influence and its ultimate control. In 37 BC, Rome appointed a client-king, Herod, to rule over Israel under Roman influence and control.

Israel was now submitted to the twin perils of Roman fiscal and economic policies and Greek culture, both of which threatened traditional Jewish culture and religion.

There were considerable, political differences between the urban ruling class of Jerusalem and peasant Jews. According to Chris Harman, who describes Jewish popular resistance in the two centuries before and after the birth of Christ, popular riots in Jerusalem and banditry in the countryside, especially in the Galilee north of Jerusalem, were frequent occurrences. (p. 89) Jews staged an unsuccessful uprising when the Roman client-king, Herod, was nearing death. Moreover, 5,000 Jews died, including 2,000 by crucifixion, when Herod's son, Archelaus, put down another uprising of Jews. In 7 AD the Romans set out to conduct a census in order to establish levels of taxation. Guerrilla warfare in the Galilee flared, led by the rebels, Judas the Galilean and Zaddok the Pharisee. There were still other clashes that displayed the resistance of the Jewish poor people towards the upper class in Jerusalem and the Roman occupiers, clashes that Harman summarizes by quoting from the contemporary Jewish historian, Josephus. The Roman rulers dealt similarly with a

> "...band of evil men who had godless thoughts, and made the city restless and insecure" as they "incited the people to insurrection...under the pretext of divine revelation." Soon afterward, "a false prophet from Egypt...succeeded in having himself accepted as prophet because of his witchcraft. He led...30,000 persons...out of the desert to the so-called Mount of Olives in order to penetrate into Jerusalem, and attempted to overthrow the Roman garrison"...."Hardly had this rebellion been put down when... a few wizards and murderers joined forces, and gained many adherents...They passed through the entire Jewish land, plundered the houses of the rich, slaying them that dwelt within, set fire to the villages, and harried the land." (p. 89)

All this was part of an apocalyptic, revolutionary atmosphere where many Jews hoped the messiah was coming soon to free the Jewish homeland. In fact, on a regular basis, such messiahs did appear, proclaimed by themselves or others as a leader who could rally the Jews to defeat their nemesis occupiers. These messiahs then met quick deaths at the hands of the Romans. To still other Jews, however, the apocalypse was to occur in the future at the end of days when God would establish heaven on earth, and the high and mighty would be pulled down to be replaced in God's favor by the humble and poor. It was in such an atmosphere that Yeshua began to preach, heal the sick, work miracles, and attract followers. Since he was crucified like so many other Jews of the period, we can assume that his actions and message as well as his following disturbed the Romans and the Jewish ruling class.

What was it precisely that brought his demise? Unfortunately, we only have religious texts to explain the events. Indeed, there is no corroborating, contemporary evidence available from non-Christian sources, even if there does exist corroborating evidence of the existence of the sect of early

Christians. Many have retrojected their own beliefs from modern times onto what they would like to believe Yeshua said and meant, did, and why. Such a process probably occurred, as well, early in the history of Christianity. Even if plausible, these explanations present no proofs; furthermore, they often contradict each other. Was Yeshua a military leader who wished to organize a violent revolt? Was he a resister to Rome, but a non-violent one who preached resistance through non-violence? Did he hold apocalyptic views of Jewish temporal power, or was his kingdom of heaven an other-worldly vision of the end of days, both common expectations in these times among Jews? Considerable effort has been devoted by theologians and other scholars to try to determine who was the historical Jesus, an enterprise that has produced results that sometimes contradict official, Christian doctrine.

American historian Robert Wilken, however, questions the whole point of the exercise of uncovering knowable beginnings since it was historical development that traced the beginnings and development of early Christianity. Documentation and opinions about the founder of Christianity kept changing and developing well after Yeshua's life and death in response to changing society and contemporary events. Wilken argues that it is this process that should be the object of historical concern. Beyond this, one enters the domain of faith, and one can only speculate without conclusive evidence about the historical Yeshua bar Yosev.

About the central tenet of Christianity, for example, what does it mean that Yeshua's followers believed that he had been resurrected from the dead? Was he actually resurrected, an impossibility to many modern minds? Or, did his followers have visions, dreams, hallucinations of his return, all fed by their disappointment at his ignoble death, or was the cause their faith in his immediate return to them, or even of an eventual return perhaps at the end of time, or was it even just evidence of how profoundly they were touched by him? The object of historians should be to study how the Christian movement developed and changed over time, and not any real, historical life of Yeshua. Historians study the written record, which does not exist with any certainty about an historical Yeshua. As for resurrection itself, for most Christians the heart of Christian doctrine, Karl Kautsky wrote the following: "It was not belief in the resurrection of Him who was crucified that created the Christian community, and lent it strength, but the converse. The vitality of the community created the belief in the continued life of their Messiah." (Book 4, II) We can only judge the veracity of Kautsky's claim itself in the light of our faith or the lack thereof.

Growth of Early Christianity

After the execution of Yeshua cum Jesus, his followers in Jerusalem gathered under the leadership of one of his followers, Simon Peter, and Jesus' brother, James the Just. Historians call these people Jewish Christians. In fact, they were one sect among many Jewish sects during these times. We know at least of five other Jewish sects. The Sadducees were upper class people focused on sacrifice at the Temple of Jerusalem and the authority of the priests of the Temple. They believed Judaism should be focused upon the ancient written texts. The Pharisees were students of Jewish law who believed that the traditions of oral interpretations and Jewish law were just as important as the written texts. Pharisaic teachings eventually were reflected in the rabbinical Judaism that emerged around the end of the second century AD. The Essenes were a sect whose members wished to avoid pollution from contact with the Greek and Roman worlds. They withdrew to the desert countryside to live ascetic lives. It was probably this community whose writings were discovered in the Dead Sea Scrolls during the 20th century. The Zealots wished to employ political and military means to separate Jews from their occupiers in order to usher in Jewish independence. Finally, there were the Galileans, who included Yeshua and his followers. Even while being religiously passionate, these Jews, according to the received religious texts, were more lax in following the minutiae of Jewish law. The Christian New Testament contains many references to conflict over religious ideas between the Galileans and the Pharisees. These may have reflected, however, the later bifurcation between early Christianity and the Pharisees who evolved rabbinical Judaism after the Temple at Jerusalem was no longer accessible to Jews. Jews had been chased from Jerusalem by the Romans subsequent to the Jewish revolts. Differences were possibly minor between the Jewish followers of Jesus and the Pharisees in the beginning, but they amplified as the two sects evolved into separate religions, Christianity and rabbinical Judaism. In fact, this process was similar to the evolution of Christian beliefs in general since Christian doctrine and dogma developed in response to evolving, contemporary needs.

During the same decade as Jesus was executed, there lived a Jewish craftsman, a tent-maker named Saul, a well-schooled Pharisee from Greek-speaking Tarsus in southeastern Anatolia. Saul was busily engaged trying to repress local Jewish Christians, who were awaiting the second coming of their Messiah at the immediately pending end of days, having already experienced the resurrection of Jesus themselves. Over time, Saul came to find his repression of the Jewish followers of Jesus pointless, untenable, and unjust. He had an epiphany in which he saw a vision of Jesus resurrected on high in the heavens to the right hand of God. He changed his name to the Greek Paulos, or the Latin Paulus, to make himself more acceptable to the non-Jewish milieu in which he started to preach the message of the Jewish Christians of Jerusalem.

Throughout the Roman empire, there were urban Jewish communities comprised of slaves, mercenaries, craftsmen, and laborers. These Jews had long left Palestine forcibly as slaves or during imperial occupations of the traditional lands of the ancient Hebrews, or to serve as mercenaries for the surrounding empires, or even just to seek a better life beyond the Holy Land. Owing to their distance from Jerusalem, their religious practices started to de-emphasize sacrifice at the Temple in Jerusalem. In their new lands, they instead formed guilds that met in their community houses, or synagogues, for purposes of worship, religious education, and socializing. Diaspora Jews were indeed numerous, in fact, many times more than the actual number of Jews living in Palestine, and included an important community in Rome itself. Julius Caesar had increased security for the Jews when he allied himself with them by ensuring their right to practice their faith everywhere within Roman territory.

Jews attracted many converts to their monotheistic beliefs and fraternal communities, which appealed to urban workers for whom the parochial gods of the provinces were increasingly irrelevant, especially since they were now in regular contact with people from the entire empire. Still other non-Jews were attracted to the synagogues and their observances and social life. They were called God-fearers who, nevertheless, were put off by traditional, Jewish dietary laws and the practice of circumcision, which appeared ghoulish to Greeks and Romans who celebrated the human body. It was these two populations to which Paul was attracted in his preaching mission: diaspora Jews and God-fearers. He de-emphasized the need to follow Jewish practices other than following the Jewish scriptures of the Tanakh. Instead, the converted only had to recognize the crucified Jesus as the Messiah, and to be faithful to his message. This put him into conflict with the original, Jewish Christians who still followed traditional Jewish practices. An early, tense consensus between the two was reached to allow Paul to preach as a follower of Jesus. Over time, this tension increased between Jewish and gentile Christians such that after the unsuccessful Jewish revolts of the first and second centuries, Christianity and Judaism separated. This was a long, arduous process that was to prove fateful for the history of the West.

In his missionary activities, Paul established groups of followers in Anatolia and Greece. In the decade of the 50s, he wrote letters to these embryonic churches that were collected in the New Testament as epistles. During the next decade, a gospel was redacted and attributed to the apostle Mark, who is reputed to have evangelized in Egypt. In the decades of the 70s and 80s, the gospels of Matthew and Luke were written, and in the last decade of the first century or in the early decades of the second century, the gospel attributed to John was written. These were recognized by the emerging, young Church as canonical, while there were many more writings that were not. Some of the latter writings became part of the controversies that we explore below regarding early heresies.

The Earliest Followers

The apostles of Jesus evangelized far and wide within the Roman empire and beyond. For instance, the apostle Andrew is reputed to have evangelized in Armenia, while the apostle Thomas apparently did so in India. At this time within the Roman empire, there was a discourse of glorifying propaganda about Caesar Augustus and his imperial successors. After the seemingly endless class conflict and murderous civil wars of the last century of the Roman republic, the era ushered in by Augustus was one of comparative peace in Rome and Italy, even if there were still local revolts such as those in Judea and Gaul. In his press, Augustus was hailed as the prince of peace, the savior of the world, the bringer of good news to the world, the son of a god, a messiah even. Christians will recognize this discourse applied to Jesus by Paul, perhaps a conscious decision made for ease of familiarity when Paul began converting subjects of the Roman empire. On the other hand, use of this language might have been a sign of rebellion by taking the propaganda descriptions of Augustus and his successors to apply them to Jesus Christ, the 'real' prince of peace, savior of the world, etc. Thus did Christianity continue in the framework of the popular resistance offered by Judaism, which was inevitable since so many of the early Christians were Jews themselves.

Christianity appealed to urban-dwellers in the empire, especially to the popular classes, even if there were also wealthy people who converted. The latter financially supported the Apostles' travels and provided places of worship and hospitality for Christian communities. As we have discussed earlier, the empire was organized to support the wealthy ruling class at the expense of the common people. Furthermore, while the empire started deteriorating in the third century, Christians were able to deal with worsening material conditions by inverting them into opportunities, even blessings. For example, as a counter-balance to ever-present realities of hunger and famine, Christianity offered the spiritually satisfying act of fasting. As a counter to the ubiquitous poverty of the times, Christianity offered positive vows of voluntary poverty; to repeated epidemics and short life expectancy during these times, Christians offered the succor of solidarity and comfort to the ill and dying, and the message that these people were leaving this life for a better one.

Christianity provided a popular counter-culture to that of imperial Rome. Christian faith also offered many strengths to its converts, which Jerry Toner describes. (p. 190–197) At a time when the state was taking increasingly more from the common people in taxes, and when wealthy patrons and the state were providing fewer public entertainments and spectacles, the Christian church was providing services, even money to faithful commoners. With recourse to the philanthropy of wealthy Christian converts, bishops were able to offer charity to the poor, the old, the sick, and the exposed, abandoned and orphaned children of the empire. While most people had always been poor, the beneficiaries of Christian welfare services now were receiving social recognition from the broader society that support must be offered to its most vulnerable members. This was a most novel, even radical idea, and it provoked wonder from Christianity's most ardent critics such as the pagan intellectual, Celsus, who marveled at the ways Christians cared for each other. Christian charity acted as a magnet for converts. The regular gatherings of *agape*, the Greek term for the social meetings and love feasts that evolved to become the sacrament of the Eucharist also were attractive. Feast days devoted to saints and the commemoration of the apostles were joyous, communal feasts that replaced the former celebrations dedicated to pagan deities. In a different order of things, holy men and ascetic monks became local heroes who delivered miracles, cures, propitious weather, and much succor and support. They provided passionate enthusiasm that could even border on heresy, but that the Church co-opted for its own purposes. Nonetheless, most noteworthy about these holy men and ascetics was their

> passion for social justice and championship of the poor and oppressed. Saints and holy men became the protectors of the oppressed—local heroes whose importance can be seen in the fierce fighting that often broke out for control of their remains. (A forerunner of the veneration of relics that was to become a motor of economic development in the Middle Ages—author) They personified Christian tenets in a way that was accessible to all. Their popularity rested on the fact that saints met many of the popular needs. The holy man's actions gained the force of charisma because they tapped in to the hidden agenda of the subordinate. (Toner, p. 192)

One of these early saints was Basil of Caesaria, a fourth century bishop of Cappadocia in eastern Anatolia. The saint wrote the following addressed to the rich.

> Which things, tell me, are yours? Whence have you brought your goods into life? You are like one occupying a place in a theatre who should prohibit others from entering, treating that as his own which was designed for the common use of all. Such are the rich...The rich man is a thief. (Ali, p. 10)

There was another important, social function that increased the store of the early Church. So as to curry public favor during the fourth century, the emperors Constantine the Great and Valentinian instituted an office to defend the urban poor called *defensor civitatis*. Within a generation or two, however, the position came under the control of local governments dominated by the local ruling classes, which meant that it lost the effectiveness it might have had originally. So, the *defensor civitatis* function was transferred to local bishops, who used their authority regularly to call to order municipalities and imperial officers when they offended the interests of the common people. The bishops also served as mediators in disputes, while the poor also had recourse to the local bishop's courts to seek justice from the state.

While the Church could not offer here on earth the kingdom of heaven, they could offer the next best thing, a chance to get there via martyrdom during local or imperial persecutions. The emperor Nero initiated persecutions of Christians by blaming them for the burning of Rome that occurred in 64 AD, the period during which Peter and Paul are alleged to have been martyred in Rome. Between the years 202–210, the emperor Septimius Severus adopted a law prohibiting the deliberate spread of Judaism and Christianity, which led to violent persecutions in Egypt and North Africa. In 250, the emperor Decius issued an edict requiring all citizens to sacrifice to the emperor in the presence of a Roman official, who would then issue a certificate called a *libellus* proving they had done so. Three years later, the emperor Valerian demanded that Christian clergy sacrifice to the Roman gods. Finally, the emperor Diocletian, who ruled from 284 to 303, pursued what is known to historians as the Great Persecution. In a series of edicts, Diocletian purged the Roman army of Christians, and demanded universal sacrifice to the Roman gods from all, including Christians. It is estimated that about 3-4,000 Christians were martyred by Diocletian, mostly in the east.

This leads us to the question of numbers of Christians killed in these persecutions. There is now a consensus that the number of Christians killed was considerably less that that evoked by promoters of Christianity. It is difficult to venture guesses on total numbers. In ancient times, people were notoriously hyperbolic and inaccurate when it came to figures. Tens became hundreds, hundreds became thousands, thousands became millions. Furthermore, while there were indeed formal, imperial persecutions, their applications were sporadic and spotty in terms of effects in the provinces. Most emperors left Christians alone, even if they might find them annoying or irreligious for their failure to worship the Roman gods that kept the world right. Even so, the cult of martyrs did prove to be an attractive element for convincing people of the rectitude of Christians. It is estimated that in the last half of the third century, the Christian population increased sixfold to six million, owing in part to the galvanizing effects of Christian martyrdom during persecutions. Nonetheless, the question of martyrdom was also to prove divisive for the early Church, as we shall see below.

Early Heresies

Understanding early heresies is important for understanding the growth of early Christianity and the heresies that emerged during the Middle Ages a millennium later. Medieval heresies offered popular resistance to the powers that existed in the Middle Ages, including the ecclesiastical authorities. There also were many different forms of Christianity in the early centuries after the death of Jesus. Scholarly opinion is divided between those who claim that the orthodox or catholic position about doctrinal matters was the majority position, which very early displayed the tenets of what might be called a proto-orthodoxy. Those of this persuasion would argue that heretical positions were always in the minority. On the other hand, some claim that the proto-orthodoxy was but one form of Christian worship among many competing forms, from which orthodoxy was hammered out as much by the Roman state after Christianity became the official state religion of the empire as by early religious convictions on the ground. In fact, early Christianity was highly enthusiastic, and resisted the early

Church hierarchy's attempt to impose central doctrine, common practice, and moderation of this enthusiasm. Even in his epistles, Paul warns about the divergences of opinion with which he was already engaged from the early days of his mission. Moreover, we've already seen that Paul and the Jerusalem community from the beginning differed on what to do about traditional Jewish practice in terms of requirements upon Christians. Jerry Toner writes about early Christians.

> The people continued to have a mind of their own about religious matters, and refused simply to follow the bidding of their new Church leadership. The proliferation of what from the Church's view were heretical teachings and ideas show that no simple consensus was established...but the Church leadership's inability to comprehend a popular need for diversity of religious expression does not alter the fact that diverse religious ideas continued to flourish in the Christian world. (p. 195)

In fact, it could hardly be otherwise, given the tremendous variety of pagan thought and practices in existence additional to those of the Roman pantheon, and given the religious fervor and superstition in the Roman world. So, while early Christianity was a form of popular revolt within the empire, so were the various divergences of Christian opinion that the Church came to identify and anathematize as heresies. These heresies were of two types: those that displayed an excess of zeal and enthusiasm in the eyes of the Church hierarchy in its early stages of development; and those that either deliberately or through well-meaning error presented doctrine that was not true in light of the young Church's perception of the Christian message. We next consider each of these in and of themselves, and as forerunners of the popular heresies of revolt in the Middle Ages.

Enthusiasm

We divide early heresies into just two groups, sufficient for our purposes since this is social history, not religious history nor theology. In actual fact, the latter two disciplines offer finer ways of categorizing and understanding the early Christian heresies, but our two categories will do for purposes of social history.

The first important heresy was promoted by a bishop from northern Anatolia named Marcion, who contended about 150 AD that the Hebrew Tanakh should not be considered a Christian holy document. Marcion argued that the Tanakh represented the teachings of the Father, which were now surpassed by those of the Jesus the Son. Therefore, the Father and His teachings were no longer relevant. The God of the Jews was replaced by the message of the God of Love, Jesus. Nonetheless, Marcion had performed the useful service of being the first to anthologize the epistles of Paul for the use of the early Church. Even so, he was declared persona non grata for his teachings, initiating a pattern with respect to several early leaders of the Church who were later anathematized for their divergences from the eventual, official Church position. Marcion was considered by the Church to have been an over-zealous advocate of the need to separate early Christianity from its Jewish roots, even as the two religions actually were in the process of bifurcating.

About AD 155 in the region of Phrygia in central Anatolia arose another heresy known as Montanism. Montanus, the leader of the heretical sect, possibly was a convert from the local paganism based on worship of Cybele, the Great Mother. Phrygians were reknowned for the ardor of their pagan beliefs and worship. Montanus, accompanied by two prophetesses, preached that the Last Judgement was nigh, and was about to happen on the peak of a specific mountain in Phrygia. Montanus also claimed to be the Paraclete, that is, one inhabited by the Holy Spirit. He and the two women would fall into rapturous trances whereby they prophesied in unknown tongues.

Montanus had an impressive following owing to his gifts of prophecy, speaking in tongues, and the alleged occupation of his being by the third Persona of the Trinity. The early Church knew of all these phenomena; in fact, Pentecost occurred when the Holy Spirit was reputed to have descended upon the apostles in order to inspire and guide them in their mission. While the common people of Phrygia yearned for the passion and spiritualism of their religious past, the Church denied that these phenomena had actually reappeared with Montanus and his followers, especially the prophecy about the end of the world and the rapture that would take place on a mountain in Phrygia. So, even if the Montanists were excommunicated, the sect continued to exist outside the Church for generations. Around 205, Montanism was adopted by a Carthaginian lawyer named Tertullian. Similarly to Marcion, Tertullian had made a significant contribution to the early Church. He was the first Latin-speaking intellectual to take up defense of Christianity, including elucidating the nature of the Trinity. Tertullian was profoundly and passionately spiritual. North Africans were similar to the Phrygians in the ardor of their religious past; their worship of Saturn had once provided occasions for wild religious celebrations of freedom and social equality. Around 206, Tertullian, concerned that the Church was becoming too lax and flabby in its practices, converted to Montanism. Tertullian attracted followers who came to be known as Tertullianists; they survived as a small sect for a time after the death of their founder.

Marcion had addressed the question of the relationship between God the Father who had created the world, and God the Word, or Jesus, who had superseded God the Father. In the second century, gnostics also addressed this question to argue that the material world created by God the Father was evil, and that only the spiritual world was good. There were several gurus/teachers around the empire who argued that Jesus had transmitted secret knowledge to this effect, and that it had come down to them. They produced bizarre schemes about reality and cosmogonies given this dual world, even while continuing to insist that they were followers of Jesus and

Christian. In a similar vein of thought, in the third century, the Church was affected by a religion that had been started by a Persian of Jewish Christian extraction named Mani. Mani added certain content to Zoroastrianism that had always taught the duality of good and evil, but Mani clearly claimed that two gods were at perpetual war in the human soul. These people were called Manichaeans, and their ideas infiltrated Christianity. In the turmoil of the third century as the Roman empire started its slow demise, many sought answers about the existence of evil in the world in spite of their Christian faith. In fact, this was a question that plagued Christians from the beginning of Christianity; theologians call this discussion about how God permits evil to exist in the world theodicy. It recurred in many forms in the early Church.

In the second century, a significant movement of ascetics emerged from Anatolia called encratites. The group professed abstinence from meat and forbade marriage for its followers; indeed, they were quite misogynistic, arguing that women were the work of Satan. One of the sub-sects of this group, the *apostolici*, also renounced and condemned private property. The apostolici lived as paupers, actually resembling the ways of the Greek cynics more than those of Christians. They professed orthodox belief, other than rejecting Paul's epistles in which the Saint had criticized gnostic tendencies in the first century. During the fourth century, they were denounced as heretics, and the emperor Theodosius pronounced a death sentence in 382 on them. In the third century, a similar group emerged in Anatolia called the apotactics, who also called themselves apostolics. These heretics condemned private property, and argued that a renunciation of property was essential to salvation. They also rejected marriage, and strove to imitate the communal sharing in which the original followers of Jesus supposedly lived. They did not accept as true Christians those Christians who had complied with the imperial order of the emperor Decius to sacrifice to the Roman gods and, thereafter, returned to the Christian fold. These people were called *lapsi*, and their treatment was an important source of disputes within the young Church. Theodosius also condemned the apotactics as heretics at the same time as the encratites, both being variants of Manichaean dualism, or so it was argued by both Church and state.

Late in the third century, the question emerged of what the Church should do with lapsed but confessing Christians who had survived the persecutions. In actual fact, most Christians did comply with the imperial dictates, so many Christians indeed were lapsed. The Church let them back into the fold via absolution and penance, sacraments of the Church. Some people did not lapse, however, and still avoided martyrdom; in fact, the number of martyrs was actually quite small. To some, the laxness of the Church was simply unholy. This led to schisms whereby entire groups of people left the Church to form their own churches. These people scholars call schismatics, many of whom also were denounced as heretics. One of these schisms occurred in Italy in the third century, under the leadership of a Roman priest named Novatian. Novationists even named their leader a rival pope. This church otherwise followed Catholic doctrine even if it did re-baptize its members into their new church.

In Carthage and Numidia, the latter a Roman province in modern-day eastern Algeria, a similar schismatic church grew under the leadership of a bishop named Donatus. Frustrated with the Church's laxness in accepting lapsed Christians, the Donatists argued that sacraments provided by lapsed clergymen were of no utility. The emperors and the Church were unable to bring the Donatists back into the fold in spite of vigorous, even vicious persecution by the state and the Church, including having their churches and properties confiscated. Around AD 340, there appeared a movement of people in North Africa called circumcellions, composed mostly of poor agricultural laborers. They were called so because of their habit of frequenting saints' tombs; they were often found *circum cellas*, or around tombs, praying ecstatically and begging for charity. Along with poor peasants, fugitive tenant farmers, and runaway slaves, the circumcellion laborers staged a popular insurrection, in the process attacking creditors and slave owners. These people were also Donatists so when Rome tried to crush Donatism by military means, the Donatist hierarchy appealed to these rebels for help. Many of the rebels were killed in the resulting Donatist rebellion, but to their survivors and successors they became martyrs. Some of these people, in imitation of the martyrs cum rebels of Donatism, practiced voluntary martyrdom whereby they would commit suicide or insist that the authorities kill them, so they might join their late, saintly predecessors. There continued to be periodic outbursts of circumcellion enthusiasm for centuries as the Donatist church survived into the seventh century, when it finally succumbed to the Muslim conquest and conversion of North Africa.

These heretics were guilty of excesses of enthusiasm, at least, according to the Church. As wealthy and powerful people joined the Church, Christianity had to come to terms with the reality of the empire, and the fact that Christianity had become its official state religion. What had been a movement of social resistance became increasingly reconciled with the material world and the Roman ruling class. In the eyes of some poor people who adopted dissenting positions, the developing Church was now subject to a number of sins: laxness in dealing with lapsed Christians; the apparent wealth and profligacy of Church leaders, which pushed many to view nostalgically the communalism of the earliest Christians; a lack of religious zeal and rigor; and a clear desire to avoid the glorious and holy end of martyrdom as well as displaying still other weaknesses. Hence, the renunciation of sex and marriage, of meat and wine, of private property and riches in favor of promoting extreme asceticism and poverty.

Starting in the third century in Egypt, two holy men, Antony and Pachomius, retired from the city to live as hermits in the desert in an effort to imitate the sufferings of Jesus, to avoid sin in the material world, and to live holy lives close to God. Tremendously popular and revered among the poor, they were soon joined by others who now formed monastic communities.

The movement spread like wildfire in the east, even if it was dangerously close to being heretical in the eyes of more conservative churchmen. Finally, Saint Basil in the east, then Saint Benedict in the west drew up common rules for these communities, which allowed the Church to reabsorb them into the fold. In the Middle Ages, monasteries even became wealthy centers of economic development and wealth creation... but once again we run ahead of ourselves. These examples of early heresies were, in fact, symptomatic of the same popular revolt that had inspired Second Temple Judaism and the early movement around the person of Jesus. In the Middle Ages, heretical movements were also to serve as means of popular resistance and revolt, often using similar language and concepts to those of early Christianity.

Excesses of enthusiasm thus could combine in a variety of ways to produce heretical movements. These features included: severe asceticism; voluntary poverty; anti-materialism; a passionate rigor of belief; a sense of being imbued with the Holy Spirit; an attraction to the idea and reality of martyrdom; anti-Roman discourse and political posture; and obsessive concern about theodicy and the Jewish roots of Christianity.

Doctrinal Disputes

From the early years of Christianity, there was a hierarchy concerned about imposing true doctrine from among the competing varieties of Christianity. This started as early as the period of the apostolic fathers early in the second century. The apostolic fathers were reputed to have known the original apostles. One of these men, Iranaeus of Lyon, wrote a critique of second-century Gnosticism. Nonetheless, it did take a long time for the Church ultimately to define what might be recognized eventually as Christian doctrine. Only in the fourth and fifth centuries were basic and formal creeds set by synods of bishops organized by the Roman state, partly to refute heresies that were current. These councils produced howling, even violent debates. The doctrine of the Trinity only appeared at the beginning of the third century; thereafter, fierce debates took place over the nature of Jesus as man and/or God. These are called the Christological debates. Catholic or Orthodox doctrine is a complex, intellectual structure. However sublime or true to a person of faith, or even obvious once learned, doctrinal arguments and positions are complex and intellectual, therefore, beyond the ken of many an uneducated or illiterate person. Thus, there was a tendency to transform doctrines into more comprehensible forms. For almost every tenet of doctrine, there was a variant ultimately defined by the Church hierarchy as heretical. For instance, some argued that Jesus was man and not God— these were the Arian heretics; others that Jesus was God and not man— these were the monophysite heretics; still others that Jesus only became the Son of God at his baptism by John the Baptist—these were the adoptionist heretics, and on it goes, such that the modern-day Catholic Church actually enumerates fifty or so heresies, even if not all of them appeared in the early history of Christianity.

The early Christian heresies were often repressed with bloodshed; in fact, many more Christians were killed in inter-Christian fighting than in the Roman persecutions. For many a modern, such debates over arcane points of doctrine can appear quite incomprehensible. However, as Karl Kautsky wrote about the doctrinal disputes:

> Thus, the clash of social contradictions came to appear within the framework of the Christian Church as a mere dispute over the words of Jesus, and superficial historians think that all the great and, so often, bloody battles that were fought in Christendom under the flag of religion were nothing but battles over words, a sad sign of mankind's stupidity. But whenever a social mass phenomenon is reduced to the mere stupidity of the men involved, this alleged stupidity merely shows lack of understanding on the part of the observer and critic, who has not been able to orient in a way of thinking that is strange to him, and to penetrate to the material conditions and forces that underlie it. As a rule, it was very real interests at play when the various Christian sects fell out over the interpretation of Christ's words. (Book 1, # III)

So, what were these material conditions and social forces that underlay these doctrinal disputes with heretical sects? After all, these are the true areas of interest for social historians. Firstly, there were regional religious antecedents that often indicated the coloring that people from a given geographic area might give to their versions of Christianity. Secondly, there were the various forms of paganism with which Christians were in contact and competition, and from which some Christians might draw inspiration. Thirdly, there was simply the matter of who got first to an area to promulgate their own brand of Christianity; for example, the first missionary to the Goths was an Arian, Ulfilas. Thus, Germans were first Arian before they became Catholic. Fourthly, diverse opinions and beliefs were promoted by people from the different capitals of early Christianity: Alexandria in Egypt, Antioch in Syria, as well as Rome, Constantinople, and Jerusalem. These churches, as American Philip Jenkins demonstrates, were ferocious competitors for doctrinal primacy. They fought internecine power struggles so the Roman state might impose their specific variety of belief. Moreover, Christians and many other people in the Roman empire believed that orthodoxy was necessary to ensure the correct operation of the state and the proper conditions for life and society. The wrath of God owing to incorrect belief might bring earthquakes, volcanoes, disease, and so many other natural or even social calamities. Heresies might also be reflections of regional revolt against the Romans who had conquered local peoples, or reflect rural-urban splits between metropolis and hinterland, or class conflicts, all of which might indicate who initiated or followed what heresy.

One final and important point should be made about the sources of our knowledge about these heresies. The accounts that have come down to us were usually written by orthodox writers since heretical tests and source documents were usually destroyed as part of the anathemas imposed by Church and state. Furthermore, the authors of early Church history were bishops and monks who, perhaps not surprisingly, focused on doctrinal, religious disputes. Nonetheless, these might have only been the tip of the iceberg of the social conflicts at play, or even might have been secondary or merely symbolic of the underlying, social conflicts. It is these social forces and conditions that make for our interest in heresies in the early Church. Furthermore, we shall see later in the chapters about the Middle Ages that heresies were to re-surface with further societal development. Indeed, they also formed some of the forms and the substance of popular resistance to social domination.

Chapter 7. The Early Middle Ages in Europe

Introduction

This chapter deals with the early Middle Ages, the period in the history of the West from late antiquity to the end of the first millennium of the common era. It covers the period from the end of urban civilization in much of western Europe around the year 500 to the renaissance of urban civilization around the year 1000. It begins with the transformation of the western Roman empire wrought by the barbarian migrations from the east into western Europe and the incursions of Germanic peoples into the western empire.

Migration of the Peoples

Among the five continents is the vast continent of Eurasia. On this continent, as the American geographer, Jared Diamond, convincingly argues: plants, crops, animals, diseases, peoples, trade, and cultures are all disposed to move on an east-west axis along the same or nearby latitudes. Thus, regions divided by hundreds or even thousands of kilometers can display similar climate, geography, natural resources, culture, and economic activity, all of which make the migrations of peoples east-west a distinct possibility. In actual fact, they are a recurring reality in both the prehistory and history of the continent. In the minds of many, Europe is commonly thought of as a continent itself, distinct from Asia. In fact, Europe is but the western peninsula of the continent of Eurasia. Europe itself is a small, peninsular landmass defined by the Black and Mediterranean seas and the Sea of Azov in the south; the North, Baltic, Barents, and White seas in the north; and the Atlantic Ocean in the west. It might be normal to expect that migrating Eurasian peoples would have a direct impact on the history of Europeans, and they indeed do.

Nonetheless, according to many traditional accounts of Western history, the invasions and migrations of the Huns, the Germanic peoples, and other peoples from the Pontic-Caspian Steppe and central Eurasia seem suddenly and dramatically to appear out of nowhere on the frontiers of the Roman empire wreaking havoc and calamity, and transforming the West forever. This version of facts, however, has two important shortcomings: firstly, Germanic peoples were already well-established within the empire before the invasions and migrations from the east began; secondly, the peoples who invaded or migrated into Europe and pushed the Germans west and south have stories themselves that need to be told if we are to make sense of the full history of the development of the West. Historians refer to the movement of peoples into Europe between 400 and 700 as the Migration of the Peoples, however, the Viking invasions of Europe began only in 797, while the Magyar or Hungarian invasions of Europe only ceased in the middle of the tenth century. Thus, it would seem reasonable to include the latter invasions as part of the Migration of the Peoples. Until the end of the first millennium, Europe was subjected to these migrations and invasions. They are, therefore, a defining element of the early Middle Ages in the West.

Germans and the Peoples of the Pontic-Caspian Steppe

Germans served in the Roman army during the last two centuries before the demise of the western empire as mercenaries in all ranks of the army from generals to private soldiers, either as permanent soldiers or as temporary additions to the Roman army for specific campaigns. There were entire army units such as regiments composed of Germanic tribes. Other Germanic tribes collected along or just within the borders of the empire with a Roman mandate to help defend Roman territory. Still others had no such mandate, but entered Roman territory anyway or settled alongside Roman borders. Thus, Germanic tribes were exposed to Roman ways including agricultural and other economic activities well before the end of the western empire. Romans also employed a practice common to the ancient world of deporting prisoners of war from one region to another, often resettling these people as farmers elsewhere in the empire, a practice that occurred among defeated German tribes. The most common means Germans entered the empire, however, was in the role of *foederati*, whereby they were placed in vulnerable areas within the empire by formal treaty, and paid by the Romans to serve as soldiers in the Roman army. According to the Wikipedia essay about foederati,

> At first, the Roman subsidy took the form of money or food, but as Roman tax revenues dwindled in the 4th and 5th centuries, the foederati were billeted with local landowners, which came to be identical to being allowed to settle on Roman territory. Large, local landowners

living in distant, border provinces or on marches on extensive, largely self-sufficient villas found their loyalties to the central authority, already conflicted by other developments, further compromised in such situations. Then, as these loyalties wavered and became more local, the empire began to devolve into smaller territories with closer personal ties.

While foederati might be settled as farming tenants on land owned by local lords, the reverse also could be true whereby local lords came to be beholden to the leaders of resettled Germanic tribes. One of the effects of this was to increase local loyalties still further at the expense of Roman loyalties, further helping the eventual transformation of once-Roman lands into discrete entities.

In Gaul, the Frankish confederation of Germanic tribes became foederati in 358. Roman armies defended the border represented by the Rhine River. Roman armies were placed south and west of the Rhine, while Frankish settlers were settled as farmers north of the Roman positions in order to constitute a buffer zone between Roman positions and possible intruders to Roman territory who might deem to cross the Rhine. In the winter of 406-407, such intruders did indeed deem to cross the frozen Rhine River. Migrating Vandals and Alans, the latter an Iranic people from the Pontic-Caspian Steppe, overran the positions of the Franks and the Roman army on their eventual way south to North Africa. To the east, the Goths entered the empire in 376 south of the Danube River to receive Roman recognition as foederati; but when promised, Roman payments were not forthcoming, the Goths rose in rebellion, defeating the Roman army in 378. In 395, the Visigoths led by Alaric began to rebel; in 410, they sacked Rome for three days. Even as late as the sixth century, Germanic foederati continued to serve in the army during the eastern emperor Justinian's attempt to reclaim the western empire.

We have seen earlier that poor oppressed Romans often helped barbarians take hold of certain regions. In fact, the opposite is also true, according to Leslie Dodd, who writes that the Roman ruling class often saw treaties with Germanic feoderati as useful for controlling the socially inferior of a region.

> For both the elites who wish to perpetuate a system of control and exploitation, and for the provincials who wish to escape that system, the barbarians present an opportunity. Wretched peasants flee to the barbarians to escape Roman injustice, while Roman nobles see in the strength of barbarian arms a means of underpinning their hold. (Paragraph 23)

The original homelands of the barbarian peoples who entered western history during the early Middle Ages were northern Europe and central Eurasia. The Goths came from Sweden. (Jordanes) Possibly owing to population growth, possibly owing to climactic cooling that might have affected their agriculture, the Goths migrated southeast to an area near the Black Sea. Another Germanic people from northern Germany, the Gepids, moved south to occupy Pannonia in modern-day Hungary along with other peoples. The Vandals moved southwest from territories around the border of modern-day Germany and Poland near the coast of the Baltic Sea. There were still other Germanic peoples we shall encounter later.

The peoples from central Eurasia present more of a mystery. Scythians and Sarmatians, Huns and Hungarians, Alans and Avars, and still other peoples appeared in the accounts of ancient literate peoples to the south; among the latter were Greeks and Romans, Assyrians and Mesopotamians. Then just as suddenly they might disappear, leaving few traces. These central Eurasian peoples came from the geographic region known as the Pontic-Caspian Steppe, a vast prairie to the northwest, north, northeast, and east of the Black Sea and the Sea of Azov, as well as the lands around the Caspian Sea and the areas to the northwest and west of the Aral Sea. Described otherwise, the Pontic-Caspian Steppe starts in the west in modern-day eastern Romania, includes parts of Moldova, the southern Ukraine, and southern Russia, and ends in the east in Kazakhstan. For purposes of simplicity, we also include among the Steppe peoples the Caucasian and other peoples indigenous to modern-day Georgia, Azerbaijan, and Armenia. The peoples of the Steppe were the originators of the languages of Europe, Iran, and northern India and, of course, the local languages of the Steppe. A competing hypothesis has it that the original source of the Indo-European languages was northeast Anatolia south of the Black Sea, but this is now considered a minority view. The Steppe is the home of the peoples who domesticated the horse, a vital part of the life of the nomadic and semi-nomadic peoples of the Steppe.

The first people of the Pontic-Caspian Steppe to be observed and labelled by literate sources was the Cimmerian people, who made their appearance in the eighth and seventh centuries BC. They were followed by the Scythians who thrived during the eighth to the fourth centuries BC. Western tribes from among the Scythians called the Sarmatians took on the leadership role among the Steppe people. The Sarmatians were first observed in the fifth century BC, and remained important for a millennium. Roman historians chronicled the activity of the Sarmatians, many of whom served in the imperial army. Between the third and sixth centuries AD, the Goths inhabited the region, as did the Bulgars, originally a people from the Ural Mountains to the east. The infamous Huns, a confederacy of Turkic peoples from central Asia, were important during the fourth to eighth centuries AD; the Alans between the fifth and 11th centuries; the Avars during the sixth to eighth centuries at the same time as the Gokturks and the Sabirs emerged further to the east; the Khazaris from the sixth to the 11th centuries; the Pechenegs from the eighth to the 11th centuries; the Kipchaks and Cumans from the 11th to the 13th centuries; and the Mongols from as far east as north of China beginning in the 13th century.

The reader might wonder how to distinguish all these peoples. In fact, these peoples were not necessarily distinct ethnic groups. For the most part, they were temporary confederacies of tribes who would unite behind a successful military leader to form a community or, in some cases, to take beginning steps to statehood. An important military defeat might end the pre-eminence of a particular tribe or confederation of tribes, then the process would begin anew. Formerly leading tribes would be absorbed into new confederacies, be chased or otherwise removed from desirable lands, or migrate voluntarily to greener, more peaceable pastures. More often than not, a vacuum created by migration of one people would draw into vacant lands another people. For instance, the Slavs moved into the lands deserted by the Goths and other German peoples after they migrated south into the Roman empire. Thus, it might be actually possible that the inhabitants of a particular locality might remain substantially the same people, but form part of several, different confederacies over the generations but with different appellations. Sometimes, the names of confederacies were actually the name of the ruling class from a tribe that ruled over other tribes. Finally, the names of the various confederacies were often derived by literate peoples to the south who had contact with peoples of the Steppe. Nonetheless, the Steppe peoples themselves might call themselves otherwise, just as the Inuit of Arctic Canada used to be called Eskimos by other peoples; Eskimo was originally a Dene name for the Inuit.

As we shall see below, there were different economies within the tribes who were sedentary and agricultural as compared to the peoples who lived nomadic or semi-nomadic lives following their flocks and herds. Horsemanship of the nomads allowed them to travel great distances in their migrations. It also permitted a particular style of mounted warfare that was to prove devastatingly effective in combats with sedentary European peoples. Around 370 BC, the nomadic Huns migrated to the Pontic-Caspian Steppe, perhaps in response to pressures from peoples further east. The Goths from what is modern-day Sweden had migrated to the shores of the Baltic Sea during the second century AD. In the latter half of the third century, some of these Goths settled within the Roman empire in Anatolia. Along with neighboring Alans, Goths fled from the Huns into eastern Europe, where they divided into two groups. The group historians call the Visigoths, or western Goths, fled through Greece and Illyrium into Italy, then finally into modern-day, northern Spain and southern France. The Ostrogoths, or eastern Goths, migrated to Italy, where they remained. The Vandals migrated from northeast Germany all the way to North Africa, looting and pillaging all the way, hence the word vandalism, finally moving to Sicily and Sardinia. The Vandals were accompanied by two other German peoples, the Suevis and the Burgundians. The former settled in northern Spain and Portugal, the latter in eastern Gaul. The Huns were defeated in the 450s in northern Gaul by a coalition of Roman and Visigoth forces, after which Attila the Hun's confederacy quickly fell apart, as was often the way among peoples from the Steppe after a military defeat.

A second round of Germanic invasions followed the demise of the western Roman empire. The Romans had already withdrawn their armies from Britain early in the fifth century. Then began the period of Germanic invasions whereby Angles, Saxons, Jutes, and Frisians migrated to Britain. Historians used to think that most of the indigenous, Celtic Britons escaped England to flee the invaders. In fact, some did move to Brittany in modern-day France and to Gallaecia in northwest Spain, while Celtic Britons from Wales and Cornwall in southwest England were able to preserve their languages and cultures where they traditionally lived. Contemporary historians now believe, however, that most of the original Celts remained in England even though the ruling class of England became Germanic. In Gaul, Franks originally from the eastern shore of the lower Rhine River, had established a kingdom late in the fourth century that received formal recognition by the Romans as a feoderatus kingdom. After Roman authority dissipated with the demise of the western empire, the Franks conquered all of Gaul except for a small region in the southeast.

A third wave of invasions and migrations into the former, western Roman territories was initiated unwittingly by the eastern Roman emperor, Justinian, in the sixth century. From 532 to 534, Justinian reconquered North Africa for the eastern empire. Emboldened, Justinian tried to do the same in Spain and Italy. He was only able to regain a small part of southeast Spain called Spania. In Italy, it took Justinian from 535 to 562 to destroy the Ostrogothic society that had been created by integration with Italians. In this process, Justinian destroyed much of urban life in Italy, and reduced agriculture to subsistence farming.

The Lombards, another German people from the north, had occupied the former Roman possession of Pannonia in modern-day Hungary. Into the breach in Italy the Lombards moved. They established a kingdom in northern Italy, since they had been pushed from Pannonia by the migrating Avars, another people from the Steppe whose original homeland might have been as far east as north of China. The Bulgars, a Turkic people also from the Steppe, divided into two groups, one group moving into the Volga River Valley of central Russia while another group settled to the west in the Balkans. The newly vacant lands of the Steppe were now occupied principally by the Khazaris, who developed a long-lasting society, economy, and culture.

Nascent States in Western Europe

The German entry to the western Roman empire might be expected to have brought with it important social transformations, and it indeed did. Roman civilization was not destroyed entirely, but it did take on new colors. For example, in the first two centuries of the millennium, Roman aristocrats had taken to country villas in order to escape the political and social tumult of Roman cities. These rural villas, even if Germans organized them in a more rudimentary and rustic fashion than the more luxurious Roman villas, suited German tribal leaders for whom a rural life of hunting, warfare, feasting, and solidarity with fellows and followers presented a better life than did urban life. In any case, towns and cities in northern Europe disappeared for the most part in the early Middle Ages, so there were few towns and cities where the new Romano-German ruling class could congregate.

The new societies of western Europe were amalgams of Germanic and Roman ways. For instance, in pre-Roman times, Germanic peoples elected kings chosen from a royal family. The king was elected as a sacral and military leader from a royal family considered to be of mythic, divine ancestry. The scions of the family would compete for the position of king. The king served as judge during the popular assemblies held by Germanic peoples, as priest during religious ceremonies, and as military commander during wars. The Germanic, popular assembly of free warriors was called a *mahal*, or *mallus* in Latin. (Musset, p. 15; in Scandinavia, the term was *thing*.)

Kings appointed nobility as a reward for services rendered. The nobles who were close to the king, in turn, appointed lower-level nobles and also served as an advisory body to the king, much as the Roman senate did in the early days of the Roman monarchies. Romans chose officials, senators, and military commanders from among the wealthy and powerful *optimates*. Local units called *pagi* in the Roman empire, often based on local marketplaces, were administered by men called *comes*. The eventual result of the Romano-German mix of ruling authorities was a two-tier nobility composed of princes, archdukes, dukes, and marquis at the top of the social hierarchy, whose ancestors might have been local kings or tribal chiefs, and a lower order of counts responsible for ruling counties that were clusters of pagi. These counts, as they were called on the continent, were called earls in Britain and *jarls* in Scandinavia. Thus, there was a marriage of Germanic and Roman customs of governance and military rule. Under Christian influence, the elected German kings evolved into monarchs with a divine right to rule; successor kings came to be chosen by primogeniture, whereby the eldest son inherited the monarchy rather than being elected by the whole tribe.

It is indeed an anachronism to speak of states during the early Middle Ages. Rather, there was a plethora of small kingdoms with personal loyalties, and a hierarchy of aristocrats who served as local military and governmental authorities. Nonetheless, we shall attempt to trace in general terms the evolution of the ancestral entities to modern-day states in western Europe since they do represent important stages in the evolution of Western society. Such nascent states were concrete signs of the emergence of class and social domination by minorities over majorities. Our ultimate aim still remains the identification and description of popular resistance to social domination. This is often difficult to uncover in the written histories of the early Middle Ages owing to their emphasis on the evolution of state and church rather than society and the popular classes. Still, proto-states were useful tools of social domination by the few over the many, leading eventually to the development of nation-states. The evolution of ancestor states is useful since it provides a framework for discussion of development in the early Middle Ages. Moreover, as we shall see later, evolution of the western state was intimately linked to the progress of the Christian churches, Catholic, Protestant, and Orthodox.

Origins

In ancient Britain, the Romans withdrew their legions during the Germanic invasions early in the fifth century as troops in Britain were needed to defend the empire in the south. The Roman population and the native Celts were left to defend themselves; the emperor, in effect, gave up on Britain. During the same century, the Picts, the indigenous population of Scotland, regularly raided the east coast of England. The solution was for the Britons and Romans to hire mercenaries from northwest Germany, that is, Angle and Saxon foederati. The latter received grants of lands and promises of payment for military service. Around 442, the German foederati mutinied since they had not been paid as promised. This was a common occurrence when Romans, increasingly constrained financially, dealt with foederati. Thus began a series of wars that continued into the next century. About 500, the Romans and Britons won a battle against the Germans in which a Roman soldier named Artorius is reputed to have played a leading role, possibly the historic kernel of the legends of King Arthur.

During the fighting, some of the indigenous Celts fled to Brittany and others to northwest Spain. Others were able to safeguard their Celtic dialects and culture away from the Germans in the southwest of Britain in Cornwall and Wales and in Strathclyde, a region in southern Scotland and northern England. It is now surmised by historians that most Celts did indeed remain in what became the seven kingdoms of England: Northumbria, Mercia, East Anglia, Essex, Wessex, Sussex, and Kent, the last kingdom being the colony of Jutes from southern Denmark. During the ninth century, in response to pressure from invading Vikings, the German-controlled kingdoms united under the leadership of Wessex and its king, Alfred the Great. They were successful in holding the Vikings at bay such that a treaty was struck eventually between the Vikings and Wessex. The treaty left northern and eastern England to the rule of the Vikings in an area known as the Danelaw. The Danelaw included Northumbria, East Anglia, and parts of Mercia in the central part of the island. The rest of the territory of Britain except for Wales became the kingdom of England. The kingdom of England fell to Viking invaders from Denmark under the leadership of King Cnut the Great in 1016. The Anglo-Saxon House of Wessex was restored to the English monarchy in 1042. Nonetheless, the last Anglo-Saxon king, Harold Godwinson, was killed in the Battle of Hastings in 1066 when the Normans, also descendents of Danish Vikings, led by William of Normandy, took England definitively from the Anglo-Saxons.

On the continent, the original inhabitants of modern-day Spain and Portugal were known as Celtiberians to the Romans, who conquered the province in the second century BC. After a period of Visigothic looting and pillaging in the empire about the year 400, the Romans set up Visigoths as foederati in a corner of land in Aquitaine in southwestern France. The Romans called on them to come to their aid to fight the Vandals, Alans, and Suevis, who invaded the Roman province of Hispania early in the fifth century. One branch of the Vandals had set themselves up with the Suevi. The latter hailed from southwest Germany in the region of Swabia. These Vandals and Suevi established themselves on lands in northwest Hispania and on the territory of the indigenous Lusitanians of Portugal. Another group of Vandals occupied the south of the province, while the Alans controlled central Hispania. Roman territory was diminished to a swath of land in northern and northeast Hispania. By the end of the fifth century, the Visigoths had helped the Romans vis-à-vis the Germanic invaders, as originally requested by the Romans. The Visigoths, however, also helped themselves in spades, conquering all of the original province of Aquitaine where the Romans first had located them, then continuing to conquer all of Hispania, save the Suevi kingdom and the tribes of northern Hispania, where lived the indigenous ancestors of modern-day Basques. The southern Vandals repaired to North Africa, while the remaining Roman province in northeastern Spain was greatly reduced in size before it was conquered completely by the Visigoths. In the sixth century, the Byzantine emperor, Justinian, was able to reconquer a small strip of land in southern and southeastern Spain called Spania. A map of Spain for the year 700, however, shows the entire Iberian Peninsula in Visigothic hands, including the north country that had previously belonged to the ancestors of the Basques, and Gallaecia in northwest Hispania, the home of the Suevi Germans and Celts originally from Britain as well as the Lusitanians.

The Franks were confederate tribes from western Germany who lived on the east side of the Rhine River in its middle and lower reaches. In the third century, they first came to the attention of the Romans when Frankish tribes began marauding in Roman Gaul. In a pattern typical of the Romans, they hired other Franks known as the Salians to serve as mercenaries to help keep out other west German tribes. The Salian Franks formed the kingdom of Tournai within Roman territory, which the Romans recognized as foederatus in 357. When Roman political and military authority diminished after the demise of the western empire at the end of the fifth century, Salian Franks began conquering other territories in Gaul. The Franks' king, a man called Clovis, initiated the conquests in 481. Conquests continued until Charlemagne's death in 814, by which time all of Gaul including Belgica had been conquered by the Franks, who located their capital at Tournai in modern-day Belgium, as well as the German regions of Frisia, Saxony, Thuringia, Swabia, Bavaria, and Carinthia. The Roman province of Belgica included the southern part of the modern-day Netherlands, Belgium, Luxembourg, northwestern France, and the German side of the northern Rhineland. The whole of the Frankish territory came now to be called *Francia*, a name that referred to territory rather than ethnic origins, similar to the term 'Romans'. The Frankish conquests also included Burgundy and Austrasia, parts of which are located in modern-day, western Germany. Dependent territories included those of the Bretons in western Francia and the west Slavs and south Slavs of eastern Europe, while the Avars of Pannonia in modern-day Hungary also paid tribute to the Franks.

The Frankish kings are known to historians as the Merovingian kings after the name of Merovech, the legendary, first king of the Franks from whom subsequent Frankish kings claimed descent. The Merovingians ruled until 751. During the reigns of the final two generations of the Merovingians, however, they were just figureheads, while actual governing was done was done by the mayors of the royal palace. In 751, the mayor known as Pépin le Bref, or the Short, decided to take royal matters into his hands by ousting the last Merovingian, then managed to get himself crowned by the pope in 754. This is the beginning of what historians called the Carolingian empire that emerged after the Frankish realm of 481–751. Pépin was the son of Charles Martel who effectively had ruled the Frankish realm without taking the title either of king or emperor. Martel had gained renown and power by his defeat of Muslim armies at Poitiers in France in 732. Pépin's son was the famed Charlemagne, who was crowned Roman emperor by the pope in 800. The Carolingian empire was divided in 842, however, when three grandsons of the late Charlemagne divided up Francia, with Charles the Fat ruling west Francia, or modern-day France; Louis the German ruling east Francia, or the German territories; and Lothair, who ruled three territories in what was called middle Francia. The territories of middle Francia included the province of Lotharingia on the French-German border in the north, the southern French province of Provence, and northern Italy. The Carolingian empire endured until the death of Charles the Fat in 888. This was the inevitable end result of a stark reality of the Carolingian period, that is, endless civil wars among royal heirs from different parts of the empire that had the effect of continually dividing the empire into smaller and smaller units wherein actual governing took place.

The era of the Holy Roman Empire began in 962 when Otto, duke of Saxony, was crowned Roman Emperor. His territory included all of Germany, the kingdom of Italy in the north of the Italian peninsula, and Burgundy in France. The empire lasted in Germany until 1806, even if as a mere union of territories wherein nobles elected a nominal emperor. The empire was actually a collection of German principalities, duchies, counties, free cities, and still other political divisions wherein real governing authorities were located, even if Otto himself originally had been a strong centralizer. In fact, this pattern of local paramountcy over central rule was a trend that bedevilled France, Germany, and Italy in the early Middle Ages, especially when compared to the original, western Roman empire. The various mountain ranges, river valleys, plains, deserts, forests, marshlands, and plateaux that divided Europe into distinct geographic regions were reflected in actual governing arrangements. Charlemagne had recognized this reality, and addressed it by means of the feudal system whereby a nobleman who ruled a territory owed allegiance to a higher nobleman and so on up to the emperor. This system later was reproduced throughout much of Europe.

Turning to the Italian peninsula, the event that many historians consider to be the formal end of the western Roman empire occurred when a Roman general, a Visigoth named Odoacer, deposed the last emperor in 476 in order to make himself king of Italy, even while still professing loyalty to the eastern Roman emperor, Zeno. Odoacer then managed to annex Sicily and Dalmatia in the Balkans to his kingdom. At that time, the Ostrogoths were then located in Thrace and Dacia, the latter a region in modern-day Romania. Led by their king, Theodoric the Great, the Ostrogoths conquered Visigothic Italy with the formal political backing of the eastern emperor to whom Theodoric professed loyalty. Theodoric ruled Italy as viceroy, and preserved the existing Italian nobility in its functions. The Ostrogothic kingdom endured from 493 to 553. At its peak, Ostrogothic territory extended from southeastern France to Serbia and included the Italian peninsula and Sicily. In the mid-sixth century, the eastern emperor, Justinian, set about to destroy the Ostrogothic kingdom of Italy in order to reclaim it for his direct rule. His campaign ultimately was successful, but it took many years of campaigning that virtually destroyed urban life and large-scale agriculture on the Italian peninsula. It also produced a vacuum on the Italian peninsula into which swept another German people named the Lombards.

The Lombards originally hailed from southern Denmark. Owing to overpopulation, a third of the Lombards had been forced to leave their homeland. They moved to the Baltic coast along the Elbe River, territory already occupied by the Vandals. None too pleased with these intruders, the Vandals chased out the Lombards, who then settled along the Danube River in eastern Europe. The Lombards then moved into Pannonia to set up a kingdom under their leader, Alboin. Once again, the Lombards were expelled, this time from Pannonia by the Avars from the Pontic-Caspian Steppe, who wished to establish themselves on the plain of what became modern-day Hungary. So, Alboin led about half a million people into northern Italy, mostly Lombards but also some other Germans such as Bavarians, Gepids, and Saxons, and even some Bulgars originally from the Steppe. The Lombards set up a state in northern Italy with its capital at Pavia. They established 36 independent duchies whose dukes often ruled by bypassing and ignoring the king. The Lombards then tried to conquer the Byzantine territories in the south of the Italian peninsula and in the duchy of Rome during campaigns that engaged them for 200 years. In the mid-750s, Pépin the Short defeated Lombard Italy. He then made the famous Donation of Pépin by which he set up the Papal States to be ruled by the pope. In 781, Charlemagne promulgated that the Papal States included the duchy of Rome, the city of Ravenna, former capital of Byzantine Italy, Corsica, parts of Tuscany, and still other parts of Italy.

One other major element needs to be introduced, even if briefly at this time, to the evolution of the political geography of Italy in the early Middle Ages: Arab Muslims. The Muslims first began raiding Lombard Italy in 652 and 669, and again more intensively, during the first half of the eighth century. They took the port city of Bari, and held it for over thirty years between 847 and 871. Bari is in the region of Apulia in southeastern Italy on the Adriatic coast. It was known to its Muslim occupiers as the Emirate of Bari. Arab Muslims also controlled all of what they called the Emirate of Sicily between 965 and 1061. By 1091, Arab Muslims were evicted from Sicily by invaders from Normandy in northwest France. A look at a map of Italy at the end of the millennium shows authority divided among the following: the Emirate of Sicily; the kingdom of Lombardy in the northwest; the marquisates of Verona and Tuscany in the north; the Papal States of the duchy of Rome and two other regions on the Adriatic coast; the republic of Venice, which included a part of Croatia and islands off the Croatian coast; the principalities of Capua, Benevoto, and Salerno; the duchies of Spoleto and Amalfi; and parts of Capua and Apulia in the south that were still Byzantine. It took until the latter half of the 19th century and many campaigns—military and nationalist—to unite the disparate regions of Italy.

The above description provides an overview of complex and complicated changes that took hundreds of years to take place. While this overview is broad and not very detailed, consideration of the political geography of western Europe is important for understanding the development of the state. We now shall attempt a similar operation for eastern and for Nordic Europe.

Nascent States in the East and the North

In the hearts and minds of moderns, it is difficult to imagine life without nation-states. We are born, live, and die within the nation-state. It is a part of our very being, our very identity. Before the modern era, however, most people lived their lives without national appartenance. The village, town, manor, and one's neighbors in the next village, town, manor, represented the limits of a person's horizons. The exceptions to these limited horizons were to be found among those whose lives included travel such as the ruling class of bishops and other religious leaders, noblemen, and monarchs, and those who served their interests; traders who travelled far and wide; and campaigning armies.

Much of historiography and history has been developed in order to tell the national story, the story of how nation-states and national identity came to be. This means there is a bias in the analysis of written documents which have been used to tell the story of the evolution of states in the West. On the other hand, the evolution of both church and state do represent important stages in the development of the West. Church and state were part and parcel of the development of social classes since kings, nobility, bishops, warriors, and scribes who ruled and represented church and state depended upon the extraction of economic surplus from the work of laboring people. Thus, one who speaks of the evolution of Church and state necessarily speaks of social class and of the appropriation of economic surplus and, hence, of the potential for resistance by the popular classes. The challenge is to tease out the active instances of this resistance when historical evidence is slanted to the views and needs of the literate people who served or formed part of the ruling classes, or who wrote accounts about them. Often, there is little direct evidence of popular resistance but only indirect evidence or even just deduced or induced propositions of popular resistance. Indeed, this is the challenge of this book itself.

Even where one might not perhaps expect it, there were actually many instances of state formation in eastern and northern Europe and in the Pontic-Caspian Steppe during the early Middle Ages even if these states often had ephemeral existences. The evolution of states in North Africa and the Middle East during the first millennium will be covered in the chapter about the rise and development of Islam and Muslim societies. Historians and social scientists speak of five broad populations who inhabited eastern and northern Europe in addition to Germanic peoples. These included peoples of the Steppe, some of them being native to the region or Iranic in origin, others who were Turkic originally from central Asia; Slavs indigenous to eastern Europe even if the location of their original homeland(s) is still debatable; Finno-Ugric peoples, among them Magyars who settled Hungary, Finns, Estonians, peoples indigenous to central Russia, and the Saami, the indigenous people of northern Finland and Scandinavia plus the Kola Peninsula of northwest Russia, all of whose languages are related; Balts, who lived along the southern and eastern coasts of the Baltic Sea; and Norsemen, or North Germans, originally from Scandinavia.

State formation varied greatly among these peoples during the early Middle Ages. In fact, the Balts did not even develop states until the emergence of the Lithuanian and Latvian states during the 13th and 14th centuries, about the same time as states also emerged in Estonia and Finland. Among the Norse were the Vikings who grew wealthy from travel, trade, and plunder. During the early Middle Ages, they were responsible for state formation in the Rus' Khaganate, Kievan Rus', and Scandinavia. From the Pontic-Caspian Steppe came the Alans, Avars, Bulgars, Khazaris, and the Magyars, the last of whom settled for a time in the Steppe before migrating to Hungary. The Slavs settled in three agglomerations in eastern Europe during the early Middle Ages: the west Slavs, the ancestors of modern-day Poles, Czechs, Slovaks, and Sorbs, the last a small minority in eastern Germany and southwest Poland; the south Slavs, ancestors of modern-day Bosnians, Croats, Serbs, Macedonians, Montenegrins, Slovenes, and even of some people in the Peloponnese and northern Greece; and the east Slavs, ancestors of modern Russians, Belarusans, Moldovans, and Ukrainians. The Slavs now draw our attention.

The Slavs

The phrase used by historians and others who study Slavic origins refers to the settling of the Slavs. This is the process by which Slavs settled permanently in eastern Europe, according to the threefold geographic division described above, during the Migration of the Peoples. Documents describing Slavs first appeared in the sixth century when they were identified as Slovenes. Their initial point of origin is a matter of contention, however, as several ideas compete in what scholars call the process of ethnogenesis, whereby ethnic groups emerge defined as such both by themselves and by others. This is a very inexact science. For example, it is speculated that the original Slavs might have appeared first either south of the Danube; or in the southern Ukraine; or in the Pripet marshes, a vast marshland and forest in southern Belarus and the northwest Ukraine 480 kilometres east to west and 225 kilometers north to south; or even along the border of modern-day Germany and Poland. Still another idea has it that Slavs were native to the Pontic-Caspian Steppe, and that they moved west after the Huns and other peoples had done so. Regardless of points of origin, we can still describe the Slavs, nonetheless, as peoples indigenous to eastern Europe alongside the Germanic peoples and the Dacs, an ancient people native to modern-day Romania. It appears that the Slavs migrated to the territories that had been occupied by the Germanic peoples who fled from the Huns into the Roman empire.

A few interesting points can be made about the ethnic behavior of the ancient Slavs. It would seem that the settling of the Slavs took place mostly by peaceful means, not military. It would also seem they had an impressive capacity to assimilate peaceably other peoples such as Balts, Finno-Ugric peoples, and peoples from the Steppes such as the Bulgars and Avars, who had migrated to eastern Europe. It was during the seventh and eighth centuries that, owing to the distances between west, east, and south Slavs, the original Slavic language split into the various Slavic languages that were ancestors to modern-day Slavic languages.

Early States

We now briefly consider the early states of eastern and northern Europe as they appeared chronologically during the early Middle Ages. They are as follows:

- the kingdom of the Avars;
- an agglomeration historians call Old Great Bulgaria;
- the principality of Serbia;
- the first Bulgarian empire;
- Khazaria, a state on the Pontic-Caspian Steppe;
- a Slavic state, Great Moravia;
- the Norse states;

- the duchy, then kingdom of Croatia;
- Hungary, settled by Magyars after they terrorized western Europe during the first half of the tenth century;
- the kingdom of Poland.

The Kingdom of the Avars

The Avars were a Turkic people who were driven west from central Asia to the Pontic-Caspian Steppe, then again further west into eastern Europe by the Persians and by other Turkic tribes. They settled north of the Danube on the Pannonian plain where, with the collaboration of the Lombards, they drove out the Gepids who had migrated to the area from their homelands in northern Germany. The next year, the Avars extended the same favor to the Lombards, forcing them into northern Italy and Dalmatia, along with other German tribes and some Bulgars. The Slavs who occupied Pannonia, in what is modern-day Hungary, were pushed into the Balkans, then forced to pay tribute to the Avars. The arrival of the Avars took place about 558; they were eliminated as a distinct people at the end of the eighth century by Charlemagne.

Old Great Bulgaria

The Bulgars were a west Turkic people of semi-nomadic tribes who occupied the land immediately north of the Black Sea between the Dniester and Volga rivers, between the Avars of Pannonia and the Khazaris of the Pontic-Caspian Steppe. In the seventh century, the Bulgar Khanate was ruled by a strong leader named Kubrat, however, his five sons departed for various parts including eastern Europe when they were unable to maintain a consensus among themselves.

Serbia

The first Serbian state was the principality of Serbia. It formed in 768 when local chiefs united under Viseslav. He was part of the Vlastimiovic dynasty, which ruled the principality for 200 years until 969, when it succumbed to Byzantine rule.

First Bulgarian Empire

Some of the Bulgars of Old Great Bulgaria rallied to Asparukh, one of the five sons of Kubrat, who led the Bulgars to eastern Europe. They settled north of Byzantine Thrace late in the seventh century along with seven tribes of Slavs from the Balkans. These two groups united with Bulgars in order to protect themselves from their mutual enemies, the Avars to their west and the Byzantines to their east. The Slavs demonstrated their capacity to assimilate peoples such as the migrating Bulgars who became, in effect, another Slavic people. The Byzantines recognized the Bulgarian empire in 681, then proceeded to help Christianize the Bulgarians. Even so, the Bulgarian empire won military victories against the Byzantines as well as battles with the Magyars, and advancing Pechenegs and Cumans from the Steppe. By the end of the eighth century, the first Bulgarian empire also controlled Epirus and Thessaly in northern Greece, Macedonia, Bosnia, eastern Hungary, and Wallachia in Romania. It stretched from the Black Sea to the Adriatic Sea. The empire fell to Byzantium in 1018. Their territory came to be controlled by the Pechenegs, another nomadic Turkic tribe from the Steppe. They, in turn, were followed in 1091 by the Cumans, still another nomadic, Turkic people who took control of Moldova and Wallachia. A second Bulgarian empire was established in 1185. Culturally speaking, the old Bulgarian language became the *lingua franca* of eastern Slavic literature. Called 'Old Church Slavonic', it became the liturgical language of Orthodox Slavs.

Khazaris

The Khazaris were originally a semi-nomadic Turkic people who had settled on the Pontic-Caspian Steppe between the Black and Caspian seas. They started expanding their territory in the seventh century, and kept extending their territory northward until, by the middle of the tenth century, it covered almost the entire Steppe, save for the westernmost reaches of the Steppe in eastern Europe. Their empire extended east to the western shores of the Aral Sea and as far north as the land of the Volga Bulgars in central Russia. At its peak, Khazari territory covered much of modern-day European Russia, the northern Caucasus Mountains, western Khazakstan, the eastern Ukraine, Georgia, the Crimea, and Azerbaijan.

In an era when peoples were warring regularly among exponents and practitioners of different religions, Khazaria was a cosmopolitan, multi-faith and multi-ethnic state comprised of Turkic, Uralic, Slavic, and Caucasian peoples. Moreover, beginning in the 670s, the Khazaris welcomed Jewish refugees fleeing from persecution in Byzantium and Islamic Persia. These Jews, who were educated, literate and well-travelled, brought knowledge of many arts and crafts to Khazaria. Among them was a guild of traders called Rhadanites, who helped the Khazaris establish important manufacturing industries. The Rhadanites had trade networks that extended as far west as Spain and as far east as China. They served as a trade link between Europe and the Muslim world, including the trade of the Silk Road. The result of the Jewish contribution and the geographic extent of Khazaria was a healthy and diversified economy where its people prospered.

About the year 800, royals, nobles, and the rest of the Khazaria upper class itself converted to Judaism, in part for the political prestige of adopting a monotheism that was, nevertheless, distinct from the Christianity and Islam that surrounded the Khazaris. Even so, they did not force the cosmopolitan population of Khazaria to convert to Judaism. There were both Orthodox and Nestorian Christians as well as Muslims in Khazaria, all of whom were free to practice their faith. Nonetheless, gradually and peacefully, much of the Khazari population converted to Islam. The reign of this remarkable people ended in the middle of the tenth century when they were beleaguered first by the Pechenegs and Alans on the Steppe, and then by Kievan Rus' when the latter's ruler Sviatoslav subjugated the Khazaris during the decade of the 960s.

Great Moravia

Great Moravia was originally a small state that comprised two small chiefdoms on either side of the Morava River in central Europe that were united forcibly by a man named Mojmir in 833. Its original extent covered territory corresponding to modern-day, western Slovakia and the Czech Republic. At its greatest extent in the 871–894 under its ruler, Svatopluk, the state covered much of the Slavic world including Slovenia, Croatia, Serbia, Poland, and the Ukraine, as well as parts of Hungary, Austria, Germany, and Romania. Even so, it was a vassal state to the Franks to whom it paid annual tribute. The social organization in the state displayed the beginnings of feudal arrangements, but the state lasted only about 70 years. Around 896, the Magyars invaded Pannonia, effectively terminating Great Moravia and causing it to disintegrate. Remnants of the state were divided then among Hungary, Bohemia, Poland, and the Holy Roman Empire.

Croatia

The Croats might have been indigenous to Dalmatia. They were an elite caste of warriors who ruled Dalmatia and parts of Pannonia. The first evidence of a Croatian state occurred in 879 when the pope recognized Branimir as duke of the Croats. In 925, the first king of Croatia, Tomislav, repelled Magyar and Bulgarian incursions into Croatia.

The Norse States

The Norsemen, native to south and central Scandinavia, terrorized Europe during the early Middle Ages. They attacked and sacked, plundered and conquered, in the process redrawing the political geography of Europe by establishing a number of states. At the same time, some became wealthy from their loot. It all began in 793 when Vikings robbed and destroyed Lindisfarne, a prosperous monastery on the North Sea coast in northeast England that had been built by Irish monks. The strikes of the Vikings in modern-day Britain continued for over a century. They conquered the indigenous, Celtic peoples of the Orkney and Hebrides islands north of mainland Scotland, coastal areas of Scotland, much of Ireland, England more than once, and Normandy, named for them, in northwest France. They also variously besieged and burnt people in the Rhine, Seine, Loire, and Rhône valleys in France as well as destroying what would become important French cities such as Rouen, Nantes, Paris, Arles, and Nîmes.

The Vikings, however, were also skilled traders and merchants. In conjunction with the local Slavic population, Swedish adventurers cum traders established what would become eventually the modern states of Russia, Belarus, and the Ukraine. When the duke and the duchy of Normandy were recognized by the king of France in 911 as legitimate local ruler and local political unit respectively, it appeared that the Vikings might be settling down to become respected and respectable elements of European civilization. Well, sort of...because in the 11th century, a Norman count conquered Sicily and parts of southern Italy. Normans also played important roles in the development of feudalism and in the Crusades to the Middle East, and in the growth of the power of medieval kings and popes. Here are brief descriptions of the states the Vikings established.

The Danelaw

Recall the Danelaw from the earlier section about the development of the state in England. The Danelaw referred originally to the laws and customs of the Danish Vikings of northern England that held sway over Anglo-Saxon customs and laws in these regions, however, the name came to be applied by the 11th century to the geographic areas and to the states that developed there, that is, the kingdoms of Northumbria and East Anglia, and parts of Mercia in central England.

Kievan Rus'

The people known as the Rus' were Vikings from southern Sweden who made their way to northern Russia, where they lived among Balts, Slavs, and Finnic and Turkic peoples. Historians call the cluster of city-states in northern Russia the Rus' Khaganate, applying the traditional, Turkic name for the region whose capital appears to have been Novgorod. Between 830 and 879, the area had a powerful ruler named Rurik, whose descendants were to rule Russia until the 17th century. In 882, Rurik's successor, Vladimir the Great, helped liberate the Slavic city of Kiev in the Ukraine from paying tribute to the Khazaris. The Rus' capital was later moved to Kiev. In 988, Vladimir the Great adopted Orthodox Christianity, and proceeded to have baptized the entire population. His son, Yaroslav the Wise, adopted a written legal code called *Russkaya Pravda*. At its peak, Rus' extended south to the Black Sea, west to the kingdom of Poland and the duchy of Lithuania, and east to the Volga River in central Russia. This state, however, divided into many distinct and competing, even warring principalities after the death of Yaroslav. By the middle of the 12th century, the influence of Kievan Rus' had waned definitively.

Norway

The small kingdoms along the coastlines of Norway were united into a single kingdom in 872 by a local man named Harald Fairhair, who ruled the kingdom until about 930.

Normandy

By a treaty in 911, King Charles of France made Rollo, the Viking leader, a French duke, and granted him a county around Rouen. Rollo was the leader who had led his people to settle in northwest France after a career of raiding and looting in the same area. Not surprisingly, the new dukes kept expanding the duchy southward until it encompassed the modern-day, French regions of Upper and Lower Normandy. The dukes were important allies of Hugues Capet and the French kings. Duke William the Conqueror of Normandy defeated the Anglo-Saxons in 1066 to assume the rule of England.

Denmark

About the year 965, Harald Bluetooth united the peoples of the Danish peninsula of Jutland, north Germany, a small coastal piece of southern Sweden, and the archipelago between the two mainlands into a single state, then initiated Christianization therein. During the first half of the 11th century, King Cnut of Denmark united under one kingdom Denmark, England, Norway, southern Sweden, and part of eastern, coastal Sweden.

Sweden

The first known king of Sweden who was neither from Norway nor Denmark was a man called Eric the Victorious, who ruled about 970-995. Interestingly, he appears to have come to power in alliance with free farmers united against the local aristocratic class of *jarls*.

The Magyars of Hungary

David Koeller provides useful information about the history of the Hungarians, or Magyars. Linguistic evidence traces this people to their ancestors among the Finno-Ugric people who occupied the forested regions between the Baltic Sea and the Ural mountains. These pre-civilization tribes lived from hunting, gathering, and fishing. Early in the first millennium AD, the Magyars moved southwest from the Urals to the Pontic-Caspian Steppe for reasons unknown. Overpopulation, climate change, famine, or flight from warfare might have been possible motivations for their migration.

Influenced by the Iranic and Turkic tribes of the Steppe, the Magyars adopted the pastoral, nomadic life of the Steppe following their herds and flocks, including the horses they adopted as a means of transport and food. As part of an extended Migration of the Peoples, the Magyars began to move west, until the ninth century when they held lands northwest of the Black Sea between the Avar and Bulgarian lands to their west in eastern Europe, and the Khazaris to their east on the Pontic-Caspian Steppe. Towards the end of the tenth century, in the pattern typical of the region, Turkic nomads from the east, the Pechenegs, forced the Magyars further west. The Magyars settled first in the Carpathian Mountains, then on the Pannonian plain around 900.

For the next half-century, the Magyars descended mercilessly on peoples with whom they came into contact in their attempt to secure a permanent home. They raided the German regions of Saxony and Bavaria from which they exacted tribute, as well as Alsace, Lorraine, Thuringia, and Swabia. They also raided southward down the Italian peninsula without settling permanently, as well as raiding the Balkans. By claiming for themselves the Pannonian plain, and by pushing its Slavic occupants south into the Balkans, they brought to an end the early Slavic state of Great Moravia. They weren't always successful in their military excursions, however, since they were beaten once and for all in 955 by the duke of Saxony, Otto, who later became Holy Roman emperor. On Christmas day in the year 1000, Hungary's king converted to Catholicism. The king, the future St. Stephen, was even given the title of apostle by the pope. The Orthodox Slavic worlds to the south, north, and east of Hungary were now permanently separated from each other by Catholic Hungary.

Kingdom of Poland

Evidence of the first Polish state appeared in 966 when a Polish ruler named Mieszko adopted Catholicism while ruling a territory similar to that of modern-day Poland. By 1025, there is evidence of a kingdom of Poland, the name of which was derived from the name of a west Slavic tribe called the Polans.

Christianity

We now turn to the second leg of state and church, the essential pillars of development in the Occident during the early Middle Ages. By extension, analyzing the development of church and state offers a framework for understanding popular resistance to social domination by the rich and powerful. This is so even if resistance is sometimes hard to identify and describe owing to the paucity and bias of sources. Moreover, reliance upon clerics as our sources skews our understanding of the Middle Ages, defined traditionally as an Age of Faith during which the Occident lived under the influence of the Christian churches, Orthodox and Catholic, and when all, save Jews and Muslims, were at least nominal Christians. In fact, there was a large secular space in the lives of commoners that, owing to the religious historical sources, is under-emphasized. Reliance on religious literature creates the impression that life, whether common or noble, was lived almost entirely in pursuit of the Christian faith. Moreover, social conflicts were sometimes reduced to their religious aspects in medieval sources even when the religious aspect might have been not so important, or was merely symbolic of a larger social conflict. Furthermore, even in the Christian faith, popular Christianity carried with it many remnants of pre-Christian paganism and adaptation of earlier myth and ritual into Christian forms. Likewise for some of the social heresies that formed part of the articulation of rebellion and revolt against authorities.

Conversion to Christianity

When Constantine converted to Christianity early in the fourth century, Christianity was still a minority religion within the empire, even if there were significant regions on the shores of the Mediterranean where much of the population had adopted Christianity through conversion, marriage, or birth into the faith. Many people in these regions were Christian, even if we do well to remember that there were many strains of Christianity: the Levant, Syria, Thrace, Greece, Egypt, Cyraenica, or eastern Libya, Tunisia, Rome, and Anatolia, where St. Paul first preached. Beyond the Roman empire, there were Christians in Ethiopia, Armenia, and Georgia. Later in the fourth century, the Ostrogoths and Visigoths were converted to Arian Christianity. By the fifth century, Christianity had spread throughout North Africa including to Egypt as well as Yemen in the south of the Arabian Peninsula, possibly assisted by trade with Christians in eastern Africa. In what was no doubt a remarkable phenomenon of growth, two centuries later, the people of many European countries had become Christian, including those of modern-day Spain, Portugal, England, Scotland, Ireland, Wales, France, Italy, Switzerland, Belgium, Pannonia, the western Balkans, and the Netherlands. During the eighth century, the slow process of converting non-Gothic Germans began as Frankish, Anglo-Saxon, and Irish monks and missionaries spread the Christian word throughout the German world. The process was often top-down since the ruler would convert, then force his population to join him. For instance, Charlemagne forced the Saxons and Frisians to convert through warfare, two examples among many of forced conversions. In the ninth century, Bulgarians and Serbs converted to Orthodoxy while, during the tenth century, Danes, Poles, and the people of Kievan Rus' began a slow process of conversion. Hungary, Norway, and Iceland converted during the next century. In the 12th century, Swedes converted, then in turn, converted Balts, Finns, and Estonians during the following century.

Even so, in spite of formal conversion, we must remember that there were many local differences among Christians based upon previous religious history and pagan beliefs. For example, the Irish practiced secret, private penance while elsewhere in Christendom, penance was a public event. Eventually, the Irish practice became the norm for penance. Thus, just as in the ancient world, there were important differences in local versions of Christianity during the early Middle Ages.

Bishops, Labor, Charity

Michel Mollat writes of the legacy of the ancient world as it concerns the poor of the early Middle Ages:

> The miseries of the aging societies of the Roman empire, and the deficiencies of the young barbarian nations were a long way from cancelling one another out; rather than mutual regeneration, the result of Rome's collision with the barbarians was an accumulation of ills, the brunt of which fell on the powerless. (p. 15)

So, while slavery was evolving into medieval serfdom, slavery did continue to exist to a certain extent during the early Middle Ages. In the previously western Roman regions bordering on the Mediterranean, in the eastern Roman empire, and among Germanic peoples, slavery continued as a method of organizing and controlling labor. Slavery in the British Isles also continued into the early Middle Ages, in fact, well into the high Middle Ages. For instance, in the Domesday Book of 1086 produced under order of William the Conqueror, a tenth of the population was recorded as slave. This possibly reflected the fact that slavery grew during the Viking invasions of the British Isles when warfare between Vikings and Anglo-Saxons, and between Vikings and the natives of Scotland, Ireland, and Wales, was commonplace.

In the east, Slavic peoples were enslaved by raids by Khazaris and other Steppe peoples to be sold thereafter in Byzantium and the Muslim world. The merchants who traded in slaves included Vikings, the Jewish merchant Rhadanites from the Iberian Peninsula, and Muslims from Europe, Asia, and North Africa. The Church was scandalized by Christians enslaving other Christians, so it was prohibited formally by the Catholic Church in 922. Christians enslaving pagans or Muslims, however, was still permitted. As for Muslims, enslaving Christians and pagans was encouraged even if enslavement of Muslims was discouraged.

Among literate people in the ancient world, physical labor and trade were viewed as beneath the man of culture. The same disdain for manual labor and for those who performed it continued to exist after the demise of the western empire. Within the Germanic world, this disdain was amplified by the preference of the ruling class for the military life. As well, there was the Christian preference for the life of contemplation and prayer rather than engagement in the material world, which affected the intellectuals and clerics who defined and transmitted the ruling ideology. As part of Christian ideology, the requirement to labor were viewed as punishment of humankind for original sin, that is, the fall of Adam and Eve from the grace of God. It took many generations for Christian ideology to develop a favorable prejudice towards manual labor and laborers and, when it did, it owed in part to the mores of Benedictine monks who valued and practiced physical labor as part of the rule of St. Benedict.

Another element of the legacy from the Roman world was the idea of Christian charity. Recall the important role of bishops in the empire where they had a formal, legally-defined responsibility to defend the poor in their role of *defensor civitatis*. Bishops also were directly responsible for charity in the diocese, and for enjoining lesser clergy to practice it in their parishes. In France, King Clovis adopted a measure that assigned a quarter of Church revenues to the poor. Bishops preached the message of charity, and often set examples with their personal wealth, which could be significant since many bishops came from the noble class. All within the Christian population who could do so were required to give alms for the poor. For the next millennium, Christian charity continued to be the norm for treating the poor, infirm, ill, old, widowed, orphaned, abandoned, and other categories of the destitute.

Popular Christianity

Conversion of whole peoples to Christianity by fiat of rulers or by warfare meant that the actual practice of Christianity among the popular classes often differed from formal Christianity. Pagan antecedents colored how Christianity was practiced among the common people, and even to a certain extent, among the nobility and lower clergy, who were often illiterate themselves. This Christianity was rife with superstition and popular misunderstandings of complex theological ideas, however, it did meet popular needs. Whereas local gods had met needs for help with harvests and with battles, illnesses and poverty, now this role was played by local saints. After his or her death, relics of the local saint were gathered, and placed at an altar in a cemetery. On this site or nearby would be built a grotto, then progressively a chapel, church, abbey, priory, or convent, and eventually perhaps, a cathedral, all as part of honoring the local saint.

A few educated clerics including bishops Claudius of Turin and Abogard of Lyon decried veneration of saints and their relics as reeking of idolatry and paganism, which it most likely did. Nonetheless, the people imposed this popular practice upon a Church that might speak, write, and preach in vain about saintliness being based upon the saint's rejection of the material and his embrace of the spiritual. What the people wanted most from saints was miracles. Writes Russian scholar Aron Gurevich:

> The most attractive thing about the saint was his ability to work miracles. The saint, connected with higher powers, employed his

magical abilities to help his worshippers, easing their lives, healing their illnesses, averting natural or social calamities, freeing the unfortunate and the powerless from oppression. (1988, p. 73)

Gurevich writes of the social miracle on behalf of the common people by saints who assisted paupers, widows, orphans, and other socially humble and destitute. So, popular veneration of saints and their relics were a vital part of popular beliefs and practices of Christianity. They were also, as we shall see below, a motor of medieval development as well as a source of popular resistance when heresies were afoot.

Monasticism

Monasticism first appeared in Syria and Egypt in the third century when a few Christians retired to the desert to live as hermits in order to avoid the evils of Roman materialism. The depths (and heights) to which some eastern Christians went to display their devotion astounds. Hermits lived in wells, tombs, caves, dungeons, deserted buildings, and even on pillar tops throughout the eastern empire in order to express their solitary, religious devotion. The needs for society brought these hermits together, however, first in small groups, then in communities, and then again in monasteries. In the fourth century, a leading cleric, Basil, wrote a rule to serve as a guide to monks in the eastern empire, which eventually served monasteries within the Eastern Orthodox and Oriental Orthodox churches.

In the west, during the fifth century, a man of noble birth named Benedict withdrew from the travails of Rome to become a religious hermit, in the process attracting many disciples. Benedict established rules for his followers who lived in monasteries, the most important being the historic monastery at Monte Cassino between Rome and Naples. The rule of Benedict came to be followed by thousands of monastic institutions in the Western world. Of note was the important requirement that Benedictine monks work physically, which had the profound effect of ennobling with the dignity of labor those who labored physically during the Middle Ages. Benedictines farmed, gardened, raised animals, and did all the cleaning, craft work, and maintenance necessary to the upkeep of a monastery, including the feeding and clothing of its members. As such, the Benedictine monastery was similar to the self-sufficient villa in Latin lands, or the manor in feudal régimes.

As the centuries advanced, however, the work of some Benedictines evolved to teaching and other intellectual pursuits. Benedictine monasteries required donations of lands by wealthy lords, who then asserted their pound of flesh in the work and control of monasteries. The result was often simony, whereby religious offices such as abbeys and bishoprics were purchased for adult offspring of local nobles. Corruption became considerable and frequent. Abbots and bishops often held sinecures where leading families came to control institutions of monks or dioceses and parishes. This problem was addressed somewhat when duke William of Aquitaine formed a monastery at Cluny, near Lyons, to be led by an abbot who ruled over related houses called priories. There were two important differences displayed by Cluny monasteries, even if they did remain somewhat Benedictine in their rule. Rather than doing physical labor themselves, these establishments hired managers and workers to supervise and perform the manual labor done normally by Benedictine monks. The second feature was that the monastery at Cluny report only to the pope, and not to local, feudal lords. Since popes were far away, in effect, the houses of Cluny were independent to pursue their goal of disciplined prayer and purity of worship. For 200 years, the Cluny movement of monks was one of the most important forces in European Christianity.

The Papacy

The monastic orders were the most important proponents of local, papal authority since it was the most useful means of asserting their independence from local, feudal lords. In fact, Pope Gregory I, Gregory the Great, who served as pope between 590 and 604, was a Benedictine. On the other hand, most popes in this era were appointed by temporal rulers, and were pawns in the politics of the early Middle Ages. This is true for the periods of Ostrogothic, Byzantine, and Frankish rule in Italy, which covered the years from about 500 to 900. This temporal control of the papacy continued thereafter during the next two centuries until the appointment of Pope Leo IX in 1049. During these two centuries, the Italian family of the counts of Tusculum including their womenfolk dominated the papacy, selecting members from their family as popes and even choosing mistresses from the family for these popes, as well as supervising popes' conduct. This period of the papacy came to be called 'the rule of the harlots'. It provoked the Gregorian reforms of the 11th century by which the Church gained some independence from secular rulers. As a result of these reforms, Church leaders even tried reversing the roles of dominance, which led to serious conflicts with the rulers in Europe.

During the early Middle Ages, the papacy was but a glimpse of what it would become in later centuries. In fact, as only one of five early patriarchs of Christianity—the others being Constantinople, Alexandria, Antioch, and Jerusalem—it is hard to perceive the bishop of Rome as having been even equal to his colleagues, let alone trying to increase his influence over the others. Quite correctly perhaps, his eastern colleagues perceived the pope as unsuccessfully trying to supervise the flock of his backwards, barbarian, boorish, barely Christian people of western Europe in face of interfering feudal rulers, who usually dictated who became pope and what he was allowed to do once he occupied the position. In spite of its hierarchy of deacons, priests, bishops, archbishops, abbots, and popes, the Catholic Church was a weak institution during the early Middle Ages that strove mightily against both popular Christianity and feudal lords and royal rulers without too much success other than within monasticism. At the same time, the Catholic Church was the only institution with an administrative hierarchy that resembled the level of organization that had existed in the western Roman empire. As such, it was a focus around which people organized human activity including socioeconomic development, as we see below.

Socio-economic Development

We have seen earlier how socio-economic conditions worsened dramatically in the latter days of the western Roman empire. The causes of this deterioration are still the object of controversy. There were probably many reinforcing factors although they are not easy to identify, let alone isolating them and determining the relationships among them. While this author is no advocate of climate determinism, the period of 300 to 700 does correspond to a dramatic cooling of the earth's temperature. This might have been one of the factors that negatively affected the organization, practices, and yields of agriculture, thus reducing the supply of food. As well, the Romans had used a two-field system of cultivation whereby one field alternately was kept fallow. During and after the demise of the western empire, this method of farming disappeared as did, in fact, the plantation economy owing to the drying up of new sources of slaves once the empire had reached its geographic limits. Much of the western world was left conducting subsistence agriculture that produced insufficient quantities of food to feed urban populations. Cities and towns and the trade they fostered thus declined. Urbanites left cities and towns to engage in subsistence farming in order to survive. Large-scale manufacturing of products such as pottery and ceramics in cities and towns disappeared, to be replaced by individual, rudimentary craft production on villas. Epidemics such as the bubonic plague possibly halved the population of the empire between the mid-sixth century and the beginning of the eighth. The city of Rome itself declined from a peak population of 500,000–1,000,000 during the first two centuries of the millennium to about 20-40,000 during the early Middle Ages.

Where large-scale agriculture did survive, it was in Byzantium and in peripheral areas of the eastern empire where there was still a significant peasantry to exploit. Agricultural development in peripheral areas was a motor of both manorial development and decentralized, feudal régimes where economic autarchy was practiced rather than trade. There was another reversal of climate during the period 700–1100 when global temperatures warmed once again, which had positive effects on agriculture. During this warm period, farming technique evolved to a three-field system rather than the subsistence farming that had appeared at the demise of the western empire. In this technique, fields were alternately planted with grains especially rye, which proved to be a hardy grain, and a second field sown with beans and peas, which fixed nitrogen in the soils, while a third field lay fallow. Families farmed small strips of land in each of the fields. The system obviously began producing surplus beyond feeding peasants since secular and religious lords took increasing shares of produce from the lands they held.

Germanic Society and Economy

One way of imagining the confrontation between the migrating and invading German tribes and Roman civilization is to think of it as an encounter between advanced and literate, urban Greco-Roman civilization and rural German societies where nomadism, hunting, and foraging were still important to survival. True, Germans within the empire and on its borders were already influenced by Roman practices, particularly in agriculture, such that they had already significantly improved their techniques with respect to growing grains. As well, Germans developed small-scale cattle raising and family farming in villages and hamlets. Nevertheless, the German tribes that moved into or near the empire as the western empire was in decline were similar to the rural peoples that the Romans had conquered and transformed in earlier days such as indigenous peoples in Pannonia, Illyrium, Dalmatia, Hispania, Gaul, and England. Now, however, with the demise of the western empire and the presence en masse of Germans within the borders of the empire, the transformations that took place were much more equal and not so lopsided in the sense of urban Romans civilizing rural societies. The reverse also took place whereby Germans helped make Roman society more rural during the early Middle Ages. The result was German ways mixed with Roman culture, ultimately producing the states and societies of western Europe.

In rural Germanic economies, the exchange of gifts, particularly among warriors, featured importantly. A gift offered meant that the recipient was expected to return a gift of equal value. In this process, status of donor and recipient as well as the nature of the gifts exchanged were important to assessing whether the exchange was satisfactory. Incorrect exchanges could lead to deadly feuds in the extreme, or to awkward social relationships in the least. Among warriors, a leader was judged by the quantity and quality of booty he was able to offer to his men. Communal feasting and beer drinking were occasions for cementing social relationships of warrior commanders and the men they led. These feasts were often the occasion for the exchange of gifts. In feudal times, the exchange of gifts was transformed, becoming the occasion when lords might expect tribute from their vassals, partly in exchange for the feast itself the lord sponsored. Another important social institution among Germans was the *weregild*, the equivalent, material value of a man who was a victim of theft, insult, injury, or even murder. Under the weregild, an offending party had to pay the offended a certain amount of wealth in cattle, furs, jewelry, land, produce, or such. This social institution, while perhaps strange to our eyes, did fill the function of helping end the ceaseless feuding that ultimately might destroy a society. The weregild of a chieftain, lord, or king could be worth as much as six times the weregild of a free warrior. Below the free man's weregild came those of the people of conquered tribes, who might have assimilated into the conquering society but not with an independent status. Still below these people were serfs and slaves.

Farming was a noble trade for a free warrior although dirty jobs such as mucking fields were reserved for slaves. The Germans did become exposed to coinage, but their use of it was quite curious. They used coins to make jewelry such as broaches, ear rings, or necklaces of gold or silver. These were highly prized evidence of social status. Only when feudalism developed towards the end of the early Middle Ages did Germans start using coins for exchange, but they were still more important for cementing feudal social relations among warriors. One curious use of coins was their burial in large hoards, the social meaning of which is still an object of speculation. Alexandra Mattison speculates that hoards could have served a practical function of safekeeping during war or social turbulence. Just as likely, however, is the religious significance of hoards, either as offerings to the gods or as part of the wealth or signs of the social status a dying warrior might want to bring to the next world. These practices do not correspond with those of a money-based, specialized economy such as imperial Rome. So, while Roman urban life, trade, and agriculture all diminished in importance during the German migrations, Romans and Germans created a more rural, subsistence, currency-less economy based upon personal relationships.

Lucien Musset describes primitive German agriculture during the early Middle Ages. (p. 14, 15) In swampy lands, Germans raised cattle that provided meat, milk, and cheese. Forest-occupying Germans used slash-and-burn techniques to carve small amounts of farmland out of the forests. Typical was the small hamlet of ten or so families that communally farmed wheat, barley, and rye. Influenced by the culture of the Pontic-Caspian Steppe, horses became important to the Goths, then to other Germans. Plowing with horses proved to be considerably more efficient than with oxen, particularly on the light soils of grasslands. Germans produced poor-quality textiles, cloth, and pottery but high-quality goldsmith products and metallurgy. They mined iron and salt, while furs, beeswax, honey, and amber were important exports to southerly peoples.

Warrior commanders built forts and fortifications on heights at river crossings. With time, they attracted merchants owing to the safety of these military installations. Fairs and markets might appear, then villages and towns might grow at sites originally chosen for their military value. A good example of this phenomenon occurred in Anglo-Saxon England during the ninth century. In order to resist invading Vikings, Alfred the Great set up fortifications manned by soldiers at ancient Roman towns. These proved to be successful in their military goals since, as the Vikings crossed England they continually had to fight the soldiers in these forts. The fortifications were called *burhs* in Anglo-Saxon English, a forerunner of the medieval burghs and boroughs. They became commercial centers that attracted traders, and became marketplaces for farmers, craftsmen, and money-changers. In a fashion similar to the commercial roles of Hudson's Bay forts in western Canada, these same processes occurred among the ancient Slavs and the Steppe peoples who migrated to eastern Europe.

Byzantium

The socio-economic situation in the eastern Roman empire during the early Middle Ages was dramatically different than that of western Europe. In fact, until the Muslim caliphates, the Byzantine economy was one of the healthiest in the world, and certainly the largest in the West. The Byzantine state's fiscal house was in good order, at least until the Arab conquests in the Middle East greatly reduced the Byzantine-held territories from which taxes and other revenues were drawn. Until that time, there was a diversified tax base of land taxes, head taxes, and import-export duties, usually 10% of the value of products traded.

Constantinople was the hub of a vast trading network that stretched over virtually the entire continent of Eurasia, including the trade of the Silk Road. There were also important regional trading centers such as Trebizond on the southeast coast of the Black Sea. Thessaloniki in northern Greece was the manufacturing hub for the supplies and weapons used by the imperial army. A large bureaucracy administered and controlled foreign and domestic trade, interest rates, guilds and corporations related to essential functions such as the supply of cereals, the setting of food prices, the organizing of public works, and imperial diplomacy and largesse, including the payment of bribes and tribute the better to control barbarian military incursions. The army and navy were important sources of economic demand for natural resources, manufactured goods, and agricultural produce. The most important items of trade probably were the cereals needed to feed the army and urban-dwellers as well as silk, even used sometimes as currency in foreign dealings. Raw silk was bought from China, and made into fine brocades and cloth-of-gold that commanded high prices throughout the world. Later, silk worms were smuggled into the empire, making the overland silk trade less important. After Justinian (mid-6th century), the manufacturing and sale of silk became a monopoly only processed in imperial factories, and sold to authorized buyers.

Besides silk and textiles, other luxury items included spices from the east and perfumes. There was a dazzling variety of goods produced and traded in Byzantium: olives and olive oil; grapes and wine; fish both salted and fresh; meat and game; vegetables and fruits; salt and iron; timber and wood; beeswax and honey; and ceramics and pottery. A major source of Byzantium's wealth before the Muslim conquests was the cereal produced in Egypt and North Africa, the granaries of the empire. Elsewhere in the empire from about 700 AD onwards, there was slow but sure progress in the volume of agricultural production as population slowly recovered from the two centuries of population decrease owing to the recurring plague that had begun during the rule of Justinian in 541-542. Gradual population increase required increased farm production, so woodlands and swamps were cleared to produce more farmland. Arab conquests in Egypt, Syria, Palestine, and Anatolia in the seventh century, however, seriously affected the economic and fiscal well-being of Byzantium, reducing the territory of the empire to a third of its earlier land base, while more than halving economic production and fiscal receipts of the state.

Byzantine agriculture was specialized by region, with coastal areas producing grapes, olives, and cereals, while inland areas in Anatolia and the Balkans produced livestock. While agricultural production did increase slowly in response to population increases, the increase did not owe necessarily to technical advances. Writes Chris Harman,

> There seems to have been virtually no advance in the techniques used to gain a livelihood by the vast majority of the population who worked on the land. The methods and instruments of cultivation showed little or no advance on ancient times. Tilling was still performed by a light plough pulled by oxen; fields were not manured systematically; and the harnesses employed until the 12th century choked animals so that two horses could only pull a load of about half a tonne, several times less than is possible with modern harnesses. (p. 118)

Agricultural land was controlled by local landowners in the provinces who were virtually independent of Constantinople. In return, Constantinople's interests mostly involved ensuring that taxes were collected, and that food was produced for city-dwellers and the army. As well, the army tried to make sure that the local autonomy of landlords did not lead to military revolt. In fact, not too successfully since civil wars, attempts at imperial usurpation, and succession crises were as common among Byzantine imperial families, aristocrats, and generals as they had been in the western empire.

At the lower end of the social pyramid were peasants, who were called *paroikoi*. They lived in villages and on estates that were dependent upon local aristocrats who collected taxes from the peasants, and offered peasants military and legal protection. The *paroikoi* were either tenant-farmers or small landholders who owed shares of their farm production to the local lord. The amounts of these shares varied according to whether peasants farmed using their own means and equipment, or those of the landlord. There was also a category of dependent laborers who were poor and landless who survived by wages paid for the work they performed for the great landowners, monasteries, and bishoprics. These people were known by a number of names including the terms *douleutai paroikoi*, a term that suggests that their social status was only a bit higher than that of slaves.

The Avar Khaganate

The Avars originally hailed from the Pontic-Caspian Steppe. They migrated to Pannonia where they ruled from 567 until their defeat and dispersal by Charlemagne in 799, after which they seem to have assimilated into the Slavic populations. The Avars ruled over the indigenous, Romanized population of Pannonia and over such German peoples as the Gepids and Lombards, as well as Bulgars and Slavs wherein, according to Tivader Vida, "political power was unambiguously reserved for the Avar elite." (Curta, 2008, p. 15) On the Steppe, the Avars had been nomadic horsemen. Once settled in Pannonia, they became more sedentary and agricultural, farming cereals and clearing the many marshlands of Pannonia. They lived in networks of small settlements built close together. There seems to have been considerable population growth, normally evidence of successful agriculture. Archaeological remains show that the society was class-based, judging from the material found in burial sites of members of the ruling class. Members of this class wore fine jewelry and belt buckles made by socially inferior goldsmiths, who may have been of Byzantine origin. The burial sites of ordinary people display no evidence of this goldsmith work. (Curta, 2006)

Slavic Society and Economy

The question of the geographic origins of the Slavic peoples is fraught with controversy since various regions are posited as the possible homelands of the Slavs. When one tries to conceive of the early socio-economic development of Slavic societies, it is well to remember that in spite of possibly a common geographic origin and ancestor language, there must have been considerable diversity in Slavic societies. Consider the vast distances dividing west Slavs, south Slavs, and east Slavs, and the different geographies in which the peoples of each agglomeration developed economies. From the Adriatic and the Black seas in the south to the Baltic Sea in the north, from the Balkans in the south to eastern Germany and Poland in the northwest, and to the northeast, the forests and taiga of north-central Russia. These were vast spaces with varying geographies: dry grasslands, forests, marshlands, mountains, river valleys, and maritime climes, both Nordic and Mediterranean.

The earliest recognizably Slavic societies in terms of chronology were the south Slavic societies of the Balkans. We have already seen how during the Migration of the Peoples, Germans fled from the invading Huns into the territory of the Roman empire. Into the vacuum of space that was created after the disaggregation of Attila's Hunnic confederacy apparently migrated the Slavs, who settled in various regions in eastern Europe, in effect, replacing the Germanic peoples who had entered the western Roman empire. About the same time, the Avars migrated to Pannonia. For almost 250 years between the mid-sixth century and 800, the Avars controlled central Europe.

Before the Avar conquest, however, Slavic tribes had invaded the Balkans, including northern Greece and the Peloponnese during the reign of Justinian of Byzantium in 527–565. The invading Slavs, apparently 100,000- strong, terrorized Roman territories in Thrace, Greece, Dalmatia, and Illyrium. They besieged and looted towns and cities including Thessalonica before settling down when there was nothing left to loot. They were the exception to the pattern whereby most Slavic tribes established themselves peacefully in the mostly empty spaces of eastern Europe. Warrior elites among the Slavs then established their rule in Serbia and Croatia. The south Slavs displayed their capacity to assimilate others when a military alliance between seven south Slav tribes and the Bulgars resulted eventually in the assimilation of the latter, previously Steppe people, into Slavic society and culture.

Unfortunately, there are few sources about the economic activities of the south Slavs in the Balkans. We do know, however, that when the Balkans were under control of Byzantium, inland areas specialized in livestock production, while coastal areas grew cereals, grapes, and olives. Perhaps this corresponded to the agricultural economy Slavs set up in the Balkans after their raiding and looting days, but this is only speculation by this author. Whatever agriculture existed in the Balkans, it would have been carved out from the omnipresent forests. A similar necessity would have applied to the forested regions of the northwestern and northeastern Slavic territories.

In the northeast, Swedish Vikings had established rule over the Rus' Khaganate, which included Baltic peoples, the indigenous peoples of what would become Russia, Turkic peoples, and Slavs. The *raison d'être* of the state was the trade in furs that the Norsemen plied on the rivers of ancient Rus'. We know that from this fur trade the Vikings earned coins of the Muslim Abbasid caliphate since thousands of Arabic coins have been discovered in hundreds of hoards in European Russia and the Baltic region. Once the capital of the state was moved south to Kiev, however, the economy of Rus' became more diversified, especially flourishing in the 11th and 12th centuries.

Among east Slavs and Swedes in ancient Rus' there developed a social class called the *druzhina*, whose individual members were called *druzhinniki*. This was a fellowship that served as a retinue for chieftains who were called *knyaz*. The druzhina was composed of two groups: the senior members, later known as *boyars*, and more junior members. The boyars were the prince's closest advisors, and also performed higher state functions. Junior members, actually common sodiers, constituted the prince's personal bodyguard. Members of the druzhina were dependent upon their prince for financial support, but they served the prince freely, and had the right to leave him to join the druzhina of another prince. As a result, a prince was inclined to seek the goodwill of the druzhina by paying the druzhinniki wages, sharing his war booty and taxes with them, and eventually rewarding the boyars with landed estates, complete with rights to tax and administer justice to the local population. This also was a pattern that had occurred among Germans, and possibly recurred with variations in the Steppe lands and eastern Europe.

It was the origin of the aristocratic class that supported the state, and even constituted the state itself in feudal times.

We have more information about the socio-economic development of Slavic societies in eastern Germany, Poland, and Great Moravia. According to the team of Broch, Crannog and Hillfort, when the west Slavic tribes settled in the sixth century, they were egalitarian societies with little or no class differentiation.

> The early Slavic self-sufficient, agricultural economy could not supply much of a surplus, which determined a relatively flat power structure. Apart from economic restraints, there were also geopolitical reasons for political retardation of the Slavs. The most important was the extensive control exerted by the Avars... (who) dominated all of central Europe. It was only after their defeat by Charlemagne in 799 that dynamic changes began to be seen among the Slavs. The collapse of the Avar empire and contacts with the mighty Frankish state, which expanded its tributary zone to the east, initiated a lively process of social hierarchization among the Slavs. (p. 1)

In other words, the simple, egalitarian societies of the west Slavs were transformed into class societies. Messrs Broch et al. continue:

> The long-lasting co-operation with the Avars, the establishment of long-distance, commercial relations, and the development of agro-technology led, around the mid-ninth century, to the appearance of local chiefdom organizations based on a redistribution economy. (p. 1)

In addition, political and military interventions of the German state in these regions also helped create local aristocracies of warriors who started demanding economic tribute from the producing class of farmers. Broch et al. see signs from archaeological evidence of the development of social class among the west Slavs. (p. 2, 3)

In southeast Poland there have been found the remains of monumental earthworks in the form of large mounds. Nonetheless, they do not appear to contain burial sites or gold and silver hoards, signs throughout eastern Europe of wealth being concentrated in the hands of a few leading warriors. They may have been sites used originally for religious purposes in the pre-Christian days since they were at higher altitudes closer to the gods. Broch et al. suggest, however, that...

> their main function was to manifest materially the ability to mobilize massive labor input. Their aim was to 'hide' the proliferating social differentiation behind the traditional symbolism of a burial mound. Such actions can be seen as a form of 'propaganda' aimed at social integration despite the progressive stratification.

It also appears that men of status may have competed with each other for the social prestige associated with symbolic mound building. In military terms, tribal chiefs and the emerging class of aristocratic warriors built up bands of armed followers as another means of increasing their personal power, maintaining the interest and loyalty of their followers by redistributing war booty.

This concentration of power, however, was offset by the democratic, tribal assemblies of free warrior-farmers. Chronicles of clerics reveal that there were two classes of independent warrior-farmers: large independent farmers and smaller, more-or-less independent farmers, while below them were classes of serfs and slaves, the latter possibly recent war captives, the former perhaps composed of whole tribes that had been made to submit at one time to their new rulers.

As we saw earlier with respect to German peoples, fortifications for military purposes also came to serve as space for storage of produce and other essential supplies extracted from farmers. These forts became trading emporia owing to the safety they offered, while also serving as central points in trading networks from which aristocrats could also extract surplus in the forms of tolls, taxes, tribute, and shares of the wealth being generated. The trade might take place over long-distance, trading networks running north-south or west-east. There were trades in slaves and in typical northern products such as furs, beeswax and honey, amber, iron, and salt. These trading emporia then also became centers for craft production. Evidence uncovered at some of these fortifications reveals dwellings, churches, and burial sites. Archaeological evidence suggests that Great Moravia featured advanced, flourishing centers of agriculture, commercial relations with Byzantium, Kievan Rus', and Black Sea communities as well craft works such as pottery, glass and jewelry making, and ironworks.

All this absconding of wealth by landowning warriors required ideological support and justification. Two means appeared: cultic practices at holy sites, including perhaps at earthen mounds, and creating ethnic myths by which the ancestors of the powerful were proposed as ancestors for the whole people, thus justifying the correct and essential roles of the powerful.

Khazaria

We have seen how Khazaria served as an important trade link between Europe and Asia, including for the traffic of the Silk Road. Owing in part to the economic and cultural infusion of the Rhadanites, the Khazaris went from being a semi-nomadic people of herders to life led as urbanites in the territories between the Caspian Sea and the Crimean Peninsula in the Black Sea. The Khazaris served as the conduit for Muslim goods going to Europe. There is archaeological evidence of considerable amounts of Arabic, Byzantine, and Frankish currencies circulating within the territory of the Khazaris. International trade was lucrative to the Khazaris, who extracted ten percent of the value of all goods travelling through its territory. Owing to the trade duties and tribute paid by subject peoples, Khazaris themselves were spared from the obligation of paying taxes to their government.

The peoples of Khazaria were diversified as reflected in economic activities within the territory of the Khazari state. There were urban Greeks in the Crimea, Turkic and Iranic semi-nomads and nomads, Finno-Ugric foragers, and Slavic farmers. There were goods produced in the north such as furs, slaves, honey and beeswax, and fish and game. From the grasslands came the products of animal husbandry and horses. There was viniculture in the south and typical agricultural production of the times especially grain, while towns and cities produced craft and industrial goods. Thomas Noonan summarizes the nature of the Khazari economy based upon archaeological findings: "The Khazari peoples had a complex economy in which specialized, nomadic pastoralism played a major role, but it was only one branch of a relatively diversified economy." (p. 342) In fact, even the pastoralists themselves during periods of increased rainfall would turn to agriculture and crafts production in order to reduce their dependence on sedentary peoples. During these periods, the nomads would live near the settled peoples of the forests or farmlands, or in towns and cities. During periods of reduced rainfall and the subsequent dry grasslands, nomadic pastoralists would return to their previous lives of nomadism and animal husbandry, sometimes even raiding their settled neighbors and travelling traders.

The Magyars of Hungary

When the Magyars moved from central Russia southwest to the Pontic-Caspian Steppe, their economy transformed from one of being nomadic, foraging tent-dwellers to one of being semi-sedentary farmers who also raised cattle, sheep, and horses. Moving to Hungary were about 400,000 people from 108 clans divided into seven Magyar tribes, as well as a few smaller tribes of other peoples from the Steppe. There were only 200,000 or so Slavs remaining from the era of the state of Great Moravia occupying Transylvania and Pannonia in sparse settlements when the Magyars entered these territories. Before settling in modern-day Hungary, however, it seems that the primary source of economic survival of the Magyars was looting and pillaging. Between 898 and 955, until they were ultimately defeated by the duke of Saxony, the future Emperor Otto I of the Holy Roman Empire, the Magyars launched 33 expeditions of pillage in Italy, Germany, France, and Byzantium. Socially speaking, Magyar society was an egalitarian assemblage of free men with few signs of social class other than Slavic slaves.

Popular Resistance

As with earlier periods, a fundamental historiographical problem when studying the early Middle Ages is that the sources were not written by commoners. In fact, during the period even aristocrats and kings were usually illiterate. Written sources came from the pens of clerics, which means that events described were seen often through the lens of religion, yielding the unfortunate impression that people mostly prayed and went to church during the Middle Ages. This belies the significant secular spaces wherein people worked and pursued normal activities of social and economic life. The other, major historiographical problem is that we only have a fleeting and probably under-estimated impression of the quantity of revolts, rebellions, riots, and other manifestations of popular resistance since accounts by people of other classes were often dismissive of such events. This leaves us with the task of describing the quality of manifestations of popular resistance even if we can't identify quantities accurately.

In this chapter we have described patterns of social development during the early Middle Ages. In summary, after the decline of Roman civilization in western Europe, roughly 500 years passed until the fabric of urban civilization was reconstituted. In the Middle East and in Byzantium, urban civilization continued to exist, but took on a dramatically different coloring with the rise of Islam. In the Pontic-Caspian Steppe, for the most part, nomadism and semi-nomadism continued to be the way of life, with the exception of those parts of the Steppe where urban Khazaris lived. In eastern Europe, the vacuum created when the Germanic peoples fled to the Roman empire in response to eastern menaces was filled by other eastern peoples: Avars, Slavs, Bulgars, and Magyars as well as Norsemen. As for the Balts and the peoples of Scandinavia, Finland, Estonia, and north-central Russia, it still would take hundreds of years more before urban civilization manifested itself in a significant fashion.

The twin pillars of the reconstitution of civilization, even where urban life did continue during the early Middle Ages, were the efforts to create and maintain church and state. The two were not mutually exclusive categories; in fact, they evolved hand-in-hand. As with other periods, development of church and state brought with it a concomitant popular resistance, even if the resistance cannot be described and analyzed, then classified according to watertight distinctions. Resistance to church was tied to resistance to state. The two categories of development taken together, church and state, explain how the processes of extraction of economic surplus were able to continue and progress over the generations. We can define at least three types of popular resistance in our period, in spite of these problems of evidence. We explore in turn: religious rebellions; tribal, proto-national revolts; and clear and evident class struggles; remembering that these categories of resistance were not completely distinct and watertight.

Religious Rebellion

As the Church developed in the early Middle Ages, there was a considerable gap between Christian ideals and practice. For one, as feudalism developed, bishops and abbots became important landowners who controlled local and regional peasant populations. These same clerics got involved in wars and earthly politics, not surprising since they often came from the same families and class as the warrior-aristocrats. Clerics were often younger sons from the nobility who couldn't go into the family business since it was the eldest son who inherited the aristocratic title, lands, and related military and governmental duties and rights. The resulting gap between ideal and practice was one of the causes of popular resistance in religious matters.

We have seen how in the popular Christianity of the times, veneration of saints and belief in the miracles they could perform on behalf of commoners were widespread. Usually self-effacing and imminently spiritual, saints were ideal Christians, even if they might hail from the ruling class. Where no popular saints were available, the common people created their own saints and, even in some cases, messiahs. This represented another source of popular, religious rebellion. Gregory of Tours, a sixth century bishop in France, records popular uprisings against wealthy, corrupt bishops who obtained their positions through bribery and gifts, or through the interventions of the powerful and wealthy. A return to primitive Christianity and voluntary poverty was the answer that saints from humble beginnings offered the people, despite condemnation by the Church hierarchy of certain holy men and women.

There were three other aspects important to the popularity of these humble saints and messiahs: firstly, the leftovers from local, pagan rituals and practices that sometimes showed up in the behavior and claims about pseudo-saints and messiahs; secondly, the millennial, apocalyptic visions of the pending end of the world whereby the wealthy and powerful would receive their comeuppance at the same time as the poor would be given the keys to heaven; thirdly, the seeming capacity of the pseudo-saints and messiahs, as with the more conventional, Church-approved saints, to perform miracles of behalf of the common people. We'll now consider some examples of these popular pseudo-saints and messiahs.

In 591, according to the chronicle of Gregory of Tours, a certain man from Bourges in France went into the forest to chop firewood. While in the forest, writes Raoul Vaneigem, the man "...experienced a kind of trauma or ecstasy upon seeing himself surrounded by a swarm of flies or wasps", seemingly a common element to many of these stories. (Chapter 26) He apparently went mad, then went wandering, finally completing his peregrinations around Arles in Provence. Dressed in bearskin, he preached as a holy man, even claiming to be Christ himself, while a woman called Mary accompanied him. He seemed to be able to prophecy, and worked miracles such as healing the sick just by his touch. When wealthy people brought him gold, silver, and clothes, he redistributed them to the poor. More than 3,000 people eventually followed him, but with the particularity that they were, in fact, an armed band that wandered from town to town, pillaging and even killing priests. The bishop of Puy, Aurelius, arranged for this alleged Christ to be killed. Thereafter, his followers were massacred, while those who weren't killed dispersed. Under torture, Mary offered that the pseudo-Christ had received his powers from the Devil. Two things strike one about this story: the extent of the popular anti-clericalism into which the pseudo-Christ tapped, and how the Church played for keeps when its position was threatened, going so far as to kill the pseudo-Christ and his followers.

This same Gregory of Tours records other incidents, including one about a man of unknown name who travelled from Spain to Gaul. Once in Paris, the man developed a following among prostitutes and commoner women. It turned out that he was found with a bag containing roots, moles' teeth, mouse bones, and bear fat that he used for making magical potions, taken as an obvious sign that the man was using witchcraft for diabolical purposes. A bishop travelling to Gaul from Spain for Church meetings eventually recognized the man as his runaway servant, which led to his capture and condemnation. The runaway servant, perhaps a slave, had fled his temporal responsibilities, then turned to witchcraft, according to the Church hierarchy.

A few years later, a man named Desiderius in Tours claimed to be able to work miracles, especially via his connections to the apostles Peter and Paul, who putatively communicated with him by messengers. He developed a large following owing to his ability to cure the ill, paralytics, and crippled. Once again according to Gregory, it was clear this man practiced black magic and sorcery in league with the Devil.

A more substantial threat to the established Church order was recorded by Boniface, the leading missionary to the Germans during the eighth century. It involved a French priest named Adalbert, who managed to seduce a large following of peasants including many women, and even managed to get himself consecrated as a bishop. Adalbert claimed to be able to see the future and read people's thoughts, telling those who came to him that they had no need to confess since he knew what they had done, and that their sins were forgiven. In fact, Adalbert went so far as to deny the need to confess, for which he was banned from preaching by the local bishop. No matter, he continued to preach in fields where small chapels were built near forests and springs, at which he erected crosses. Three synods of bishops finally concluded that Adalbert was mad, so he was sent to prison where he died. His writings, including a biography in the tradition of a saint's hagiography, were burnt by the Church. Adalbert's use of sacred springs, stones, trees, brooks, forests, and other elements of nature as sites for prayer and worship demonstrates how certain pagan rites and rituals had survived despite conversion to Christianity. This probably was the greatest danger that Adalbert represented to the established Church.

A contemporary of Boniface and Adalbert was an Irish priest named Clement. Clement had two bastard sons, putting into practice his teaching that the Church command that priests be celibate was irrelevant. He also promoted a Jewish practice whereby a man should marry his brother's widow. His most dangerous opinion, however, was that Jesus had saved all who had died including sinners, thereby contesting the doctrines of original sin and redemption. Clement was excommunicated at the same time Adalbert was declared mad.

Many of the followers of pseudo-saints and messiahs were women but, furthermore, some of these holy people actually were women. In the ninth century, a prophetess from German-speaking Switzerland named Thiota began prophesying the imminent end of the world in 847. She developed a following even among clerics. At a synod of bishops, she confessed that she had only made up her predictions in order to obtain money and other gifts. She was publicly flogged and shamed, after which she ceased preaching and prophesying.

Finally, there was the example of a man from Champagne called Leuthard. In the year 1000, Leuthard apparently saw the light, and left his wife. He broke into the local church and destroyed the crucifix. He preached the need to return to the simple virtues that the Apostles had displayed. He argued that the Old Testament was no longer relevant and, what is even more interesting, that payment to the Church by parishioners of *dîmes*, or tithes, was not necessary. Furthermore, the words of the Prophets and Gospels needed corrections that he was willing to provide. Bishop Gébuin of Châlons-sur-Marne convinced Leuthard of the error of his views and even of his insanity. Indeed, the possibly mad Leuthard eventually did end his life by throwing himself down a well.

These examples of false saints and messiahs showed the persistence of popular paganism despite conversion to Christianity. They also showed the popular need for miracles in light of the calamities that beset the lives of commoners, for which even false saints and messiahs sufficed. They also demonstrated a widely-held, apocalyptic belief that the end of days was nigh. Most importantly, they demonstrated the active streak of popular anti-clericalism that challenged the authority and even the necessity of the Church. These characteristics permit us to describe these examples as manifestations of popular resistance to the rich and powerful.

Proto-national Revolts

By no means did the imposition of Christianity, often by force, go unchallenged. Popular resistance to the imposition of Christianity by Charlemagne and the Franks showed up in tribal revolts among the Frisians in the Netherlands and the Saxons of northwest Germany. The Saxons' resistance was led by a legendary, shadowy figure named Widukind who led the resistance in 782. After the victorious Charlemagne organized Saxony as part of the Frankish state, the emperor ordered the forced conversion of pagan Saxons to Christianity. So, Widukind led the Saxons in revolt once again between 782 and 784 until, finally, Charlemagne was once again victorious. Charlemagne had Widukind baptized in 784, even serving as his godfather, then had him imprisoned in a monastery. Then, to signal his victory even more clearly, Charlemagne had thousands of Saxons massacred.

From the ninth century onward, Widukind was idealized as a hero of popular resistance about whom legends proliferated. Subsequent German monarchs, in fact, even strove to claim Widukind as an ancestor.

The Frisians murdered the first bishop of Frisia, Boniface, as part of pagan resistance to Christianization in 754. During 782-785, the Frisians allied unsuccessfully with the Saxons in resistance to forced Christianization. As a result of this resistance, thousands of Frisians were killed by the Franks as had already had among Saxons. Finally, in 793, a popular rebellion led by the Frisian dukes, Onno and Eilrad, was sparked when Frisians resisted conscription to the Frankish army to fight the Avars of Pannonia.

The Carolingian state, the Rus' Khaganate, and Kievan Rus' all encountered considerable resistance to Christianization from Slavic peoples. As the Carolingian state pushed to the east, it came into conflict with Slavic tribes. For instance, under the leadership of Ljudovit Posavaski, duke of the Croats of Pannonia, the Croats unsuccessfully tried to establish an empire of south Slavs in revolt against the Franks, who had defeated and crushed the Avar Khaganate of Pannonia that ruled over local Slavs. The biggest uprising of the Slavs against the Holy Roman Empire, however, occurred in 983. This revolt, which historians call the Great Slav Rising, combined elements of tribal, religious, and class conflict. It involved the Lutici, or Wilti tribe, in collaboration with the Odobrite tribe, whom Otto had subjugated in 955. These peoples lived east of the Elbe River in what is modern-day, eastern Germany. The Franks set up several bishoprics and a monastery in the region, and set to converting pagan Slavs to Christianity, while also turning them into serfs. The Slavic uprising was successful. From 985 onwards, the Franks in collaboration with Polish princes, Miezko and Boleslaw, unsuccessfully tried to subdue the rebel Slavs. In 1003, the Holy Roman ruler, Henry II, reversed previous policy, and allied with rebel Slavs in order to fight against Poland. For 200 years, German expansion east of the Elbe was halted. The Germans recognized the independence of the Slavs, who remained pagan. When the Germans continued their territorial expansion eastward 200 years later, it was done this time in collaboration with Slavic princes.

We know only a little in the French-language or English-language literature about a revolt by Slavs against the Swedish rulers of the Rus' Khaganate in 860. Led by a legendary Slavic figure, Vadim the Bold, Slavs in northern Russia rebelled against Rurik, the Viking ruler. It seems that Vadim was an older cousin of Rurik. As such, he might have had a stronger claim to the throne of the Khaganate since leadership was not inherited by sons but by the eldest male relative, or the cognatic system of inheritance. In his ultimately unsuccessful claim, Vadim had the support of the Slavs, so the dispute might have had a popular, proto-national character, that it might not have been just a dispute between related but rival noblemen over succession to the throne.

The Drevlians, originally a forest-dwelling Slavic people of the northern Ukraine, between the sixth and tenth centuries resisted attempts by Kievan

Rus' to conquer them. In 883, the Viking Prince Oleg of Novgorod managed to compel the Drevlians to pay tribute to Kievan Rus'. After Oleg's death in 912, the Drevlians stopped paying. In 945, Oleg's son, Prince Igor, tried once again to levy the tribute. That was Igor's mistake, because the Drevlian Slavs rebelled and killed him. In revenge, Igor's widow, Olga, wreaked a serious and pitiless revenge upon the unfortunate Drevlians, destroying their capital and killing their nobility.

These tribal rebellions by the Saxons, Frisians, Croats, Lutici, Odobrites, and Drevlians demonstrate popular resistance to the formation and institutionalization of states that imposed Christianity and serfdom on rural, tribal peoples among whom class differentiation was previously non-existent or still incomplete. We now turn to conflicts during the early Middle Ages that can be seen more clearly as class revolts even if tribal or religious aspects might still be present.

Class Conflicts

We know of only a few popular revolts of direct and obvious class conflict during the early Middle Ages. The most well-known is the Stellinga revolt in Saxony between 841 and 845. This author also has been able to inventory six others even if little precise information in English or French is available about these popular revolts during the period. Possibly, there are many others that haven't been documented, for example, disputes among the nobility or military campaigns that contained important components of popular resistance, but that are missing from our knowledge owing to the sources having been written by clerics, a problem about early medieval evidence to which we have referred previously. As rural societies with little class differentiation were transformed into states supported by warrior aristocracies and church hierarchies, the means of gaining riches changed from warfare, conquest, and plunder to more regular absconding of economic surplus by clerics and aristocrats from wealth created by agricultural, crafts, and trade activity by peasants, artisans, and merchants respectively. Rather than resistance through military means, resistance took the form of revolts and rebellions against tithes, taxes, corvée labor, lordly injustices, and the like by the lower social orders.

Beyond the evolution toward medieval statehood, more direct information allows us to discuss but a few cases of readily apparent class conflict. For instance, in 579, King Chilperic of the territory of Neustria in western France was most unpopular owing to high taxes and corruption in the Church whereby bishoprics were sold to the highest bidders, and many wills were being assigned directly to bishoprics and abbeys. This provoked a popular revolt in western France in the region between the Loire and the Seine rivers. (Vangeim) Unfortunately, we know little about the course of this revolt other than its existence itself.

The Stellinga revolt occurred when the *frilingi* and the *lazzi*, the two lowest, non-slave social orders in Saxony tried to recuperate the rights they had held as free pagans before forced Christianization by the Franks. Throughout all of Saxony, the power of the slaves rose up against the nobles of the land. The latter were violently persecuted and humiliated by the lowest orders among Saxon freemen. Louis the German, the ruler of the Germans, however, marched against the Saxon free men, crushed them ruthlessly, and sentenced the ringleaders to death. Then, the Saxon nobility joined the festivities in the onslaught against the rebels.

In 859, peasants in Neustria in western Gaul swore a collective oath to resist the Norman raiders who were terrorizing the Seine Valley. This led them afoul of their local nobility who, apparently more afraid of a militarized peasantry than Viking raiders, wiped out the peasant conspirators.

In Byzantium, Basil the Copperhand was a rebel leader in Bithynia in northwest Anatolia in the years between 928 and 932. An initial revolt that he led resulted in his capture and the removal of his hand in punishment. He must have been a skilled artisan or, at the very least, he knew one since he made or had made a hand of copper holding a large sword. Nonetheless, he gathered a following of poor and destitute people. They seized a military stronghold in Anatolia, and used it as their base for plundering the countryside. The rebels were defeated eventually by the Byzantine army, then Basil was burnt at the stake. Nevertheless, this manifestation of peasant discontent apparently resulted in a program of agrarian reform instituted by the Byzantine state in 934. The reform prohibited lay noblemen and Church officials and monasteries from acquiring property owned by peasants through any means. (Thomas et al.) As such, the revolt of Basil did lead to positive results for the lower classes even if at the cost of Basil's life and possibly of the lives of many of his followers.

In 955, serfs in Mecklenburg in eastern Germany rebelled. This author has found several references to this rebellion, however, no further information could be found regarding the causes or outcomes of the rebellion in the secondary literature in English or French.

About 970, the first king of Sweden about whom something is known for sure came to power. His name was Eric the Victorious, and he came to power with the support of the free farmers in conflict with the aristocratic *jarl* class. He then proceeded to limit the power of the nobility. In fact, this was not unusual during the Middle Ages as kings, often from foreign lands, were often in league with the common people against the native aristocratic class. This will be explored later more fully.

Finally, around 997 and 998, there occurred a most impressive revolt by Celtic peasants in Normandy against the local nobility of Viking extraction. It happened during the reign of the fourth duke of Normandy, Richard II. Peasants began the revolt by refusing to honor seigneurial rights. They then overran seigneurial pastures, woodlands, fisheries, and waterways, claiming them for themselves. They organized local conventions that made laws and appointed representatives to a larger regional assembly. All meetings were open and public in this minor but instructive economic democracy. Richard's uncle, Rollo, count of Évreux, however, was sent to put down the revolt, which he did with ruthless efficiency. The local conventions and regional assemblies thus ceased, quickly ending a noble experiment in local and regional anarchy.

Summary

This chapter covers the period in Europe between the demise of the western Roman empire and the end of the first millennium of the common era. During these five centuries, much of city life disappeared in western Europe even if it continued to exist elsewhere in the West. Europe of the former western empire was subjected to invasions and migrations by the Huns, Germans, nomadic peoples of the Pontic-Caspian Steppe, Norsemen, Magyars, and, as we shall see later, Muslim Arabs and North African Berbers. Often, it meant the confrontation of nomadic foragers and hunter societies with sedentary agriculturalists and the urban societies that were remnants of Roman times. Eventually, these peoples were forged into the peoples that formed the basis of the states founded on Christianity. These states and near-states introduced greater social differentiation and class relations to what had been egalitarian tribal societies based on agriculture or foraging. Aristocrats, kings, abbots, and bishops now ruled large swaths of land. Manor-organized agriculture and monastic economies slowly replaced subsistence peasant farming. At the same time, the positive attitude of Benedictine monks towards work and those who performed it did reflect an increase in the social status of laboring people.

In Byzantium, the economy continued to be one of the largest in the world before the ascension of the empires of the Muslims. The new economic systems of the early Middle Ages brought new forms of popular resistance to the extraction by other classes of economic surpluses produced by laboring people. Although written evidence is scarce or biased, it is still possible to glean some evidence from secondary sources of popular resistance in proto-national rebellions, popular religious revolts, and obvious class conflicts.

Chapter 8. Islam in the Middle Ages

Introduction

The Middle Ages witnessed the explosive combination of religion, imperialism, warfare, societal transformation, and culture that was Islam. Just as Judaism and Christianity have merited our attention in this study, we now turn our attention to the final monotheism to make its appearance during the Middle Ages. This was the last entry of what we argue was an extended Axial Age, during which humankind tried to temper the violence and brutality of the Iron Age and its aftermath.

Some readers might be puzzled about the extent to which we emphasize religion in a study of development and social domination and popular resistance thereto. While the same readers might not be as surprised at the importance of religion to the history of development and social domination, reading together religion and resistance might strike readers as novel. In fact, religion was as much a tool of popular resistance by the ruled in the pre-modern world as it was an element of social domination by the ruling classes. This affirmation is clear with respect to the Muslim world in the Middle Ages. In its very essence, Islam was a religion preoccupied with social equality and justice that spawned virtually endless rounds of popular resistance to social inequality and domination. At the same time, its rapid geographic spread owed as much to states that conquered non-Muslim peoples as to the religious fervor of its faithful. This same religious fervor, sometimes even revolutionary, often made targets of the Muslim states that led to the spread of Islam in the first instance. As such, the Islamic paradox resembles somewhat the complicated and complex relationship of Christianity to the Roman empire, and the conflict between the spiritual and temporal domains that played itself out in so many facets, even if the details and language of the Islamic paradox are also unique.

Comparing Islam to Christianity

In some ways, Islam and Christianity present mirror images of each other. For one, each has been divided over the years by schisms and heresies into principal branches and smaller, offshoot sects. For instance, Christianity is comprised of its three branches of Catholicism, Orthodoxy, and Protestantism as well as peculiar, related churches such as Mormonism. Islam is divided into the majority Sunnis and important minorities of Shi'ites and Sufis, with each branch being further divided into sects and schools of thought, and with peculiar, related sects such as the Druze of Lebanon and the Yazidis of Iraq. Such divisions, beyond religious explanations, are understandable sociologically given the broad range of societies and historical periods in which each faith set down roots.

Both Christianity and Islam possess theological texts that purport to explain their beginnings but, in fact, about their founders and the circumstances in which the faiths were founded, more is unknown than is known with certainty. Each faith was transformed and developed over the first generations, even centuries, until it emerged in forms recognizable to a modern. Thus, while at the cores of Christianity and Islam are theologies for which there is sometimes little corroborating evidence from other sources, the details of each faith, the 'fleshing out', if you will, emerged through processes of historical development that can be studied fruitfully.

Of course, there are important differences between the two faiths, but this is a book of social history, not an exercise in comparative religious studies. Undeniably, however, each faith, as per the first major monotheism, Judaism, is committed in its ideals to social justice and equality of all in the eyes of God. Just as importantly, nonetheless, each of the great monotheisms struggles with the reality of life in the temporal realm wherein faith falls considerably short of ideals, partly owing to the history of conquest and imperialism in the name of each faith. The monotheisms, it must be stated, have produced their share of "killing in the name of God", to quote an American ethicist, David Perry.

Beginnings of Islam in Arabia

Sources about the beginnings of Islam include the biographies of Muhammad's life; oral traditions about his life and times, sayings, and actions of Muhammad and his original companions; and the Qur'an, purportedly the documentation of the instructions of God to his messenger, Muhammad, allegedly transmitted by the archangel Gabriel in visions during the last 22 years of Muhammad's life, beginning in 610. Each source is highly problematic.

Firstly, the earliest biographies were written long after the deaths of Muhammad and his contemporaries. Ibn Ishaq's *Life of God's Messenger* was written in 767, 135 years or about six generations after Muhammad's death in 632. The author based his book on oral traditions about his subject. The book is written somewhat in the style of a Christian hagiography wherein the life of the saint and his or her accomplishments are described in most positive and glowing, even miraculous terms. These hagiographies were extremely popular in the Christian world; they possibly served as a model for Ibn Ishaq. The next life of Muhammad was written 200 years after Muhammad's death, and was based on the first biography, while still more biographies were written later in the ninth century. The fact that later biographies added material not included in the original documents suggests that creative editing, redaction, and composition were taking place in subsequent biographies.

Secondly, not only are there problems with the source materials for these documents, having been published long after the events surrounding Muhammad and his times, they were also published during the Abbasid caliphate when the Muslim empire covered thousands of square kilometres of territory, well beyond the Arabian peninsula where Islam had originated. There were important political imperatives for the production of impressive, awe-inspiring origins to match the scale of the growing and powerful Muslim empire. The tardiness of basic documents about the founding of the faith is not surprising in the context of the ancient world that was just ending when Islam appeared. Consider that it took until the fifth century before the basic doctrine, beliefs, and origins narrative were established definitively for Orthodox and Catholic Christianity. The Jewish Tanakh, or the Christian Old Testament, which related the stories of the Hebrew patriarchs and prophets from hundreds of years earlier was assembled during and after the Babylonian captivity of the sixth century BC, according to current historical consensus. To take another example, during the reign of Augustus Caesar the poet Virgil wrote his *Aeneid*, wherein he glorified the ancestors of the Romans as being descended from a great Trojan warrior, Aeneas. The epic served to glorify what were actually the humble origins of Rome as an Iron Age hamlet, as well as justifying the contemporary policies of Augustus, and the actual course of Roman history and development. As far as it concerns Islam, the story of the redaction of the Qur'an and its origins is indeed muddled and confused, and it is unclear when the first versions actually did appear. As evidence of this, Ibn Mujahid, a ninth-century Islamic scholar from Baghdad, selected seven of the-then fourteen versions of the Qur'an extant in the ninth century as being canonical, that is, to be officially recognized by Muslims.

So, with original sources about Muhammad and the beginnings of Islam being so iffy, let us see what we might be able to discern with some sense of historical rectitude about the origins of Islam. Some background information about Arabia is in order, information that provides valuable context for the life and times of Muhammad and the beginnings of Islam. In fact, understanding the context of the Arabian Peninsula can go a long way in explaining how Islam came to be.

The Arabian Peninsula showed the first signs of permanent, human habitation around 2000 BC. Arabia is an arid, originally volcanic land with three deserts in the interior. Along the western shore are mountains from which a plateau slopes gently eastward, which comprises most of Arabia. Agriculture developed in Arabia mostly around oases and springs, and in the more humid coastal or mountainous areas, where villages and towns developed based on an economy of farming and trade. Only about a sixth of Arabs lived in towns during the seventh century when Muhammad lived, while the remainder were pastoral nomads, the reknown Bedouin. Throughout their long history, the Bedouin survived in harsh lands, dependent upon herds of sheep, goats, and camels, while surplus meat, dairy products, hides, and wool were sold to town-dwellers. The Bedouin held their grazing lands collectively without individual ownership; these lands included summer and winter camping grounds. The desert Bedouin also controlled trade routes, and escorted, guided, or drove trade caravans for economic reward when they were not plundering or taxing travellers. In difficult times, they raided settlements and caravans to collect tolls, so often that these activities were not even considered criminally or morally wrong. In fact, in this aspect, the economy of the Bedouin was similar to the economic basis of the nomadic societies that inhabited the Pontic-Caspian Steppe.

There were two main stocks of Bedouin. The Yamanis first settled in the mountains of southwest Arabia. The second group of Bedouin, the Qaysis, first settled in northern and central Arabia. As early as the 13th century BC, the mountains and relatively wet climate of Yemen permitted the Yamanis to develop a sedentary agricultural and urban civilization. In central and northern Arabia, nomadic Bedouin were able to settle only around oases and springs where they cultivated grains and dates and other fruits. The towns that grew around springs and oases also served as trading centers for the caravans that transported spices, gold, and ivory from the Far East and Africa via southern Arabia to the lands of the Fertile Crescent.

The customary law of the ancestors of the Bedouin, called the Sunnah, regulated affairs of Bedouin society, which was characterized by a fierce and demanding loyalty to family, clan, and tribe that often provoked blood feuds and revenge killings whereby relatives of a murdered man were required to kill the man's murderer or one of the murderer's relatives in revenge. The negotiated acceptance of blood payments as compensation for the murder victim was the only way to stop the killing from escalating into endless feuds. These payments were similar to the weregild among Germanic tribes. Warfare among the tribes was perennial. In spite of this warfare, there also were highly developed codes of hospitality and generosity to travellers among the Bedouin, understandable since the harsh nature of the land made mutual aid vital to the survival of its inhabitants.

Most Arabs were either animists or polytheists. Arab animists worshipped at springs, trees, mountains, or other natural features. For polytheists, one of the most important settlements was Mecca owing to its Ka'ba, a cube-shaped shrine built around what was probably originally a meteorite. Arabic myth had it that the site of the first cube shrine had been built by Adam, and it was reputed to have been a site of prayer and veneration also used by Abraham. The meteorite Ka'ba, as if fallen from heaven itself, served as a pilgrimage center for Arabs who worshipped idols of about 360 local and pan-Arabic gods, goddesses, and spirits. According to Piero Caruffi, a Stanford academic, in the fourth century AD a man named Qusayy "...gained control of Mecca, collected the nearby idols, created a monopoly of pilgrimage, and established the Quraysh as wardens of the shrine", making his tribe the tribe of Allah, an important Arabic god. Moreover, by agreement among Arab tribes, antipathies and conflicts among them would be suspended once their members were in Mecca for religious observance. With the perennial influx of pilgrims, Mecca became a wealthy town that made some members of the Quraysh very rich. So much so that this wealth was an object of consternation to Muhammad, who was also a member of the Mecca tribe though from a different clan. This Quraysh wealth was, in fact, a motivating factor for Muhammad's political and religious campaign of aggressive monotheism combined with a program of social justice and equality since the wealthy of the Quraysh subjected their poorer neighbors to maltreatment and oppression, at least in the opinion of the Prophet.

An important element of Arab culture was the poetry that sang of love, nature, tribe and clan, gods and goddesses, and heroic figures. Poets were respected members of Arab society. Some poets composed verses, while others were tasked with memorizing and reciting these poems. One of Muhammad's mentors was a poet named Zayd bin Amr, who was a member of the Hanif, monotheists indigenous to Arabia. Even if they were neither Jews nor Christians, the Hanif still thought of themselves as descended from a common patriarch, Abraham. Muhammad's father had been a member of the Hanif. Muhammad was a poor orphan raised by an uncle, his father's brother. As a young man, he married a successful and powerful, older business woman with whom Muhammad became wealthy. His poor origins, however, weighed heavily on him. Meanwhile, Zayd bin Amr condemned the polytheism and idolatry and wealthy of Mecca for their oppression of the poor, which brought upon him the wrath of the Meccans. He was forced to exile himself in a cave on Mount Hira near Mecca. There were still other dispirited souls who joined Zayd bin Amr in their criticism of Meccan ways. As he reached middle age, the equally forlorn Muhammad joined with Zayd's group to pray and meditate. It was possibly Zayd and not the archangel Gabriel who told Muhammad to recite, and helped the illiterate Muhammad do so. Muhammad's recitations, apparently ultimately from Allah, were assembled and redacted by his followers during his life and the years after his death.

As Zayd had done, Muhammad angered his fellow tribesmen with his preaching about their evil ways, so he too was forced to flee to a neighboring town called Medina. There, Muhammad encountered a much more positive response to his preaching. Medina had a substantial Jewish population of refugees from the Roman destruction of Jerusalem and the expulsion of Jews during the Roman-Jewish wars of the first and second centuries AD. Villages of Jews were also found at oases surrounding Medina. Nearby were several monasteries of Christian monks. In point of fact, on the Arabian Peninsula, there were also Christian communities in Yemen, Bahrain, and Oman during the life of Muhammad. According to the Library of Congress essay about Saudi Arabia,

> Najran, a city in the southwest of present-day Saudi Arabia, had a mixed population of Jews, Christians, and pagans, and had been ruled by a Jewish king only fifty years before Muhammad's birth. In sixth-century Najran, Christianity was well-established, with a clerical hierarchy of nuns, priests, bishops, and lay clergy.

The existence of prior groups of monotheists in Arabia must have influenced Muhammad and his original followers, and made the environment in Arabia propitious to the preachings of the Prophet. As well, many of the respected poets of Arabia were monotheists who rejected the materialist and idolatrous ways of the wealthy Quraysh tribe that controlled Mecca. From this movement of social protest emerged Muhammad and his radical monotheism.

The Arabian Peninsula was subject to cycles of drought and overpopulation. During some of these periods, some Arabs had moved into the Fertile Crescent. The Nabatean tribe settled near Judea with their capital carved out of rock at Petra, in modern-day Jordan. In the Syrian Desert, the Arab town of Palmyra flourished during the third century AD until the Romans destroyed it. There were also two Bedouin tribes who served as soldiers in the rival Byzantine and Persian armies. A Christian Monophysite, so-called Ghassanid state of Arabs in the valley of the Yarmuk River, a tributary of the Jordan River, served the Byzantines, while a Christian Nestorian tribe of Arabs called the Lakhmid was based in the southern Euphrates Valley, and fought on behalf of the Persians. It was, in part, among this Arab diaspora that Islam was first able to take root outside the Arabian Peninsula.

What else do we know with some degree of certainty about the beginnings of Islam? About the belief system of Muhammad, there are two principal elements that were drawn, in fact, from ideas then current among Jews, Christians, and the Hanif. The first was a fierce and implacable monotheism. To these monotheists, the source of the evils of Mecca was idolatry and polytheism. Secondly, Muhammad held apocalyptic views since he was convinced that the end of the world and the Last Judgement were nigh, a view also held by the Zoroastrians of Persia and other peoples in those days. Similar to the message of the Hebrew prophets, Muhammad's message was that:

> God is one...all-powerful, he is the creator of the universe, and that there will be a Judgement Day when those who've carried out God's commands will enjoy paradise in heaven, and those who have not will be condemned to hell. (Library of Congress study, Saudi Arabia)

There were two other, basic points to Muhammad's beliefs: his commitment to social justice and equality among Arabs, and his methods of spreading Islam by waging holy war against infidels and his use of other military or political means.

We shall consider the latter point first. Very early, Muhammad's leadership of Medina brought him into conflict with Mecca, owing to his preachings about the evil of Mecca that had led to his forced exile from his home town. In 624, Muhammad's force intercepted a caravan from Syria on its way to Mecca in order to disrupt the economic activity of Mecca, and to distribute the cargo among his followers, most of whom were poor. By using this tactic, Muhammad was only doing what poor Bedouin had done from time immemorial. In the same year, Muhammad decided that that his followers, rather than praying in the direction of Jerusalem as prescribed originally by Muhammad, would now pray in the direction of Mecca towards the Ka'ba. This would lead eventually to a demonstration of Muhammad's singularity of purpose, if not obsession with undoing the worship of Arab spirits and gods at the Meccan shrine. Muhammad continued to harry commercial traffic to and from Mecca, with the result that Mecca fell to Muhammed in 630 with little military resistance. He then won over Meccans to his side by ordering a general amnesty rather than punishment, even if he also destroyed the idols at the shrine at the Ka'ba.

Muhammad proceeded to spread his belief system beyond Medina and Mecca throughout Arabia using political, diplomatic, and military means. These included the methods that had always been employed by the tribes of Arabia, inter-tribal warfare and disruption of trade caravans. An American military historian, Richard Gabriel, writes that Muhammad led his troops in eight major battles and 18 raids, and helped plan another 38 military operations executed by others.

While a fine general, Muhammad also displayed considerable political skills, allying with some tribes, threatening others, playing off one against the other, and convincing still others through argument, among other peaceful tactics. His troops were from the poorest of the Bedouin tribes and clans. They were only too happy to share in the booty from raids upon the caravans of enemy tribes and clans. He molded these poor men into an army of thousands organized into infantry and cavalry. For the traditional communities of tribes and clans, Muhammad substituted the *Umma*, the community of believers as the rallying-point of Arab society. Refusal to adopt the monotheism espoused by Muhammad was taken as a virtual slap in the face to people raised on concepts of tribal loyalty and honor. Thus, he translated inter-tribal competition and warfare into expressions of support or rejection of his beliefs. 'Either you were with 'im or agin' 'im', as the popular expression goes. In fact, the Qur'an is a mixture of beautiful prose almost poetic in its reverence for God and nature, joined to what appears to be instructions drawn from military manuals. According to the basic document of Islam:

> When you encounter the unbelievers, blows to the necks it shall be until, once you have routed them, you are to tighten their fetters...Thereafter, it is either gracious bestowal of freedom, or holding them to reason until war has laid down its burdens. (Holland, p. 301)

With such a philosophy, by the time of his death in 632, Muhammad had convinced or forced all of Arabia to join his movement.

Social Justice and Islam

The final pillar of Islam was the commitment to social justice and equality evinced by Muhammad at the beginnings of Islam. In one sense, the commitment to social justice and equality is the content, the 'what' of Islam, while the fact that it was spread as much by warfare as any other method represents the 'how' of Islam. Muhammad's followers were principally composed of poor Bedouin tribes and clans of Arabia to whom his social message was highly motivating. Muhammad used the same methods that the Bedouin had always employed, that is, raiding caravans and conducting inter-tribal warfare, so use of these methods must have appeared most reasonable to Arabs, helping ensure the acceptance of Muhammad's message among the poor of Arabia. The message of Islam also was simple, especially when compared to the complex doctrines of Christianity. Being a Muslim required that one accept that there is one God whose messenger is Muhammad, the last in the line of prophets; that one pray five times a day in the direction of Mecca; that one give alms for the poor and unfortunate; that one fast during the lunar month of Ramadan from dawn to dusk; and that, if possible, one should make a pilgrimage at least once to Mecca. The simplicity of these requirements must have been another cause of their acceptance, especially among the poor and illiterate.

The third requirement of Islam was called the *zakat*, the giving of alms. This was a poor tax, expiation for the bounty a person had received from God and donated, in return, to God. Originally a donation based upon the tenets of Islam, it was very early translated into being a legal tax paid to the state. According to authors Irani and Silver, under the régimes of Muhammad and the first four caliphs, the zakat was distributed thus among the following: the poor and needy; officials who gathered the zakat; recalcitrant Meccans whose hostility had to be bought off, in effect, bribes for some Meccans to accept the peace of Muhammad; certain slaves to help them buy their freedom; individuals who had incurred bad debts as a result of self-sacrificing, benevolent acts; the state in order to arm soldiers for holy wars against infidels; social institutions established to serve Allah, for example, public works, charities, and mosques; poor travellers. The scriptures of Islam also suggested giving voluntary contributions called *sadaqua* to the public treasury, the *Bayt al-Mal*. All this giving by the wealthy to the less fortunate, as has been argued by Islamic scholars, was indeed done during the eras of Muhammad and the Rashidun caliphates, the first, 'rightly-guided' caliphs, as they are known to Sunni Muslims. Muhammad and the first caliphs also sequestered lands to make them available to the poor for pasture of their animals, in effect, establishing public ownership of some land, which also must have appealed to the Bedouin who held their lands collectively. Given these dispositions, one can see how the message of Islam appealed to the poor. In one particular example concerning the disposition of lands, the caliphs refused to make available to wealthy Arabs lands conquered in Mesopotamia and Syria, preferring to establish small farmers in villages on conquered lands.

The constitution of Medina that Muhammad developed shortly after his flight from Mecca in 622 established the first Islamic state. Muhammad's constitution established the following: the security of the community; religious freedoms; the role of Medina as a *haram*, or sacred place barring all violence and weapons; the security of women; stable tribal relations within Medina; a tax system for supporting the community in time of conflict; parameters for exogenous political alliances; a system for protection of individuals; a judicial system for resolving disputes. Most notably, Muhammad's constitution provided for a system of payments to the state in retribution for acts of bloodshed rather than permitting blood revenge and endless feuding among families, clans, and tribes.

Muhammad's laws made for considerable social advances for women. The Prophet outlawed the practice of *wa'd*, or female infanticide, apparently a common occurrence in pre-Islamic Arabia. Early Islam also increased the legal status of women as legal persons with respect to divorce, inheritance, and family law, including controls and limits on polygyny and polygamy, while offering societal respect for motherhood and for women generally. During this period, many women, witness Muhammad's own wives and daughters, played important roles in the economy, religion, politics, even warfare of Muslim society.

The apocalyptic world-view, the holy war method of spreading the faith, and the social message of Islam was combined with the inspiring message of the Qur'an to the effect that those who oppress the weak will answer for their crimes at the final resurrection by facing everlasting punishment. The poor of Arabia and elsewhere in the Muslim world can only have felt justified by this message. In fact, Muhammad and the coming of Islam wrought nothing less than a social revolution. This is the view of a leading American scholar of Islam, Bernard Lewis.

The new faith, hot from Arabia, overwhelmed existing doctrines and churches; its new masters who brought it overthrew an old order, and created a new one. In Islam, there was to be neither church nor priest, neither orthodoxy nor hierarchy, neither kingship nor aristocracy. There were to be no castes nor estates to flaw the unity of believers; no privileges, save the self-evident superiority of those who accept to those who willfully reject the true faith. (1973, p. 273)

The Pattern of Muslim Conquest

While the social promise of Muhammad was indeed revolutionary, Chris Harman reminds us that Muhammad was also successful

because he was able to build a core of young men committed to a single world view, while forming tactical alliances with groups whose purpose was very different: with townspeople and cultivators who wanted peace, with merchant families who relished the profits a powerful Arab state would bring them, and with tribal leaders hoping for loot from fighting for his cause. (p. 125)

Immediately after Muhammad's death in 632, less committed Arabs fell away from Muhammad's movement, thinking they might avoid paying taxes to a central authority, especially if their adherence to Muhammad's cause had been less than enthusiastic or even forced. Recalcitrant Arabs also were inspired by a raft of prophets who sprung up like mushrooms on the Arabian Peninsula, and whose messages competed with that of the deceased Muhammad, men such as Tulayha, Musaylimah, Aswad Ansi, and a woman named Sajjah, virtually a prophet for each tribe. This would have been hardly surprising after all since tribes had always had their own gods and spirits. Muhammad's successor, the elderly Abu Bakr, the Prophet's father-in-law, was chosen by consensus among the deceased Muhammad's companions and family members. Abu Bakr sought to return apostate tribes to the fold using force with a military campaign called the *Riddah*. Between Muhammad's use of military means and his successor's tribal warring, a pattern emerged of spreading the Islamic faith militarily. There would be easy military conquests and some more difficult; some conversions to Islam were voluntary, while others were forced.

At the time of Abu Bakr's selection as successor to Muhammad, or *caliph*, some of Muhammad's family and entourage favored a young man for the position named Ali, who was Muhammad's cousin and son-in-law married to the Prophet's daughter, Fatima. While Ali rallied to the choice of Abu Bakr, the question of whether or not Ali, after all a member of the Prophet's family, should succeed Muhammad proved to be pregnant with consequences. The next two choices as caliph put forward by the Prophet's followers, Umar in 634 and Uthman in 644, also bypassed the *shiat Ali*, or party of Ali. Ali was finally named as the fourth caliph in 656, but he was killed shortly after during a civil war, which we discuss below. This ended the short period when the entire Muslim community recognized one caliph. By now, the promise of peace among Arabs as well as the social message with respect to the poor and unfortunate were indeed being lost in translation to Arabic power. The new reality among Arabs was a series of succession crises, civil wars, rebellions and revolts, and outright imperialism.

Arab conquests beyond the Arabian Peninsula started as tentative probes to neighboring regions, partly to deflect the warring energies of the Bedouin who had been fighting for over a decade on behalf of Muhammad and Abu Bakr. Almost a millennium later, the Muslim empire had conquered a good portion of the world. By way of summary, here is a list of some Muslim conquests before 1492 that were relevant to the West, along with the dates of the conquests.

- 636—Palestine and Iraq
- 637—Syria
- 639—Armenia and the Sinai Peninsula
- 642—Egypt and Persia
- 643—Cyraenica and Tripolitania (Libya)
- 652—Carthage (Tunisia) and Numidia (eastern Algeria)
- 654—Cyprus
- 667-699—the Maghreb (western Algeria and Morocco)
- 711-718—Al-Andalus (Portugal and Spain, except for Celtic Gallaecia in northwest Spain and the Basque country in the north)
- 720—Septimania (southern France)
- 736—Georgia
- 820—Crete
- 827—southern Italy
- 831-878—Sicily
- 1060-1350—Anatolia
- 1350—establishment of Ottoman empire in Anatolia
- 1371—Ottomans conquer Thrace and Macedonia
- 1382-1422—Ottomans conquer Bulgaria
- 1385-1501—Ottomans conquer Albania
- 1453—Constantinople falls to Ottoman empire
- 1460—Greece falls to Ottomans
- 1482—Ottomans conquer Bosnia and Herzegovina

The Bedouin, whose perennial warfare in the early days of Islam had helped destroy the Arab economy, began making probing attacks and raids into Mesopotamia in search of booty during the reign of Abu Bakr. They were struck by the ease and success of these attacks, and were encouraged as well by Arabs who had previously settled in Mesopotamia. Abu Bakr lent his support to Bedouin warriors by declaring a holy war upon the infidels of the Middle East. The prime states in the region were Byzantium and Persia, empires that had been warring incessantly with each other such that both were exhausted militarily, psychologically, and economically. Persian society had been further weakened by the control exerted by its landowning class of aristocrats who ruthlessly exploited other classes. In Byzantium, potential Byzantine resistance to Muslim Arabs was compromised by a lack of enthusiasm for Constantinople from its subject peoples, owing to the oppression of Jews and non-orthodox Christians—Monophysites, Nestorians, and Arians—to which the Byzantines subjected constituent peoples in the Middle East. In fact, conquest by the Arabs was greeted by Byzantine subject peoples as a relief from the religious ministrations of Constantinople.

Abu Bakr, just before his death in 634, sent troops northwest into Palestine. At Ajnadia, thirty kilometers west of Jerusalem, the Arabs defeated a Byzantine army, thus bringing much of Palestine under Arab sway. Abu-Bakr's successor, Umar, began his rule by successfully besieging Damascus in Syria. As well, an Arab victory at Qadisiya permitted the Arabs the run of Mesopotamia such that, in 638, the Arabs took Ctesiphon, the Persian capital in Iraq. In the same year, the Arabs also took Jerusalem and Caesarea Maritima, the port city in Palestine. The conquest of Iran, divided into many principalities under the ruling Sassanid empire, proved to be more time-consuming and arduous. It took years before the Arabs were able to subdue the eastern peoples of the Persian empire. To the west, the peoples of the Byzantine empire, however, welcomed the Arab conquerors, who Christians and Jews practice their religions in peace provided they paid the tax that non-Muslim peoples were required to pay to their Arab conquerors as well as commercial and property taxes. In fact, forceful conversion of these peoples by the Muslims would have been counter-productive since the Arab conquerors would have foregone revenues. The religious situation in Persia with respect to Zoroastrians was different when compared to that of Jews and Christians. According to Frank Smitha:

> Zoroastrianism was doomed as a great religion. In response to conquest by Islam's armies, the Zoroastrians would foment rebellions, and the conquering Muslims responded. In many provinces, Muslims forced Zoroastrians to convert to Islam, while many Zoroastrians adopted Nestorian Christianity instead. Here and there, Zoroastrianism would survive but in coming centuries, conversions to Islam would leave Zoroastrians a small minority.

There were other reasons for the success of the initial Arab forays into the Middle East, in addition to the facts that Byzantium and Persia had exhausted themselves fighting each other, and that the Arabs permitted the conquered peoples of the Byzantine empire to practice their religion freely. The Arabs created the impression, in the words of Smitha, "...that they were warring against the Byzantine empire rather than against local people." The Arabs plundered the homes and lands of the wealthy who had retreated to Constantinople from the Roman provinces. They left the local poor mostly undisturbed; the poor had little to plunder in any case.

For the most part, it was Arab policy to leave intact local communities and their laws, even local upper classes, as long as taxes were paid. Moreover, early caliphs had a policy of segregating Bedouin warriors in Iraqi garrison towns such as Basra and Kufa so that they not mix with conquered, local populations. This policy was set in the hope that the warriors would not assimilate to conquered peoples; intermarriage might mean conversion of wives and children to Islam which would mean loss of taxable subjects. Thus, the idea that holy wars were all about forced Muslim conversion of infidels was not true, at least in the early Arab conquests. The Arab policy of segregation of soldiers from the surrounding communities was doomed to failure, however, as the Bedouin did indeed intermarry, thus increasing the chance of conversion to Islam by conquered peoples. This was to prove a source of considerable discontent in the near future, as we shall see later in the section about popular resistance.

Evidence of immediate discontent in the present was the fact that other than the elderly Abu Bakr who died peacefully, the next three caliphs—Umar, Uthman, Ali—were all killed in office. After the last caliph died, at no further time did all Muslims follow the same leader. Umar was murdered by a mad slave from Persia; Uthman was killed by disgruntled Arabs who had fought in Egypt; and Ali died in a war with the Arab governor of Syria, a man named Mu'awiyah, a cousin of Uthman. Mu'awiyah was determined to seek revenge for the death of Uthman, at the behest of the latter's widow, and in the name of the Umayyad clan to which they belonged. The irony was that it was the Umayyads that had been the most oppressive clan in Mecca; it was against the Umayyads that Muhammad had fought most intensely. It was, in fact, a return to the blood feuds of the desert that the succession problem occasioned. Furthermore, to Mu'awiyah, Muhammad was a prophet like any other. The caliph treated Jews, Christians, Samaritans, and Manicheans as equal to the followers of Muhammad, all of whom were part of the faithful. This also might indicate that Islam was still far from fully developed as a distinct religion from its regional cousins in terms of its doctrines and narratives.

Mu'awiyah died in 680, and the caliphate passed to his son, Yazid, whose mother was a Christian. Many resisted this succession, including an Arab named Abdullah ibn Zubayr, who led a rebellion against the Umayyads. There were also three others who claimed the caliphate, if indeed the principle of succession was that leadership was going to pass to sons of previous rulers: Hussein, the second son of Ali; Abu Bakr's son; and the grandson of Umar. Hussein was killed in battle at Karbala in Iraq against troops of Yazid, and he was buried there at what came to be the holiest of Shi'a shrines. Hussein's death outraged supporters of Zubayr in Medina. Yazid tried to reconcile with Zubayr, but he was rebuffed by the latter, so Yazid's 12,000 troops from Syria conquered Medina in August of 683, in the process killing the leaders of the Zubayr rebellion including many noblemen. Zubayr repaired to Mecca, which Yazid's army besieged for two months beginning in September of

683. Frank Smitha relates the following incident during the siege of Mecca: "Rocks from catapults fell into the sacred Ka'ba; to the horror of believers, the Ka'ba caught fire, burned to the ground, the sacred black stone split, and fell from its socket." Zubayr and the Meccans won a reprieve from destruction when Yazid's generals learned that caliph Yazid had died in November of 683, and the Syrian army returned home. Yazid's sick teenaged son succeeded as caliph, but died a few weeks later. The senior member of the Umayyad clan, Marwan, claimed the caliphate. The Zubayr-led Arabs and the Syrians fought a great battle east of Damascus, with Marwan defeating the forces of Zubayr. Marwan was recognized ruler of Syria, then extended his rule to include Palestine and Egypt by persuading Arabs in Egypt to support him rather than Zubayr. After just nine months as caliph, however, Marwan was struck down in May, 685 during an outbreak of the bubonic plague. His son, Malik, succeeded him as head of the Umayyad forces. For seven more years, civil war raged between Zubayr, leading the Arabs, and Malik, leading the Syrians. Finally, in 692, Malik's forces took Mecca, killed Zubayr, and ended this episode of civil strife.

The conflict between the Umayyads and the supporters of Ali was, of course, political in nature, involving the question of succession to the leadership of the Prophet. The question was who would be caliph, whether it was a man chosen by an ill-defined consensus of the faithful, or a man who was a descendant of Muhammad, even if the ancestral link might be tenuous or tangential. Over time, the division of opinion between the two political camps took on theological and philosophical aspects. Shi'a proponents argued that their candidates inherited the mystical properties of Ali since they were relatives or descendants of Muhammad. This was interpreted to mean that caliphs might continue to receive divine instructions other than those received by Muhammad. The majority, Sunni view, however, held that Muhammad alone received divine guidance, as evidenced in the various versions of the Qur'an that various sages and scribes were assembling.

> Disagreements among Shi'a over who of several pretenders had a truer claim to the mystical powers of Ali produced further schisms. Some Shi'a groups developed doctrines of divine leadership, far removed from the strict monotheism of early Islam, in hidden (occulted) but divinely chosen leaders with spiritual powers that equalled or surpassed those of the Prophet himself. The main sect of Shi'a became known as the 'Twelvers' because they recognized Ali and eleven direct descendants as Imams. (Library of Congress country study, Saudi Arabia)

Other Shi'a groups recognized six descendants or even four as legitimate imams, and there were still other derivations of belief among the Shi'a. All these divisions translated what might have been a practical, political, and peaceful choice of leadership succession into an issue fraught with religious and philosophical overtones that revealed significant class and ethnic divisions among the faithful. We'll consider these differences of religious opinion later since they do reflect tangibly different social interests.

The Umayyads concentrated their rule in Damascus rather than in Medina or Mecca, even if the two Arabian cities retained their religious auras. This was to be the pattern in the future: temporal power concentrated in cities outside Arabia in Cairo, Baghdad, Toledo, Samarkand, and other cities in the Muslim world. The Umayyads concentrated power, wealth, and influence among members of the caliph's family in the manner of kings with aristocratic retinues. They also employed a professional army of Syrians, many of whom had Christian or pagan origins, rather than employing Bedouin fighters. The latter came to feel cheated of the spoils of victory, the booty that had been shared traditionally among victorious tribes in Arabia. The caliphs responded with two strategies. Firstly, they encouraged the restart of civil strife among the Arab tribes, including the traditional conflict between the Yamanis and the Qaysis, the southern and northern Arabs, by playing off one against the other. Secondly, they initiated new rounds of military expansion with new promises of booty and riches for conquering soldiers.

Muslim conquests had already taken on different colors. By way of summarizing the evolution of these conquests, at first, the campaigns of Muhammad and Abu Bakr were religious movements with powerful social messages on behalf of poor Bedouin tribes. Their methods, however, resembled nothing less than the traditional tribal warfare that Muhammad wanted to arrest at the same time as he employed these same military methods himself. After Arabia was secured, conquests were the result of tentative probes into weakened states in search of booty and riches, campaigns that were also organized and fought to deflect the military ardors of the Bedouin soldiers. Arabs had been fighting now for a decade during which the Arabian economy had gone to waste owing to the negative impacts of constant warfare on trade and agriculture. Furthermore, they were encouraged in their probes into Byzantine and Persian-held lands by their Arab cousins who had long since moved to southern Palestine, Syria, and Mesopotamia, and who had been misused and abused by both Persia and Byzantium. Forays into Mesopotamia put the invading Arabs in conflict with the Persians who ruled Iraq. This put the Muslims on a course of invasions eastward into Iran and other Persian-ruled territories in central Asia. Under the Umayyads, the caliphate had become more materialistic and concerned with temporal power than religious matters. One of the concerns behind new conquests was to deflect the growing discontent of the Bedouin under Umayyad rule, discontent that was to manifest itself in both the civil wars of succession and popular rebellions and revolts that we inventory and analyze below.

Conquests of Egypt and North Africa

After initial conquests in familiar lands involving more or less familiar people, the Muslim armies turned west to cross the Sinai and take on Egypt. Irish writer Eamonn Gearon describes Muslim motivation:

> Initially reluctant to risk an invasion of Byzantine Egypt, Umar was eventually persuaded to do so by the military governor of Palestine... Amr ibn al-'As. Like Muhammad...Amr was a member of the Quraysh... Having already secured Palestine and the Levant, and with serious Muslim incursions harrying Byzantine forces in Anatolia, Amr successfully argued that not only was the time right to invade Egypt, but also that such a move would secure the southern borders of the nascent Muslim empire by attacking those Byzantine lands from which the Arabs expected they themselves would otherwise be threatened.

In 639, the conquest of Egypt began; by 646, all of Egypt had succumbed to Muslim armies. Egypt was a vital prize since it was a land of considerable wealth and the bread basket of the Byzantine empire that imported much of its grain from Egypt. Moreover, the country was held in reverence and awe by most peoples during these times owing to Egypt's mythic, legendary past including the mysterious building of the awesome pyramids. Egypt was held to be the fount of ancient wisdom.

Many Egyptians greeted their new masters positively since the Byzantines oppressed the Monophysite Coptic majority, menacing them with forced conversion to Christian orthodoxy. The Muslims let Benjamin, the Monophysite patriarch of Egypt, know that his people could worship as they wished in peace, indeed as they had done under previous Persian masters. In fact, in military campaigns against the Byzantines, Benjamin would pray for Muslim victory against his fellow Christians, so pleased were the Copts to recover their religious freedom. Furthermore, Egyptian peasants were oppressed by their mostly Greek landlords, so they too felt liberated by the Arab victors, who judiciously left control of farmlands and governmental administration in the hands of locals. As per elsewhere, the Arabs had no interest in converting Egyptians to Islam since it would have meant a loss of tax revenue, which would have contradicted one of the main motivations of conquest.

Amr then turned his acquisitive eyes southwards to Nubia, the modern-day Sudan. The Nubian invasion turned into an unmitigated disaster, so Amr re-directed his armies west. On a thousand-mile march with the aim of securing his western borders, Amr's forces raided into what is modern-day Libya. In 647, the third caliph, Uthman, launched the first, full-scale invasion of North Africa west of Egypt. Gearon notes an important fact about North Africa.

> Byzantine grip on the region was never as strong as that of Rome and, as a result, oppression, revolts, and insurrections characterized Berber-Byzantine relations. (Author's note: The Berbers were the disparate,

native tribes of North Africa.) This century of animus saw the slow collapse of Byzantine influence in the region.

So, in a manner similar to that of their subjects in the Middle East, the Byzantine ruling class's actions, in fact, eased the way for Arab conquests in North Africa. Moreover, North Africa still held Donatist Christians who were continually at loggerheads with the Church at Rome and the emperor at Constantinople, which further weakened the resistance by North Africans to the Arab conquerors.

In 647, an Arab army of 10-20,000 soldiers left Egypt on a 15-month campaign through Libya and Tunisia. In southern Tunisia, the Arabs convincingly defeated a Byzantine army. Over the next twenty years or so, the Arabs fought with local tribes for shares of formerly Byzantine lands and riches. During this period, there began a slow process of conversion to Islam from the Christian, Jewish, and pagan roots of the Berber population, even if all were not were converted to Islam until the 12th century. (Library of Congress country study, Algeria). There were two more Arab invasions before the Berbers were finally conquered, and in 682 the Muslims reached the Atlantic Ocean in Morocco. It had taken two generations, 43 years, for the Arab Muslims to conquer all of North Africa from Egypt to Morocco. This had been a difficult process since the native tribes put up persistent resistance to the invaders, even if it was true that the two parties did collaborate to oust the Byzantines from North Africa in the first instance. In the process, the Arabs established three capital cities: Fustat in Egypt, which was to become Cairo; Kairoun in Ifriqiya (Tunisia and eastern Algeria); and The Fes in the Maghreb (western Algeria and Morocco).

New Conquests

The Umayyad caliphs continued their conquests in new territories during the eighth century. In one sense, these campaigns were about protecting their new acquisitions from reprisals from the Byzantines and the Persians by guarding and extending borders preemptively. In a more fundamental sense, however, they were acts of imperial aggression with the aim of increasing the wealth and power of the Arab ruling class just as any empire might have acted.

In the west, a combined Berber-Arab army crossed the Straits of Gibraltar in 711 to begin the conquest of the Iberian Peninsula. Eventually, the Muslims controlled most of the Iberian Peninsula, except for the northwest of the peninsula and the Basque country in the north. The invaders then crossed into southern France, however, their advance into central France was checked in 732 at the battle of Poitiers by Charles Martel, leader of the Franks and grandfather of Charlemagne, even if the Muslims continued to occupy Septimania for decades longer. The Muslims also organized a navy to fight the Byzantines. By the early decades of the ninth century, they had conquered Cyprus, Crete, Sicily, Malta, and Sardinia as well as the Balearic Islands near Spain.

In the east, early in the eighth century, the Umayyad caliphs began the conquest of central Asia beyond Iran. They first conquered the region known to historians as Transoxania, which lies between the Oxus and Jaxartes rivers in central Asia. These rivers flow northwest to the Aral Sea, the Oxus emptying in the then-southwest corner of the Aral Sea, the Jaxartes in the then-northeast corner of the Aral Sea. Between 706 and 738, the Umayyads exercised a loose control of Transoxania, which was consolidated in 740 by Nasr ibn Sayyar. The vast Islamic empire was now as large as the Roman empire had been. It had been conquered in a little more than a century from the time of Muhammad's conquest of Mecca. While Mecca and Medina remained holy cities to the Muslims, Umayyad temporal power was concentrated in Damascus where a bureaucracy, often manned by former Christians and Jews, tried to maintain central control over the empire.

> The empire was very much an Arab conquest state. Except in the Arabian Peninsula and parts of the Fertile Crescent, a small, Arab Muslim aristocracy ruled over peoples who were neither Arab nor Muslim. Only Muslim Arabs were first-class citizens of this great empire. (World History Project)

In 750, a new régime replaced the Umayyad caliphate following the Abbasid revolution, which we describe below. In 751, this new régime defeated the equally expansionist, Buddhist Tang dynasty of China in the battle of Talas River, fought near the border of modern-day Kyrgyzstan and southern Kazakhstan. The Chinese then withdrew from the region, leaving the Turkic and Iranic peoples who lived there to convert slowly but inexorably to Islam. The Kazakhs and other Turkic peoples on the central Asian and Pontic-Caspian steppes, as well as the Iranic peoples, began to convert to Islam late in the 700s. In 922, the Bulgar state in the Volga Valley converted to Islam, making it the first state of what is modern-day, northern Russia to do so. By the tenth century, most Turkic and Iranic peoples had converted to Islam.

Turkic and Mongol Empires

The first of the Turkic, Islamic convert peoples to affect the West in an important way were the Seljuks, named for their ruler, whose homelands were in Transoxania. The Seljuks were related to the Turkmen of central Asia and to the Kipchaks, Turkic people who were in the process of displacing the Pechenegs, another Turkic people, in southern Russia. About 950, Seljuk's people migrated to a land then known as Khwarezm, the easternmost Muslim territory that corresponded to parts of modern-day Kazakhstan, Turkmenistan, and Uzbekistan. In 1037, Seljuk's grandsons, Tughril and Chagri, conquered Iran and Azerbaijan, thus ending Arab control of these lands. In 1039, the Seljuks took Syria and Palestine, then Iraq in 1055. In 1064, Georgia and Armenia were added to Seljuk control. In 1071, at the battle of Manzikert in eastern Anatolia, Chagri's son, Alp Arslan, defeated the Byzantines. This was indeed a crucial turning point since almost all of Anatolia, with the exception of Cilicia in the south, was now in the hands of the Seljuks. The Seljuk Turkic people conquered what had been traditionally Greek lands for over 1,500 years.

Another wave of conquerors from the Asian Steppes to affect the West directly came from the Mongol Empire. In 1206, Genghis Khan succeeded in uniting Turkic peoples and Mongol peoples native to Mongolia, north of China. Then began a seemingly unstoppable series of conquests on the central Asian and Pontic-Caspian steppes, in the Middle East, and even eastern Europe. Upon his death, Genghis Khan's will decreed that the Mongol empire be divided among four of his surviving sons. Of particular relevance to the West were the Mongol régimes known to historians as the Il-khanate in the southwest portion of the empire and the Kipchak Khanate in the northwest part of the empire. The latter included parts of modern-day Russia, the southern Ukraine, the Crimea, and Alania, homelands of the Alans on the Pontic-Caspian Steppe. About 1240, Mongols of the Kipchak Khanate were busy invading and terrorizing parts of eastern Europe: Poland, Hungary, Lithuania, Croatia, Wallachia in modern-day Romania, Thrace, Bulgaria, and Serbia. In December of 1241, however, the Mongol supreme leader, the Agakhan Ogedia, son of Genghis Khan, died in Mongolia. Mongol rulers were recalled to elect a new agakhan, and to deal with the inevitable succession crisis; this brought an end to Mongol threats in eastern Europe.

During the reign of Uzbeg during the period 1312–1341, the ruler of the Kipchak Khanate, so-called since the majority of people under Mongol rule were Kipchak Turks, converted to Islam, a case of a ruler being assimilated by the Muslim population he governed. At the height of its power, the Kipchak Khanate covered most of eastern Europe from the Ural Mountains in modern-day, central Russia to the southern banks of the Danube River. On its southern borders were the Black Sea, the Caucasus Mountains, and the Il-khanate, the southwestern portion of the Mongol empire. At the end of the 15th century, the northern state of Muscovy, a Kipchak vassal state, succeeded in terminating the Tatar Yoke, the Muscovite term for rule by the Mongols and Turks over Slavic Russia. Even so, remnants of the Turco-Mongol rule known as the Great Horde continued to exist on the Pontic-Caspian Steppe until 1502. Thereafter, small khanates also remained among the Volga Bulgars, in the Crimea, and in Astrakhan, the land immediately northwest of the Caspian Sea in the lower Volga valley and delta.

In the Il-khanate, during the 1250s, a grandson of Genghis Khan, Hulagu, received instructions from Agakhan Mangu to complete what had been but a perfunctory, nominal conquest of Persia. This Hulagu did with a vengeance. Before he was finished, Hulagu had conquered Iran, Iraq, Syria, Azerbaijan, Georgia, Armenia, Turkmenistan, eastern and central Anatolia, and western and southwestern portions of modern-day Afghanistan and Pakistan respectively. These conquests were disastrous for their Muslim population since the ruling Mongols persecuted the Muslims, while at the same time they favored Buddhists and Christians. In 1295, however, the Il-khanate became officially Muslim. The shoe was now on the other foot as Muslims now received favorable treatment from the Mongols, while Buddhists and Christians now received short shrift. Furthermore, Muslim leadership now passed from the original Arabs and Persians to the Turkic and Mongol peoples of the Steppes. At the turn of the 14ᵗʰ century, Mongols ruled lands stretching from Korea and China in the east as far west as the eastern borders of Hungary, and from Siberia in the north to Burma in the south. This was the largest empire to ever exist at that time, to be surpassed in geographic extent eventually only by the British empire of the 19ᵗʰ century.

Another Turkic Muslim people to affect the West was the Mamaluke Sultanate that ruled Egypt, the Levant, Syria, and western Arabia between 1250 and 1517. The Mamalukes were originally Turkic slaves employed as soldiers by the Muslims. They eventually became essential to the Muslims, so much as to become the effective rulers of Egypt and the Middle East even before the Mamaluke Sultanate was organized formally. The Mamalukes drove the Christian crusaders out of the Levant in 1291 and 1302, the latter being the last crusade to the Middle East.

At the turn of the 14th century, an Anatolian aristocrat named Osman established a state that came to be known as the Ottoman empire. It lasted until after WWI when the modern state of Turkey was formed from the ashes of the empire; modern Turkey includes Anatolia, Thrace, and Constantinople, the great city having been renamed Istanbul after the Ottoman conquest of 1453. At its largest extent towards the end of the 16ᵗʰ century, the Ottoman empire covered important parts of eastern Europe (see earlier chronology) as well as still other parts of eastern Europe: modern-day southern Russia, Moldova, Romania, Slovakia, and eastern Hungary, as well as Armenia, Syria, Palestine, Egypt, and North Africa as far west as Algeria.

The Muslim Economy

Even before the advent of the Mongol and Ottoman empires, Muslim-held territories were immense, covering an area running east to west from the borders of China to Portugal. These included central Asia, parts of the Indian sub-continent, Anatolia, the Middle East, North Africa, most of the Iberian Peninsula, southern Italy and France, and the major Mediterranean islands of Cyprus, Malta, and Sicily among other Mediterranean islands. Between the 8ᵗʰ and 13ᵗʰ centuries under the Abbasid and Fatimid caliphates, the Muslim economy was the largest in the world, bypassing even that of Byzantium. While there were economic generalities applicable to the entire Muslim world, there were also particularities to the different régimes and societies, which we explore further below. Nonetheless, there are five general components that contributed to the economic development and remarkable success and prosperity of the Islamic world: trade, agriculture, industry, science and knowledge, and collectivist, social institutions. We now explore each of them.

Trade

Trade constituted the most important source of wealth in the Islamic world. Muhammad himself had been a trader, while trade was the prime source of wealth on the Arabian Peninsula. Muslims developed a merchant capitalism of trade in goods and products from almost the entire, known world: spices and silk from the east; furs, beeswax, honey, and wood from the north; ivory, gold, and minerals from the south, among others. All this trade was supported by infrastructure such as regular fairs, caravan stopover places called *caravanserai*, merchant hangars, and warehouses; states' fiscal policies that usually excluded taxing Muslim production; and well-established trade routes. All these indicated that the Muslim world was indeed mercantile in economic organization and intent.

Muslim merchants developed commercial innovations still being used today: bills of exchange, promissory notes, savings and deposit banks, partnerships, accounting methods, credit and lending arrangements, and cheques (itself an Arabic word), to name but a few. A cheque drawn upon a bank in Baghdad, for instance, could be cashed in Morocco or anywhere else within the Islamic world. This commercial capitalism spread over such a vast geographic territory included large cities that served as centres of commercial enterprise: Damascus, Baghdad, Cairo, and Cordoba and Toledo in Spain. These great cities as well as smaller cities and towns were all designed with commerce in mind, and led and controlled by merchants. Each urban agglomeration included bazaars, industrial and craft production areas, commercial infrastructure, and universities that were loci of economic development.

One of the principal commodities of Muslim trade was the commerce in slaves. The basis for the trade in slaves was not religious, nor was it based upon a religiously-sanctioned, racial hierarchy. To Muhammad, all races were equal. The only permissible, hierarchical difference among people was the difference between the faithful and infidels, a statement observed often in its breach, but one that did mean, nonetheless, that prisoners taken during the frequent Muslim warfare with non-Muslims could be enslaved by the victors. Furthermore, as the slave trade became well-established and lucrative, there were incentives to conduct raids and other forays into enemy lands with the explicit aim of adding slaves to be traded within the Muslim world. Slaves came from the following peoples: Slavs and other eastern Europeans, Mediterranean peoples, western Europeans, Turks, Persians, Caucasians, that is, Georgians and Circassians, Christians and Jews from the Middle East and North Africa, and Africans from eastern Africa and sub-Saharan Africa. The extent of the slave trade was geographically vast. The ninth century Muslim geographer, Ibn Kurradadhbeh, described slave-trading, Jewish merchants from southern France

> who speak Arabic, Persian, Greek, Frankish, Spanish, and Slavonic. They travel from west to east and east to west by land and sea. From the west, they bring eunuchs, slave girls and boys, brocade, beaver skins, sable and other furs, and swords. (Madany, p. 1)

All these slaves helped make Islam what Bernard Lewis calls the first universal civilization. Numbers enslaved are difficult to estimate. If one considers just the African trade, one credible source suggests that 17 million Africans were enslaved in the Islamic trade, comprised of four million via the Red Sea trade, four million via the Indian Ocean trade further south, and nine million via the sub-Saharan trade. (M'bokolo) This figure compares to an estimate of 22 million Africans captured for the Atlantic trade with Europe and the Americas. Estimating numbers of non-African slaves, however, is a mug's game, impossible to do. Suffice to say that it was not a trivial number since conquests of non-African populations provided the original sources of slaves for the Muslim world.

What work did Muslim slaves perform? Men worked as servants, soldiers, and laborers in mines and on irrigation works and plantations. Some slaves were skilled craftsmen who introduced new techniques to the Muslim world. For instance, at the battle of Talas River when the Abbasid régime defeated the Chinese Tang army, among the prisoners taken were Chinese paper makers. Thereafter, the use of paper spread throughout the Muslim world, reaching Egypt by 800 and Spain by 900. (Madany, p. 1) It should be stated that unlike the Atlantic trade where men were more highly valued than women owing to the nature of the work they were destined to perform in the Americas, the Muslim slave trade seems to have valued women more highly. While women often worked as servants, many were actually concubines in harems. Perhaps a useful generalization might be that slaves in the Muslim world were more oriented for use in consumption, while slaves in the Atlantic trade were destined more to serve in production.

As per latter-day Roman slavery, manumission was a common procedure in Islamic societies, originally encouraged by Muhammad himself. Masters and slaves might even sign deeds whereupon after a certain amount of time or work, a slave could gain his freedom. A person born of a slave woman and free man was born free, even where concubinage defined the relationship between parents. There were so many people born to slave women that it was hardly to one's discredit in Muslim society to be born of a slave woman. Many such people rose to positions of prominence and stature in Muslim societies. As well, *sharia* law helped ensure the permanence of slavery as an institution by regulations that conferred legal status to slaves. In fact, slavery continued in many Muslim countries even into the 20th century. Slavery continues today in certain Islamic countries in spite of years of abolition efforts and international legal advance about slavery. One should have no illusions, moreover, that being a Muslim slave was life in Paradise for, as we shall see below, the treatment of conquered peoples and slaves who converted to Islam was indeed problematic. In fact, the ill treatment of slaves and slave-born progeny led to continual revolt and revolution in the Muslim world.

The Islamic Agricultural Revolution

In 1974, an economist at the University of Toronto named Andrew Watson suggested that Arabs and Muslims created during the Middle Ages an agrarian revolution that greatly improved agricultural productivity world-wide. He argued that the Islamic world was responsible for introducing and for distributing certain crops via the vast Muslim trade networks. Watson "... listed 726 plants that have been given Latin names derived from Arabic origins." (Safieh, 3.10) This revolution introduced to the world such vegetables as spinach, eggplant, and artichoke, among many others; fruits such as mangoes, bananas, and oranges and other citrus fruits; and such staples as durum wheat, sugar, and cotton. In 2009, an historian at the University of South Florida, Michael Decker, argued using ancient written sources that, in fact, cotton and durum wheat, the hard wheat used to make pasta, were long-known in the ancient Roman and Persian worlds, and that the Muslims did not develop these crops first. The point is moot, however, since it is important that even if Muslims didn't first farm these crops, the vast trade network of the Muslims was responsible for diffusing these crops on a broad basis. The introduction and spread of these new foods also resulted in the development and diffusion of new cuisines, confections, and culinary techniques.

In addition to diffusing new crops, Muslims introduced new techniques to increase agricultural productivity. Muslim agronomists in the Middle Ages wrote about tree planting, types of soils, use of fertilizer, control of crop diseases, medicinal qualities of plants, the use of spices such as saffron, thyme, and aniseed, and the aromatic qualities of flowers such as roses, camellia, and jasmine. There were also advances to existing agricultural technologies in hydraulics, irrigation, and mills which the Muslims were responsible for developing and diffusing. Finally, there were advances in the organization of land tenure systems whereby large landholdings were divided into smaller lots farmed by individual owners and inhabitants, which resulted in more productive use of farmlands. (Safieh)

Industry

Thomas Glick, historian at Boston University, has written about the spread of technology throughout the Muslim world and into the West.

In general, the movement of technological diffusion in the high Middle Ages followed a trajectory from China and India to the West through the mediation of Persia, which was also a hearth of technological innovation...There tended to be substantial lags between the invention of a technique in China and its eventual arrival in the West; after the Arab conquests, however, eastern techniques diffused much more rapidly once they gained the borders of the Islamic world.

So, while some techniques took up to a millennium to move from China or India to the West as was the case for many foundry techniques, after the Arab conquests techniques such as paper making and the use of Arabic (Indian) numerals spread to the West in a matter of decades. The rapidity of technological diffusion throughout the Muslim world and the West seems to have been a function of trade networks, local resources, and whether or not there were existing technologies that might be further developed and refined. Most crafts and industrial production were based on families of craftsmen, therefore, they were somewhat resistant to innovation. Nevertheless, under the pressure of conquest, demand from large cities, and the migration of artisans sometimes even organized by states, family crafts production based on age-old, sometimes secret techniques was affected by technical innovations. (Glick) Ancient technologies were refined and developed further, or reintroduced anew. These included such hydraulic innovations as mills, water turbines, water-raising machines, mill gears, and dams. Techniques eventually were brought westward, or introduced to the West after improvements by Muslim craftsmen and engineers. It should be pointed out that the Islamic view of manual labor meant that physical work was held in higher regard than it had been among ancient civilizations, a factor that further encouraged technical improvements.

One industry in the Islamic world was the motor of much economic development. Textiles in the Islamic world were like the petroleum industry today in terms of their importance and essential nature. States did not always leave the textiles industry to small craft families. They often organized private or public monopolies. Women played a key role in the production of cloth, textiles, and clothing, doing such work as weaving, spinning, dyeing, and embroidery. There is no direct evidence for the existence of structured women's guilds, nonetheless. The segregation of sexes in medieval Islam was the rule, whereby women worked in family groups in private homes since they could not gather in public in the presence of men in marketplaces or bazaars or public work spaces. Their production was ordered, directed, and sold by male agents in what appears to have been an outsourcing system. (Shatzmiller, p. 357, 358) Nonetheless, according to Maya Shatzmiller, historian at the University of Western Ontario who has studied the organization of labor in the medieval Muslim world, "...the limited participation (of women) in economic activities and in the labor force can no longer be upheld." (p. 39)

As for men, craftsmen were organized into guilds as has been the case almost from the beginnings of urban life generally. Important guilds were the associations of *warraqeen*, people who worked with paper. The warraqeen were vital to the extension of knowledge in Islamic societies. The website Master Artisan describes the roles of the warraqeen.

> Early Muslims were heavily engaged in translating and absorbing all knowledge from all other known civilizations from as far away as China. Critically analyzing, accepting, rejecting, improving, and codifying knowledge from other cultures became a key activity, and a knowledge industry as presently understood began to evolve. By the beginning of the ninth century, paper had become the standard medium of written communication. Most warraqeen were engaged in paper-making, book-selling, and taking the dictation of authors to whom they were obliged to pay royalties on works, and who had the final discretion on the contents. As the standard means of presentation of a new work was its public dictation in the mosque or madrassah in front of scholars and students, a high degree of professional respect was required to ensure that other warraqeen did not simply make or sell copies, or that authors did not lose faith in the warraqeen or this system of publication.

The warraqeen guild system began late in the ninth century, and continued well into the 15th century. According to one author, a warraq doing good translations could be paid as much as 500 gold dinars per month, an amount currently equivalent to about $25,000 U.S. (Bennison, p. 185) Countless numbers of works were produced and published by these craftsmen. The expansion of scientific knowledge in the Middle Ages would have been impossible without their work.

Science and Knowledge

The Islamic world in the Middle Ages produced countless advances in science and human knowledge, which the warraqeen helped diffuse. We've already seen some of their advances in agronomy and agriculture. As was the case with technologies, Muslims either elaborated existing knowledge or made breakthroughs. This was the case even in arts such as painting, music, and poetry. In fact, there is conjecture to the effect that the troubadour tradition that emerged in southern France during the high Middle Ages was a product of Muslim influence via Spain.

In addition to the arts, Muslims made breakthroughs in philosophy, theology, law, zoology, geography, cartography, architecture, and astronomy. In mathematics, Muslims introduced or refined algebra, algorithms, trigonometry, and geometry including applied geometry as seen, for example, in Muslim mosaics. They also pioneered the use of Arabic numerals, zero, and the decimal system. In chemistry, Muslim scholars isolated arsenic, alcohol, ethanol, and several acids—nitric, sulfuric, chlorohydric—as well as petroleum products such as kerosene, naphtha, tar, and gasoline.

Furthermore, they introduced 2,000 chemical substances used in medicine. Still in medicine, Islamic scholars identified and wrote about smallpox and the measles, and the defensive role fever played. They also made medical breakthroughs in pharmaceuticals, surgery, medicinal qualities of certain plants, optics and ophthalmology, and human anatomy including describing the blood circulation system.

The Muslim wise man was known as a *hakim*. These men were knowledgeable in medicine, astronomy, and mathematics. One such hakim important to the West was Avicenna, who rehabilitated Aristotle. The philosopher's works had a profound effect on scholasticism in the West, the effort to reconcile Christianity and science as represented by Aristotle. (Arberry) In fact, during the high Middle Ages, Muslims were responsible for re-introducing to the West its patrimony of ancient Greek knowledge about astronomy, geometry, poetry, and philosophy. Part of the explanation for this intellectual effervescence lay with the religious controversies and different sects that demonstrated there were divergent ways to be a Muslim, even if these differences might imply political disturbances or even political violence. These divergences provided intellectuals with liberty and incentives to seek out the truth, which led to scientific and artistic advances. Moreover, the whole pursuit of knowledge in medieval Muslim societies, in fact, was inspired by faith. In a manner that reveals the religious context to the search for scientific truth, the Muslim philosopher Avicenna wrote:

> There is a natural hierarchy of knowledge from the physics of matter to the metaphysics of cosmological speculation, yet all knowledge terminates in the Divine. All phenomena are creations of Allah...Nature is a vast unity to be studied by believers as the visible sign of the Godhead, divine nature or essence. Nature is like an oasis in the desert; the tiny blades of grass as well as the most magnificent flowers bespeak of the Gardener's loving hand. All nature is such a garden, the cosmic garden of God. Its study is a sacred act. (Wye)

This philosophy inspired Thomas Aquinas in the 13th century with regard to his development of a proof of the existence of God. (Arberry)

The Islamic world held important public and private libraries at a time when, in Christian Europe, books were a rare commodity. Libraries, in addition to the stand-alone facilities that sometimes were architectural marvels, were attached to mosques, madrassahs, and to *bayt al-hikma*, medieval research institutes that attracted scholars from the length and breadth of the Islamic world. (Spiegel) There were 3,000,000 books at the library in Tripoli and 2,000,000 at the Cairo library. During the tenth century in Cordoba, there were 70 libraries, the largest of which held 600,000 documents, while in mid-13th century Baghdad there were at least 36 libraries. In al-Andalus alone 60,000 books were published each year. Muslim libraries introduced public lending and the use of library catalogues. Unfortunately, millions of books produced in the Islamic world were destroyed by the Mongols in the 13th century invasions, or by Christians during the Crusades and the final

Christian takeover of Muslim Spain towards the end of the 15th century. (Wye)

Collectivist Institutions

The Islamic world created social institutions that both increased and redistributed the fruits of its prosperity. These collectivist organizations went back to the time and example of Muhammad himself. After the death of the Prophet, social institutions were formalized by the first four caliphs, especially the second caliph, Umar, who is revered by most Muslims for his holiness and charity towards others. There were more social improvements made during the reign of the Umayyad caliphs. We have already considered the requirement upon Muslims to contribute *zakat*, charitable donations based upon individual wealth collected by medieval Muslim states. Two more social institutions, the *waqf* and the *bayt al-mal*, deserve consideration. The waqf was a trust established by individuals to be used for the building and operation of religious institutions such as mosques, or for social institutions such as madrassahs, hospitals, and other charitable organizations. The wealthy could make contributions to the waqf from their wealth including gold and silver, cash, land, wills and estates, and still other forms of wealth. The waqf was introduced by Caliph Umar, who also introduced the bayt al-mal, the public treasury responsible for the administration of taxes including the zakat. Wealthy Muslims were also encouraged to make contributions to the bayt al-mal additional to the zakat called *sabaaqa*. It was from the bayt al-mal that soldiers were paid. It was also the fund used to pay pensions to the elderly, the poor, disabled, widows, orphans, and the unemployed. Pensioners included non-Muslims. The bayt al-mal was also used to stockpile foodstuffs for general distribution during famines. Umar even used the bayt al-mal to pay minimum incomes to the poor. Begging and inactivity were not permitted for poor pensioners, however, who were expected to contribute to society, even if they could not work gainfully. Later, Umayyad caliphs instituted the payment of guide persons for the blind and of servants for the disabled as well as general disaster relief and pensions for injured soldiers. Islamic societies were, in fact, social welfare states well before they became the norm in Bismarck's Germany or elsewhere in the West during the 20th century.

Particular Muslim Régimes

So much for generalities about the medieval Muslim economy that covered a good portion of the globe for almost a millennium. Obviously, there would have been differences in the economic development of the empires and dynasties that comprised Islam in the Middle Ages, some of which we now consider. This will also permit us to illustrate and amplify certain aspects of the Islamic economy and society. We now consider particularities about the

Umayyad and Abbasid caliphates, the Volga Bulgars, the Fatimids of Egypt, the Seljuk Turks, and the Mamalukes in Egypt and the Middle East.

Umayyad Caliphate

The Umayyads came to power with the third Rashidun caliphate under the rule of Uthman. Uthman is notable for having continued the imperial march of Islam into North Africa. Uthman ruled from 644 to 656, and was succeeded by Ali, cousin of Muhammad, who was from the same clan as the Prophet, the Hashemites. It was after the succession and rule of Ali, however, that the Umayyad dynasty began in earnest in 661. The dynasty lasted until 750, when it was replaced by the Abbasid régime, which endured until 1258. The Umayyads' capital was at Damascus; the Abbasids' capital was at Baghdad. The Umayyads extended Islam into Pakistan, into central Asia in Transoxiana and Afghanistan, and on the Mediterranean islands of Crete and Rhodes. After the Abbasids came to power, an Umayyad scion escaped mass assassinations of Umayyads to initiate a Muslim régime in Spain, which itself eventually became a caliphate.

There was no small irony in the accession to power of the Umayyads, who had been Muhammad's antagonists in Mecca. This rich clan became even wealthier with the Muslim conquests and the resulting tax revenues paid by Christians, Jews, and other non-Muslims under Umayyad rule. Although the dynasty was responsible for introducing additional social measures, for the most part, the régime was secular, mostly concerned with the administration of temporal power and expanding Muslim rule. The Islamic ideal of frugality and simplicity was replaced by the enjoyment of lavish wealth and luxury that made the Umayyad dynasty resemble more the Byzantine court or the court of any other royal dynasty than it did poor Bedouin societies. In fact, the latter were excluded increasingly from the exercise of power to be replaced by Christians, Jews, and ex-Zoroastrian Persians. This was a source of social tension that periodically erupted, as we shall see later in this chapter.

Abbasid Caliphate

The initial assembly and redacting of the Qur'an might have started in the time of Muhammad himself. It is most likely that Muhammad was illiterate, but the community of monotheists with which the Prophet associated included poets and scribes who might have recorded bits and pieces from memory and oral tradition that eventually became part of the Qur'an. Under the Rashidun caliphs, the first successors to Muhammad, the assembly of materials into written form began, even if there were more than one version of the Qur'an. Early in the Abbasid régime, Islamic scholars began the process of developing more formally the written documentation of the Islamic message, theology, and philosophy in the form of *hadiths*, the purported sayings of Muhammad. These served as a more substantial guide to the development of the religion, while the *sharia* provided formal codes of Islamic law. According to Chris Harman:

> Today, these codes are often presented in the West as expressions of pure barbarism as opposed to the allegedly humane and civilized values of Judeo-Christian tradition, but in the ninth and tenth centuries the codes represented, in part, the values of traders and artisans who sought to free themselves from the arbitrary rule of imperial officialdom and landed aristocrats, and did so in ways that stood in marked contrast to what prevailed in Christian Byzantium, let alone in the developing feudal system of western Europe. (p. 130)

In effect, sharia law provided a more socially egalitarian ethos, based on contract and social and geographic mobility, which referred to Islam for religious and political legitimation. The traders and artisans who benefited from the mobility and equality inherent in Islamic law and philosophy produced immense prosperity in a society that was indeed cosmopolitan. For instance, bazaars in Abbasid Baghdad offered goods from the entire, known world.

> There were spices, minerals, and dyes from India; gems and fabrics from central Asia; honey and wax from Scandinavia and Russia; ivory and gold dust from Africa; goods from China including silks, musk, and porcelain. In the slave markets, Muslim traders bought and sold Scandinavians, Mongolians, and Africans. (World History Project, The Abbasids, Zenith of Islamic Civilization")

The trade networks of the merchants—not just Muslims but merchants of other faiths as well—who assembled these products ranged over vast territories.

> Merchants travelled to India, Sri Lanka, the East Indies, and China, giving rise to settlements of Arab merchants in the south China cities. Trade also extended up the Volga into Russia—with hoards of Arab coins found even in Sweden—through Ethiopia and the Nile Valley into Africa, and via Jewish merchants into western Europe. (Harman, p. 129)

In Canton, there was a merchant community of about 100,000 Arabs, Persians, and Jews who had sailed on Muslim ships across the Indian Ocean. (Smitha)

The Abbasid civilization represented the golden age of Islamic society. Nonetheless, like all empires, it was not to last. Beginning in mid-tenth century, local governors increasingly held the real power, while caliphs were reduced to reigning as figureheads and religious symbols. In 756, an escaped member of the Umayyads who had fled for his safety after the Abbasid revolution established a separate régime in Iberia. The countries of North Africa also gained independence from Baghdad, while eastern Persia came to be governed by rulers who offered just nominal allegiance to the Abbasids.

In the tenth century Ismaili Shi'ites established a caliphate with a capital at Cairo. Known as the Fatimid Caliphate it ruled Syria, the Levant, and Egypt. In the 11th century, Seljuk Turks from Transoxiana migrated to Abbasid-held territories, then converted to Islam. They conquered Iran, then Baghdad and Iraq in 1055. Thereafter, the Seljuk Turks took Syria and Palestine from the Fatimids and most of Anatolia from the Byzantines. In 1258, the Mongols captured Baghdad, formally ending the Abbasid régime. Another group of Turks known as the Mamalukes also had an important role in the disintegration of the Abbasid régime. They were Turkic slaves from the Caucasus and the Pontic-Caspian Steppe who were trained from an early age to serve the caliphate as soldiers. The use of these Turks was an attempt to employ people other than the unruly Bedouin as soldiers since the latter were always susceptible to revolt if they became displeased at the turn of events in Muslim society. The Fatimids used the Mamalukes in important roles. Eventually, they began to be the real governing force in Egypt. They rebelled and began to rule Egypt much as German soldiers had done with respect to the ancient Romans. The Mamalukes, in turn, fell eventually to the Ottomans, Turks who hailed from central Asia and had migrated to Anatolia.

The Volga Bulgars

The Volga Bulgars converted to Islam in 922. Analyzing their development is interesting for the information it provides about the economic workings of a northern Islamic society, in fact, the first Islamic society in central Russia. A.A. Rorlich is our source of information about the Volga Bulgar economy. With respect to state taxation, as per elsewhere in the Islamic world, agricultural production was exempt from taxation. Most state revenue came from taxes on trade. While there were no tariffs on trade within most Muslim states and empires, there was a 10% tax on all goods traded within Volga Bulgaria, whether by local or foreign merchants. There were also taxes on weddings and on booty absconded during warfare, as well as an annual tax on sable pelts. In fact, furs were such important items of Bulgar trade that they were sometimes used as currency, similar to the historic use of pelts by the Hudson's Bay Company in Canada.

Agriculture, cattle and grain production were indeed successful; in fact, surplus was exported. Travellers reported glowingly about the fruit orchards and walnut groves found in the Volga Bulgar lands. Abu Hamid al-Garnati, a 12th century Arab geographer, reported that "...they have so many fruits that it is impossible to find more than this elsewhere." (Rorlich)

Bulgar craftsmen both in town and country were skilled producers of goods of outstanding quality. They were particularly skilled at processing pelts and hides derived from cattle breeding, hunting, and trapping. Their fame spread far and wide, so much so that a certain type of leather was known as *Bulgari*.

As per elsewhere in the Islamic world, trade produced considerable economic prosperity. The Volga Bulgars engaged in domestic and foreign trade, as well as dominating transit trade since they were able to take advantage of the many navigable rivers in their territory and their location at the crossroads of Asia and northern Europe. From Muslim lands to the south, Bulgar merchants imported spices, gems, rugs, gold, silver, and other luxury items. To more southerly lands, Bulgar merchants sold grains, honey, beeswax, felt, furs, bulgari, and slaves. As per elsewhere in the Islamic world, trade defined the urban geography of cities. Writes Rorlich:

> It was the intense trade activity that was responsible for the emergence of fairs and marketplaces throughout the territory of the Bulgar state. Aga-Bazar on the Volga was perhaps the most famous, but there were fairs and markets in the cities and countryside alike. The economic function of the cities—their emergence as trade centres—had a tangible effect on their physical development. Caravanserais catered to the needs of the eastern merchants became fixtures in Bulgar towns. The main function of the caravanserai was that of an inn, but most often it doubled as a combination inn, warehouse, and cultural center that provided merchants with food and shelter, storage facilities for their goods, and mosques...Christian merchants lived on the outskirts of town in segregated quarters...

Fatimid Caliphate

Trade and agriculture also were prime sources of wealth under the Fatimid Caliphate. The Fatimid Caliphate derived revenues from customs duties on foreign goods. Moreover, the extent of the Fatimid state and its collective institutions required an expansion of the tax base. This was achieved through the *ikta*, estates granted to entrepreneurs by public auction for four-year periods. The ikta-holder paid to the state a fixed sum comprising rent on land and taxes to be collected. Surplus revenue constituted profit for the ikta-holder. (Hassam) State wealth was also increased by the gold the Fatimids had at their disposal from trans-Saharan trade routes, North Africa, and the mines of the northern Sudan. The gold coinage used by the Fatimids was highly prized. The gold trade was part of Fatimid trade networks that ran from Spain to India and China and other points east. The Cairo economy was described by the contemporary Afghani scholar, Nasir Khusraw,

> I estimated that there were no less than 20,000 shops in Cairo...Every sort of rare good from all over the world can be had there. I saw tortoise shell implements such as small boxes, knife handles, and so on. I also saw extremely fine crystal, which the master craftsmen etch most beautifully...I saw the following fruits and herbs in one day: red roses, lilies, narcissus, oranges, citron, limes and other citrus fruits, apples, jasmine, basil, quince, pomegranates, pears, melons of all sorts, bananas, olives, plums, fresh dates, grapes, sugarcane, eggplants, fresh squash,

turnips, radishes, cabbage, fresh beans, cucumbers, green onions, fresh garlic, carrots, and beets...all types of porcelain, so fine and translucent that you can see your hand behind it when held up to the light...glass so pure and flawless that it resembles chrysolite (green and gold gems of volcanic formation—author). (Hassam)

The Seljuk Turks

The Seljuk empire provides valuable illustration of two key points: how steppe nomads from central Asia became sedentary, civilized people, and how the Seljuks used ancient trade routes to become a trading society. Our source is Stanford Shaw, an American historian of Turkey. When the Seljuks conquered Byzantine Anatolia, conditions were ripe for economic prosperity. There was a vigorous agricultural economy; there were centuries-old traditions of mining and metallurgy that went as far back as the ancient Hittites of eastern Anatolia as well as ancient trade routes that had been established millennia earlier. However, there was a major economic challenge in that the nomadic Seljuks' culture and economy was based, in part, on raiding civilized communities. The challenge was to wean Turks from raiding farms, villages, and towns in Anatolia. The solution was the ikta system we saw with respect to Fatimid Egypt, employed to collect taxes in a manner somewhat comparable to a feudal fief in Europe. Ikta-holders now had an interest in ensuring the continuing prosperity of their tax fiefs, and in transforming themselves from aggressive nomads into sedentary, civilized people.

Trade routes criss-crossed medieval Anatolia. They ran north-south, east-west, and on diagonals. In addition, there were important port cities on the Mediterranean and important inland towns and cities. There were also traditional trading routes: the Tin Road, the Silk Road, the Assyrian trade road, the Persian Royal Road as well as the more recent Crusades road. These routes permitted Seljuk trade to prosper. They merit our attention for the examples they provide of the type of trade routes that multiplied throughout the Muslim world.

In the ancient world, tin had been a valuable commodity when alloyed with copper to produce bronze. The use of bronze characterized civilization in the third millennium BC during the Bronze Age. The main source of tin in the ancient world was Afghanistan, from where it was shipped overland through Iran to Mesopotamia. Mesopotamian merchants acted as middlemen for the trade of tin into central Anatolia in return for Anatolian gold and silver. The tin then was moved to the port of Ugarit in northern Syria, from which it was shipped throughout the lands of the Middle East.

The famed Silk Road that linked Europe to China may have been created by merchants in the wake of Alexander the Great's eastern conquests. This trade route linked the Chinese civilization of the Yellow River Valley to central Asia, northern India, and the Parthian and Roman empires. In the Middle Ages, the Chinese sent silk westward in return for medicines, perfumes, and slaves, and received furs through a linked northern route from Russia. While the precise routes of the Silk Road are still a matter of conjecture, we do know that the Silk Road linked ultimately with Mediterranean port cities in Anatolia.

The Assyrian trade route went from northern Mesopotamia into Anatolia. Its use seems to have begun after the initiation of the Tin Road. In Seljuk times, there was a vast commercial fair called *yabanlu pazari*, or the bazaar of the foreigners, held for forty days each year at a point where the various caravan routes converged, not far from the site of a Bronze Age Hittite trading post dated to about 2,000 years BC.

The Persian Royal Road had been established during the fifth century BC in order to connect the Persian cities of Susa and Persepolis to the Anatolian port city of Sardis. It ran from Sardis in Anatolia east through Anatolia to the old Assyrian capital of Nineveh near present-day Mosul in northern Iraq, then south to Babylon, near Baghdad. It is believed then to have split in two, with a northeastern route to China and an eastern route to Susa and Persepolis in Iran.

Finally, the crusaders developed among wealthy Europeans a taste for luxury goods from the east. So, goods passed through Anatolian port cities on the Mediterranean and by overland routes to Constantinople to be distributed eventually in Europe. Thus did Europeans come to know Muslim carpets, textiles, ivory, metalwork, ceramics, and glass as well as silk from China and other trade goods from central Asia and India. All these important trade routes as well as the local trade routes of Anatolia permitted the Seljuk economy to develop and thrive.

Along this highly-developed network of trade routes, the Seljuks exported sugar, soap, horses, livestock, fruits, grains, olives, wheat, salted fish, textiles, carpets, chemicals, minerals and metals such as silver, lead, tin, zinc, copper and iron, leather, wool, mohair, timber, and Kipchak and Circassian slaves to Egyptians who became servants and slave-soldiers in the Mamaluke régimes. Among Seljuk imports were spices and cotton from Egypt; woolens and perfumes from Baghdad; glass from Syria and Iraq; silk, pearls, paper, sandalwood, gun powder, jade, and porcelain from China; gems from central Asia; pepper, spices, pharmaceuticals, and perfumes from India; and furs from the Caucasus and Russia.

The Mamaluke Régimes

The Muslim régimes did not know unending prosperity. In fact, they all eventually collapsed, even the most successful economically, as is the ultimate fate of all dynasties and empires. The Mamaluke collapse is most instructive since it highlights the role played by economic deterioration in the collapse of a society. Our sources are Wan Kamal Mujani and Bethany Walker. As we've seen earlier, the Mamalukes were originally slaves sold by the Seljuk Turks to Egypt to serve as slave-soldiers. There were two sources, both from the Pontic-Caspian Steppe: Kipchak Turks from southern Russia, and Circassians from the North Caucasus region. For more than 250 years, the Mamalukes ruled Egypt, the Levant, and Syria. The Mamaluke rulers were ex-slaves or sons of slaves whose military importance in the region came to be so important that they dethroned the Ismaili Fatimid Caliphate. Historians divide the Mamaluke rule into two periods: the first period from 1250 to 1382, the Turkish Mamaluke period, and the second period, the Circassian Mamaluke period from 1382 to 1517, at which point the Mamalukes fell to the Ottoman empire. The principal claim to the military fame of the Mamalukes was that they halted the Mongol advance in the Middle East, defeating the Mongol invaders handily and repeatedly. Economically speaking, according to Mujani,

> there is universal agreement among historians that the Mamaluke state reached its height under the Turkish sultans, and then fell into a prolonged phase of decline under the Circassians. The Circassian Mamalukes experienced a critical, economic period before their downfall. Internal and external problems have been identified as the causes of the economic decline.

Nonetheless, Walker also proffers as explanations for the economic decline natural disasters such as earthquakes, droughts, locust infestations, floods, and the bubonic plague and other epidemics as well as political factionalism in Cairo, currency devaluation, and the region's unruly Bedouin "...who are said to have been eager to devour villages once the garrisons protecting them pulled out..." Between 1468 and 1517, civil strife and coups d'état were the order of the day. Seven incompetent sultans were installed during this period of civil war and political instability. The military absorbed almost all the public treasury, and tax increases and confiscations of wealth were undertaken to pay for wars. During this period, agricultural output declined while imports of food increased owing to failure to maintain irrigation systems, technical stagnation, and unfair taxes on the peasantry. Industrial factories closed, while imports of goods increased. According to Mujani:

> The main factor that led to the decline of industry was the Mamalukes' attitude towards this sector. They monopolized...industries, and imposed heavy taxes on the civilian industrialists in their own interests. The decline of industry was also due to technical stagnation. When there was no more free competition, or the competition had been much weakened, there was no need to improve production methods. This led to competition from Europe, where technological innovation had been in progress from the end of the eighth century up to the 14th century in various industrial sectors. The superiority of European industrial products and their cheaper price affected Mamaluke industry. The recurrences of the plague... caused a dearth of workers, which led to an increase in labor costs and in the prices of industrial products...

Finally, trade produced fewer revenues owing to monopolistic practices by the state, unproductive policies, increased tax rates, and increased imports. Thus, economic decline helped precipitate the end of the Circassian Mamaluke empire and conquest by the Ottoman régime early in the 16th century.

Popular Resistance under Islam

The onset of Islam wrought a revolution in the Arabian Peninsula and the lands where Islam spread. Even as Muslim states became absorbed with the exercise of temporal power, there continued to be:

> ...a revolutionary strand in the Islamic political tradition although, as has been the case with most such ideologies, it has remained the ideology of the opposition, and not that of the establishment in the Muslim world. This was particularly true as long as political power continued to remain in the hands of Muslim rulers, and before the Muslim world fell under the political subjugation and military domination of European powers. Movements of social and political protest during the first millennium of Islam invariably took on a religious character. (Ayoob, p. 1)

The revolutionary form of Islam with its roots in the social message of Muhammad persistently conflicted with the conservative, authoritarian message of the Islamic states and their ruling classes, comparable to the dialectic that existed in Christianity.

> Thus, the history of both Christianity and Islam, can be thought of as a continuing struggle between the revolutionary-democratic and conservative-authoritarian interpretations...Against the revolutionary interpretation, the popes, emperors, kings, caliphs, sultans, and the main body of the clergy and the *ulama* have constantly restated the conservative-authoritarian interpretation; insisted that this is the true Christian or Muslim faith, and that the revolutionary interpretation is heresy; and burned, hanged, tortured, imprisoned, and made war on those who thought otherwise. (Hodgkin, p. 140)

Moreover, in the opinion of Hodgkin, the ruling class employed an important *modus operandi* in order to preserve its interpretation and power. It argued that the future kingdom of heaven was not to be achieved on this earth as the revolutionaries presented but only in the afterlife. Nonetheless, for the popular classes, radical religion was a vital tool of resistance to the ministrations, religious or otherwise, of the ruling class here on earth. The words of Marx describe this role of religion as "the sigh of the oppressed creature, the heart of a heartless world...the spirit of a spiritless situation." (Hodgkin, p. 139) Hakim Bey describes the mechanism by which popular religion historically turned the tables on the conventional role of religion as a conservative force and how, in reaction to this conservatism, popular religion served to defend and promote the interests of the socially lowly.

If religion has always acted to enslave the mind, or to reproduce the ideology of the ruling class, it has always involved some form of entheogenesis, birth of the god within or liberation of consciousness; some form of utopian proposal or promise of heaven on earth; and some form of militant and positive action for social justice as God's plan for the creation.

Early Years of Islam: Endemic Civil Strife

Muhammad died suddenly in 632 without having established a process for his replacement. This created a seemingly endless series of succession crises marked with civil strife and clan and tribal conflicts during the early years of Islam. While the search for power, glory, and wealth were indeed at the heart of these crises and conflicts, there was, nevertheless, still a social element, an attempt to relive and renew Muhammad's message of brotherhood and equality, which we now explore.

We already have seen that immediately after the death of the Prophet, much of Arabia apostasied, partially to avoid paying the *zakat*, the redistributive taxes that Muhammad had promoted. The prime mission of Caliph Abu Bakr was to fight the *riddah* wars to bring the Arabs forcibly back to the Islamic fold. As for the recalcitrant Arabs themselves, they were inspired by a series of prophets rival to Muhammad: Tulayha in eastern Arabia, Dhu'l-Taj in Oman, Qais bin Abd Yaghus in Yemen, and the prophetess Sajjah, a Christian who married Musaylimah from central Arabia, the most prominent of the rival prophets. Musaylimah actually controlled more territories and properties than did Muhammad before the latter's death. He held discussions with Muhammad, to whom he had offered himself unsuccessfully as Muhammad's successor. He even suggested his own personal divinity. Perhaps, his popularity was helped along by his promotion of free sex and alcohol consumption, and his desire to abolish prayers, this in marked contrast to the puritanism of Muslim leaders. Even though Musaylimah and his followers did convert to Islam, twenty years later, some of his followers again apostasied, and were executed for it.

The second caliph, Umar, was lionized in his time for his holiness and establishment of the Islamic welfare state. Nonetheless, Umar was mortally wounded while he was leading prayers at a mosque in Medina by a Persian Christian named Abu Lulu Firoz, a craftsman who had been captured and enslaved during the Arab conquest of Persia, then brought to Medina to serve his Arab master. The caliph's killer thought his master's exigencies too stringent, so he asked Umar to intervene, which the latter refused to do, leading to the assassination. So, in 644, the followers of Muhammad once again faced the problem of succession. Umar had named a council of six called the Eminent Companions of Muhammad to name the successor. Ali, Muhammad's cousin and son-in-law, was married to a daughter of the Prophet named Fatima, and was once again a candidate for the position of caliph. Ali was a Hashemite, a member of the same clan as Muhammad. The council of six, however, passed over Ali to pick the merchant Uthman, like Umar, a member of the increasingly wealthy Umayyad clan, the rival to Muhammad's Hashemite clan. Uthman did introduce some social measures similar to those of Umar but, as with the latter, Uthman also continued to appoint members of his clan to important positions such as regional governors. This, along with a few other features of Uthman's rule, was to prove his undoing. Moreover, as Frank Smitha writes:

> In the first half of his eleven-year reign, he was popular enough, but paying for continuing wars against resistance in Persia and Armenia, while receiving no compensation in the form of booty or increased taxation drained his government's treasury. Building a navy with which to protect Islamic rule in Syria and Egypt was also costly, as was his successful naval operation that seized the island of Cyprus, and delivered defeats to Constantinople's navy.

Uthman named a committee to codify officially the teachings of Muhammad in the form of the Qur'an, while ordering the burning of rival collections that had emerged. Uthman also tried to centralize decisions that had hitherto been within the bailiwick of the Arab tribes. The sudden increase of wealth that accompanied Arab conquests brought with it increased coinage without a concomitant increase in production, which resulted in a general inflation that hurt the poor most. Then, there was the problem of nepotism which aggravated many. Uthman had to deal with the complaints of a man named Abu Dharr al-Ghifari, one of the earliest converts to Islam. A popular holy man and ascetic, Abu Dharr is regarded by Muslim scholars as a proto-socialist. He complained of the distribution of booty from conquests to Uthman's officials, and of the pursuit of material wealth that seemed to be the priority of Uthman's caliphate.

In the year 656, five hundred Arab warriors from Mesopotamia were returning from battles in Egypt on behalf of the caliph. Claiming divine guidance, they argued that Ali should have succeeded Umar, that Uthman was a usurper, and that naming Ali would permit the return to life of the Prophet himself. They demanded Uthman's resignation in Medina even as none of the local commoners rose to defend the caliph. So, the warriors killed Uthman, while other members of the Umayyad clan fled for their lives. Ali was proclaimed caliph, a proclamation that was particularly popular among the poor owing to his commitment to Muhammad's values of social equality and brotherhood among the faithful. The nomination of Ali, however, was challenged by several factions, a challenge that manifested itself in civil war, what Muslims call the first *fitna*.

The early military successes of the Muslims had papered over traditional divisions among Arab tribes and clans, between the cities of Mecca and Medina, between north and south Arabs, and between Syrians and Iraqi Arabs. As well, there were differences of opinion about the division of booty from Arab conquests. After Uthman had been killed, the wealthy demanded punishment for his assassins, but Ali's poor supporters would not permit it. The first to challenge militarily Ali and his supporters was a faction led by Aisha bint Abu Bakr, daughter of the first caliph and Muhammad's third wife, purportedly Muhammad's favorite. She was joined in this challenge by al-Zubayr ibn al-Awwam, one of Muhammad's early companions, and by Talhah ibn Ubayd-Allah, one of Ali's rival caliphal candidates. This last faction demanded that Ali punish the assassins of Uthman, which the faction itself proceeded to do itself by killing the assassins of Uthman. It then chose to meet Ali, ultimately unsuccessfully, in battle at Basra in Iraq.

A second challenge came from a man named Mu'awiyah, an Umayyad cousin of Uthman and governor of Palestine and Syria. Mu'awiyah refused to offer homage to Ali unless he was given autonomy over the region he governed, a demand to which Ali would not acquiesce. The two camps skirmished but, owing to the reluctance of Ali's army to continue to fight, Ali agreed that the question of who would be caliph be submitted to arbitration, as per a suggestion of Mu'awiyah. This process resulted in Mu'awiyah being named caliph, in effect, beginning the Umayyad dynasty in earnest. The fortunate victor then continued to build support in places such as Yemen and Egypt.

The third challenge to Ali came when a group of schismatics, unhappy with the result of the arbitration that chose Mu'awiyah, turned against Ali himself, eventually mortally wounding him in 661 in Kufa in Iraq. These schismatics, known as Kharijites, will receive further consideration below. They argued that Ali should have taken Mu'awiyah to an ultimate battle, the outcome of which would have been determined by Allah himself in warfare, rather than submitting the choice of caliph to the arbitration panel, an artificial human method. The Kharijites were to remain an important and powerful force in Islam for generations. We can see that while the succession conflicts were indeed inter-tribal and inter-clan power struggles, also at work was how to pursue the legacy of the Prophet with respect to questions of social equality and brotherhood.

The Second Fitna

The second fitna took place in the last two decades of the seventh century after the death of Caliph Mu'awiyah. After Ali had been killed by a Kharijite, Ali's followers proclaimed his first son, Hasan, as successor, a role which the reluctant Hasan refused owing to intimidation by Mu'awiyah's supporters. So, Mu'awiyah was succeeded as caliph by his son, Yazid. Ali's second son, Husayn, refused to recognize Yazid, and set out for Iraq to raise an army, however, Husayn's party was killed at Karbala in Iraq in 680. From this event, the split between the majority Sunni Muslims and the minority Shi'a Muslims became definitive. In fact, the latter commemorate the killing of Husayn each year at Karbala, one of the holiest sites for Shi'ites.

Another rebel in these times was Ibn al-Zubayr, the son of a man who had been part of the triumvirate that had resisted Ali's caliphate after the death of Uthman named al-Zubayr ibn al-Awwam. Mu'awiyah's son and successor as caliph, Yazid, was viewed by the more ascetic Muslims as being profligate and illegitimate. Ibn al-Zubayr led a campaign of resistance by this faction from his home region of the Hejaz in western Arabia, gaining widespread recognition as an anti-caliph in 683. The rebel caliph built support in Iraq, southern Arabia, Egypt, and Syria. Yazid died suddenly, and was succeeded by his cousin, Marwan ibn al-Hakam, who managed to recover territories lost in the Zubayr revolt. In a side campaign, Ibn al-Zubayr defeated another man named al-Mukhtar in 687, who was a Shi'ite ruler who called for the caliphate to go to the third son of Ali, the unenthusiastic Muhammad ibn al-Hanifiyah. Even if a hero to Shi'ites, al-Mukhtar is known to Sunni Muslims as the Deceiver since he was accused of opportunism. While in Kufa in Iraq, he had seized the local public treasury, and distributed millions of coins to the poor. As well, slaves who supported al-Mukhtar in the Iraqi city of Nisibis brought that city temporarily under their control, only to be defeated eventually then executed. According to the Encyclopedia Britannica online essay about al-Mukhtar:

> In his call for revolt, Mukhtar appealed to the pro-Shi'ite sentiments of Iraq's Arab tribesmen. He also rallied the *mawali*, non-Arab, mainly Persian Muslims of Kufa, to his cause by preaching the imminent coming of a *mahdi*, or savior, who would wipe out ethnic and class differences, and implant the egalitarian society of believers envisioned in the Qur'an...As a promoter of the idea of the mahdi and of the equality of Arab and non-Arab Muslims, Mukhtar influenced the course of later Shi'ite Islam and is, thus, more important than his brief success as a leader of an egalitarian, revolutionary movement would indicate.

Returning to Ibn al-Zubayr, the rebel was isolated in the Hejaz when Kharijites established an independent state in central Arabia called Najdat, then rebelled against both Marwan and Ibn al-Zubayr. Marwan lived only briefly after coming to power, and was succeeded by his son, Abd al-Malik ibn Marwan, whose army finally killed Ibn al-Zubayr in 692. This reunited the Islamic empire once again under Umayyad rule, and ended the civil, social tumult for a couple of generations.

At the turn of the eighth century, an Iraqi Arab general named Ibn al-Ash'ath led a three-year rebellion against the Umayyad régime in Syria. As with al-Mukhtar, this was a rebellion by the Iraqi *mawali*, who attempted to earn socio-economic and political rights similar to those held by Muslims of the Arabian Peninsula, as per the teachings of Islam. The rebellion also manifested the strong anti-Syrian feeling of Iraqi Arabs and their alienation from a local, tyrannical Umayyad governor.

The Abbasid Revolution

The Umayyad régime ultimately was short-lived since another civil war, the third fitna, shook Islamic society once again. In fact, the Umayyads represented the symbol of the vices against which Muhammad had fought when he created his religious movement with its message of social equality and brotherhood. To many Muslims, the fact that the Umayyads had been among the direct antagonists of the Prophet was too much of a bitter irony. Chris Harman comments that social rebels during the Umayyad caliphates were reacting with outrage at this bitter irony when they:

> ...harked back to Muhammad's own time, regarding it as a model of purity that had since been corrupted. Again and again in subsequent history, the cry for a return to the time of Ali or of the first two caliphs has been a call for revolt against the existing state of affairs from one social group or another. It still motivates fundamentalist organizations today. (p. 127)

Only three generations or so after his death, the memory of al-Mukhtar and his opposition to the ruling Umayyads was resuscitated in the Abbasid Revolution. The revolution reflected at a profound level the social divisions that accompanied the growth of Islam from being a local sect in Medina in Arabia to becoming the faith of an imperial power with a sudden influx of riches. There were tensions among the Arabian tribes, between nomad and agriculturalist communities, between city and country-dwellers, between Arabs and non-Arab Muslims, and among the social classes, all of which were wrapped up in the religious conflict between the Sunni establishment and the Shi'ite opposition. As well, economic growth during the Umayyad caliphates accentuated the class differences between the wealthy and the rest of Islamic society. The actual catalyst came in the middle of the eighth century. More than 50,000 Arab warriors had been settled near the oasis community of Merv, in modern-day Turkmenistan. Contrary to the Umayyad policy of separating warriors from local populations, many soldiers had married into a local community that resented the dictates of distant Damascus, the Umayyad capital. As well, the soldiers felt they did not receive their fair share of booty from years of military conquest. When Damascus tried to introduce new troops to the Merv region to silence opposition from the Arab soldiers, the revolt was on throughout eastern portions of the Islamic empire.

The Abbasids were descendants of Muhammad's Hashemite clan via one of Muhammad's uncles, Abbas. As part of their plotting for power, they mandated one of their freed slaves, Abu Muslim Khorasani, to build secret, underground support for the Abbasids in Khorasan and Iran, where Muslims in one area after another declared their support for the Abbasids. After going from one victory to another in the easternmost portions of the empire, Abu Muslim defeated the Umayyads in a major battle in the Euphrates Valley that allowed the Abbasids to take over the caliphate. The Abbasid revolution brought the Hashemite clan back to power in the Muslim world. In addition to the Hashemites, the Abbasids initiated to power many Persians who had been second-class citizens under Umayyad rule. Frank Smitha describes the early days of the Abbasids.

> They began ruling with a show of Islamic piety, and they talked of reforms. They gave prominence in state affairs to Islamic theologians and experts in Islamic law. Under the Abbasids was a skilled bureaucracy and professional army, manned to a large extent by those who helped the Abbasids to power. Many of them were Persian. At the Abbasid court were Persian refinement and urbanity, Persian titles, Persian wives and mistresses, Persian wines and garments...

The Indian scientist and inventor, Nazeer Ahmed, describes the actual mechanics of the transfer of Hashemite power from the Alawis, descendants of Ali, to the Abbasids. Recall the rebel al-Mukhtar who claimed he revolted in the name of the son of the fourth caliph, Ali, a man named Muhammad ibn al-Hanifiyah. The latter's mother was one of the wives Ali had married after the death of his wife, Fatima, the Prophet's daughter. After Muhammad ibn al-Hanifiyah died, his son, Abu Sulaiman Abdullah, inherited the title of imam, but he was poisoned by the Umayyad caliph, Sulaiman. Nazeer Ahmed writes:

> As he lay dying, Abdullah looked around for someone from his family to pass on the imamate. As no one from his immediate family was available, he found a Hashemite, Muhammad bin Ali Abbas, in a nearby town. Muhammad bin Ali Abbas was grandson of Abbas, uncle of the Prophet. Thus, through a twist of historical circumstances, one branch of the imamate passed from the children of Ali ibn Abu Talib to the children of Abbas. This branch is referred to as the Abbasids. It was the Abbasids who established their caliphate in the year 750, and ruled from Baghdad the vast Islamic empire for more than 500 years until the Mongols destroyed Baghdad in 1258.

Sound like a flimsy basis for erecting an empire that ruled a good portion of the world for hundreds of years? Indeed, just as flimsy as the bases for medieval European monarchies. Nevertheless, Muhammad bin Ali Abbas skillfully and diplomatically developed a network of supporters for the Abbasids, especially in the east. His son, Ibrahim, next in line for the imamate, gained further support for the notion that the caliphate rightfully belonged to the Hashemite clan, of which the Abbasids were the logical heirs. The Umayyad Caliph Marwan, feeling the heat from the Abbasids, had Ibrahim killed. Before the latter died, however, he managed to name as Abbasid imam his brother, Abul Abbas Abdullah, who became the first Abbasid caliph in 750. Yet another flimsy thread of justification for the Abbasid Imperial rule? Furthermore, as Nazeer Ahmed writes:

> The ideological basis for Abbasid rule was not provided until a generation after they gained power. It was the Caliph Mansur who

provided this ideological basis in 770 in response to a question from a Kharijite. According to this position, since the Prophet left no sons, and lineage passes from father to son, children of Fatima had no claim to succession. Accordingly, succession had to be through the male progeny of the Prophet's uncle, Abbas.

In actual fact, leadership passing to the eldest living man, or cognatic succession, was a common form of succession among tribal societies, especially in light of the uncertainties involved with leaders who might or might not be fortunate enough to have sons.

Once in power, the Abbasids were as autocratic and oppressive of the common people as had been the Umayyads, in spite of the popular support the Abbasids had used to gain power. In fact, as we shall see below, the Abbasid régime's autocratic ways wrought considerable revolutionary ferment. It was more than just ironic that they themselves had come to power in a revolution whereby they had skillfully developed allies among the common people and the Shi'ites. The actual revolutionary leader of the Abbasids, Abu Muslim Khorasani, was killed by the Abbasids shortly after they came to power on the premise that the popular leader was plotting against the Abbasid caliph.

There were still other periods of fitna in medieval Islamic society. Canadian journalist Tarek Fatah reports the following.

> Between 700 and 900, the period when *Sharia* law was created and the *hadith*, the sayings of the Prophet Muhammad were compiled, about 45 Muslim versus Muslim wars, assassinations, revolts, and counter-revolts took place...an incident of violent conflict every five years. (p. 214)

There were, furthermore, many other movements of opposition and popular resistance in the medieval, Islamic world, which we now consider.

Movements of Popular Resistance

Economic development in the Islamic world made many in the mercantile and ruling classes wealthy, even as the gap between them and the poor widened. The resulting social tensions regularly broke out into movements of revolution or other forms of popular resistance in the Middle Ages. These revolts took place irrespective of whether or not a local political régime was waxing or waning in its political saliency. The section that follows covers the major moments of popular resistance and a few, though certainly not all, of the minor moments of resistance. Sometimes, the social message of equality and brotherhood espoused by Muhammad and inherent to Islam was the inspiration for popular resistance to oppression and exploitation, especially owing to the differences between the original spiritual message and to the too-bitter temporal realities. At other times under Islamic rule, people resisted the imposition of the religion itself, especially where there existed strong forms of existing religion in a particular region. At still other times, the revolt involved tribal or proto-national forces resisting central rule. In spite of all this persistent popular ferment, Nazeer Ahmed insists that:

> ...all Muslims believe in the Qur'an and the Sunnah (traditions) about the Prophet, and disagree only in the unfolding of Islam in the matrix of human affairs. Like the branches of a mighty tree, the various schools of *fiqh* (jurisprudence) shade the Muslim *ummah* (the faithful), and Islamic history would not be the same without any of them.

The various movements often left their remnants in various religious forms or sects of Islam. Ours is not to enter in detail into these religious differences since this a work of social, not religious history. Therefore, we shall try to concentrate on the political and social elements of social protest. Enough to say that, despite Nazeer Ahmed's assertion above about the essential unity of Islam, differences among the various schools of thought and sects are so dramatic as to make one wonder whether they all can really qualify as being descended from the words and deeds of the Prophet. For unlike Christianity with its Orthodox and Catholic churches, and to lesser an extent, Protestantism and their hierarchies, clergies, doctrines, dogmas, and temporal power, under Islam there was no such enforcement of a similar, common religious discipline upon the Ummah. Furthermore, in its essence, Islam itself was revolutionary, a fact that was demonstrated repeatedly throughout the Middle Ages.

Kharijites

The Kharijites first appeared during the first fitna, the battle for supremacy between the fourth caliph, Ali, and Mu'awiyah, governor of Syria and Palestine and Umayyad cousin of the assassinated third caliph, Uthman. In 657, Ali's followers and those of Mu'awiyah met in battle. Mu'awiyah had repeatedly resisted attempts to make him recognize the caliphate of Ali. Facing the possibility of a quick defeat owing to the military superiority of Ali's forces, Mu'awiyah ordered his men to put pages of the Qur'an on the ends of their lances before a military engagement. This caused consternation among many of Ali's soldiers since Muslims were not supposed to make war upon other Muslims. So, Ali's soldiers reacted positively when Mu'awiyah proposed arbitration to determine who should be caliph, especially since they were confident that Ali would be the fortunate choice. They refused to fight, forcing Ali to accept the arbitration idea. All in all, it appears that Ali's troops really did not want to fight. One excuse was as good as another. Furthermore, in actual fact, they were sure that the proposed arbitration would result in a decision favouring Ali. All were surprised when the arbitrators ruled against Ali.

Now, many of Ali's men, especially those from two Arabian tribes, turned against the decision to have submitted the issue of the succession to the caliphate to arbitration in the first place. They cited the Qur'anic verse about no rule but that of God, arguing that Ali had no business agreeing to the arbitration solution; that this was a decision that belonged to the entire Ummah subsequent to Allah's chosen outcome in a battle between the two armies. In the eyes of the rebels, the arbitration business showed Ali acting as an imperial monarch rather than as a humble Muslim. The rebels left Ali's army, which then pursued the rebel army of 12,000 to Nahawand, east of the Tigris River, where Ali's forces defeated them the following year. The victory, however, was pyrrhic as the slain became martyrs to the Kharijite cause that continued to be a force within Islam. Moreover, in 661, a member of one group of the surviving Kharijite rebels fatally wounded Ali.

The ascetic and uncompromising attitude of the Kharijites over time led to splintering into many sub-sects, each one more extreme than the others. Still, Kharijites expressed the revolutionary idea that any Muslim could become caliph or occupy office in Islam provided he be pure and holy. This differed greatly from the old tribal notion that only a Hashemite or Umayyad Arab could lead the Muslims. The Kharijites believed that only Abu Bakr and Umar had been legitimate caliphs, and that correct belief and action must accompany Muslim faith. All Muslims were equally capable of such behavior, which helped the Kharijites plant roots among non-Arabic peoples such as the Persians and the Berbers of North Africa. One sub-sect of the Kharijites even believed that women could be imams if they were holy and just. Nonetheless, they also believed that mortal sinners among Muslims were on a par with infidels such that they could be attacked physically with impunity, thus justifying the extreme terrorism of some of their members. This caused irreparable damage to the Kharijites and to their case, perhaps otherwise acceptable to other Muslims. In the opinion of Thomas Hodgkin,

> ...their basic principle, 'judgement belongs to God alone', showed the tendency which has been characteristic of radical movements throughout history to move towards an anarchist viewpoint, the rejection of government as such. The caliphate, the crucial Islamic institution...could only be justified on utilitarian grounds. If the people were sufficiently mature and virtuous to ensure the application of the Shari'a, the divine law, there would be no need for a caliph. If there had to be a caliph, the Kharijites insisted on the maximum popular participation in his election, and on the right of the community to depose him for errors, particularly for oppression or corruption. (p. 142)

The Kharijites continued to be a force during the first three centuries of Islam, offering an alternative to the establishment Sunnis Muslims and the opposition Shi'a minority, while now and then managing to raise revolts against the two main expressions of Islam. They settled in Oman in 686, then became influential eventually in North Africa and in eastern Africa. In 695, two Kharijite holy men, Salih ibn Musarrih and Shahid bin Yazid, led an initially successful but brief revolt in northern Iraq. Earlier in the same decade, Najdah ibn 'Amir led a breakaway Kharijite state in central and eastern Arabia before being murdered by one of his own men. In the spring of 745, two Kharijites, Sa'id ibn Bahdal and Al-Dahhak ibn Qays, led a major revolt in Iraq and western Iran during a power dispute between rival Umayyad governors. Their initial success and the attractiveness of Kharijite doctrine drew to them an army of 120,000 soldiers, however, they were subdued eventually in 747. The Kharijites did eventually run their course as an influential force, but their Ibadi descendants, even if less extreme than ancestor Kharijite sects, continue to worship today in Oman and in parts of Africa.

Zaydis

The initial rebelliousness of the Shi'ites did not last forever. The fifth and sixth imams, spiritual fathers of the Shi'a, took a decidedly non-political stance in their position as imams in order to concentrate on the pursuit of knowledge and holiness. The fifth imam, Muhammad al-Baqir, and his son, the sixth imam, Ja'far al-Sadiq, not only rejected the idea of armed rebellion but, in fact, deplored politics. To the brother of the former imam and uncle of the latter imam, the time was ripe for open revolt against the Umayyad caliphate, and for pressing the claims of the Hashemite clan to the caliphate. Zayd ibn Ali was a great-grandson of Ali and a grandson of the martyred Husayn. Zayd sought support for over a year among the Arab tribes at Kufa in Iraq, which had been Ali's capital and the site of Husayn's revolt of 680. The Umayyads, however, got wind of the plot, and defeated Zayd's army, killing him in battle. Zayd's revolt became the inspiration for the Zaydi sect of Shi'ites, who held that any learned Hashemite descendant of Ali could press his claim to the calpihate by fighting for it; this alone made this person an imam. This contrasts with other Shi'ites who maintained that an imam had to be appointed divinely. In practice, this meant direct descent from the Prophet and from Ali, which applied to the first twelve imams, starting from Ali. Only these men could demonstrate *huija*, or proof of God's existence to humankind, owing to the knowledge held by the Prophet and Ali of God and God's will and words.

While Zayd's revolt was spectacularly unsuccessful, it did inspire other successors of the Hashemite clan to do likewise. One example of this was a revolt in 744-748 just before the Abbasid revolution led by a man named Abdallah bin Mu'awiyah, who was a great-nephew of Ali descended from Ali's brother, Jafar. Abdallah commenced his revolt in Kufa among Iraqi Arabs who had been only superficially Islamicized, including among them a strong contingent of Zaydis. The rebel then set up his rule in western Iran. After his defeat by the Umayyads, Abdallah fled to Khorasan, where he was eventually executed by the Abbasid revolutionary, Abu Muslim Khorasani. Coming only a few years before the successful Abbasid revolution, Abdallah's revolt was, in fact, a precursor of the later, successful revolution despite Khorosani's treatment of Abdallah. Another example of a Zaydi revolt was that of Muhammad al-Nafs az-Zakiyya, who led a revolt on the Arabian Peninsula against the Abbasid caliphate in 762. Muhammad was a direct descendant of the Prophet by Fatima, the Prophet's daughter married to Ali. Many felt he was destined for greatness owing to his lineage, so Muhammad was forced to live much of his life travelling in disguise to avoid the political authorities who distrusted him and his possible political aims. They were well to do so since the rebel finally made his move in 762, after having assembled a large army in western Arabia. His army took Yemen and Mecca then Medina, where the rebel ultimately was killed. In an example of a more successful revolt, an army led by a Zaydi family from the Caspian Sea region called the Buwayhids took the Abbasid capital, Baghdad, in 945. The Buwayhids and their descendants were the effective rulers of the caliphate between 934 and 1055, even if they did maintain the Abbasid caliphs as religious figureheads.

The Zaydis' example reveals a pattern that repeated throughout Islamic history during the Middle Ages. A popular rebellion in the name of the true Islam and Muhammad's social message erupted and, even if defeated by the ruling political powers, might result in the establishment of a sect or sub-sect. As well, sometimes political arguments over who was to succeed to the Sunni caliphates or the Shi'ite imamates also might result in the establishment of new sects or sub-sects. Eventually, a successful revolution might be undertaken by the successors of the original rebels in the name of the relevant sect or sub-sect. This would lead to the establishment of new autonomous states and empires that might include vast territories, even replacing the original, imperial authorities. In the Middle Ages, Islam appeared to be in a state of permanent revolution, if we may borrow Trotsky's term for the phenomenon from another, different context.

Mazdakism: Revolutionary Iranian Antecedents

Ancient Persia or Iran admittedly does not constitute part of the West as we have defined it. Nonetheless, for an understanding of the revolutionary Islamic movements that affected Western history in the Middle Ages, it is important that we understand the revolutionary strains of Islam that developed in Iran. These revolutionary movements recalled a pre-Islamic, Iranian movement historians call Mazdakism, after the name of its two founders, each named Mazdak. Mazdak the Younger was a Zoroastrian mobed, or priest, who was active in the early part of the sixth century, about a hundred years before Muhammad. Mazdak was a religious reformer and a proto-socialist who preached a reformed view of Zoroastrianism, combined with Manicheism and Gnosticism. There had been an earlier Mazdak the Elder, who preached of altruism mixed with hedonism. It was this doctrine that was further developed by Mazdak the Younger. According to the Wikipedia essay about Mazdak, the elder philosopher directed his followers to enjoy the pleasures of life, and satisfy their appetite in the highest degree with regard to eating and drinking in the spirit of equality and friendly intercourse; to avoid dominating one another; to share in women and family; to aim at good deeds; to abstain from shedding blood and inflicting harm on others; and to practice hospitality without reservation. (Yarshater, p. 995-997)

Mazdak's religious teaching aimed at reducing the formalities of religion and the power of the Zoroastrian clergy who oppressed Persians and induced poverty. Mazdak called for social revolution. Mazdak taught that God had originally placed the means of subsistence on earth, so that people should divide them equally among themselves, however, the strong had wronged the weak, seeking domination, and causing the contemporary inequality. To prevail over these evils, justice had to be restored, and all must share excess possessions with his fellow men. Mazdak allegedly planned to achieve this by making all wealth common and by redistributing it. It is possible that Mazdak took measures against the widespread polygamy of the rich and reulting lack of wives for the poor, a notable symptom of too much inequality in society.

A Persian king named Kavadh ruled from 488 to 531. He converted to Mazdakism, and encouraged Mazdak's program of social reform, pacifism, anti-clericalism, and social aid to the poor. His followers apparently raided the palaces and harems of the rich, and seized the valuables to which they believed they had equal rights. Indeed the stuff of revolution, to which the powerful and wealthy reacted by massacring Mazdak and his followers, then restoring traditional Zoroastrianism. The ideas of Mazdak lived on, however, among small groups of supporters in remote areas where Mazdak's doctrines mixed with those of Shi'ites. Mazdakism then resurfaced in new forms among other Muslim movements, the Khurramites and the Qarmations, whom we consider below. During the Middle Ages, Islamic scholars used the term 'Mazdakist' in a pejorative sense to describe the subsequent radical, egalitarian movements in Muslim Iran.

Zoroastrian Revolutionary Sects in Islamic Iran

In the 400 years or so prior to the conquest of Iran by Arab Muslims, Zoroastrianism had become a stale religion whose clergy that oppressed the laity, especially the poor. Islam, with its stirring social message, provided a serious challenge to the Zoroastrian priesthood. In response, there appeared what might be called neo-Zoroastrian movements that combined the social and political message of Islam with the native religion of Iran, simplified and reformed, contrary to the priest-led Zoroastrianism that had become complex and ritualistic. At the same time, Zoroastrian resistance to the onset of Islam in Iran led to Arab attempts to wipe out Zoroastrianism completely.

In this complex environment lived and preached early in the eighth century in Khorasan a self-designated prophet named Behafarid, who combined Zoroastrianism with elements of Islam. In 745, about the same time as the Khorasani rebels, Haret bin Sorayj and Joday bin Ali Kermani, were harrying the Umayyad authorities, Behafarid led a religious peasant rebellion against the Umayyad authorities. Among Behafarid's social measures that appealed to the poor was his proposal of a one-time tithe of a seventh of people's wealth to be used for the construction of public works, nursing the sick, helping the needy, and performing other charitable works. Nonetheless, Abu Muslim Khorasani had Behafarid killed as an unwanted competitor, while Behafarid's movement was snuffed out in favor of the Muslim Abbasids, who were at the time themselves preparing to rebel and seize power from the Umayyads. In fact, Behafarid and other, similar Khorasani rebels were precursors to the Abbasid revolution that started in Khorasan and eastern Iran in 747. Once again, a similar pattern reappeared. Although Behafarid's rebellion was short-lived and unsuccessful, the movement outlasted its founder by two centuries. (Encyclopedia Iranica essay about Behafarid). It also inspired other related rebellions. In 758-759, two men named Ishaq Tork and Baraz led Zoroastrian revolts against the Abbasids in Transoxiana. In 767, a man claiming to be a prophet named Ostadhsis amassed an army of about 300,000 soldiers in Afghanistan and Turkmenistan. He won an initial battle against the Abbasids but, in 768, lost a major battle against the son of the Abbasid caliph, which cost Ostadhsis 70,000 soldiers killed in battle, while another 14,000 were taken captive. Thereafter, Ostadhsis was executed.

Khurramites

The Khurramites were an influential religious sect and political movement in the eighth and ninth centuries in Greater Iran. They were active in such areas as Azerbaijan, Armenia, Khorasan, Kurdistan, Iraq, and Iran proper. Recall the murder of Abu Muslim Khorasani in 754 by the newly-minted Abbasid régime centered in Baghdad. To the Khurramites, Abu Muslim was not definitively dead; they believed he would return some day as a savior to Muslims. The first figure to lead a reaction in protest of the murder of Abu Muslim was a Persian cleric named Sunpadh, who led a revolt in 755 of Persian Shi'ites, Zoroastrians, and Mazdakists. Sunpadh's preaching mixed Islam with Zoroastrianism. He vowed to go to Mecca to destroy the sacred Ka'ba, but he and his revolt were snuffed out in only 70 days. (Wikipedia essay about Sunpadh)

The second, major Khurramite figure was a man named Hashim al-Muqanna, a clothing worker from Turkmenistan who claimed to be a prophet, even an incarnation of God. He claimed he inherited the prophet role from Abu Muslim, Ali, and, ultimately, from Muhammad himself. His movement took place in correspondence with an unsuccessful revolt on the shores of the Caspian Sea in Iran during 778–779, more or less a generation after Sunpadh, by a group known as the Red Banner Batenites, a group of neo-

Zoroastrians who followed many tenets of Mazdak. Even so, al-Muqanna's sect continued to exist well into the 12th century.

The most successful leader of the Khurramites was a man named Babak Khoramdin, a Persian from Azerbaijan who, for 23 years early in the ninth century, held the Abbasids at bay fighting in central and western Iran and in Azerbaijan. Beginning with Babak's attacks in 816, the Khurramites fought successfully with Abbasid forces. A peasant movement, the Khurramites demanded the breakup and redistribution of great land estates, a perennial and omnipresent demand of the socially lowly especially peasants, and an end to despotic Arab rule. Babak's forces defeated four Abbasid armies with the aid of Byzantine support. When the Abbasids finally suppressed the rebellion, many Persian and Kurdish Khurramites fled to Byzantium to join the Byzantine army under the leadership of a general named Nasr, who was baptized and took as a Christian name of Theophobos. This might suggest that at least some of his Khurramite forces also may have adopted Christianity once in Byzantium. In 839 towards the end of Babak's resistance, an Iranian aristocrat and ardent Zoroastrian named Mazyar unsuccessfully resumed the Khurramite resistance to the Abbasid régime. The Khurramite sect did not disappear, nonetheless, because spiritual descendants of the Khurramites in Azerbaijan were instrumental in the installation of the Safavid ruling régime in Persia. Thus, the familiar pattern: while the original movements of resistance in the Islamic world ultimately might fail, they eventually did produce successful movements that would result in social change, including changes of political régimes.

Shi'ite Rebellions

Not all the eastern revolutionaries were Zoroastrians or others of the ilk. Shi'a Muslims also revolted in the ninth century against the Abbasids. One imam, Muhammad ibn Qasim, led a short-lived Shi'ite revolt in northeast Afghanistan. Muhammad was captured but managed to flee, never to be seen again. In 864, another imam named Yahya ibn Umar began a Bedouin revolt in Kufa in Iraq, a revolt that also gained support among Zaydis. Although Yahya won a significant initial battle against the Abbasid forces, he was soon defeated and killed on the battlefield in August of 864.

Slave Rebellions

It would be hardly surprising with the extent of slavery in the medieval Islamic world that there be evidence of slave revolts, regardless of the availability and quantity of manumissions or the existence of other legal protections for slaves. For one, the Arabs took so many prisoners of war that there was virtually an endless entry of new slaves to the Muslim society and economy. One early such rebellion of POWs destined to be sold as slaves took place in the Iraqi town of Nisibis during the first fitna, after the death of the Umayyad caliph Mu'awiyah, in 686–687. This rebellion was associated with that of Al-Mukhtar, whom we met earlier.

The next important rebellion of Muslim slaves took place between 820 and 835 in southern Iraq among slaves brought to work breeding water buffalo in the marshlands of southern Iraq. Writes Indian human rights activist, Ranbir Singh,

> the Arabs brought tens of thousands of Indian peasants from the Indus region as slaves to be settled in Iraq. The Zotts (Arab name for Roma, or Gypsies—author) became powerful enough to challenge the Abbasid caliphate, hence, Baghdad sent its forces against them in 820. The Zotts were defeated in 834, and their entire population deported to Syria.

During the reign of the Abbasid Caliph al-Mu'tasim during 833-842, the Abbasids tried to overcome the problematic reliance upon Arab tribes as a source of soldiers since the Arabs inevitably demanded their traditional share of booty from the defeated during conquests. So, POWs taken from among the Turks of central Asia or from the Caucasian peoples on the Pontic-Caspian Steppe were turned into slave-soldiers called *ghilman* in order to serve as the caliph's personal bodyguard. One group of these soldiers was so abusive of the local Arab population of Baghdad, however, that after riots directed against the ghilman, Mu'tasim had to relocate his capital to a site north of Baghdad on the Tigris River. The slave-soldiers soon became so powerful that, beginning in the 860s, they began to make and unmake caliphs, who became simply figureheads. The ghilman assassinated four caliphs in their new location until they returned the capital to Baghdad in the 880s. From then on into the tenth century, the ghilman were the real force behind the Abassid caliphate. They eventually established the independent dynasty known as the Ghaznavids that ruled a territory in central Asia that included parts of Afghanistan, Iran, Khorasan, northern India, and Transoxiana between 962 and 1186.

One famed slave revolt, known as the Zanj revolt in southern Iraq, took place between 869 and 883. Tens of thousands died in a revolt of half a million lower class people in southern Iraq who worked in the sugar plantations, salt mines, and land reclamation efforts in the marshlands of the Tigris and Euphrates delta. Their principal leader, Ali ibn Muhammad, was the son a slave from Bahrain on the Arabian Peninsula. He preached the Kharijite doctrine that any qualified man could reign as caliph, even if he were slave and not Umayyad, Hashemite, nor a descendant of Ali, the fourth caliph. Ali ibn Muhammad's slave supporters were able to gain their freedom by making war against rich Arab landowners and slaveholders. While many slaves joined the revolt, in fact, revised historical opinion has it that the actual revolt took place first among poor clients—laborers, peasants, and craftsmen—of rich Arabs, who were then joined by slaves from eastern Africa, likely from the Sudan. (Talhami, p. 460) Bedouin warriors were the soldiers in what became a long guerrilla war by Zanj rebels against the Abbasid régime.

Finally, attention must be drawn once again briefly to the Mamaluke slave-soldiers of the Fatimid caliphate who eventually took command of Egypt, the Levant, and Syria between 1250 and 1517. Like the earlier ghilman, the Mamalukes were Turks from central Asia or Caucasians from the Pontic-Caspian Steppe.

Qarmatians

The episode of the Qarmations represents one of the most revolutionary and violent sects of Islam in the Middle Ages. In fact, many historians qualify the state they established in Bahrain in eastern Arabia as proto-communist. The Qarmatians were Ismaili Shi'ites, that is, followers of the same brand of Islam as the Fatimid caliphate of Egypt, although they differed in that Qarmations did not recognize the first Fatimid caliph as being a legitimate imam. Throughout medieval Islamic history, Shi'ite Muslims differed about the recognition of this or that imam as being legitimate for either political or religious reasons. Thereafter, a new lineage of imams would be established since the imamate was passed from father to son, while a new sect or sub-sect would emerge. Theological and political differences would then grow among the new groups, distinguishing them further from other Muslims. To non-Muslims, the explanations for differences among sects appear to be indeed murky and arcane. Suffice to say, however, that resulting political and social differences among the sects were and are indeed still real. It is these that concern us rather than the theological differences among the various stripes of Islam. The dramatic irony with respect to the Qarmations is that by the end of their period of dominance, they had turned bitterly anti-religious, turning against all forms of monotheism including Islam.

The Qarmatians were active in the 10th and 11th centuries in Iraq, Syria, and Palestine and, especially, in Bahrain. Their Bahraini state was egalitarian with respect to sect members even if it was still a slave-holding society. There were Qarmations found in all regions influenced by Ismaili missions: Yemen, northern India, Khorasan, Transoxania, and North Africa. The Qarmations undertook successful military campaigns against both the Abbasid and Fatimid caliphates. They were influenced by Manicheism and Mazdakism. For them, social inequality among free men was intolerable, a position they pursued with messianic passion. As with other Ismailis, the Qarmations' beliefs were gnostic and tinged with neo-platonism; also as with other Ismailis, the Qarmations developed an esoteric line of interpretation of the Qur'an rather than holding to the literal meaning of the scriptures. It was their social message, however, that was revolutionary since they argued for a just redistribution of lands and the holding of property in common. The founder of the Qarmation sect was an Ismaili laborer from Kufa named Hamdan Qarmat.

We have already seen that the Abbasid caliphate brought with it considerable economic development that benefited the merchant class and the courtiers. The influx of gold and the increase of credit brought a dramatic inflation of prices since production was still mostly an affair of family-operated, craft industries or businesses wherein productivity could increase only slightly to meet increased demand resulting from the increase in coinage. Production could not keep pace with the amount of new currency. The result was a general impoverishment of the working population, while the ruling class grew wealthy from taxes and their control of banks. According to Raymond Debord, a ninth century family needed annually 360 dinars, dinars being the Muslim currency, to survive. A soldier received about 500 dinars per year, while a religious official might receive a few thousand dinars annually, and a vizier, a high-ranking government official similar to a modern-day prime minister, might receive several hundred thousand dinars. Such apparent inequality was further aggravated by the fact that most common people did not receive even the basic minimum needed to support a family.

About 875, Ismaili missionaries began to spread among rural people and the Bedouin messianic propaganda about the pending arrival of a savior in the form of a hidden Mahdi. (See Mahdism section below.) This Mahdi would bring social equality and the holding of property in common. In 890, Hamdan Qarmat began preaching among peasants and workers in southern Iraq. Within a movement of strikes and social revolts, the Qarmations developed a new doctrine focused on individual freedom and the rejection of Islamic law in opposition to the ideas held by the Muslim ruling class. Like other millennial movements, the Qarmations harkened back to a simpler, happier time for humanity. (Debord, p. 2) Hamdan Qarmat's involvement with the new movement, however, was short-lived, for he soon repented of his radical views to return to the Ismaili fold.

Even so, the movement he helped initiate was still known as Qarmation. Its new leader was a man named 'Abu Sa'id al-Jannabi, whom Hamdan Qarmat had delegated earlier to Bahrain, where Jannabi founded a Qarmatian state in 899. This Qarmation state then began a political movement that could be characterized as being openly anti-Islamic, in fact, even anti-religious. They rained upon Arabia and southern Iraq what might be qualified as a century of terrorism. Eventually, evevn considering the pilgrimage to Mecca a pointless superstition, the Qarmations ambushed pilgrimage caravan in 906 returning home from Mecca, killing in the process about 20,000 pilgrims. From 923 to 944, al-Jannabi's son, Abu Tahir, ruled the Qarmation state. In 930, the Qarmations sacked Medina and Mecca, stealing the black meteorite from the Ka'ba, which they only returned to the Abbasids in 952 at a handsome ransom of 50,000 dinars. While one might imagine the scandal among Muslims at these actions, in actual fact, the Qarmation ideology also was about building a society based upon reason and equality. All property was divided equally among initiates who had passed through an initiation ceremony in seven stages. This society resembled somewhat the Spartan society of extreme communism, at least, in its outward ideological expression, however, the Qarmation state eventually grew wealthy, collecting tribute from both the Abbasid and the Fatimid caliphates. The state also grew

> ...vast fruit and grain estates...cultivated by some 30,000 Ethiopian slaves. The people... were exempt from taxes. Those impoverished or in debt could obtain a loan until they put their affairs in order. No interest was taken on loans, and token, lead money was used for all local transactions. (Nakash)

Recall that the Spartan state under Lykurgus had also used lead money, worthless outside Sparta, as a means of discouraging the pursuit of gold and silver.

The sack of Mecca was part of a millenarian fever that gripped the Qarmation state. The year 931 was 1,500 years after the death of Zoroaster, which Abu Tahir believed corresponded to the end of the Muslim era and the beginning of the final religious era, the arrival of which was to be marked by the advent of the Mahdi. Abu Tahir believed the Mahdi was a young Persian by the name of Abu'l Fadl al-Ishafani. The young man turned out to be a neo-Zoroastrian who re-instituted Zoroastrian rituals based on fire, forbade Islamic law and worship, burnt Muslim holy books, cursed imams and the prophets, and proclaimed a religion based upon Adam, the first man. Abu'l Fadl reigned for only eighty days before Abu Tahir's mother, Farha, exposed the young man as a fraud, while the ruler's brother, Sa'id, killed the alleged young Mahdi. (Cortese and Caldirini, p. 26) The whole episode embarrassed the Qarmations, who never recovered to become the scourge of the Middle East they had once been, becoming in the 11th century just another local power. After the death of Abu Tahir in 944, the Qarmation state was rent by succession crises and assassinations. In 976, the Abbasids handed an important military defeat to the Qarmation state. Tribute payments to the state by Iraqis and by Arab tribes were then terminated. In 1058, the islands of Bahrain returned to orthodox Fatimid rule, as did the eastern coastal regions of Bahrain on the Arabian Peninsula. By the middle of the 11th century Qarmation communities in Iran, Iraq, and Transoxiana had re-integrated the Fatimid orbit, or just plain disappeared. Nonetheless, the Qarmation episode demonstrated that radical, revolutionary programs under Islam were not necessarily doomed to failure, and could continue to survive many years. Moreover, according to Raymond Debord,

> The exceptional duration of the Qarmation episode demonstrates that it is not inevitable that the dominant classes always dominate. The episode also shows how egalitarian and revolutionary aspirations are not just products of the 20th century, but instead, that they are endemic in history, and can be found in all civilizations. (p. 4) (Author's adaptation of original French-language version)

Mahdism

In both Sunni and Shi'a doctrine, there is a belief in the Mahdi, a messianic figure who, alongside Jesus, will appear at the last Judgement to purify the world and bring justice to all, especially to the most humble. While this was an interesting idea to Sunnis who awaited such a time at the end of days, to many medieval Shi'ites the concept was literal. Throughout the Middle Ages, Shi'ite Islam experienced men claiming to being the Mahdi, or who others thought were the Mahdi. The Mahdi figure appeared in periods marked by millenarianism as part of a response to the social injustices of the day.

In the Middle Ages, there were five such mahdis, three of them active among the Berber tribes of North Africa. In the eighth century in North Africa, Salih ibn Tarif was the second king of the Berghouata Berbers. He founded a Berghouata state that resisted Arab conquest. Salih's religion looked suspiciously like Islam. The differences with Islam, in fact, were used as a means of national distinction, and became part of the rebellion. Between 909 and 934, another mahdi, Ubayd Allah al-Mahdi Billal, with the help of Berber tribesmen, acceded to the Ismaili Fatimid caliphate in North Africa and Egypt. In 1125, the Moroccan Abdallah ibn Tumart, another alleged mahdi, led what is known as the Almohad revolt in Morocco. He died in 1130, but his successor, Abd al-Mumin, did establish a successful sultanate. So, among Shi'ites, contrary to the Sunni view, the concept of the mahdi was that of a temporal power who rebelled and established greater justice in the here and now on earth, rather than being a religious concept relevant to a vaguely-defined future, perhaps at the end of days at the last Judgement. There were two other mahdis relevant to our period. In 777, Shi'ites from Iraq established Abdallah ibn Mu'awiya as a mahdi and an imam. He managed to control western Iran for two years until the Abbasids defeated him. Finally, to the main group of Shi'ites known as the Twelvers, the 12th and final imam was Muhammad ibn al-Hasam al-Mahdi, born in 869. He is reputed to never have actually died, but rather was occulted by God, hidden away eventually to return to purify the world and to bring justice to all. The occulting and return of this Mahdi seems to this author to have taken us a long way from the implacable monotheism of Muhammad.

Persistent Revolt among the Berbers

Within the Muslim world, popular resistance occurred within many ethnicities—Arabs, Persians, Turks, Egyptians—to name a few. There is one group of people, however, that demonstrated a particular and persistent predilection for popular rebellion over several centuries. These were the Berber tribes of North Africa and the Iberian Peninsula. The relationship between conquering Arabs and the Berber peoples is complicated and complex. For our purposes, it is the instances of popular revolt among Berbers that concern us most, to which we now draw attention.

Irish writer, Eamonn Gearon, summarizes the exasperation and frustration of the Arabs with respect to the Berbers.

> For years, Berber revolts continued to trouble the Arabs, leading one governor to declare despairingly: "The conquest of Ifriqiya is impossible; scarcely has one Berber tribe been exterminated than another takes its place." The Roman term of opprobrium for any non-Roman, 'barbarian', had now morphed into an Arabic, Berber identity of a united people rather than disparate desert tribes.

So, just as the Romans had often defined peoples into existence even if only by their resistance to Rome, so the Arabs did with the Berbers. Clans and tribes that forever had been at loggerheads now confederated to stall or even defeat outright the Arabs in their march to the west. Moreover, Berber resistance to the Arabs was fueled by the Muslim religion itself which, at least in its ideology, promised equal treatment for all in the eyes of God. In the first instance, the Berbers resisted the imposition of Islam by collaborating with the Byzantines to defeat the Arabs then, working with the Arabs, to defeat the Byzantines. Berber converts to Islam inconveniently insisted on a literal observance of the words of the Prophet about social equality and brotherhood.

The first source of Berber popular resistance was led by a Christian named Kusayla, who led the Awraba tribe and a confederation of Berbers in collaboration with the Byzantines with the goal of arresting Arab expansion into North Africa during the 680s. Originally successful, Kusayla and the Awraba tribe were defeated ultimately by an Arab army in 690.

The next great Berber leader was a woman, al-Kahina, a Jewish or Christian leader who died fighting the Arabs about 700. Al-Kahina is a legendary figure who has been turned into a mythic hero by feminists, Berber nationalists, and anti-colonial activists. The demise of al-Kahina and her army helped ensure Arab control of North Africa after the Arabs had ousted the Byzantines from Carthage. The Arabs then established four provinces in North Africa: the Maghreb, modern-day Morocco and western Algeria; Ifriqiya, modern-day eastern Algeria, Tunisia, and Tripolitania, or western Libya; Cyraenica, or eastern Libya; and Egypt.

In 710-711, the Muslims began their conquest of Iberia, taking advantage of a civil war in Visigothic Spain. The Muslim armies were led by a Berber freedman, Tariq ibn Ziyad. Even so, Berbers in Iberia rebelled several times against the Arabs for perceived injustices in the 740s and in 768, and then again, several more times in the first half of the ninth century. (Glick, Chapter 5) Nor did conversion to Islam, moreover, ensure peace between Arabs and Berbers in North Africa. The former treated the latter to unfair taxation and tributes of slaves, contrary to Muslim law. So, Berbers grew receptive to the blandishments of Kharijite holy men who preached the equality of all under Islam, including the idea that anyone, irrespective of appartenance to the Umayyad or Hashemite clans, could become caliph. This led to what historians call the Great Berber Revolt of 739–740 under the leadership of a man called Maysara, from the tribe of the Matghari. A man of low social status, apparently a poor water-carrier for the Arab army, Maysara led the popular revolt of four tribes in western Morocco: the Gomara, Berghouata, Miknasa, and the Matghari. Maysara began his rebellion in 740, when the Arab army of Ifriqiya was off on a military campaign in Sicily. Maysara's army quickly killed a particularly offensive governor of western Morocco before submitting the entire region to their control. With the west under their control, the front of the war with the Arabs then moved east to the territory of the Zenata tribe, who won two more victories over the Arabs. The Arabs then left the lost territory to the Berber tribes, who proceeded to exact revenge on Berber notables who had collaborated with the Arabs. In the wake of the Berber victories over the Arabs, the Berghouata tribe withdrew from the successful confederacy to establish an independent state. In 744, the second king of the new state, Salih ibn Tarif, started a new religion that we described above, and that lasted into the 11th century.

Early in the 10th century, Ismaili Shi'ites established themselves in North Africa, particularly among the Kutama tribe. This tribe overthrew the ruling Abbasid dynasty that had governed North Africa during the ninth century, in the process creating a military and religious base for the Fatimid caliphate of Egypt. One of the Fatimid provinces was Sicily, which installed a Fatimid governor in 909, however, an independent régime under a man named ibn Khorab was installed in Sicily in 913, which led to Berber revolts on the island in 915, 937, 940, and 941. The Fatimid general who finally quelled the Berbers bragged of having killed 600,000 rebels.

In 944, the first Fatimid Caliph, al-Mahdi, died. This was the signal for a man named Abu Yazid, a Berber from the Banu Ifran tribe and a Kharijite, to lead a revolt against the Fatimids from a base in the Aurès Mountains in Tunisia. The rebels won considerable support among Berber peasants revolting against big Shi'ite landowners. Abu Yazid had several military successes, including in the cities of Tunis and Kairouan, the Ifriqiyan capital 160 kilometers south of modern-day Tunis, before being defeated finally by the Fatimids in 947.

Our final example of Berber rebelliousness in the Middle Ages in North Africa came in 1125 in the person of a rebel named Abdallah ibn Tumart. From the Masmuda tribe of the Atlas Mountains, ibn Tumart, a deeply religious man, led a movement aimed at reforming North African society. The Almohads, as Tumart's followers are known to historians, believed in a unitary concept of God rather than in the anthropomorphic concepts that had developed in North Africa. This idea of the unity of God, after all, was one of the inspirations that had guided the Prophet himself. Like many a reformer in tribal societies, for example, men such as Solon and Lykurgus among the ancient Greeks, ibn Tumart aimed to replace the traditional divisions of family, clan, and tribe with social divisions organized by trade and occupation as a means of re-ordering the social solidarity of the Berber peoples. It was apparently an unsuccessful effort for it failed to take root in North Africa during the life and times of ibn Tumart, who died in 1130. (Le Tourneau et al., p. 76-77)

Islamic Guilds

The Islamic world included guilds of craftsmen as did all urban civilizations prior to modernity. Their influence spread far and wide; arguably, a case might even be made for the Islamic guilds serving as an inspiration for the European guilds of the Middle Ages. Our sources about the Islamic guilds include Tahir Abdullah, G.G. Arnakis, and Bernard Lewis (1937).

It is probable that the conquering Arabs at the beginning of Islam continued to permit the existence of Roman guilds in Byzantine Syria and Egypt since their initial policy was to disturb existing cultures and practices as little as possible provided, of course, that Muslim taxes were paid. Thus, Byzantine guilds of the seventh century were probably left intact by the Arab conquerors. It should be noted that these guilds were not independent organizations representing the interests of working people, but were rigid corporate organizations that formed part of the state apparatus for ensuring the provision of food and other essentials for Byzantine cities. By the tenth century, it appears the Muslims themselves had instituted similar guilds but, once again, as tools of state control of essential craft production.

Bernard Lewis reminds us of the Muslim movements of popular resistance in his introduction to the Islamic guilds. (p. 22-23) During the first half-century or so of Islam, the Sunni form of orthodox Islam was the religion of the state and its ruling Arab notables. The Sunnis were viewed by the popular classes as being symbolic of a foreign, privileged ruling class far removed from their interests. The religious inclinations of the masses were found among the various popular and sometimes mystical, even heretical movements—Shi'ites, Kharijites, Khurramites—and still others. According to Lewis,

> These sects were almost all characterized by a syncretistic philosophy, containing elements borrowed from pre-Islamic systems especially neo-platonism, Manicheism, and Mazdakism, by a revolutionary and equalitarian social philosophy, and by a secret, quasi-masonic organization, usually inter-confessional, with graduated ranks of initiation. (p. 22)

Recall that the Abbasid régime of the tenth and 11th centuries produced a high level of economic development based on mercantile capitalism and concentrations of capital and labor in major cities. The resulting social inequalities contributed to continuing social rebellion, including the emergence of the Ismaili Fatimid caliphate and the Qarmation movement and state. The opinion of Lewis with respect the latter was most laudatory. He described the Qarmations as being

> ...characterized by an extraordinary liberalism. It appealed to all the innumerable religions and sects of the Muslim world—Sunnis, Shi'ites, Christians, Jews, Zoroastrians alike—in the name of intellectual liberty and social justice....It was a form of rational idealism, recognizing the relativity of all religions, rejecting the formal law of Islam, and basing itself on a system of justice, toleration, and complete equality. (p. 23)

The Qarmations used the guilds to help forge the working class into a force with the ultimate aim of overthrowing the Abbasid caliphs, hence their attempt to organize artisans into professional fraternities. As well, under the Fatimids, guilds had been encouraged and supported, while after the Kurd Saladin recovered Egypt for Sunni Islam, guilds were once again submitted to rigorous state control. After the Mongol conquest of the mid-13th century, Sunni, Shi'ite and all other stripes of Islam were subjected to foreign control by a hostile power, at least until the Mongol ruling class converted to Sunni Islam. This fact meant that Sunni Islam became not necessarily the Islam of the ruling class but instead a form of Islam acceptable to the majority of Muslims, including to the lower social classes. Nonetheless, guild members came to associate themselves with mystical Sufi brotherhoods, who sometimes verged on the edge of Muslim heresy.

Craftsmen also came under the influence of a movement known as the *futuwwa*, groupings of young men who observed a strict religious and social code of duties and responsibilities including military service to the cause of Islam, along with ceremonial initiation and gradation procedures. The futuwwa code was similar to the codes of chivalry for European knights; in fact, some even have suggested a link between the two. According to Lewis, the association between crafts guilds and the futuwwa first began in 13th century Anatolia after the Seljuk régime had been destroyed by the conquering Mongols. There were also youth associations among craftsmen known as *akhis*, whose code was solidarity and hospitality, with the slaying of tyrants and their minions being their task. The akhis were social political, military, and religious confraternities of artisans who provided some social solidarity in the chaos after the Mongol conquest of Anatolia. Despite not being religiously mainstream, they continued to exist until the Ottoman conquest. Until then, the akhis spread throughout the Islamic world especially in Iran, Iraq, Syria, and Egypt. (Lewis, p. 29)

Another group important to the development of futuwwa associations among craftsmen were the *ayyars*, volunteer warriors from the lower classes who defended the Abbasid Sunnis against their Shi'ite and Kharijite adversaries. The ayyars, under the leadership of Ya'qub bin Layth al-Saffar, created the Saffarid dynasty that ruled in eastern Iran, Khorasan, and Afghanistan between 861 and 1002, however, their origin was as

> ...groups of poor young men who occupied the urban slums of Iran and Baghdad. These clubs of young men were often involved in careers as

sportsmen, tradesmen, and cavalrymen, and would come together in the form of brotherhoods of hospitality where communal meals and socializing would take place. Additionally, these clubs often maintained their martial character, often bearing arms, allegedly to defend, as needed, their futuwwa brethren. (Abdullah, p. 6)

By way of summary, we can say that Islamic guilds displayed five broad characteristics:

- an abiding hostility to states and their ruling classes, hostility that the Muslim states usually reciprocated;
- absence of the journeymen craftsmen who, in 15th century Europe, entered into conflict with masters, since Islamic guilds included only apprentices and masters;
- unlike in Europe, Muslim guilds were often inter-confessional wherein Jews and Christians might also participate, while some guilds were even primarily non-Muslim;
- the strong moral and religious codes made guilds in medieval Muslim states sometimes less like European guilds and more like Catholic confraternities, or *confrèries*;
- the important role guilds played in the physical organization of an Islamic city, organized as it was according to needs of merchant and artisan guilds. (Lewis, p. 20, 36, 37)

Conclusion

At the same time that much of Europe was trying to recover from the loss of civilization and urban life that accompanied the invasions and migrations from the north and the east after the demise of the western Roman empire, to the east, the last entry of what we have argued was an extended Axial Age appeared in the form of Muhammad and his monotheistic faith of submission to God. The aim of the faith, as per the other religions founded during the Axial Age, was an attempt to replace the violence and brutality that accompanied the Iron Age and its wake with values of fraternity, equality, and social justice. The Arab proponents of this faith were able to defeat the weary Byzantine and Persian empires that had been weakened by years of imperial warfare.

At the same time as the social message of equality, justice, and brotherhood inflamed Bedouin warriors, the results of the Arab conquests included states and empires that, even if they were able to bring considerable socio-economic and intellectual progress, settled down to oppress the poor as most states and empires usually had done. In response, the Middle Ages saw persistent rounds of popular resistance to the social domination of the ruling classes and the states that had been organized in the name of the same Islam that inspired continuing social revolt. Hence, the abiding paradox of medieval Muslim civilization.

Europe, moreover, was affected by the cultural, economic, and scientific advances of the Islamic world. In the following chapters about the Middle Ages in Europe, we shall learn more fully how the development of Christian Europe was affected by the progress of Islam.

CHAPTER 9. CASTLES/CRUSADES — COMMUNES/CATHEDRALS — CRISES/CALAMITIES

Introduction

This chapter describes the framework of development that included the popular resistance of the Middle Ages. Our concerns are the periods known as the high Middle Ages from 1000 to 1300, and the late Middle Ages from 1300 to 1500. While they are often studied separately, this chapter treats both periods together. Phenomena common to both periods such as feudalism and manorialism occurred between the years 1000 and 1500 in both western and eastern Europe. Some historians have observed a phenomenon whereby elements of the development of western Europe during the high Middle Ages seem to occur only during the late Middle Ages in eastern Europe. This apparent cultural lag has appeared to some as an objective phenomenon. In actuality, western Europe and eastern Europe are so intertwined that the apparent developmental tardiness of eastern Europe, when studied more closely, can be quite illusory. For example, consider the migrations westward of the Huns and the Avars along with other peoples from the Pontic-Caspian Steppe. From this perspective, we can observe that certain elements of development began first among the eastern peoples before they affected western Europe. Indeed, we have analyzed these migrations in just this manner. Moreover, while some states did emerge comparatively later in eastern Europe, Byzantium did rule southeastern Europe, Anatolia, Syria, the Levant, and Egypt, which had states with long existences both prior to and as part of the western Roman empire. The eastern Roman empire continued intact until the eve of the modern era, even if reduced in size and importance. Furthermore, while it is indeed true that certain states in eastern Europe did emerge later than did states in western Europe, the same thing also applies within western Europe itself.

The general observation about the developmental lag of eastern Europe when compared to western Europe turns out to be, in fact, not very important nor useful. More important are the individual histories of the various geographical entities that became states. There are more useful methods of analyzing the emergence of these geographic entities cum states other than the division into western and eastern Europe. More specifically, we employ an analysis based on development, or societal transformation including the evolution of Church and state, social class, class conflict, and popular resistance as dynamic forces at work in each geographic entity.

In the previous chapter, we argued that Islam was the last entry of an extended Axial Age by which humankind strove to control the violence and brutality of the Iron Age and its aftermath. We have argued, furthermore, that the *force motrice*, the dynamic of development of Islamic society, was the contradiction between the states that spred the religion and culture of Islam and the radical social values of Islam itself. Periodically and persistently, the lower social orders revolted against the states and ruling classes that had spread Islam in the first instance by referring to the tenets of Islam itself to maintain that these states were betraying the spirit, faith, and ideals of Muhammad.

In the next two chapters, we shall see that the same work of taming and controlling the violence, brutality, and warfare of the Iron Age and its aftermath continued in Europe during the Middle Ages, well beyond the period of the initial spread of Islam. In fact, reigning in the power of aristocratic descendants of the medieval warrior class in Europe continued even into the post-WWI period, well after the liberal, bourgeois revolutions of the modern era. Only in the 20th century did the governing role of nobility and royalty in Europe finally become for the most part irrelevant, even if they continued to serve as historical symbols of tradition and symbolic heads-of-state in the constitutional monarchies of Great Britain, Spain, Belgium, The Netherlands, Scandinavia, and four small principalities: Andorra, Liechtenstein, Monaco, and Luxembourg.

The mission of confronting, resisting, and reducing the sway of the nobility of Europe during the Middle Ages was undertaken by all social classes, sometimes united, sometimes divided one against another. This resistance to the nobility came from several sources in terms of social class. Firstly, there were the kings, often foreigners to the lands they were trying to govern, whose strategy was to develop centralized states that might reign in indigenous, local aristocracies. Secondly, the Catholic Church sought to control the warrior class. Thirdly, there were the townsfolk, including the *bourgeoisie*, the merchants whose *raison d'être* and source of power was the wealth created by trade. Fourthly, there were the popular classes composed of craftsmen, peasants, laborers, serfs, and slaves. Medieval peasants were sometimes free, but were usually serfs tied to the land they worked, and to the noble or ecclesiastical landowners who extracted economic surplus from their labor. All classes had an interest in trying to bring to heal the aristocratic class over the course of the Middle Ages. In fact, this phenomenon was the principal dynamic of development, the *force motrice* of the Middle Ages.

State Formation

We have seen in earlier chapters how Mediterranean civilization was subjected to destabilizing migrations from the north and the east at the end of the ancient era during the early Middle Ages. By the end of the millennium and the inception of the high Middle Ages, the migrations of these peoples in Europe finally ran their course. Huns; Germanic peoples; Avars, Bulgars, Pechenegs, Cumans, and Kipchaks, all of whom were Turkic peoples from the Pontic-Caspian Steppe or central Asia as well as the Iranic Alans; Slavs; Muslim Arabs and Berbers; Norsemen; Magyars, all had settled in new territories that began to crystallize into hundreds of statelets.

Where these people were once tribal in organization and led by warrior chieftains who garnered wealth for distribution to retinues of warrior-followers by looting, pillaging, enslaving, and raiding other peoples, now these same people and their descendants ran out of people and lands to plunder. Moreover, their societies and economies underwent important transformations such that warrior leaders became noblemen whose wealth now came from the economic surplus farmed by peasant labor in conquered lands. It eventually became pointless and unproductive to pillage and loot indiscriminately from peasants whose economic surplus became the source of the wealth of the warriors cum nobility. The latter had to be careful not to draw from the well so often that it would run dry, but it took time and much pain before this seemingly obvious lesson was learned. The old habits of the warrior nobility were unlearned only with the assistance of resistance from other social classes.

Typical migrants in Europe were tribal peoples comprised of armies of freemen led by chieftains acclaimed by a popular assembly of freemen. Clan leaders assembled in advisory councils to the kings. Generals were selected from the noble retinue of the kings, and were often clan leaders themselves. The law was one of custom, ancient law venerated and interpreted by priests and rulers. Political power in the tribe was focused on clan leaders. Members of a clan often descended from a common great-grandparent, while the clan itself was usually led by the eldest man considered to have the finest qualities of leadership, provided he be of the same blood as the long-ago relative. During the course of the Middle Ages, however, power, wealth, and land came to be transmitted by inheritance to the eldest sons of tribal chieftains rather than from among the oldest clan leaders. This was the inheritance and property system known as primogeniture. It represented, at the same time, a transfer of power from clan leaders to tribal leaders, which also represented sort of a centralization of power. Previous, non-primogeniture forms of succession are called cognatic. As the Middle Ages proceeded, increasingly primogeniture defined the succession of leadership, whereby power in a tribe fell to the eldest son of the fallen or dead leader rather than a worthy elder from among the clan leaders.

Contact of these tribal people with the nearby or bordering empires— Roman, Frankish, Carolingian, Byzantine, Abbasid—was a source of new wealth for migratory tribes. The new wealth came from raiding within the borders of the empire; from transmission of improved agricultural techniques from empire to periphery; from serving in imperial armies either as individuals or in discrete units; from tribute or protection money paid to peoples by the threatened empires; from services or produce sold by the migratory tribes to the empires and their armies. All this generated circulation of imperial coinage among the tribes, which resulted in increased wealth, inflation, debt, and social inequality. Essentially egalitarian societies were transformed into class societies in which some tribal chieftains became local kings who were served by warrior clan leaders who eventually became landholding nobility. There were lower classes comprised of freemen, of peasants tied to the land, and of slaves captured in warfare or sold into slavery.

Many states such as Poland, Greater Moravia, and Bohemia, were ruled in a process called royal itineration whereby the king moved from region to region, receiving his due homage, food, and other essentials from the local economy, peasantry, and lords. According to the British scholar Peter Heather, "[I]t's a broad rule of thumb that an early medieval ruler really governed only where he regularly travelled. All our evidence suggests itineration was the key method of government in the new entities of northern Europe and eastern Europe." (2010, p. 529) In some cases, warfare and permanent military occupation by a centralized state eventually destroyed local cultures and rulers. The emergence of Kievan Rus' as a recognizable state was the result of still another kind of process. Up the river valleys the Viking raiders cum traders travelled south, establishing among the Slavs

> ...not so much a state, as a glorified Hudson's Bay company, composed of essentially independent trading operations located at various centers along the main river routes, loosely linked together by having to pay protection money to the most powerful among them...The Rus' state began life, therefore, as a hierarchically organized umbrella organization for these merchants, no doubt established originally by force. (Heather, 2010, p. 536)

Positing the conflict of other classes with the nobility as being a *force motrice* of the Middle Ages might appear reductionist. In fact, we do not preclude other dynamics that also influenced development in the Middle Ages. Marxists might well speak of the extension of the forces of production, in effect, the evolution of technology as part of the process of accumulation of capital. Students of military history might argue that the motivating force of social development was the development of military technique and technologies that formed part of the history of warfare. Historians of religion might study the Middle Ages as being an Age of Faith. All these emphases have explanatory value for comprehending the Middle Ages in Europe. However, the most useful prism for studying popular resistance to the extraction of economic surplus from the labor of working people by other classes is to study the popular resistance to those who profited most from these economic arrangements. For the most part, this was the aristocracy of warrior-chieftains that evolved to become the landholding nobility in the Middle Ages.

Among the first people to resist the landholding nobility were the kings who tried to develop centralized states, a painstaking process that took hundreds of years to work out before Europe came to be composed of centralized competing and collaborating nation-states. The work of the late American sociologist, Charles Tilly, is most useful when considering the historical processes of creating centralized monarchies. Firstly, with respect to the character of these centralized monarchies, while uniting diverse local populations into a centralized state sometimes was a dignified and peaceful effort, for the most part, centralized European monarchies were created by warfare. One of Tilly's best-known aphorisms is that war makes states, and states make war. Warfare, which Tilly places on a continuum with "... banditry, piracy, gangland rivalry, and policing...", was the principal means medieval Europeans used to created centralized monarchies even if, at times, less violent means also were employed such as marriage, alliance, threat, land swaps, diplomacy, or inheritance. (1985, p. 170) Secondly, most attempts to create lasting, centralized states ultimately failed. In 1500, there were about 500 states of various forms and sizes in Europe, about which only a tenth of that number survive today. Once again, according to Tilly: "The enormous majority of the political units which were around to bid for autonomy and strength in 1500 disappeared in the next four centuries, smashed or absorbed by other states-in-the-making." (1985, p. 38) Among the medieval states that disappeared eventually were not just tiny principalities but immense, powerful states such as the Byzantine, Ottoman, and Holy Roman empires; the Pecheneg and Kipchak khanates of the Pontic-Caspian Steppe; the Cordoba Caliphate in Spain and Portugal; the German State of the Teutonic Order in the Baltic region; Kievan Rus'; and the Grand Duchy of Lithuania.

While state-making was difficult and most medieval states ultimately failed, the effort to reign in the warrior-aristocrats in centralized monarchies, nevertheless, did succeed in a general sense. Once again, in the words of Charles Tilly:

> The Europeans of 1500 had a tradition of kingship which stretched back in diverse ways to Roman times. Just behind them lay 700 years of king-making experience which, for all its chaos, had resulted in almost every European being at least nominally subject to one crown or another. (1985, p. 25)

According to Tilly, while both the rise of the nation-state and the long hegemony of Europe might appear to be natural phenomena, in fact, they only came into being during the Middle Ages. "The hegemony of a dense and uneven urban network with a division into numerous, well-defined and more or less independent states eventually set off Europe from the rest of the world ", a distinction that, in fact, makes it one of the defining characteristics of the West. (1989, p. 563)

As part of the research for this chapter, this author conducted an informal survey of how Western states emerged during the Middle Ages. Within the modern-day countries that constitute the West—minus, of course, the Americas, which only entered Western history after the European contact initiated by Christopher Columbus—seven countries emerged by a process of a local ruler of a county or duchy expanding his rule to a territory more or less analogous to the existing modern nation-state. This was the case for Algeria, Tunisia, Morocco, Denmark, France, Lithuania, and Poland. Another five states emerged when a foreign ruler turned unorganized tribal territory into a state under foreign rule. Such states included Estonia, Finland, Gibraltar, Latvia, and Monaco. Iceland was an unoccupied territory organized into a state under foreign rule. For other modern-day nation-states in the West, the role of foreign conquest of a then-existing medieval state was primordial. The appendix to this chapter lists modern-day statelets formed by foreign conquest during the Middle Ages. In this informal survey, as with this book itself, the West is defined to include Europe as far east as the Ural Mountains in Russia, the Middle Eastern and North African countries with Mediterranean coasts, and the Mediterranean islands.

By no means did the landholding nobility simply acquiesce, however, to the rule of kings, foreign or local. We now consider three examples of conflict within the ruling class when the aristocracy was able to limit the control of centralizing monarchs, foreign or native, by obtaining formal, legal declarations that limited the power of the king. Perhaps the best-known case to English-language readers is that of England, which took an important step towards becoming a limited, constitutional monarchy in the Middle Ages with the signing of *Magna Carta*, by which the English nobility subjected John, the Norman prince ruling England, to limitations such as the right to trial of the nobility and churchmen by juries of their peers. This has come down in the English-speaking world as the right for all to trial by jury. The principle of limited monarchy owes, in actual fact, to still earlier charters in English history. In 1093, King William II, son of William the Conqueror, issued a charter lost to history that is thought to have freed prisoners, forgiven debts, and assured that holy and good laws would be maintained. Nonetheless, when the brother of William II, Henry, was crowned king of England in 1100, he issued a written proclamation, forced upon him by Church officials and secular noblemen, called the Charter of Liberties or the Coronation Charter. The Charter addressed royal abuses of power by his predecessor, including an alleged over-taxation of the barons and royal misuse and abuse of Church offices. Among other things, the Charter guaranteed that the king could not abscond with vacant lands that had been occupied by deceased churchmen or secular lords. The later Provisions of Oxford in 1258 forced King Henry III to submit to rule by a council of lords, while the next decade saw the development of the parliament of Simon de Montfort which created a place in government for representatives of the local knightly and bourgeois classes.

Elsewhere in Europe, a similar document, the Golden Bull of 1222 in Hungary, may have been inspired by Magna Carta since the proponents of the Hungarian document had met during the Crusades with Robert Fitzwalter, an exiled English baron who had been instrumental in the proclamation of Magna Carta. The Hungarian edict, signed by King Andrew II, required that all noblemen be treated equally by the king, and that noblemen had the right to resist the law, a right known as *jus resistendi*, if the king acted contrary to law. It also freed the nobility and Church from the imposition of royal taxes and from the obligation to fight or finance foreign wars of the king. These were charters that extended rights to lords in their opposition to kings trying to extend central power. We should have no illusions that they also applied originally to commoners. In fact, in Denmark, the nobles' charter, called the *Haandfaestning*, actually diminished the power of peasants and the local assemblies of freemen called *things*. The document, issued by King Erik V in 1282, limited the king's power by recognizing aristocratic power in return for aristocrats' support for the king. The document forbade the king from arresting lords arbitrarily, and required the king to call an annual meeting of the *Hof*, a national parliament composed of Church prelates and aristocrats that also functioned as the highest court in the land.

So, while it took hundreds of years to do so, centralized states eventually did get the better of the local nobilities, in the process submitting the descendants of tribal warrior leaders. At the same time, however, in the words of one internet source who employs the moniker *Beastrabban*...

> The Middle Ages had succeeded in establishing constitutional limits to the power of monarchs and the authority of councils to represent the wider people based on ideas of popular sovereignty, partly based on the arguments of theologians such as St. Augustine and Thomas Aquinas and developed by canon (Church) lawyers from the conduct of ecclesiastical councils, and on ancient Greek and Roman political theory.

Church versus Nobility

Centralizing kings had an important ally in their long term campaign to reign in the warrior class. This was the Catholic Church, even if there were also well-known disputes between kings or emperors and Church, which we examine later. The extension of centralized monarchies and the growth of Christianity went arm-in-arm. Polish scholar Michal Tymoski describes the relationship between the two phenomena.

> The emergence of states was a fundamental, deep transformation. It was brought about by external pressure...but also by the attraction of the external state models. Adoption of the model was tantamount to the adoption of Christianity, which legitimized the political order of the state. If Christianity was rejected, adoption of the model became impossible, and military pressure left no time for the development of a local system. As a result of invasion, the invader's state was created. This was the fate of the tribes and early state organizations of the western Slavs...as well as most of the Balts.

In fact, the same situation also applied to Scandinavians and to German peoples such as the Saxons and the Bavarians.

The Church employed three strategies to try to bring to heal local warlords. The first was confronting directly the warrior class about its intolerable behavior; the second involved developing local Church structures and hierarchy and the papacy as counterweights to the warrior class; the third involved moral and intellectual reforms meant to change medieval society from top to bottom, including orienting the actions of the landholding class.

This is work that took the Church hundreds of years to accomplish, in fact, a millennium from the demise of the western Roman empire to the onset of European imperialism in the Americas and elsewhere. When one speaks of Church strategy, it is not necessarily to imply a conspiracy of the Church, even if it might have appeared so to early Protestant reformers. Moreover, while it is true there were great leaders who directed the affairs of the Church during the Middle Ages, popes such as Gregory I (the Great) and Gregory VII, or Leo IX and Innocent III, it is also true there were dud popes whose rule, in effect, countered the work of these great Church leaders. What was at work, however, in the strategy of the medieval Church was the long-term evolution and execution of a class interest. Such a statement admittedly might under-estimate the extent and sincerity of the passions and visions at work in the evolution of the Church, the travails of sinners and saints, of martyrs and mystics. Execution of Church interests was anything but a series of cold-hearted calculations. Nonetheless, Church interests did bring the Church to confront the warrior class by supporting the centralizing Christian monarchs. In a similar fashion, as we shall see later, the Church might support the popular classes in their struggles, even while oppressing and exploiting the common people at the same time. The working out of these relationships, their zigs and zags as Friedrich Engels called them, constituted a part of medieval development and of the class dialectic.

The Church and Christian Monarchs

It is useful to consider some examples of how the centralization processes of Christian monarchs and the spread of Christianity complemented each other. Written about the ancestor-states of the Czech Republic and Slovakia, respectively Bohemia and Great Moravia in medieval times, these words also apply generally to state formation in the Middle Ages.

> Christianization was inseparably linked to the process of the creation and building of the polity. This is not because the Church was a 'state' church but, because in many respects, it was identical with the polity or state. Christianity, understood as a new life order, offered the intellectual justification for the radical changes in society that accompanied the creation of a newly united and organized state. Just as the creation of the new political order was probably accomplished by force...so too the installation of Christianity was made essentially from above. (Berend, p. 251)

In the case of medieval Bohemia, in order to foster the extension of royal power against the power of local noblemen, Bohemian kings encouraged large-scale immigration of German lords and clergy in an effort to counter the influence of their Bohemian counterparts. Thus, in some cases, it was not just foreign Christian kings who conquered foreign lands, but sometimes conquest might also involve clergy, missionaries and nobility from the conquering societies. Nora Berend summarizes the relationship between foreign conquest and the imposition of Christianity in northern and eastern Europe as being part of long term processes that resulted in both the dominance of Christianity as the religion of European societies and a system of states as the political structure of these societies. (p. 8, 9)

These processes started before the high Middle Ages and continued after the late Middle Ages into the modern period. For instance, the Holy Roman Empire was established during the first millennium at the same time as Germany became Catholic. At the end of the first millennium, Christianity and monarchy were established in concert in Hungary. There the Magyars formed a Christian monarchy recognized by the pope as part of a process marked by violence and warfare.

About the same time as Hungary became a Christian monarchy, in Iceland, the Norwegian Christian, King Olaf Tryggvasson, used intimidation, murder, and economic blockades to convince the Icelanders to adopt Christianity rather than maintaining their ancient, Norwegian pagan beliefs. Thus, they avoided civil war with Icelandic Christians. Iceland had been colonized mostly by Norwegians in the ninth and tenth centuries. These people continued to worship traditional Norse gods. On the other hand, a minority of Icelanders originated from the British Isles; they had been converted to Christianity by Irish monks and missionaries.

In the case of Finland, several Christian states tried for years to colonize the Finns, who were ruled by local tribal chieftains with no central authority. Finally, in the second half of the 13th century, the Swedes won out in the competition to Christianize and colonize the Finns in competition with Denmark, Novgorod, in northwest Russia, and German crusading monks.

Lithuania provides the exception to the rule of foreign conquest combined with conversion to Christianity. Local pagan rulers continued to expand and consolidate their power during the Middle Ages, turning Lithuania into an important pagan power during the 14th century. Lithuania only became Christian late in the 14th century when the Lithuanian leader, Jagiello, was baptized in 1386 in order to marry Queen Hedwig of Christian Poland, in the process creating a state based on the personal union of the rulers of Lithuania and Poland. (Berend, p. 34, 35)

Medieval Warfare

Even as the warrior-leaders of the tribes of Europe settled from their nomadic patterns to become the peasant-exploiting, landholding nobility, it was still not easy to turn off the tap of perennial violence and warfare. In confronting the phenomenon, nonetheless, the Church employed three tactics. Firstly, through such means as the development of codes of chivalry partly inspired by Muslim examples and partly by the Peace of God and the Truce of God movements, the Church tried to orient the behavior of the nobility to more peaceful actions. Secondly, the Church tried to deflect the military energies of the nobility through Crusades—to the Middle East and northern Europe—against heretics such as the Cathars in southern France or other small-scale, local heretics. The aim was to control the perennial warfare in Europe that might have destroyed all including the Church. Thirdly, the Church itself joined in the parade of warriors by creating orders of warrior-monks to do the work of the Church as well as serving as examples of holy warriors that might influence the conduct of other warriors. Before considering in more detail these Church tactics, however, let us examine the more fully the nature of the military violence of the Middle Ages.

The warfare of the Middle Ages had several sources. Firstly, there were the wars among polities as small as towns or counties and as large as immense empires, and everything in between. The geography of the European peninsula is indeed varied with mountain ranges and valleys, river valleys, plains, plateaux, deserts, and coastal regions. Sometimes, it appeared that each geographic region merited its own medieval state that would come to blows invariably with its neighbors owing to different interests partly created by geography itself. Since there were hundreds of these states, at any time in medieval Europe there might be several wars being waged simultaneously, either as discrete, contained campaigns or as wars of coalitions and alliances of polities that sometimes might be fought on several fronts. According to Charles Tilly, there were up to 500 medieval states being created, formed, and defined by warfare. Then, there were the wars of succession when royal lineages ran out of sons to succeed as kings, or when war erupted among rival armies controlled by royal siblings and relatives in conflict, or among local nobility vying for royal, ducal, or county thrones. These were civil wars, but there were also wars fought between states about royal successions, or even about successions in third-party polities in which belligerents defended their perceived interests.

Major examples of such wars of succession during the years 1337–1453 occurred in the Hundred Years War between the kingdoms of England and France over the question of accession to the French throne and control of France. Actually three long wars separated by significant truces, the Hundred Years War did much to define the political geography of western Europe. Finally, the French did win control over most of France. The wars were important for the emergence of popular nationalism among both the French and English peoples, who now no longer identified themselves as only being from a given locality, but also as forming part of the French or English nations. Moreover, since the war was fought on the continent, it was especially calamitous for France. Campaigns would end and truces, temporary or otherwise, would be signed while troops, defeated or victorious, would simply be left on their own to return home by surviving off the land, in actual fact, on the backs of French peasants. For about a century, these *écorcheurs*, as they were called evocatively, roamed France wreaking havoc either individually or in bands and armies, with respite given to the unfortunate French only when these men were hired once again by military campaigners. Ultimate relief only came after the Hundred Years War when French merchants accepted payment of a regular, permanent tax for royal coffers called the *taille des gens de guerre*. This permitted the state to pay soldiers and officers to serve in a regular army that could bring to heal other loose, unemployed soldiers. This phenomenon of out-of-control soldiers wreaking havoc was one of the elements that inspired the popular French nationalism around the person of Joan of Arc.

Medieval wars were lengthy affairs that might drag on inconclusively for years. There were other examples of these lengthy medieval wars. The Thirteen Years War in mid-15th century was fought between the German State of the Teutonic Order in the Baltic on one side, and the Prussian Confederation and Poland on the other. This war was followed immediately by the equally long 'War of the Priests' fought between 1467 and 1479 about the independence of the Prussian state of Warmia, ruled by its bishop, vis-à-vis its erstwhile ally, the kingdom of Poland.

As the Middle Ages advanced, combatants came to involve more than just the knightly class. Commoners also served as soldiers, fighting in ways that modified the traditional, medieval warfare of armored knights on horseback. As well, a considerable element of armies was now mercenary. These soldiers fought for whatever polity might pay them, sometimes switching sides in the middle of a war, other times fighting on behalf of their own interests. While some mercenary forces were originally engaged directly by states, there also were private mercenary armies for hire that just as readily could and did wreak havoc and random violence.

One of the best examples of private mercenary armies was the Catalan Company, whose history is worth a brief exposition. The Catalan Company was founded by Roger de Flor early in the 14th century, an Italian defrocked Templar and ex-crusader who was also the count of Malta. De Flor recruited soldiers who had been dismissed after a peace settlement between the kingdom of Aragon in northern Spain and the Anjou dynasty of France. With the connivance of the king of Aragon, who also ruled Sicily and the southern part of the Italian peninsula, de Flor offered the services of his Aragonese soldiers in 1303 to the Byzantine emperor fighting the Turks in Anatolia. The Aragonese state was anxious to rid their Italian and Sicilian territories of these unemployed, unruly soldiers. So, they equipped de Flor with 39 galleys and transports carrying about 1,500 knights and 4,000 almogavars, infantrymen employed by the Aragonese.

Once the Catalan Company arrived in Constantinople, the Byzantine emperor, at the further instigation of the Aragonese, displayed his gratitude to Count de Flor by marrying him off to his niece, who also happened to be the daughter of the czar of Bulgaria. The fortunate bridegroom then went to work defeating the Turks in Anatolia, however, his soldiers then engaged in widespread looting and pillaging of the Byzantine inhabitants whom they were purportedly protecting from the Turks. Furthermore, the Catalan Company hired 3,000 Turkic horsemen, which helped create the perception among Byzantines that the Company was now little more than a troop of brigands.

De Flor also sought to establish a separate state in Anatolia that he would rule, a challenge that meant war with Byzantium. The latter handed the Company a defeat, this time with the help of Alan mercenaries. They slew de Flor on April 30, 1305, along with 300 knights and 1,000 infantrymen. A depleted Catalan force of only 206 horsemen and 1,256 infantrymen with no real leader, however, still managed to defeat a larger army led by the son of the Byzantine emperor in July, 1305. For two more years, the Company proceeded to devastate Thrace and Macedonia. Since the Company was such a powerful force in its own right, several European states offered to employ it. In 1310, a new Company leader, Roger Deslaur, also a Catalan, offered the services of the Company to the duke of Athens. The Company defeated the duke's enemies, but the latter refused to pay his hirelings or was unable to do so, so the Company then eliminated the duke of Athens and his army in March of 1311. The Company now controlled the duchy of Athens and the city of Thebes. In 1318, it expanded its power into Thessaly in northern Greece, and took control of the duchy of Neopatria in central Greece, a duchy that had been established by crusaders after the western conquest of Byzantium during the Fourth Crusade early in the 13th century. Company rule of Neopatria lasted until 1390, when it was finally defeated by the Navarrese Company, another mercenary army of Catalans hired by Florentines and Corinthians. The Corinthians then controlled the Catalan Company until 1456, when it was defeated in battle by the Ottoman Turks. It then proceeded to fade out of history, as was the case with the other medieval, mercenary armies.

It was in medieval Italy that the use of private mercenary armies became most widespread. Called *condottieri*, the leaders of these armies were employed by the papacy and the north Italian city-states. The latter included such states as Venice, Florence, and Genoa, made wealthy from trade but which, nevertheless, fielded only small armies. The first source of mercenary soldiers came from the returning veterans of the Crusades. Unemployed, desperate men, they often behaved as brigands until rehired. Other soldiers came from all over western Europe to serve in these private armies, men from Spain, France, Germany, England, Bohemia and, of course, Italy. They served in armies with such names as the Company of the Dove, the Ventura Company, the Great Company, the Company of St. George, the White Company, the Star Company, the Little Hat Company, and the Company of the Rose. From the 15th century onwards, most leaders of these armies were landless Italian nobles who chose the profession of arms as a livelihood and way of life. A well-paid profession, even non-officer mercenaries were paid as much as half of what officers were paid, which made this employment most interesting to commoners. Still, the leaders of these armies had little in common with their soldiers. Most were armored cavalrymen whose greed was legendary. They were ready to switch employers without notice for higher pay. Condottieri often waged what were little more than mock battles so that no combatants actually got hurt, while the real aim was to capture prisoners who might draw lucrative ransoms or bribes. Battles were often as bloodless as they were theatrical. Splendidly equipped armies were known to fight for hours with hardly the loss of a man. Mercenary captains were treacherous, tending to avoid combat and to resolve fights with bribes. A prisoner was always more valuable than a dead enemy.

The end of condottieri fighting in Italy came in 1494 when the French royal army defeated the mercenary forces of the Italian city-states during a successful invasion of the Italian peninsula. Thereafter, condottieri leaders served throughout Europe as commanders of public armies. The Vatican's now-largely ceremonial Swiss Guards descend from a medieval mercenary army to which members still come from all over the world to serve the pope. These private armies often were out of control, and wont to loot and pillage towns and peasants just as much as they served their employing states.

A final type of medieval warfare were the private vendettas and feuds among noblemen that grew to become veritable wars. These had innumerable causes—personal slights, family squabbles, economic competition, blood vendettas over murdered relatives—that could result in private wars that would spill over to affect the common people, the innocent peasant and townsfolk bystanders. These wars were legion in the Middle Ages, occurring from the early Middle Ages to the end of the late Middle Ages.

Here is an example of one of these private wars. Friesland is the northwesternmost region of the Netherlands. Throughout the 14th and 15th centuries, the region was the site of persistent warfare between two noble families, the *Vetkopers* and the *Schieringers*. The Vetkopers were based in the eastern part of Friesland, the Schieringers in the west. There was a peculiarity to the conflict, moreover, since each side was associated with rival monastic orders; the farming Cistercians supported the Schieringers, while the Norbertine monks, who raised livestock, supported the Vetkopers. This suggests that there might have been at base an economic competition between the two antagonist families of some unknown nature.

What is most important is that without a strong central authority, rival noblemen were free to make their own law. The Friesland conflict went on for almost two centuries until a visible government set laws, peace, and taxes, but only at the end of the 15th century and with much difficulty. As the late Middle Ages proceeded, moreover, private warfare among nobles actually increased in some lands, for example, in the Germanies. The Israeli scholar, Gadi Algazi, provides a most interesting analysis of the phenomenon, perhaps applicable to the Frisian example above. Private warfare among the nobility, according to Algazi,

> was not a mere remnant of a more primitive age but a prevalent, codified practice which had little to do with the early medieval blood feud. In the 15th century, feuds seem to have increased. Every properly-conducted feud enabled the warring parties to open a series of well-rehearsed moves, beginning with a formal declaration, then openly raiding villages, plundering livestock and any movable property, burning down villages, and raping peasant women. The parties did not take unnecessary risks... the warriors never encountered each other on the battlefield. They focused on exhausting their rivals' economic and human resources by raiding their peasants, and waited for the counter-attack to take place until the conflict was resolved, sometimes with a compromise restoring their honor. (p. 254-255)

Algazi argues that the whole process seems to have served the purposes of keeping peasants in their place, making them "... recognize who they really were by reversing a process of material accumulation and social transformation." (p. 254) Indeed, the social and economic position of the common people vis-à-vis the nobility improved greatly after the Black Death during the mid-14th century. Lords' private warfare seemed to play a role of safeguarding their social position by justifying the perceived necessity for protection for commoners while, at the same time, attempting to reverse the economic advances of the common people.

The Peace of God/Truce of God Movements

By the end of the first millennium, the prospects of social change associated with the high Middle Ages were in the air. The first, underlying social problem, however, was to limit or control the warfare endemic to the period. In 989, the Church began what is known as the Peace of God movement in an attempt to control medieval warriors. The movement began in southern France, where chaos reigned after the collapse of the Carolingian empire. Local lords and knights fought with reckless abandon trying to establish control over southern France. In response to clerical invitations to the Benedictine abbey of Charroux, a great crowd of people gathered. They brought body parts and relics of saints to an assemblage of local clergymen who were determined to apply spiritual sanctions to out-of-control warriors. Excommunication from the Church and its grace and sacraments were to be the lot for warriors who attacked or robbed peasants, who struck, robbed, or seized clergymen or nuns, who invaded churches, who beat the defenseless, or who burnt property and homes. Later on, women and children were added to the list of people protected by the Peace of God, as were merchants.

The movement soon spread throughout Europe. In 1027, there also began an associated movement known as the Truce of God in Catalonia and southern France, which aimed to limit warfare among Christians by setting aside certain days of the year where violence was not permitted such as Sundays, holy days, Fridays, and Lent. This movement too spread throughout Europe; the two movements came to be viewed as one, part of a régime of protection by the Church of the socially inferior that lasted into the 13th century.

Unfortunately, the Peace of God and the Truce of God were observed mostly in their breach. They were impossible to enforce without arms or centralized states with real authority and jurisdiction. A sign of this is that they had to be renewed continually since they were so often ignored or defied. Nevertheless, they set a precedent to be followed by other measures of Church sanctions to out-of-control warriors. They also contributed to creating public zones of safety around Church properties. These safe zones permitted the erection of villages and towns that benefitted from local protection provided by the Church.

Medieval Chivalry

The codes of chivalry developed during the Peace and Truce of God period were another means of orienting the military, social, and religious behavior and obligations of the lordly and knightly classes. According to the Catholic Encyclopedia, New Advent:

> In early Christianity, although Tertullian's teaching that Christianity and the profession of arms were incompatible was condemned as heretical, the military career was (still) regarded with little favor. In chivalry, religion and the profession of arms were reconciled.

Even before the Peace/Truce of God period, the first abbot of the French monastery of Cluny, St. Odo, had written about the capacity of the sword to be used for sacred purposes in his hagiography of St. Gérard of Aurillac. This new attitude was enforced with the Peace/Truce of God movement and with the Crusades, when the Church urged upon the warrior class the taking and defense of the Holy Land as a sacred mission. The Church had a role in conferring knighthood since anything in the Middle Ages that involved swearing oaths, as men had to do when they joined the knightly ranks, required the participation of the Church. The Church took this chance to get knights to swear to ten things, the so-called 'ten commandments' of knighthood. They included the following: believing the teachings, and observing the directions of the Church; defending the Church; respecting and defending the weak; loving one's native land; facing the enemy directly without shirking; making war against the Infidel (Muslims and pagans); performing one's feudal duties completely; telling the truth; being generous; and being the champion of the right and the good in the battles against injustice and evil. (Medieval Spell, p. 1)

> The most important and most sacred of them was the first commandment. The thought of God filled knights' hearts, and the main part of the medieval knight's service was due to the Church. He was brought up in the use of her sacraments, and in obedience to her precepts and reverence for her ministers. The crusader, the Templar, the Hospitaller were champions of the Church against the Infidel. The knight's consecration to chivalry was after the form of a sacrament, and to defend the Church was part of his vow of initiation. (Medieval Spell, p. 2)

After the Crusades, the religious aspect of chivalry came to be downplayed as chivalry came to be part of secular social, courtly, and romantic lore and codes of behavior. Codes of knightly chivalry also came to be surpassed by the evolution of military practices. During the Hundred Years War, infantry grew to be a more important element of warfare than mounted cavalry. At the battles of Crécy and Agincourt, fought respectively in France in 1346 and 1415, English commoner archers destroyed the best of French knighthood. Similarly, in Switzerland in the 14th and 15th centuries, peasant armies were able to win their freedom in battle against Austrian and Burgundian nobility and knights.

The great medieval writers, Chaucer and Cervantes, especially the latter in his *Don Quixote*, subjected the knightly class and its codes of chivalry to satire, making them the object of buffoonery. (New Advent, p. 4, p. 5) This perhaps signaled that the Church's actions had contributed to social change since the warrior class did experience some domestication.

Crusades

> The most important attempts to orient the behavior of the warrior class were the Crusades. First preached by one of the leading churchmen of his time, St. Bernard of Clairvaux, a French Cluniac monk, as well as the popes, the aim of the Crusades was to free the Holy Land of Muslim rule, for which the crusaders were promised absolution from their sins, and were guaranteed entry to heaven if they died in battle.

> Other motives, of course were added to religious ones: the spirit of adventure; the hope of carving out new estates and principalities, especially attractive to younger sons of the feudal nobility, who were

largely disinherited by the principle of primogeniture; the diplomacy of the Byzantine emperors, who needed military help against the Turks; the commercial ambitions of a few Italian towns all contributed to the Crusades... (McNeill, 1986, p. 277)

While the Crusades were the best example of the Church's attempt to orient the military class to holy purposes, it is also true that the Crusades had enormous consequences for the economic and social development of Europe, which we explore below. The Crusades to the Middle East are the best-known, however, there were still other Crusades preached by the Church that affected the behavior of the warrior class: the northern Crusades, the Albigensian Crusade against exponents of the Cathar heresy in southern France, and still other minor, local crusades preached against heretics. The northern Crusades, first preached by Pope Celestine III in 1193, had the object of converting the pagan tribes who lived on the shores of the Baltic Sea. They were conducted during the 12th and 13th centuries by the Christian kingdoms of Denmark and Sweden, to whom the prospect of new colonies was an equal motivation, and by two orders of north German, Christian warrior-monks. The Germans included the Teutonic Order, which first fought in the Crusades in the Middle East, and the Livonian Brothers of the Sword, founded in 1202 in Latvia for the purpose of creating a lasting Christian presence in the Baltic region. There were even unsuccessful campaigns against Orthodox Russians conducted by Swedish and German Catholic armies. Against their will and with much bloodshed, indigenous Baltic tribes; the Old Prussians, the indigenous people of Prussia; the Slavs of northeast Germany; and the Estonians and the Finns were all converted to Christianity.

The Albigensian Crusade was preached by Pope Innocent III. It was an attempt to eliminate a heresy known as Catharism that had grown up in southeast France as part of the popular dissatisfaction with the temporal power and wealth of the Church. Catharism was a sect with a Manichean philosophy that was an offshoot of the similar Bogomil church in the Balkans. It might have been introduced to France by returnees from the Middle East Crusades. The 20-year campaign against the Cathars was taken up by nobility and kings from the north of France between 1209 and 1229. While Innocent III's ambitions were religious with respect to Catharism, this was less the case for the northern French nobility. They seized upon the opportunity to bring lands under their control that had been hitherto under Catalan and Aragonese control. Sadly, the crusade also greatly diminished the distinct Occitan culture of southeastern France, even if the crusade did encounter resistance from the people of the region.

Joining the Fray—Christian Warrior-Monks

Another tactic employed by the Church in its effort to control the warrior class was to join the fray of knighthood itself. This involved the creation and sanctioning of warrior-monk orders established to do the Church's bidding, and to serve as examples of chivalrous, just, and Christian behavior by the knightly class. We've already met two of these orders when discussing the northern crusades, the Livonian Brothers of the Sword in Latvia and the Teutonic Order from northern Germany, in addition to the well-known Templars and the Hospitallers that were created for the Middle East crusades. In actual fact, there were thirty or so of these orders of military monks established during the period, 1000–1500. The first such order, established in 1075, only ceased to exist in 1459. This was the Order of Saint James of Altopascio in Tuscany that served the *Via Francigena*, the pilgrimage route from Canterbury, England through France, Switzerland, and Italy ending in Rome. In addition to its mission of protecting pilgrims, the Order also operated hospitals. The last military order to be introduced during the Middle Ages was the Order of St. George, founded in Rome by Pope Alexander VI in 1498. According to the website of the Canadian priory of the Order of St. George, the original, five-year mission of the Order of St. George was to defend the Papal States on the Adriatic coast from pirates.

Church Structures and Hierarchy

An even better bet for both spreading and protecting Christianity and for confronting the warrior class was the development of the Church's own structures and hierarchy. These might help the Church escape the control and blandishments of local warlords. Recall from earlier chapters the development of early Church structures. The office of presbyter or elder or priest did not exist in early Christianity. Local churches were led by bishops, assisted by deacons who helped with services or administration. Bishops were elected by local Christians. From the beginning, the Church and its bishops had temporal powers, partly owing to their charitable and social missions, partly owing to the bishop's role as *defensor civitatis* within the Roman empire, partly owing to the imperial support of Christianity from the fourth century onwards.

Even before the Church became the imperial religion, however, ascetics in Syria and Egypt withdrew from the urban society where Christianity was first established to live alone in the desert with the aim of returning to a purer Christianity untainted by temporal concerns. Individual hermits such as St. Anthony were joined by followers. Pachomius of Egypt established rural communities of men devoted to the same pursuit of a purer Christianity, but supported by the benefits and solidarity of groups. A similar process occurred among women under the leadership of the sister of Pachomius, Marie, who established three convents in Egypt. ("Pachomius: 292-346")

In Europe during the fourth century, the first monastery was founded by Martin of Tours, a former Roman soldier in southern France. More or less against Martin's will, awed local Christians named him bishop. This was representative of the way Christianity grew early in the first millennium.

Local missionaries or bishops or other holy people were first revered by local Christians. After the death of these people, their bodies or parts thereof, or even objects that came into contact with the holy person, were regarded as holy relics with mystical, miraculous powers. Tombs of the saints or their remains became sites of shrines in the pagan manner of establishing shrines at holy places in nature such as at sacred trees, rocks, waters, etc. The shrines would become sites for local pilgrimage by people praying for favors from the dead saint. In time might be added altars, chapels, churches, abbeys and convents, and even cathedrals eventually, all to serve as sites of reverence for the local saint. As the number of churches multiplied and villages were established, bishops and deacons could not meet all local needs, so the position of parish priest became important, serving as a focus for the Church and for offering services including the Eucharist and other sacraments. While these priests might sometimes be intelligent, educated men, for the most part parish priests were uneducated, rural bumpkins who learned the sacramental Latin rites by rote without understanding their meaning or content. Nonetheless, parish priests became essential elements in the organization of the Church in the West, supervised and led by local bishops that came to be appointed by the Church hierarchy and not by local parishioners.

At the most senior level of the Church was the bishop of Rome, the Pope, who tried to assert his ascendancy over all Christianity, an assertion that was rejected nonetheless by the bishops of Antioch in Syria and Alexandria in Egypt, each of whom held jurisdiction in their regions. These bishops were joined later as metropolitans by the bishops of Constantinople and Jerusalem, and then from still other capitals as Orthodoxy spread in eastern Europe. This division of jurisdiction became the kernel from which the Orthodox churches and other eastern Christian churches evolved.

Improving the saliency of the bishop of Rome and the ultimate objective of the supremacy of a universal, Catholic Church ran into another formidable obstacle, the control of the position of pope by the Roman nobility. In particular, the papacy came to be controlled by the counts of Tusculum, the most powerful secular lords in Latium, near Rome, from the 10th to the 12th centuries. In the 11th century at the beginning of the high Middle Ages, the counts of Tusculum arranged for several popes to be selected from their ranks. They created and perfected the formula of noble-papacy whereby the pope was arranged to be elected only from the ranks of the Roman nobles. This was also the period of papal history known as the Pornocracy, the period of influence by powerful female members of the Tusculum family, who also chose and supplied papal mistresses.

Known subsequently as the 'rule of the harlot', the Tusculum papacy came to an end with the appointment of Pope Leo IX in 1049. In reaction to the Tusculum period, the Church embarked on the Gregorian reform in the latter half of the 11th century. With this reform, both the papacy and the Church at local and state levels conspired to escape the clutches of control by secular warlords and rulers. Leo IX, himself an Alsatian nobleman, initiated the reforms by insisting that his appointment as pope by the Holy Roman emperor be confirmed by the people and clergy of Rome in order to become legitimate. Leo tried to reinstate the principle of clerical celibacy to preserve clerics from temporal temptations and concerns, and tried to arrest the practice of simony whereby Church offices were sold to the highest bidder, usually noblemen or their adult offspring. In 1059, the Burgundian Pope Nicholas II established new rules for the election of popes including creating the College of Cardinals. This body of leading bishops united in Rome in a conclave at the death of a pope to elect their new leader, rather than being beholden to the local lords in Rome for the selection of the pope.

The same struggle to free the papacy of the control of Italian nobility proceeded apace at the local level in Europe. Bishops were often chosen by local secular noblemen such as the local count or a regional duke or even the king. One possible avenue for countering this control was the monastic movement. Of course, from its beginnings, monasticism was an implied criticism of the temporal power and worldly wealth of the Church. In the sixth century, the rule of the Italian, St. Benedict, spread into hundreds of monasteries and convents of western Europe, just as the rule of St. Basil had done in Byzantium. The Benedictine reform contained much that was social in nature, including the requirement that monks had to work and its communal organization, in addition to the asceticism and prayer normally associated with monasteries. According to Robert Nisbet, an American sociologist,

> We should find it very difficult to account for the fertility of Christianity in producing its great complex of reform and even revolutionary movements, apart from the ethic of brotherhood, community, and service to the social order that sprang, in the first instance, from the rule though which the great Benedict sought to show and preserve what he regarded was the very essence of the Christian community. (p. 146)

This was all well and good for the beginnings of the Benedictine movement but at the same time during the first millennium, Europe was being subjected to attacks from Magyars and Vikings. Moreover, since the feudal system developed in the absence of central state authority, local warlords grew to have an inordinate role in the selection of churchmen, including abbots and abbesses of monasteries and convents. This owed to the fact that the lords came to control the ownership and disposition of local lands. As well, the Church often received the movable wealth of the community to protect it from plunder by raiders, which added to the need for the Church to seek protection from local warlords. Thus, bishops and abbots came under even more pressure to be selected by these warlords, who often named their daughters and younger sons disenfranchised by the practice of primogeniture to positions in the Church hierarchy. So, just as the leaders of monasteries and convents might serve as lords of a locality, they were often also feudal vassals of the local, secular nobility.

This seemed to be the case throughout much of western Europe regardless of when areas became Christian. For instance, in sixth century Ireland, the local chieftains who became the local nobility controlled monastery leadership, just as this also was happening in France and elsewhere on the continent. (Sorabella) During the beginnings of Christianity in 12th century Denmark, the same situation of control of the local Church by secular nobility existed, at least until the 13th century when local clergy started confronting the Danish state and nobility.

A potential solution to this problem came with the Cluniac monastic movement. The movement was initiated by a man known as William the Pious, duke of Aquitaine in southwest France, who established the first monastery near Cluny with the unusual stipulation that the monastery report directly to the pope rather than to the local lord, actually William himself. This guaranteed the practical independence of the monastery since it was far from Rome, even while the Cluny monasteries received the strong support of Pope Urban II, the same pope who preached the first Crusade. Over a thousand daughter-houses of Cluny were established in France, England, Spain, and Italy wherein ultimate authority rested with the Abbot of Cluny rather than with local noblemen. The Cluniacs were strong supporters of the Peace of God and Truce of God movements. Unlike earlier Benedictines, however, rather than performing manual labor themselves, the Cluniacs hired workers and stewards in order to preserve themselves for prayer, contemplation, and intellectual pursuits, among them, the development of a rich liturgy that used vessels of gold, fine tapestries, and stained glass to fill their churches. Partly owing to this, the Cluniacs became wealthy. This inevitably provoked a reaction from some who wanted to return to the poverty and manual labor of the original Benedictines. So, in 1098, St. Bernard of Clairvaux and 21 monks from Cluny established another order of monks on marshland at Cîteaux in France, and founded the Cistercian order. The Cistercians were followed by still more orders who found the Cistercians still not ascetic enough, for example, the Carthusians. So on and on the process continued of creating new orders or offshoot orders in the Middle Ages, in fact, right into modern times, always with the aim of returning to the seemingly fleeting goal of holy poverty. Nonetheless, the Cluniacs had established a principle that monasteries, henceforth, could be independent from local lords, reporting only to the popes. This also helped increase the power of the papacy.

The Gregorian Reform

As part of its effort to free the papacy from the clutches of the Roman nobility, the Church sought a strategic alliance with the German Holy Roman Empire, an echo of an earlier alliance between the Church and the Carolingian empire. However, soon afterward, the emperor began selecting popes, and otherwise interfering with the work of the Church. The Gregorian reform of the latter half of the 11th century aimed at ending this interference, establishing once and for all the independence of the Church, and even proclaiming superiority over secular structures such as the state. One of the most important proponents of these reforms was Ildebrando Benizi, son of a Tuscan blacksmith. He became a leading papal administrator then pope with the papal name of Gregory VII. His work during his reign as pope between 1073 and 1085 was based on his conviction that the Church was founded by God, and entrusted with the task of embracing all mankind in a single society in which divine will is the only law. God is supreme over all structures, including the secular state; the pope is the vice-regent of God on earth, so that disobedience to the pope implies disobedience to God or defection from Christianity.

In practice, Gregory accepted that states did have a role to play, but they were inferior ultimately to the Church and the papacy. His 1079 papal bull, *Libertas ecclesiae*, insisted upon Church independence from secular authorities. In his *Dictatus papae* in 1075, Gregory claimed that:

> The Roman pontiff alone is rightly called universal; he alone has the power to depose and reinstate bishops; he alone may use an imperial insignia; all princes shall kiss the foot of the pope alone; he has the power to depose emperors; he can be judged by no one; no one can be regarded as Catholic who does not agree with the Roman Church; he has the power to absolve subjects from their oaths of fealty to wicked rulers. (Baldwin, p. 182, 183, as quoted in the World History Project, "The Church in the high Middle Ages")

For obvious reasons, secular rulers from counts to kings and emperors, were extremely displeased with Church claims. From the time of the fourth-century emperor, Constantine the Great, rulers had selected churchmen, everyone from bishops and abbots and abbesses to popes, metropolitans, and patriarchs. The most important of these rulers was the Holy Roman emperor who ruled Germany and northern Italy. As far back as Otto the Great in the tenth century, the emperor emphasized his dual leadership of Church and state. Otto argued that he was the "...successor of Augustus, Constantine, and Charlemagne." (World History Project, as per above) In Germany, the practice of feudal lords and kings naming Church officials was most advanced, so much so that "the German church, in essence, was a state church."(Source as per above) In 1075, Pope Gregory formally prohibited lay investiture of churchmen, and threatened both rulers and clergy with excommunication if they dealt in the practice. The battle was joined with German emperor Henry IV. The popes finally did manage to increase the store of the papacy after the struggle had continued for years without resolution. In 1122, the issue was finally resolved with the Concordat at Worms in Germany whereby...

> The Church maintained the right to select the holder of an ecclesiastical office, but only in the presence of the king or his representative. The candidate...was invested by the king with the scepter, the symbol of his administrative jurisdiction, after which he performed the act of homage, and swore allegiance as the king's vassal. Only after this ceremony...was the candidate consecrated by the archbishop, who invested him with the ring and pastoral staff. (Source as per above)

This arrangement had already been accepted by the kings of England and France, and it now was accepted by the emperor of Germany and northern Italy. The Concordat dramatically increased the independence and legitimacy of the Church vis-à-vis lay rulers. By the turn of the 13th century, papal power reached its zenith. Pope Innocent III, originally an Italian aristocrat named Lotario dei Conti, who had been a Church lawyer and administrator, so successfully wielded his spiritual, administrative, and political power that the rulers of many European states actually became his vassals. He won major power struggles with Prince John of England and King Philip Augustus of France. He intervened in a civil war about succession to the Holy Roman throne, eventually securing the election of his ward, Frederick II. The administrative and legal systems of the papacy under his reign were far advanced of those of secular states, and he had skilled and mobile manpower to effect local political and religious decisions. His most powerful weapons, however, even if spiritual in nature were excommunication and interdict. The latter denied services and sacraments to the faithful in polities where rulers offended Rome. "Pope Innocent III successfully applied or threatened the interdict 85 times against disobedient kings and princes." (Source as per above) Until the end of the 13th century, the Church continued to grow in power and wealth, eventually possessing about a third of lands in Europe, while controlling the lives of the peasant-serfs who farmed these lands, so much so that it would eventually provoke popular resistance.

Medieval Churches in Eastern Europe and the Middle East

Entirely different dynamics obtained in the relationships of church, state, and the nobility in the east. The Orthodox Church and the eastern Roman empire were united under an ideology called *symphonia*, whereby the two institutions were to play complementary, interdependent roles where mutual respect was to be displayed with regard to the responsibilities of each institution. In actual practice, the emperor convoked councils of churchmen, resolved theological and other disputes including guiding the thorny Christological debates, and enacted Church laws and policies. This state-church relationship dated to Constantine himself when Christianity was on its way to becoming the official religion of the empire. The relationship lasted mostly undisturbed until the tenth century.

As for the nobility, while Byzantium did have an aristocracy as did all Middle Ages societies, the number of nobles, in fact, was quite small. One estimate has it that there were only 145 aristocratic families in the Byzantine empire during the 11ᵗʰ and 12ᵗʰ centuries. Noblemen from these families were engaged in civil administration or military leadership on behalf of the empire. Many of the emperors themselves came from aristocratic ranks, even if they might have come to imperial power by such actions as *coups d'état*, local rebellions, or palace revolutions. There were few indigenous, independent noblemen striving to dominate the Church locally as there were in western Europe. For the Orthodox Church in Byzantium, the most important relationships were with the central state. One dynamic that brought change to these relationships was the movement for independence from the empire that occurred in Serbia and Bulgaria. Thereafter, pressures were applied for the independence of local churches even if communion within the Orthodox Church was maintained. Thus, so-called autocephalous, Orthodox churches were first established in Serbia and Bulgaria, a pattern that was to be repeated for the countries that developed from the shell of Kievan Rus'— Russia, Belarus, and the Ukraine—as well as Romania and Georgia.

The Church of the East that resulted from the Christological dispute with Nestorius is not really a factor in the medieval history of the Occident, even if its geographic breadth at its greatest range stretching from the Mediterranean to China including India, central Asia, and the Mongol world was truly awesome. This is because the fifth century dispute between Church and Nestorius led to most of the Syriac followers of Nestorius being exiled from the eastern Roman empire to Persia, where they joined with existing Christians in Mesopotamia to form what is known in modern times as the Church of the East. There, the principal dynamic at play during the Middle Ages was survival as a minority, even if usually protected in the Islamic world. When political conditions became more unfavorable in the late Middle Ages, however, the Church was reduced from its impressive geographic range to small, remaining communities in Upper Mesopotamia and India.

A similar dynamic was at play with the autocephalous churches of the communion of Oriental Orthodoxy such as the Copts of Egypt, the Syriac Orthodox Church in Syria, and the Armenian Apostolic Church. The tendency that came to be known as Oriental Orthodoxy resulted from a Christology distinct from that of Catholics, Orthodox, and the Church of the East. For these churches, the driving medieval problematic was survival in a minority situation in the Muslim world. Most of the time, they were respected as people of the book, *dhimmi*, who had to pay a special tax, and were not allowed to engage in converting others to their faith. For the most part, while their rights normally were respected, they could be subjected to persecution from time to time when relations soured with the Muslim majority, including being subjected to conversions to Islam, sometimes forced or encouraged by the state.

Intellectual and Moral Reform

With its campaigns of intellectual and moral reform, the Catholic Church thoroughly changed European society, making it Christian through and through save for areas under Muslim control and for Jewish minorities, the latter often embattled and persecuted. In terms of intellectual developments, we must mention canon law; the emergence of universities originally associated with cathedrals; scholasticism, the effort to align reason and divine revelation; the Church and education; and the creation of the Dominican and Franciscan orders of friars, among other similar orders.

Canon law applied to clergy but also to lay society since it dealt with such matters as apostasy, simony, heresy, administration of the sacraments, and matters where the swearing of oaths was involved. The last of these responsibilities meant that the Church adjudicated matters of marriage, inheritance, disputes among the clergy or lay faithful, and even appointments to knighthood and monarchy. The development of canon law also served as a guide to the development of secular, civil law.

Universities were first established as cathedral schools for the training of clergy. Their physical association with the Church afforded them protection from the secular nobility. Universities may have been inspired by the Muslim example of *madrassahs* associated with mosques. In fact, the first degree-granting institution in the West was Al Karaouine in Fez in Morocco, established in 859. In 1150, the Sorbonne was established in Paris, while Oxford had already opened in 1096 for the study of theology, philosophy, and preparation for the priesthood. University education ultimately led to an overall improvement in the quality of the priesthood including parish priests. Rebel scholars from Oxford founded Cambridge University in 1209. Early in the 14th century, Oxford housed about 1,500 teachers and students, among them 84 Franciscan and 90 Dominican friars, the latter order being especially committed to learning and debate. One Oxford Franciscan was Roger Bacon, a leading scientist and mathematician of the 13th century. (Somerville) The University of Bologna was established in 1088 to specialize in the study of civil law rather than philosophy or theology.

The Church's sway over education meant that it would teach the coming generations of nobility in order to make them more amenable to the needs of the Church and Christian society. The Church also was a leading contributor to the cultural renaissance of the 12th and 13th centuries. Arts such as poetry, literature, music, and architecture were imbued with the Christian spirit as were intellectual pursuits in science, philosophy, political theory, theology, and law.

In 1231, Pope Gregory IX arranged for the independence of cathedral universities from all control, secular or ecclesiastical, other than from that of the pope himself. The circumstances of the reform were most unusual. The Sorbonne was one of the oldest universities in Europe, founded for the study of theology. Its students were under the administration of the Church, and were treated as clerics not subject to the laws of the king or the city of Paris. Students at the Sorbonne were often rowdy; many were adolescent sons and young men of the nobility. They often engaged in age-old activities of university students, drinking and partying. In March of 1229 during a drinking bout on Mardi Gras in a Paris suburb, a dispute about a bill between partying students and a tavern operator led to a fight whereby the students were beaten and thrown into the streets. In revenge, the students returned the next day with clubs, broke into the tavern and destroyed it, beating their rivals from the night before, and damaging neighboring shops in an ensuing riot. The Church protected their charges, but the regent ruling France during the childhood of the future King Louis IX authorized the city guardsmen to punish the students. The guards found a troop of students, and killed several students none of whom had been involved in the riot. In response, the university went on strike by closing for two years, thus depriving the local economy of the considerable spending and consumption of masters and students. Finally, the pope, himself an alumnus of the Sorbonne, issued a bulla that guaranteed civil and ecclesiastical independence for the university, even authorizing university masters to initiate strikes for a wide range of offences against the institution and its students and masters.

The moral reform of Christian society affected all manner of endeavor: private, public, and social. In addition to its traditional role of providing charity, social services, and hospitals, the Church continued to encourage pilgrimages such as the treks to Rome and to Santiago de Compostella in northwest Spain, alleged site of the remains of the apostle James. We've already discussed the moral reform by which the Church tried to suppress clerical concubinage and simony. The Church also sanctioned the Dominican and Franciscan mendicant orders that had been created to live and work in towns and cities in response to criticism about Church wealth and power. Development of reverence for Mary, the mother of Jesus, as a guiding light to knights suffused warriors and civil society with nobler ideas about women. The Age of Faith was also reflected in the annual calendar whereby social, cultural, and work life was organized around the liturgy of holy days and saints' days, and in the construction of the numerous parish churches and magnificent cathedrals for religious devotion, as well as being works of art themselves.

A special tool for exacting correct Christian behavior and belief was the infamous Inquisition, a special papal court established in 1233 to combat heresy. The World History Project describes its workings.

> Those accused were tried in secret without the aid of legal counsel. Those who confessed and renounced heresy were reconciled with the Church on performance of penance. Those who did not confess voluntarily could be tortured. If that failed, the prisoners could be declared heretics, and turned over to the secular authorities, usually to be burnt at the stake. A rationalization for torture was that the soul was considered incomparably more important than the body, therefore, it was believed

that torturing a suspected heretic was justifiable if confession could save the soul. (p. 4)

The inquisitors proved to be none other than members of the Dominican order, which had been created to use learning and debate to counter the plague of heresy in urban areas. While the Church did not have the power of secular governments, it usually could find secular rulers willing to execute the faithless or heretical on behalf of the Church, even if it was often for their own non-religious, more political purposes. In fact, beginning in the 13th century, if its spiritual tools were inadequate to the job of enforcing the will of the Church, the pope even had access to mercenary armies, while many bishops also engaged their own armies. One example of many such bishops was Albert of Riga, whose German army at the turn of the 13th century was useful in forcibly converting Latvian tribes to Christianity.

By the end of the high Middle Ages, the Church was not the timid and submissive institution vis-à-vis European states and noblemen it had been during the early Middle Ages. It was a feared and wealthy power that had transformed European society from top to bottom as part of its mission of Christianization. This same wealth and power, however, was to prove the cause of much popular resistance in the Middle Ages, as we shall see in the next chapter.

Medieval Economic Development

The European warlords and their power and wealth came to be overwhelmed by the forces of development of the medieval church and state. In addition, the European warlords of the Middle Ages eventually were overwhelmed by the forces created by medieval economic growth and social change during the Middle Ages, which we now consider.

Proto-Feudalism

The Middle Ages featured the social organization commonly known as feudalism, however, before considering the nature of feudal society and its economy, we should recall some of the roots from which feudalism developed. Australian medievalist Paul Budde is useful for this purpose. Budde relates that the Roman emperor Diocletian had organized certain public responsibilities incumbent upon wealthy landowners such as administration of justice and tax collection while, at the same time, peasant farmers increasingly were being tied to the land they worked for fiscal and economic purposes. As the western Roman empire was declining, Franks and other German peoples adapted elements of Roman rule. The administrators of local districts, *comes civitatis*, evolved to become counts, responsible for local rule. The military leaders known by the Latin term *dux* evolved to become medieval dukes, while some tribal chieftains became kings. The nobles closest to the kings and the most powerful were those who were able to supply the kings with warriors. They also grew to be the wealthiest owing to lands granted as gifts for military services rendered. A bishop had an official, public role as *defensor civitatis* under Roman rule. Bishops continued to have civil and legal responsibilities for their dioceses after the Germanic peoples became Christian. Warlords and knights who held land in return for military service probably numbered in the thousands in western Europe if one considers the geographic extent of the Carolingian empire. After the empire crumbled, these warlords then had to deal with the Viking and Magyar invaders, who eventually settled down to possess and govern their own lands.

There were feudal antecedents, as well, in eastern Europe during the early Middle Ages, especially among the peoples of the Pontic-Caspian Steppe. The Hun invaders of the fifth century, the Avars who settled in Pannonia to rule over local Slavs, and the Khazaris all displayed elements akin to medieval feudalism such as local chieftains distributing land in return for services provided. In the early Russian states of the Rus' Khaganate and Kievan Rus', as well as in early Poland, the *druzhina* was a retinue of warriors who guarded and served chieftains known as *knyaz*, helping them rule a principality. Senior members of the druzhina advised the prince and performed important state functions on his behalf. In Russia, these people were called *boyars*; they evolved to become the most important Russian aristocrats, owning the largest estates along with rights to tax and to administer justice to local populations. Junior *druzhinniki* were common soldiers who served as the personal bodyguard to the prince. Members of the druzhina were dependent upon the prince for financial support, but they were free to leave to serve any other prince. Thus, princes were inclined to maintain the support of druzhinas by paying wages and by sharing war booty and taxes with them, as well as rewarding them with land. Druzhinas existed in various forms into the early modern era in Czarist Russia. Similar personal retinues were also found among early Germanic tribes and in Scandinavia.

As we have seen in the early Germanic world, the exchange of gifts and service was a vital element cementing social relationships among warriors. These customs continued into the Middle Ages, even if the payment of gifts and services evolved to become formal rights and responsibilities. Writes the Russian medievalist, Aron Gurevich,

> For medieval seigneurs, exchange of gifts was no less important than the question of donations to the Church for the purpose of saving souls... Generosity is an inseparable trait of the monarch as, in general, of any great lord...As we are told in the *Romance of Lancelot*, the ruler must distribute horses and gold, raiment, prime revenues, and rich lands whereby "he loses nothing but will gain in all." In the Arthurian cycle, generosity and gifts appear as the sole factors making for cohesion among knights. (1985, p. 252)

Feudal Economy and Society

One systematic analysis of feudalism appeared in a 1956 publication edited by Rushton Coulborn. For Coulborn and his fellow writers, feudalism was a political phenomenon, a system of government rather than a socio-economic system. To Coulborn et al., the fundamental social relationship of the Middle Ages was one of lord and vassal whereby political authority was the property of an individual person, rather than that of an abstract, centralized state. Stephen Sanderson, moreover, adds that feudal relationships were associated with the creation, then political disintegration of the Carolingian empire when the empire created by Pépin disaggregated. Feudal relationships also flourished in a period that was characterized by barbarian attacks on Europe and a low level of commercial activity. (p. 136)These all contributed to the emergence of feudal relationships in western Europe towards the end of the first millennium. Moreover, medieval feudalism fused the economic and the political. "Feudalism combines landlordship with military service and, as such, leads to a political arrangement in which authority is fragmented among a variety of lords, and is thus highly decentralized." (Sanderson, p. 137) As such, necessity was the mother of invention of feudal relationships among warriors, whereby kings were able to defend their sovereignty only by sharing it along with wealth-producing lands with lower-ranking lords. This was one reason for the inherent instability and perennial warfare of the Middle Ages in Europe. Holding on to one's personal lands, wealth, power, and authority was a chancy proposition dependent upon the good faith of others. Feudal relationships first appeared in northern France; they later developed with local and regional variations in southern France, Italy, Spain, Portugal, Germany, England, Scotland, Scandinavia, and in parts of eastern Europe such as Poland, Hungary, and Russia.

During the early Middle Ages in the Slavic, Germanic, and Scandinavian worlds, river crossings were attractive trading sites for people who had settled alongside rivers. On heights near these crossings, warriors erected primitive forts such as wooden palisades around earthen mounds to serve both as lookout points and as defensive positions. During the Middle Ages, these primitive installations were improved with stone castles that housed local warlords and served to defend positions, as well as reminding the local population, peasant or otherwise, who indeed ruled should the more lowly members of the local population develop contrary notions.

Historians and lawyers in the early modern era, in attempting to understand the social functioning of feudal relationships, drew elaborate schema and definitions whereby sovereignty was shared between lords and vassals and, then once again, further down the line to lower-ranking vassals. The various ranks of the medieval nobility were well-defined in this hierarchy. It was argued that fealty was sworn by vassals to lords who granted lands to vassals while, between lord and vassal, complex contracts of loyalty were entered. This came to be the view, the prism through which the Middle Ages was analyzed.

About fifty years ago, however, this view was challenged by an American historian at the City University of New York, Elizabeth Brown. She argued that there were many regional and local differences in medieval documents and practices; that simple land ownership was widespread and sanctioned by local use and customs rather than there being a general land tenure system of fiefs granted from social superiors; that legal and semantic differences among terms were too important to allow one to generalize for the whole of Europe; and that an abstract 'ism' was not useful for analysis when historians rather should be studying the differing, concrete realities and social relationships on the ground. This was an argument amplified a generation later by an Oxford historian, Susan Reynolds. (Cheyette and Hyams) Moreover, it would be most important to include in any idea of feudal society the role of chaos and brute force by the fact of lords commanding regions and localities, states, and other polities, whether local inhabitants liked it or not. Aron Gurevich writes of the brutal exploitation of the peasantry by the warrior class extracting economic surplus in the form of rents, taxes, tolls, duties, corvée labor, etc.

> Often the poorest peasants were driven to ruin and desperation. Nor did it take the nobility long to decide to lay its hands on the wealth of townspeople as well. Medieval knights saw nothing disgraceful in relieving others of their wealth; indeed, they often boasted of their predatory skills and exploits. Respect for other people's property was not uppermost in their minds. The history of the Middle Ages is one of interminable wars and civil strife. Each and every campaign...was accompanied by pillage and rape. The seizure of wealth was followed by its distribution among one's comrades-in-arms, the bestowal of gifts upon vassals and companions, and the ostentatious consumption of whatever was left at feasts. (1985, p. 252)

Even if Brown and Reynolds might be right in questioning the validity of the concept of feudalism to define generally the society of the Middle Ages, nevertheless, we can still speak of the feudal economy and society in the Middle Ages when we consider the subjugation of the popular classes to the landowning aristocracy. Moreover, even if fiefdom in the sense of a higher noble granting land to a lower-ranking nobleman was not necessarily a frequently-used form of land tenure, vassalage might be a useful term to describe the military relationship of some warriors with their superior lord.

As one example of a society where feudal relationships occurred, 14th century England receives a useful treatment by J. P Somerville. There were about 200 lords, secular or religious. King and nobles, bishops and abbots were landlords for about 75% of England's lands. During the same period, about a thousand knights might have owned about 5% of the land. Somerville continues his description:

The other class of freemen were sokemen. Roughly, one in six of the population were sokemen, and they owned about 20% of the land...they had security of tenure provided they carried out certain defined services often including light labor services, while paying a fixed rent. Their land was heritable.

The largest class of serfs was comprised of villeins, about 40 % of the population, who did not own land, but could farm the land they occupied in exchange for labor services and shares of their production paid to the landlord. While there were regional and local variations, Somerville estimates that villeins had to work about half the time for their lords, and still more during harvest time. During the 12th century, payment of money started to replace labor services and payment of rents by shares of farm and crafts production, even if the latter did still remain as one form of payment. Lords and peasants both found it useful to convert labor services and production shares to money as agricultural wealth increased during the high Middle Ages, landlords owing to reasons of efficiency and their need for cash, peasants owing to the increased freedom offered by payment in cash.

Another lower-ranking form of serf was called a bordar or cottar. They might have numbered about a third of the population, but farmed only a small portion of the land in return for labor services. They were, in effect, virtually landless laborers. According to William the Conqueror's Domesday Book, at the very bottom of society were landless slaves called *nativi*, who numbered about 10% of the population of England at the end of the 11th century. In the next century, nativi were turned into bordars whereby they, and not their owners or landlords had the responsibility of feeding and clothing themselves and their families. Among the lower social ranks, however, there were both upward and downward social mobility depending upon changing conditions. Even knighthood was not necessarily heritable, and depended on actual prowess in battle and horsemanship.

Medieval Agriculture

The high Middle Ages produced a notable rise of agricultural productivity owing to a confluence of positive factors. There was a large population increase in western Europe which incited increased production, and resulted in more people living and thriving owing to the increased amount of food. Population doubled and even tripled in some places. Two examples: the population of what came to be modern-day France rose from about 12 million to 17 million, while the English population might have increased by as much as from about two million to possibly seven million. (Somerville) Historians and scientists describe the years 800–1300 the as the Medieval Warm Period, when temperatures rose in comparison to the previous periods. Temperatures decreased again during the period 1300–1450, a factor that helped provoke what historians call the crises of the late Middle Ages. From 1450 to 1650, temperatures rose again during the early modern period and the Renaissance, only to be succeeded in the latter half of the 17th century by a cold period known as the 'Little Ice Age'.

Contact with the more economically advanced Muslim civilization in the Iberian Peninsula, southern Italy, the Muslim-controlled Mediterranean islands, and the Middle East, exposed European agriculture to new techniques and technologies. Contact with the Muslim world also brought new markets for European production, first exploited by the city-states of northern Italy. New crops were either introduced to western Europe from the Muslim world, or were broadly diffused in the case of crops known in Europe but seldom cultivated. Just as important to European economic growth were the new attitudes and tastes in Europe owing to contact with Muslim science and culture.

There were also important agricultural innovations that helped spur increased agricultural productivity. This allowed a greater economic surplus to support urban mercantile and crafts development. For instance, in the latter centuries of the first millennium, peasants began using the three-field method of farming. Different crops were planted in two fields, while one field was left fallow. Crops and field use were rotated the following year. This meant in simplest terms that 2/3 of arable land was being used at any one time rather than half as in the two-field system of ancient times, while some land was still left for natural regeneration. Peasants also discovered that planting legumes such as peas and beans helped restore the nitrogen supply in soils.

From the Pontic-Caspian Steppe and central Asia came new techniques for horse collars and harnessing which permitted the use of horses for plowing rather than the slower and cumbersome oxen. From the Slavs came iron plows useful for the heavy soils of northern Europe, a technique that spread throughout western Europe during the last centuries of the first millennium. Increased planting of oats used for livestock production meant more meat and dairy protein in European diets as well as additional production of hides and wool. Livestock production was also a source of manure that came to be used widely as fertilizers in grain production. The wheelbarrow, a technology first seen in ancient China and possibly ancient Greece, came to be used in mining, construction, and agriculture in the late 12th century in England, France, and the Low Countries. By the late 15th century, its use seems to have become widespread in Europe. Wheelbarrow technology might have been diffused in Europe owing to contact with Muslims, who were also responsible for the spread in Europe of water-raising machines, widely employed in Muslim agriculture and milling. Historians debate whether windmill technology used for milling grains originated in the Muslim world during the first millennium, or was an indigenous development in northwestern Europe towards the end of the 12th century.

One of the greatest factors affecting agricultural growth was the increased supply of arable lands. Population increase forced Europeans to clear woods, swamps, and marshes that had hitherto been considered wasteland in order to increase the amount of arable land. Beneath these former wastelands were to be found some of the most fertile soils created by natural cycles of rotting vegetation. Nonetheless, perhaps the most important cause of the increased arable land was the increase in the size of civilized, Christian Europe. From the 11th to the mid-13th century, western Europe's frontiers expanded via the *reconquista* of Iberia; the conquest of the Muslim-held Mediterranean islands; the Norman conquest of Sicily and southern Italy; the Crusades that brought French control over Syria and Palestine; the English conquest of Wales and Scotland; and the Christian conquest of the Scandinavian, Baltic, and northwest Slavic peoples. (Wallerstein, 2011, p. 38, 39)

This expansion of civilized Europe owed to the Church-inspired efforts vis-à-vis the warrior class of calling for crusades to the Middle East, Iberia, and northern Europe. So, the class that dominated western Europe, whose persistent, endless warfare almost destroyed western Europe, was distracted and reoriented successfully by the Church to conducting warfare in other lands. In addition to the increased lands conquered and made available for western European agricultural and economic development, one shouldn't discount the benefits to Europeans of the simple absence of many of their warlords on crusades, leaving others greater freedom to pursue their own interests including economic prosperity.

In the 13th century, perhaps enabled by all this increasing agricultural productivity, great estate owners, both lay and ecclesiastical, began organizing agricultural production for sale in urban markets. Labor services extracted from peasants were increased, even doubling in some cases. In 13th century England, peasants never had been quite so exploited. Immanuel Wallerstein qualifies this period as the beginning of capitalist agriculture, which resulted in early pools of private capital for investment in economic development. The Church had been involved in economic development during the early Middle Ages by way of the relic trade, pilgrimages, and the construction of chapels and churches, monasteries and convents. During the high Middle Ages, much of increased agricultural development resulted from innovations and improvements put into place by farming and livestock-raising monasteries and convents. In addition to improved techniques, monastic institutions effected major improvements in such domains as viniculture, dairy production and cheese-making, grain production, baking, and brewing, and the treatment of wool and hides. Monastic institutions may also have been involved in the organization of guilds in Europe. Church institutions employed stewards who specified requirements for products grown or made by local populations. Establishment of local standards might have encouraged local producers to ban together to share in natural resources and markets, in effect, the beginnings of medieval guild structures. Church lawyers were important in reviving Roman law as far as land and property ownership, equality before the law, and contract law were concerned. This was to prove invaluable in assisting medieval agricultural progress and economic development generally.

The Church's contributions to the medieval economy and agriculture were important, but then so was the extraction of economic surplus from increased agricultural production. In addition to taxes paid by some kings to the papacy, the local parish structure was well-placed to benefit from the increased productivity of the peasant class through payment of regular tithes. Secondly, monastic institutions enserfed many peasants. This was the case especially for institutions such as the Cluny priories that were dedicated to prayer and intellectual pursuits rather than to labor by the monks themselves, as the original Benedictine institutions had been. Thus, the essential work of production for survival of monastic institutions and monks themselves came to require either hiring for money or enlisting local peasant labor via serfdom to the institutions.

Manorialism is the term used to describe the organizing principle for the agricultural economy during the Middle Ages. In manorialism, peasants farmed lands belonging to a lord, occupying land for which payment was made to landlords for the right to farm. As we saw earlier, while some land was held by lords in fief, that is, as a result of a land grant from a higher-ranking nobleman or Church official, there were still considerable lands owned allodially, that is, outright ownership by their occupants, whether lords or peasants. Local custom, traditions, and history played an important part in determining who occupied what lands as well as tenure arrangements of local land ownership. Generally speaking, the roots of the manorial system were the Roman *villas* owned by wealthy Romans. The villas were often accompanied by plantations, *latifundiae* worked by slaves or coloni; the latter were often ex-soldiers. Roman administrations had tried to freeze socio-economic structures as new slave sources dried up when Roman conquests were ending. The aim was to stabilize the economy and the imperial tax base in order to support the costs of the military and the ever-growing civil administration. Roman legislation had been adopted that forced sons and even sons-in-law to occupy trades worked by their fathers or fathers-in-law. Nominally free coloni were not permitted to leave their land, while their status merged with that of slaves to produce the medieval serf. Moreover, during the last three centuries of the first millennium, German, Norse, and Magyar warlords occupied and took over Roman villas and the peasants who farmed them, often using brute force or the threat thereof to seal their new ownership arrangements. Furthermore, according to a thesis of the Belgian historian, Henri Pirenne, when the Muslims closed Mediterranean and eastern trade to western Europeans, a spur was produced to both feudal relationships and autarchic manorialism in the Carolingian empire, whereby self-sufficiency on the manor came to be the rule.

A manor, or the French term, *seigneurie*, was divided into several parts according to the land tenure of its occupants. One part, the demesne, was the seigneur's land, which was farmed by the villeins who owed labor or payments-in-kind such as a portion of a harvest to the lord. With the rest of their time, serfs could farm their own land. As the high Middle Ages proceeded, both lords and serfs had incentives to commute payments-in-kind or labor services to money payments.

Typically, the manor was farmed in several fields where certain strips of land were owned by the lord and others by his serfs. A serf might have access to about 10–15 acres of land spread over several fields to plant grains and other crops for his family and himself. Livestock, livery stables, equipment, machinery, mills, wine-presses, bakery ovens, and breweries were communal property that, in actual fact, might provide additional income to the lord. For instance, grinding one's wheat at the communal mill might mean that the lord would receive a certain amount of the flour as payment for use of the mill. Sometimes, labor services were actually delivered in the form of craft work such as cobbling or smithy work. With respect to the use of communal property, it is also important to recall the prevalence of extended families that shared land, labor, and tools. The lord was the law on the manor, so fines for legal or customary offences also went to his pockets. Manorialism outlasted feudal relationships; inb fact, the manorial form of organization could support, in addition to the peasant occupants of a manor and medieval warlords, capitalist landlords such as the English gentry of the early modern era. Thus, the manor could aim at the practical self-sufficiency of its inhabitants, or it could be aimed at market production as per the Wallerstein thesis, and it could even serve as a cash-producing, capital investment for its owners.

Crises of the Late Middle Ages

By the turn of the 14th century, the economic growth of the high Middle Ages began to sputter and slow. The 14th and 15th centuries were periods of crises in agriculture and other facets of economic life, and in society in general. The initial trigger might have been the end of the Medieval Warm Period that had lasted from about 800 to 1300. This climactic change occasioned a series of famines caused by deadly cold winters and cool, wet summers. Added to these were rampant respiratory diseases and the Black Death of 1348, the infamous bubonic plague initially imported from Asia on Italian trading ships. There were now hundreds of famines, either local or generalized, that became commonplace as crops failed repeatedly. There were 95 such famines in England and 75 in France in the late Middle Ages. Perhaps as much as half the European population disappeared during the 14th century, while as many as 2/3 of the French population, in particular, was lost. Another important factor contributing to the economic and agricultural disarray and to depopulation was the persistent, seemingly endless warfare. During the 14th century, there were seven decade-long wars in Europe, while there were 16 such conflicts in the 15th century. This compares to a total of 19 decade-long wars in the previous three centuries.

The Great Famine of 1315–1325 marked the definitive end to increasing prosperity, both agricultural and otherwise. It affected the continent as far east as the borders of Russia and as far south as the Alps and the Pyrenees. Particularly hard hit were Britain, northern France, the Low Countries, Germany, Scandinavia, western Poland, and the western Baltic region. Famine brought with it such social ills as infanticide, cannibalism, theft, rape, murder, and other aggressive, criminal behavior. During the spring of 1315, unusually heavy rain began in much of Europe. Throughout the spring and summer, it continued to rain, and the temperature remained cool. These conditions caused widespread crop failures. Straw and hay for animals could not be cured, so there was no fodder for livestock. The price of food rose, doubling between spring and midsummer. Salt, the only way to cure and preserve meat, was difficult to obtain because it could not be evaporated in the wet weather. During the summer of 1317, the weather dried, but people were still weakened by respiratory illnesses. Much of the seed stock had been eaten. Even while a subject of historical debate, there are estimates that as much as 10% to 25% of the population in towns and cities died during the Great Famine. Then, there were the local famines; for example, there were local famines during the 14th century in France during the years 1304, 1305, 1310, 1330–1334, 1349–1351, 1358–1360, 1371, 1374–1375, and 1390.

State actions were of little use during periods of famine. Governments instituted measures that prohibited exports of foodstuffs. They condemned black market speculators, set price controls on grain, and outlawed large-scale fishing. At best, these measures proved mostly unenforceable and, at worst, they contributed to a continent-wide, downward spiral. Any grain that could be shipped eventually was taken by pirates or looters to be sold on the black market.

There also was a rise in rents and fines as landlords struggled to preserve their standard of living, adding to the travails of peasants. The crises also instigated a rise in aristocratic gangsterism and private warfare in England, Sweden, France, Germany, and Denmark as lords fought to maintain their social superiority over the lower classes. (Wallerstein, 2011, p. 47)

Towns and Cities

It would behoove us to consider once again the Muslim influence upon medieval Europe before considering the renewed urbanization in western Europe of the high Middle Ages. We've seen the effects of Islam upon the organization of medieval agriculture during the early Middle Ages, especially from the perspective of the Pirenne thesis according to which autarchy emerged in Europe because European trade westward was blocked by the Muslim presence. The Muslim effect on the rise of medieval towns and cities in Europe is more direct and evident. The work of the Korean, Jihoon Ko, is most useful when considering the Muslim effects on European towns and cities and their economies. We've argued that as much as any other effect of the Muslim influence was the change in European attitudes wrought by contact with Islam. By re-introducing ancient Greek knowledge to western Europe, the Muslims paved the way for the Renaissance that began in northern Italy during the latter half of the 15th century. In addition, Europeans were affected by Muslim advances in fields such as philosophy, art, poetry, music, architecture, mathematics, geography, medicine, anatomy, optics, chemistry, and geology. There was also the diffusion in Europe of Muslim technology such as machines used for raising water and milling as well as navigation aids such as the astrolabe and the sextant.

Advances in Muslim commerce were transmitted in Europe partly via the Jewish merchants in Islamic Iberia, the Rhadanites, who travelled far and wide. Merchants in tenth century Venice also took advantage of the trade opportunities afforded by contact with Muslims. The Venetians were followed in this trade by merchants from Genoa. Owing to the Crusades, Italian merchants were able to establish monopolies in the trade of luxury items such as silks, spices, sugar, and many other products from the Muslim world. In return, Italian merchants exported from western Europe natural resource products such as timber and minerals—gold, silver, iron—an excellent example of a metropolis-hinterland relationship between western Europe and the Muslim world. Italians also became the bankers of Europe with the wealth earned from Muslim trade. Arguably, the European bourgeoisie was partly a creation of Muslim influence. For their part, Italian noblemen rushed to make their fortunes in the growing towns and cities of Italy, forsaking their rural, agricultural life, in the process helping free manors for capitalist agriculture.

Rising agricultural productivity during the high Middle Ages meant better diets and increased longevity, including for expectant and birthing women. Thus, population doubled in western Europe. Even so, Charles Tilly reminds us of an important reality about European towns and cities.

> Although cities grew with the European population as a whole, and the number of urban places therefore multiplied, the proportion living in cities did not rise dramatically until the 19th century. The share in places of 10,000 people or more ran around six percent in 1000 and (was) still six percent in 1500...(1989, p. 572)

In other words, most people continued to be rural throughout the Middle Ages despite the continuing progress of urbanization.

The dramatic increase of agricultural productivity meant a greater economic surplus which, while it did lead to increased wealth for the aristocratic descendants of medieval warlords, also meant more resources for trade and crafts, most of which took place in urban settings. So, townspeople were able to buy farm produce brought to urban markets by peasants and their landlords, and to sell to rural people the products of urban merchants and craftsmen. Coinage became a regular method of exchange rather than payment by exchange of services, while the advent of banking meant lending, investing, depositing, and other services were now being offered in towns and cities. As well, towns and cities were magnets for runaway serfs who, if they lived for a year and a day in a town, were then deemed to be free of any masters. A German medieval saying had it that town air made one free. Town and city residents did their utmost to resist the blandishments of lords who still tried to preserve their social control over the lowly. This urbanites accomplished by the establishment of guilds and commune governments, often in return for financial payments to lords. In this resistance to medieval lords, urbanites often could count on support from kings who were happy to increase urban freedoms to help counter the sway of local lords.

There were other merchants other than those of the northern Italian towns who became great traders owing to Muslim contacts; other centers of urban proto-capitalism were found in the Low Countries, London, and northern France in such towns as Paris, Rouen, and Provins. The Flemish towns of Bruges, Ypres, and Ghent were linked to the northern Italian towns via the mountain passes through the Alps and the rivers of western Europe such as the Rhine, Seine, Weser, and Meuse. Italian-made or imported goods from Muslim lands such as silks, spices, and sugar were sold in Flanders in return for Flemish cloth that had been imported from England as wool, then transformed in Flanders. Baltic furs, honey, and timber and English tin were also exchanged for Flemish cloth. Another important Flemish industry was the curing and salting of fish. There was capitalist-controlled, cloth manufacturing in Antwerp factories as early as 1200. In Liège, Namur, and Hainault, there were businesses devoted to iron smelting and coal mining where production methods went beyond traditional craft methods. In Florence at the end of the 14th century, 200 workshops employed a total of about 30,000 workers, about a quarter of the work force of the city. (Sanderson, p. 143) By the turn of the 13th century, the city of Venice featured markets, shops, warehouses, commercial fairs, and a mint, commercial infrastructure facilities similar to those that had been initiated centuries before in Muslim towns and cities.

The positive influence of Muslim civilization upon the development of an early type of capitalism in western Europe constitutes one view held by historians. This was a so-called exogamous cause for the emergence of early capitalism. Other historians, however, maintain that it was rather the contradictions and class struggle within feudal and manorial society that led to the development of proto-capitalism as the Middle Ages progressed; this represented an endogamous cause. In response to the increased exploitation by landlords of the peasant class as the Middle Ages advanced, peasants fled from the land to the thriving towns in order to gain their freedom. The emergence of factory production controlled by merchants, of market sale of surplus farm produce, and increasing occupation of land for commercial purposes were all signs of the development of capitalism where economic and social relations occurred not only between lord and peasant but between urban masters and journeymen/apprentice craftsmen. These journeymen and apprentices became wage workers in the modern era. Once again, as with other historiographical disputes involving either/or choices, there is no reason that the facts on the ground can't prove the ultimate applicability of both theoretical explanations in the endomagous vs exogamous debate, even if there are regional variants where one or the other theory might be more applicable to given regional situations.

The Medieval Hunger for Freedom

A driving force animating townsfolk, as seen in the flight of oppressed and exploited serfs from the land to the town, was the search for freedom from the dictates of medieval landlords. Townsmen had recourse to several tools to increase their freedom. One of the earliest tools were the annual or semi-annual fairs organized to permit merchants from different locations to exchange their wares. During the high Middle Ages, fairs in Champagne in France were among the most important for the meeting of Italian and more northerly traders. Fairs were often festive and popular community affairs, during which...

> the feudal law of the region was set aside...and in its place was substituted a new commercial code called 'merchant law' (*loi marchande* in French—author). Special courts, with merchants acting as judges, settled all disputes. In England, such courts were called pie-powder courts, from the French *pied poudre*, meaning dusty feet... (of travellers, merchants, and other fair attendees—author) (World History Project, Towns in the Middle Ages, p. 1)

The importance of this seemingly innocuous point about legal jurisdiction resting with participating merchants at a fair rather than with local lords cannot be under-estimated for it gave a taste to merchants of legal control over their own interests. It is ironic that many medieval fairs actually launched by noblemen anxious to earn cash payments for granting the rights to merchants to hold fairs; in fact, this was one of the early steps in the eventual decline of the nobility.

Animated by this taste of self-government, urban merchants took steps to organize medieval *communes*, as they were known in French. Communes were self-governing municipalities where merchants administered their own courts, levied their own taxes, and issued their own coinage. Sometimes, such privileges could be purchased from the ruling lord; at other times, they were obtained through successful, violent struggles. In still other cases, kings granted communal charters with the aim of increasing their wealth and tax base, thus facilitating the development of capital. Some of this capital might then be lent with interest to kings, the better that they might pursue their conflicts and wars, often against local lords. Communes collected the king's taxes in return for local government and legal powers, including the right to select their own mayors and aldermen. As well, some kings and lords even got into the urban planning and development business, building and organizing towns for merchants and other inhabitants, while offering financial inducements to settle in these new towns. Thus, town building came to be another money-making proposition for cash-hungry lords and kings.

Antony Black proves to be a useful guide to the progress of communes. About 1070 in the Rhine Valley, oath-bound, civic communities appeared where residents vowed to defend their towns and each other in the event of military or bandit attack. Known by the Latin term, *coniurationes*, they next appeared in northern Italy, then the most populous part of Europe, during the next decade. Over the next three generations, they spread further into northern France and the Low Countries, followed by the German territories and Spain and, eventually, everywhere in Europe, from the shores of the Baltic to the Mediterranean.

> They varied in size from the great Italian and Flemish cities to the numerous small towns of Germany. Towns varied in type between those concentrating upon long-distance commerce such as Venice, Lubeck, and Genoa, those producing for export, especially of cloth, such as Florence and Cologne and the towns of the Low Countries, and... the great majority of smaller towns producing for their region. (Black, p. 45)

To what tasks did the communes set themselves? Usually, the first task was protection from warlords and bandits, often one and the same, usually behind the fortified walls of the commune. They raised citizen armies, or mercenary armies in the case of Italian cities. They taxed, minted their own coins if they were important cities, negotiated with outside authorities, wrote and amended their constitutions, administered justice, civil or otherwise, chose mayors and aldermen, and planned the further development of their towns. Some communes passed economic measures with respect to guilds, wages, and prices as well as developing policies about the supply and use of grains and farm produce from the local countryside or from abroad, or about the use and distribution of natural resources. Certain communes even operated breweries, factories, mills, or granaries. In the social area, municipalities in conjunction with the Church and guilds operated hospitals, hostels, poorhouses, schools, and universities. With respect to the last category, there were important municipally-founded universities at Basel, Cologne, and Bologna. Communes sometimes even defined their legal relationship with the local Church and its institutions. (Black, p. 46, 47)

The commune was one type of association; a second type of associations that flourished within communes were guilds, both merchant and craft. Guilds played central roles in the government of the communes. Although there seems to be little written evidence, as we argued in an earlier chapter, some sort of guild organization probably existed in Europe during the early Middle Ages. Such a proposition is reasonable if we consider the need to transmit artisan knowledge from one generation to the next in contexts where members of extended families worked in the same trades. According to the website, Medieval Spell, there is evidence that as far back as the seventh century in Merovingian France, goldsmiths and bakers were organized in associations. Guilds began to appear regularly in northern Italy during the high Middle Ages at the same time as the communal movement, that is, late in the 11th century. The first guilds were merchant guilds that

> ...ensured a monopoly of trade within a given locality. Alien merchants were supervised closely, and made to pay tolls. Disputes between merchants were settled at the guild court according to its own legal code. The guilds also tried to make sure that the customers were not cheated. They checked weights and measures, and insisted upon a standard quality for goods. To allow only a legitimate profit, the guild fixed a just price that was fair to both producer and consumer. (World History Project, 'Towns in the Middle Ages', p. 2)

Merchant guilds dominated communal government, which provided further incentive to craftsmen to form their own guilds in order to increase their own political power within towns. Craft guilds performed similar functions to the merchant guilds but in specific trades, one to each guild, whereas merchant guilds united all merchants in a town. Both types of guild played important social roles by offering charity for destitute members and their orphans and widows; by donations to hospitals, churches, and charities; and by organization of correct and dignified burial ceremonies for guild members. In ancient Rome, the members of craftsmen's colleges had worshipped patron gods or goddesses whose myths most resembled the narratives surrounding the practice and nature of individual crafts, a role that was taken over during medieval times by patron saints, for example, St. Joseph with respect to carpenters.

Legal endorsements for guilds came from European monarchies struggling to become centralized states. For instance, in 1261 the king of France appointed a wealthy bourgeois, Étienne Boileau, provost of Paris, to undertake a codification of guild practices. He arranged for the inscription of the customs and usages of guilds by interviewing senior guild members. He then described and amended the practices in the *Livre des métiers*, the Book of Trades, which then gained legal currency once approved by the king. Merchants held a privileged position in the document, which was arranged according to a hierarchy of precedence among drapers, grocers, mercers, furriers, hatters, and goldsmiths. In London in 1375, an ordinance of King Edward II required every citizen to join a trade. The regulation also transferred the right to select guild officers from ward aldermen to trading companies called livery companies operating among grocers, fishmongers, drapers, goldsmiths, and other occupations. By this, the king effectively removed some power from the municipality in order to give it directly to guild members.

Finally, the commune offered new social opportunities to women. Some medieval townswomen operated businesses and crafts organized by their own guilds, especially in such fields as brewing and weaving. Other opportunities also opened for women in towns and cities. Religious women assumed increased social roles as nuns working in various trades such as teaching, nursing, and providing charity. Still other urban holy women even became well-known mystics, visionaries, scribes, and spiritual guides.

Communes' Drive to Confederate

There was another political tool at the disposal of communes that helped increase their freedom of action relative to local lords and to kings or emperors. Communes could unite in alliances or confederations to increase their political sway. The first such known grouping was the Lombard League of northern Italian cities formed in 1167 in order to counter the influence of the Holy Roman Emperor Frederick, who was trying to assert imperial control in Italy. Member communes of the Lombard league variously included such cities as Cremona, Milan, Genoa, Bologna, Padua, Venice, Verona, Parma, and Siena, among others. This was the period of the investiture struggle between the pope and the emperor, so the pope gave his support to the Lombard league in the hope of weakening his imperial opponent. At the battle of Legano in May of 1176, the Lombard league defeated Frederick. As a result, a peace was reached whereby member communes of the league agreed to remain loyal to the German emperor in return for him accepting local control over communes. The league was revived in the first half of the 13th century when Frederick's namesake son once again tried to increase his power at the expense of the Lombard league cities and the pope. Ultimately, Frederick II was unsuccessful, getting defeated at the battle of Parma in 1249 by the northern Italian communes. The next year, the Lombard league was dissolved when the emperor died since it had outlived its purpose. Some of the member cities, however, became powerful city-states owing to their leadership in the league. Moreover, Pisa, Genoa, Milan, Florence, and Venice were able to absorb smaller communes to become independent city-state republics and regional powers. Venice remained a powerful republic with its own empire well into the early modern era after its armies conquered part of Byzantium.

Another prominent example of alliances of medieval communes is the Old Swiss Confederation. What was to become the territories of modern Switzerland were united during the 11th century under the rule of German Holy Roman emperors. Nonetheless, according to the Britannica online encyclopedia essay about Switzerland, owing to Swiss remoteness and to the gradual decline in real power of the emperor, four competing families of the local nobility gradually assumed administrative and legal responsibilities in the Swiss lands. As part of the competition among the noble families, each founded monasteries and towns to stimulate local trade and to profit from the growing European trade of merchants who travelled over the Alps through Swiss lands. By the middle of the 13th century, two noble families became extinct owing to the absence of male heirs, while the Hapsburgs of central Switzerland chased the remaining Savoy family from the Swiss lands, making themselves effective rulers of the territory. Hapsburg influence and power grew when their scion Rudolf was made Holy Roman emperor. Even after the Hapsburg power base moved eastward when they became dukes of Austria, they still wished to maintain and consolidate their lands and rights and revenues from trade through the Swiss territories. In 1291 when Rudolf of Hapsburg died, some Swiss towns were afraid that the imperial successor or his governor might try to remove the traditional rights of the towns. So, three communities—Schwyz, Uri, and Unterwalden—swore an oath of mutual defense and support in order to counter this possibility. According to an historical website of the Swiss department of foreign affairs, "similar alliances had been sworn by the various communities in central Switzerland, but this is the first one whose text has been preserved."

The Confederation reached two most interesting agreements late in the 14th century that deserve mention. The *Pfaffenbrief* of 1370 ensured free passage through the Saint Gotthard Pass through which much trans-Alpine trade travelled. It also addressed the problem of private warfare as well as submitting religious authorities to the dictates of the Confederation. The *Sempacherbrief* of 1393 imposed common rules on its member communes about the conduct of war.

The confederation ultimately was successful in its resistance to Hapsburg claims over central Switzerland. The Confederation won military victories over Austrian Hapsburg armies in 1315, 1386, and 1388. During the forty years after its first military victory, the confederation expanded to include towns such as Lucerne, Zurich, Glarus, Zug, and Bern. The Confederation was known to contemporaries by its rather prosaic name of Eight Old Places. From 1353 to 1481, membership in the Confederation remained unchanged. Each confederate commune administered its own affairs, while joint meetings were held to deal with common interests and issues. The Confederation was unique it that it eventually also included rural communities in addition to its urban members.

As we've just seen, the Confederation was obtained not just by legal and administrative means. The achievement also involved passions and warfare. It produced legendary figures in Swiss history such as the world-renown William Tell, whose story has inspired historical chronicles, plays, and music in the modern era. Tell was a legendary figure who symbolized the struggle for liberty in Switzerland. In actual fact, Tell's reputed exploits are disputed by historians who, in fact, can't even find evidence of his existence. The legend has it that Tell was a peasant who defied the authority of a much-despised Hapsburg official. As punishment, he was made to shoot an apple from the head of his son, which Tell did successfully. Marksmanship in archery is a recurring theme in medieval tales of popular heroes, as in the Robin Hood tales. In response to his forced marksmanship, Tell then threatened the governor's life, a threat eventually executed after a number of trials and tribulations. Tell's resistance to the Hapsburg authority, which is supposed to have taken place in 1307, allegedly helped spur Swiss resistance to the Hapsburgs.

At the very least, the tale of William Tell is part of Swiss political mythology somewhat similar to such English popular heroes as Robin Hood and King Arthur, even when the actual existence of these legendary heroes remains uncertain, or their actual exploits, if they did exist, have been greatly exaggerated. Comparable, modern examples can be found in the legends of the American West. For instance, the legendary U.S. army scout, Kit Carson, is reputed to have said about his overblown reputation something like: "I might 'a done all the things I'm supposed to 'a done, but I don't recall 'em."

Further to the north within the Holy Roman Empire, German towns and cities confederated in what were called *stadtebunde*, or town leagues. They were commonplace institutions in medieval Germany between the 13th and 15th centuries, continuing to form and evolve in spite of imperial opposition. They were, in fact, illegal as early as 1231 owing to regulations of Emperor Henry VII. The most documented imperial attempt to arrest the development of the leagues was the Golden Bulla of 1356 issued by Charles IV, by which many stadtebunde were dissolved, some even forcibly. Where this happened, the law did favor the interests of local lords as well as the emperors. Nonetheless, according to the Finnish historian, Ossi Kokkonen, "these and other restrictions, however, did not have much effect in practice as the towns broke them time and again." (p. 3) Moreover, emperors sometimes created their own pro-imperial leagues, of which a good example was the Swabian league, a confederation of towns in southern Germany. In fact, pro-imperial leagues provided examples of emperors breaking their own laws against the formation and operation of inter-town leagues. According to Kokkonen, the leagues

> ...guaranteed mutual economic benefits and legal standing of towns and burghers. Leagues were often formed in times of social instability as during the rule of a weak ruler or crown vacancy. Sometimes, the aim of the league was to act against lords and knights, and a recurring theme was the maintenance of the security of trade routes, travelling burghers, and towns. (p. 3)

Leagues often formed among free imperial cities, an urban category that deserves some explication. By the end of the Middle Ages, there were about 4,000 towns or cities in the Holy Roman empire, 90% of which held fewer than a thousand inhabitants. Most of these centers were subject to the legal rule of a local lord, but about 200 were under the direct control of the emperor, which gave them a different status and more legal independence than other towns or cities. Among these German cities are to be found many whose names the reader might recognize: Lubeck, Augsburg, Cologne, Strasbourg, Aachen, Worms, Regensburg, Nuremburg, Hamburg, Frankfurt, and Muhlhausen. These cities had acquired this status partly by payment to the emperor. First administered by royal representatives, the cities came to be directed eventually by local burghers who assumed local administration and justice. In non-imperial cities, the local bishop, abbot, or archbishop often was the lord from whom burghers gradually won independence. Imperial cities might even wage war or make peace in addition to controlling trade and municipal administration. Some favored cities gained a charter by gift. Others purchased them from a prince in need of funds. Some won it by force of arms. Some cities became free through the void created by the extinction of dominant families.

With their republican form, free imperial cities were usually oligarchies ruled by a governing council composed of a hereditary, wealthy elite called a *ratsverwandte*, or city council families. They ruled a larger class of burgher-citizens that held varying amounts of political rights and powers according to the town or city. Burgher status was heritable, but could also be purchased. Below the burghers in the social hierarchy were people called residents or guests who held no formal political power. These included visitors but also such permanent inhabitants as small artisans, street vendors, laborers, servants, and the poor. In general, these people could number as much as half of the urban population of the empire.

The first, important German league was the Rhine league of 1254–1257. Despite its short duration, the Rhine league served as a model for other confederations. It was formed as the ruling, imperial Hohenstaufen dynasty was in its death throes owing to persistent conflict with the popes. The conflict led to a widespread popular sentiment of continual, endless warfare in a land where there was little social and legal order. The league formed in July of 1254 at the behest of the city of Mainz under the leadership of a burgher named Arnold Walpot. The league also included three bishop-lords and local secular lords and knights, even if its true leaders were the cities of Worms, Strasbourg, Speyer, and Basel. Its stated objective was "... to maintain the peace and stop the excessive use of violence. In order to do this, the league forbade its members to collect unjustified taxes, and asked them to hold to their traditional rights...as communes)" (Kokkonen, p. 5) The league also maintained a common army to protect itself from lords and knights; it fought several battles against noble-led armies.

About the same time, Mainz formed separate, bilateral alliances with Worms, Oppenheim, and Bingen as much as to resolve inter-city disputes as to protect the peace that the emperors seemed unable to do. (Kokkonen, p. 7) In 1261–1263, the city of Strasbourg formed distinct leagues with each of Nuenburg, Colmar, and Basel. At issue was the new bishop of Strasbourg, Walter of Geroldseck, who tried to reclaim for himself powers and rights previously granted to the towns. The league handed the bishop a military defeat in March, 1262. Even after the bishop's death in 1263, moreover, Strasbourg still formed three other alliances to defend against the family of the late bishop. In addition, the towns agreed to swear "...loyalty only to a new bishop who promised to act according to their rights." (Kokkonen, p. 9) Elsewhere, to the northeast, from 1346 to 1815, the Lusatian league included five towns in Germany and one town now in Poland. The league had the stated purpose of protecting against the depredations of wandering warriors.

That the league lasted so long bears witness to its effectiveness in protecting the member towns, and in promoting their political and economic interests.

The most famous and powerful of these inter-city leagues was the Hanseatic League, initiated in northern Germany by cities near the shores of the Baltic and North seas. The league was founded in 1259, and endured into the middle of the 16th century, when the league's economic and political clout was overtaken by Dutch cities. Its main purposes were to share the risks and hazards of business travel, to protect and promote trade and economic growth, and to deal with quarrelsome lords. In its time, the league had member cities and operated facilities in the territories that now form part of Germany, Great Britain, Belgium, Poland, Latvia, Estonia, Lithuania, Russia, Belarus, and the Scandinavian countries. Initial leadership came from the burghers of Lubeck and Hamburg. Other participating cities included merchants and their guilds from London, Cologne, Danzig (Gdansk), Riga, Krakow, Bruges, Antwerp, Bremen, Berlin, Utrecht, Novgorod, and Bergen, as part of a variable roster of 70 to 170 towns and cities. The member cities maintained facilities that resembled Muslim *caravanserais;* these included churches, dwellings, warehouses, offices, and other business facilities available to travelling merchants from league cites.

The league was a confederation in that member communes maintained their own legal, political, and administrative systems, even though there was a common diet, or assembly, that met to discuss common issues. The league's cities played a role of metropolis to the northern hinterland regions where they monopolized trade with the Baltic and North Sea regions. Typically, league cities exported manufactured goods such as cloth, textiles, luxury goods, ships, and the salt that was vital for the salt fish trade. Besides fish, the league cities imported and distributed from more northerly regions such products as furs, timber, honey and beeswax, amber, resin, rye and wheat, and iron and copper.

The league maintained a powerful fleet to ship its goods as well as warships to fight pirates and to defend its interests militarily, which it was not shy to do. The league fought a successful war with the Denmark-Norway state in the 1360s, eventually winning the right to free passage in the sound that lies between Denmark and Sweden, as well as an incredible but real veto over the Danish choice for king. The military victory was achieved by the creation of another alliance among league cities known as the confederation of Cologne, which included Amsterdam even if it was not a member of the Hanseatic League. The confederation of Cologne endured from its founding in 1367 until 1385.

In the middle of the 15th century, a confederation of 19 Hanseatic communities and 53 clergymen and secular nobles formed the Prussian confederation in order to oppose the rule of the German Teutonic Order over Prussian territory. Under the leadership of Hanseatic towns such as Danzig, Elbing, Thorn, and Konigsberg, a successful alliance was struck with the king of Poland. As a result of the military victory of the Prussian confederation and Poland, western Prussia became part of Poland while still maintaining rights of local autonomy. The Teutonic Order did manage to maintain control of eastern Prussia but only as a vassal to the king of Poland.

Not all Hanseatic League wars met with success. As a result of their war with the league, Dutch cities won free access to the Baltic Sea trade during the war of 1438–1441, thus breaking a league monopoly in the region. Even in wars in which it was not directly involved, the league played an important role as banker. For instance, merchants from Cologne financed the military campaigns of the English King Edward III in the 14th century during the Hundred Years' War with the French. While it was Dutch cities that succeeded the league as the economic powerhouse of Europe, it was actually the evolution of the centralized nation-state, wherein states learned how to control the warring, banditry, and gangsterism of the European nobility that ultimately made the Hanseatic League and other urban confederations superfluous.

Medieval Socio-Economic Development in North Africa

We've made the argument in a previous chapter about why our definition of the West must be broader than the typical definitions of the Occident. Many discussions about the medieval economy and society concentrate on western Europe, meaning France, Germany, England, northern Italy, the Low Countries, and sometimes Spain and Portugal. Recall that our definition of the West includes Europe as far east as the Ural Mountains in Russia and the Caspian Sea, as well as Turkey and the Middle East, Egypt, and North Africa. While feudal and manorial societies and the pattern of medieval urban development of western Europe do indeed apply elsewhere than in western Europe, there are important differences that require explanation if we are to understand the context and patterns of development throughout the medieval West.

In the chapter about medieval Islam, we discussed socio-economic conditions in the medieval Muslim lands of Turkey, Syria, the Levant, Egypt, and North Africa, so we need make just a few more salient points. Recall that the Fatimid caliphate that ruled from Syria to Tunisia was centered in Egypt. The successor régimes included rule by two Mamaluke dynasties. The first dynasty under Turkish Mamaluke rule was a time of economic growth and prosperity. The second period, under the Circassian (Caucasian) Mamalukes, however, saw a reversal of the positive trends of the Turkish period. We've described some of the causes of this economic deterioration in the previous chapter. It also should be noted that during the 14th and 15th centuries, Egypt knew calamities possibly worse than those that occurred in northern Europe. The bubonic plague struck a year earlier than it did in Europe in 1347, while there were also important plagues in 1388–1389 and 1397–1398. In the next century, another dozen major epidemics of the plague struck. Under such conditions, the socio-economic and political deterioration in Egypt during the late Middle Ages might have been understandable.

To the west of Egypt, the easternmost portion of Libya was known as Cyrenaica. While the Egyptian rulers claimed suzerainty over Cyrenaica, their political control was nominal. In actual fact, the land was controlled by Bedouin tribes from Arabia whose main source of income came from offering protection to caravans and traders who travelled west from Egypt, or by robbing those who refused to pay for this protection. This was typical of tribal economies as existed for centuries among nomadic peoples such as the Bedouin or those of the Pontic-Caspian Steppe. To the southwest of Cyrenaica, the land of the Fezzan which juts southward into the Sahara was controlled by the chieftains of an indigenous tribe known as the Banii Khattab. Their income derived from control of the oases on the trade routes over which caravans carried gold, ivory, and slaves from the Sudan north to Mediterranean coastal communities. The exception to the prevalence of tribal economies was found in the towns of Tripolitania in northwestern Libya where merchants succeeded in reviving trade during the late Middle Ages.

To the west of Libya were the Muslim-held lands of the Maghreb with coasts on the Mediterranean, that is, modern-day Tunisia, Algeria, and Morocco. In historical debate, the Maghreb economy of the Middle Ages has been often characterized as not very productive. Maria Vidiassova nuances this portrait, however, dividing the medieval economic history of the Maghreb into two phases. In the first phase during the high Middle Ages, the agricultural economy in the Maghreb was productive owing to Muslim innovations in irrigation and the introduction of Asian crops suited to Maghreb conditions such as rice, cotton, and sugar cane. Agricultural production in the Maghreb of such crops as olives, wheat, barley, peas, and beans actually exceeded that of western Europe during this period. Trade also was healthy in terms of exports of silk, textiles, iron, lead, and mercury. During the late Middle Ages, in a pattern in accord with the thesis of Immanuel Wallerstein, the Maghreb assumed a hinterland role vis-à-vis western Europe, a role that emerged during the reconquest of the Iberian Peninsula by western Christians during the 15th century. There was an increase in exports from the Maghreb of unfinished raw products as well as diminished agricultural production. Irrigation works were abandoned and not maintained, while there was ecological damage owing to dessication of farmlands and reduction of soil fertility. Innovative economic growth was limited to seaside towns rather than in the inlands of the south.

Medieval Socio-Economic Development in Eastern Europe

Feudal and manorial social arrangements gradually came to an end in western Europe during the late Middle Ages. We read the words of Friedrich Engels.

> The feudality of all western Europe was in full decline during the 15th century. Everywhere, cities with their anti-feudal interests, their own law, and their armed citizenry had wedged themselves into feudal territories...Through money, in part, they had established their social—and here and there even their political—ascendancy. Even in the countryside, in those areas where agriculture was favored by special circumstances, the old feudal ties began to disappear under the influence of money. (p. 3)

Even so, the lords of western Europe did not give up their wealth and power without a fight. American historian Robert Brenner provides us with two examples, England and Catalonia, where nobles fought a strong rearguard action against the social transformations that occurred after the Black Death of 1348–1349. (p. 51, 52) As a result of the plague, the number of serfs and other producing people in Europe was greatly reduced, perhaps by as much as a third, so the bargaining power of members of the lower classes increased dramatically. In response, nobles undertook a strategy of trying to control the geographic and social mobility of peasants by increasing manorial fees and rents, and by charging peasants for the right to leave their lords. In England, the Statute of Laborers of 1351 tried to roll back wages to pre-plague levels. A British Liberal MP, Thorold Rogers, wrote in 1879 that this dynamic was a motivating theme of English history in the six centuries following the Black Death during which English lords, gentry, and capitalists tried to roll back workers' and peasants' gains obtained subsequent to the Black Death. Nevertheless, through revolt and flight, the common people did obtain their freedom such that serfdom ultimately did die out in England during the 15th century.

Similar restrictive laws to those of England were adopted in Catalonia in the 14th and 15th centuries. Writes Brenner about Catalonia:

> By the early 15th century, this legislation had proceeded a good distance with apparently significant success...It provoked a response of a high level of peasant organization and, in particular, the assembling of mass peasant armies...Only a series of violent and bloody confrontations ultimately assured peasant victory. Armed warfare ended finally in 1486 with the Sentence of Guadeloupe by which the peasantry was granted in full its personal freedom, the full right in perpetuity to its property, and... full right to those vacant holdings they had annexed in the period following the demographic catastrophes.

The social situations in eastern Europe and Scandinavia differed. Admittedly, the same classes of tribal chieftains cum kings, clan leaders cum nobility, warriors cum knights, peasants, craftsmen, laborers, slaves, and merchants as seen in medieval western Europe also existed in eastern and Nordic Europe. Nonetheless, the relationships among classes differed substantially from those in western Europe. During the high Middle Ages, 1000–1300, the vast lands of eastern and Nordic Europe were lightly populated. While it was still common to see slaves working the farmlands held by their social superiors long after slavery had died in western Europe, peasants mostly were allowed personal freedom and geographic mobility since they had considerable bargaining power vis-à-vis lords. During the late Middle Ages, 1300–1500, while feudal and manorial arrangements including serfdom were drawing to an end in western Europe, in eastern Europe and Scandinavia, however, rulers and lords rolled back peasant gains in an attempt to increase their power and wealth. Lords got legislation passed to restrict movements of peasants who worked lords' lands. Lords took by force some peasant lands, and imposed heavy labor obligations on the peasants who occupied land already owned by lords. For instance, in Poland, peasants owed their lords only a few days of labor each year during the 13th century. This increased to one day per week in the 14th century, then to almost 6 days per week during the 18th century. They lingered into 20th century, in fact, during WWII, more precisely on September 6, 1944, folwarks finally eliminated for good in Poland by the Polish Committee of National Liberation.

Starting during the late Middle Ages and into the early modern era, hereditary serfdom was established and reinforced legally in Prussia, Hungary, Austria, the Polish-Lithuanian Commonwealth, and Russia, while rights of autonomy and self-rule of cities and towns also were being limited. In some of these countries, legally enforced serfdom persisted into the 19th century. Serfdom typically had not been a reality in Scandinavia, but it became so in the 14th century, remaining in effect into the early modern era.

The incentive for such a major social shift, once again as per the Wallerstein thesis, was the inclusion of eastern and Nordic Europe as hinterlands for the nascent capitalism of western Europe. For example, Polish lords expanded their grain production not for local use but for export westward. In Hungary and the Balkans, silver, iron, and other mining operations produced for export westward. An important factor in this socio-economic transformation was the significant migration eastward, with the active encouragement of local lords and rulers, of German peasants, knights, and lords searching for new lands, which meant both an increased population and an importation of western European ways and mores even as natural resources from eastern Europe were being shipped west. Politically speaking, weak kings could not resist the demands of local lords in eastern Europe while, at the same time, the opposite phenomenon was occurring in western Europe whereby centralized monarchies were becoming stronger in opposition to local lords. (McKay, p. 1) So much for a general portrait. It will be now useful to examine some of the local realities of the medieval socio-economic order in eastern Europe, the Baltic region, and Scandinavia.

Byzantium

When one considers medieval socio-economic conditions in the eastern Roman empire, one is immediately struck by what must have been devastating effects of the continual loss of territory over the years. Obviously, there was the loss of territory to the Muslims and the ultimately successful independence campaigns of the Bulgarians and the Serbs. Even so, Constantine V launched successful economic reforms in the eighth century that brought a revival of fortunes to Byzantium that continued into the beginning of the 13th century. Visitors to Byzantium between the 10th and the end of the 12th century were overwhelmed by the impression of luxury and wealth in Constantinople. The state's control and direction of trade made Constantinople the most important commercial city in Europe until the rise of the northern Italian cities during the high Middle Ages. Then came the disaster of the crusade in 1204 when western European warriors sacked Constantinople, literally removing most of the city's wealth. It was an economic blow from which Byzantium could not recover. In addition, the western warriors established so-called Latin territories in what had been formerly parts of Byzantium. By 1330, the empire was now limited to a small northwestern corner of Anatolia and the greatly diminished capital city of Constantinople and its surrounding territory in Thrace as well as Macedonia and parts of northern Greece.

In terms of social structure, unlike western Europe, there had never been historic and traditional land bases for autonomous lords who might challenge and restrain emperors. During the high Middle Ages, most Byzantine aristocrats held no power other than honorific titles bestowed upon them for being related to the emperors, the exceptions being noblemen involved in the military or in imperial administration. In the middle of the 11th century, however, noblemen began plotting against the emperors, even proclaiming their rule over certain parts of the empire. So, at the end of the same century, emperors began distributing lands under state control to aristocrats called *pronoiai*. This had the aim of getting aristocrats out of Constantinople in order to stop their political intrigues. During the 12th century, aristocratic soldiers also started to receive pronoiai in return for the responsibility of collecting imperial taxes, while being allowed to keep a certain portion of the money collected for themselves. In fact, it resembled the ikta system employed in the Muslim world, particularly in Anatolia and Egypt. Holders of the pronoiai might also be allowed to collect portions of harvests and revenues from trade and transit traffic, and to exercise and control hunting rights. Emperors could request military service from these aristocrats who, however, could not compel local taxpayers to serve in the military. After the Byzantines recaptured Constantinople in 1261, pronoiai holdings became heritable; pronoiai holders could even distribute holdings to military followers. As the ever-impoverishing empire produced fewer taxes, pronoiai holders began to extract rents from the occupants of the land. All this meant that Byzantium began to resemble somewhat a feudal/manorial régime *à l'Occidentale* as the empire drew closer to its ultimate demise during Ottoman military conquests in the 15th century.

Under the Byzantine medieval social régime, commoners were known as *paroikos*. They included occupants of villages and estates under the legal and fiscal responsibility of the pronoiai holders. They were free even if they owed obligations to pronoia holders rather than directly to the state. They included both property owners and tenant-farmers, and were further categorized according to the amounts of land they worked and the portions of harvests they owed to landholders. Still socially inferior were the people who owned or leased no land, but survived on wages for work done for landowners or for monasteries or other Church properties. These people were called by various names including *douleutoparoikoi*, and lived lives of poverty even if they were spared from paying taxes. Nonetheless, if they cultivated the same land for thirty years, they might acquire the status of permanent tenant-farmers even though they still owed labor and services to their erstwhile employers. Christian slaves were unknown in medieval Byzantium, but there were non-Christian slaves who were either Muslim or pagan.

Agricultural progress in the medieval period was slow even if continuous. Coastal areas concentrated on production of grains, grapes, and olives while interior lands in the Balkans and Anatolia concentrated on livestock raising, a pattern that had always existed in the eastern Roman empire. Moreover, according to Chris Harman,

> There seems to have been virtually no advance in the techniques used to gain a livelihood by the vast majority of the population who worked on the land. The methods and instruments of cultivation showed little or no advance on ancient times. Tilling was still performed by a light plough pulled by oxen, fields were not manured systematically, and the harnesses employed until the 12th century choked animals so that two horses could only pull a load of about half a tonne, several times less than is possible with modern harnesses. (p. 118)

After the conquest of Byzantium by the crusaders in 1204, there was little or no land clearance to create more arable land. Epidemics were common, peasants became increasingly impoverished, and more wealth was concentrated in the hands of big pronoia holders and monasteries, neither of which were innovative in terms of agricultural productivity.

The second economic pillar of Byzantium had always been trade since Constantinople stood at the crossroads of Europe and Asia. After the sacking of the capital by the crusaders in 1204, however, emperors lost their capacity to control and tax trade, which was taken over by Italian merchants and their city-state, republican governments. In the last days of the empire just before the Ottoman conquests, imperial officials had lost control of all economic levers, even the export of precious metals and the minting of coins.

The Pontic-Caspian Region

The Pontic-Caspian Steppe was occupied and governed by a series of evolving tribal confederacies during the Middle Ages. During the early Middle

Ages, the prime ruling group of the region was the Khazari. During the high Middle Ages, Khazari pre-eminence was succeeded by the domination of the Pechenegs, then of the Cumans and the closely-related Kipchaks, all of which were Turkic confederacies. In the mid-13th century came the conquering Mongols from north of China who had united with Turkic peoples from the same region. Over time, the Mongols were assimilated to the majority Turkic population as the upper class of what came to be known as the Khanate of the Golden Horde, or the Kipchak Khanate since the majority of people were Kipchaks.

Before the Mongol conquest, the local Turkic populations of the Pontic-Caspian Steppe had been nomadic, following their herds of horses, cattle, sheep, and goats on the grasslands of the Steppe, even if there were sedentary farmers normally subservient to their nomadic neighbors. The nomads also hired themselves as guides to the Silk Road traffic north of the Black Sea. As with other nomadic peoples of the era, local nomads reserved their right to tax and rob traders if the latter did not pay their due.

Urbanization was limited to Kiev, the Crimean peninsula, and the Genoan cities on the shores of the Black Sea. Once the Mongol invaders settled down to rule their new possessions in the West, however, they successively established two capital cities in the Volga Valley, each called Sarai. Both the later city to the north of the original city and the original capital had populations of over half a million, making them among the largest medieval cities. Trade was important to the Kipchak Khanate, with peoples from Europe, the Mediterranean and Black Sea regions, the Levant, Rus', and Asia all constituting trading partners. Exports included furs, fish, especially sturgeon, livestock and meats, salt, and honey. The Kipchak Khanate also displayed crafts typical to the medieval period. Farming of crops such as millet, rye, wheat, barley, oats, and peas was well-developed, while livestock meats rather than game were important in the local diet, normally a sign of sedentarization of the population. (Nedashkovskii)

The countries immediately south and east of the Black Sea include Armenia, Georgia, and Azerbaijan. Each of these countries' economies was affected by successive onslaughts of invaders. During the early Middle Ages, the Arabs controlled the region, having taken it from the Persians, after which the Byzantines regained parts of it, to be followed by the Seljuk Turks and then, finally, the Mongols. Each conquest meant a cycle of economic devastation followed by recuperation and flourishing, then economic disruption once again, and so on. Under the indigenous Bagratid kingdom, east-west trade flourished so much along the Silk Road that the kingdom was known as the Great Armenian Highway. In addition to the transit trade through Armenia, there were native crafts industries and exports to Rus', Byzantium, the Arab countries, Iran, central Asia, and the Black Sea ports. The products exported included textiles, metal works, arms, jewelery, horses, cattle, salt, wine, honey, timber, leather, furs, wool, silk, and carpets.

As a result of this trade, new towns and cities were founded that rivaled those of western Europe for population size and dynamism. On the other hand, agriculture was organized in feudal-type arrangements that were indeed oppressive to the common people. The livestock raising and farming peasantry was composed of both tenant farmers and slaves. Peasants paid high taxes to the state and to the Armenian Apostolic Church, an Oriental Orthodox Church, which provoked popular resentments and a series of peasant uprisings during the medieval period. Finally, the Mongol conquest produced high levels of taxation that weighed heavily on the possibilities of Armenian economic recovery. Armenia also was affected by the new sea routes the Portuguese were discovering at the end of the late Middle Ages, which offered an alternative to transit trade through Armenia for oriental trade, including to that of the Silk Road traffic.

On the western shore of the Caspian Sea, Azerbaijan also benefited greatly from the transit trade of the Silk Road through its territory. The result was the erecting of several cities in Azerbaijan devoted to trade that numbered populations in the tens of thousands. The agricultural economy of Azerbaijan, as with Armenia, was organized on feudal-like lines. The land of the indigenous people of Azerbaijan had been known as Caucasian Albania in ancient times. It was then conquered by the Persians in the early centuries of the first millennium before being conquered by the Muslims during the early Middle Ages. During the high Middle Ages and the late Middle Ages, Azerbaijan was ruled by the Shavanshah dynasty of Persianized Arabs. This dynasty ruled either independently, or as vassals to a progressive line of dynasties and empires, including the following: the Ghaznavids from northern Afghanistan; the Seljuk Turks; the Khwarezmid empire of Mamaluke Turks who had previously served the Seljuks, but then came to rule greater Iran; the Mongols; and, finally, the Turko-Mongol régime of Timur Lenk, a ruler of mixed Turkic and Mongol heritage who hailed from Transoxiana in modern-day Uzbekistan. Each time it was conquered, Azerbaijan's economy suffered correspondingly, so much so that it is difficult to imagine that medieval Azerbaijanis could have lived in prosperity.

Probably the most powerful régime in the region was that of the Georgians whose land borders on the eastern shore of the Black Sea. During the 12th century, Georgia prospered as an independent regional power. This followed a period of devastation so complete at the hands of the Seljuk Turks that by the 1080s, there were more Seljuk Turks living in Georgia than native Caucasians. Some Georgian independence was regained under the leadership of the Bagatrid royal family of Armenia. In order to repopulate the land after the Seljuk Turks had departed, Georgian rulers invited to the country about 40,000 Kipchak warriors and their families, Alans from north of Georgia, and mercenaries from Germany, Italy, and Scandinavia. In the 1220s, Georgia fell to the invading Mongols, then once again to the forces of Timur Lenk, who invaded Georgia eight times. Each time Georgia would be conquered in a manner similar to the Armenians and Azerbaijanis, Georgians would rebuild their economies only to have them destroyed once again along with much of the indigenous population in the next round of invasions. Once the Ottoman régime came to power in the 15th century, Georgia was a small Christian enclave in a Muslim world separated by far from distant European Christendom.

Bulgaria

There had been a Bulgarian empire in the early Middle Ages that eventually succumbed to the eastern Roman empire. In the 11th century, there were two major attempts to regain Bulgarian independence, each of which ultimately failed: in 1040–1041 under the leadership of Peter Delyan and again in 1072 under the leadership of Georgi Voiteh. The spark for each revolt seems to have been Byzantine taxation. Finally, in 1185–1186, under the leadership of the brothers, Peter and Asen, a new dynasty was established in what is known as the second Bulgarian empire subsequent to a successful revolt once again sparked by Byzantine tax increases. The second Bulgarian empire displayed a typical medieval economy based upon agriculture, forestry, metallurgy, mining, and trade and crafts in the urban centers. During the 14th century, Bulgaria succumbed to the Ottoman onslaught along with all the Balkans except for Croatia and Wallachia in modern-day Romania.

The Ottoman Empire

The Ottoman régime was born in 1299 in northwest Anatolia when an alliance of Turkish tribes united under the leadership of an aristocrat named Osman. In the first seven decades of the 14th century the Turks captured the Balkan countries to either rule them directly or as vassal-states. These lands were briefly lost by the Turks, but eventually recovered over the course of the next century. In 1376, Bulgaria's rulers accepted vassal status to the Ottomans. In 1387, the Turks took Thessaloniki in northern Greece. The Turks' victory at the battle of Kosovo in 1389 effectively ended Serbian power in the region. Early in the 15th century, Thessaloniki, Macedonia, and Kosovo were temporarily lost by the Turks, but they were recovered in the mid-15th century. In 1417, Wallachia became an Ottoman vassal-state. In 1453, the eastern Roman empire finally succumbed for good when Constantinople fell to the Ottoman Turks. In 1475, an Ottoman protectorate was organized in the Khanate of the Crimea, which included the Crimean peninsula and the land around the Sea of Azov north of the Black Sea. By the end of the late Middle Ages at the turn of the 16th century, the Ottoman empire included most of Anatolia except for the southeastern portion of the peninsula. Early in the next century, all of greater Syria including northern Mesopotamia, Kurdistan, and the Levant fell to Ottoman rule. The Balkans were called Rumelia by the Turks, *Rum* being the Turkish word for Rome. Rumelia included Greece, Macedonia, Albania, Herzegovina, Serbia, Bosnia, Bulgaria, Thrace, and Constantinople, the last renamed Istanbul by the Ottomans.

In the Ottoman economic mind basic concepts of state and society and economy were all closely closely related. The ultimate goal of a state was consolidation and extension of the ruler's power, and the way to reach it was to get rich resources of revenues by making the productive classes prosperous. The ultimate aim was to increase the state revenues without damaging the prosperity of subjects to prevent the emergence of social discord, and to keep the traditional organization of the society intact. The philosophy was thus conservative. The Ottoman mind would not have understood the emerging capitalism that was developing in western Europe. Nonetheless, the Ottomans did promote trade including international trade. The successive, Ottoman capital cities of Bursa in northwest Anatolia, Adrianople in Thrace, and Constantinople were made into thriving commercial and industrial centers in which the activities of merchants and craftsmen were encouraged. The Turks also encouraged immigration of Jewish merchants, who were oppressed and harassed in western Europe. This immigration had salutary economic effects for the empire. The Ottomans also allowed relatively free reign to Christians of the Orthodox Church, which constituted an improvement in the eyes of local Christians over persistent harassment by the Catholic Church and Catholic Venetians who were prominent in the region prior to the Ottoman conquest.

Organization of professional guilds within the empire only began in the 16th century but, before that, many artisans assembled in the Muslim fraternity known as the Ahi Brotherhood, which was closely related to Sufi religious orders. While trade and manufactures were encouraged, nonetheless, agriculture was seen as being more important to the economy. Ultimately, the main source of wealth was military conquest to increase the fiscal basis of the state. Nevertheless, the Ottoman empire was mostly an agrarian economy where the land was rich even if labor and capital were scarce. The majority of the population earned its living from small family holdings, which contributed 40% of the empire's taxes. Fams were organized around crop agriculture and livestock for milk, wool, and hides. The régime encouraged the expansion of arable lands by clearing wastelands.

Small farmers were subjected to a particular régime of land/fiscal grants known as the *timar*. Similar to the Byzantine pronoia and the Egyptian ikta, the timar was a grant of land made between the 14th and 16th centuries to soldiers in lieu of pay. These grants were given to cavalrymen and military slaves, the well-known janissaries, or to state administrators. The grantee then controlled arable lands possessed by peasants as well as vacant lands, wastelands, fruit trees, forests, and waters found within the territory of the timar, from which the grantee had to collect a certain amount of taxes for the state, beyond which wealth obtained could remain with the timar holder. There were several purposes of the system: to encourage increased agricultural production, held to be the prime source of wealth for the state;

to produce tax revenues for the state; to avoid having to pay soldiers directly; to increase the number of cavalrymen by using the possibility of a timar grant as an incentive to fight for the state; to gradually bring conquered lands directly under Ottoman control; and to centralize the authority of the state by removing from political, military, and economic authority existing feudal nobility and rulers left over from conquests. Timar holders often engaged stewards known as *voyvoda* to collect taxes, and to do the actual administration of their lands. Timar holders were rewarded for bringing new lands under cultivation, but punished for the abandonment of farmlands. It should be noted that the state maintained ownership of all land, that timars could not be inherited, and that the timar was contingent upon a minimum of active military service every seven years.

Slavery played an important role in the medieval Ottoman state; in fact, slavery continued to exist in the empire into the 19th and early 20th centuries. There were some agricultural and domestic slaves as well as concubines in harems, including many in the imperial household, however, it was in government and the army that slaves were most prominent. Many government officials had been bought as slaves, then raised free in order to serve the state; this guaranteed their fierce loyalty as employees of the state. As much as a fifth of the population in Constantinople was slave. In the mid-14th century, the Sultan Murad created an army of slaves called the *Kapikulu*, who were reminiscent of the ghilman and the mamalukes wherein many Turks had served. The Sultan's rationale was that he had a right to a fifth of war booty, interpreted to mean slaves caught in battle. The Turks also employed a particular method of military recruitment known as the *devsirme*, which might be translated as blood tax or child collection. Young Christian boys from the Balkans and previously Byzantine Anatolia were taken from their homes and families, taught and converted to Islam, and enlisted as special soldiers known as janissaries. These boys were raised to be military leaders and imperial officials, while some even became *de facto* rulers of the empire. From the Crimean Khanate, a massive slave trade was maintained with the rest of the Ottoman empire. Many slaves were Slavic peasants captured during raids in Russia and the Ukraine. It is estimated that as many as ¾ of the Crimean population consisted of slaves, making the Crimean Khanate a slave economy if ever there was one.

Hungary

The Magyars conquered what was to become Hungary around the turn of the tenth century, then joined with indigenous Slavs and Avars from the Pontic-Caspian Steppe to produce the Hungarian population. The Magyars were patrilineal families, clans, and tribes organized into a confederacy ruled by a grand prince who was a descendant of Arpad, the Magyar leader when they entered Pannonia. Originally nomadic, the Magyars did adopt farming ways once they had completed their raiding in western Europe, and had settled in Pannonia. The land was only sparsely populated, perhaps about four or five people, or one peasant family per square kilometre. Throughout the medieval period, as a matter of state policy, Hungary was a recipient of European immigration of all classes to fill the largely empty land. From western Europe came Germans, Italians, Frenchmen, Flemings, and Walloons. Cumans and Alans came from the Pontic-Caspian Steppe; Moravians, Slovaks, and Poles came from north of Hungary; Croats and Serbs came from the south; while Roma and Jewish and Muslim merchants also immigrated. Merchants were attracted to Hungary since the land was a crossroads of international transit trade. Besides being a multi-ethnic state from its beginnings, medieval Hungary was a large state, geographically speaking. In addition to Hungary proper, it included at various times Dalmatia, Croatia, Bosnia, Herzegovina, and Serbia in the Balkans, and the lands that comprise modern Romania, that is, Wallachia, Transylvania, and Moldavia.

King Stephen introduced Catholicism to Hungary about the year 1000. He pursued a vigorous policy of forced Christianization, overseeing the installation of Benedictine monasteries, dioceses, and parish churches, one parish church for each ten villages. He strove to support Christian marriage as opposed to polygamy or other, traditional Magyar customs, even trying to change customary pagan fashions. Not surprisingly, this policy did meet with resistance including a major pagan revolt in 1044–1046. In spite of being an officially Catholic state, medieval Hungary also included Orthodox Christians, Jews, Muslims, and pagans.

In terms of social organization of the Hungarian classes, we earlier made the point that eastern Europe differed from western Europe. Hungary is a case in point. Unlike western Europe where foreign monarchs had to contend with a native nobility in order to create a centralized state, in Hungary the quantity of royal estates was so great that the land, for the most part, belonged to the king and state, while there was only a small, local nobility mostly descended from the Avars. On royal lands lived a class of commoners known as *udvornici* who provided services to the king such as provisioning royal properties with food and other essentials. The king organized counties centered on fortresses and castles administered by a royal official called an *ispan* whereas, in western Europe, local lands were controlled by indigenous aristocrats.

The medieval historical dynamic in Hungary, moreover, was the opposite of that of western Europe. Over time, an increasingly powerful and wealthy landed nobility in Hungary emerged to limit the Hungarian king's power. When this happened, it also meant that freemen living in formerly royal lands lost their free status to become vassals of the large noblemen, as did ecclesiastics and lesser nobility as well. After the destructive Mongol invasion of 1240–1241, the king granted still more estates to his noble supporters. By the time King Andrew III died early in 1301, there were about a dozen important lords who had achieved de facto independence from the monarchy in the lands they ruled. For example, Slovakia and Transylvania were each ruled by virtually independent lords.

Another important difference in the social organization of Hungary as compared to western Europe was the prevalence of slavery as a way of commanding labor rather than serfdom, according to James Wilson. Slavery had long been established among the Magyars, not just among war captives but also among native Magyars. Belonging to a clan guaranteed freedom to a Magyar warrior. Those who did not belong to a clan for whatever reason could be and often were enslaved. Furthermore, Magyars also dealt in the slave trade, selling their indigenous slaves. The number of Hungarian slaves was increased by the addition of the Avars and indigenous Slavs of Pannonia who had resisted the Magyar conquest. In fact, obtaining more slaves was one of the motives for the Magyar terror in western Europe during the first half of the tenth century. The sparse population of Hungary meant that slaves were needed to work the land on behalf of Magyar lords. This situation continued throughout the high Middle Ages, well into the 13th century. The early, legislating monarchs of Hungary—Stephen, Ladislas, Coloman—passed copious laws to organize the treatment of slaves, including prescribing enslavement as punishment for crimes. Slavery disappeared for use in agricultural production only late in the 13th century after the Mongol invasion, although slavery continued for household purposes. Immigration of western Europeans en masse helped change social mores such that feudal social relations including serfdom eventually appeared to be more natural and profitable than slavery, after it had long disappeared in western Europe.

Economically speaking, during the late Middle Ages, Hungary developed as a hinterland for western Europe as per the Wallerstein thesis. This could be seen in three aspects: in the Hungarian role as recipient of surplus population from western Europe, which doubtless encouraged the adoption of feudal relations including serfdom in Hungary; in the Hungarian role as a market for finished goods from western Europe; and in the Hungarian role of providing gold and silver, raw materials needed for western Europe's increasing reliance on coinage as a medium of commercial exchange. Arguably, Hungary came to be one of the proving grounds for what was to become Western imperialism vis-à-vis the Americas and the rest of the world in the modern world. Gold and silver mining as well as salt mining became prominent in Hungary during the 14th century. Hungarian mines produced about 30 % of the world's production of gold and silver until the Spanish conquests in the Americas. King Charles' Hungarian state took its share of mining revenues needed to fund its large army, while Charles also authorized landholders to retain 30% of the income from mines on their estates. Even so, most profits from the mines were transferred to Italian and south German merchants because the value of imported fine textiles and other goods always exceeded the price of cattle and wine exported from the kingdom.

As the number of German merchants and other people from western Europe increased in the few Hungarian cities, the number and legal status of these urban centers increased and improved during the 14th and 15th centuries. At the same time, peasants from Hungary, Croatia, and Slovakia also were drawn to the towns and cities and the advantages urban life offered. Nevertheless, Hungary continued to display a mostly rural, agricultural economy throughout the Middle Ages. Most people were peasants who grew wheat and barley, and millet and oats used in animal husbandry. Fishing and hunting provided protein. In fact, commoners were allowed to hunt in royal forests, a privilege that was guarded jealously by kings and noblemen in western Europe. Even if the latest agricultural techniques such as iron plows were available and used, there was so much unoccupied land in Hungary that peasants were able to move to new lands when their own land became exhausted. They were encouraged to do so by the new, noble landholders of hitherto royal lands who offered attractive financial conditions to encourage peasants to move to their land. In their new homes, peasants built villages of side-by-side, multi-room, timber houses on equal parcels of land, which were improvements upon traditional huts.

The Mongol invasion was indeed destructive; about one in six Hungarians were killed, while the economy was devastated. The state was not destroyed, however; some fortresses were still holding off the Mongol invaders when the death of the Great Khan Ogedei obliged the invaders to return home to choose another great khan. Thus was Hungary able to pursue its development after the Mongol invasion.

Poland

The entry of the Polish state to the historical record coincides with the Christianization of the country in the Catholic rite. As with other parts of central and eastern Europe, Poland was sparsely populated, which led to relative freedom for Polish peasants other than the craft work and services they were obliged to provide to local lords. The local aristocracy resembled contemporary feudal lords in western Europe in terms of their political and economic power. Until the end of the 12th century, however, slavery was common in medieval Poland, used especially in agriculture. Even after the end of slavery in Poland, there was still a transit slave trade in the country during the Middle Ages.

Beginning in the late Middle Ages, Poland was brought into the emerging agricultural capitalism of western Europe by the Polish nobility. The results were catastrophic for the Polish peasantry. Polish noble landowners started producing grains for export westward on large latifundia worked by serfs. Rather than receiving money-based taxes and feudal rents from peasants as was happening in western Europe, Polish lords enserfed peasants for agricultural work on what were known as *folwarks*. Late in the 14th century, laws were adopted regulating and enforcing serfdom that prevented peasants from leaving the land, and that outlawed the sale of farmlands to townspeople, in effect, making for forced labor on the farms noblemen held and operated for profit as a monopoly. The first folwarks appeared on Church lands, but the system was soon taken up by the Polish noblemen known as *szlachta*. Folwarks were the basis of the power and wealth of the Polish nobility well into the 20th century, being abolished finally only during WWII by the conquering Soviet Union and indigenous communists. So, as serfdom was drawing to a close as a form of organizing agricultural labor in western Europe, Polish serfdom was reinforced and extended during the late Middle Ages into the modern period. During the same period, the only form of social progress for working people were the urban guilds that formed in spite of the limited rights of towns and cities. In addition, German merchants also immigrated to Polish towns and cities to engage in trade as they did in Hungary. These merchants also demanded and obtained rights similar to medieval merchants elsewhere.

Lithuania

The Grand Duchy of Lithuania was one of the most important European states in the Middle Ages. It was also pagan until the end of the 14th century when, as part of the arrangement for the royal marriage of the Lithuanian ruler with the Polish queen, Lithuania converted to Christianity, in the process finally appeasing the Catholic Church which had regularly referred to the country as the 'Spawn of Satan'. At its greatest extent in the 15th century, Lithuania included Latvia and Belarus and parts of modern-day Russia, Moldova, Poland, and the Ukraine, stretching from the Baltic Sea to the Black Sea. It joined formally with Poland in the early modern era to form the even larger Polish-Lithuanian Commonwealth, even if each country did maintain considerable political, legal, and administrative autonomy.

Lithuania encouraged merchants from Germany, Rus', and Poland to immigrate to towns and cities to engage in trade, especially in the chief city Owing to its geography of dense forests and difficult wetlands and river systems, Lithuania was immune to attempted conquest by the Germans when they moved into the Baltic region, and to attempted conquest by princes from Rus' and the Mongols. In fact, early in the 14th century, when the Mongols retreated from Rus', the Lithuanian state expanded to the south and east, such that it conquered Kiev in the Ukraine in 1323.

Historians know little about Lithuania during the high Middle Ages. It is thought that, as with the Slavic world, Lithuanian society was governed by a loose association of clans who occupied hilltop fortresses wherein some trade took place, and from which plunder of neighbors was organized. Clan leaders evolved to become noblemen, one of whom became the overall Lithuanian leader. According to James Wilson, slavery was a common means of organizing medieval agricultural labor in Lithuana. Early in the 14th century, the Lithuanian state invited and capital, Vilnius. In spite of papal disapproval, trade flourished between pagan Lithuania and Catholic Europe. In the 15th century, the folwark system emerged for organizing agricultural production for export westward, as had begun in the previous century in Poland, along with the accompanying tightening of the serfdom of peasants. The folwark system continued to be used into the modern era in Lithuania and in the subsequent Polish-Lithuanian Commonwealth.

The Baltic Region

The Baltic region was exposed to conquest by German and Scandinavian invaders spreading Christianity during the High Middle Ages. Then came the state ruled by the Teutonic order of German knights as well as economic penetration by the Germans owing to the Hanseatic League. The Baltic countries were so dominated by Germans that, in the opinion of Kristian Gerner:

> Towards the end of the Middle Ages, the Baltic region was a German region in terms of trade, urban culture, and common language. As was the case with the Vikings, one cannot speak of an empire but certainly of dominance and political hegemony. The Middle Ages saw a functional German empire in the Baltic region. (p. 60)

Scandinavia

During the high Middle Ages, the Scandinavian countries relied greatly on slaves for economic production. James Wilson explains why:

> Within the Scandinavian communities, the principle of individual, private property was very slow to take hold. Until the later Middle Ages, most Scandinavian settlements were populated by free peasants organized into clan units, with all important property being held by the clans. The Scandinavians thus had neither the complex system of property ownership necessary to create dependent tenancies nor a money economy in which a landowner could hire wage laborers to work his land, leaving slavery as the only way to convert wealth into labor.

Furthermore, slaves were an important item of booty and trade for the roaming Vikings.

After the Black Death, the positions of peasants and monarchs in Scandinavia worsened, while those of nobility and clergy improved, contrary to what happened in western Europe. Moreover, as with the Baltic countries, Scandinavia played a hinterland role vis-à-vis the German merchants of the Hanseatic League. The latter occupied towns and cities such as Stockholm in Sweden, and profited from Scandinavian exports of metals, timber, furs, hides, and herring and cod that was salted in Germany before distribution throughout Europe. Finished goods, in return, were imported to Scandinavia from the Hanseatic League cities, a good example of both a metropolis-hinterland relationship and of the extension of capitalism from western Europe to other parts of Europe, once again as per the Wallerstein thesis.

Russia

Finally, we examine the medieval economy and society of the Russian principalities in the land bounded by the Carpathian Mountains in the south to the Baltic Sea in the north; or stated otherwise, the valleys of the Don, Dnieper, Dniester, and Volga rivers. The reader might recall that during the ninth century Viking trader-warriors ruled the land known as Rus' from its capital city of Kiev in the Ukraine. The Vikings traded on the rivers that flowed south towards the Black and the Caspian seas. Their particular interest was furs which they trapped and/or absconded from local Slavs, then traded in Byzantium along with other goods from the north. The Vikings also adopted the Orthodox Church along with many of the cultural and artistic ways of the Byzantines. The original Viking ruler of the Slavs was a man named Riurik. His princely descendants ruled the various regions of what are the modern-day Ukraine, Belarus, and Russia until the Romanovs of Russia came to the throne in the early modern period.

The social organization of Kievan Rus' differed from the feudal-manorial society of western Europe. At the top of the social order in Rus' were the Riurikid princes who had assimilated into the families of Slav chieftains. William Stevens describes the lower ranks of Rus' society:

> Below the princes, came the merchant-soldier landowner class of boyars, then landowning peasants, tenant farmers, and slaves. Kievan peasants were, as a whole, free to buy, sell, and inherit property, and owed no special allegiance to the landowners. Kievan law recognized few class differences, and with the exception of slaves, most citizens were equal in the eyes of the law.

More about the class structure of Rus'. The boyars, the upper nobility, were either Slavic chieftains or Viking soldiers whose descendants had a long history of dominating the eastern Slavic countries. The relative freedom of peasants in Rus' compared favorably to the situation of peasants in western Europe owing to the vast distances in Rus' with sparse populations where peasants, grouped into traditional clans and tribes, were free to roam and settle where it was advantageous. The relative equality and democracy of the tribal warriors were similar to the tribal societies that had existed in Germany, Scandinavia, and on the Pontic-Caspian Steppe. Nonetheless, slavery also was an important economic institution in the Rus' lands. Slaves represented as much as 10% of the population during the late Middle Ages and well into the early modern era. (James Wilson)

Kievan Rus' developed a successful and complex economy including use of money and credit. By the 11th century, particularly during the reign of Yaroslav the Wise, Kievan Rus' displayed an economy and achievements in architecture and literature superior to those that then existed in the western part of the continent. Of particular importance was Rus' control of three major trade routes: the Volga Valley trade route from the Baltic Sea eastward; the Dnieper Valley route between the Baltic and the Black seas; and the trade between the Khazaris of the Pontic-Caspian Steppe and the Germans. On the eve of the Mongol invasions in the 1230s, Kievan Rus' included about 300 towns and cities. Kiev had a population of about 50,000, while two more northerly towns, Novgorod and Chernigov, each had populations of about 30,000.

As the Middle Ages proceeded, there developed in Rus' a more hierarchical, class-based society, and greater competition and conflict among the various regions ruled by the princely descendants of Riurik. These princedoms had emerged by a coalition of traditional, patriarchic family communes joined in an effort to increase the applicable workforce and expand the productivity of the land. As these communes got larger, the emphasis was taken off the family holdings, and placed on the territory that surrounded them. As Wikipedia says, "This shift was known as the *verv*'. The change in political structure led to the...development of the *smerdy*, free unlanded people who found work by laboring for wages on the manors" that began early in the 11th century. The smerdy, initially given equality in the Kievan law, were theoretically equal to the prince, so they enjoyed as much freedom as can be expected of manual laborers, however, in the 13th century, they began slowly to lose their rights and to become less equal in the eyes of the law.

The competition and conflicts among the principalities might have contributed to their inability to unite to fend off the Mongol invasion in the 1230s. Particularly hard hit by the Mongols were the regions of the Pontic-Caspian Steppe, while more northerly regions such as Novgorod, Tver', Iaroslavl', and Rostov escaped destruction. Southern regions such as Riazan', Vladimir, Chernigov, and Kiev were mercilessly destroyed, as were their populations and economies. The population of Kiev diminished from about 50,000 to 2,000. Villages and farmlands surrounding the towns and cities were also destroyed. As well, laborers and craftsmen were deported to build new Mongol cities in the lower Volga Valley. Many were enslaved or sold into slavery abroad, while slaver raids into Slavic territories by Mongols continued to be typical throughout the Middle Ages. The minting of coins in the Russian principalities ceased for about a century. Even so, the Mongols occupying the Pontic-Caspian Steppe collected taxes, customs, tolls, and tribute, and conducted hostage-taking for ransoms, expropriations, and extortion of silver and other wealth from Russian lands.

Turco-Mongol society was called 'Tatar' by the Slavs. It emerged during the invasions by the Mongols, who formed a ruling class governing Cumans and Kipchaks. The Mongols remained nomadic and devoted to their raising of livestock, even if they did incorporate some sedentary, farming people among indigenous Steppe peoples. The Khans, who ruled from two cities named Sarai on the lower Volga River, were descendants of Ghenghis Khan, the original Mongol conqueror. Two other important cities the Mongol ruling class absorbed were Bulgar-on-the-Volga, the original homeland of the Bulgars, and Khwarezm in modern-day Uzbekistan. The khans issued lands to subordinates, who were then required to raise and lead cavalry armies. During the reign of Khan Uzbek, 1313–1314, the Mongol ruling class converted from paganism, shamanism, and even Christianity and Buddhism, to Islam thereby adopting the faith of the Turkic and native Caucasian peoples they ruled.

The khans granted a right to the Russian princes to rule their domains as Mongol vassals called *iarlyk*, for which princes travelled to the Mongol capitals in order to obtain these rights, to establish embassies, and to pay homage to their overlords. As early as the 1350s, however, some Russian princes started to organize resistance to their Mongol overlords, although most princes continued to serve the Mongols as tax collectors, while even performing other official duties on behalf of their overlords. In fact, it was the Russian lower classes rather than the princes and aristocratic families who bore the brunt of the Mongol economic yoke. Writes historian Charles Halperin:

> The peasantry...suffered the most from the Mongol campaigns and slave-raiding expeditions, and paid the greatest part of the tribute...the aristocracy were the chief beneficiaries of the commerce with the Orient. The princes...profited handsomely... (p. 85)

> Indeed, the Russian princes profited from the exploitation of their people. The grand princes were in charge of collecting tribute for the Mongols. This proved so profitable that the throne was more than worth the large bribes the khan required before awarding it...The princes manipulated the allocation of the tax burden. They exempted the crown lands from paying tribute altogether. It was the Russian elite who made the tribute regressive, forcing the poor to pay the most. (p. 78)

The southwestern portions of Rus' conquered by the Mongols eventually fell under the influence of the Poles and Lithuanians. These lands correspond roughly to the modern-day Ukraine and Belarus. In the northwest, the republics of Novgorod and Pskov continued independent existences into the early modern era. To the northeast, the Grand Duchy of Muscovy came to dominate what became the modern state of Russia. Moscow is located on the river of the same name which is a tributary of the Oka, itself a tributary of the Volga, the largest river in Europe. This gave the future capital access to trading wealth. By conquest, purchase of lands, marriage, strategic alliances, and diplomacy, the Grand Duchy of Muscovy, ruled by descendants of the original Viking ruler of the eastern Slavs, Riurik, grew in size and wealth during the late Middle Ages. Muscovy was one of the principal vassal-states of the Mongols, but it was also the head of a coalition that finally ousted the Mongols late in the 15th century from Russia. Ivan III, nicknamed 'the Great', saw himself as the leader of a national state for all Russians, historical descendants of what had once been Kievan Rus' during the high Middle Ages and the Kaghanate of Rus' during the early Middle Ages. As well, "he saw his newly independent realm as the successor to the recently vanquished Byzantine empire. He married Sophia, niece of the last emperor, and adopted the Byzantine double-headed eagle as his royal symbol." (Stevens) His successor, Ivan IV, nicknamed the 'Terrible', assumed the title of czar, derived from the caesars of the Roman empire. The Grand Duchy of Muscovy inherited much of the governmental and administrative apparatus of the Mongols including taxation, treasury and fiscal systems, customs, and tolls; military organization, armaments, and methods; bureaucratic language and diplomatic forms; and postal and justice systems.

Contrary to other parts of eastern Europe such as Hungary and Poland, the Russian economy did not hold a hinterland position vis-à-vis the emerging agricultural capitalism of western Europe, as per the Wallerstein thesis. Its farm crops were used internally, not for export westward. While it did trade eastward with Asian régimes, most trade was internal. The Moscow state regulated the economy with a view to keeping out foreign economic influence during the late Middle Ages. (Halsall) It was also a prosperous economy in part owing to its becoming a center for settlers from the northeast of Russia migrating toward Moscow and its countryside, and to its central position for overland and transit trade on the rivers of Russia. (Pitts, p. 3)

Russia was both a supplier and user of slave labor well into the early modern era. The peasantry was mostly free as per the rest of eastern Europe until the end of the 15th century and the modern era, when feudal relationships and serfdom *à l'Occidentale* came to Russia. Under Ivan III, laws were passed to restrict the movements of peasants, who became formally enserfed in the 17th century, a civil and legal status that endured into the mid-19th century. Boyar landlords also came to control their peasant tenants by means of credit and debt. This trend did not go unchallenged for, beginning in the 14th century and continuing afterwards, many of the descendants of erstwhile free peasants who were being enserfed ran away to the Pontic-Caspian Steppe where they survived as nomads by hunting, fishing, and raiding, joining with the local peoples of the region. A similar phenomenon occurred among Ukrainian serfs escaping economic exploitation by lords in the Polish-Lithuanian state. These were the famed Cossacks who offer, in fact, a prime example of popular resistance to exploitation via migration. It was a mass flight of peasants and other commoners who organized distinct communities. (Kimball)

Conclusion

The aim of this chapter has been to present the framework of development—political, social, and economic transformation—in which popular resistance to the ruling classes occurred during the high and the late Middle Ages, 1000–1500. Thus, we have described the development of church and state, and society and economy as well as the framework of class and class relations in this period in the West.

We found important diversity in the patterns of medieval development of the West. Thus, while feudal relationships and manorialism are useful tools for understanding medieval development, they are not concepts without difficulties, if only for the diversity of the manifestations of the two concepts. In some lands, in fact, they hardly apply at all even if, broadly speaking, most societies displayed the same social classes, that is, kings, princes, or emperors, lords, warriors, clergy, merchants, peasants, craftsmen, and laborers. Relationships among these categories of class varied so much that, in some cases, feudalism and manorialism are useful terms only by opposition to socio-economic realities on the ground. Still, the terms do serve as starting-points for the discussion of these diverse realities.

Chapter 10. Popular Resistance in the Middle Ages

Introduction

Barrington Moore describes the nature of the authority of rulers over the ruled.

> Authority is a reflection of the fact...that human society is, in part, a set of arrangements through which some human beings manage to extract an economic surplus from other human beings, and turn it into culture. (p. 17)

Among the products of that culture are ideological justifications that 'grease the wheels', as it were, of the extraction of the economic surplus of producers. Ideological justifications explain the origin and justify the maintenance of this extraction process. At the same time, just as in physics, actions produces equal and opposite reactions. Producers resist both the extraction of economic surplus iself and the ideological justifications that grease the wheels of this extraction: racism, sexism, patriarchy, to name a few. Resistance in the present requires that producers draw from memories of acts of resistance in the past by previous generations in order to motivate and inspire them. So, while rulers create ideology to justify and support extraction of economic surplus from producers, so do popular classes develop their own distinct culture, which includes both ideologies and attitudes towards ruling authorities.

> Popular attitudes towards authority ... are shot through with ambivalence, and in many cultures, there is evidence for a powerful undercurrent of egalitarianism, of resistance to and suspicion of all forms of subordination of one human being to another. (Moore, p. 24) A very small degree of social support...is sufficient to shatter the mystique of oppression and deception, and to permit a critical response to surface. (Moore, p. 116)

It is to these incidents of critical response in the Middle Ages that we now turn. There are two types of popular resistance, implicit and explicit. Implicit resistance refers to acts that do not confront the ruling classes overtly and directly. These include such acts as flight or migration to sites where conditions are more amenable. A good example of such mass movements occurred with the Cossacks. Fighting to maintain and restore, when necessary, the balance between demands for production and reproduction can represent another type of implicit resistance. Expressions of solidarity among immediate and extended family, clan and tribe during periods of social crisis or emergency can serve to provide another form of implicit resistance or, at least, mitigation of the negative effects of social domination. Students of slavery recognize instances of implicit resistance by slaves at work such as poor workmanship, foot-dragging, theft, and still other actions.

As interesting as implicit forms of resistance might be, we are more concerned with explicit and direct acts of medieval resistance such as riots, rebellions, revolutions, strikes, battles, wars, political actions, and religious dissent whereby the ruled confronted ruling classes overtly. Most useful is a concept of popular resistance suggested by the German scholar, Peter Blickle. Explicit popular resistance includes "...all forms and levels of conflicts, individual and collective, with subsidiary terms such as rebellions, riots, risings, uprisings, conspiracies, disturbances, and popular movements employed interchangeably." (Samuel Cohn, 2013, p. 27, footnote # 98) Furthermore, Samuel Cohn makes a further, useful distinction in his study of popular resistance in medieval English towns. Even where there existed considerable possibilities for legally recognized, collective action by the popular classes, Cohn is most concerned with "...collective action that took place only after such legal means had faltered, and the aggrieved had formed illegal assemblies, or had planned tactics rulers called conspiracies, or had engaged in collective action against rulers and their symbols of power." (2013, p. 26, 27) This type of popular action is the concern of this chapter, that is, explicit, extra-legal activities.

Popular Resources

People of the popular classes in the Middle Ages led difficult lives. Their short lives were punctuated by regularly occurring famines caused by poor harvests and by crop and animal disease, by illnesses and epidemics such as the bubonic plague, by persistent warfare among their social superiors for which innocent commoners often paid the price, by the ubiquitous social controls of their social superiors, and by superstitions and demons deemed to be everywhere haunting them. Most of all, there were the oppression and exploitation, and extraction of the fruits of their labors by people other than themselves. The latter included landlords, both secular and ecclesiastical, the rulers of Church and state, and the patrician, bourgeois elements governing the towns and cities to which commoners had migrated during the Middle Ages in order to improve their lives.

At the same time, commoners had at their disposal resources or strengths which they could plumb in order to inspire, motivate, and enable popular resistance. We've identified six wells from which the common people could draw, which we proceed now to elucidate. The first involved the traditions and customs that informed the lives of commoners; second, new attitudes to labor that emerged in the Middle Ages; third, legal advances in the Middle Ages; fourth, collective institutions that served or represented the popular classes; fifth, the emergence of centralized states; and sixth, alliances with other classes during conflicts of the latter amongst themselves, during which commoners often were able to advance their own situation.

The first source included the traditions and customs of the hamlets or villages in which most peasants lived. These were communities based on extended families from a given clan and tribe that occupied common fields, forests, marshes, and bodies of water from which peasants made their living. These commons might be subjected to takeover by other classes during the Middle Ages, but they were the bedrock of common agricultural life. Hence, they were both a common cause to be defended, and a resource and strength of the common people. In addition, left over from the days when tribes grouped all freemen-warriors in decision-making bodies were democratic assemblies where collective issues could be debated and decided. Among Germanic, Scandinavian, and even some Celtic peoples, these popular assemblies were called *things*. In fact, there are still linguistic relics in German and English, and in the Scandinavian and Romance languages of the ancient terms used for such an assembly, or for the location of an assembly, or for legal concepts derived from the existence of these assemblies. In England, a *folkmoot* was just such a popular assembly of freemen, leftover from pre-Norman, Anglo-Saxon times. Among Slavic countries, the popular assembly was called a *veche*, which might have been inspired by the example of the Vikings who colonized ancient Rus'.

It was possibly from memories of such primitive forms of democracy among freemen-warriors that the popular classes drew inspiration to develop councils, parliaments, estates, and the like in medieval times. One example of ancient popular assemblies surviving well into the Middle Ages occurred in Frisia, where geographic isolation meant that government by king and counts was only nominal. Instead, it was local councils of freemen who actually ruled. "Frisia in the 13ᵗʰ century consisted of about 25 de facto independent, 'peasant farmers' republics'." (Henstra, p. 85) For the most part, feudal social relationships never developed in Frisia. Rather, "...without counts or representatives of the king, the Frisians started to rule themselves in local and regional committees (where) decisions were made by the people." (Henstra, p. 161) A final source of custom and tradition defining popular life was the Church and its rituals, ceremonies, and liturgy of saints including local saints by which the annual calendar of peasant communities and their agricultural activities of sowing, harvesting, and the like operated. The difficult peasant life of seemingly endless labor, in fact, was broken up by the liturgy of holy days, saints' days, and celebrations that brought respite and joy into the lives of commoners. Appeal to customs and traditions was a powerful rallying-cry and point of reference for commoners defending themselves against other classes seeking to extract increased economic surplus, or to modify or remove customs beneficial to commoners.

A second source of strength among the popular classes was the new attitude towards labor that developed in the Middle Ages. This mew attitude differed from the negative social attitudes towards work that had existed from the onset of civilization itself. Even for early Christian thinkers, work was one of the inevitable effects of the original sin of Adam and Eve that defined and limited humankind. During the early Middle Ages, however, new ideas about the place of work and those who worked emerged. Now, the prevalent social régime within Christianity had it that there were three orders of society. Members of each order served God and society in their own way: those who prayed, those who fought, and those who worked. During the high Middle Ages, social thought with respect to labor evolved still further.

> A theology of work was developed. Work is pleasing to God. The first worker was the Creator himself, *summus artifex*, architect of the world. In the cathedral at Laon, God is portrayed as a worker...and is shown resting after completing his work. Representations of various trades and crafts are frequent in medieval cathedrals... Not infrequently, productive work is glorified in iconography devoted to religious subject-matter; for example, Noah's construction of the Ark, or the building of the Tower of Babel...The fact that agricultural occupations and crafts could be portrayed in such sanctified surroundings bears witness to general recognition of the value of labor as a divinely appointed institution, one of the ways to salvation... (Gurevich, 1985, p. 265)

A third, perhaps surprising resource for the popular classes involved the development of law, both of the Church and civil society, partly inspired by the rediscovery of ancient Roman law that civil jurists used to elaborate medieval property and contract law. Although this law was immediately advantageous to the landowning classes and the bourgeoisie, it also came to serve the popular classes in their advancement. In order to understand the resuscitation of Roman law during the Middle Ages and its positive effects on the common people, we quote Friedrich Engels.

> These new jurists...were predominately bourgeois, but not only that. The law which they studied...and practiced had an essentially anti-feudal... bourgeois character. Roman law is...the classic juridical expression of the living condition and frictions of a society in which the dominating concept is one of pure private property... Bourgeois property in the Middle Ages, however, was still permeated with feudal limitations; it consisted...largely of privileges...The further historical development

of bourgeois property could only be in the direction of pure private property....It was a mighty advance when a system of law was established that did not rest on feudal relations, and that fully anticipated modern ideas of private property. (p. 6)

Along with expressions of private property came the acceptance and general use of ideas that became part and parcel of commerce such as contract, partnership, pact, trust, credit, billing, and many other ideas that were Muslim in origin, and that were indispensable to trade and the bourgeoisie. In turn, these ideas rested on a basic concept of equality in legal rights, which goes as far back as the writings of Cicero in ancient Rome. This concept of equality of rights began to permeate all social layers during the high Middle Ages as lower classes also demanded their share of the legal rights and equal treatment being gained by the bourgeoisie. Writes James Thompson:

It is evident that by the 11th century, something like a revolution in political and social ideas was being generated in Europe. The older theories and principles...commenced to lose their force. Men were beginning to be impatient of the eschatological point of view and apocalyptic motif... and to demand something more practical and concrete, something more capable of terrestrial application. (p. 596)

These new legal ideas and commercial notions contributed to the prosperity and economic growth of the high Middle Ages. At the same time, advances in law also led to political change. The investiture struggle between the Holy Roman Emperor, Henry IV, and Pope Gregory VII produced arguments from the papal side to the effect that secular rulers ruled in a pact, a contract with the ruled in which rulers committed before God and the ruled to rule in a just manner. Should rulers abuse their power, they broke their contract with the ruled. The latter then could refuse to provide feudal service, while even deposing the ruler, if necessary. The divine right of kings had been limited first by secular lords and ecclesiastical officials. These same limitations, including the idea of the right of resistance by the ruled, percolated downwards in society to the bourgeoisie and then to the popular classes, so that these ideas became part of popular consciousness. As such, they became another resource available to the lower social classes for the defense and promotion of their interests.

The fourth resource of the popular classes included the collective institutions the lower social classes were able to develop themselves, or the collective institutions that other classes developed to address the needs of the lower social orders. This was part of a reliance upon collectivism rather than individualism and civil society. According to Antony Black:

The correlation... (of) property, security of person, legal equality, individual diversity... is mirrored in counter-schemes for redistribution of wealth, the abolition of private ownership, greater social conformity, and a tightly-knit, warm, charismatic community... or fraternity.

> Collectivism has...provided the counter-culture to civil society to which it poses a constantly unsettling threat. (p. 43)

We have already described some of these collective institutions: communes, confederations and alliances of communes, merchant guilds, and craft guilds. Another institution, seen particularly in the Holy Roman Empire in the late Middle Ages, was the village *gemeinde*, a democratic council that administered many local affairs previously occupied by lords as the latter devolved certain responsibilities onto the peasants, even as their demands on peasants increased. In a positive sense, this village government experience put peasants in western Germany and Switzerland in a good position to increase their political power. (Brenner, p. 58)

We've seen that as the Middle Ages proceeded, craft guilds were able to insinuate themselves and their working-class members into roles of greater importance in municipal governments and in society more generally. Around the end of the high Middle Ages in late in the 13th century, economic growth and prosperity started to wane, part of the coming crises of the late Middle Ages. Some guilds then began to display "...a transition from social to economic priorities, and a move away from social solidarity to mere collective self-interest within the group (and), about the same time, a change from liberal policies to protectionism and over-regulation..."(Black, p. 8) At the same time as guilds became less interested in promoting the concerns of customers and the equality of lower-ranking members of guilds, they became more interested in promoting monopoly control in their respective industries.

It has to be said, however, that actual behavior of guilds of all types is a matter of historical debate, with some historians arguing that guilds continued to play a positive social role during the late Middle Ages, rather than just defending the narrow interests of guild masters. At the very least, there were probably considerable local and regional differences in guild behavior across Europe. Nonetheless, many master craftsmen did become employers interested in suppressing wages and other conditions of employment of journeymen and apprentices. Journeymen responded by creating their own organizations, often extra-legal or secret, that municipalities sometimes prosecuted as conspiracies. So, workers responded once again by forming religious confraternities of journeymen called *compagnonnages* or *confrèries* in French, organizations that also served economic or social functions on behalf of journeymen.

These organizations often crossed city lines to include workers in entire regions. In part, this was a reflection of the reality that employment such as the building of castles, palaces, churches, monasteries, and cathedrals took place over more than one generation, whereby work and craft were handed down from father to son. These grand building projects might also require the services of workers from several locales since there simply weren't enough craftsmen in individual cities or towns to meet all local needs. Journeymen organizations served these migrant workers, offering them such services as reasonable accommodation, social support, and economic protection. These organizations were to play important roles in the social movements of the 14th and 15th centuries.

We've seen earlier that merchant and craft guilds and journeymen's associations offered charity to members such as burials, widows' and orphans' pensions, and the like. Some guilds also offered social services to the broad public. Nevertheless, the chief source of charity and social services had always been the Church since the beginning of Christianity, well into the Middle Ages. Almoners whose mission was to distribute charity to the poor worked in monasteries, abbeys, convents, dioceses, parishes, and among mendicant orders of friars.

Moreover, the Middle Ages saw the emergence of *béguinages* that grouped lay people in towns and cities who lived and worked communally, and who prayed and contemplated together. These people did not take religious oaths, but they did provide charity to the poor, and they often included wealthy men and women. Men in these lay groups were called *beghards*, while women were called *béguines*, with many being crafts people. As we shall see later, béguinages were a serious concern of the Church since they sometimes included spiritual advisors and leaders operating outside ecclesiastical boundaries, including some mystics who drew impressive urban followings. In fact, some béguinages and their members were judged by Church authorities to have crossed the boundary into heresy.

The granting of charity and social aid also went beyond almonry from religious sources, even while the religious benefits of providing Christian charity remained a motivation for rulers, communes, and secular lords who offered charity and social aid to the poor. As the Middle Ages proceeded, municipal institutions such as almshouses, hospitals for the lame and ill, and even public stores of food in towns and cities became commonplace. Among the services these institutions sometimes offered were short-term loans and other forms of easy credit for the poor such as pawnshops.

A fifth source of strength for the popular classes was a by-product of the successful development over time of the centralized monarchies that ruled national or proto-national states. Even though the growing states imposed taxes that often became the objects of protests by the lower classes, it is also true these same taxes paid the national armies that kings fielded in their attempt to control local lords. These armies included peasants and urban-dwellers from the lower social orders. Friedrich Engels described the process of how these new armies rang the death-knell of feudal armies composed of knights on horseback.

> In England, the gradual disappearance of serfdom gave rise to a numerous class of free peasants, yeomen or tenants and, therewith, to the new material for a new infantry practiced in the use of the longbow, at the time, the English national weapon. The introduction of these archers... was the occasion for an essential change in the tactics of the English

armies. From the 14ᵗʰ century on, the English knighthood preferred to fight on foot...Behind the archers who started the battle and softened up the enemy, the dismounted knights awaited the enemy attack in a closed phalanx, or waited for a favorable opportunity to break out with an attack themselves. Only part of the knights remained on their horses to help in...flank attacks. (p. 8)

Only when the French hired mercenary Italian archers could they counter the impressive English victories on French soil during the Hundred Years War. Mercenary armies became the modus operandi of European armies as the late Middle Ages gave way to the early modern era. Furthermore, the introduction from Iberian Arabs of gunpowder and cannon that could breach the walls of castles of knights and lords also contributed to making knights and lords in their castles militarily superfluous towards the end of the Middle Ages.

We saw earlier that the evolution of military tactics in the ancient world led to political changes that increased the power of citizen-warriors, as had occurred in ancient Athens and Sparta; witness the social and political ramifications of the Greek phalanx and of the Athenian trireme. Furthermore, the development of new citizen-armies provided another source of strength for the popular classes. These were the trained soldiers who sometimes led popular protest in military battles, and even drafted knights who were drawn into leading former infantrymen and archers in these same conflicts. These, in addition to the skilled soldiers that filled the private, mercenary armies, and helped lead popular medieval protests in Flanders, Switzerland, northern Italy, and the Holy Roman Empire.

The final source of strength for the popular classes in their attempt to advance socially involved alliances with other classes as part of conflicts between Church and state, king and noble, noble and Church such that popular interests might be served. There were endless zigs and zags in the relationships of the non-laboring classes, however, laboring people did know their interests and when uniting with other classes might serve their interests. This was popular agency at work, that is, the lower social orders choosing to advance their interests by their own actions. Thus, the common people might unite with the Church and king who were developing centralized states since this meant reducing the sway of local lords. Alternatively, in other instances the lower classes might ally with other classes to resist the imposition of state taxes. Or still, they might ally with secular powers to reduce the import of the Church, whose representatives actually might be the landlords of peasants and local rulers. On and on it went during the Middle Ages. Societal development meant a continuing kaleidoscope of changing class relationships in which popular classes played their part. Never were the poor—slaves, peasants, craftsmen, laborers—mere victims of their plight.

We now move on to consider popular resistance to each of the socially dominant classes: nobility, clergy, kings, and the urban patriciate-bourgeoisie.

Popular Resistance to the Nobility

There had always been popular uprisings, even if limited to specific locales, directed against particularly unpopular or ruthless lords. As the Middle Ages advanced, however, there were mass movements covering entire regions. The classes targeted by these popular revolts also evolved in conjunction with the march of medieval development. During the high Middle Ages at the zenith of the social power of local feudal lords, secular lords were the targets of popular revolts. Sometimes, the common people allied with Church and kings who were also trying to reduce the power of local, secular lords for their own reasons. In the late Middle Ages when centralized, proto-national monarchies emerged, kings and states became the targets of popular revolt, especially when new taxes or other state obligations were imposed on the common people. During this same period, ecclesiastical officials also became the target of popular protest as their temporal power and wealth increased with the progressive Christianization of Europe, and when lords ruling over the common people often were priors, abbots, bishops, or archbishops.

Some popular revolts were unsuccessful in the sense that their goals were not achieved, while rebellions sometimes were brutally suppressed by the lords who were the targets of popular protest. On the other hand, others were successful. Witness the long term success of the communal and guild movements. Generally speaking, there were increased liberty and social and economic possibilities for the popular classes as the Middle Ages proceeded. In the opinion of Samuel Cohn: "Late medieval revolts...were neither infrequent nor suicidal, ending inevitably in brutal suppression. Instead, regularly their leaders could cut favorable deals with their social betters and, more than occasionally, win outright their demands." (p. 316, 317) Moreover, in spite of the failure of some large-scale popular revolts...

> What was successful...was the less spectacular but, ultimately, more significant process of stubborn resistance village by village, through which the peasantry developed its solidarity and village institutions. It was on this basis that peasants...were able to limit considerably the claims of the aristocracy and, ultimately, dissolve serfdom and forestall seigneurial reaction. (Brenner, p. 59)

A similar claim can be made for the towns and cities where gradually urban residents successfully limited the power of the local nobility.

Quantifying medieval popular revolts is a difficult task that would require access to primary archival sources. An attempt at quantification is beyond the scope of the present work which mostly employs secondary sources. In fact, nowhere have we found secondary sources that provide such information, with the exception of Samuel Cohn's 2013 work about late medieval, popular revolts in English towns and cities, which we analyze later in this chapter. Nonetheless, a qualitative approach can help uncover patterns among the causes and effects of revolts, the course of events, gains and losses for rebels, popular leadership, and subsequent repression. Peter Blickle describes some of the causes of medieval revolts.

> A basic motive behind the numerous agrarian revolts... (was) resistance to... increasing dues and services restricting peasant autonomy, common lands and the use thereof... (1979, p. 225, footnote # 11)

Furthermore, once again according to Blickle,

> There seems to be, in fact, no revolt mentioned in the sources for the late Middle Ages in which the original motive was not protest against increased dues. Even if the peasants only demanded restoration of customary practices, closer investigation reveals, in all cases, an increased economic burden on the peasantry. (p. 231)

Another pattern seen in revolts in the West was that they were usually led by peasants or craftsmen rather than by representatives of other classes. The leaders of these revolts were peasants, butchers, carpenters, weavers, sailors, and other workers and craftsmen. There was still another pattern in the late Middle Ages: popular revolts were part of the long term emergence of proto-capitalism, part of:

> ...the long transition from functional feudalism with its social hierarchy based on an agricultural foundation to parliamentary democracy based on egalitarian and capitalist foundations. (Blickle, 1979, p. 226)

Anti-nobility Revolts in France

Feudal social relations developed precociously in France owing to the formation then disaggregation of the Carolingian empire towards the end of the first millennium. Nobility came to rule the various regions of France during the early Middle Ages, while the central state was weak. Thus, it might be expected that we might see considerable anti-nobility rebellion and revolt in France, which we indeed do. What follows are some examples of this ferment during the high Middle Ages.

In 998, early in the reign of the fourth duke of Normandy, Richard II, Norman peasants revolted against exorbitant seigneurial dues. They resisted the exercise of seigneurial rights, proceeding to take command of the fields, waters, and forests over which the lords claimed ownership. In what might be cited as an example of self-managed, anarchist communities, the peasants established local law-making councils. Moreover, each council sent two representatives to a regional council, hailed by anarchists as an example of bottom-up federalism. (Fremion, p. 15) In actual fact, Norman peasants might have been resuscitating the Norse tradition of the *thing*, the democratic assembly of freemen warriors. In fact, Normandy had been conquered only four or five generations previously by Viking invaders. Nevertheless, the outraged Norman lords, led by the duke's uncle, the count of Évreux, Rollo, reinstated their rule with a vicious and bloody repression of the rebellion. During the 12th century, a Norman poet named Wace wrote about the rebellion in a poem entitled *Le Roman de Rou*, written in old Norman French and commissioned by King Henry II of England, who wanted a chronicle of the Norman dukes. We can read two excerpts of this poem drawn from secondary sources that relate the events of 998–999.

The villeins and the peasants held several parliaments. They spread out this command: He who is higher, he is the enemy and many of them made an oath that they would never agree to have lord and master. (Harman, p. 150)

Moreover, of the lords and masters...

> Woe betide them should they come face to face with thirty lads in the bloom of youth! Not one of them can stand against us if we all set about him with clubs, great staffs, bludgeons, bows, arrows, and axes, and, for the weaponless, stones. Then, we will be able to go into the woods to fell trees, and take what we will, and take fish from the ponds and venison from the forests. And we will have our way with everything, with the woods, fields, and meadows. (Fremion, p. 16, Author's translation into English)

Almost two centuries later, the 12th century war for the succession to the French crown wreaked havoc. There was much brigandage by lords and their soldiers in one region in particular, the Auvergne, in south-central France, where the Church responded to out-of-control aristocratic warfare and violence by organizing the Peace of God and Truce of God movements.

The clerics who led these movements, in fact, were responding to social pressures from the lowly. There was at least one peace movement initiated by the poor themselves. In 1182, a carpenter named Durand Dujardin from the town of Le Puy in the Auvergne reported receiving visions from the Blessed Virgin Mary to the effect that he create a brotherhood of peace. The resulting confraternity of people of lowly social rank swore oaths to attend mass, and to follow more closely the tenets of their Catholic faith. The members of the confraternity, called *caputiati*, wore white hoods with Latin inscriptions and portraits of Mary and the Christ Child. Their numbers swelled to include poor people in the surrounding regions of central and southern France in the Berry, Limousin, Gascony, Aquitaine, and Provence regions. The cause struck a responsive chord among rebellious laboring people grown weary of out-of-control violence by lords and their soldiers.

During the next year, the caputiati organized militia that defeated several armies of brigands. The caputiati broadened the targets of their actions to include social superiors whom the Caputiati attacked and killed. "Flushed with success, the Caputiati extended their definition of plunder to include prelates and nobles who exploited their serfs; they even invoked Adam and Eve as proof that all should be free and equal." (Landes, p. 170) Alarmed local aristocrats and brigands sought revenge by smashing the caputiati militarily.

The successful avengers were led by a nobleman named Hughes of Noyers, who became the local bishop in 1183.

The Black Death wrought by the bubonic plague struck the West during the years 1347–1351. The plague had a motivating effect on popular protest. Even before the Black Death, however, there had been incidents of popular revolt, especially in the form of riots directed against local nobility. Revolts were a frequent occurrence in several regions in France: Normandy, Picardy, l'Île-de-France, where Paris and Orléans were located, and the Champagne and Lyonnais regions southeast of Paris. Several towns and cities experienced more than one revolt over the years, among them: Lyon, Béziers, Carcassonne, Mont-Brison, and Saint-Galmier. The leading communities in this regard, however, were the ever-tempestuous people of Paris, Provins, and Rouen. The latter two cities experienced at least six popular revolts directed against local noblemen prior to the Black Death. There were also similar popular revolts in Calais in 1298, in Beauvais in 1305, in 1308 in Saint-Malo, in Brittany, where the sole revolt and attempt to form a commune in the region failed miserably, as well as in Saint-Quentin in 1311. (Bourin, p. 55, 56, 61)

Some explanation is in order with respect to the Black Death, the social and economic consequences of which were enormous. The Black Death was believed by both Muslims and Christians to be of divine origin. Moreover, owing to the Christian doctrine of original sin, the plague was held by many to be God's punishment for humans being born in sin. Even though the personnel of monasteries, convents, and churches struggled mightily to treat the ill, with many religious people dying in the process, popular trust and faith in the Church were shaken to the roots. This later contributed to the popular revolts against the Church and its ecclesiastics. According to an American historian, Walter Zapotoczny,

> It is estimated that between 1/3 and ½ of the European population died from the outbreak. As many as 25% of all villages were depopulated, mostly smaller communities, as the few survivors fled to larger towns and cities. The Black Death hit the towns and cities disproportionately hard. Some rural areas, as in Poland and Lithuania, had such low populations, and were so isolated that the plague made little progress. Larger cities were worse off as population densities and close living quarters made disease transmission easier. Cities were also strikingly filthy, infested with lice, fleas, and rats... (and) subject to diseases related to malnutrition and poor hygiene... The influx of new citizens facilitated the movement of the plague between communities, and contributed to the longevity of the plague within larger communities. (p. 1, 2)

From the same source come examples of population loss in the Middle East. In 1348, about 10,000 died in Gaza, while 500 per day died in Aleppo in Syria in the same year. In Damascus, at the peak of the fury of the disease in the months of September and October, about 1,000 died each day, with a total estimated population loss of 25-38% for 1348. By March, 1349, Syria had lost 400,000 people. Some European examples of population loss: in Bremen in Germany, 7,000 of a total population of 12,000 died; in Florence, nearly 40,000 of 90,000 died; in Siena, in Italy, 2/3 of the population died; finally, Paris lost 50,000 from its population of 180,000. (p. 2)

As a result of the plague and the attendant population loss, the economy of the West was greatly transformed. There were more arable lands available with fewer people to farm them. Thus, lords were forced to make their lands more attractive to peasants. Rents extracted from tenants decreased, services and dues paid to landlords were lightened, while cash was used increasingly rather than payments-in-kind; as well, more freedom and autonomy were granted to peasants. All this at the same time as grain prices diminished owing to decreased demand. This exerted a downward pressure on the incomes of the nobility.

It also represented, for the most part in western Europe, the beginning of the end for feudal relationships. Peasants migrated in great numbers to towns and cities, attracted by rising wages, sometimes five times pre-plague levels. (Zapotoczny, p. 2) While per capita wealth increased since there were fewer people to use available resources, profits actually declined owing to increased wages. French historian Michel Mollat provides some examples of wage increases for workers. (p. 199, 200) In Paris, wages for masons and roofers working on the building of a hospital doubled between 1348 and 1453. In Florence, wages doubled after the plague, while wages for construction laborers quadrupled in the years after the plague. In England, wages for journeymen masons increased 20%, while agricultural day laborers' wages more than doubled after the plague compared to wages at the beginning of the century. This was also the case throughout much of Europe including in such countries as Navarre, Poland, and Germany.

Lords responded by getting governments to pass legislation to control and limit wages to pre-plague levels, measures that met with little success. Among the most notorious of these measures was the Statute of Laborers of 1351 in England. Municipalities and states tried to regulate wages, prices, guilds, mobility of workers, unemployment, and begging. Local governments tried to limit wages such as occurred in the towns of Amiens in France and Metz in Germany, and in Flanders and Hainault counties in the Low Countries. In July, 1349, the Aragon government set maximum wages for tailors, tanners, blacksmiths, carpenters, quarrymen, ploughmen, shepherds, and domestic servants. These workers were asking to be paid four or five times pre-plague wages. (Mollat, p. 200, 201) In such an atmosphere, class conflict was overt, and led to some major popular revolts against French secular and ecclesiastical lords during the period from the 1350s to the 1380s. We consider next the most significant anti-seigneurial revolt of the post-plague period in France.

The Great Jacquerie

The Great Jacquerie was a peasant revolt that took place on the plain surrounding Paris in late May and early June in 1358, a decade after the Black Death. It started in a village in the Oise Valley named Saint-Leu d'Esserent, and led to similar movements in Picardy, Champagne, Normandy, and l'Île-de-France. The term 'jacquerie' derived from a nickname of derision used by the upper classes for the peasants whom the former called Jacques Bonhomme, Jacques being a common given name of French peasants. By way of analogy, it might be comparable to a contemporary, English-language name for blue-collar workers, 'Joe Lunch-bucket'. Jacquerie has become a term used generally by historians for violent peasant revolts.

As background for the events, French historian Monique Bourin cites several factors: the Hundred Years War, which left unemployed mercenary soldiers to wreak havoc looting, raping, and plundering, violence the French nobility seemingly was incapable or unwilling to arrest; the destabilizing political rivalry for the French crown between the Valois family and Charles of Navarre (Navarre was a kingdom in the Basque country in northern Spain and southwest France) after the extinction of the Capetian line of royal male descendants; the French state's increased financial requirements owing to war with England; the unjust rule of the governing oligarchies in the towns and cities of France; and the economic difficulties associated with the crises of the late Middle Ages. (p. 50) Add to this the general ill health of the populace after the plague. More specifically, in September of 1356, the French king, John II, was taken captive at the battle of Poitiers during which French nobles surrendered their king, only one of several disgraceful performances on the battlefield by knights and nobles in 14th century France. The country and the estates, the legislative representatives of commoners, clergy, and nobility, were divided between their support for Charles of Navarre and the king's son and future king, Charles V, such that there was really no effective government in the country.

The actual sparks for the jacquerie were the requirements that peasants pay increased taxes including the *taille*, a regressive head-tax, and that they provide unpaid corvée labor to repair war-damaged aristocratic properties such as castles and manors. On May 28 in Saint-Leu, a group of 70 or so peasants were meeting to commiserate about these burdens when two young aristocrats led a small troop of knights and squires who came to organize the corvée. The peasants killed the aristocrats and nine soldiers, and the rebellion was on.

The rebels conscripted as their captain a seemingly reticent peasant named Guillaume Carle, who appears to have had military experience, along with several knights whom the peasants drafted, possibly against their will. In towns such as Beauvais, Senlis, Rouen, Amiens, and Meaux, burghers and the urban underclass supported the peasant rebels. The rebels set about destroying castles and houses of noblemen, about 150 in all, murdering their occupants, and sacking towns. On June 6, the rebels struck an arrangement of support with Étienne Marcel, a rich bourgeois who was the *prévôt des marchands* in Paris, an office similar to mayor. Marcel was leading an anti-royal revolt in Paris in an attempt to apply constitutional limits to the monarchy. (More about Marcel later) The rural rebels and 800 Parisians took a castle at Ermononville, near Paris. Three days later, however, Charles of Navarre, accompanied by a few nobles, put a bloody end to the revolt. Carle received a promise of a truce and a pardon, and was invited to the camp of the nobles, where he was summarily decapitated.

In the aftermath of the rebellion, nobles and knights roamed through the countryside, lynching peasants at will. About 20,000 peasants were killed in reprisals even if it is estimated that only about 5,000 peasants and 800 Parisians actually took part in the Jacquerie. The campaign of terror by the nobility continued throughout the summer. One massacre even occurred at Reims where there had been no rebellion, while French knights and nobles were joined in the festivities by their noble and knightly brothers-in-arms from the Low Countries. As brutal as was the repression and punishment of the rebels after the Jacquerie, the mere mention of the word continued to send chills down the spines of French aristocrats even well after the French Revolution into the 19th century.

Anti-seigneurial Revolts in the Low Countries

The ecclesiastical principality of Liège in modern-day Belgium provides an almost perfect example of the social forces at work in western Europe during the late Middle Ages. Our source is Alphonse Le Roy. For 38 years beginning in 1297, two groups of noblemen known as the *Awans* and the *Waroux* fought a seemingly never-ending, private war, the putative start of which involved a romantic elopement. The war cost 30,000 lives. The ruling bishop was unable to bring the war to an end, a fact that diminished significantly his legitimacy as well as that of the local nobility. Against this background, partly inspired by the example of successful guilds in nearby Flanders, Liège workers started agitating for rights. In 1302, the ruling council of Liège signed a declaration in which they granted the guilds a veto over the raising of taxes and public expenditures, including for purposes of raising a militia or for making municipal grants to the bishop. No sooner had this veto been granted than the bishop and the local council reneged on the offer to the workers. The wardens of the local cathedral, however, led the workers in resisting the wealthy. The latter responded by setting a trap for the rebel workers by inviting them to a conference in August, 1305, for which the noblemen were prepared militarily. Nonetheless, the local workers showed up in a disciplined, armed force led by an educated burgher named Arnould de Blankenheim. The workers successfully insisted on the maintenance on their new rights. Two years later, the bishop once again formally recognized the popular rights gained by the citizens of Liège.

Five years later, the aristocratic and democratic forces once again had a major disagreement, this time over the appointment of a regent to represent the bishop during his absences. The person chosen was none other than the leader of the popular party, de Blankenheim. The nobles, however, wished to name a nobleman to the post. As had happened five years earlier, the nobles proposed a great regional assembly to resolve the difference of opinion. At the same time, however, they hatched a secret plot to be put into effect during the regional assembly. At the regional meeting, the democratic forces held their own, refusing to yield to the demands of the lords, who were frustrated mightily. Their secret plot had it that 400 knights would invest the city of Liège in the middle of the night, occupy strategic posts, and set the butchers' shops on fire. In the confusion, an army of knights would deliver the fatal blow to the popular forces.

Somehow, de Blankenheim got wind of the plot. That night, the butchers prepared in the dark in the building that housed their shops. When the knights penetrated the building, the butchers let out a loud roar, setting upon the knights with knives and other tools of their trade. At the same time, the town bells rung, signalling to the vintners, drapers, tanners, and other craftsmen to join in the attack on the knights. All night long, the battle raged. Come dawn, the knights fled in a fighting retreat to a nearby mountain. During the pursuit of the knights, de Blankenheim was killed, which seemed to rally the noblemen, who were further encouraged by the coming of reinforcement knights. The popular side seemed to be losing finally, when a clamor arose as local peasants and rural coal-miners joined the fray alongside the workers of Liège. The knights scattered to and fro, finally ending in Saint-Martin church where 200 of them sought refuge. When the popular army discovered this, they set flame to the church, killing all inside. The common people then went on a bloody rampage, destroying the houses of knights and those of the ruling council, while also taking the lives of their occupants. The mayor of Liège and the wardens of the cathedral tried in vain to calm the ardors of the populace. The Liège knighthood was completely domesticated after this battle, known in the local dialect of the time as the *male de Saint-Martin*. A peace treaty the next year made it impossible for aristocrats to sit on the ruling council unless they were also members of workers' guilds. Liège was now governed as a democracy rather than an oligarchy.

The county of Flanders was a French territory in the Low Countries, part of modern-day Belgium. It contained both French and Dutch-speaking communities. The county was a hotbed of anti-nobility sentiment and political action during the late Middle Ages. Sometimes, the French king and state were the targets, especially since French control over the county had only been established at the end of the 13th century. At the same time, there were local, longstanding, popular customs that needed defending, a role which the local nobility sometimes claimed. At still other times, the local bourgeoisie was the target of popular resentment and political action.

Flanders was one of the most advanced parts of Europe in terms of economic and urban development. Local merchants and patricians had won significant power, which sometimes clashed with popular interests. Important popular revolts occurred during the years 1323–1328.

With borders on the shore of the Atlantic Ocean, Flanders traditionally had close economic relations with England. English wool was imported to Flanders, then woven into cloth, and exported throughout Europe. In English-French conflicts, the people of Flanders, as well as their counts and members of the ruling class, often sided with England. In 1322, the Flemish count Robert III died, and was succeeded by his grandson, Louis of Nevers. By marriage and upbringing, Louis was thoroughly French, in fact, he was one of the most powerful noblemen of France. As count of Flanders, Louis adopted a pro-French, anti-English policy, which made him unpopular with the common people of Flanders. After poor harvests in 1323, the imposition of a county tax along with increased Church tithes provoked popular resentment among peasants. Two farmers, Zegher Janssone and Nicolaas Zannekin, led a revolt which successfully won over community after community. Count Louis arrived in Flanders in January of 1324. With no army, he was forced to negotiate with the rebels. In April, the rebels won their legal points against the new French count and his tax collectors.

The next year, rebellion occurred in the cities of Flanders. The actual spark was the murder of a laborer by knights, and the related arrest of six burghers of Bruges by Count Louis. The people of Bruges took up arms. After the town of Courtrai was burnt by Count Louis, he was captured by citizens of the burnt town. Burghers from Ypres and weavers from Ghent joined in the now-regional rebellion. The urban-rural collaboration of the rebels was notable. The city-dwellers were led by a weaver from Bruges, Jacob Peyt, and the mayor of Bruges, Guillaume de Deken. The king of France, Charles IV, suggested that the Count and the popular party submit their respective griefs to the king for his resolution, which the popular party refused to do. In response, the Church issued an interdict on Flanders, and the king's army defeated the rebels in a battle near Assenede. Just before Christmas of 1325, the Count was finally liberated by his captors from Courtrai. In February of 1326, Count Louis pardoned the rebels, and promised to respect the liberties and customs of the Flanders communes. The king ratified the arrangement, while the Church's interdict was finally lifted on April 26.

The French king died in 1328, and was succeeded by Philip VI. Shortly thereafter, popular rebellion began anew. At Count Louis' request, Philip ordered a campaign of pillage in western Flanders. The Flanders communes were defeated in August of 1328. In the defeat Zannekin was killed. The king returned to France with 1,400 hostages in tow chosen from the burghers of Bruges and Ypres. The Count undertook the arrest and execution of the rebel leaders, while their properties were distributed to his followers. Urban privileges were revoked, and the towns were made to pay heavy fines as punishment for their misdeeds, while the fortifications of Bruges, Ypres, and Courtrai were destroyed. This was a clear case of the French state and its county representative, Louis of Nevers, establishing the preeminence of the state over French territory including Flanders, regardless of the contrary perception of the economic and political interests of the people of Flanders.

The revolt known as the 'Bread and Cheese' revolt was a peasant revolt that took place in 1491–1492 in West Frisia and Kennemerland, in North Holland. An economic crisis caused by poor harvests, an epidemic of the plague, and the tax policies of the local count, Jan III of Egmond, provoked the rebellion. Jan had raised taxes to support his army. The rebels travelled to The Hague to demand tax relief, but this pressure only resulted in the addition of another new tax. The rebels then sacked two castles of Count Jan, then travelled from town to town successfully gaining the support of local burghers. In their travels, they carried banners with emblems of bread and cheese, while carrying the same two foods around their necks. This leads one to suspect that the lower classes might have been hungry owing to famine, and that the taxes imposed by the local lord were the final straw that provoked them to rebel. The count referred disparagingly to the whole business as the 'bread and cheese game', hence, its historical title. The rebels eventually were defeated soundly by an army of the count and the local governor, the duke of Saxony, Albert III, whose troops were equipped with cannon. They managed to kill over 200 rebel peasants, and executed still more rebels. As well, rebel towns were constrained to pay severe financial penalties, and were deprived of their urban rights and privileges for many years. (Budde) In 1497, the same duke of Saxony put down another peasant revolt in Frisia, this time led by one Shaard Ahlva, in which peasants tried unsuccessfully to resist the imposition of feudal obligations. Recall that for many years the peasants of Frisia had lived de facto free lives in spite of nominal rule by distant noblemen.

Anti-noble Revolts in Spain

The territory that comprises modern-day Spain provides several examples of medieval popular revolts against local lords. As with other parts of western Europe, local seigneurs in Spain were powerful, while monarchies were weak and unable to govern their kingdoms without sharing sovereignty with local warlords. In fact, this phenomenon might have even been more acute on the Iberian Peninsula where Christian kingdoms were established during the high Middle Ages on a piecemeal basis as part of the *reconquista* of Islamic Iberia that took place over hundreds of years. The solutions for common people to the problem of strong local lords resembled those used by the common people of the Holy Roman Empire, that is to say, development of autonomous communes and confederations and alliances among communes for purposes of socio-economic development and resistance to the aggressions and claims of noblemen.

The medieval kingdoms of Castile, Leon, and Aragon were no match for the warlords who controlled the countryside. So, brotherhoods of townsmen and peasants called *hermandades* were formed to maintain the peace. The first instance occurred in northern Spain where a brotherhood was formed in the 12th century to protect pilgrims from roving bands of robber knights on the famed route of pilgrimage to Santiago de Compostela in Galaecia in northwest Spain. It should be noted that this was not just a humane nor religious impulse on the part of the brotherhood since the pilgrimage was vital economically to the towns on the pilgrimage route. This initial, temporary example was repeated throughout the Iberian lands, such that the brotherhoods became a common and permanent feature of medieval Spain, in fact, right into the modern period. The local brotherhoods also included small organizations meant to maintain the peace in small towns and villages, among them, market towns that served peasant farmers. These small brotherhoods federated with larger organizations into fraternities known as *hermandades generales*. (Brunel/Brunet, p. 96, 97)

The hermandades eventually became involved in national political questions such as royal successions. Spanish historiography includes debates about whether the brotherhoods were genuine instruments of popular resistance to the nobility, or merely tools in the hands of the various pretenders to the crown or other politicians. In fact, as with most such either-or historical debates, both arguments are true. (Brunel/Brunet, p. 95) The brotherhoods were allies of the centralizing monarchs who also sought to control local lords. At the same time, locally speaking, the brotherhoods became responsible for many state justice activities. Abuses of power were common, so popular demands eventually grew to reign in the authority and scope of brotherhood activities. A similar mixed assessment can also be rendered about one of the most important national uses of the brotherhoods. As one of the first acts after the War of the Castilian Succession, King Ferdinand and Queen Isabella established a centrally organized, efficient *Santa Hermandad*, or holy brotherhood, with themselves at its head. They adapted the existing form of the hermandad to the purpose of creating a general police force endowed with large powers of summary jurisdiction, even in capital cases. The rough-and-ready justice of the Santa Hermandad became famous for brutality.

In fact, one of the missions of the Santa Hermandad was to limit opposition to Ferdinand and Isabella, for which the brotherhood was well-funded with taxes including special wartime taxes the organization was able to collect from resistant individuals and communities by force, if needed. Thus, the story of the hermandades provides a good example of social development during the Middle Ages. Originally a grassroots, peasant response to the lawlessness of local warlords and knights, the brotherhoods allied themselves with kings trying to strengthen the monarchy in resistance to their mutual enemy, the local warlords. Eventually, the state took over the brotherhoods, turning them into organs of administration of the emerging national state.

A Galaecian variant of the Castilian hermandades was the *Irmandino*, which occurred in two stages, from 1431 to 1435, then again a generation later between 1467 and 1469. The irmandinos were self-defense fraternities that emerged in response to feudal exactions by secular and ecclesiastical lords from peasants and burghers. Galaecia was part of the united kingdoms of Leon and Castile, however, its geography and economy gave it unusual features. Very much an agricultural economy exploited by lords, Galaecia's location near the sea isolated by mountains meant that local lords were more or less free to do as they wished with their subject populations. The Wikipedia essay describes the Irmandino revolts. The first revolt took place in response to cruel treatment meted out by the lord of Andrade, one Nuno Freire. A confraternity called the *Irmandade Fusqunelha* was created among peasants. From its inceptions in two regions, the revolt spread to three bishoprics, including to Santiago de Compostela. The leadership for the revolt was provided by a knight named Roi Xordo, who was killed in noble reprisals when the revolt was suppressed in 1435. In the 1460s, another knight named Alonso de Lanzos created a larger brotherhood called the *irmandade xeral* to defend against the feudal lords. This organization had the direct support of the king and several municipal councils. The actual inception of the Irmandinos revolt occurred during years of poor harvests and episodes of the bubonic plague. At its height, the Irmandinos numbered about 80,000 troops drawn from a broad class base: peasants, townsmen, knights, and some clerics who even financially supported the rebels. They were led by three knights who divided up the military tasks: de Lanzos, who fought in the northern reaches of Galaecia; Pedro de Osorio, who fought in central Galaecia around Santiago de Compostela; and Diego de Lemos who led the forces in the south. Their opponents were the heads of the main churches and monasteries in the region and the secular noble families, in particular, the Andrade, Lemos, and Moscoso families.

At first successful, the rebels destroyed about 130 forts and castles, and forced the local nobility to flee to Portugal but, in 1459, a nobleman named Pedro Madruga returned with a force from Portugal equipped with arqebuses that joined forces with the army of the archbishop of Santiago de Compostela. The rebels were defeated, while their leaders were captured and executed. Although immediately unsuccessful, two decades later, the monarchs Ferdinand and Isabella created a justice system independent of local lords whereby officials reported directly to the crown. As well, the Galaecian monasteries now were required to follow the decisions of their respective Castilian orders. Madruga and other powerful lords were executed by the monarchs, with seigneurial lands being redistributed to the crown. The authority of the Santa Hermandad also was extended to Galaecia. Finally, the royal couple definitively abolished any remnants of serfdom in

1480. Thus, over the long term, the Irmandinos did succeed in their ambition to limit the power of local lords.

The region of Catalonia in northeast Spain, which formed part of the medieval kingdom of Aragon, also saw its share of lower-class, social revolts. Ultimately, these rebellions succeeded in dismantling the serfdom that had existed for about 400 years in the region. Around the end of the first millennium, Frankish peasants had settled in the Spanish March, the border area dividing what were eventually Spain and France. Small farmers, these Catalonian peasants were confirmed as the owners of their property, land, and persons by the justice court of the local count about the year 1000. Elsewhere in western Europe during the high Middle Ages, the common people were beginning to gain their freedom from warlords in order to advance their social and economic interests. The situation in Catalonia was quite the opposite. During the period 1030–1060, local agents of the count of Barcelona began establishing themselves as independent lords in the countryside of Catalonia. In effect, they were erecting the social and economic structures of feudal arrangements as they applied to peasants. Around 1100, a system known as redemption serfdom came into being. Peasants became *pagesos de remença* tied to the land they work, which they could not leave without the permission of their lords, that is, without redemption by their masters, usually obtained by hefty payment to the lords. The status of remença was passed from father to son. Thus, lords began the long process of extracting economic surplus from the labor of peasants, even absconding the land itself, traditionally occupied and worked by peasants. The lords exacted dues and rights in return for the peasants' right to survive on their own customary land.

In 1150, by a document known as the Customs of Barcelona, the process of broadening the definitions of seigneurial rights began in earnest. In addition to the right of redemption, seigneurs gained several new rights. Lords could abscond with part of a peasant's land if the peasant died without progeny, in a portion that was equal to what would have been the son's share if he had existed. If a peasant died without having made a will, the lord could assume a third of the late peasant's land if he left a widow and orphans, or half the land if there were no heirs. Even more bizarrely, the lord could abscond with half the property of an adulteress who cuckolded her husband, or with all her property if the husband acquiesced in her infidelities, indeed a blatant example of patriarchy that encouraged husbands to control their wives under the risk of serious financial penalty. A woman who expressed her illicit, amorous desires paid financially for her indiscretions, a cost that might even involve her life itself if she was left with no land to support herself. If a peasant's farm buildings burnt, the lord could claim a third of the peasant's land as punishment for putative neglect of the property or possible malice by the peasant. As well, a peasant also had to pay the lord for the right to marry. During the 13th and 14th centuries, the lord's rights over the life, family, and land of the peasants were further extended in terms of practices of justice, permitted movements of peasants, prohibition of the sales of peasants' lands without seigneurial approval, and even prohibiting the possibility of peasants taking holy orders as monks, priests, nuns, etc... (Organizing Committee...) The lives of peasants were fully circumscribed in terms of their marrying, loves, family, labor, and even death, all part of the processes of ensuring the transfer of economic surplus from one class to another, and ensuring the continuing availability of peasant labor to create that surplus.

In 1333 there began a long period of famine as well as epidemics including the bubonic plague, which produced increased mortality. Many peasant farms became simply unused and abandoned. The diminished peasant population increased the bargaining power of the lower class vis-à-vis the nobility, as per elsewhere in western Europe while, at the same time, noblemen strove to circumscribe even further the lives and labor of peasants. This was the signal for overt class war and popular resistance to the nobility. The latter tried to install what the peasants called *malos usos*, additional services to be provided to the lords, thus ensuring the availability of labor on lords' estates or financial payments in lieu thereof. Around the turn of the 15th century, spontaneous resistance started to appear. There were riots, crops burnt, and threats issued to lords by peasants who dug symbolic graves and erected crosses at the future, threatened burial sites of the lords. Aragonese kings such as Marti, Alfons, and Joan tried to promulgate measures favorable to the peasants, measures that the lords resisted. Among the measures instituted by King Alfons was the right of peasants to form a peasants' union, but the king soon reversed his position in response to noble pressures. Nonetheless, peasants held assemblies and created organizations of self-defense.

Social tensions grew further. In 1462, there were riots, part of a peasant-nobility civil war that coincided with a war between King Joan II and the nobility. The king's armies fought on the Mediterranean coasts while, in the mountainous interior of Catalonia, a popular movement led by a peasant named Francesc Verntallat fought the noble armies for a decade. The king won the war, but failed to deliver on his promise to the peasants of ending feudal abuses, even if he did institute minor reforms such as creating the position of Viscount of Hostoles for Verntallat himself. A generation later, the nobles forced the king to re-establish the feudal rights of the seigneurs. Open warfare broke out in 1484 under the leadership of a lawyer named Tomas Mieres and a priest named Joan Sala. Sala was a true revolutionary, more radical than Verntallat; the latter seems to have been more of a reformer. To Sala, it was self-evident that feudal dues should be abolished, and that peasants should own the land they worked. Sala was defeated in 1485; however, during the next year after another rebellion, King Ferdinand II of Aragon passed measures that outlawed feudal abuses, including reducing the redemption payment to the relatively small amount of 60 *sous* that freed the peasantmore or less from feudal exactions on his land and on his person.

The kingdom of Aragon also included the Balearic Islands in the Mediterranean. Over the course of the 14th and 15th centuries, conditions for peasants on the largest Balearic island of Mallorca deteriorated greatly. There were poor harvests and increased taxation of the peasants, who were called *foraneos*, as well as stringent land tenure conditions by the rulers of the main port of Palma, who owned most of the land on the island. These oligarchs also controlled the ruling council of the island. In 1450, a major revolt began with a tax strike by Church leaders joined by the peasants, then by the lower classes from the small port towns. The rebels succeeded in gaining control of the island, and laid siege to the capital; however, they were defeated in 1452–1453. The king responded to the rebellion not by decreasing the requirements of serfdom, but by decreeing permanent serfdom for all rebels. A second peasant revolt on Mallorca was also repressed in 1462–1463, as was also a major rebellion on the second Balearic Island in terms of size and importance, Menorca, between 1462 and 1466. Unlike the mainland, peasant revolt on these islands was met with bloodshed and the strengthening of feudal obligations upon the peasantry.

The Holy Roman Empire

The Holy Roman Empire also knew its share of anti-noble popular revolts during the late Middle Ages. The empire was a unified entity in name only. The many member states and principalities of the empire were ruled by counts, dukes, princes as well as by bishops, archbishops, and abbots. Clergy ruled many states that were actually ecclesiastical entities. With such decentralization of authority, it is easy to understand how local rulers were the antagonists of the peasantry in the rebellions. The causes of the revolts were multiple: warfare, taxes, serfdom, Church exigencies, arbitrary justice systems, and seigneurial limitations on hunting, fishing and other rights to the bounty of the forests, especially firewood. These were reflected in the demands of peasant rebels. While it appears that most of the targets for these rebellions might be described as ecclesiastical, there were indeed some régimes ruled by secular lords that were subject to peasant uprisings.

The most cataclysmic events of peasant-seigneur conflict in Germany took place early in the modern era beyond the period covered in this book. Known as the German Peasant War, the conflicts of 1525–1526 cost the lives of 100,000 peasants. Nonetheless, during the late Middle Ages, there were precursor revolts and attempts at revolution in the empire. Austrian historian Christina Linsboth enumerates 44 peasant uprisings during the late Middle Ages before the period of the German Peasant War: four in the 14th century, 15 between 1400 and 1450, and 25 in the next half-century, with another 18 during the first quarter century of the early modern period. Peter Blickle has mapped these uprisings as being concentrated for the most part in four contiguous regions of the empire: the Swiss lands, the Austrian lands,

Swabia in southwest Germany, and the upper Rhine valley in southern Germany. (1979, p. 227)

Interesting to note is the relative absence of peasant revolts east of the Elbe River. Robert Brenner offers a useful explanation for these differences. (p. 56, 57) West German peasants had over many generations developed democratic village institutions that took on many tasks such as maintaining the local peace. In addition, these village councils oriented agricultural practice such that communal organization of peasant farmlands became the norm. This provided an institutional base from which peasants could resist the aggressions of the lords during the crises of the late Middle Ages when class conflict over the division of the economic surplus became most acute. According to Brenner:

> Most fundamental was the need to regulate co-operatively the village commons, and to struggle against the lords to establish and to protect commons rights: common lands for grazing and so on, and the common field organization of agricultural rotation.... Issues of a more general economic and political character (also) tended to be raised. The peasants organized themselves in order to fix rents and to ensure rights of inheritance...They fought successfully to replace the old, landlord-installed village mayor...by their own village magistrates. In some villages, they even won the right to choose the village priest. All these gains the peasants forced the lords to recognize in countless village charters...through which the specific concerns of the peasantry were formally institutionalized.

In eastern Germany, however, a different pattern obtained. Settled en masse much later, east German communities were often colonies founded by lords who directly sought out peasants to work their lands. The lords and their officials directed the administration and government of lands and villages. In eastern Germany, direct, allodial ownership by lords was more common than the age-old, customary occupation and ownership of farmlands by the peasantry in western Germany. There were fewer village charters and institutions of peasant solidarity and self-management in eastern Germany. There were also fewer common lands and fewer instances of common field agriculture as compared to western Germany. All this meant that east German peasants had a less effective base from which they could resist seigneurial demands.

Two particular periods of anti-nobility conflict within the empire draw our attention: the Carinthian peasants' revolt of 1478 in Austria and the Bundshuh movement in Germany during the late 15th and early 16th centuries. The peasant revolt in Carinthia took place in the context of Turkish raids into Austria. There were five such raids during the decade of 1473–1483 during which much murder and mayhem occurred. The local nobility was so overwhelmed by the scale of the Turkish raids that they retreated into their castles. At the same time, local clerics fortified their churches and monasteries to protect themselves. The peasants were left without the protection that the nobility was supposed to offer the common people according to the traditional justification for the wealth and power of the nobility vis-à-vis commoners. In 1478, a peasant named Peter Wunderlich led the creation of a Carinthian farmers' league. The peasants formed an army of 3,000 to face the Turks. The Turkish army of 20,000 men, mostly cavalry, however, frightened off the majority of the peasants. The rebelling peasants were accused by the authorities of treachery, the rebellion was suppressed, and Wunderlich was publicly dismembered. A small force of Slovenians led by a man named Matjaz, nonetheless, decided to meet the Turks in the fields near the village of Kokovo, modern-day Coccau, in Italy. The 600 poorly-armed peasants and miners were massacred in the battle, after which the Turks continued their campaign of plunder throughout the region. The battle spawned a myth among the Slovenes that the 600 peasants and their King Matjaz did not die, but actually sheltered in the nearby Urslja Gora Mountain, and are still sleeping there. They will wake up once the king's beard has encircled the stone table by which he rests nine times, after which he will walk outside, and happy times will come for Slovenians.

The direct precursor to the Great Peasant War of 1525–1526 was the Bundshuh movement of loosely related peasant rebellions in western Germany that occurred between 1493 and 1517. The movement took its name from the rebels' flag with the emblem of the laced shoe worn by peasants in contrast to the boot worn by members of the nobility. The flag was first used by the peasants and townsmen who defeated the army of the French count of Armagnac in Upper Rhineland in successive battles in 1439, 1443, and 1444. During the famine of 1493, peasants and other poor people in Alsace formed a secret society. Even some wealthy burghers, including the mayor of Sélestat, as well as some local knights joined the organization. Its aims were revolutionary: a jubilee year as per the practice among the ancient Hebrews during which all debts would be cancelled; the ending of customs and excise duties and other taxes; the end of ecclesiastical and nobles' courts; the right to vote about taxes; reductions in priests' salaries; the right of communities to elect their own leaders; and finally, what was to be one of the ugliest and cruelest legacies of the Middle Ages, the proposed-then executed pillage and extermination of Jews, among whom local money-lenders in Germany were concentrated.

The plan was to take the castle of Sélestat, and to confiscate the treasuries of the town and of the local monastery, then proceed to spread their revolt to all of Alsace. Just before the execution of this plan during Holy Week, however, the authorities got wind of the secret project. They captured, tortured, and decapitated the would-be revolutionaries. Many of the would-be rebels fled to Switzerland and southern Germany, where they continued their secret agitation. In 1502, in the diocese of Speyer, a similar conspiracy of 7,000 lower-class people prepared a plan comparable to the Alsatian plan. This time additional conspirators came from the north in the lower Rhine Valley. Their demands: abolition of all feudal dues, custom duties, Church tithes, and personal taxes paid to nobles, priests, and princes; abolition of serfdom; and confiscation of Church properties and their redistribution to the poor people. As part of their demands, the common people would have no master except the emperor, and would be subjected to no justice other than to that of God. Unfortunately, the movement was betrayed by a priest who revealed the contents of a confession of one of the conspirators. Nonetheless, the Bundshuh continued its secret existence, including organizing three more public manifestations of the movement during the next generation early in the modern era, all of them unsuccessful. (Engel, 1850)

The English Peasants' Revolt

Many in the English-speaking world are familiar with the English Peasants' Revolt of 1381. It is one of the best-known of the medieval popular revolts, taking place a generation after the Black Death. In 1351, the Statute of Laborers was adopted by the English government in response to pressure by lords, both secular and ecclesiastical. This law tried to peg wages of workers to pre-plague wages, even as wages were rising in light of the shortage of labor after the plague. As well, the shortage of peasants to farm the lords' lands also presented opportunities for rural commoners to improve their economic and social lot. Many more fled to towns and cities, while others successfully bargained better arrangements with their lords. Trying to administer unpopular laws and regulations to control workers and peasants was virtually impossible in light of what was actually happening on the ground in thousands of daily transactions among lords and their social inferiors. Nonetheless, there were officials who tried mightily to do so, in the process further antagonizing the common people.

The Peasants' Revolt occurred against the background of the Hundred Years' War and the financial exactions necessary to fund English armies. Between 1377 and 1381, there were three attempts to collect poll taxes, per capita taxes of an equal amount to be taken from all adults, rich or poor, male or female, whether women were married or single. This latter point was to prove vital since women played an important role in the revolt. The poll tax was collected from them whether they were married or not, employed or not, and whether or not they had the financial means to pay. The poll taxes then were spent quickly on fruitless military campaigns. The English Peasants' Revolt was sparked by the third attempt at collecting a poll tax in 1381.

There were several contemporary chronicles of the revolt. Even if they were not at all sympathetic to the cause of the commoners, they do provide detailed information about the revolt, including names of rebels and their leaders. When combined with court records and Church archives, the result is a treasure trove of historical and archival information about the English Peasants' Revolt, about which much data has been published in secondary sources.

The term 'peasants' is actually somewhat of a misnomer since many of the rebels were craftsmen or other workers from villages, small towns, and market towns in southeast England or from London itself. Local priests also played leadership roles even if targets of the revolt included high-ranking churchmen. There were even some merchants and successful farmers who took up the rebel cause as did many of the poor of London. Finally, certain government officials such as bailiffs and aldermen also played leading roles.

Wat Tyler was the most important leader and public spokesman of the revolt, while a priest named John Ball played the role of leading propagandist and ideologue. Even so, the leadership of the revolt was manifold and broad, both geographically and socially speaking. Moreover, we know many of the rebels by name and occupation including those of the leaders. Tyler himself was a worker from Kent, southeast of London, perhaps a tiler-roofer who had served in the French wars. Geoffrey Litster, a weaver or dyer from East Anglia, northeast of London, earned the title 'king of the commons' for his leadership role. William Corre was a tailor from Cambridgeshire, while Thomas Baker was a cook from Essex. Among the farmers who played leading roles were William Gildeborne, John Cook, Thomas Engilby, and Thomas Samson. Robert Westbrom was a merchant, Geoffrey Denham a squire, Henry Bakere a bailiff. Geoffrey Cobbe and John Hanchach were successful farmers from Suffolk and Cambridgeshire respectively. John Home was a London alderman who arranged for the gates of London to be opened to the rebels.

There were many other leaders whose occupations this author did not find in secondary literature, men such as Alan Threder, William Hawler, William Bokenham, John Brux, Robert Cave, Abel Ker, Thomas Brembole, and Thomas Harding. In some cases, we don't know the trades of rebel leaders, but we do know whence they hailed. John Hales and John Ferrour were from Kent, while Essex man John Starling bragged about beheading the archbishop of Canterbury, Simon Tybald of Sudbury. Thomas Farringdon, Henry Baber, and Adam Mitchell also were from Essex, while Jack Straw also seems to have been one of the Essex leaders. John Greyston was from Cambridgeshire; Thomas Halesworth was from Bury Saint Edmund's; William Grindcobbe led the revolt in St. Alban's.

Women were central to the revolt in leadership roles, and not merely as voices in the crowd. Among women leaders were Katherine Gamen, Margaret Starre, and Margaret Wright. Gamen was involved in the capture and execution of the chief justice of the realm, Sir John Cavendish. There were at least 70 women rebels from Suffolk. The most important woman leader seems to have been Joanna Ferrour, wife of John Ferrour, who were leaders of the rebellion in Kent. Mrs. Ferrour was also involved in the burning in London of Savoy Palace, the most impressive mansion in London and property of the influential lord and politician John of Gaunt. Joanna Ferrour was also involved in the summary executions of the Archbishop of

Canterbury, the Royal Treasurer, and the king's physician /tax collector for Kent.

Priests played important ideological roles in the English revolt. John Batisford, Geoffrey Parfrey, and Nicolas Frompton were among the twenty or so clerics who helped lead the rebellion. The two most important priest-rebels were John Wrawe from Essex and the afore-mentioned John Ball. In June of 1381, Wrawe led rebels from Essex seeking to foment rebellion in neighboring Suffolk. On June 12th, Wrawe's force destroyed a local lord's property in Overhall. The next day, the force reached Cavendish and Bury St. Edmund's in western Suffolk. Along with Suffolk leaders, Wrawe's force attacked the local priory, whose leader, John Cambridge, was most disliked among locals. Two days after the attack on the priory, Cambridge was found and executed. Rebels moved north, and tracked down Sir John Cavendish, who was chancellor of Cambridge University in addition to being chief justice in the land, then executed him. On June 15th, revolt broke out in Cambridgeshire, led by Wrawe and local leaders. There must have been a longstanding town-gown quarrel between the locals of Cambridge and the university's priests as the rebels burnt the Cambridge charter since it was perceived by the rebels as being the source of the university's unpopular and unfair privileges. At the university, Wrawe's rebels ransacked Corpus Christi College and the campus church, and burnt the institution's library and archives. The next day, according to the Wikipedia essay about Wrawe, the university was forced to agree to a new charter minus its erstwhile, royally-granted privileges. The rebels then moved north to Ely where they executed a justice of the peace, and opened the local jail, freeing its prisoners.

John Ball had already been imprisoned for his radical, apocalyptic preachings. Ball publicly preached...

> that in the beginning, all human beings had been created free and equal. It was evil men who, by unjust oppression, had first introduced serfdom against the will of God. Now was the time given by God when the common people...could cast off the yoke they had borne so long, and win the freedom they had always yearned....The great lords, the judges, and the lawyers, all these must be exterminated, and so must everyone else who might be dangerous to the community... (Norman Cohn, p. 199)

A French chronicler of the revolt, Jean Froissart, put these words in the mouth of Ball as being typical of his sermons.

> If we are all descended from one father and mother, Adam and Eve, how can the lords say that they are more lords than we are, save that they make us dig and till the ground so that they can squander what we produce? They are clad in velvet and satin set off with squirrel fur, while we are dressed in poor cloth. They have wine and spices and fine bread, and we have only rye and spoiled flour and straw, and only water to drink. They have beautiful residences and manors, while we have the trouble and the work, always under rain and snow. It is from us and our labor that everything comes, with which they maintain their

pomp.... Good folk, things cannot go well in England nor ever shall until all things are in common, and there is neither villein nor noble, but all of us are of one condition. (Norman Cohn, p. 199)

This was indeed the stuff of revolution, and John Ball was its leading ideologue.

We shall now trace the actual evolution of the revolt and its aftermath using several secondary sources that are listed in the accompanying reading list: Samuel Cohn (2013), Halesworth, Hogeboom, Milone, Mollat, Simkin. As mentioned above, the actual spark for the revolt was the third poll tax. Returns were less than what the government expected. On March 16, 1381, the king's tax collector for the county of Kent, Sir John Legge, suggested that Parliament compare tax payment lists to population lists with a view to compelling payment. In Norfolk, there were 8,000 people who had evaded the tax while, in Suffolk, the figure was 13,000. Judges were sent to punish tax evaders. In some villages, government agents were reputed to have inspected young girls to determine if they were still virgins since, if not, the poll tax would apply to them as they would be considered adults. On May 30, government agents travelled to Brentwood to collect the poll tax. Thomas Baker led local men in refusing to pay the tax. They were joined by about a hundred men from nearby communities. The government agents tried to arrest the men, but the rebels drove the officials out of town. Baker then sent the men off to other nearby villages and towns to spread the word to not pay the poll tax. The rebels armed themselves with scythes, axes, and knives, and the revolt began in the region. On June 2nd, a judge named Robert Belknap arrived in Brentwood to summon jurors to try the recalcitrant tax evaders. He could not raise the jurors; furthermore, the community forced him to swear an oath not to try to do so again.

On June 7, the rebels from Kent chose as their leader Wat Tyler. The next two days, the rebels went to work, attacking castles, manor houses, and lords' houses, in the process destroying documents relating to serfdom, taxes, and judicial proceedings against serfs. They broke open prisons freeing prisoners, one of whom was the priest, John Ball. On June 10, Tyler and the rebels reached Canterbury in the middle of Mass. They demanded that the monks choose another archbishop of Canterbury since the current man, Simon Tybald of Sudbury, was a traitor according to the rebels. Indeed, Simon was chancellor for the king, sort of a royal advisor. Several local officials in Canterbury also were attacked and killed. Lords' houses were destroyed including that of Sir Robert Hales, treasurer of the realm. Lords were forced to issue charters granting freedom to their serfs. On June 11, the Kent rebels started advancing toward London, in the process destroying more manor houses and freeing imprisoned serfs. The next day, Kent rebels reached Blackheath outside London, while Essex rebels reached Mile End, also near the capital. Revolts were now spreading throughout England. Rebels were arriving in the capital from Surrey, Sussex, Suffolk, Norfolk, Cambridgeshire, Buckinghamshire, and Hertfordshire. Tyler's force probably numbered about 30,000, while there might have been a similar number of rebel supporters in the capital itself. Norman Cohn explains that there was a considerable urban proletariat in London, similar to those in France, the Holy Roman Empire, and the Low Countries. This proletariat included

> ...journeymen who were excluded from the guilds and, at the same time, were forbidden to form organizations of their own; unskilled workers and worn-out soldiers and deserters; a surplus population of beggars and unemployed; in fact, a whole urban underworld living in great misery, perpetually on the verge of starvation, and constantly swollen by the flight of villeins from the countryside. (p. 204)

London mayor William Walworth ordered the rebels to disperse, an order the rebels ignored. In fact, with the connivance of a London alderman, John Home, access to the city for the rebels was granted via London Bridge during the afternoon of June 13. Early that same day, it became clear to the king and his advisors that they would have to negotiate with the rebels. The king and his court of seven or eight noblemen had retreated from Westminster Place to the Tower of London. There were about 1,200 troops nearby available to the king and his government, but the loyalty of these men could not be trusted since it was feared it might actually lie with the rebels. The young king was all of fifteen years of age, and only recently governing at the end of the regency during his minority. He decided to talk with the rebels, the first of several meetings between Richard II and Wat Tyler. So, during the morning of the 13th, Richard talked to the rebels for the first time from the Tower of London. Tyler asked for a meeting, a request to which the king acquiesced. From the relative safety of a barge, the king and his advisors parlayed with the rebels on shore, who demanded the execution of John of Gaunt, then in Scotland, Simon Tybald of Sudbury, Robert Hales, and John Legge. The frightened royal party refused to disembark, and returned to the Tower of London, however, the king agreed to meet the rebels the next day at 8 am at Mile End, just outside the city walls. This was to be the third discussion between the king and the rebels, at which time Tyler presented his demands: the end of all feudal services serfs were required to provide their lords; the freedom to buy and sell any and all goods; and a pardon for offences committed by the rebels during the revolt. The king agreed to these demands, and arranged for signed charters granting freedom to all serfs. Tyler pressed his advantage, and suggested that the administrators of the poll tax were corrupt and should be executed, to which the king replied that all people found guilty of corruption would be tried and punished by law.

After the signing of the charters granting freedom to the serfs, many of the rebels returned home satisfied, however, there remained a considerable force of angry rebels still committed to the cause. Later that afternoon, John Starling led 400 rebels into the Tower of London where they summarily executed Tybald, Hales, and Legge, then proceeded to loot wealthy properties and to burn Savoy Palace and the temple of the Knights Hospitallers of St. John, an organization led by Hales.

By this time, Mayor Walworth had managed to raise an army of 5,000 men. The king sent a message to the rebels that he wished to meet Tyler again the next day, June 15, at Smithfield, near London. Tyler arrived alone only lightly armed. He made further demands: the end of tithes paid to the Church; the removal from office of all bishops, to be replaced by one bishop for the entire kingdom; redistribution of wealth; equality of all before the law, and freedom to hunt in the forests. The king asked Tyler to leave London with the rebels, which led Tyler to suspect the sincerity of the king, interpreted by royal supporters present as a sign of disrespect for the king. Walworth was outraged, and began arguing with Tyler. The mayor stabbed and killed Tyler. Then, some of Walworth's men beheaded Tyler, brandishing his head on a pike for all the rebels to see. The intimidated rebels were surrounded by Walworth's force, but the king allowed the rebels to disperse, which they now did, the rebels deprived of their principal leader and spokesman.

Over the next week, the king in council with his advisors decided to renege on his promises to the rebels. On June 23rd, the king announced his new position, and marched with an army into Essex where there still were rebels active. Five days later, Richard II defeated the Essex rebels; 500 rebels were slain in a battle while survivors dispersed. On July 5th, William Gildeborne and Thomas Baker, both from Fobbing, were executed along with other rebel leaders from the area. A week later, the king and his government finally managed to restore order. The time was now ripe for a general repression. John Ball and Jack Straw had been in hiding in Coventry when they were captured and executed. Ball was hung, drawn, and quartered, as was William Grindecobbe from St. Alban's. There were still echoes of rebellion in the south of England as late as the end of September under the leadership of Thomas Harding, but these disturbances were short-lived after their leaders were executed. There seems to be no evidence that Joanna Ferrour was ever convicted for her part in the rebellion. Cleric John Wrawe appears to have escaped execution by denouncing co-conspirators. By the end of the year, the king had issued many pardons, and ordered a general amnesty for other rebels. Interestingly, the Cambridgeshire tailor, William Corre, escaped the royal repression along with nine other men in order to live in the countryside by banditry, surviving from their plunder for a year until October of 1382.

The Peasants' Revolt of 1381 might appear to have been a failure at first glance. It was indeed so in the sense of the bloody repression and the temporary tightening of feudal arrangements with respect to workers and peasants following the revolt. In another sense, however, the revolt was part of a process of inevitable, long-term social development. By the end of the 14th century, official attempts to enforce the Statute of Laborers were ended since it was a fruitless exercise. Serfdom faded away, leading to a form of proto-capitalism at the end of the late Middle Ages, in no small part caused by the direct resistance of the lower classes to the constraints of feudal society. Nonetheless, the violence of the repression following the revolt, as was the case with many of the revolts during the late Middle Ages, demonstrates how the ruling class was able to use state violence and terror to maintain a social order favorable to its members.

The Uprising of Ivaylo in Bulgaria

There were other popular revolts against secular nobility in Scandinavia and eastern Europe. One of the most successful of these revolts was an uprising led by a peasant named Ivaylo in northeastern Bulgaria during the years 1277–1280. Ivaylo was a swineherd who managed to convince his fellow peasants to follow him into battle by claiming to have received messages from God. The Bulgarian state and nobility during this period were engaged in the erection of oppressive feudal obligations upon the common people. As well, the Mongols were continually raiding in northeastern Bulgaria, activity that the local nobility and a usurper emperor named Constantine Tikh could not seem to arrest since state authority had diminished in the region.

In the spring of 1277, Ivaylo's army twice defeated Mongol forces. By the fall, Ivaylo had chased the Mongols completely out of Bulgaria. His popularity reached untold heights, so much so that Ivaylo was proclaimed emperor by the peasants in areas under his control. Towards the end of 1277, Constantine Tikh raised a force against the peasant rebels. The imperial force was defeated, while Ivaylo himself slew Constantine Tikh, whose army then joined Ivaylo's rebels. The rebels proceeded to take the fortified towns and cities of Bulgaria. Only the imperial capital, Tarnovo, remained in the hands of the nobility. In a stunning turn of events, one of Constantine Tikh's widows offered her hand in marriage to Ivaylo so that she might remain in power. Ivaylo accepted this arrangement in order to avoid further bloodshed in a fight for the capital and the imperial crown. In the summer of 1278, Ivaylo entered the capital to be proclaimed emperor.

From the south, however, came a new threat, the Byzantine empire. Ivaylo's ascendancy had foiled Byzantine interventions in Bulgarian politics. Furthermore, there was a risk that Ivaylo's successful class war might spread south. The Byzantines sent several armies to face Ivaylo, but the latter's army managed to defeat them during the summer and fall of 1278. The Bulgarian nobles rallied, however, and chose one of their own number as a rival emperor to Ivaylo. The Byzantines successfully urged their new Mongol allies to resume their attacks on Bulgaria. The combined armies of Mongols, Bulgarian nobles, and the Byzantines were too much for Ivaylo, whose armies and peasant supporters became exhausted by the continual warfare. By the end of 1280, Ivaylo was defeated, then killed by the Mongols. Ivaylo had not had the time nor the liberty to install a new social régime, what with all the warfare. Nonetheless, to Bulgarian peasants, he was a popular hero devoted to social justice and equality. In his memory, pseudo-Ivaylos afterwards appeared several times in the Balkans to lead popular revolts. Ultimately,

Ivaylo's revolution offered proof that a medieval peasant army could defeat imperial armies and nomadic raiders if it was well-led and inspired by the pursuit of popular justice.

The Zealots of Thessalonica

In the first half of the 14th century, Thessalonica was one of the wealthiest and most populous cities in Byzantium, second only to Constantinople. During the same period, however, the Byzantine empire went into decline owing to civil war in the 1320s and foreign invasions. As a result, the whole empire was beleaguered and impoverished. This was especially the case among the lower classes when compared to the aristocracy of town and country in whom most wealth was concentrated. The leader of the nobility was a man named John Kantakouzenos. Opposed to Kantakouzenos was the *megas doux*, the grand duke, Alexios Apokaukos, admiral of the Byzantine navy. The latter led a legitimist faction that supported the imperial crown in a civil war against the aristocracy. The conflict between the two sides degenerated into a class war whereby the wealthy aristocrats were confronted by other social classes supporting the crown. The political divisions were also exacerbated by each of the two camps receiving the support of rival groups of differing religious opinions. In Thessalonica, the workers were led by longshoremen and sailors, especially a man named Michael Palaiologos. The workers took control of the highly prized, second city of Byzantium in a bloody revolution. They roused up the people against the aristocracy and, for two or three days, Thessalonica was like a city under enemy occupation, and suffered all the corresponding disasters. The victors went shouting and looting through the streets and night, while the vanquished hid in churches, considering themselves lucky to be still alive. Then followed a hunt for all the members of the upper classes. They were driven through the streets like slaves with ropes round their necks. Here a servant dragged his master, there a slave his purchaser, while the peasant struck the *strategos* (general), and the laborer beat the land-holding *pronoiars*. When order returned, the Zealots, suddenly raised from penury and dishonor to wealth and influence, took control of everything, and won over the middle class.

The workers' city supported the crown during the civil war. Thessalonica was governed as a commune and a popular republic. The possessions of the noblemen were confiscated and redistributed to the common people. The tide of the civil war, however, eventually turned in favor of the nobility. The erstwhile leader of the crown faction turned against the Zealots, and had Michael Palaiologos killed in order to take control of Thessalonica himself. Once again, the common people, led by another longshoreman named Andreas Palaiologos (unrelated to Michael), retook the city, in the process killing about a hundred aristocrats, then plundered their property. The Zealots then held Thessalonica until the end of 1349, when they were defeated finally. The next year, the emperor and the Orthodox Church patriarch returned triumphantly to Thessalonica after having reconciled successfully with the noble faction and its leader, John Kantakouzenos. Nonetheless, as was the case with Ivaylo of Bulgaria, the common people of Thessalonica, at least for a certain time, had succeeded in establishing popular rule by mean of a successful revolution.

Anti-noble Revolts in Scandinavia

During the late Middle Ages, the Nordic countries including Finland, then part of Sweden, were ruled by a common monarch, even if local political institutions were respected by the crown. Unlike western Europe where feudal obligations on peasants and townsmen gradually were ending, in Scandinavia during the 15th century, local noblemen and magnates were attempting to impose such obligations on other social classes. Predictably, such attempts met popular resistance. We consider two peasant rebellions against the intentions and plans of the nobility: David's uprising in Finland during the 1430s, and a peasant rebellion in the Danish region of North Jutland during the next decade. In the first rebellion, a wealthy peasant named David led peasants to revolt against local taxes and lordly incursions into what had been traditionally peasant economic space: fisheries, meadows, and forests. Peasants traditionally used the ancient method of creating farmland out of forests by using slash-and-burn techniques. Now, however, changing economic conditions allowed aristocrats to claim their due over the unimproved wilderness. (Katajala, chapter 3.) David led peasants in the revolt; unfortunately, there exists little information in the secondary literature in English or French about the actual events of the revolt and its results and aftermath.

We know more about the contemporary revolt in Denmark. Noblemen in Denmark were engaged in a similar operation to Swedish lords in Finland in the much less remote and more populous, settled farmlands of Jutland, trying to extend their economic sway over the land. The new king of Scandinavia, Christopher of Bavaria, had just put down a peasant revolt on the Danish island of Funen, east of the mainland in the Baltic Sea, one of his first acts upon assuming the crown. Christopher then followed up on his campaign on Funen by moving against a major peasants' revolt in North Jutland in the north of mainland Denmark. This peasant force proved to be formidable. It was led by a man named Henrik Reventlow, who managed to assemble an army of 25,000 peasants. In one of the most legendary of peasant military battles, Reventlow's army built a fortress of wagons arrayed three layers deep in front of which was a huge bog. The peasants knew the local noble army that formed up to fight the rebels would come at them directly from the direction of the bog. So, the peasants placed tree branches on the bog, then covered it with earth so it might appear to be solid ground. The nobles' army, led by a man named Eske Brok, confidently charged the peasants' fortifications on May 3rd, 1441, only to become mired helplessly in the bog. The peasants then closed in and slaughtered the knights. Brok was killed and dismembered, then his parts were sent as warning to other lords in nearby communities.

The peasants next burnt the most important lord's manor in the region, forcing its owner and occupant to flee with nothing but his life. Soon, however, the king rode north with his own army to confront the rebels. On June 8th, King Christopher's army defeated the peasants in a ferocious battle in which thousands of rebels were killed. Survivors were fined heavily, and were now permitted to own no weapon bigger than a small knife. Most importantly, serfdom was extended to the whole realm, so that the erstwhile free farmers of Denmark, the proud descendants of Vikings, now became feudal serfs.

The Merfold Rebellion in England

The middle of the 15th century presented trying economic times in England. Historians refer to the period 1440–1480 as the Great Slump, essentially brought on by the seemingly endless Hundred Years' War. England suffered from economic blockades and loss of markets for its wool trade, partly owing ironically to English predations in war-torn France. The king of England at the time was Henry VI, whose mental grip on reality was tenuous, to say the least. In fact, in 1454, the king went completely insane. Before that happened, however, his government was one of the most unpopular ever seen in the land. In June of 1450, a veteran of the French wars named Jack Cade led a revolt against the king and his government in the same county of Kent where the Peasants' Revolt of 1381 had started. Cade's rebellion, however, was directed against the poor government of the king and the corrupt officials who directed it. In fact, in one declaration, Cade specified that his revolt was not against the established social order but rather only against those lords and gentlemen, lawyers and judges, bishops and priests, and government ministers and officials who were guilty of malfeasance and corruption. Shortly after, Cade was killed and the rebellion was defeated; the reprisals of the king and government that followed were ruthless in spite of the king having issued pardons to the rebels, pardons that were quickly revoked.

Later that summer, discontent and grumbling grew once again among the lower classes. At the end of July, two brothers, independent farmers named John and William Merfold, from Sussex, made a public declaration in a marketplace to the effect that the king was mad and, as such, should be deposed. At the end of August, a certain William Howell encouraged local men to join him in a rebellion. All through the fall, men congregated, armed for war with clubs and bows and arrows. In a tavern in October, John Merfold declared that the rebellion would leave no survivors among the gentlemen of the land. The local lords, particularly the unpopular duke of Suffolk, were targets for the rebels who beat noblemen and clergy, then pillaged from their unfortunate social superiors. Contrary to Cade's rebellion, the Merfold rebellion was definitely class-based. The ultimate aim was to destroy the social order, not just to demand reforms. The demands of the rebels included termination of feudal exactions and duties paid to lord,s and payment of fines and taxes paid to the state. The rebels stopped paying these monies, partly since they simply did not have funds to do so. They demanded the deposition of the king, and advocated the murder of all lords and high clergy. In their stead, the rebels proposed that a government of twelve rebels be appointed to rule the land. Most tellingly, they advocated that all property be held in common. In the spring of 1451, men once again began congregating for action in Sussex and Kent. While there were some agricultural laborers and farmers among the rebels, most were young craftsmen: carpenters, skinners, masons, dyers, tailors, smiths, cobblers, weavers, tanners, butchers, and other tradesmen. This time, the authorities moved swiftly. They arrested the rebels, and hanged four rebel leaders from Sussex; thus was the rebellion quelled.

Success and Failure of the Anti-noble Rebellions

To some, the violent, popular revolts against the nobility proved to be pointless. According to this view, since the rebels knew violent ends during the periods of repression and reprisals from their social superiors that followed peasant rebellions, the latter were but instances of temporary madness afflicting the common people. Furthermore, the latter were often led to revolt by leaders from other classes misleading the lower social orders for their own diabolical purposes. In fact, this is a view often found in the contemporary sources written by clerics or government officials.

To historians influenced by this view, any success the rebels might have known was only the result of secular trends that were going to result in social change, regardless of the actions of the common people. These arguments are easily countered by a brief review of the patterns in the above cases. Firstly, most of the leadership in Europe of popular uprisings against secular lords came from the common people themselves. As for long-term trends pushing social changes, in fact, popular rebellion was indeed one of the factors creating secular transformations. Viewed in a long term over centuries, ultimately all anti-seigneurial revolts were successful, if only for the fact that the noble class was eventually replaced as the ruling class in the West, whether by its destruction in revolution or its evolution to irrelevancy other than in symbolic, traditional roles.

In a more limited sense, however, even if we look at the cases described above with respect to results obtained during medieval times, we still find an optimistic record. Some of the anti-noble efforts saw immediate success, as in Liège, the Hermandades in Castile, and the revolts in Catalonia. Other revolts produced temporary successes even if the final results were repression and temporary return to the old social order. Witness the revolts of the Caputiati in southern and central France as well as popular revolts in Flanders, Bulgaria, and Thessalonica. Other revolts, even if immediately suppressed by the ruling classes, did result in popular demands being met within a generation or two of the initially unsuccessful revolts, as seen in the aftermaths of the English Peasants' Revolt or that of the Irmandinos in Galaecia. Finally, the examples of anti-seigneurial revolts cited above provide evidence of the historical agency of the popular classes, that is, peasants and workers self-consciously trying to improve their lot and those of their children and grandchildren by undertaking political actions. As such, these revolts provide evidence of the continuing and persistent nature of class conflict throughout medieval history.

Moreover, the fact that popular rebellion in the Middle Ages led to brutal repression and reprisals lends proof to the idea that the medieval social order could only be maintained through the use of armed force or the threats thereof. One more point needs to be made, that of necessity. Sometimes rebellion happened because the common people had no choice, that their backs were to the wall, that rebellion was better than waiting for a perceived destruction and disappearance without resistance. Hence, even if the risks of political action were great, sometimes political inaction or apathy would have been even more dangerous to the popular classes when faced with the predations of the seigneurs.

Popular Revolts against Ecclesiastical Lords

Perhaps as much as a third of the land in medieval Europe was the property of the churches, Catholic and Orthodox, and their institutions: abbeys, priories, bishoprics, archbishoprics, convents, cathedrals, chapters, universities, churches, and presbyteries as well as the papacy and the Orthodox patriarchies and metropolitan sees. This meant that in many cases, the lords to whom the peasants and townsfolk were beholden were ecclesiastical. This was the case in several lands in particular: England, the Holy Roman Empire, the Papal States in Italy, Armenia, and parts of France, Macedonia, and the Baltic region. In these areas, popular revolts against ecclesiastical lords were commonplace during the Middle Ages. We now consider some of these anti-church, popular uprisings.

Tondrakians

The Tondrakians were a heretical sect centered on the city of Tondrak in western Armenia. They came into existence at the beginning of the ninth century, and endured despite state harassment and repression into the 11th century. The genesis of the movement came during the many peasant revolts in early medieval Armenia. The movement was strongly anti-clerical as seen in its rejection of the validity of the sacraments and of fundamental Christian doctrines. The Tondrakians organized their communities in a communal manner, as reputedly had done the original Christians, in which women were treated as equals with men. They rejected the feudal obligations of landlords, secular or ecclesiastical, upon peasants for whom the Tondrakians urged full property rights. Contemporary accounts related how Tondrakian peasants fought against feudal lords, destroying their castles and properties.

An important episode occurred after the construction of the Tatev monastery in 906. By a special edict, ownership of the nearby villages was transferred by the state to the monastery, a measure which met with the instant objections of local peasants. War with the monastery ensued during which peasants attacked the monastery. The movement was repressed for a brief period, but rebellions continued throughout the tenth century until 990, when the local king burnt the last rebellious village, disarming its inhabitants. This ended the first Tondrakian movement, but the movement re-emerged during the next century in Armenian villages. This second instance led to repression by regional Byzantine and Muslim authorities. Thus, the movement was defeated a second time, after which many Tondrakians were deported to Thrace. In 1045, Byzantium conquered the Bagatruni kingdom of Armenia, which provoked a third resurgence of the movement including in the cities where it received the support of knights and local priests. This suggests the movement might have acquired a nationalist tinge in addition to its social and religious aspects. Perhaps owing to resulting internal tensions among members of the Tondrakian sect, however, the movement split into three doctrinal sub-sects, one of which even advocated atheism.

The Commune of Rome

The conflict about the Commune of Rome occurred during the first half of the 12th century. At this time, there were two important political issues in Italy. One was the successful effort of the towns and cities of Lombardy in northern Italy to gain municipal autonomy from their feudal lords, ecclesiastical or secular. The second was the lay investiture controversy, the struggle for temporal power between the Church and the Holy Roman emperor. This latter issue revolved around the Gregorian reforms that aimed at establishing the independence of the Church from control of secular lords, including from that of emperors and kings. For centuries after the conversion of the Roman emperor, Constantine the Great, Rome had been the site of conflicts between the administrators and governors of the city and the bishop of Rome, who was none other than the pope himself. Over time, the papacy came under the control, however, of formerly rural noble families who had installed themselves in their urban castles and hotels in Rome. As well, these same nobles controlled many of the Church cardinals, who themselves came from noble families. This control by the nobility of the Church and its temporal sway over politics in Rome met with the disapproval and resistance of the lower classes and the burghers of Rome. Owing to this conflict, it even became commonplace for the pope to live elsewhere than in Rome because popes feared for their personal safety. (Cistercian website)

In 1144, social tensions in Rome escalated into revolution. The popular forces established a communal government based on the ancient Roman republic. They set up a government ruled by a senate with 56 members elected in an equal number from fourteen districts. The senators then elected as leader Giordano Pierleoni, a local notable, and gave him the title of *patricius*. In order to protect and promote its autonomy, the city government declared itself for the emperor in the imperial-papal conflict. The city then demanded that newly-elected Pope Lucius II renounce his temporal power, and that he assume the papacy in the role of priest rather than as the ruler of Rome. Lucius refused this entreaty. In fact, he then formed an army to attack Rome itself. In the process, Pope Lucius was killed, while the republicans were victorious over the papal force. The late pope was succeeded by Eugene III, a man who was not even a cardinal. In fact, he was elected by the cardinals without him having any prior suspicion or knowledge. The fact was no cardinal wanted the position during a period of such dangerous social turmoil. (Cistercian website.)

As the conflict proceeded, intellectual, ideological, and spiritual leadership of the commune fell to an already-controversial religious rebel named Arnold of Brescia. An Augustinian priest, Arnold became the leader of a priory in Brescia. He became involved in a local land dispute with the ruler of the county, the bishop of Brescia. Arnold preached that the Church should renounce temporal authority over city government and property, and that it should return to the alleged poverty of the early Christians. The Church condemned his teachings, so he exiled himself from Italy to Paris, where he studied under the reformer and philosopher Pierre Abélard. Arnold then drew the condemnation, however, of the leading French cleric of the day, Bernard of Clairvaux, for his views. So, he had to flee once again. He took refuge first in Switzerland, then in Bavaria. About 1145, he returned to Rome, where he became the most influential spokesman for the commune. In 1146, he had the pope driven into exile, for which he was excommunicated by the Church in 1148. In 1155, the new Pope Adrian IV, in a stunning reversal of policy, convinced the famed emperor Frederick Barbarossa to invade Rome, which he did successfully in order to restore social order. Then, Adrian placed the city under an interdict during the Holy Week leading up to Easter, no less. Arnold of Brescia was captured and tried as a rebel. He refused to recant his views, however, which made him even more of a popular hero. He was hanged, then burnt, with his ashes thrown into the Tiber to prevent any relics from being discovered so that he might not be venerated as a martyr.

Even though the commune had been defeated, in 1188 Pope Clement III concluded an agreement with the people of Rome called the Concord Pact. This allowed that, even if the emperor could name a prefect for Rome, the pope would retain sovereign rule over the Papal States, while the city of Rome would govern itself, including making declarations of war and peace. Civil government, henceforth, was in the hands of the citizens of Rome rather than the pope, the emperor, or the local nobility. So, while the commune of Rome met an initially disastrous outcome, a generation later the Roman citizens' right to their own municipal government was confirmed. Thus, the commune of Rome produced a delayed victory, as occurred with many other popular revolts during the Middle Ages.

Éon de l'Étoile

Éon de l'Étoile was born Eudo to a Breton noble family. 'Éon de l'Étoile' was a religious affectation he adopted. He entered the Augustinian order as a monk, but left soon after to live as a hermit in the Breton forest. He lived in an abandoned convent at a former Druid holy site. Claiming to be both a messiah and a prophet, the illiterate Eudo started gathering about him a following of faithful. He must have impressed one local seigneur, who built Eudo his own monastery. Eudo preached that the Church and its sacraments, offices, and wealth were worthless. This attracted to him many peasants and poor people. They formed a band that pillaged churches and monasteries in the region, terrorizing monks in Brittany and Normandy between 1140 and 1148. His band was organized into a hierarchy of followers known as angels and apostles, whose individuals had names such as Knowledge, Wisdom, Judgement, and the like. Eudo's pillaging of monasteries brought him enormous wealth, which he redistributed to his followers in the manner of a tribal warrior chief. Thus, in addition to claiming to be a prophet, Eudo was sort of a Breton Robin Hood, robbing from the rich and giving to the poor, similar to the English legends. Gradually, Eudo's violent, anti-clerical movement became a real religion with considerable followers, including in an important, regional Breton town, Saint-Malo, and in Gascony, in the south of France, in addition to its origins in rural Brittany.

Church authorities became nervous about this heresy, so Pope Eugene III asked the duke of Brittany to arrest him in order to bring him to a Church synod being held in the French city of Reims. The synod was being organized to deal with the growing problem of medieval heresies. It held Eudo to be guilty of heresy. Under torture, he confessed and repented for his errors, including his notion of himself as a prophet and messiah. The archbishop of Reims then sent him to an abbey, where he died in 1150. His followers, however, continued the sect Eudo had initiated in Brittany. They refused to repent and renounce Eudo, even when they were being burnt at the stake as heretics. A local bishop had Eudo's monastery destroyed, leaving untouched only its chapel. By this action, the Church hoped to erase even the memory of Eudo's heretical movement. The movement, however, was only one of many such heresies to appear during the Middle Ages, including many that displayed social and political elements that appealed to peasants and poor people. As for Eudo's movement itself, it might also have echoed ancient Druid culture and influences since the Bretons were a Celtic people.

The Stedingers

Stedingen is an area on the North Sea coast in the delta of the Weser River in northwest Germany. In medieval times, the area was under the authority of the archbishop of Bremen to the south. Early in the 12th century, the area was settled by a small community of Dutchmen originally from the delta of the Rhine River to the southwest of the Weser delta. They made an arrangement for paying annual taxes and shares of crops and livestock to the archbishop that was indeed favorable to the Dutchmen when compared to contemporary feudal demands on peasants elsewhere in western Europe. The attractive terms drew still more Dutchmen who reclaimed the delta and its marshland while creating a strong agricultural community alongside native Frisians. Compared to other medieval peasants, the Stedingers were free.

In order to establish veritable control over the area, however, the ruling Archbishop Gerhard built two fortresses in Stedingen. The soldiers and knights who occupied the fortresses demonstrated their character by kidnapping local women in order to earn healthy ransoms. At a local *thing* in 1204, it was determined that Gerhard's fortresses would be destroyed, and the transgressors be punished, a clear sign that the tribal, Germanic order had prevailed over the medieval, feudal order. Gerhard was succeeded as archbishop by another man also named Gerhard who decided to enforce feudal obligations once again upon the Stedinger peasants. He built a castle manned by his noble brother. Towards the end of 1229, however, during a battle between the archbishop's army and the Stedingers, the brother of Gerhard was killed as his knights fled. In the spring of the following year, Gerhard convened a synod of leading local clergymen in order to excommunicate the Stedingers. The archbishop successfully pleaded with the pope that the latter call for crusades against the offending peasants, crusades which were organized by the count of Holland and the duke of Brabant. The crusaders were successful. Ultimately, 5,000 Stedinger peasants were slain in bloody battles. The pope then reversed the existing order of excommunication in return for the remaining Stedingers repenting and confessing. Legitimate feudal authority was then re-established over the region. (Knight)

The Commune of Laon

Laon is a town in the French region of Picardy, on the plain north of Paris, south of modern-day Belgium. During the early Middle Ages, it was bustling and prosperous. A market and cathedral town governed by a bishop, Laon was as turbulent as any other town in the Middle Ages. One writer describes the social situation in Laon:

> The nobles and their servitors, sword in hand, committed robbery upon the burghers. The streets of town were not safe by night nor even by

day, and none could go out without running a risk of being stopped and robbed or killed. The burghers, in their turn, committed violence upon the peasants who came to buy and sell at the market town. (Morris, p. 2)

In 1106, after the bishopric had been vacant for two years, a Norman priest named Gaudry who was more of a soldier and a hunter than a cleric purchased the vacant holy seat from the king. Gaudry proved to be a violent and unsavory man who displayed a genuine lack of justice and respect for the Church and the local community, all social classes included. During a temporary absence in England, local burghers successfully bribed the clergy and knights who were replacing the bishop into accepting the establishment of a local commune in which the burghers could choose their own government and administrators. Upon his return, Gaudry was outraged, but the burghers placated him with still more bribes. This, the burghers reinforced by offering still more bribes to the king to confirm the communal status of Laon with a royal charter in return for modest annual dues to be paid to the king.

Three years later, the bishop and his faction were out of money, so they invited the king to celebrate Holy Week in Laon in the hope of getting him to renounce the communal charter. Sensing that something was afoot, the burghers offered 400 *livres* (French pounds) to the king in order to maintain their communal status, but the bishop's party countered with an offer of 700 livres to undo the commune. The king accepted the latter offer, then fled Laon on Good Friday to avoid the wrath of the local populace. The local population went on strike the next day. Locals further nursed their anger when they heard rumors to the effect that the bishop was now also going to extract from the burghers the money the latter had offered the king. The burghers met, and forty of them swore to kill the bishop. Three days after Easter, popular anger finally boiled over. The common people appeared on the streets shouting "'*Communia! Communia!*'...armed with swords, lances, axes, bows, and clubs...", as Charles Morris describes it. (p. 7) Rioters burst into the bishop's palace, while his protecting knights rushed to defend him. The locals disposed of the knights with despatch, but the bishop fled to the cellar of the cathedral, where he hid among some empty barrels and casks. A local social bandit named Teutgaud discovered Gaudry, who begged unsuccessfully for mercy with predictable, negative results. During the following years, the people of Laon continued to fight for their legal and political rights. They finally won a new communal charter in 1128. They were able to maintain the commune without interruption for two centuries, at which time French communes were dissolved to be replaced with royal administrators as France proceeded on its path to royal absolutism. (Morris, p. 9)

In 1295, there was another social disturbance in Laon, even if not as dramatic as the 12th century events. (Denton) This riot revealed the subterranean conflict that had continued between the populace and Church institutions, a conflict that occasionally bubbled to the surface. In fact, the king had even assigned armed protection for the bishop and other

Church officials. In February, two knights affected to the protection of the bishop, Jean de Faucoucourt and Jean de Lanzous, got into a fistfight with the deputy-mayor of Laon and his domestic servants. Fearing the popular reaction to this transgression, the two knights along with a student cleric at the cathedral, a brother of de Faucoucourt, hid in the cathedral for safety. All night and through the next day, locals gathered, growing increasingly angry at the cathedral officials who continued to protect the three men who refused to leave the cathedral. Finally, at 3 pm, the townsmen closed the town's gates, rang the bells summoning the locals, and began shouting, "Communia! Communia!", the rallying-cry of the community. The burghers rushed the cathedral, then grabbing the three men over the vain protests of cathedral officials, led their prisoners to the house of the deputy-mayor. There their captors invited anyone from among the onlookers to beat them, which the latter obliged by stoning the prisoners, and by attacking them with knives and swords. The de Faucoucourt brothers were left half-dead in the streets, while de Lanzous was thrown into prison, where he died a few days later. (Denton, p. 81) A year later, the pope issued a sentence of enormous financial repairs to be paid to the local Church institutions and officials of the commune of Laon as punishment for the riot, a sentence which the king duly enforced.

Only a few years later, however, the underlying town-church conflict resumed over new issues, which came to the surface again within the next generation. During the 1330s, an important movement occurred throughout France to reduce the communal rights granted during the early Middle Ages. The Church institutions in Laon agreed to pay the king the enormous sum of 20,000 livres to terminate the communal privileges of Laon. At the same time, local Church institutions received 12,000 livres in payments from locals to end their serf status vis-à-vis ecclesiastical lords. In the spring of 1338, the local social conflict worsened as serfs stopped paying the *taille*. By July, 5,000-6,000 peasants from 24 surrounding villages gathered in Laon, armed themselves, and attacked the cathedral and its officials, who fled for their lives. The king's reprisals were swift. Nine men taken from seven villages were executed, while six rebel women were branded on their face with hot irons. Two years later, however, the king adopted measures to remove some of the more offensive legal powers from local church officials, which represented but a small part of the gradual liberation of French serfs.

The Appenzell Wars

The Appenzell wars were a series of armed conflicts and related legal wrangling between the abbot of Saint-Gall in Switzerland near Lake Constance and his noble supporters, among them the dukes of Austria, versus the peasants in the surrounding countryside known as the Appenzell, who allied eventually with workers from the neighboring town of Saint-Gallen. Inspired by the successes of the Old Swiss Confederation, the

Appenzell peasants argued with their feudal masters during the course of the 14th century about grazing rights, taxes, and tithes. Finally during the 1390s, the peasants simply stopped paying feudal duties including tithes, to which the abbot responded by successfully negotiating a military arrangement with the Hapsburgs, then ruling the duchy of Austria. The actual spark for war occurred in 1403 when an official working for the abbot demanded that a dead body be dug up so he might have the corpse's clothes. Deeply offended by this outrage, in 1403 the Appenzell declared itself ready to fight the abbot with the support of two Swiss cantons, Schwyz and Glarus. In May of 1403, the abbot's army met the Appenzeller army in a mountain valley. A small force of eighty Appenzellers initiated an attack from a nearby hill, while 300 men from Schwyz and 200 from Glarus moved around the flanks of the abbot's army. It was a trap whereby the attackers' cavalry unknowingly charged up the hill, where they were met by 2,000 Appenzellers. In the retreat, 600 horsemen and many of the 5,000-strong infantry force of the abbot's army were killed by the peasant army.

As part of the ensuing peace treaty, the abbot was forced to give up some of his land in the Rhine Valley and around Lake Constance. So, the abbot next negotiated successfully with Frederick IV, duke of Austria, to provide two armies to deal with the Appenzellers. The Austrians, however, were defeated in a bloody battle in June, 1405 by the Appenzell peasants. Afterwards, the city of Saint-Gallen and the Appenzellers formed an alliance known as the *Bund ob dem See*. The Bund started collecting member communities, in the process taking sixty castles and destroying thirty others. In response, the Austrian nobility was emboldened into creating their own order of knights called the Order of St. George's Shield in order to fight the rebellious Bund. In 1407, the Order besieged a community that was a member of the Bund. In revenge, in January of 1408, the Bund force attacked the Order, but it proved to be a disaster for the popular army. In the resulting peace treaty, however, the abbot of Saint-Gall was forced to give up the Appenzell land even if he still insisted on the payment of past monies due. During the 1420s, the Appenzellers once again refused to pay the abbot his money. In response, the Church placed the offenders under an interdict. In December of 1428, the Order met the Appenzellers in battle and defeated the peasants. In the peace of 1429, the Appenzellers were forced to meet their financial obligations to the abbey, but the latter lost ultimate control over the Appenzell in the future. The peasants had finally won their freedom from the abbey. They then drew closer to the Old Swiss Confederation of autonomous cantons, which they finally joined in 1513.

The Revolt at Bobâlna

The revolt at Bobâlna was a peasant revolt in 1437–1438 in northern Transylvania. Our source is Laszlo Makha. Now part of modern-day Romania, Transylvania was then part of the medieval kingdom of Hungary, then a large multi-ethnic state. Among Transylvanian peasants there were Hungarians, Saxons, and Vlachs, indigenous Romanians. In the 15th century, the Hungarian nobility and the Catholic Church were busily initating feudal obligations upon the hitherto more or less free peasantry. Peasants now also were being forced to serve in the military in the wars with Turkey when for centuries, military service had not been required of the peasantry. Moreover, lords were establishing measures to impede the geographic mobility of their peasant serfs as well as also increasing rents, tithes, and taxes. Faced with this growing feudalization, peasant discontent started to grow. An important insult occurred when the Catholic bishop of Transylvania ruled with royal approval that Orthodox Vlach peasants would have to start paying tithes to the Catholic Church. Most peasants simply stopped paying tithes. The bishop of Transylvania responded by placing an anathema on the peasants, in effect, excommunicating them. Then in 1436, the amount of tithes was raised once again.

The following spring, an army of Hungarian and Vlach peasants erected a military encampment at a hill at Bobâlna, where they were joined by petty noblemen and priests. Their leaders included a Vlach peasant, three Hungarian peasants, and a burgher. The leader of the rebel army was a Hungarian petty nobleman named Antal Nagy de Buda. The peasant army sent a delegation to the local governor to demand the lifting of the anathema, resolution of the issue of the Church tithes, and the free movement of peasants. The governor, however, had the peasant emissaries killed, and launched an unsuccessful attack on the peasant army. As a result of its defeat, the nobility now was forced to negotiate with the rebels. Feudal obligations were greatly diminished, leaving only small cash levies to be paid to the noblemen. The peasants' right to free movement was guaranteed; furthermore, the nobles recognized the right of the peasants to meet annually at Bobâlna to review seigneurial compliance, and to punish abusers if necessary, which offered clear evidence of class consciousness and effective agency among the peasants. In part, peasant success owed to support from petty noblemen such as Antal Nagy and local burghers. The former were angered when the bishop demanded tithes from knights as well as from peasants, while townsmen were upset at new custom duties applied to their trade and crafts.

Hungarian aristocrats responded to the popular success by forming a union with upper class Saxons and the Szekeleys, who were freemen descendants of the Huns from a millennium earlier. The union was aimed at protecting Hungary from attacks by the Ottomans and the Tatars but most importantly for our purposes, protecting the upper classes from the lower classes. In January, 1438, the aristocrats won a decisive military victory over the popular army, such that previous popular advances were reversed by the victors. By way of conclusion, Makkai writes:

> Although the rising ended in failure, it had revealed profound changes at the grassroots. The emergence of a market economy helped the peasantry to develop a sense of its collective interests. Their goal was

economic independence and production for the market. The proposal to turn the Bobâlna assembly into an annual event indicates the emergence of a collective peasant consciousness.

Hans Bohm

Hans Bohm was a street musician and shepherd born in a village in Franconia, a region of southern Germany. In 1476, while in the town of Niklashausen, Bohm had a vision of the Blessed Virgin Mary tell him to preach about social equality and the virtues of a life of poverty. Thus inspired, the musician burnt his musical instruments in a bonfire of the vanities, a medieval ceremony where people threw their possessions into a bonfire to indicate their adherence to God and to a life of poverty. After this expression of his faith, Bohm began to preach, attracting poor followers from across Germany to witness his miracles, at the height of his popularity, as many as 40,000 people. The Virgin Mary had told Bohm that, in the future…

> there would no longer be any emperors, princes, popes, nor any other spiritual or temporal authorities. Men would be brothers who would gain their daily bread by their labors, while none would possess more than his neighbors. All feudal obligations, corvées, custom duties, and taxes would be ended forever, while forests, rivers, and prairies would be everywhere free to all. (Engels, 1850, p. 58)

One day at the end of his preaching, Bohm invited the men in his audience to return the next Saturday with candles and weapons. In fact, among Bohm's converts were the parish priest of Niklashausen and two local knights who had been preparing a military action. This was to be the signal for a revolution to begin. Nevertheless, the night before the planned insurrection, the bishop's knights captured Bohm. The day of the planned insurrection, 34,000 armed men reported as requested. Disheartened by the news of the capture of Bohm, the majority of the would-be peasant army dispersed. An army of 16,000, however, led by the knights, gathered at the castle where Bohm was being interned. The bishop parlayed with leaders of the peasant force such that most of the men began to disperse. Just then, however, the bishop's knights attacked the peasants, in the process routing them. Bohm and other prisoners were killed. Pilgrimages of the poor to Niklashausen continued for a time, but they were forbidden ultimately. The peasant movement had been suppressed.

Anti-clerical Revolt in England

As was the case with the Holy Roman Empire, the target of much popular revolt in England was the Catholic Church and its manifold institutions. Local lords were often bishops, abbots, university chancellors, and so on. Unlike the rest of Europe, however, revolts against ecclesiastical lords in

England usually met with failure. Kings and the state in England, centralized long before other states in Europe, usually supported ecclesiastical lords in their conflicts with local secular nobility or with burghers. Our guide to the English situation is a recent work of Samuel Cohn, published in 2013, in which the Glasgow scholar draws comparisons with the rest of Europe as a tool for analyzing popular revolts in England. In continental Europe, the Black Death was the signal to launch popular revolts. The common people benefited from the shortage of labor and loss of population resulting from the Black Death to drive a hard bargain with lords, whether secular or ecclesiastical. In England, by contrast, popular revolts against ecclesiastical lords had begun during the early Middle Ages. Popular revolts against Church lords were concerned with feudal economic obligations upon social inferiors, and not about theological heresy. Heresies in England only manifested themselves well after the Black Death during a period in which heresies were declining elsewhere in Europe.

The English state was perhaps the first successful example of a centralized monarchy in Europe. People contesting local lords had at their disposal a number of courts and commissions of inquiry and other tools of justice by which commoners might seek redress for wrongs committed against them by their lords. This might lead one to think that recourse to violence and extra-legal mean of redress for commoners might have been less necessary than they were on the continent. Nevertheless, Samuel Cohn draws an impressive list of these extra-legal disputes with English Church institutions. Referring to towns and cities where there were at least ten such revolts during the Middle Ages, Cohn counts 51 such incidents in Oxford, possibly among them town-and-gown conflicts. Other leading centers of popular rebellion directed at local Church institutions included: London—39; Bristol—36; York—28; Norwich—27; Yarmouth and Lincoln—16 each; Cambridge—14; Northampton and Canterbury—12 each; Exeter—11; Newcastle, Carlisle, Shrewsbury, Coventry, Worcester—10 each, all these in addition to many other communities where there were less than ten medieval conflicts with the Church. (p. 14, 15)

In continental Europe, popular revolts were led by peasants and workers, sometimes allied with bourgeois or low-ranking noblemen or clergy. On the other hand, English revolts against the Church were usually led by burghers, often the wealthiest and most powerful among them. Rebel leaders also included mayors and bailiffs; sometimes, even noblemen led popular forces against Church lords and the kings who supported them. The reasons for the revolts:

> More crucial was the high number of English revolts against the Church, struggles for liberties by burgesses over jurisdiction in urban neighborhoods, rights to hold courts, fairs, and markets, to patrol and to guard town gates, and above all else, to elect their own mayors, aldermen, coroners, and other officials...Monastic boroughs were not the only, or even primary arenas for these contests...More protests, and ones which

were just as violent, raged between burgesses and bishops, priories, canons, universities in towns that were not monastic boroughs. (p. 12)

Success rates and regularity of reprisals from social superiors vary, as well, between England and elsewhere in Europe. Professor Cohn counts successes among popular revolts against the Church on the continent as often as 70 % of the time. In England, popular revolts against the Church usually failed.

> Burgess insurrections that challenged the privileges of monasteries, priories, bishops, canons, and parish priests and their jurisdictions within towns invariably failed. Ecclesiastical lords appealed to the king, his courts, and special commissions, resulting in swift reprisals, stiff fines, and often capital punishment by drawing, quartering, or even death by fire. (p. 321)

Finally, as we saw earlier with the English Peasants' Revolt of 1381, the role of women in popular rebellion was vital in England when compared to the rest of Europe where women were seldom mentioned as leaders and participants in popular rebellions. (p. 319)

Analysis of Anti-clerical Popular Revolts

Among the examples of the anti-clerical, popular revolts described above, there were revolts that knew partial or temporary success before the inevitable repression and reprisals from social superiors. This applied to the revolts in Armenia among the Tondrakians, in Brittany to Éon de l'Étoile and his followers, to the Stedingers of Frisia, and to Transylvanian peasants in the Bobâlna revolt. In other examples, the Commune of Rome, the revolts in Laon in Picardy, and in the Appenzell in the Swiss lands, the revolts met with immediate failure but success a generation or two later when aims of the revolts were resolved in favor of the common people and their demands. In all cases, popular revolts against Church lords involved alleged abuses of the temporal power of the Church. Moreover, in some cases, for example, among the Tondrakians of Armenia, the Commune of Rome, the Stedingers, and in the case of Éon de l'Étoile, the causes of the revolt involved not just abuses by the Church but the existence itself of the temporal power and wealth of the Church. The rebels argued that as matters of doctrine, the clergy should be poor, and it should not exercise temporal power.

These opinions were heresy as the Church defined it. Understanding medieval heresies is not merely a matter of understanding arcane theological disputes. Understanding heresies gives us a portal into the social conflicts of the day, including class disputes and rebellions of the lower social orders against their social superiors. The contemporary chroniclers of medieval heresies were usually monks and priests, in some locales and periods the only literate people. The tendency was to record and describe and analyze social conflicts as theological disputes when theological arguments might only have represented the tip of the iceberg. Often at the base of heresies were political and economic disputes that were expressed in religious terms since for a society shot through with and organized and defined by religion, there was no discourse, no *langage*, other than religious discourse. Absent were secular definitions of liberal rights such as the right to free speech, etc.

In fact, during the Middle Ages, these rights were still centuries away from being typical elements of discourse commonly understood. Even more so for the modern 'isms' of popular political movements such as trade unionism, socialism, anarchism, etc., which only came into existence during the industrial revolution of the 19th century. In order to understand heresies, we need to consider the way of thinking of heretics and their religious arguments, which might include expressions built upon the recurring theme of worship of the Holy Spirit manifesting itself in the world, or excessive religious zeal and enthusiasm as seen, for example, in the Crusades and the anti-Jewish pogroms. It is also important to note that not all critiques of the temporal power and wealth of the Church came from people defined as heretics but also from holy people within the fold of the Church such as Francis of Assisi and Dominic, who were even canonized later by the Church.

Popular Resistance to the Imposition of Christianity

Before considering the nature of the heresies, however, it is important to note that the imposition of Christianity often resulted from foreign, military force against pagan societies. This imposition of Christianity met popular resistance, which we now examine.

The kingdom of Poland had become Christian in 966 beginning with the so-called baptism of Poland during which the first king of Poland, Mieszko, under the influence of his Christian wife, Dobrowa of Bohemia, had the royal court baptized. Over the coming years, the population of Poland gradually Christianized but with considerable popular opposition. During the 1030s, King Mieszko II was overthrown in a civil war with his brother, Bezprym, after which Mieszko II fled to Bohemia. This civil war, in fact, was only one of several social conflicts wrapped in one, which also included a military invasion of Poland by the duke of Bohemia, Bretislaus, and an anti-Christian uprising in which churches and monasteries were destroyed, and priests were killed. At the same time, there was a peasant uprising against the nobility that was imposing feudal obligations upon the Polish peasantry. About 1040, the son of Mieszko II, Casimir the Restorer, reunified the Polish lands into one centralized state that eventually became thoroughly Catholic.

During the 1040s, a similar popular, anti-Christian revolt took place in Hungary. Christianity had been introduced to Hungary by King Stephen at the beginning of the second millennium. After his death in 1038, Stephen was succeeded by his nephew, Peter Urseolo, a nobleman from Venice. Peter proved to be unpopular with peasants owing to tax increases and his foreign adventures. The latter led the populace into thinking that he was trying to insinuate Hungary into the Holy Roman Empire. Ultimately, this did occur, which provoked a popular rebellion by the pagan populace led by a nobleman named Vata. During this rebellion, King Peter was killed, while a number of bishops and priests also were slain. The monarchy eventually fell to a second cousin of King Stephen, Andras, who rose to power with pagan support. Once in power, however, Andras distanced himself from Vata and his pagan supporters, even if he did not mete out the expected capital punishment to the pagan rebels for the crime of regicide.

There were similar rounds of pagan resistance from the common people to the imposition of Christianity elsewhere in Europe: among the Swedes towards the end of the 11th century, who resisted Christianity being imposed by the Danes; among the native tribes of Prussia who, between 1260 and 1274, resisted Christianity as imposed by conquering Germans; among Estonians who, during the years 1334–1346, resisted the imposition of Christianity by the Danes and Germans; and during the first half of the 15th century among the tribes of Lithuania that rose up against Polish christianizers. It should be noted that these pagan rebellions were complex phenomena that make them difficult to categorize. The religious aspects of these rebellions were combined with opposition to feudal obligations lords were imposing on commoners along with political, proto-national elements of resistance to foreign rulers. (Guoga)

Internal Calls for Church Reform

For all its impressive hierarchy and temporal power and wealth, the medieval Church was not a monolith. The debate and contradictions between a church of wealth that supported the social order versus a church of poverty and social revolt extended from early Christianity in Roman times through the Middle Ages into the modern era. We'll briefly consider some of the medieval forms of this debate before concerning ourselves with some of the most radical movements of the Middle Ages, that is, the popular heresies.

We've already examined the ever-reforming waves of monasticism in opposition to the Church hierarchy, extending almost from the beginning of Christianity well into the medieval period. There also were other movements that emphasized the necessity of Church poverty and a return to the purer form of Christianity of the earliest years of the Jesus movement. Even as the Catholic Church was standing up to the warrior class to become the institution par excellence of temporal power and wealth in western Europe, by no means was this the case for all of Christianity. In eastern Europe, Orthodox Christianity, with its priests and monks led by a hierarchy of bishops, metropolitans, and patriarchs, developed on a different course than the Catholic West. Moreover, there were several points of dispute between western and eastern Europe whereby religious differences grew into immutable cultural divergences. These differences of opinion hardened permanently during the Fourth Crusade in 1204 when crusaders sacked Constantinople for little reason other than greed, in the process stealing

Orthodox relics and riches, while humiliating and massacring eastern Christians. This led to an understandable Orthodox resistance to Catholicism in medieval Byzantium, Bulgaria, and Romania as well as the Balkans and the Russian principalities. Additionally, in lands such as Armenia, Syria, and Egypt, another strain of orthodoxy with another Christology called Oriental Orthodoxy held sway.

Internal resistance to the Catholic hierarchy sometimes came from the low-ranking clergy of parish priests and wandering preachers. An incident of this resistance took place in Milan around 1066 when low-ranking clergy led a popular movement called the *pataria.* This movement grew from popular resistance to a Church hierarchy accused of concubinage and simony, that is, clergy openly living with women and the buying of Church offices respectively. This form of resistance was mostly seen, however, in medieval England. We've seen how the Peasants' Revolt produced ideological leaders from parish priests and itinerant preachers, men such as John Ball and the twenty or so other priest-leaders of the popular rebellion. Moreover, there were many other local popular rebellions in England led by clerics. Samuel Cohn lists two pages of these local, popular rebellions led by priests during the 14th and 15th century. (2013, p. 326, 327)

As well, there were several movements of opposition to the Church hierarchy led by intellectuals such as John Wycliffe and William of Ockham in England, Jan Hus in Bohemia, and Marsilius of Padua in Italy, that proved to be most dangerous to the Catholic hierarchy, even comprising a sort of proto-protestantism. These men argued that the Church was not just the clergy but rather included all the faithful. It is beyond the point of this work to delve into the course of these philosophies, but we merely point out three intellectual movements that followed from these philosophies. The first two movements were Christian humanism and the Renaissance; the latter started in Italy to spread throughout Europe. A third movement known as conciliarism directly affected the Church hierarchy. To proponents of this movement, Church government should not issue just from the pope and the higher clergy but from an ecumenical council that included lay people and representatives of lower-ranking clergy. Conciliarism emerged in reaction to the temporal power and wealth of the Church, especially of the popes and cardinals after the Church had successfully struggled to earn autonomy from secular rulers.

The Church of the early Middle Ages was rural, hardly surprising since cities were rare during the period. During the high Middle Ages, however, towns and cities sprang up throughout western Europe, and then again during the late Middle Ages elsewhere in Europe. The Catholic Church was ill-suited by its philosophy and structures to serve urbanites. Moreover, some urban intellectuals including many women developed new forms of spiritual mysticism whereby, it was argued, it was possible to know God directly without the interventions of sacraments dispensed by clergy. As far as the Church hierarchy was concerned, these forms of spirituality teetered dangerously on the edge of heresy, if not being clearly heretical, even when their proponents claimed to be entirely faithful.

In terms of popular revolt against the Church hierarchy, the religious movements that are most relevant to this study are those that proposed voluntary poverty as a viable and holy way of life in contrast to the wealth and temporal power of the Church hierarchy. They included loyal mendicant orders within the Church such as the Franciscans and the Dominicans, and lay movements that issued from outside the Church hierarchy. These latter movements were known as béguines, among women, and beghards, among men, and they emerged respectively among women and working class men in the later years of the Middle Ages.

The careers of Francis and Dominic bear testimony to the lack of success of the Church in reaching the new urbanites created by societal transformations during the Middle Ages. That they could succeed with their message of the spiritual value of poverty proved that the message struck a note in harmony with popular concerns of the day. The Church could ignore the successes of Francis and Dominic at its peril, even if their message was so obviously at odds with the wealth and temporal power of the Church hierarchy. Francis was the son of a wealthy Italian bourgeois made rich from the clothing trade. As a young man, Francis experienced a growing contradiction between his material wealth and his spiritual quest. So, he rejected the material world including even his clothes to live as a hermit in the poverty in which Jesus was alleged to have lived. His preaching resonated with popular views such that, by 1210, he had a small group of followers for whom Francis eventually had regulations written, much as Basil and Benedict had done centuries earlier. Pope Innocent III acknowledged the legitimacy of Francis, and his movement became known as the Franciscans. This was all quite against the original intentions of the humble Francis. Nonetheless, by the time of his death in 1226, there were more than 5,000 Franciscans, with another thousand waiting to gain entrance to the order. While Francis was not the least heretical, there was, nevertheless, an evident irony. According to Steven Kreis:

> The strength of his movement was that people were appealing to his order for spiritual guidance. This clearly shows that, first, the Church was clearly losing ground in providing its flock with necessary spirituality. Second, it shows an amazing spiritual vitality among the people...The people did not reject Christianity. What they were rejecting was the way the Church hierarchy had interpreted and manipulated Christian dogma...Dominicans and Franciscans could only exist and flourish because they told the people what they wanted to hear. (p. 5)

Thus, the Church hierarchy, at odds with Francis's rejection of property as a requirement to join the order, arranged for the future saint to step down as the head of the Franciscans. A new rule more acceptable to the hierarchy was written in which the antipathy of Francis to the idea of the Franciscans owning property was softened. This enraged many followers of the future saint who subsequently became known as Spiritual Franciscans. Meanwhile, the hierarchy was blessed with a new head, Bonaventure, while a new officially-authorized hagiography of Francis was produced. Once again, all was well within the realm of the Church with the majority of Franciscans co-opted by the Church hierarchy.

Another order of friars that proposed voluntary poverty was founded by an educated Spaniard named Dominic, who had preached against heresy in southern France. From this experience, he proposed that the new order devote themselves to preaching the true doctrines of the Church, even while espousing voluntary poverty as the holiest form of existence. Dominic proposed learning as a form of service whereby the learned man conveyed his learning to others, including to the urban poor whose lives his followers should imitate. There was one significant feature common to both Franciscans and Dominicans.

> The principle of fraternity so essential to their definition accorded with the horizontal forms of solidarity prevalent in the cities, and particularly respected by the poor. The traditional ecclesiastical model was vertical and hierarchical. The preaching of the prelate filtered down to his flock. This was now supplanted by a model of reciprocity, or charitable sharing. This tendency had first begun to develop a century earlier in the communes and confraternities. (Mollat, p. 125)

The message and zeal of the Dominicans and Franciscans did much to provide necessary leadership at a time when the Church was under profound criticism from the popular classes for its wealth and power. It was more than ironic that Dominicans, however, went on eventually to lead the Church's charge against heretics in the Inquisition. Nonetheless, both Dominicans and Franciscans eventually produced intellectuals including university professors dedicated to education and to service to the Church. In the process of becoming part of the hierarchy, nonetheless, friars lost much of their original simplicity and novelty. (World History project, "The Church in the High Middle Ages", p. 5)

Béguines and beghards were Catholic lay communities active in cities in the 13th and 14th centuries. These women and men lived in loose, semi-monastic communities, without formal vows binding them permanently to their vocations. Béguines first emerged early in the 12th century in the Low Countries while the first Crusades were unfolding. Beguine women lived on the edges of towns, devoting themselves to prayer and good works on behalf the poor and others in need. The Crusades produced many single women and widows, some of whom were widows or daughters of crusader knights and noblemen. About 1200, some women grouped their houses together, or began to live together in communities or béguinages. The béguinages were not convents, nor were its members nuns. They took no vows, could rejoin the broader community at will, and could marry. They did not renounce their property; in fact, it was from their wealth that many béguines practiced charitable works. Other poorer béguines survived by manual labor or by teaching. They did not beg for alms. There might be a head mistress in the béguinage. The women lived together for mutual aid and support, common worship, and solidarity among co-workers. There weren't central rules or orders for béguines, although some adopted the Spiritual Franciscan ways as guidance, which made them appear suspicious to the Church hierarchy. Some béguinages catered exclusively to upper class women, others to workers and poor women while, most commonly, communities grouped women of all classes. Béguinages were particularly commonplace in the Low Countries. According to the Wikipedia essay about the subject:

> There was a béguinage at Mechlin as early as 1207, at Louvain in 1234, at Bruges in 1244, at Brussels in 1245; and by the close of the century, there was hardly a commune in the Low Countries without its béguinage, while several of the great cities had two or three or even more... Several béguinages, like the great béguinage at Ghent, numbered their inhabitants by the thousands. (p. 2)

It was to these lay communities that the common people increasingly turned for spiritual sustenance rather than to rural monasteries, rural parish priests, or the Church hierarchy. About the year 1300, some béguines took to begging rather than working, while engaging in intellectual pursuits and religious speculation that went beyond Church conventions. Some béguinages produced mystics who argued that it was possible to learn to know God by prayer, meditation, and reflection without the dispensation of Church sacraments or offices. The Church establishment found this heretical and dangerous, perhaps even providing unfair competition for the souls of urban-dwellers. In the 14th century, some béguinages were prosecuted for heresy, while still others were absorbed into more conventional and acceptable monastic or mendicant orders. In the 15th century, Pope Eugene IV rehabilitated the béguinages. This religious participation, especially leadership by lay women, evidently presented problems for the Church hierarchy. The béguinages represented a challenge not only from wealthy women but also from working class and burgher women.

Just as the era produced béguinages, the Middle Ages saw the development of similar communities of men called beghards who, nonetheless, displayed several important differences from their feminine counterparts. Beghards usually renounced personal property, and lived under one roof with common finances and meals. There were hundreds of these male communities, always lay, usually tied to the crafts guilds in which their members worked. Beghards were weavers, dyers, fullers, and other workers, particularly in the textiles industry. To become a beghard in Brussels, one had to become a weaver. This was quite common across western Europe. In fact, the terms weaver and beghard almost became synonymous. Even if the initial purpose of these communities was spiritual, they did solve a practical, social problem of caring for old or injured workers. As with béguinages, beghard communities produced mystics who exceeded official Church doctrine and control in their worship. The beghards were working class through and through, however, which perhaps helped them resist Church attempts to regulate and control them. The highest number of beghard communities was found in Belgium where there were 94 communities at their peak. By the close of the Middle Ages, however, both béguinages and beghard communities had started to fade away, although some were incorporated into Church-sanctioned organizations even as their numbers dwindled in the modern era. By 1631, there were only 2,487 members left living in Beghard communities.

Béguines and beghards, Franciscans and Dominicans, and still other mendicant orders of friars were examples of alternative religious communities that emerged because the Church was not meeting the needs of townsfolk, especially of the poor and of workers. They initially presented no direct doctrinal challenge to the Church, but met human needs for worship and solidarity as well as practical, social needs for housing and the like in urban areas. Even so, they did present challenges to the temporal power and wealth of the Church, even if for the most part they were loyal Catholics in communion with the Church.

Medieval Popular Heresies

Catholic or Orthodox dogma and doctrine, the basic beliefs of Christianity, form a complex edifice indeed. The Christian churches of the Middle Ages took centuries to evolve. Their construction involved the talents, logic, intellects, and passions of the best brains in the West. In fact, especially in western Europe, the Church was the only social institution to employ the owners of those brains, and to provide the only locus of literacy and intellect. Moreover, from the beginnings of Christianity, certain points of orthodox doctrine had always been contested as to their veracity. Indeed, wholly different forms of Christianity had emerged contemporaneously with early Christianity to what eventually became orthodoxy. For example, in contrast to the doctrine of the fall of humankind from God's grace which affected all humans, the original sin of Adam and Eve as elucidated by St. Augustine, there were early Christians who argued that humankind, at base, was good and not tainted with sin. A wholly different theology then resulted. These doctrinal arguments continued into the Middle Ages.

These religious debates produced heresies based on theological differences. These are not our immediate concerns, even if they are the object of specialist fields of study. We're less interested in doctrinal differences between orthodox theology and heresies as the latter were defined by the Church, than we are in heresies that were of popular origin, and that overlapped with the social unrest of the Middle Ages. Such heresies inspired and animated disputes between rulers and ruled. The particular problem, of course, as per forever, was the temporal power and wealth of the Church hierarchy in contrast with the poverty of the common people. The Church hierarchy was the first and best organized social institution of the Middle Ages. It was also one of the principal beneficiaries of the economic surplus produced by laboring people since it owned roughly a third of the land in Europe. The actual mechanisms of what we'll call social heresies might involve an understandable lack of comprehension of complex doctrines by illiterate people; or they might involve exaggeration of a particular item of doctrine or its application to extremes of zeal; or they might involve differences of Church doctrine with existing, pre-Christian religious beliefs. In actual fact, social heresies often employed the language of the doctrines of the Church itself to contest orthodox Christianity.

The social heresies of the poor contained a strong element of millenarianism, that is, the belief that the end of days was approaching, and that the poor had a responsibility to bring about conditions that might favor the second coming of Christ, at which point the evil rich of the world would be punished, while the lowly would be rewarded for their travails. Norman Cohn's description of the coming salvation for the popular classes is useful, for it was to be:

collective, in the sense that it was to be enjoyed by the faithful as a collectivity;

terrestrial, in the sense that it was to be realized on this earth, and not in some other-worldly heaven;

imminent, in the sense that it was to come both soon and suddenly;

total, in the sense that it was utterly to transform life on earth, so that the new dispensation would be no mere improvement on the present, but perfection itself;

miraculous, in the sense that it was to be accomplished by, or with the help of supernatural agencies.

In the final apocalyptic massacre, perhaps to be perpetuated by the poor themselves, evil as personified by Jews and Muslims, clergy and the wealthy and powerful, demons and devils, would be exterminated, so that the poor might then set up their own kingdom of heaven on earth. (Cohn, as per above)

An unfortunate impression one can get from reading the histories of medieval heresies can be an uncomfortable feeling of superiority and disdain from the present and current, modern, safe, and knowledgeable position of looking back on the childish, insane, or bizarre misconceptions of reality and truth as expressed in the medieval heresies. Nonetheless, to the contrary, popular religion that differs from official, conventional religion actually is part of the inevitable clash of culture between rulers and ruled. This clash should be understood in terms of the absconding by non-producers of the economic surplus created by producers, and the religions that either support or reject this process. That medieval heresies employed the language of Christian dogma and doctrine is not surprising since Christianity was so all-pervasive and important in the medieval world. Furthermore, the secular language of popular protest was only being developed and established in the

Middle Ages. So, from the point of view of the poor and downtrodden, which was most of the medieval population, popular heresies were reasonable responses to oppression and exploitation, rather than being irrational and senseless.

According to Steven Kreis, "just as there were sound theological reasons why one person might become a heretic, there were equally sound political, economic, intellectual, and social causes...Heresy meant something more than just doctrinal error. Although there were numerous heresies which appeared in the 12th and 13th centuries, some characteristics were common to them all: a desire to return to the apostolic practices of early Christianity; a need to free Christians from their enslavement to a material world; a protest against the concentration of authority in the Church; a challenge to the sacraments, especially baptism; and an emphasis on chastity, preaching, communal life, and moral purity." (p.1)

Of the many medieval heresies, we shall consider two before examining a more general species of heresy wherein the alleged intervention of the Holy Spirit was a central element. The first emerged in southern France in Lyons during the decade of the 1170s. A rich bourgeois whose name is believed to have been Pierre Valdo, in a manner similar to Saint Francis, sold his belongings and gave the proceeds to the poor. Valdo began promoting two ideas: that voluntary poverty was the only way to reach perfection; and that his followers needed a bible in the local dialect to benefit from the Gospel, so he arranged for a local cleric to translate the Gospel into Provençal. Valdo's followers, dubbed the 'Poor Men of Lyons', took to preaching voluntary poverty and condemning the clergy. They developed their own hierarchy of deacons, priests, and bishops. They preached against relics and the cult of saints including praying to them, and they preached against the use of churches or cathedrals. For the Waldensians, as they came to be known, the only necessities were a bible, prayers, and songs, all in the vernacular, along with their own schools and missionary work. Not surprisingly, the local bishop condemned the Poor Men of Lyon, so in 1179, Valdo went to Rome to seek approval for his movement. The pope confirmed the Poor Men of Lyons' right to practice voluntary poverty, but denied them the right to preach. Too late, for on his way to Rome, Valdo had preached to the textile workers of Lombardy in northern Italy, who readily adopted his ideas, with the addition that members of the Lombard movement should survive by manual labor. Valdo's movement spread throughout Europe. The Waldensians continued to inspire similar movements throughout the Middle Ages. In fact, they survive even today as a Protestant sect. (Kreis, p. 2, Manteuffel, p. 2-6)

The second movement we consider, the Taborites of Bohemia, was considerably more violent. In fact, the movement was born in an environment of war and violence and, eventually, was destroyed by the same war and violence. As background, we need to examine the proto-national and social context in Bohemia. According to Norman Cohn,

There was no part of Europe in which the usual criticisms could be brought against the Church with greater conviction than in Bohemia. The wealth of the Church there was enormous; one-half of all the land was ecclesiastical property. Many of the clergy, especially, the great prelates, lived decidedly worldly lives, while the Curia (Vatican) was constantly interfering in the affairs of the country, and was also extracting from it great financial profits. (p. 205)

Moreover, there was a decidedly ethnic or 'national' element in the social structure of the country and its organization of religious expression. Even if Bohemia was part of the German-speaking Holy Roman Empire, the majority of its population was Slavic. For 200 years, there had been a strong German presence in Bohemia among the ruling class, including its nobility and higher clergy. These people continued to speak German, and to preserve their German character. In fact, they were largely responsible for the spread of feudal structures in Bohemia that oppressed the once-free commoners to such an extent that Bohemian Slavs believed that feudalism was uniquely a German phenomenon.

These social tensions underlay the religious warfare that burst into the open early in the 15th century. The catalyst was a Bohemian priest, intellectual, and university professor named Jan Hus, who criticized the Church for its temporal wealth and power, arguing further that the Church was not just the clergy but rather the faithful, much as the English intellectual, John Wycliffe, had done. The clerical and political authorities came down hard on Hus, who was essentially a loyal, would-be Catholic reformer, and had him hanged.

In the national and social context of Bohemia, virtually the whole country was outraged. Hus's cause became a national one involving most of the population. Although the actual course of events was complex with many twists and turns, there were two principal movements, each one supported by distinct social classes. The bourgeoisie dominated the cities as patricians and heads of the merchant guilds. They formed a moderate party whose members followed the teachings of Hus fairly closely. They sought reform while hoping to leave intact most of the hierarchy and liturgy of the Church. The moderate reformers were especially pleased that the Church cease being paid for sacraments, rents, loans, and other sources of Church revenue so that this money remain in the hands of bourgeois themselves.

A second tendency in Bohemia, the radical tendency, splintered into several strands over time. This latter movement enjoyed the support of the craftsmen and urban poor as well as the peasantry. The lower class of Prague—the low-paid journeymen, unskilled laborers, servants, prostitutes and the criminal underworld as well as unemployed, landless peasants who had drifted into the city— comprised as much as 40% of the population of the capital. (Norman Cohn, p. 209) These people, led by craft guilds, constituted a revolutionary party that wished to eliminate both the higher clergy, and the bourgeois who controlled economic activity. In the countryside, traditional rights of peasants were being eliminated by German lords who were trying to make peasants more dependent. These peasants too formed part of the revolutionary followers of Jan Hus. This revolutionary wing sought to return the Church to its alleged condition of poverty during the early years of Christianity. The existing Church hierarchy had to be removed from office, while Church properties should be secularized. Radicals preached a doctrine of *sufficientia legis Christi*, the divine law or the Bible (as) the sole rule and canon for human society, not only in the Church, but also in political and civil matters. They rejected everything that they believed had no basis in the Bible such as: veneration of saints and images, fasts, superfluous holidays, the swearing of oaths, intercession for the dead, auricular (oral) Confession, indulgences, the sacraments of Confirmation and Anointing of the Sick. This left few offices for the Catholic clergy to perform. They also admitted laymen and women to the preacher's office, and chose their own priests.

Furthermore, the radicals rejected the idea of Purgatory and capital punishment. At first, these radicals resembled the Waldensians, but as events unfolded, the radicals became more and more revolutionary, in the process leaving behind less radical fragments. This process was helped along, no doubt, by the fact that the Vatican organized no fewer than five unsuccessful crusades against the Bohemians. As the movement advanced, it also became more millennarian and apocalyptic. The revolutionaries founded communities in the countryside comprised of townsmen and peasants who lived outside the feudal order, and who "...attempted to regulate affairs on the basis of brotherly love instead of force." (Norman Cohn, p. 210) The most important of these communities was renamed Mount Tabor. This was reputedly the name of the hill where Christ had ascended to heaven, to which he would return at the Second Coming. Hence their name, chosen at a site that was also judicious since it was the site of gold mines that came under the control of the revolutionaries. For about a generation, the Taborites were a significant political, social, and religious force in Bohemia.

Once the foreign military interventions in Bohemia had all been defeated, Bohemians proceeded to turn on each other. At the battle of Lipany on May 30, 1434, the Taborites were soundly defeated by the moderate Hussites, so much so that about 2/3 of the Taborite army was killed. Three years later, the Taborites signed a treaty with the Czech king, Sigismund, by which the movement was all but eliminated. Twenty years later, some exponents of more pacifist Taborite theological thought re-emerged in a denomination known as the Unity of the Brethren, or the Moravian Church, as it is known to English-speakers.

We've briefly described the Taborite and Waldensian movements, each of which had complex histories covering many years. In fact, we're only touching the surface of the many medieval heresies. There are, in fact of fifty or so Christian heresies. The New Advent Catholic Encyclopedia essay about heresy reveals just how widespread heresy was in the Middle Ages. Many of them were fleeting movements named for their leaders that only lasted a few years, and were without major consequence or interest save to specialists of Church history or theology. Our concern, in any case, are the social heresies, the popular heresies that mixed with the political movements of the common people.

One such species of social heresy involved movements in which the third persona of the Holy Trinity, the Holy Spirit, was believed to be present and acting in the political and social interests of workers, peasants, and the poor. One such case involved a monk known as Tanchelm of Antwerp. Between the years 1112–1114, Tanchelm preached in the Low Countries, gathering a considerable following for his heretical teachings. This was the period when communes were being formed in western Europe whereby commoners in towns and cities gained certain freedoms from their lords, including from ecclesiastical lords. Preaching in open fields with the physical allure of a holy man, Tanchelm first preached against the parish priest in Antwerp, who lived openly with a woman. His preaching then turned to clerics as a whole. He taught that sacraments were invalid if administered by unholy men. Even further, he preached that all sacraments were invalid, while churches were meaningless buildings similar, in fact, to brothels. Moreover, Tanchelm caught the spirit of the day in terms of contemporary social conflicts when he preached that the payment of Church tithes by peasants was quite unnecessary. Tanchelm also preached that he was inhabited by the Holy Spirit just as Jesus had been. He thought himself, in fact, a messiah, so much so that he distributed his bath water to his followers as a substitute for the Eucharist. One of his followers, a smith named Manasses organized a fraternity of twelve male followers as per the example of the Apostles, while one woman follower represented the Virgin Mary. Tanchelm was eventually imprisoned by the archbishop of Cologne in 1113–1114, but he was released. He was later killed by a priest in 1115. (Norman Cohn, p. 46-49) Tanchelm and movements such as the Waldensians and the Taborites proposed voluntary poverty as an alternative to the established Church and its temporal wealth and power.

They were, however, movements of opposition rather than movements offering alternative philosophies. In the second half of the 12th century emerged alternative ideas from a man known as Joachim of Fiore, an abbot from Calabria in southern Italy who was a mystic, hermit, and popular preacher. (Manteuffel, p. 5) The abbot taught that world history was divided into three stages. The first age was the age of the father, the God of the Jews, of the Hebrew Tanakh. The second age was the age of the Son, which corresponded to the period of Christianity and the New Testament. The third age would be that of the Holy Spirit, during which a new gospel would appear to replace that of the Catholic Church. Society would become egalitarian and be organized on a utopian, monastic basis. Joachim calculated that each division of world history would endure 42 generations, which was the duration of each of the first two ages. This meant the age of the Holy Spirit would begin roughly a century later in 1260 with the coming of the Antichrist, an essential step before the utopian third age could begin. Various interpretations of when this new age would begin were applied by different schools of thought. Many seemed to fall on Joachim's writings themselves as being the new gospel predicted by the abbot. Some even have argued that this type of thinking has influenced thinkers such as Hegel and Marx, and perhaps others who divided history into distinct phases. What is most important is that Joachim's ideas did fall on fertile ground in the Middle Ages, influencing many who were trying to reform or even eliminate the Church as an article of faith of the popular, revolutionary, heretical movements.

Another movement inspired by the idea of the Holy Spirit was that of the Franciscan Spirituals. Recall that even while Francis of Assisi was still alive, the question of whether voluntary poverty was a necessity for his followers was already an issue. Even while Francis was alive, the Church hierarchy worked to soften the requirements of voluntary poverty to bring the Franciscans in line with the rest of the Church. This disposition, however, met with the objections of a considerable element of Franciscans who disagreed vehemently, wishing to follow more closely the precepts of voluntary poverty as they had been espoused and lived by their patron saint and hero. They were the Franciscan Spirituals, many of whom were charged eventually with heresy by the Church establishment. Many of these Franciscans came from the dominant classes in Italy. They renounced their wealth and power to become as poor as beggars. The age of the Holy Spirit meant to them that people should live in mystical contemplation and prayer in preparation for the Second Coming of Christ.

At the same time, however, workers, peasants, and the poor were deriving more violent forms of political and religious actions that might be categorized as anarchistic and revolutionary. A Franciscan from the Languedoc region of southern France named Pierre Jean Olivi was one of the intellectual leaders of the Franciscan Spirituals. Influenced by Joachim of Fiore, Olivi proposed that bishops themselves live in voluntary poverty. Furthermore, Olivi argued that the pope himself did not even have the authority to amend the Franciscan Order to differ from the rule of St. Francis himself. This had the double effect of bringing the Church hierarchy down hard on Olivi and his associates, while increasing simultaneously the popularity of these people among the poor and the rest of the populace.

In the same era, a man from Parma in northern Italy named Gherardo Segarelli, a man of low birth and little education, was rejected for membership in the mainstream Franciscan Order, as it had been reorganized by the Vatican. Segarelli decided to devote his life to restoring what he believed had been the ways of the Apostles. In 1260 or thereabouts, he sold his house and gave away the resulting money, then set out to preach repentance throughout Lombardy. He developed followers whom he labelled Apostolic Brethren, who survived by begging. The Church hierarchy came down hard several times on the Apostolic Brethren over the next decades since only the mendicant orders with Church authorization, of which there were now no shortage, were permitted to preach. Finally came a period of outright persecution. In 1294 in Parma, four members of the Brethren were burnt, while Segarelli himself was condemned to perpetual imprisonment. Six years later, he was burnt, ostensibly for relapsing into heresy.

The Brethren now came under the sway of a man named Fra Dolcino, who had joined the group about 1290. Inspired by St. Francis, Dolcino was also a supporter of many of the ideas of Joachim de Fiore. To Dolcino, the current age of the Holy Spirit meant the end of the Church hierarchy; the return of the Church to its supposedly original poverty; the end of the feudal system; human liberation from any restraint or entrenched power; creation of an egalitarian society based on mutual aid and respect, the holding of property in common, and the equality of men and women. Any self-respecting, modern-day anarchist might look favorably upon these ideas of the would-be medieval monk.

After the Church's suppression of the Brethren, Dolcino reunited them about 1303. He also met a woman named Margherita Boninsegna, from Trento in Italy, and she became Dolcino's lover, his 'sister in spirit', as he called her. Early the next year, three of Dolcino's followers were burnt at the stake at the request of the Inquisition. So, Dolcino fled with his followers to a mountain near his home town, where he led a guerrilla campaign against the crusaders sent by the Church to defeat him and his 1,400 surviving followers. Cold and hunger got the better of the rebels, however, since they seemed to be unable to obtain the material support of the local inhabitants. A guerrilla campaign without the support of locals is bound to fail, as modern-day experience has shown. In 1307, Dolcino and Margherita along with 150 followers were captured by an army of the bishop of Vercelli. They were brought to the town of Biella, where Margherita was burnt at the stake. Dolcino watched Margherita's death, and was then taken to Vercelli. He was tortured; his fingers, nose, and ears were amputated; and his tongue and eyes removed. When they reached Vercelli, he was burnt at the stake.

A third example of the influence of the Franciscan Spirituals occurred almost a century later in the decade of the 1340s. A common man named Nicola di Rienzi was born to an innkeeper in Rome. Somehow, he gained an education, becoming particularly influenced by ancient Roman writers such as Cicero and Seneca. Di Rienzi was beguiled by the idea of the ancient empire centered on his hometown of Rome, which he contrasted to the decay represented by contemporary Rome ruled by local nobles who continually fought amongst themselves, destroying innocent commoners in the process. One of these innocents was his own brother, after which di Rienzi vowed to restore the greatness of ancient Rome by bringing local nobles to heel. In order to do so, he had to gain the support of other commoners, which he now set out to do in the manner of an ancient tyrant as per the classical days of Greece. In 1343, he impressed the pope with his eloquence when describing the oppression of Roman commoners. So, the pope named him to a political position in Rome, which he used to conspire to obtain popular support.

On May 19, 1347, di Rienzi assembled the population of Rome, and revealed his plans to a public that granted him support for his agenda that was aimed at bringing the hated noblemen under control. These plans involved the creation of a communal militia to resist the armies of the noblemen; punishing noblemen who had previously enjoyed immunity from prosecution for their crimes; placing nobles' castles at the disposal of the community and its militia; imposing special taxes on nobles, while also depriving them of tolls they charged, which added greatly to food prices; and instituting an austere moral program to suppress gambling, blasphemy, and corruption. Just as significant was his choice of the day for his coup d'état, Pentecost, when the Holy Spirit is reputed to have descended upon the Apostles. This corresponded to the new age of the Holy Spirit, of which di Rienzi's ascension to power was a part. A true showman and doubtless megalomaniac, in addition to being named tribune of the people, di Rienzi assumed as titles the following: *Candidatus Spiritus Sancti, Imperator Orbis, Zelator Italiae, Amator Orbis, and Tribunus Augustus.* (Nominee of the Holy Spirit, Emperor of the World, Italian Patriot, Lover of the Universe, August Tribune—Author's adaptation)

Di Rienzo's stay in power lasted only a few short months, however, before the nobility organized a counter-revolution with the support of the Church hierarchy. Di Rienzi's régime of pomp and bombast soon fatigued even his commoner supporters, especially when new taxes had to be collected to pay for his extravagance. The successful coup by the local nobility forced him into hiding with the Franciscan Spirituals. Rome then returned to its previous state of noble-induced terror. So Di Rienzi was received once again in triumph in Rome on August 1, 1354, lasting again only two months in power owing to the imposition of still more taxes and the same old bombast from the now-just-plain dictator. More popular violence resulted, and di Rienzi was slain on October 8. (Catholic Encyclopedia, New Advent essay and Mollat and Woolf, p. 100–103)

There were still other movements in the Middle Ages in which the devotion towards the Holy Spirit, and the alleged presence of the Holy Spirit played an important part. These movements, however, touched less the popular classes than they touched members of the upper classes, including many women. The movements addressed the need for a new kind of spirituality which brought people closer to God. The Church establishment seemed unable to address this spiritual need in the new towns and cities of the Middle Ages. The tenets of these movements were sometimes quite arcane and mystical, but they did draw upon the teachings of Joachim of Fiore whereby the age of the Holy Spirit was judged to be the current age as opposed to the past ages of the Father and the Son. Where they did run parallel to the complaints of the lower classes was in their difficulties with the Church hierarchy, and its temporal power and wealth. Many of these people, in fact, were also determined by the Church to be heretical, as were the fates of many of the social heretics among the lower classes. As for the popular classes, the alleged age of the Holy Spirit, in its crudest form, had working people choosing the third persona of the Holy Trinity as their favorite in comparison to those of the Father and the Son, whose ages were things of the past. It was the Holy Spirit that seemed to offer the most succor and hope to the poor.

Tangents of Popular Hyper-religiosity

A recurring dynamic of religion in the West has been the conflict between two kinds of religion. On the one hand, there is the religion of power that justifies class domination by the few over the many, and forms part of the ideology of domination. On the other hand, there is the religion of the lower classes and the dominated, religion that is part of the culture of the poor, religion that justifies, supports, and inspires popular resistance by the many to social domination by the few. This dynamic, which has displayed itself throughout the history of the West, can be seen in the three, great monotheisms, the first of which appeared about three millennia ago among the ancient Hebrews. There was the dynamic between the tribal Judaism of the Temple and its priests and ruling class focused on worship at the Temple and other long-existing, local gods, versus the Judaism of the prophets who bemoaned the lack of justice and social equality among Hebrews. The prophets sought to restore belief in the one true God as inspiration for the pursuit of social justice and equality among the Hebrews. Similarly, within Islam, there was the Islam of the wealthy and powerful states and empires created by Muslim warriors versus the Islam of social equality and revolution as first espoused to the Arabs by Muhammad. Within Christianity, there have been two kinds of religion throughout the two millennia of its existence. On the one hand, there is the Church that, as early as the fourth century, had become an institution of temporal, urban wealth and power that helped unite and govern the diverse, immense Roman empire. On the other hand, as early as the third century, Christian hermits and monks withdrew to the countryside in order to express a different kind of religion in opposition to the temporal wealth and power of the Church in the Mediterranean region. These two forms of Christianity played out in political, ideological, and theological movements and debates, albeit often about issues and over choices of words that can appear arcane in retrospect to moderns, in fact, sometimes even pointless. Nonetheless, the dialectic is real and important and meaningful to people of faith.

During the high Middle Ages, the Catholic Church successfully strove to become independent of the warlords, kings, and emperors ruling western Europe. The result, whether or not intended by Church reformers, was a powerful and wealthy institution that came to possess as much as a third of the land in Europe, in some regions even more. Even as this was occurring, counter-movements emerged that challenged the right of the Church to its temporal power and wealth when the Church, after all, was supposedly a spiritual body concerned with saving souls. There were several ways this antagonism to the wealth and temporal power of the Catholic Church manifested itself. Firstly, there were the clear manifestations of class revolt by peasants and townsmen against their landholding, feudal lords, who were often abbots, priors, bishops, and archbishops, positions often held by younger sons of the secular nobility. Secondly, there was the resistance in pagan countries against the initial imposition of Christianity and its clerical hierarchy, institutions, and temporal power and wealth. Thirdly, there were within the Church itself movements of opposition to the temporal power and wealth of the Church as seen in new forms of monasticism such as the Cistercians, described in an earlier chapter. As well, saints such as the Italian Francis of Assisi and the Spaniard Dominic challenged the Church since they and their followers chose to live in voluntary poverty as it was believed Jesus and his disciples had done. Some movements of voluntary poverty were judged to conform to Christian doctrine, while others went beyond the pale to be judged by contemporary churchmen as heretical. The line between the two was thin as it concerned these movements of voluntary poverty, which were very popular among the lower social classes whose poverty was quite involuntary. These movements could even acquire a revolutionary character dangerous to the social order and the ruling classes and, thus required suppression, according to the authorities.

One particular species of heresy recurred throughout the first 1,500 years of Christianity. These heresies provided pride of place to the third persona of the Trinity, the Holy Spirit, working his way in the material world, sometimes even being present in a particular person who inspired radical forms of Christianity. These movements were often judged by the Church hierarchy to be excessive and wrong-headed.

Finally, there were the tangential movements of popular hyper-religiosity that deviated from the original aims of the Church hierarchy, and that might acquire strange forms indeed. Writes Chris Harman:

> Direct displays of class militancy were not the only way people responded to the devastation of their lives. There was a long history of millennarian movements in medieval Europe, which combined popular bitterness against the rich with the religious expectation of the Second Coming of Christ and, often, hatred of outsiders. The official Crusades of the popes prompted unofficial crusades of the masses—the People's, Children's, and Shepherds' Crusades. Heretical preachers gained enormous support by proclaiming themselves the successors to Jesus. Typically, masses of people would march from town to town, looting and gathering popular support. They would direct their bitterness not against the feudal ruling class as such, but against corrupt priests and, especially, Jews...an easy target. They (Jews) were the only non-Christian group in a society where Christianity was the all-pervasive religion... (p. 151)

Thus, we need to examine the unofficial crusades of the poor that were tangential to the Crusades as first preached by Pope Urban II in 1095, as well as movements that were themselves tangential to the popular crusades, most especially, the anti-Jewish pogroms. Norman Cohn is most useful when describing the original aims of the Crusades, and how the Crusades came to be distorted by the tangents of popular hyper-religiosity.

> The main object of Urban's famous appeal...was to provide Byzantium with the reinforcements it needed in order to drive the Seljuk Turks from Asia Minor, for he hoped that, in return, the eastern Church would acknowledge the supremacy of Rome so that the unity of Christendom would be restored. In the second place, he was concerned to indicate to the nobility, particularly of his native France, an alternative outlet for martial energies, which were still constantly bringing devastation upon the land. (p. 61)

In actual fact, the council of Clermont, where Urban made his famous appeal, attracted hundreds of knights and noblemen in addition to clergymen in order to discuss the Truce of God with the objective of containing feudal warfare and other feudal violence. The pope and bishops returning from the council of Clermont went about France for several months preaching the necessity of the Crusade.

At the same time, however, popular preachers in the forms of ex-monks and hermits went about France, Flanders, and the Rhineland preaching the necessity of the common people joining the Crusade, that it was not just the nobility, knighthood, and monarchs of western Europe who were being summoned to Crusade. Among the most important popular characters was a severe ascetic from Amiens named Peter the Hermit, who fascinated and dazzled the poor with miracles and holiness, and a French nobleman named Walter Sans-Avoir, as well as a German count from the Rhine Valley named Emicho of Flonheim. Emicho recounted a story to the effect that Christ had appeared to him. Infused with the teachings of the Gospel of Luke, Emicho was chosen to fill the end-of-times prophecy. Emicho envisioned that he would march on Constantinople, and overcome the forces there, taking over the title of 'Last World Emperor'. In accordance with canonical, prophetic tradition, all Christian armies, Latin and Greek, would then unite, and march to seize Jerusalem from the Saracens (Muslims), thus prompting the Second Coming.

The masses who joined what historians call the People's Crusade sought salvation during a most difficult time in western Europe when there had been years of floods, droughts, famines, and epidemics. In 1095, heavenly events such as episodes of the Northern Lights, comets, meteors, and a lunar eclipse indicated favorable omens for a crusade. Moreover, travelling to the Holy Land to the heavenly city of Jerusalem was as good as any other religion-inspired solution to the poverty and destitution being experienced by the poor. In fact, Jerusalem had long been a site of pilgrimage. The bands of Peter the Hermit and Emicho met in the Rhineland early in April, where they proceeded to conduct anti-Jewish pogroms, before heading east through Hungary and Byzantium, then into the Holy Land. In southern France, poor people joined the army of the count of Toulouse, Raymond, to comprise a force as hyper-religious as the bands of poor people led by the itinerant preachers. The army of Walter Sans-Avoir, a few thousand strong, had left France even before Peter the Hermit, arriving at the Byzantine border early in May. This was still over three months before the official, authorized army of noble crusaders was to leave France in mid-August. Forty thousand crusaders, all but a few thousand of whom were skilled knights with retainers and squires, were much more than what the pope had expected. In fact, they were also more than what was also expected in Hungary and Byzantium on the road to the Holy land. Not knowing what to do with Walter's army, who arrived first near the border of Byzantium, the local military commander refused entry to the Frenchmen, who then had to pillage the countryside in order to survive. In fact, this became a typical pattern whereby western Europeans sent east to help fellow Christians ended up making war upon the latter. The popular army of Peter the Hermit and the Germans under Emicho now had to fight their way through Catholic Hungary, since the cat was now out of the bag with respect to the crusaders. Most of the poor crusaders never even made it to the Holy Land. Of those who did, facts and legends mixed to produce people known to contemporaries as *tafurs*, the term for the bands of vagabonds from western Europe who had survived the journey east to reach Syria and the Holy Land.

> Barefoot, shaggy, clad in ragged sackcloth, covered in sores and filth, living on roots and grass and also, at times, on the roasted corpses of their enemies, the tafurs were such ferocious bands that any country they passed through was utterly devastated. Too poor to afford swords and lances, they wielded clubs weighted with lead and pointed sticks, knives, hatchets, shovels, hoes, and catapults. When they charged into battle, they gnashed their teeth as though meant to eat their enemies alive as well as dead. (Norman Cohn, p. 65)

While their social superiors regarded the tafurs with embarrassment and apprehension, Muslims regarded them as living devils. Moreover, European noblemen made sure to be well-armed when near the tafurs for fear that the latter might turn on their social superiors, not just on the enemy. When tafurs were involved in capturing a city or village, they were known to offer local Muslims the choices of immediate conversion to Christianity, death, or slavery. The tafurs looted, raped, and carried out indiscriminate massacres, even cannibalism, which the European lords were unable or unwilling to arrest. (Norman Cohn, p. 66-67)

Nevertheless, in spite of all the travails, the First Crusade, both in its official, knightly and lordly capacity, and that of the People's Crusade, was ultimately brutally successful. Symbolic Jerusalem fell to the Europeans, after which most Muslim occupants of the Holy City were killed, except for the Muslim governor who bought his way to freedom. Around the Jewish

Temple, there was so much blood that horses waded in blood to their knees. A number of the city's Jews collected in a synagogue, then died when the building was set afire. A few locals had arranged for their safety by paying a large ransom to Tancred, a noble leader of the expedition, but crusading soldiers scaled the walls of the mosque where refugees were hiding in order to behead all of them, save for those who jumped from the roof of the mosque to their death. (Norman Cohn, p. 68)

In 1212, another popular crusade known as the Children's Crusade started out from France and Germany. In actual fact, it is not certain that the purported events actually even occurred. Legends, myths, and facts seem to have mixed to produce widely-varying accounts. It appears there might have been actually two movements, one each from France and Germany. In both of them, young boys or adolescents under the influence of visions of Jesus seem to have inspired movements that grew to be as large as 30,000-strong, comprised mostly of poor, young people. Neither movement reached the Holy Land; each knew disastrous ends.

In the early spring of 1212, Nicholas of Cologne, a shepherd from the Rhineland, led young crusaders across the Alps and into Italy with the intention of converting Muslims peacefully. Nicholas promised his followers that the Mediterranean would part before them, allowing them to walk safely to the Holy Land. In actuality, two-thirds died in Europe, while many returned home. About 7,000 reached Genoa in late August, and proceeded immediately to the harbor, expecting that the sea would part as promised by Nicholas. When the division of the waters did not occur some accused Nicholas of betrayal, while many squatted, waiting for God to get around to the job. Genoese authorities were impressed with the faith and sincerity of the young people, so they offered them citizenship, an offer that most of Nicholas' followers accepted. Nicholas continued, however, with an ever-shrinking band to Pisa, then on to Rome, where Pope Innocent III treated them with kindness, exhorting the good boys and girls to return home. Nicholas did not survive the return trip through the Alps, however, while a group of his followers wandered into southern Italy.

In June, a second movement started from France. Another shepherd, a 12-year-old named Stéphane of Cloyes, claimed that he had a letter from Jesus addressed to the king of France. Large numbers of children, some with alleged miraculous powers, were attracted to Stéphane, such that his following of children and adults grew to number about 30,000 when they headed off to Paris to meet the king. Both the king and University of Paris scholars, however, advised the troop to return home, half of whom followed this sage advice. Stéphane and his now small following, wandered about France still preaching the need for a crusade. His following, who survived by begging, had halved by the end of June when he finally reached Marseilles, where the would-be crusade ended ingloriously in a whimper.

Speaking of shepherds...In fact, there were two more crusades that involved young shepherds. Each was called a crusade of the *Pastoureux*. The first took place in 1251, the second in 1320. In 1248, King Louis IX of France, after death canonized as Saint-Louis, went on a crusade to the Holy Land. He was defeated in battle in February of 1250, taken prisoner, then managed to buy his freedom. He apparently wanted to continue fighting, for he sent word home with his brothers to send more troops to the Holy Land. The French nobility demurred, however, which infuriated the poor people, who revered the king. Peasants and workers rose in revolt against the nobility and the Church hierarchy. Around Easter in 1251, a mysterious, old man called the 'Master of Hungary' began preaching the necessity of a crusade without the authorization of the Church. His initial audience came from the shepherds of northern France, but the movement spread rapidly throughout Flanders, Brabant, and Hainault in the Low Countries, and Lorraine and Burgundy in eastern France. An army of 30,000 men soon proved themselves hostile to a Church hierarchy that was apparently uninterested in following the king or the Pastoureux to the Holy Land. Instead, an underground movement of criminal lowlife joined the Pastoureux. In the spring, they entered Paris to hear their religious leader publicly preach in the garb of a bishop. Writes Louis Bréhier:

> Clerics and monks were hunted, slain, and thrown into the Seine, and the bishop of Paris was insulted...The Pastoureux then left Paris, and divided into several armies that spread terror everywhere. At Rouen, the archbishop and his clergy were expelled from the cathedral on June 4th. At Orléans, a large number of university clerics were killed and thrown into the Loire on June 11th. At Tours, the Pastoureux took by storm the convent of the Dominicans, and desecrated the churches...When they reached Bourges, the clerics and priests had fled, whereupon they seized the possessions of the Jews, sacked the synagogues, and pillaged the city. (p. 1)

A number of burghers from Bourges responded to the assaults by hunting down and killing the Master of Hungary, after which his followers dispersed.

The mystical anarchism of the Pastoureux raised the level of paranoia among some clergymen who even suspected the most ironic possibility that the Pastoureux had concocted a secret plan with Muslim leaders to subject Christians to Islam and Muslim rule.

> It is said that they have resolved first to exterminate the clergy from the face of the earth, then to suppress the religious and, finally, to fall upon the knights and nobles in order that the country, thus deprived of defense, may be more easily delivered up to the errors and incursions of the pagans. (Bréhier, p. 2)

The second Pastoureux episode of 1320 was just as chaotic. Former clerics preached the need for a crusade in the face of the indifference of the ruling class about the fate of the Holy Land. Numbers of poor people, including the now-obligatory shepherds, reached a total of perhaps as many as 40,000 poor people looting and pillaging throughout France. At Verdunsur-Garonne, 500 Jews hiding in a dungeon felt compelled to strangle each other rather than fall into the hands of the Pastoureux. The Pastoureux received the support of the bourgeoisie of many towns and cities, including for their anti-Jewish activities. The pope, at the time based in the French town of Avignon, excommunicated the Pastoureux, who then decided to pay the pope a visit. The pope's army, however, drove the would-be crusaders into the marshes surrounding Avignon, where many of them starved to death. Others, nonetheless, continued to ravage the south of France. Once again writes Norman Cohn,

> Many were killed in battle at various points between Toulouse and Narbonne, or captured and hanged from trees in twenties and thirties. Pursuits and executions continued for 3 months. The survivors split into small groups, and crossed the Pyrenees to kill more Jews, which they did until the son of the king of Aragon led a force against them and dispersed them. More than any earlier crusade, this one was felt... to threaten the whole, existing structure of society. The Pastoureux of 1320 struck terror into the hearts of all the rich and privileged. (p. 104)

The Anti-Jewish Tangent

The Crusades were, in and of themselves, clear expressions of the violence of western Europeans wreaked against almost everyone. Victims of the crusades included the pagan societies of northern Europe; people expressing a Christianity judged by Church authorities to be heretical or schismatic; enemies of individual members of the ruling class; victims of military sallies by the nobility dressed in the garb of religious debates; Orthodox Christians and their clerical hierarchy, as well as the Orthodox Christians of southeastern Europe and Byzantium; the people of the Holy land, whether Muslim or Jew, and still other Christians. Call for Crusades and their execution were perversions tangential to the original message of Christianity. The popular derivations of the Crusades as seen in the People's, Children's, and Pastoureux crusades, were themselves tangential to the original call for the crusades by the Church hierarchy and pope. Finally, in a similar fashion, the anti-Jewish pogroms in western Europe in 1096 were even tangential to the popular crusades.

In 1096 anti-Jewish pogroms began, even as the official First Crusade was being organized, first in Rouen, then in other French communities. They continued while the People's Crusade was making its way east to the Rhineland, adding along the way peasants and workers, the indigent, and even some low-ranking knights and their retinues. It was in the Rhineland, where Jewish communities were long established with an economy and successful social integration based on commerce and crafts, where the most destructive expressions of anti-Jewish violence occurred.

Norman Cohn maps out the grim travelogue. (p. 69-70) At the beginning of May, 1096, crusaders under Peter the Hermit and Emicho planned to attack the Jews of Speyer in their synagogue on the Sabbath, but they were only able to kill a dozen or so in the streets. The local bishop hid the rest of the Jews in his castle, then later even had some of the popular crusaders punished for murder. In Worms, the local bishop again hid local Jews in his castle when locals joined with the crusaders to sack the synagogue, loot houses, and kill Jews who refused baptism. Some children were killed, while others were captured then baptized. The bishop offered to baptize the Jews he had hidden in his castle in order to save their lives, but they refused the offer, preferring to commit suicide rather than become Christians. In total, 800 Jews died at Worms. The Jews of Mainz, the largest Jewish community in Germany, numbered about a thousand dead. The same pattern obtained at Trier, Metz, and Cologne. In mid-June, the crusaders turned east, forcibly baptizing Jews in Regensburg and Prague. Norman Cohn estimates 48,000 Jews dead in May and June. Other estimates range from 2,000 to 10,000. Still another estimate has 10,000 murdered Jews during the January-July period of 1096, representing a quarter to a third of the Jewish population of northern France and Germany.

Norman Cohn recounts another popular crusade at the time of the Second Crusade two generations later. In 1146 as the French king and nobility were preparing a crusade, desperate commoners started killing Jews in Normandy and Picardy. A monk named Rudolph travelled from the Low Countries to the Rhineland, calling for the crusade to begin by murdering Jews. In episcopal cities, the ground was fertile for anti-Semitism in Cologne, Mainz, Worms, Speyer, Strasbourg, and Wurzburg. The Jews turned to wealthy burghers and bishops for protection, but popular fury was at a revolutionary pitch. The would-be crusaders proposed to Jews that they get baptized, then join them in the destruction of Islam. The lack of appeal of this proposal to German Jews is easily understandable. Other popular crusaders held even cruder positions. Why go all the way to the Holy Land to kill infidels when there were infidels living right among them, that is, Jews? According to the Gospels, ancestors of medieval European Jews had crucified Jesus Christ. Moreover, commoners were just as likely as burghers or kings or nobility to owe money to Jews since the latter formed part of the bourgeoisie; they often lent money as capital or even for the basics needed for human survival. (p. 70)

The Black Death of 1347–1351 provoked still more pogroms. Jews, lepers, and foreigners were all singled out this time as causing the plague. Once again, the pope and Church authorities tried to stop the pogroms with only modest success.

> By 1351, sixty major and 150 smaller Jewish communities had been exterminated, and more than 350 separate massacres had occurred...An important legacy of the Black Death was...the eastward movement... of north European Jewry to Poland and Russia... (Zapotoczny)

The typical view of historians is that, for the most part, campaigns of anti-Semitism issued from the lower classes, at least on the continent. Samuel Cohn makes the case that the opposite occurred in England, that is, the pogroms issued from the Church hierarchy and state and king. This also might have happened more often on the Continent than is generally presented, certainly among the nobility and the bourgeoisie, who were often debtors to Jewish money-lenders, and thus often joined in the pogroms. In England, it was upper class people who initiated anti-Jewish campaigns. In fact, Jews were expelled formally from England in 1286. Samuel Cohn writes:

> The bulk of the English evidence... challenges these longstanding generalizations of hate percolating from below. Threats of excommunication by the bishop of Hereford afford glimpses of Christian-Jewish relations that point to an intermingling, even friendship between Christian commoners and Jews that alarmed authorities, especially those at the top of the ecclesiastical hierarchy...A bull of Pope Honorius... instructed the archbishop of Canterbury "...to check the familiar intercourse between Christians and Jews..." It pointed particularly to shameless conviviality between Christian and Jewish women...On the eve of the Jews' expulsion, this bull was circulated throughout England, suggesting that...interfaith tolerance and friendship may not have been exceptional. The Church hierarchy at its highest levels, starting with the pope, had led the charge against Jews. (2013, p. 281-282)

Perhaps the jury is still out. The source of anti-Semitism in terms of social class varies per region, city, town, or village according to the evidence. Can one even make broad statements about the relation between social class and anti-Semitism? A pamphlet that presented a dazzling study of anti-Semitism in European history was written by Jean-Paul Sartre. Published in October, 1944, only two months after the liberation of Paris, this suggests that the great philosopher might have been working on it, in fact, during the years of WWII. Sartre argued that, broadly speaking, in modern times anti-Semitism is an ideology of the petite bourgeoisie, or the middle class, used to affix social blame for social ills rather than recognizing class relationships as a cause of social injustice or even as a motor of development in the West. According to Sartre, the petite bourgeoisie has been horrified at the prospect of a general proletarianization that might eventually include it. It was easier, therefore, to affix blame for injustice to a scapegoat such as Jews rather than dealing with the root causes of exploitation and oppression, or by even avoiding the latter discussion altogether. Thus the appeal of both fascism and anti-Semitism to the petite bourgeoisie, the two ills often occurring together in Western history.

At the same time, Sartre also wrote magnificently and convincingly about how anti-Semitism is broader than contemporary manifestations of WWII and the lead-up to the conflagration and subsequent manifestations. Sartre demonstrated that they were part and parcel of the cultural fabric of European history. In the post-Holocaust era, we can perhaps understand the why and how and what of medieval, anti-Jewish pogroms in France, England, and Germany. Nonetheless, can we even begin to understand, however, the madness that has been anti-Semitism throughout the history of the West? This represents an important challenge for all in Western society including, most particularly, to intellectuals.

Popular Revolts against King and State

The Middle Ages saw the development of some states that eventually formed the basis of modern nation-states. The prime obstacle to be overcome for this development to take place, at least in western Europe, was local control by warlords cum feudal lords. In their effort to create centralized states, kings, emperors or princes, often foreign to the land they occupied or desired, united with indigenous classes—clergy, peasants, workers, bourgeoisie—to overcome the power of the local nobility.

In eastern and Nordic Europe, a different situation obtained. Tribal and clan societies continued well into the high and late Middle Ages, societies in which commoners were freer than their western counterparts owing to the vast, empty spaces that made it difficult for nobility and monarchies to establish control. As well, there were different concepts of property, custom, and law operating than in western Europe, and that provided bases for the emergence of centralized states. The exception to both western Europe and the rest of Europe, however, was the centralized state of Byzantium that continued to exist, albeit in much reduced extent, wealth, and power, until the Ottoman conquest in the 15th century. In general, however, the relationships between medieval classes in the West were complex, ever-changing, and often unstable. Moreover, it took hundreds of years before centralized nation-states came to be. Charles Tilly reminds us that:

> The state makers only imposed their wills on the populace through centuries of ruthless effort...The state makers frequently found the traditional authorities allied with the people against them. Thus, it became a game of shifting coalitions: kings rallying popular support by offering guarantees against cruel and arbitrary local magnates, or by challenging their claims to goods, money, services; magnates parading as defenders of local liberties against royal oppression, but not hesitating to bargain with the crown when it appeared advantageous. (cankaya. edu.tr)

Throughout the Middle Ages, popular classes revolted against king and state when new taxes were introduced, taxes such as those on consumption of specific goods. Some examples of these were the French *gabelle* on consumption of salt, a vital commodity owing to the increase in meat and fish consumption in medieval towns and cities. As well, states imposed customs and duties on trade, income and wealth taxes, and poll taxes on individuals. These taxes were essential to pay for centralized state administration and the conduct of diplomacy and warfare. Moreover, wars among centralized states wreaked calamity upon both combatants from the popular classes and non-combatants. In addition, when states imposed centralized justice such as Roman law, the common people often rose up to protect ancient, customary privileges and laws. In summary, there were many reasons for popular discontent and protest against the development and operations of centralized states. At one and the same time, there were also reasons why, in other circumstances, commoners might support a central state in conflict with local aristocrats. (Bourin et al., p. 89)

Some historians are reluctant to see links among the various popular revolts that occurred during the Middle Ages, arguing that they were particular to specific localities. Nevertheless, one aspect of the development of Western society during the Middle Ages was increased communications among regions. This owed in large measure to the development of the centralized state. Consider monarchs travelling with courts within the states they ruled, or the emergence of mass armies composed of soldiers from many places of origin. In fact, through the persistent conduct of long-lasting wars, disgruntled commoners including soldiers might hear of political actions taken in other parts of Europe by their popular brethren. The growth of the Catholic Church and the Orthodox Church and their central administrations, hierarchies of clerics, and monastic orders; travelling preachers including sometimes even heretical preachers; crusades and pilgrimages; cathedral building projects taking generations to complete that would require importing craftsmen from hither and yon—all these led to increased communications and popular knowledge of developments elsewhere in the West. In addition, journeymen craftsmen were called such because that's exactly what they did to exercise their crafts. In France, this travelling was called the *Tour de France*; in the Holy Roman Empire, it was called the *Wanderschaft*. There were also the travelling merchants such as the Radhanites, the Jewish merchants from Spain; the German merchants of the Hanseatic League; merchants from Italian city-states; and merchants who accompanied and supplied crusaders and pilgrims. Finally, consider knights errant in search of lords and ladies to serve and wars to fight.

The point is that the Middle Ages produced considerably increased communications by which the popular classes could learn of and imagine possibilities for rebellion. Historians employ as evidence the contemporary chronicles and histories usually written by clerics as well as Church records and local archives. Some might point out that one can't make an historical argument using lack of evidence about apparently absent links among rebelling commoners. Social scientists including communications theorists are not so constrained, however, since they can use comparative evidence and theory from modern sources. Thus, it is easy for them to imagine how a peasant apparently limited to his village or hamlet could still be influenced directly by developments and occurrences elsewhere in Europe, including understanding the benefits and possibilities offered by revolt and social solidarity of the popular classes. We now turn to popular revolts against king and state in the Middle Ages in order to determine commonalities and patterns in this popular resistance.

The Kievan Rus' Uprisings

The popular uprisings in Kiev in 1068–1069 and 1113 against the monarchs of Rus', the predecessor state of what are now the Ukraine, Belarus, and Russia, are indeed interesting. They combine anti-royal elements with popular resistance to the imposition from on high of Christianity upon pagan Slavs, and the imposition of feudal obligations upon the common people. Our principal source is the Great Soviet Encyclopedia. In 1068, Kipchak Turks defeated Kievan Rus' in a battle southeast of Kiev. Thereafter, the Turks continued to raid the region. The common people of Kiev and the surrounding countryside held a traditional, popular assembly called a veche in the local marketplace, at which they decided to request arms and horses from the monarch to continue the fight against the Kipchaks. Fearing an armed populace, the grand prince denied the veche request. So, the people freed an imprisoned prince from another royal lineage to name him grand prince while, in the countryside, anti-feudal revolts erupted, often led by pagan priests called volkhvy. Meanwhile, however, forces loyal to the deposed grand prince returned to power. These feudal lords then promulgated new laws known as the Code of the Iaroslavichi that increased punishments for attempts on the lives or property of feudal lords or other property owners.

In 1113, the lower classes of Kiev once again revolted against the ruling grand prince, his policies, and the royal administrators. The latter were growing rich by speculating in salt and bread, thus driving up prices on essential foods. Other sources of popular disaffection were debts and usurious interest rates. Inability to repay debts resulted in enslavement of debtors to creditors, many of whom were bourgeois Jews. The combination of issues meant that the lower classes of Kiev, the peasants surrounding Kiev, and the slaves known as kholopy proceeded to destroy the property of local boyars and Jewish creditors. Soon after these events, the grand prince of Kiev died. The frightened nobility convinced a popular nobleman named Vladimir Monomakh to become ruler of Kievan Rus'. The new prince passed a law that placed limits on interest that could be collected on debts. This did succeed in providing some level of comfort to the common people, thus helping put a halt to the popular rebellions even while producing a real gain for commoners.

Tumult in Flanders

The high Middle Ages had seen considerable class conflict in Flanders between peasants and the nobility, and between the patrician bourgeoisie and urban workers. Early in the 14th century, this conflict amplified when the French monarch, Philippe le Bel, took over the county of Flanders, and lent his support to the local bourgeoisie. This French takeover was celebrated with much pomp and ceremony by the new king ruling Flanders, who then rubbed salt into the wound by demanding that Flanders communes foot the bill for the royal celebrations. This was only the straw that broke the camel's back, however, for the socio-economic growth brought by the textiles industry serving all of Europe, much as also happened in northern Italy, already had led to increased class conflict. On one side, the wealth of the textiles industry created a ruling class that severely exploited its workers, and monopolized economic activity and municipal and county politics. On the other side were the craft guilds and their members who lived in poverty, and were subject to heavy taxes and to an overbearing and unfair system of justice.

Workers of the Flemish towns and cities staged an initial revolt, which the French king quickly suppressed. Philippe le Bel imposed a soldier as governor, a dictatorial man named Jacques de Châtillon, to impose royal discipline in the county. In response, however, Flemish workers produced a true popular leader, a weaver of modest means from Bruges named Pieter de Coninc. Apparently blessed with a silver tongue, de Coninc also "...had real political sense and breadth of vision; he was thus able to impart to the movement he had initiated a wider bearing" beyond the weavers and textile workers who comprised his first followers. (Mollat and Woolf, p. 58) After a first rebellion at Bruges the captured de Coninc was freed from prison by his followers. De Coninc quickly won over to his cause the workers of Ghent and even the count of Flanders, Gui de Dampierre. In the first insurrection of 1301, the workers of Bruges and Ghent pillaged the property of the patricians in both cities. Some of these unfortunates were burnt alive, while others literally were forced to run the gauntlet between two ranks of workers. Those who survived these trials were then banished from the two cities.

With the count on his side and the count's grandson, Guillaume de Juliers, de Coninc led a popular movement tinged with anti-French elements. At daybreak on May 18, 1302, royal soldiers were awakened from their sleep as the second wave of the Flemish revolution began. The spark was lit throughout the county from the Atlantic Ocean in the west, inland to its eastern boundary. De Coninc controlled Bruges and launched a mass killing of the king's soldiers known to historians and to locals still today as the *mâtines brugeoises*.

The king sought revenge for what was the third phase of the revolution in Flanders. He sent an army to meet the Flemish revolutionaries in an open field near the town of Courtrai on July 11, 1302, after unsuccessfully besieging the town for two days. The French army had about 40,000 men, including thousands of knights and noblemen. The Flemish had about half that number of troops, and only twenty knights. The actual conduct of the battle of Courtrai made it difficult for the French cavalry owing to the layout of the field which was crossed by numerous ditches and streams. The large French infantry force leading the initial attack went well, but the

French commander, Count Robert II of Artois, recalled the infantry, so that the noble cavalry might claim the victory. Hindered by their own infantry and the tactically sound position of the Flemish militia, the French cavalry was an easy target for the heavily-armed Flemish. When they realized the battle was lost the French fled, only to be pursued over ten kilometers by the Flemish force. Contemporary accounts placed the total number of dead and wounded at 10,000, with at least 1,000 of them being French knights. In that era, knights and noblemen used golden spurs to ride, while wealthy bourgeois used silver spurs. The Flemish collected 700 of these golden spurs to hang them in Notre-Dame church in Courtrai, hence, the name commonly used for the Battle of the Golden Spurs.

In the aftermath of the battle, the repressive labor regulations of the urban merchant guilds were ended. Guilds of weavers, fullers, dyers, and other workers won the rights to procure necessary raw materials, shops, and tools, and to sell their products beyond city walls. In order to serve in public office, one now had to be a member of a crafts guild, effectively excluding the patricians from office. The battle is a landmark of Flemish and later Belgian independence, celebrated annually as an official holiday. It was also one of a series of other European battles such as Crécy and Agincourt where infantry armies from the lower social classes defeated mounted cavalrymen and noblemen, which eventually helped lead to a transformation of military strategies and tactics in the West. Finally, it was a sterling example of a successful popular revolution against a monarch and a bourgeoisie he supported, one more example of the shifting class coalitions in the Middle Ages.

Étienne Marcel

As per the examples of the northern Italian cities, the cities of the Low Countries, and the cities of the Hanseatic League, the cities of northern France grew in wealth and political saliency during the Middle Ages owing to the shift in economic development based upon ownership of rural lands to urban commerce. The chief urban beneficiary in France of this transformation was Paris. An important political and economic position in Paris was held by the *prévôt de Paris*, the chief merchant who was sort of like a mayor. Étienne Marcel served in this position during years of political crisis provoked by the Hundred Years War. Born to a family of wealthy bourgeois who made their money in the textiles industry, Marcel served as a representative of the cities in the third estate, which ostensibly represented the common people, that is, people who were neither nobility nor clergy. In reality, however, the third estate represented the wealthy bourgeois on the royal council, people who were summoned periodically to grant finances to the king, and to advise on matters of war and government. The other estates represented on the royal council were the nobility and the clergy.

The estates of 1355 dealt with control of taxes and expenditures; the estates of 1356 with the levying of new taxes to fight the war with the English; the estates of 1357 with payment of the ransom to the English for the return of the French king known as the Jean le Bon. All these became important constitutional issues. Marcel was the head of a reforming movement that attempted to institute political controls over the French monarch similar to those that had been instituted in England at the end of the 11th century/ beginning of the 12th century. Marcel also led the popular forces of the poor, craftsmen, and small shopkeepers, who were quite disgruntled at the prospect of new taxes and royal devaluations of French currency in order to improve royal finances by diminishing the real value of royal debts owed by the monarchy. Marcel also backed the rebelling peasants of the Great Jacquérie, which occurred about the same time, so as to increase his chances of success with constitutional reforms. In addition, he promoted his reforming movement in other French cities such as Arras, Toulouse, Rouen, Amiens, and Laon as well as in Flemish cities.

Marcel's downfall, however, was his involvement in the shenanigans and machinations about the royal succession by the Dauphin Charles, son of King Jean le Bon, the English King Edward III, and King Charles of Navarre, all of whom could advance somewhat legitimate claims to the French throne. In fact, Marcel was sort of an anglophile as might be seen in his attempted monarchical reforms inspired by English examples, reforms that eventually failed. He was ultimately killed by Parisian supporters of the Dauphin, who were concerned that Marcel was plotting to deliver Paris to the English. Historical consensus has it, in fact, that Marcel died trying to organize a French Revolution about 450 years before its time.

After Marcel's failure at reforming the French monarchy, the kingdom resumed its path towards the monarchical absolutism of the modern era. Nevertheless, France saw another attempt as reducing the power of the monarchy a generation later during the revolutionary years, 1378–1383, when all of western Europe experienced the convulsions of popular revolution and, once again in 1413, when the Cabochien rebels in Paris unsuccessfully tried to rein in the French king. The position of prévôt in Paris was thereafter reconstituted but only as a royal position that reported to the king. Perhaps if Marcel had stuck to his alliance with the urban poor and craftsmen and the rural *Jacques*, rather than his dalliances with the English and Navarrese kings, he might have achieved his aim of a constitutional monarchy for France. This eventually occurred only briefly in the aftermath of the French Revolution at the end of the 18th century when all the medieval powers—monarchy, nobility, clergy—were not only submitted to somewhat of a democratic control, but deposed and killed, as well. Later in the 19th century, French historiography turned Étienne Marcel into an anachronistic, revolutionary hero in the eyes of French republicans, similar to the post-facto, nationalist treatment reserved for Joan of Arc in medieval times, and for Vercingetorex, a rebel leader of the Gauls, during Roman times.

The Revolt of Seyh Bedreddin

At the beginning of the 15th century, the conquests of Timur Lenk in the Ottoman empire resulted in a civil war among Ottoman princes. A Sufi intellectual named Seyh Bedreddin rose to serve one of the contesting princes as his chief jurist in the Balkans. Bedreddin was of mixed parentage, his father being a high-ranking government official of Muslim Turk origins, his mother a Greek Orthodox Christian. While the exact circumstances are murky, Bedreddin led a popular revolt against the high taxes of the Ottoman imperial government. His followers included nomadic Turks, Christians in the Balkans especially Bulgaria, and Muslims in the western portion of Anatolia. The Muslim rebels were eventually concentrated in the region of Karaburum, the westernmost part of Anatolia that juts into the Aegean Sea in the modern-day Turkish province of Izmir at the site of the ancient Greek city of Smyrna. Bedreddin's vision was of a society where all were equal and property was held in common. For this reason, he and the revolt he led are considered, even in modern-day Turkey, to have been expressions of a proto-socialism. The revolt was crushed, thousands of insurgents were killed, and the leader of the revolt was hanged.

Popular Rebellions in Scandinavia

In the 15th century, the countries of Scandinavia were ruled by the king of Denmark who united Norway including Iceland, and Sweden which included western Finland, into what was known as the Kalmar Union. In actuality, many political decisions in Scandinavia were made locally. In Sweden, there was a Council of the Realm, which included representatives from four estates: nobility, clergy, burghers, and peasants, although most local government was conducted by the first two estates. In 1434, the king was Eric of Pomerania, a German prince. Eric's continual warfare in northern Germany upset the Swedish economy, largely based on iron exports to Germany, even as high taxes were being collected by the Danish monarchy. This enraged Swedish peasants while, at the same time, the Swedish ruling class was suspicious of the Danish centralization plans that would have curbed Swedish autonomy. King Eric refused to negotiate with the four estates assembled for a diet in Sweden, which sparked a rebellion. Rebellious peasants and miners took out their anger by burning and assaulting castles in the summer of 1434. A nobleman with the majestic moniker of Engelbrekt Engelbrektsson emerged as the popular commander.

In August of 1434, negotiations with King Eric yielded nothing. In January, 1435, Engelbrekt summoned the four estates to a special diet, where he was voted Captain of the Swedish Realm, in effect, the leader of government but not its monarch. King Eric offered some changes which, by the next spring, still did not seem to be forthcoming. So, on April 27, a rebel army collected in Stockholm but here, the situation became muddy. The people of

Stockholm included a strong Danish presence who were supporters of the king. Furthermore, some Swedish nobles and clerics in Stockholm backed a competitor to Engelbrekt, a man named Karl Knutsson Bonde. In a twist of fate, the stalemate between the rival camps of Swedish rebels broke when Engelbrekt fell sick, then was murdered on May 4 over an unrelated personal conflict. This left the field open to Knutsson, who eventually became King Charles of Sweden in 1448. Another nobleman with the not-so-majestic moniker of Erik Puke tried to pick up the rebellion where Engelbrekt had left it, but he was unsuccessful, and paid for it with his life.

In 1434, Engelbrekt had encouraged the peasants of Denmark and Norway to rebel against the king and his local officials. In fact, even after the death of Engelbrekt, other Scandinavian peasant rebellions did occur. Rebellions against the king and his officials began in eastern and central Denmark, where peasants burnt castles as part of their opposition to taxes. The antipathy between the Danish and their king became even more acute in 1439 when the Danish Council of the Realm began negotiating with another German nobleman, Count Christopher of Bavaria, to become the new king of the Kalmar Union. This change in monarchs did come to pass in 1440, but the unrest among peasants continued. Very soon after his coronation, Christopher went to war with the Netherlands, which required another special levy of taxes. In the spring of 1441, peasants in northern Denmark rebelled against the new tax by burning royal castles and manors. This time a local lord named Henrik Tageson assumed military command of the peasants' army. After initial popular successes, King Christopher assembled an army, ventured northward, and defeated the peasants. Tageson was executed on June 12, 1441, according to the Finnish historian, Kimmo Katajala. (chapter 3)

According to Katajala, during the first few decades of the 15th century, there were about twenty popular uprisings in the most densely populated areas of western and eastern Norway. They were usually squabbles between local clergy and the common people of their parishes. The quarrels were settled by local assizes of the bishop or by royal representatives. Inspired by the Swedish peasants, Norwegian peasants rose in arms in 1435–1437, choosing as their leader a local nobleman named Amund Sigurdsson Bolt. The peasants demanded political reforms and evictions of foreign officials, priests, and bishops. The demands were met only partially, so tensions simmered. A similar revolt occurred among the peasants who lived west of the Oslo Fjord, led by a man named Halvard Gratopp. (Katajala, chapter 3)

Even if generally unsuccessful, the rebellion of Engelbrekt and similar rebellions in Norway and put Norway and Sweden on the road to national sovereignty. Furthermore, after Engelbrekt's death, a democratic diet was held in Sweden in 1436 where representatives of peasants and burghers sat as legitimate members of the four estates, which constituted a major step on the road to democracy in Scandinavia.

Popular Tax Revolts in Lyon

The decade of the 1430s in Lyon in France produced several revolts against royal taxes. The most violent and widespread socially was the *Rebeyne* of 1436, a term in the local, medieval dialect that is still used by modern-day historians to label the revolt. The immediate cause was the imposition of new head taxes and salt taxes by the monarchy, which provoked the people of Lyon to pick up arms to revolt. The 1436 revolt, however,

> presented many differences when compared to the earlier revolts of the 1430s. It mobilized many people; the most numerous of them comprised beggars, peasants who had fled to the city to escape feudal wars, low-ranking workers such as domestic servants, journeymen, and apprentices. Their leaders were master craftsmen, chiefly butchers, cutlers, and barbers. (Author's note—Since these artisans worked with sharp instruments that also could be used as weapons, they often took the popular lead in violent political actions.) Others who took part in the revolt included shoemakers, tailors, weavers, fishermen. The rebels targeted royal officials such as tax-collectors, the wealthy who avoided paying taxes, and creditors who became wealthy by charging high rates of interest. (Novopress-Lyons, author's adaptation from the French version)

The revolt occurred against the background of the Armagnac-Burgundian civil war in France about control of the French crown, which started in 1407 and finally ended only in 1435. The war produced food shortages, increases in food prices, and stoppages in trade and employment. Peace left roving bands of unemployed soldiers looting and pillaging, as often happened in medieval times. Then, there were the increases in royal taxes. The local communal council took the habit of calling popular assemblies when the royal administration sent officials to explain the tax increases. The assemblies often intimidated bureaucrats who would flee for their lives. In April, 1436, such an assembly was organized that resulted in the royal official granting a delay for payment of the taxes.

In May, the Lyon council declared that it might collect the new taxes, but the commoners insisted that the wealthy, fiscal deadbeats pay first. To further emphasize their point, the lowest social orders pillaged the hotels and properties of the wealthy during a five-day period near the end of May. On May 25, the people of Lyons learned that there would be no royal reprieve regarding the new taxes. So, the lower classes called their own meeting independent of the Lyon communal council, where they vowed that no new taxes would be paid by the people of Lyon. Now, the Lyon council started to organize military defenses against what was starting to appear to be a social revolution. This must have had a tamping effect on the popular fury for by June 6th, all parties alike were promising mutual pardons. Lyon council sent letters to the king, asking for his clemency. Instead, the Lyon rebels received repression. "All the leaders of the Rebeyne were incarcerated, three were decapitated, 150 were banished from Lyon, and one had his wrist cut off." (Novopress-Lyons—author's adaptation) It appears that when tax resistance overflowed into social revolution, the notables of Lyon and the monarch managed to put a brake on the popular turmoil.

Jack Cade's Uprising

By the mid-15th century, the endless wars with France left the English people almost as exhausted as were the French, on whose lands the battles actually were fought. In addition to the loss of English lands in France and the human and social costs of the wars upon commoners, there were the economic and fiscal strains upon England and its treasury.

> Heavy taxation was the result, but added to the burden of this taxation was the greed of royal officials, who lined their own pockets at the expense of proper administration of the tax system, ... forced labor, corrupt courts, and the seizure of land by nobles. (Ross, p. 1)

In the county of Kent, an ex-soldier named Jack Cade, organized local people in protest. He and his followers drew up 'The Complaints of the Poor Commons of Kent' about the failings of the administration of King Henry VI. Although Cade mostly represented peasants, his followers did include some craftsmen, shopkeepers, landowners, knights, members of Parliament, and even some important clerics. While Cade and his followers did not aim at the monarchy itself as an institution, their list of complaints goes on to charge King Henry VI of injustice in that he chose not to impeach his underlings and lords, even though they were guilty of treason or unlawful acts. In essence, the rebels were angry due to the injustices in the government, and decided to revolt against the king unless he agreed to fix and punish the wealthy men who deserved it.

Early in June of 1450, about 5,000 of Cade's rebels, who also included soldiers and sailors returning from campaigns in France, assembled southeast of London. While the king fled London, Cade set up headquarters at Southwark, at the southern end of London Bridge. On July 3rd, the rebels crossed into London with the assistance and support of sympathetic Londoners. They stormed the Tower of London to make known in full their demands. There they captured some of the king's closest advisors, including the archbishop of Canterbury and the lord high treasurer of the realm. The royal advisors were beheaded, with their heads ignominiously placed on pikes, and made to kiss each other. Cade's force then proceeded to loot and plunder in London.

In the evening following the return of Cade's rebels across London Bridge to Southwark, a battle broke out between Cade's army and an army organized by London officials. The battle lasted until 8 o'clock in the morning, during which Cade's force endured many casualties. A truce was arranged at which Cade presented his demands as well as a list of his followers to be granted pardons, to which the Lord Chancellor, Bishop John Kemp, agreed. Cade's army dispersed after Kemp's promises of pardons and agreement to his demands. Neither the king nor Parliament, however, accepted the Cade-Kemp arrangements. In fact, the king demanded Cade's arrest, so the latter fled London. He was captured, then mortally injured. Once returned to London, Cade died, then his head was placed on a pole near London Bridge after he had been hung, drawn, and quartered. While most of the 5,000 rebels were indeed pardoned as promised by Kemp, 34 of Cade's lieutenants were killed. Cade's rebellion had failed dismally, while the abuses of which Cade's army had complained continued unabated. Owing to the actions of the government after the rebellion, however, another popular revolt led by the Merfold brothers, as described earlier, broke out, but this time with more radical, revolutionary demands.

The Cornwall Rebellions

Cornwall is the southwesternmost region of England. For centuries, its population were tin miners, among the poorest people in England. In the Middle Ages, the Cornish spoke a Celtic language similar to that of the Welsh. When the Welsh House of Tudor came to power following the War of the Roses in the person of Henry VII, father of the famed King Henry VIII, Cornish expectations were high. Henry VII named his first son the duke of Cornwall, an act of respect to the Cornish, but the actual behavior of Henry VII and his government brought the Cornish down to earth in a rude way. In 1497, the king proposed to raise a special tax to finance a war against Scotland in response to some bizarre local intrigues against the English monarch. The Cornish argued that the war with the Scots had nothing to do with them, so they refused to pay the tax. About 15,000 men proceeded from Cornwall to advise the king that he had been misled by corrupt advisors, with the intent of explaining why they refused to pay the tax. The Cornish were led by a blacksmith named Michael Joseph and a lawyer, Thomas Flamank. For the most part, the Cornwall petitioners proceeded without violence. Along the way, the Cornish acquired still another leader, an accomplished but disaffected soldier and baron, James Touchet. The Cornish were now led by two political leaders, Touchet and Flamank, while Joseph remained in charge of the army, what was a common occurrence among rebel or revolutionary forces, that is, a triumvirate of leadership.

On their way to London, the rebels proceeded peaceably enough, with new rebels occasionally joining them. The king, however, demonstrated little desire to meet the rebels or to recognize their demands. Flamank conceived of the idea of proceeding through the county of Kent since, historically, it had been a socially volatile region. The people of Kent, however, were quite uninterested in the Cornish cause. Some even offered to fight on behalf of their earl against the rebels. The rebels then split in two. Some drifted away from the cause to return home. Others, however, determined they were going to have to fight the king himself to win their cause. In the meantime, Henry VII mustered an army of 25,000 men, which met the ill-experienced and poorly equipped army of Cornish rebels, 9–10,000 strong, in several battles. The results were never in doubt. In defeat, up to 2,000 Cornwall men were killed, while the leaders were captured. All three leaders were put to death. In the aftermath, severe monetary penalties extracted by crown agents pauperized sections of Cornwall for years to come. Prisoners were sold into slavery, and estates were seized and handed to more loyal subjects. The remaining rebels that did escape went home, ending the rebellion.

Years of Revolution

Without doubt, the most revolutionary period in western Europe in the Middle Ages occurred in a seven-year period between 1378 and 1385. There were revolutions in Portugal, Catalonia, Germany, and Flanders, with turmoil in the Low Countries lasting from September, 1378 to December, 1385. There were the Peasants' revolt in England in 1381, and the Ciompi revolt in the summer of 1378 in Florence of the lower classes against the local bourgeoisie. In northern Germany, there were social upheavals in Danzig in the summer of 1378, in Brunswick in the summer of 1380, and in Lubeck in December, 1380 and September, 1384.

Popular agitation was most intense in France. The principal issue was the re-institution of custom duties and the gabelle, the hated salt tax, after the previous king, Charles V, had abolished them on his deathbed. There were popular uprisings in April, 1378 in Le Puy and Nîmes; in the fall of 1379 in Montpellier and Alès; in the fall of 1380 at the Sorbonne in Paris, and in Saint-Quentin, Compiègne, and Laon; and in May, 1381 once again in Saint-Quentin. In February and March of 1382, there were tax rebellions in towns and cities throughout Normandy, Picardy, and Champagne. (Mollat and Woolf, p. 138–141, Bourin et al., p. 54)

The most noteworthy and best-documented popular revolts took place in Rouen, Paris, and the Languedoc region of southern France. There were several pre-existing social conditions in the latter half of the 14th century that served as background for tax revolts: endless war with England; successive famines and economic crises; increasing poverty and deteriorating living conditions; craftsmen being forced to hire out their labor rather than working independently; and an influx of unskilled labor from the countryside to the towns and cities forming an under-employed lumpenproletariat. The actual leaders of the revolts indeed reached down low into the social orders; they included poor textile workers and other poor craftsmen, laborers, and beggars. (Mollat and Woolf, p. 176–177)

The first violence began in Rouen, with the disturbances called the *harelle*. Ancient Norse freemen used to indicate their approval of courses of collective action such as decisions to go to war or to go 'viking' by banging their swords on their shields while shouting "Haro! Haro!." This came to be known in the medieval Norman dialect as the *harelle*. On February 24, guildsmen led by a draper, Jean le Gras, sounded the bells of the commune to announce publicly that they were not going to pay their taxes. They closed the gates of the city, while protestors from the poorest parts of town filled the streets. A local chronicler described them with the unflattering term of *la merdaille*, or the shit people, which reveals more about the chronicler than the people he was describing. The poor began looting and destroying the property and buildings of the wealthy and of communal councillors, tax collectors, churches, and convents. Every major building was looted, including those containing archives where evidence of rents, lawsuits, debts, and feudal rights and privileges were destroyed.

The rebels then attacked the local abbey of Saint-Ouen in order to recover the city's communal charter, which had been obtained from King Louis X in 1315 during the communal movement. While the abbot escaped, much of the abbey itself was destroyed. The 1315 charter had granted rights to individuals that were rarely observed. The charter then was attached to a pole, and paraded around the city. City leaders were rounded up and made to swear to abide by the charter. For three days, the riots continued. The local archbishop, who held feudal rights and privileges in Rouen, was captured then forced to renounce them. Thus, what started as a tax revolt among craftsmen grew into a social revolution that affected the entire society of Rouen.

The kingdom was being ruled at this time by the regent, the duke of Burgundy, uncle of the young king, Charles VI, who was all of twelve years old. The duke and the king set out with a small army from Paris to contain the revolt in Rouen. Only two days passed before the royal party learned of a revolt in Paris, so they returned to the capital without even having reached Rouen. At the beginning of March, tax collectors had set up their booths in the Paris markets, but 500 men attacked them, beating several to death. The revolt spread to the streets of Paris. At city hall, the rebels found a cache of 3,000 lead mallets called *maillots*, which were used to strike invaders in medieval warfare attempting to scale city walls and gates. Contemporary chronicler Jean Froissart called these men *maillotins*, a term which has been used ever since by historians. Similar to what had already happened in Rouen, the revolt spread throughout Paris into the wealthy sections of town. Major buildings were looted and destroyed. Bourgeois were attacked, including Jewish money-lenders. In fact, the rebellion turned into a pogrom whereby hundreds of Jews were murdered, while some Jewish children were baptized forcibly. The city's officials and royal administrators in Paris, with the exception of one small garrison left at a royal property, fled the city to meet the royal party returning from the road to Rouen. On March 5, the duke of Burgundy began negotiating with popular leaders located on the walls of Paris. The duke refused outright the peoples' demands to abolish all royal taxes, and to pardon all Parisians involved in the revolt. Violence once again erupted, and the remaining garrison within the walls of Paris was attacked, during which several soldiers were killed. The people then opened the prisons to release prisoners, many of whom likely were debtors.

Overnight, the guilds took hold of the situation while the people dispersed to sleep. In the morning, the guilds still refused to open the gates to the royal party. On the other hand, they did seek to negotiate with the duke of Burgundy, who responded by seizing military posts overlooking the city, and by stopping river traffic into Paris, thus denying the city of food. The dukes of Brittany and Anjou sent armies to join the duke of Burgundy in an attempt to end the revolt in Paris. Now, revolts similar to those in Rouen and Paris broke out across the country. The same pattern of violence obtained, including in the south of France. Only in the regions where royal taxes were not collected—Provence, Brittany, Burgundy—were there no rebellions.

With tax collection impossible in the realm, raising an army to put down the revolution also became impossible. So, royal administrators were obliged to concede. The taxes were repealed, and amnesty offered to most of those involved in the insurrection. Nonetheless, after the royal party finally gained admission to Paris, the leaders of the Paris revolt were captured and executed. Having learned of the royal retribution in Paris, the leaders of Rouen decided not to resist the royal army. When the king arrived at Rouen on March 29, the city gates were opened. While only twelve leaders of the revolt were executed, the city's bells were confiscated, while the gates of the city were destroyed. A 100,000 franc fine was imposed, the communal charter was revoked, while Rouen put under the administration of a royal governor.

In the Languedoc, the rebels were known as *tuchins*. *Touche* was a term in the local dialect for woodlands. The tuchins were peasants and craftsmen who took over the defense role that seigneurs were supposed to provide as part of feudal arrangements. The tuchins defended their lands against roving bands of unemployed English soldiers. They survived in the countryside by brigandage and by close links with townspeople, who resisted royal tax collectors and seigneurs who served the king. The tuchins were also under the influence of a Spiritual Franciscan priest named Jean de Roquetaillade, who was a visionary and tribune for the poor of the Languedoc. (Mollat and Woolf, p. 179) Among the feats of the Tuchins at their peak of influence was capturing seigneurial storehouses of salt and wheat, then redistributing them to surrounding villages. French historian Vincent Challet summarizes the role of the tuchins:

> firstly, a spontaneous reaction to the chaos in the Languedoc, and the incapacity of both king and seigneurs to provide for the defense of the region. It was both an opposition movement against royal taxes, and part of a crisis of the emergence of the modern state...The multiplication of fiscal demands by the French state, and the unwillingness of the nobility to pay their part of taxes had already, a generation earlier in the 1350s, created ruptures in the social fabric, uniting seigneurs with their feudal dependents. (Bourin et al., p. 31—Author's adaptation into English)

Popular Revolts against the Bourgeoisie

Workers, peasants, and the poor often collaborated with merchants in their conflicts with lords, both secular and ecclesiastical. However, once merchants came to power in communes which they governed, previously collaborating classes began to clash since their interests came to differ. We shall consider examples of these clashes along six axes:

- communal government and the efforts of the lower social orders to gain entry to municipal office and administration;
- the local economy and workplace;
- social conflicts between rich and poor;
- emergence of proto-national, centralized monarchies, and the administrative roles played by bourgeois therein;
- indebtedness of workers and peasants to bourgeois including bourgeois from certain ethnic groups such as Jews, Flemings, and Italians;
- the control the bourgeois tried to effect over the peasants of the countryside surrounding towns and cities, which were what medieval Italians called the *contado*.

Communal Government

Burghers had come to power in towns and cities by allying with the poor and the craftsmen to limit the power of the secular nobility and ecclesiastical lords. The allied parties were able to establish municipal governments and courts of justice. It was normal at the outset of these communes for all citizens to participate in the choice of their politicians, judges, and administrators. Nonetheless, over time, a patrician class of wealthy merchants came to dominate election to municipal office to the exclusion of the lower classes.

Mollat and Woolf describe some of the mechanisms at work whereby wealthy merchants dominated municipal office. (p. 28-32) In the Holy Roman Empire, democratic, communal elections gave way to systems of officials choosing their own replacements. Retiring councillors won the right to choose their successors in 1263 in Strasbourg, followed by similar manoeuvres in Augsburg, Vienna, and Hamburg. In Cologne, each of the 15 councillors gained the right to choose their successors from among family members. Ambitious men who wished to gain access to municipal office might even marry into patrician families in order to ensure their selection. Elsewhere in western Europe, similar provisions existed. Ghent in Flanders came to be ruled by 39 people. If one of them died, his companions would co-opt a successor into the exclusive club. Arras was ruled by twelve councillors, four of whom were replaced every four months by co-opting successors to the vacant posts. Thus, over a year, the council would renew itself completely by internal selection rather than by open elections. In Rouen, an oligarchy known as the 'Hundred Peers' annually chose the aldermen and city councillors, and nominated three candidates for the position of mayor, who would be elected by the populace at large. In Provins in northern France, the mayor drew up a list of his representatives as successors to the positions of municipal office, which the count of Champagne would then ratify.

The result of all these manoeuvres was a limited number of men and families who held municipal office even after blood had been shed for these principles by democratic, popular forces. In Liège, in the century between 1214 and 1312, only nine families provided the municipal aldermen. In Lille in northern France, ten patrician families dominated municipal office. It was commonplace for the same family names to appear over and over again in lists of medieval municipal politicians. In Rouen, five families dominated the office of mayor during the 13th century, including the Val Richer family that provided twenty mayors over the course of a century.

Towards the end of the 13th century, the excluded common people began to address the situation in Flanders and France. (Mollat and Woolf, p. 44‑47) In Flanders, workers sought out an alliance with the count of Flanders in order to bring the communal oligarchies under control. In 1275, commoners forced the ruling 'Council of the Thirty-Nine' in Ghent to completely reform its practices. The workers of Ghent demanded a place in municipal council for representatives of craftsmen; abolition of hereditary succession to municipal office; popular control over the justice system; and suppression of the monopoly of imports of raw wool by the guild of Flemish merchants. In 1276, the common people of Douai arranged for magistrates' unfavorable legal sentences against craftsmen to be reversed.

About 1280, workers stopped making peaceful demands. They turned to violence to press their case for reforms to municipal government. Violence occurred in Tournai, Douai, Ypres, Bruges, and Ghent. In the summer of 1280, textile workers in Ypres revolted, while Bruges workers revolted in May and September of 1280. Fullers and weavers led the charge on behalf of the workers. According to Mollat and Woolf...

> Violence degenerated into pillage, murder, and the desecration of churches. Eleven of the sixteen magistrates of Douai were assassinated. The rebels, as usual, went for the archives, which recorded the titles to positions of control. (p. 46)

In Liège in 1287, workers opposed the imposition of a tax on consumption that workers called the *maltôte*. They obtained the elimination of the tax as well as a reform of the judicial system. In Arras in 1285, a popular leader named Jean Cabos inspired the people to pillage the houses of the wealthy, for which Cabos was imprisoned, while the most violent rioters were hanged. In response to these events, however, the local count ordered an inquiry into the workings of the local patricians.

Elsewhere, Provins had experienced an economic decline owing to a decline in the importance of its commercial fairs. In reaction, an unpopular mayor named Guillaume Pentecôte proposed to increase taxes and to add an hour to the length of the working day. In protest during January of 1281, thousands of workers attacked and killed Pentecôte, then pillaged his property as well as the homes of several magistrates and wealthy bourgeois. Days later, at the beginning of February, a similar thing happened to the mayor of Rouen. Echoes of these disturbances occurred again in Rouen a decade later over fiscal questions.

Local Economy and Workplace

Much of the wealth of the high Middle Ages came from the development of the textiles industry, particularly in England, France, northern Italy, and the Low Countries. With this economic development came new organizational forms whereby merchants employed craftsmen as their workers rather than contracting them as individual entrepreneurs. This led to labor strife between merchant guilds and workers' guilds. In Flanders, some workers' guilds were declared illegal in Arras in 1233, while workers struck in Douai in 1245. During the decade of the 1270s, textile workers rose in revolt in Douai, Bruges, Ypres, and Ghent, when wool imports were interrupted from England. During the next two decades, similar labor strife took place in Provins, Tournai, Douai, Bruges, Ypres, Ghent, Arras, Damne, Lille, Cambrai, Brussels, Liège, Rouen, Laon, Saint-Omer, Calais, and Saint-Quentin. An impressive list indeed that tells of changes in the organization of work in one of the most important industries of the day; this situation foreshadowed the serious labor strife of the type seen in modern, industrial times.

One of the best-known and well-documented popular revolts in the Middle Ages occurred during the heady, revolutionary years around 1380 in western Europe. It was known as the revolt of the *ciompi*, and it took place in Florence in the summer of 1378. The ciompi were lower-class textile workers who did wool carding work, that is, combing wool to produce straight strands of fiber that could then be further worked. The ciompi had no guild, thus, no representation in communal government. Florence was dominated by the *Arte della Lana*, wool merchants, and other important guilds known as the *Arti maggiori*. During the spring of 1378, the upper class of Florence was divided between the parties representing the papal power and the Holy Roman emperor, the recurring conflict of the day. One side appealed to the lower classes for support at the end of June. The lower classes profited from this appeal to demand changes in fiscal policies and the right to form guilds with a role in the government of Florence. On July 22, the lower classes forcibly took over municipal administration with the support of the usually powerless, minor guilds, and placed a wool carder named Michele di Lando as head of justice in the commune. Di Lando and his followers then created three new guilds to represent the poorer workers.

For one of the first times in Europe, a communal government represented all classes in society. Nevertheless, conflicts soon appeared between the more revolutionary poor people and the minor guilds. Setting up a base in a Dominican priory, the most revolutionary group selected eight men to represent the poorest members of society, the so-called 'Eight of the Santa Maria Novello', or simply the 'Eight'. The Eight gained control of certain offices in the communal administration, then appealed to di Lando for legal recognition of their decrees. Di Lando refused, so street fighting broke out on August 31st between the combined forces of the major and minor guilds and the poor followers of the Eight. Di Lando's force won, after which the lowest-ranking guild was disbanded. All this in-fighting among the democratic forces proved to be pointless for, by 1382, rule of Florence by the major guilds and the local aristocrats was re-established, while the two new guilds representing the lowest workers gradually went into decline.

Rich and Poor

The Middle Ages saw direct conflicts between rich and poor that developed into open, violent confrontations such as riots and pitched battles. One such conflict took place in the high Middle Ages in London near the end of the 12th century even if, generally speaking, there were few examples of anti-bourgeois conflicts in England. The contemporary source for the events was an English historian named William of Newburgh, whose bias against the rebels and their leader, William fitz Osbert, makes it hard to know exactly what transpired in the spring of 1196. Although fitz Osbert came to be seen as the champion of the poor of London, we don't know why this apparent member of the ruling class did so. Apparently a striking figure, fitz Osbert held municipal office. He was university-educated, cultivated, eloquent, and witty, and had fought in the crusades to the Holy Land. Nonetheless, he delivered stirring speeches to the poor that aroused his audience against the wealthy of London.

He wore a long, black beard, thus earning the nickname of William Longbeard, in imitation of the manner of the Anglo-Saxon English as opposed to the normally clean-shaven, Norman ruling class. This was not a trivial matter; in fact, it was a political statement, which leads this author to suggest that he might have been Anglo-Saxon rather than Norman. To counter accusations of disloyalty to the crown, however, Fitz Osbert went to Normandy to attest his loyalty to the king of England, Richard the Lion-hearted. Still, fitz Osbert gathered thousands of loyal followers, who were reputed to have stashed weapons across the city as part of their readiness for an armed rebellion. The English regent, Hubert Walter, the archbishop of Canterbury, summoned fitz Osbert to a meeting, but the latter killed one of the two noblemen sent to bring Longbeard to Walter. Fitz Osbert then fled to a local church where he organized fortifications. His followers were afraid to fight near or in a church, so Walter easily had his way, and had his men burn the church. Fitz Osbert escaped from the burning church, but was stabbed by the son of the slain nobleman. He was then hanged, drawn and quartered, along with nine followers. (Keene) Fitz Osbert was treated as a martyr by the poor of London, which suggests that the movement he led also might have had religious overtones. The spot where he was hanged became a daily place of gathering. Objects associated with his execution were venerated. Even the dirt at the spot where he died, now presumably holy, was collected, resulting in the creation of a pit. Eventually, armed guards were put in place to keep people away.

The second half of the 13th century produced conflicts between rich and poor that amplified during the late Middle Ages, especially during the crises of the 14th century. Recall that the Low Countries saw considerable popular agitation during the high Middle Ages. In the 1250s, there were clear signs of poor-rich conflict in Liège that culminated in 1254 when a bourgeois named Henri de Dinant led a popular insurrection. Once in power, de Dinant levied a tax on the wealth of the rich. For the rest of the century, popular agitation continued in Liège and elsewhere throughout the Low Countries.

There were also riots of poor people caused by food shortages and rising food prices at the mid-13th century throughout Italy: in Piacenza in 1255, in Bologna in 1256, in Milan in 1258, in Siena in 1262, and in Venice in 1268. (Mollat and Woolf, p. 38, 158) In France, the last two decades of the 13th century and the first half of the 14th century produced famine every second year. In fact, the 1280s were particularly trying throughout western Europe. There were related riots and insurrections by the poor in such cities as Rouen, Cologne, Arras, Douai, Tournai, Ghent, Bruges, Ypres, and Barcelona as well as in central Italy. A generation later, there were still more general insurrections by the poor in Flanders. French cities experienced riots by the poor right up to the time of the Black Death in 1348, and again in 1413 and 1418 in Paris when popular forces lined up with the Burgundian party in the fight against the Armagnac party for control of the French monarchy. The poor were also involved in the rebeyne in Lyons that occurred in 1423, 1424, 1430, 1435, and 1436.

Monarchies and the Bourgeoisie

During the late Middle Ages, towns and cities took over more roles that would eventually accede to states and national governments such as the administration of courts and the justice system; the operation of military forces, often manned by mercenary armies, and the building and maintenance of town and city defensive walls; the conduct of foreign relations such as sending ambassadors abroad, receiving foreign delegations, and striking alliances; the collection of taxes and the raising of loans both for urban administration and bureaucracies but also on behalf of the rising national states; and the operation of customs duties and excise taxes, and related regulation of trade within towns and cities. At the same time, urban centers were usually governed by patricians who were the wealthiest merchants from the oldest and most salient guilds, who adamantly resisted entry to municipal government of the lower social orders.

Now, this increase in financial burdens, an outcome of economic expansion, brought social discontent into the open. What kind of taxes should be levied; how should the burden be distributed; and how should the money be expended in a useful way and so as to avoid abuse and wastefulness? Such problems appeared everywhere; their outcome explains the passions that were aroused. (Mollat and Woolf, p. 33)

Debt

While many popular rebellions by peasants, workers, and the urban poor against wealthy bourgeois took place in the 14th century during the crises of the late Middle Ages, in actual fact, rebellions caused by the level of debt of the lower social classes began as early as the 13th century. One such rebellion took place in Barcelona in 1285 under the leadership of a commoner named Berenguer Oller. (Bensch) Oller may have captured control of the mayoralty, since he seems to have had the support of the communal council. Workers, craftsmen, and small shopkeepers were groaning under the weight of debt in the form of regular annuities paid to lenders during the spurt of economic expansion of Barcelona. Somehow, Oller and his supporters organized the cessation of payments for debts to the Church, the local bishop, and wealthy bourgeois. In the spring of 1285, rumors circulated to the effect that Oller's followers were going to attack the local wealthy, the Jews, and the clergy on Easter weekend, with a view to killing them and confiscating their wealth, unless they were prepared to acquiesce to Oller. The details of the story of Oller are not too clear owing to the bias of the prime chronicler of the events, a Catalan named Bernat Desclot. On the other hand, there does exist good evidence that Oller and seven of his supporters were captured by the Catalan ruler, King Pedro III, then hanged. Some 600 Oller supporters fled Barcelona, but 200 were arrested, among them many artisans.

Bourgeois and Peasants

Here are two examples of peasants revolting against local bourgeois attempting to impose their requirements, often related to commerce, upon the peasants of the surrounding countryside. Late in the 15th century, the principal export of the city of Haarlem in the Netherlands towards the end of the 15th century was a beer brewed with herbs called Koyt. It was sold throughout western Europe, including in Frisia, a region which throughout the Middle Ages managed to avoid foreign rule, as we saw earlier. The region effectively came to be ruled by its local merchants, who imposed stiff duties on imports and exports. In 1487, the largest city in Frisia, Leeuwarden, banned all sales of foreign beer within its borders including Koyt in order to protect the sales of local brewers. One innkeeper, however, in order to serve his loyal customers, continued to offer Koyt. When communal authorities came to confiscate the beer, a major brawl broke out with Koyt customers. During the action, these customers fled to the home of a local devotee of the brew, where the beer's loyal customers were besieged. In the local countryside, a peasant army started organizing in opposition to the merchant-rulers of Leeuwarden. A few days later, an army of 8,000 men marched into Leeuwarden to demand their beer and fair trade in other goods, as well. This leads one to suspect that this was a long-brewing (pun intended) issue involving more than just the distribution and sale of beer but trade in other goods as well. The peasants rescued their trapped friends still being besieged by the town's officials, then sacked the entire city. After this, sales of Koyt beer were allowed once again, while trade duties on other goods were lowered. This was a blow to local merchants who, furthermore, lost local control when the Hapsburg Emperor Charles V took over Frisia early in the 16th century. (Focusing Fluid website)

A second example of a peasant revolt against the local bourgeoisie involved a man named Hans Waldmann. Waldmann was born to peasant parents in Switzerland. He married well above his social station such that he became wealthy. As a general, he led the 12,000-men confederate army from the Swiss cantons in wars with the duke of Burgundy, defeating the forces of Charles the Bold. This he parlayed into becoming the mayor of Zurich during the 1480s, where he served the interests of the urban patricians of the Swiss Confederacy. His dictatorial rule and imitations of aristocratic excesses were legion, but the straw that broke the camel's back was his attempt to impose increased taxes on the peasantry in the countryside surrounding Zurich. In Knonau, a village east of the city of Zurich, 500 peasants gathered and proceeded to topple Waldmann forcibly from office in 1489. He was beheaded on April 6, 1489, after being accused of financial corruption, questionable foreign connections, and sodomy.

Summary

Half a millennium is a long time in human history. The high Middle Ages and the late Middle Ages cover the period from 1000 to 1500. During these 500 years, there were important social transformations in the West. As development proceeded, so did the evolution of the nature of popular resistance to the extraction of economic surplus by classes other than producers. As the first millennium was ending, the economic base of tribal and clan warlords evolved from nomadic raiding and theft to a more sedentary extraction of economic surplus by what might be characterized as extracting protection wealth from the farming population. This further evolved into a system of landlords extracting feudal rents and labor on land subjected to the hereditary 'ownership' of lords. These lands had been traditionally worked by peasantry, and were peasants' principal means of survival.

In opposition to the lords, the stratagem of the common people became one of gaining as much freedom as possible from feudal burdens in order to pursue an agenda of their own economic prosperity. This commoners did by violent rebellion and revolution, by negotiation, by pursuing alliances with Church and monarchy, by gaining legal recognition for the customary ownership of land by the peasantry and for the peasant organization of hamlets and villages, and by offering cash payments to lords rather than working for landlords, among other tactics. Most important was the long-term development of towns and cities where merchants and craftsmen might engage in their trades and businesses aimed at profit and prosperity, and where they gained legal authority to govern themselves, often in return for payments of cash once again to lords.

Around the end of the 11th century / first half of the 12th century, as part of the movement known as the Gregorian reform, the Church undertook a process of obtaining liberty of action from the control of warlords cum feudal lords, kings, and emperors. During this process, the Church greatly increased its intellectual and moral authority, and its temporal wealth and power by becoming an important landlord, with its institutions eventually owning as much as a third of European land. Popular resistance grew to this growth of Church sway, both against the temporal wealth and power of the Church as landlords, and against the intellectual and moral authority of the Church. The former was manifested in anti-landlord actions similar to the actions taken against secular lords; the latter was manifested in medieval heresies or attempts to reform the Church.

Throughout the Middle Ages, Church, peasantry, and monarchs, the last of these often foreign to the land they were attempting to govern, worked in concert to reduce the sway of indigenous warlords cum feudal lords. Eventually, kings succeeded in bringing the nobility under their control, even if kings more often now issued from the indigenous nobility rather from foreign lands. The results were centralized monarchies where the role of local nobles changed from one of opposition to the king to one of performing administrative work on behalf of king and state, such as tax collecting and raising and leading armies, acting as regional governors or royal representatives. The target of popular rebellion then became kings and proto-national states, and their local noble agents. The causes, the issues being addressed in these anti-state revolts involved taxes and warfare, the latter both in its demands upon commoners and in its effects on non-combatants.

Finally, the burghers who struggled mightily for their liberties against lords, both secular and ecclesiastical, had included both merchants, some of whom became wealthy businessmen who now dominated municipal governments, and workers including craftsmen, laborers, and the indigent. These former allies now evolved to become classes in opposition even if, sometimes, old alliances still held firm. Thus, popular revolt was also aimed at the bourgeoisie in the late Middle Ages.

Obviously, the above is but a general schematic. Sometimes, more than one class or issue were the object of popular revolt. Sometimes, one might place examples of popular resistance in other categories than those we have employed or, for that matter, in more than one category, but the above summary does serve as a brief guide to understanding the evolution of popular resistance during the Middle Ages.

EPILOGUE

Within the pages of this book, we have studied two inter-related phenomena: development and popular resistance. On one side of the equation is development, the process of societal transformation through time. It includes political, social, economic, and cultural change within societies. Among the defining elements of any society is the production of economic surplus beyond the immediate needs of producers, and the extraction of portions of that surplus by those who do not produce it. This defining element gives rise to social classes.

As in physics whereby actions produce reactions, extraction of economic surplus by non-producers leads to reactions by those who produce the economic surplus. The latter react by resisting the extraction of the surplus by plumbing their own culture for examples of previous events of resistance. This resistance takes many forms, and changes over time as methods of extracting economic surplus also evolve with development. In order to grease the wheels of the extraction processes, cultural components such as religion and ideology justify the extraction as being normal and natural. These cultural components also change over time, in response to which the culture of producers also changes over time, including patterns of resistance.

These phenomena can be observed as early as the beginnings of complex civilization in ancient Mesopotamia and Egypt. We have recounted them through various Western civilizations right up to the conclusion of the Middle Ages, when the early modern period began with the start of European Imperialism in the Americas and elsewhere in the world.

Civilizations have always included religions that served important roles in justifying the contemporary organization of society, including the favored, privileged position of the ruling classes. Popular resistance, however, includes the popular forms of religion that inspired working people to imagine a different organization of society, whereby the extraction of economic surplus by other classes would not take place, or would take place to a lesser degree, subject to the control of working people. In other words, society would be more equal, just, and equitable for working people. It might become a City of the Sun. This contradiction between the two sides of religion is seen in all three of the main, Western monotheisms: Judaism, Christianity, and Islam. Since secular societies in the West only emerged after the liberal, democratic revolutions of the modern era, a study of development and popular resistance during the pre-modern eras must emphasize the evolution of the social role of religion as well as the religious contradictions described herein.

There is a feedback loop between popular resistance and development, such that the former helps orient and motivate the latter. This does not preclude other inter-relationships or factors. Societies also change as a result of technological changes and the ever-increasing forces of production, as per the Marxist proposition, or of the evolution of ideas, or of the evolution of warfare, or perhaps of still other factors of change that orient and motivate development. Nonetheless, contrary to what conservative historians have asserted, regardless of the era—the ruled, common people, the poor, working people—have not simply acquiesced to social domination by ruling classes. Well before modern-day unions, political parties, co-operatives, and other modern tools of popular defense, lower social orders resisted, and where they could not successfully resist, it was usually a function of rulers having access to sufficient prisons, armies, laws, and state terror to maintain social order and discipline. Even these tools of social control by rulers were resisted by the socially dominated in the pre-modern West.

This book, with recourse only to secondary sources, with the exception of a few primary sources mostly from the ancients, has found evidence of popular resistance throughout pre-modern times. We also know that popular resistance has continued throughout the modern era in the West. It is reasonable to suggest that popular resistance probably shall also continue through the post-modern period during the third industrial revolution that we are living today. This will be so even if methods of extraction of the economic surplus by non-producing classes will continue to change over time, as will also change the methods and forms of popular resistance to extraction of economic surplus by other classes.

FIN

Historiography

A coda in music provides an additional structure to the piece that also serves as a conclusion. This section provides a historiographic discussion that might be familiar terrain to the historian but that, it is hoped, provides some useful information about methodology that addresses issues and questions that might be asked by the lay reader as a coda to this study.

Modern Hunter-Gatherers

Among the sources of information about hunter-gatherer societies are the hunter-gatherer societies that continue to exist in Africa, the south Pacific islands, and the Amazon. Some question the utility of these comparisons. Several limitations have been advanced, including the following arguments.

- It is difficult to find pure examples using modern peoples since many are actually in contact with civilization either indirectly or via other peoples who are regularly in touch with civilization;
- Similarly to neolithic, semi-sedentary peoples, modern-day hunter-gatherers may farm, practice animal husbandry, or trade with civilized people;
- Modern foragers might consume game as a larger element of their diet than did ancient hunter-gatherers, who might have hunted mainly as a sideline to their pursuit of plant food;
- There may have been substantial physical differences between ancient hunter-gatherers and modern hunter-gatherers resulting from evolution or from increased population, which might have accelerated evolutionary change in more recent times.

These points are all valid. Our interest, however, lies more with social behavior and group dynamics such as the imparting of tool use, language, and social mores than with biological evolution. We conjecture that social and cultural behavior is more likely to have remained relatively unchanged among modern foragers, making them comparable to ancient hunter-gatherers. This makes it possible to maintain that ancient, simple hunter-gatherers on the balance of probabilities—the judgement of which, after all, is ultimately, the task of historians—were egalitarian, non-sexist, and mostly peaceful. C. R. Hallpike, a Canadian anthropologist, writes:

> Studies of modern, hunter-gatherer societies in many parts of the world show that there are basic similarities between them, and we are entitled to assume that these would have applied to ancient hunter-gatherers as well. The very low population densities, the difficulty of making permanent settlements, and the equal availability of resources to all meant that groups were small; private property was limited to a few personal possessions; and any social inequality could only be based on age and gender, not on inherited wealth or power. (p. 30)

Romans

There are difficulties inherent in collapsing two millennia of Roman history into a few pages about the development of ancient Rome. A similar difficulty plagues attempts to describe the demise of the western Roman empire, usually described as the fall of the Roman empire. The historical giant who affected all subsequent history about Rome was the Englishman, Edward Gibbon, with his publication, *The History of the Decline and Fall of the*

411

Roman Empire, released during the period 1776–1789. Gibbon was greatly influenced by the Enlightenment and the revolutionary era in which he released his masterpiece. His study and his conclusions were based on primary materials from contemporary Roman times, rather than the secondary literature that had previously illuminated writing about Roman history. He set a new standard of scholarship for gathering evidence and providing sources, a standard that is also employed in academic disciplines other than history.

Gibbon's explanation for the fall of Rome was mostly moral as he argued that the old values of traditional Rome were lost to new values, especially those of Christianity, and that it was this change that brought the demise of Rome. In more recent times, historiography has concentrated more on social and economic factors that led to the demise of Rome. Furthermore, for Gibbon, the fall of Rome was a catastrophe with continuing negative effects. For many scholars today, the empire did not even 'fall' so much as it was transformed. It is argued the so-called 'fall' was not even felt as such by contemporaries, but rather as people doing what they have always done, that is, trying to improve their lot in life for themselves and their children and grandchildren. The Germanic tribes who eventually ended the western Roman empire perceived themselves as participants in the continuation of the Roman history of western and Christian Europe, a view that many modern historians also share.

On the other hand, the whole idea of a decline and fall of civilization has become something of a constant in western thought, discourse, and logic, sort of an archetype. It was originally central to conservative political thought, but it is also a pattern of thought seen on the political left. We have argued herein that the transformation of the Roman empire was partly explained by the changes in the methods of extraction of economic surplus by Rome's ruling class. As well, popular resistance to the methods of extracting economic surplus was a factor in them running their course and evolving to new social forms, for example, from Roman slavery to European serfdom.

The English scholar, Peter Heather, concentrates on one important element in particular to explain the demise of the western empire, the Germanic incursions. "It is impossible to escape the fact that the western empire broke up because too many outside groups established themselves on its territories, and expanded their holdings by warfare." (2006, p. 436) These outsiders stripped the western empire of its centuries-old tax base. (2006, p. 432) This no doubt had profound economic, fiscal, and social effects on the capacities of the western empire. According to Heather, "by virtue of its unbounded aggression, Roman imperialism was ultimately responsible for its own destruction." (2006, p. 459)

Early Middle Ages

The commonly used definition of the early Middle Ages is mostly focused on western Europe, a focus that raises several historiographical issues. Firstly, while cities and towns disappeared or greatly shrunk in size, importance, and economic activity in western Europe after the demise of the western Roman empire, this was not the case for the lands bordering on the Mediterranean. Roman civilization continued to exist, even if transformed, in Italy, southern France, and parts of the Iberian Peninsula. Furthermore, the eastern Roman empire continued to exist through the early Middle Ages well into the late Middle Ages until the Ottomans finally defeated Byzantium in 1453 when Constantinople fell to the Turks. Thus, urban life persisted in the Middle Ages in the Balkans, Greece, Thrace, Anatolia, Syria, the Levant, Egypt, and North Africa. This was still the case after the Muslim conquests of Byzantine territory reduced the eastern Roman empire to a shadow of its former self limited to southeastern Europe and western Anatolia. Finally, the Khazari society of the Pontic-Caspian Steppe included a continuing urban phenomenon during the early Middle Ages. Hence, a limitation in the commonly used definition of the early Middle Ages involves the continued existence of towns and cities during the period.

Secondly, for a long time, the period from the demise of the Roman empire to the reprise of cultural and intellectual activity in the Renaissance was known to English-language scholars as the Dark Ages; French-speakers spoke of l'Âge de l'Ignorance. A whole millennium of development was dismissed as a dark period scarcely worthy of study except by a few dedicated scholars. In one sense, scholars were responding to a shortage of written sources when compared to the literate Greco-Roman era. As well, nostalgia for the Roman empire as a high point of Western civilization led to dismissive judgements about the Middle Ages. After considerable research, however, archival and other sources from the Middle Ages have been uncovered, and analyzed by historians, archaeologists, and social scientists. It has become clear there were actually renaissances of cultural, intellectual, and economic activity under the Carolingian empire in 9th century France, Germany, and northern Italy; again during the period of the communal revolution that began in the 11th century when autonomous municipal life in Europe resumed relatively independent of kings and nobility, secular or religious; and finally, during the early stages of the Holy Roman Empire under the rule of Otto I. The territory of the Holy Roman Empire was enormous including much of Europe corresponding to the modern-day states of Germany, Austria, Slovenia, the Czech Republic, Switzerland, Liechtenstein, the Netherlands, Belgium, and Luxembourg as well as much of eastern France, northern Italy and western Poland. Thus, the so-called 'Dark Ages' produced several periods of renaissance applying to large parts of Europe. Scholars no longer speak of the 'Dark Ages' since we now know much more about the Middle

Ages. Thus, most now use the more neutral, precise, and less emotionally charged term, the Middle Ages, divided into early, high, and late stages.

Thirdly, in and of itself, contact between the advanced urban civilization of the Romans and the barbarian societies during the early Middle Ages is a phenomenon of historical and social science interest that merits study, to which we attempt to give its due importance. (Heather, 2013) It is hardly scientific to dismiss whole periods of history because of a bias about a supposed lack of cultural achievement of the people of those periods.

Fourthly, the concentration of historical studies upon western Europe has meant that eastern Europe, the Middle East, and North Africa have received short shrift in the study of Western history, even if all three areas were part of the Roman empire during antiquity and, thus, were part of the ancient West. In part, the explanation for this shortcoming is that since the Middle East and North Africa fell to Muslim control beginning in the seventh century, scholars have been reluctant to consider them part of the West. This rather specious reasoning ignores the fact that such European lands as Spain, Portugal, southern Italy, Sicily, Cyprus, and Sardinia and other Mediterranean islands became Muslim during the early Middle Ages. As well, many parts of eastern Europe were held by Muslims when the Ottoman empire advanced into Europe as far west as Vienna before its expansion in Europe was halted in 1529, and then again in 1683. Moreover, the cultural, intellectual, and economic development of Islamic society itself directly influenced the course of European history, including the course of popular resistance of the many to social domination by the few. In our study, we include eastern Europe, the Middle East, and North Africa as part of the West. This is not a question of political rectitude but one of fact if we are to understand the development of the West and, within it, the phenomenon of popular resistance to social domination. The history of the West is much more than the history of Christendom.

A fifth and final point needs to be made. Part of the reason for the transformation of the western Roman empire owes to the migration of Germanic peoples into the empire. These peoples, in response to population pressures and the need to flee from invaders from the east, seem to barge into Western history seeking survival and security within the Roman empire. In actual fact, the Germanic presence within the empire was already well-established before the demise of the western empire. We have described the evolution of the peoples of central Asia who applied pressure on the Germanic tribes to seek safe haven within the borders of the Roman empire. Thus, the Huns and other peoples from the Pontic-Caspian Steppe also form part of the history of the West owing to their impact upon Europe, but also because these peoples command interest in and of themselves.

Islam as Part of the West

Western scholarship has traditionally assigned the study of Islam to the domain of oriental studies. In the late 1970s, a Palestinian scholar, Edward Said, argued that this orientation was itself part of the ideology of Western imperialism. Qualifying Islam as belonging to the eastern world of the Indian sub-continent, central Asia, the Arab world, eastern Africa, etc. marginalizes a religion and culture that are, in fact, central to the history and development of the West. Therefore, the whole enterprise of including Islam as being only part of the Orient, according to Said, is an exercise of dubious intellectual value and veracity. Even without affirming one way or another the intellectual right of orientalists to study Islam, there are practical reasons for including Islam when studying the Middle Ages in the West, among them the following.

- Mideastern Asia is the home of the three great monotheisms; no one contests the fact that Judaism and Christianity, central to the culture and history of the West, first emerged in the Middle East; a similar argument can apply to Islam, which first emerged in Arabia, then flowered and grew in the Middle East and Europe.
- Islam, once out of Arabia, spread rapidly in many lands that had been part of the Roman and the Greek-speaking world, thus, part of the Occident: North Africa, Egypt, Syria, the Levant, and Anatolia.
- Geographically speaking, during the Middle Ages, Islam spread in western Europe into what we know as Spain, Portugal, southern France, southern Italy, and Sicily and other Mediterranean islands; into Thrace, Greece, the Balkans, Hungary, the Aegean islands, the Pontic-Caspian Steppe, and eastern Europe, including the Tatars in Russia, advancing in early modern times under the Ottoman empire as far west as the gates of Vienna.
- We also may observe the influence of Islamic culture on the Western economy and culture through such elements as the spice and silk trades and Muslim economic growth; architectural elements such as the pointed arch and Gothic architecture; the re-introduction to the West of Greek philosophy, science, and geometry; the introduction to the West of algebra, trigonometry, and Arabic numerals, originally an Indian innovation, as well as the development and use of zero and the decimal system; and still other cultural and scientific advances.

So, while orientalists may continue to study Islam as part of their bailiwick, for our purposes, it is important to study Islam as a vital and essential part of Western history and development. As well, we shall see later that Islamic culture also brought its own unique forms of popular resistance. Finally, the idea of a clash of civilizations between Islam and the Judeo-Christian world by which the former is seen as mysterious, exotic, inscrutable, unknowable, and dangerous, and utterly opposed to the West, is just plain inaccurate and ahistorical, and not very useful to our study.

The High and Late Middle Ages

During the half-millennium covered in this chapter, there were hundreds, if not thousands of acts of popular resistance, even if evidence is sometimes slight, or biased against the common people where evidence does exist. Inevitably, a taxonomy is necessary for organizing data prior to attempting to advance theoretical understanding of these phenomena and providing evidence related thereto. There is likely more than one way of categorizing resistance, for example, according to the types of action, violent or non-violent, rebellions or revolutions and such; or chronologically; or geographically, to name a few. We have chosen to employ as categories for analyzing resistance the target classes against which the popular classes, which includes slaves, laborers, peasants, and craftsmen, undertook actions of popular resistance. Thus, we analyze actions of popular resistance undertaken against warriors cum lords, against the Church, against kings and emperors and the states they led, and against the bourgeois who came to power in medieval towns after they had gained powers and rights during the high Middle Ages.

It will become clear when we examine the evidence for medieval popular resistance that these certainly are not watertight categories, and that some acts of resistance arguably might be placed in another category other than the one we have used or, for that matter, in more than one category. This might be true, but some taxonomy is still needed *a priori* to organize and study the considerable evidence of popular unrest. Furthermore, the context of medieval development as we described it in the previous chapter leads us to using target classes for popular resistance as the best method of organizing the data, especially since it was these non-producing classes that benefited from the extraction of the economic surplus of producers.

Further Reading

Abdullah, Tahir, "The Origin and Meaning of Al-Futuwwa", Sankore: Institute of Islamic-African Studies International, February, 2012, available on the internet at ibnfodio.com.

Abun-Nasr, Jamil, *A History of the Maghreb in the Islamic Period*, Cambridge University Press, 1987.

Adler, Eric, *Valorizing the Barbarians: Enemy Speeches in Roman Historiography*, University of Texas Press, 2011.

Ahmed, Nazeer, "The Abbasid Revolution", available on the internet at www.historyofislam.com.

Al-Faruque, Muhammad, "The Revolt of 'Abd al-Rahman ibn al-Ash'ath: Its Nature and Causes", *Islamic Studies*, 25:3, 1986, available on the internet at iiu.edu.pk.

Algazi, Gadi, "Pruning Peasants: Private War and Maintaining the Lords' Peace in Late Medieval Germany", in *Medieval Transformations*, editors, Esther Cohen and Mayke de Jong, Leiden: Brill, 2000.

Ali, Tariq et al., *The Verso Book of Dissent*, London: Verso Books, 2010.

Al-Oadah, Sheikh Salman, "The Story of Zayd bin Amr bin Nufayl", Islam Today website, July 15, 2010.

Applebaum, Herbert, *Work in Non-market and Transitional Societies*, Albany: SUNY Press, 1984.

Applebaum, Herbert, *The Concept of Work: Ancient, Medieval and Modern*, New York: SUNY Press, 1992.

Arberry, Arthur, "Avicenna (980-1037)", available on the internet at libertyfund.org.

Arkenberg, Jerome, "The Complaints of the Poor Commons of Kent", modernized version, Paul Halsall, *Internet Medieval Source Book*, January, 1999, available at halsall@fordham.edu.

Arnakis, G. G., "Futuwwa Traditions in the Ottoman Empire: Akhis, Bekhtashi, Dervishes, and Craftsmen", *Journal of Near Eastern Studies*, volume 12, no 4, October, 1953, available on the internet at aub.edu.lb.

Arnold, Jeanne, "Labor and the Rise of Complex Hunter-gatherers," *Journal of Anthropological Archaeology*, 1993, p. 75.

Aslan, Reza, *Zealot: The Life and Times of Jesus of Nazareth*, New York: Random House, 2014.

Aungier, George, *French Chronicle of London*, 1844, available on the internet at google.ca.

Austin, M.M. and Pierre Vidal-Naquet, *Economic and Social History of Ancient Greece: An Introduction*, University of California Press, 1997.

Ayoob, Mohammed, "The Revolutionary Thrust of Islamic Political Tradition", *Third World Quarterly*, volume 3, no 2, April, 1981.

Baldwin, M.W., *Christianity through the Thirteenth Century*, New York: Harper and Row, 1970.

Bamyeh, Mohammed, *The Social Origins of Islam*, University of Minnesota Press, 1999.

Bauer, Walter, *Orthodoxy and Heresy in Earliest Christianity*, Philadelphia: Fortress Press, 1971, (first published in German in 1934).

Beastrabban weblog, "The Medieval Christian Origins of Western Democracy", available on the internet at WordPress.com.

Bennison, Amira, *The Great Caliphs: The Golden Age of the Abbasid Empire*, Yale University Press, 2009.

Bensch, Peter, *Barcelona and Its Rulers, 1096-1291*, Cambridge University Press, 1995.

Bercé, Yves-Marie, *History of Peasant Revolts*, Malden, Massachusetts: Polity Press, 1990.

Berend, Nora, *Christianisation and the Rise of Christian Monarchies: Scandinavia, Central Europe and Rus', c 900-1200*, Cambridge University Press, 2007.

Bernal, Martin, *Black Athena*, volume 1, Rutgers University Press, 1987.

Bernbeck, Reinhard, "Class Conflict in Ancient Mesopotamia", *Anthropology of the Middle East*, volume 4, no 1, Spring, 2009, available on the internet at ingentaconnect.com.

Bey, Hakim, "Religion and Revolution", Dublin, 1996, available on the internet at hermetic.com.

Black, Antony, *Guilds and Civil Society in European Political Thought...*, Cornell University Press, 1984.

Blackwell, Amy, "Slaves and Slavery in Ancient Europe", in Peter Bogucki, editor, *Encyclopedia of Society and Culture in Ancient Europe*, New York: Facts on File, Inc., 2008, available on the internet at fofweb.com.

Blackwell, Christopher, "Athenian Democracy: A Brief Overview", in Adriaan Lanni, editor, "Athenian Law in its Democratic Context", Harvard Center for Hellenic Studies, On-line Discussion Series, 2003.

Blake, William, *The History of Slavery and the Slave Trade, Ancient and Modern*, New York: Haskell House of Publishers Ltd., 1969, (first published in 1858).

Blickle, Peter, "Peasant Revolts in the German Empire in the Late Middle Ages", *Social History*, volume 4, no. 2, May, 1979.

Bloch, Marc, *Feudal Society*, University of Chicago Press, 1961.

Bloch, Marc, *Land and Work in Medieval Europe*, New York: Harper and Row, 1969.

Boehm, Christopher, "Egalitarian Behavior and Reverse Dominance Hierarchy", *Current Anthropology*, volume 34, issue 3, 1993.

Boehm, Christopher, *Hierarchy in the Forest: The Evolution of Egalitarian Behavior*, Harvard University Press, 1999.

Boone, Marc, "Le comté de Flandre dans le long XIVe siècle: une société urbanisée face aux crises du Bas-Moyen Âge", and Monique Bourin, "Les révoltes dans la France du XIVe siècle: traditions historiographiques et nouvelles recherches", in Monique Bourin et al., *Revolte urbane e revolte contadine nell'Europa del Trecento: un confronto*, Firenze University Press, 2008, available on the internet at unifi.it.

Borg, Marcus, *Jesus: Uncovering the Life, Teachings and Relevance of a Religious Revolutionary*, San Francisco: HarperCollins, 2006.

Borg, Marcus and John Dominic Crossan, *The First Paul*, New York: HarperOne, 2009.

Boyer, Richard and Herbert Marais, *Labor's Untold Story*, Pittsburg: Communist Party USA, 2000.

Bradley, Keith, *Slaves and Masters in the Roman Empire*, Oxford University Press, 1987.

Bradley, Keith, *Slavery and Rebellion in the Roman World, 140 BC–70 BC*, Indiana University Press, 1998.

Brahic, Catherine, "Human Exodus May Have Reached China 100,000 Years Ago", New Scientist website, August, 2014, available on the internet at newscientist.com.

Brather, Sebastien, "The Beginnings of Slavic Settlement East of the River Elbe", *Antiquity*, June, 2004.

Bréhier, Louis,"The Crusade of the Pastoureux", *Catholic Encyclopedia*, 1913, available on the internet at newadvent.com.

Brenner, Robert, "Agrarian Class Structure and Economic Development in Pre-industrial Europe", *Past and Present*, no. 70, February, 1976.

Brierbrier, Morris, *The Tomb Builders of the Pharoahs*, New York: Scribner, 1984.

Broch, Crannog, and Hillfort, "Early Slavic States and Strongholds—Early Middle Ages", available on the internet at mitchtempparch.blog.com.

Brooke, Rosalind and Christopher, *Popular Religion in the Middle Ages*, New York: W.W. Norton and Co Inc., 1985.

Brown, Elizabeth, "The Tyranny of a Construct: Feudalism and Historians of Medieval Europe", *The American Historical Review*, volume 79, no. 4, October, 1974, available on the internet at isites.harvard.edu.

Brown, Peter, *Power and Persuasion in Late Antiquity: Towards a Christian Empire*, University of Wisconsin Press, 2007.

Brown, Robert, "Lecture Notes: The Legacy of the Roman Empire and the Middle Ages in the West, (AD 500-1450/1500)", University of North Carolina at Pembroke, available on the internet at uncp.edu

Brunel, Ghislain and Serge Brunet, editors, *Haro sur le seigneur! Les luttes anti-seigneuriales dans l'Europe médiévale et moderne*, Toulouse: Les Presses universitaires du Mirail, 2009.

Brunt, p. A., *Social Conflicts in the Roman Republic*, New York: W.W. Norton, 1971.

Budde, Paul, "Paul Budde's History Files", available on the internet at paulbuddehistory.com.

Burford, Alison, *Craftsmen in Greek and Roman Society*, Cornell University Press, 1970.

Burg, David, *A World History of Tax Rebellions*, New York: Routledge, 2003.

Calafeteanu, Ion, "The History of Romania, Part 2: The Medieval Wallachia, Moldavia, Transylvania", available on the internet at romania.org.

Calmet, Augustin, *Histoire universelle, sacrée et profane...*, volume 8, 1747, available on the internet at books.google.ca.

Cambanis, Thanassis, "Islam's Beginnings", *Boston Globe*, May 2, 2010, available on the internet at boston.com.

Carr, Edward Hallett, *What is History?*, New York: Random House, 1990.

Castelneau, Jacques, *Étienne Marcel: Un révolutionnaire au XIVième siècle*, Paris: Librairie Académique Perrin, 1973.

Cauvin, Jacques, *Naissance des divinités, naissance de l'agriculture*, Paris: CNRS Éditions, 2013.

CBC-TV, Canadian Broadcasting Corporation, "The Human Odyssey, Part 3", The Nature of Things, broadcast February 26, 2015.

Challet, Vincent, "Tuchins et brigands des bois: Communautés paysannes et mouvement d'autodéfense en Normandie pendant la guerre de Cent Ans", November 17, 2010, available on the internet at archives-ouvertes.fr.

Chelaru, Ana, "Recent Studies on the Indo-Europeans' First Contact with the Romanian Neolithic Cultures", Zamolxis: Comparative Mythology, available on the internet at Anarchelariu.wordpress.com

Cheyette, Fredric and Paul Hyams," Internet Medieval Sourcebook: Two Reviews of Susan Reynolds' 1994 Fiefs and Vassals", Fordham University, 1998, available on the internet at fordham.edu/HALSALL.

Cistercian French-language website, "Information complémentaire: Arnaud de Brescia et la Commune à Rome", available on the internet at citeaux. net.

Cochrane, Charles, Christianity and Classical Culture, Oxford University Press, 1944.

Cohen, Ronald and Elman Service, Origins of the State, Philadelphia: Institute for the Study of Human Issues, 1978.

Cohn, Norman, The Pursuit of the Millennium, Oxford University Press, 1970.

Cohn, Samuel, A Lust for Liberty: The Politics of Social Revolt in Medieval Europe, 1200-1425, Harvard University Press, 2007.

Cohn, Samuel, Popular Protest in Late Medieval English Towns, Cambridge University Press, 2013.

Collingwood, R.G., The Idea of History, edited by J. van der Dussen, Oxford University Press, 1993.

Cone, James, God of the Oppressed, New York: Seaburgh Press, 1975.

Coppens, Philip, "Old Europe", available on the internet at philipcoppens.com.

Cornford, Francis, From Religion to Philosophy, Mineola, New York: Dover Publications Inc., 2004, (originally published in 1912).

Cortese, Delia and Simonetta Calderini, Women and the Fatimids in the World of Islam, Edinburgh University Press, 2006.

Coulborn, Rushton, editor, Feudalism in History, Princeton University Press, 1956.

Crossan, John Dominic, The Historical Jesus: The Life of a Mediterranean Jewish Peasant, San Francisco: HarperCollins, 1993.

Crossan, John Dominc, The Birth of Christianity, San Francisco: HarperCollins, 1999.

Csaplar, Richard, "1,400 Years of Christian-Islamic Struggle: An Analysis", available on the internet at www.cbm.com.

Curp, David, "War Without End: A Brief History of the Muslim Conquests", 2006, available on the internet at http://islam-watch.org/.

Curta, Florin, *Southeastern Europe in the Middle Ages, 500-1250*, Cambridge University Press, 2006.

Curta, Florin, editor, *The Other Europe in the Middle Ages*, Leiden: Brill, 2008.

Daly, L.J., *The Political Theory of John Wyclif*, Chicago: Loyola University Press, 1962.

David, Marcel, *Les travailleurs et le sens de leur histoire*, Paris: Cujas, 1967.

Davidson, Morrison, *Four Precursors of Henry George*, New York: Kemikat Press, 1871.

Davis, David, *The Problem of Slavery in Western Culture*, Cornell University Press, 1966.

Davis, Leo, *The First Seven Ecumenical Councils, 325-787: Their History and Theology*, Collegeville, Minnesota: Liturgical Press, 1990.

D'Avout, Jacques, *Le meurtre d'Étienne Marcel*, Paris: Gallimard, 1960.

Debacq, Gabriel, *Libéraux et démagogues au Moyen Âge...*, Paris, 1872, available on the internet at googlebooks.com.

Debord, Raymond, "Le mouvement Qarmate, apogée des révoltes communistes aux premiers temps de l'Islam", August, 2003, available on the internet at le-militant.org/

Decker, Michael, "Plants and Progress: Rethinking the Islamic Agricultural Revolution", *Journal of World History*, volume 20, no. 2, June, 2009.

De Labriolle, Pierre, *La crise montaniste*, Paris: Leroux, 1913, available on the internet at archive.org.

De Laet, Sigfried, *History of Humanity: Prehistory and the Beginnings of Civilization*, New York: UNESCO, 1994.

Délisle, Léopold, *Étude sur la condition agricole et l'état d'agriculture en Normandie*, 1906, available on the internet at www.persee.fr/

Della Monica, Madeleine, *La classe ouvrière sous les Pharaons*, Paris: Librairie d'Amérique et d'Orient, 1975.

Denton, Jeffrey, "The Second Uprising at Laon and its Aftermath, 1295-1298", Bulletin—John Rylands Library, University of Manchester, available on the internet at manchester.ac.uk.

Derry, T. K., "Late Medieval Scandinavia: Some Economic Features" in chapter 4, *A History of Scandinavia*, University of Minnesota Press, 2000.

De Ste. Croix, Geoffroy, *The Class Struggle in the Ancient Greek World*, Cornell University Press, 1989.

Devisme, J.-F.-L., *Histoire de la ville de Laon*, available on the internet at archive. org.

Diamond, Jared, *Guns, Germs, and Steel: The Fates of Human Societies*, New York: Norton, 1997.

Dickson, Gary, "Flagellants of 1260", *Journal of Medieval History*, volume 15, issue 3, September, 1989.

Diodorus Siculus, *The Slave Revolts in the Roman Empire and Sicily*, Books 34/35, 2.1-48, available on the internet at fordham.edu/HALSALL.

Dodd, Leslie, "*Romans, Barbarians and Provincials*", Glasgow: *eSharp*, no.3, Autumn, 2004, available on the internet at www.gla.ac.uk.

Dollinger, André, "The Admonitions of Ipuwer", ReShafim Kibbutz, Israel, 2000, available on the internet at reshafim.org.il.

Dommanget, Maurice, *La Jacquerie*, Paris: François Maspero, 1971.

Donald, Leland, *Aboriginal Slavery on the Northwest Coast of North America*, University of California Press, 1997.

Douglas, David, *The Norman Fate*, London: Eyre Methuen, 1974.

Duchatel, Frédéric, "La Grande Jacquerie, 28 mai - 9 juin 1358", available on the internet at saintleudesserent.fr.

Dungen, Wim van den, "The Instructions of Khety to Merikare", Antwerp, 2010, available on the internet at www.maat.sofiatopia.org/merikare.

Dungen, Wim van den, "Ancient Egypt: The Impact of Ancient Egypt on Greek philosophy," (as per above information; see "hermes1.htm.").

Durant, Will, *Caesar and Christ: A History of Roman Civilization etc.*, New York: Simon and Shuster, 1944.

Earl, D.C., *Tiberius Gracchus, A Study in Politics*, Brussels: Collection Latomus, 1963.

Eco, Umberto, *The Name of the Rose*, New York: Harcourt Brace, 1984.

Eduljee, K.D., "Zoroastrian Heritage: Zoroastrianism in Post-Arab Iran", 2013, available on the internet at heritageinstitute.com.

Elbahnasawy, Reda, "Islamic Golden Age", 2010, available on the internet at elbahnasawy.com.

Engels, Friedrich, "Prodromes de la Guerre des Paysans entre 1476 et 1517", chapter 3 in *La Guerre des paysans en Allemagne*, 1850, available on the internet at http://www.uqac.uquebec.ca/.

Engels, Friedrich, "The Decline of Feudalism and the Rise of the Bourgeoisie", 1884, *Monthly Review*, April, 1957, available on the internet at archive. monthlyreview.org/.

"Éon de l'Étoile: le premier communiste français?", available on the internet at http://numeriphot.chez-alice.fr/eon.htm

Epstein, Steven, *Wage Labor and Guilds in Medieval Europe*, University of North Carolina Press, 1991.

Ertman, Thomas, *Birth of the Leviathan*, Cambridge University Press, 1997.

Esmark, Kim, "Spinning the Revolt: The Assassination and Sanctification of an 11th Century Danish King", Pisa University Press, 2009, available on the internet at cliohworld.net.

Fatah, Tarek, "Part Two: The Genesis" in *Chasing a Mirage*, Mississauga: Wiley Canada, 2008.

Federbush, Simon, *The Jewish Concept of Labor*, New York: Torah Culture Department of the Jewish Agency, 1956, available on the internet at abebooks.com.

Fenner, Julian, "To what extent were economic factors to blame for the deterioration of the Roman empire in the third century AD?" available on the internet at www.roman-empire.net/articles.

Figes, Orlando, *A People's Tragedy*, Penguin Books, 1996.

Fischer, David Hackett, *Historians' Fallacies: Towards a Logic of Historical Thought*, New York: Torchbooks, 1970.

Flannery, Kent and Joyce Marcus, *The Creation of Inequality*, Harvard University Press, 2012.

Focusing Fluid blog, "Koyt: A Beer Worth Fighting For", originally printed in the April, 2000 issue of *Saveur*, February 7, 2006, posted by 'joefriday', available on the internet at focusingfluid.blogspot.com

Follett, Ken, *The Pillars of the Earth*, New York: Penguin Books, 1989.

Forbes, R.J., *Man the Maker: A History of Technology and Engineering*, New York: Abbelard-Schuman, 1958.

Fremion, Yves, *Orgasms of History: 3,000 Years of Spontaneous Insurrection*, Oakland: AK Press, 2002.

Frend, William, *The Donatist Church: A Movement of Protest in Roman North Africa*, Oxford University Press, 1971.

Frey, John, *Craft Unions of Ancient and Modern Times*, Washington: American Federation of Labor, 1945.

Fustel de Coulanges, Numa Denis, *The Ancient City*, New York: Doubleday and Co. Inc., 1956, (first published in 1864).

Gabba, Emilio, "The Collegia of Numa: Problems of Method and Political Ideas", *The Journal of Roman Studies*, 74, 1984.

Gabriel, Richard, "Muhammad: The Warrior Prophet", 2007, available on the internet at historynet.com.

Garnsey, Peter, editor, *Non-slave Labor in the Greco-Roman World*, Cambridge Philological Society, 1982.

Gearon, Eamonn, "Arab Invasions: The First Islamic Empire", *History Today*, volume 61, issue 6, 2011.

Gerner, Kristian, "Networks, States and Empires in the Baltic Region", in Witold Maciejewski, editor, *The Baltic Sea Region: Cultures, Politics, Societies*, Uppsala: Baltic University Press, available on the internet at diva-portal. org.

Giescke, Annette, "Homer's Eutopolis: Epic Journeys and the Search for an Ideal Society", *Utopian Studies*, spring, 2003.

Glick, Thomas, *Islamic and Christian Spain in the Middle Ages*, "Part Two: Movement of Ideas and Techniques", and "Part Five: Ethnic Relations", Library of Iberian Resources Online, University of California, available on the internet at uca.edu.

Glotz, Gustave, *Ancient Greece at Work*, New York: Barnes and Noble, 1965, (first published in 1926).

Golden, Peter, "The World of the Steppes", excerpted from *An Introduction to the History of the Turkic Peoples*, Wiesbaden, 1992, available on the internet at msu.edu.

Gozzoli, Roberto, "History and Stories in Ancient Egypt and the Myth of the Eternal Return", IBAES, Das Ereignis, p. 103, available on the internet at gozzoli_ibaes10.pdf.

Graeber, David, *Debt: The First 5,000 Years*, Brooklyn: Melville House Publishing, 2011.

Granier de Cassagnac, Adolphe, *Histoire des classes ouvrières et des classes bourgeoises*, Paris: Auguste Desrez, Éditeur, 1838.

Grant, Michael, *A Social History of Greece and Rome*, New York: Macmillan, 1992.

Grant, Robert, *Augustus to Constantine: The Rise and Triumph of Christianity in the Roman World*, Westminster: John Knox Press, 2004.

Great Soviet Encyclopedia, 3rd edition, The Gale Group, 2010, available on the internet at the website, TheFreeDictionary.

Guoga, Aurimas, "The Last Pagans in Europe", Kenneth Humphreys' website, available on the internet at jesusneverexisted.com.

Gurevich, Aron, *Categories of Medieval Culture*, Boston: Routledge and Kegan Paul, 1985.

Gurevich, Aron, *Medieval Popular Culture: Problems of Belief and Perception*, Cambridge University Press, 1988.

Gutiérez, Gustavo, *The Power of the Poor in History*, Maryknoll: Orbis Books, 1983.

Haldon, John, "Iconoclasm in Byzantium: Myths and Realities", available on the internet at

http://www.Isa.umich.edu/.

Hall, Joseph, "The Peasant Revolt of Bobâlna, 1437-1438", *Slavic Review*, volume 36, no. 1, March, 1977.

Halliday, Stephen, "The First Common Market? The Hanseatic League", *History Today*, vol. 59, no 7, 2009.

Hallpike, C.R., *How We Got Here*, AuthorHouse, 2008.

Halperin, Charles, "Economic and Demographic Consequences", chapter VII, *The Mongol Impact on Medieval Russian History*, Indiana University Press, available on the internet at google.ca.

Halsall, Paul, "Summary of Wallerstein on World System Theory", August, 1997, available on the internet at byu.edu

Hands, A.R., *Charities and Social Aid in Greece and Rome*, Cornell University Press, 1968.

Hansen, Mogens, *The Shotgun Method: The Demography of the Ancient City-State Culture*, University of Missouri Press, 2006.

Harman, Chris, *A People's History of the World*, London: Verso Books, 2008.

Harris-Greenwell law firm, "The Tale of the Eloquent Peasant", http://www. harris-greenwell.com/HGS/TheTaleoftheEloquentPeasant, (see file about the art of law), Corpus Christi, Texas, 2006.

Harrison, Dick, "Murder and Execution Within the Political Sphere in 15th Century Scandinavia", *Scandia 2008*, available on the internet at www. scandia.hist.lu.se.

Hassam, Sadru, "The Socio-economic Aspects of the Fatimid Caliphate", available on the internet at simerg.com.

Heather, Peter, *The Fall of the Roman Empire*, Oxford University Press, 2006.

Heather, Peter, *Empires and Barbarians: Migration, Development and the Birth of Europe*, London: Pan Books, 2010.

Henrotte, Jean-Georges, *Entre Dieu et hasard: Un scientifique en quête de l'Esprit*, Paris: Éditions L'Harmattan, 2002.

Henstra, Dirk, *The Evolution of the Money Standard in Medieval Frisia*, doctoral dissertation, Groningen, 2000.

Hickson, Charles and Earl Thompson, "A New Theory of Guilds and Economic Development", *Explorations in Economic History*, 28, no 2, April, 1991.

Hildinger, Erik, *Warriors of the Steppe*, Cambridge, Massachusets: Da Capo Press, 2001.

Hill, Christopher, *The World Turned Upside Down*, London: Penguin Books, 1971.

Hilton, Rodney, *Bond Men Made Free*, London: Temple Smith, 1973.

Hilton, Rodney, *The English Peasantry in the Later Middle Ages*, Oxford University Press, 1975.

Historia Spécial, "Spartacus: l'esclave qui fait trembler Rome", no.5, May-June, 2012.

Historical Atlas of the Mediterranean website, "The Birth of Islam in Arabia", available on the internet at explorethemed.com/mohammed.asp.

Hitchcock, Don, "Sungir-Sunghir" available on the internet at donsmaps.com.

Hobsbawm, Eric, *Primitive Rebels*, University of Manchester Press, 1963.

Hodges, Richard and David Whitehouse, "The Abbasid Caliphate", chapter 6 in *Mohammed, Charlemagne and the Origins of Europe*, London: Duckworth, 1983, available on the internet at msu.edu.

Hodgkin, Thomas, "The Revolutionary Tradition in Islam", *History Workshop Journal*, volume 10, no 1, 1980.

Hogenboom, Melissa, "Peasants' Revolt: The Time When Women Took up Arms", *BBC News Magazine*, June 14, 2012.

Holland, Tom, *In the Shadow of the Sword*, London: Little, Brown Books, 2012.

Hopkins, Keith, *Conquerers and Slaves: Sociological Studies in Roman History*, volume 1, Cambridge University Press, 1979.

Hopkins, Keith, "Murderous Games: Gladitorial Contests in Ancient Rome", *History Today*, volume 33, issue no. 6, 1983.

Hosseini, Dustin, "The Effects of the Mongol Empire on Russia", *Vestnik, The Journal of Russian and Asian Studies*, December 12, 2005, available on the internet at sras.org.

Howard, Michael, *War in European History*, Oxford University Press, 2001.

Hughes, Philip, *A History of the Church to the Eve of the Reformation*, volume 2, 313-1254, available on the internet at franciscan-ofs.net.

Hunter, Bill, "In Defense of the Peasants' Revolt", June, 1981, available on the internet at billhunterweb.org.uk.

Ibrahim, Mahmood, "The 1327 Silk Weavers' Rebellion in Alexandria...", Middle East Documentation Center, University of Chicago, 2012, available on the internet at uchicago.edu.

International Standard Bible Society, "Crafts in the Bible Encyclopedia", available on the internet at bible-history.com/isbe/C/CRAFTS/.

Irani, K.D. and Morris Silver, *Social Justice in the Ancient World*, Westport, Connecticut: Greenwood Publishing Group, 1995.

Jones, A.H.M., *The Later Roman Empire*, volume 2, University of Oklahoma Press, 1964.

Jones, Rhys, "Early State Formation in Native Medieval Wales", *Political Geography*, vol. 17, no. 6, 1998.

Johnston, Ian, translator, "Homer, The Iliad, Book 2 ", etext available on the internet at viu.ca.

Jonsson, K.M., *History of the Egyptian Religion, part III*, "Instruction of Duauf", available on the internet at http://www.philae.nu/akhet/index.html.

Jordanes, *The Origins and Deeds of the Goths*, translated from the original Latin by Charles Mierow, available on the internet at ucalgary.ca.

Jenkins, Philip, *Jesus Wars*, New York: HarperOne, 2010.

Juliusson, Arni Daniel, "Peasants, Aristocracy and State Power in Iceland, 1400-1650", *The CAHD Papers*, Issue 2, 2007, www.akademia.is/CAHD, available on the internet at axelkrist.com.

Kamali, Masoud, "Conceptualizing the Other: Institutionalized Discrimination and Cultural Racism", available on the internet at ser_racism_kamali_session2.pdf

Kampen, Natalie, *Image and Status: Roman Working Women in Ostia*, Berlin: Gebr. Mann Verlag, 1981.

Kasem, Abul, "Who Authored the Qur'an—An Enquiry", April 11, 2004, available on the internet at mukto-mona.net

Kajala, Kimmo, editor, *Northern Revolts: Medieval and Early Modern Peasant Unrest in the Nordic Countries*, Helsinki: Finnish Literature Society, 2004.

Kautsky, Karl, *The Foundations of Christianity*, New York: Russell and Russell, 1953, (first published in 1908), available on the internet at http://www.marxists.org/archives.

Keen, Maurice, *The Outlaws of Medieval Legend*, University of Toronto Press, 1977.

Keene, Derek, "William fitz Osbert", *Oxford Dictionary of National Biography*, available on the internet at oxforddnb.com Kelly, Robert, *The Foraging Spectrum*, Washington: Smithsonian Institution Press, 1995.

Kimball, Charles, "A History of Russia, Chapter 1: Medieval Russia, 862-1682", available on the internet at faithweb.com.

Kloppenborg, John and Stephen Wilson, *Voluntary Associations in the Graeco-Roman World*, London: Routledge, 1996.

Knapp, Robert, *Invisible Romans: Prostitutes, Outlaws, Slaves, Gladiators, and Others*, Harvard University Press, 2011.

Knight, Kevin, editor, *New Advent: Catholic Encyclopedia*, "Chivalry" and "Stedingers", available on the internet at newadvent.org.

Ko, Jihoon, "Economic Impact the Islamic World Had on Christian Europe, (11th-14th Century)", available on the internet at zum.de.

Koeller, David, "The Magyars", 2003, available on the internet at http://www. thenagain.info/webchron/easterneurope/magyars.html.

Kokkonen, Ossi, "Understanding Peace in 13th Century German Culture: Were the Rhenish League and the Town Leagues *Coniurationes?*", PDF available on the internet at ennenjanyt.net.

Kreis, Steven, "Lecture 27: Heretics, Heresies and the Church", *The History Guide: Lectures on Ancient and Medieval European History*, 2013, available on the internet at historyguide.org/.

Kropotkin, Petr, *Mutual Aid: A Factor in Evolution*, Montreal: Black Rose Books, 1989, (first published in 1902).

Kuhn, A.B., *Shadow of the Third Century: A Re-evaluation of Christianity*, Kessinger Publishing, 1997.

Lambert, Malcolm, *Medieval Heresy: Popular Movements from the Gregorian Reform to the Reformation*, Oxford: Blackwell Publishing, 2002.

Lambert, Tim,"Viking and Medieval Ireland", and "A Brief History of Iceland", available on the internet at localhistories.org.

Landes, Richard, "Capuciati", in William Kibler et al., editors, *Medieval France: An Encyclopedia*, London: Routledge, 1995.

Landtman, Gunnar, *The Origin of the Inequality of the Social Classes*, University of Chicago Press, 1938.

Langston, John Mercer, "The World's Anti-slavery Movement; Its Heroes and Its Triumphs", Oberlin, Ohio: Oberlin College, available on the internet at oberlin.edu.

Latouche, Robert, *Les origines de l'économie occidentale (IV-XIième siècles)*, Paris: Albin Michel, 1956.

"Le comté de Flandre au Moyen Âge: Révoltes et conflits", in Les Belges, leur histoire et celle de leur patrie, la Belgique website, available on the internet at histoire-des-belges.be.

Le Goff, Jacques, *Hérésies et sociétés dans l'Europe pré-industrielle, 11e-18e siècles*, Paris: Mouton et compagnie, 1968.

Le Patourel, John, *The Norman Empire*, Oxford University Press, 1977.

Le Roy, Alphonse, "Arnould de Blankenheim", *Bibliographie nationale de Belgique*, available on the internet at wikisource.org.

Lesko, Leonard, editor, *Pharoah's Workers*, Cornell University Press, 1994.

Le Tourneau, Roger et al., "Revolution in the Maghreb", in P.J.Vatikiotis, editor, *Revolution in the Middle East*, Totowa, New Jersey: Rowman and Littlefield, 1972.

Levasseur, Pierre Émile, *Histoire des classes ouvrières et de l'industrie avant 1789*, Paris: Slatkine, 1981, (first published in 1858).

Lewis, Bernard, "The Islamic Guilds", *Economic History Review*, volume 8, no.1, November, 1937.

Lewis, Bernard, *Islam in History*, London: Alcove Press, 1973.

Leyre, Rafael, "An essay on violence, tradition and modernity", 2007, available on the internet at Rafael_Leyre@yahoo.com.

Library of Congress Country Studies, "Saudi Arabia", "Hungary, Early History", "Algeria: Islam and the Arabs, 642-1830", "The Bohemian Kingdom", Washington, available on the internet at Icweb2.loc.gov.

Lindsay, Jack, *The Normans and Their World*, New York: St. Martin's Press, 1974.

Linsboth, Christina, "Peasants Versus the Lords of the Manor", The World of the Habsburgs website, available on the internet at habsburger.net.

Lintott, Andrew, *Violence, Civil Strife and Revolution in the Classical City*, London: Crook Helm, 1982.

Ludemann, Gerd, *Heretics*, Norwich: SCM Press, 1995.

Macartney, C.A., *Hungary: A Short History*, Edinburgh University Press, 1962.

MacCulloch, Diarmaid, *Christianity: The First Three Thousand Years*, New York: Viking Press, 2010.

MacMullen, Ramsay, *Roman Social Relations, 50 BC to AD 284*, Yale University Press, 1974.

Madany, Shirley, "Arabs and Slave Trade", available on the internet at http://www.answering-islam.org/ReachOut/slavetrade.html.islam.org/.

Makkai, Laszlo, "The Hussite Movement and the Peasant Revolt", *Transylvania in the Medieval Hungarian Kingdom*, available on the internet at oszk.hu.

Manadian, Hagop, *The Trade and Cities of Armenia in Relation to Ancient World Trade*, Lisbon, 1965.

Manteuffel, Tadeusz, *Naissance d'une hérésie: Les adeptes de la pauvreté volontaire au Moyen Âge*, Paris: Mouton et compagnie, 1970.

Markoe, Glenn, *Phoenicians: Peoples of the Past*, London: British Museum Press, 2000.

Martin, Janet, *Medieval Russia, 980-1584*, Cambridge University Press, 2008.

Martin, Michael, *Working Class Culture and the Development of Hull, Quebec, 1800-1929*, annex entitled "A Genealogy of Workers' Organizations", Manotick, Ontario: ArchiveCDBooks.ca, 2015.

Martin Saint-Léon, Étienne, *Le compagnnonage*, Paris: Librairie Armand Colin, 1901.

Martin Saint-Léon, Étienne, *Histoire des corporations de métier*, Paris: Félix Alcan, 1922, (first published in 1896).

Master Artisan website, "Guilds—An Early History", available on the internet at Masterartisan.com , 2006.

Mattison, Alexandra, "Re-interpreting Ninth and Tenth-century Hoards in England", *TrackChanges*, issue 1, summer, 2011, available on the internet at http://trackchanges.group.shef.ac.uk/

Maugis, Édouard, "Mélanges et documents: La journée de huit heures et les vignerons de Sens et d'Auxerre devant le Parlement en 1383-1393", *Histoire du Parlement de Paris*, Paris: Augustin Picard, 1914, available on the internet at free.fr.

Mayfield, James, "History of the Tatar Muslims in Eastern Europe...", European Heritage Library website, 2008, available on the internet at euroheritage. net.

M'bokolo, Elikia, "La dimension africaine de la traite des Noirs", *Le Monde diplomatique*, April, 1998, available on the internet at www.monde-diplomatique.fr.

McCarthy, George, *Marx and the Ancients*, Totowa, New Jersey: Rowman and Littlefield, 1990.

McKay, John et al., *A History of Western Society*, Boston: Houghton Mifflin, outline for chapter 17, "Absolutism in Eastern Europe to 1740 ", 2007.

McNeill, William, *The Rise of the West*, University of Chicago Press, 1963.

McNeill, William, *The Pursuit of Power*, Oxford: Blackwell, 1983.

McNeill, William, *History of Western Civilization: A Handbook*, University of Chicago Press, 1986.

Medieval-spell website, "Medieval Code of Chivalry" and "Medieval Guilds", available on the internet at medieval-spell.com.

Meeks, Douglas, *God the Economist: The Doctrine of God and Political Economy*, Philadelphia: Fortress Press, 1989.

Meiggs, Russell, *Roman Ostia*, Oxford: Clarendon, 1973.

Micallef, Charles, *Ancient Labor's Untold Story: Evidence of Workers' Organization from 3000 BCE to 550 CE*, doctoral thesis, University of Michigan, 2005.

Miller, Daniel and Christopher Tilley, editors, *Ideology, Power and Prehistory*, Cambridge University Press, 1984.

Miller, Daniel et al., editors, *Domination and Resistance*, London: Routledge, 1989.

Milone, Kim, "The English Peasants' Revolt of 1381", available on the internet at loyno.edu.

Mitchell, Richard, *Patricians and Plebians: The Origin of the Roman State*, Cornell University Press, 1990.

Mollat, Michel, *The Poor in the Middle Ages*, Yale University Press, 1986.

Mollat, Michel and Philippe Woolf, *Popular Revolutions in the Late Middle Ages*, London: Allen and Unwin, 1973.

Moore, Barrington, *Injustice: The Social Bases of Obedience and Revolt*, White Plains, New York: M.E. Sharpe, 1978.

Moret, Alexandre, *Le Nil et la civilisation égyptienne*, Paris: La Renaissance du livre, 1926.

Morey, William, *Outlines of Roman History*, New York: American Book Company, 1901, available on the internet at www.forumromanum.org.

Morris, Charles, "The Commune of Laon", The Baldwin Project website, available on the internet at mainlesson.com.

Morfill, William, "A Brief History of Medieval Russia", excerpted from Morfill, "History of Russia", in Morfill and Charles Frye, *Russia and Poland*, New York: P.F. Collier & Son, 1913, available on the internet at shsu.edu.

Mossé, Claude, *The Ancient World at Work*, New York: Norton, 1969.

Mujani, Wan Kamal, "The Economic Decline of Circassian Mamluks in Egypt, 1468-1517", 2004, available on the internet at www.ehs.org.uk/ehs/conference2004/.../mujani.

Muraskin, Bennett, "The Prophetic Tradition: Is It Ours?" *Jewish Currents*, February 7, 2013.

Nakash, Yitzhak, *Reaching for Power: The Shi'a in the Modern Arab World*, Princeton University Press, 2007.

Nazeer, Ahmed, "The Abbasid Revolution", *History of Islam*, available on the internet at historyofislam.com.

Near East Foundation, "Social Justice in Islam", available on the internet at neareast.org.

Nedashkovskii, L. F., "Economy of the Golden Horde Population", *Anthropology and Archaeology of Eurasia*, volume 48, no 2, fall, 2009.

Nederhof, Mark-Jan, "The Tale of the Eloquent Peasant", 2009, available on the internet at mjn.host.css.st-andrews.ac.uk

Nederman, Cary, editor, *Policraticus, by John of Salisbury*, Cambridge University Press, 1990.

Nesbit, Robert, *The Social Philosophers*, New York: Washington Square Press, 1982.

Newsome, James, *The Hebrew Prophets*, Louisville, Kentucky: John Knox Press, 1984.

Neyrey, Jerome, *An Ideology of Revolt: John's Christology in Social Science Perspective*, Augsburg: Fortress, 2007.

Noonan, Thomas, "What Can Archaeology Tell Us About the Economy of Khazaria?" in Bruno Genito, editor, *The Archaeology of the Steppes: Methods and Strategies*, Naples: Instituto Universitario Orientale, 1994.

Nooruddin, Ubai, "Orientalism and Islamic Philosophy", available on the internet at muslimphilosophy.com.

Novopress-Lyon, "La Rebeyne de 1436", June, 2009, available on the internet at lyon.novopress.info.

Noyer, Rolf, "Proto-Indo-European Language and Society—Late Neolithic in the Pontic-Caspian Society", available on the internet at ling.upenn.edu.

Oesterdiekhoff, Georg, *Mental Growth of Humankind in History*, Norderstedt, 2009, available on the internet at www.bod.de.

Oesterdiekhoff, Georg, *The Steps of Man Towards Civilization*, Norderstedt, 2011, available on the internet at www.bod.de

O'Neal, Michael, "Government Organization in Ancient Europe", in Peter Bogucki, editor, *Encyclopedia of Society and Culture in the Ancient World*, New York: Facts on File, Inc., 2008, available on the internet at fofweb.com.

Organizing Committee ..., "Beginning and Aggravation of the Redemption Problem", available on the internet at remencas.com.

Ota, Hidemichi, "The Ancient Mediterranean World Structures", in Toru Yuge and Masaoki Doi, editors, *Forms of Control and Subordination in Antiquity*, Brill, 1988.

Owensby, Walter, *Economics for Prophets*, Grand Rapids: Eardmans, 1988.

"Pachomius: 292-346", available on the internet at scourmont.be.

Panichas, George, *The Simone Weil Reader*, New York: Mackay, 1977.

Parenti, Michael, *The Assassination of Julius Caesar: A People's History of Ancient Rome*, New York: New Press, 2003.

Paris, Robert, "Révolutions de l'Antiquité", livre 3, chapitre 2, 2011, available on the website, Matière et révolution at www.matierevolution.fr.

Payne, Stanley, "Castile and Aragon in the Late Middle Ages", chapter 8 in Stanley Payne, *A History of Spain and Portugal*, volume 1, Library of Iberian Resources Online, University of California, available on the internet at uca.edu.

"Peasants' Revolt, 1381", from the website, A History of Halesworth, Suffolk, UK Through the Ages, available on the internet at quovari.co.uk.

Perry, David, "Killing in the Name of God: The Problem of Holy War", Santa Clara University, available on the internet at scu.edu/ethics

Perry, Michael, *Labor Rights in the Jewish Tradition*, New York: Jewish Labor Committee, 1993.

Pitts, Forrest, excerpts from "The Medieval Trade Network of Russia Revisited", *Social Networks*, 1978/1979, 1: 285-292, available on the internet at analytictech.com.

Polopolus, Leonidas, "Athens, Greece: A City-state...", available on the internet at http://www.clas.ufl.edu/users/kapparis/AOC/

Prak, Maarten, *Early Modern Capitalism: Economic and Social Change in Europe, 1400-1800*, London: Routledge eBook, 2000.

Putnam, Bertha, *The Enforcement of the Statute of Laborers* etc., 1908, available on the internet at archive.org.

Raaflaub, Kurt, editor, *Social Struggles in Archaic Rome*, University of California Press, 1986.

Rambaud, Alfred, "Rambaud on the Kievan Rus' in the Appanage Period etc.", excerpted from *Russia*, volume 1, New York: Collier, 1900, available on the internet at shsu.edu.

Réville, Albert, *Le soulèvement des travailleurs en Angleterre*, 1898, available on the internet at abebooks.com.

Richardson, Gary, "Medieval Guilds", *E.H. Net Encyclopedia*, editor, Robert Whaples, 2008, available on the internet at http://eh.net/encyclopedia/article/richardson.guilds.

Rodriguez, Junius, *Encyclopedia of Slave Resistance and Rebellion*, Westport, Connecticut: Greenwood Publishing Group, 2007.

Roemischer, Jessica, "A New Axial Age", *Enlightenment*, December, 2005-February, 2006, available on the internet at www.enlightenext.org/magazine/j31/armstrong.asp

Rogers, Thorold, *Six Centuries of Work and Wages*, London: Macmillan, 1879.

Rollason, David, *Saints and Relics in Anglo-Saxon England*, Harvard University Press, 1989.

Rorlich, Azade-Ayshe, "The Bulgar State" and "The Mongol Conquest", excerpted from *The Volga Tatars: A Profile in National Resilience*, Hoover Institution Press, 1986, available on the internet at kroraina.com.

Rosenbaum, Stanley, *Understanding Biblical Israel*, Mercer University Press, 2002.

Ross, David, editor, "Jack Cade's Rebellion, 1450", Britain Express website, available on the internet at britainexpress.com.

Rostovtzeff, Mikhail, *The Social and Economic History of the Roman Empire*, Paris: Biblo-Moser, 1926.

Rostovtzeff, Mikhail, *Social and Economic History of the Hellenistic World*, volume 2, Oxford University Press, 1957.

Safieh, Jaser Abu, "Gleanings from the Islamic Contribution in Agriculture", available on the internet at www.muslimheritage.com.

Sander, Oral, "The Complexity of the Process of Civilization", available on the internet at http://dergiler.ankara.edu.tr/

Sanderson, Stephen, *Social Transformations: A General Theory of Historical Development*, Totowa, New Jersey: Rowman and Littlefield Publishing Inc., 1999.

Sartre, Jean-Paul, *L'Antisémitisme*, Paris, October, 1944.

Schaps, David, *Economic Rights of Women in Ancient Greece*, Edinburgh University Press, 1979.

Scaruffi, Piero, "A History of Islam...", 2010, available on the internet at scaruffi. com.

Schmidt, Alvin, *Fraternal Organizations*, Westport, Connecticut: Greenwood Press, 1980.

Scolnic, Benjamin, "The Prophets and Social Justice", Ziegler School of Rabbinic Studies, American Jewish University, available on the internet at www.aju.edu/

Scott, James, *Domination and the Arts of Resistance, Hidden Transcripts*, Yale University Press, 1990.

Scullard, H. H., *A History of the Roman World, 753-146 BC*, London: Methuen, 1980.

Searl, Edward, "Martin Luther King Jr. and the Prophetic Tradition," available on the internet at http://searlsermons.blogspot.com

Selbin, Eric, *Revolution, Resistance, Rebellion: The Power of Story*, New York: Zed Books, 2010.

Sennett, Richard, *The Craftsmen*, Yale University Press, 2008.

Shahadah, Alik, "African Holocaust: Not Just History but Legacy", July, 2012, available on the internet at www.africanholocaust.net.

Shatszmiller, Maya, *Labor in the Medieval Islamic World*, Leiden: E.J.Brill, 1994.

Shaw, Brent, "Bandits in the Roman Empire", *Past and Present*, no. 105, 1984.

Shaw, Stanford, "The Seljuk Empire, 1040-1157", excerpted from *The History of Modern Turkey*, volume 1, available on the internet at tripod.com.

Shipley, Graham, *The Greek World After Alexander, 323-30 BC*, London: Routledge, 2000.

Shotwell, James, *An Introduction to the History of History*, Whitefish, Montana: Kessinger Publishing, 2007, (first published in 1922).

Simkin, John, "Chronology of the Peasants' Revolt", from the website Spartacus Educational, August, 2013, available on the internet at schoolnet.co.uk.

Singh, Ranbir, "Color Prejudice in India: A History", 2012, available on the internet at hinduhistory.info.

Sizer, Michael, "The Calamity of Violence: Reading the Paris Massacres of 1418", *Proceedings of the Western Society for French History*, volume 35, 2007, available on the internet at umich.edu.

Smitha, Frank, "Islam, Power and Empire to 677", and "Islamic Empire and Disintegration", 2007-2011, available on the internet at www.fsmitha.com.

Snell, Melissa, "The F-word—The Problem with Feudalism", available on the internet at about.com.

Somel, Selcuk Aksin, "Revolt of Seyh Bedreddin", *Historical Dictionary of the Ottoman Empire*, Lanham, Maryland: Scarecrow Press, Inc., 2003.

Somerville, J.P., "Medieval English Society", and "The Medieval English Church", available on the internet at wisc.edu.

Sorabella, Jean, "Monasticism in Western Medieval History", New York Metropolitan Museum of Art, available on the internet at metmuseum.org.

Sox, David, *Relics and Shrines*, London: Allen and Unwin, 1985.

Spiegel, Nancy, "Library History and Architecture: Medieval Islamic Librairies", *University of Chicago Library News*, April, 2011, available on the internet at uchicago.edu.

Stark, Rodney, *Cities of God*, San Francisco: HarperOne, 2007.

Stearns, Peter, "Islam from the Beginning to 1300", World History International website, available on the internet at http://history-world.org/islam.htm

Stephenson, Carl, *Medieval Feudalism*, Cornell University Press, 1967.

Stevens, William, "Medieval Russia, 900-1600", available on the internet at www.humanities360.com.

Stevenson, Graham, "Spartacus and Class Struggle in Ancient Rome", available on the internet at http://www.grahamstevenson.me.uk/.

Stoyanov, Yuri, *The Hidden Tradition in Europe: The Secret History of Medieval Christian Heresy*, New York: Penguin, 1994.

Svajcner, Janez,"Military History of Slovenians", available on the internet at nato.gov.si.

Tacitus, Cornelius, *Agricola*, 31, available on the internet at sacred-texts.com

Talhami, Ghada Hasham, "The Zanj Rebellion Reconsidered", *The International Journal of African Historical Studies*, volume 10, no. 3, 1977, available on the internet at ualberta.ca.

Tarnas, Richard, *The Passion of the Western Mind*, New York: Ballantine Books, 1993.

Telushkin, Joseph, *Jewish Literacy*, New York: William Morrow, 1991, available on the internet at www.jewishvirtuallibrary.org/

"The Bedouin of Arabia", available on the internet at angelfire.com.

Thomas, John et al., editors, "Byzantine Monastic Foundation Documents", *Dumbarton Oaks Studies, no. 35*, Washington: Dumbarton Oaks Research Library and Collection, 2000.

Thompson, E.P., *Customs in Common*, London: Merlin Press, 1991.

Thompson, James, "The Development of the Idea of Social Democracy and Social Justice in the Middle Ages", *American Journal of Sociology*, 1923.

Tilly, Charles, "War Making and State Making as Organized Crime", in Peter Evans et al., editors, *Bringing the State Back In*, Cambridge University Press, 1985, PDF available on the internet at static.ow.ly.

Tilly, Charles, "Reflections on the History of European State-making", available on the internet at cankaya.edu.tr.

Tilly, Charles, "Cities and States in Europe", *Theory and Society*, volume 18, no. 5, September, 1989.

Toner, Jerry, *Popular Culture in Ancient Rome*, Malden, Massachusetts: Polity Books, 2009.

Tuchman, Barbara, *A Distant Mirror: The Calamitous 14th Century*, New York: Knopf, 1978.

Tymowshi, Michal, "State and Tribe in Medieval Europe and Black Africa—A Comparative Approach", *Social Evolution & History*, volume 7, no. 1, March, 2008, available on the internet at socionauki.ru.

UNRV-Roman Empire website, book review by 'Pertinax', available on the internet at http://www.unrv.com/book-review/famine-food-supply.php", also article by 'Caldrail' about mutiny in the Roman army at the same website.

Valla, François et al., "From Foraging to Farming: The Contribution of the Mallaha (Eynan) Ecavations, 1196-2001", *Bulletin du Centre de recherche français à Jérusalem*, 10, 2002, available on the internet at bcfrj.revues.org

Vanderbroeck, Paul, *Popular Leadership and Collective Behavior in the Late Roman Republic, c. 80-50 BC*, Amsterdam: J.C. Glieben, 1987.

Vaneigem, Raoul, *The Resistance to Christianity*, chapters 31 and 34, published in French by Fayard in 1993, translated into English by 'NOT BORED!' available on the internet at notbored.org.

Van Nijf, Onno, *The Civic World of Professional Associations in the Roman East*, Amsterdam: J.C. Glieben, 1997.

Van Zanden, Jan and Maarten Prak, "Towards an Economic Interpretation of Citizenship: The Dutch Republic between Medieval Communes and Modern Nation-States", *European Review of Economic History*, 10, 2006.

Vidiassova, Maria, "Le Maghreb médiéval: mercantilisme parisitaire ou société productrice", available on the internet at revistas.ucm.es.

Von Harnack, Adolf, *The Mission and Expansion of Christianity in the First Three Centuries*, 1908.

Wade, Nicholas, *Before the Dawn*, New York: Penguin Books, 2006.

Wade, Nicholas, *The Faith Instinct*, New York: Penguin Books, 2009.

Waite, Charles, *The History of the Christian Religion to the Year 200*, Chicago: C.V. Waite, 1900.

Walker, Bethany, "Mamluk Investment in Transjordan: A 'Boom or Bust' Economy", *Mamluk Studies Review*, VIII-2, 2004, Middle East Documentation Center, University of Chicago.

Wallerstein, Immanuel, "Islam, the West and the World", 1997, available on the internet at binghampton.edu.

Wallerstein, Immanuel, "The Medieval Prelude" in *The Modern World-System I: Capitalist Agriculture and the Origins of the European World-Economy in the Sixteenth Century*, 2nd edition, University of California Press, 2011, available on the internet at google.ca.

Walter, Gérard, *L'histoire des paysans de France*, Paris: Flammarion, 1963.

Walter, Gérard, *Les origines du communisme*, Paris: Payot, 1975.

Waltzing, Jean-Pierre, *Étude historique sur les corporations professionnelles chez les Romains*, Bologna: Forni Editore, 1968, (first published in 1899).

Ward, Osborne, *The Ancient Lowly*, volume 1, Chicago: Charles Kerr, 1907.

Weidemann, Thomas, *Greek and Roman Slavery*, Johns Hopkins University Press, 1981.

Weisfeld, Israel, *Labor Legislation in the Bible and Talmud*, New York: Yeshiva University, 1974.

Weiss, Johannes, *Earliest Christianity: A History of the Period A.D. 30-150*, New York: Harper's, 1959.

Westermann, William, *The Slave Systems of Greek and Roman Antiquity*, Philadelphia: American Philosophical Society, 1955.

White, Matthew, "Body Count of the Roman Empire", 2002, available on the internet at http://users.erols.com/mwhite28/romestat.htm

White, Michael, *From Jesus to Christianity*, HarperSanFrancisco, 2004.

Wikipedia.org, numerous essays and articles.

Wilken, Robert, *The Myth of Christian Beginnings: History's Impact on Belief*, London: SCM Press, 1979.

Wilson, James, "*Sinespe libertatis*: Slavery in Hungary under the House of Arpad", master's thesis, Central Eurasian studies, University of Indiana, November, 1998, available on the internet at indiana.edu

Wilson, Peter, "Secrets of the Assassins", available on the internet at hermetic.com.

Wittfogel, Karl, *Oriental Despotism*, Yale University Press, 1957.

Wischnitzer, Mark, *A History of Jewish Crafts and Guilds*, New York: Jonathan David, Publishers, 1965.

Woodward, E.L, *Christianity and Nationalism in the Later Roman Empire*, London: Longmans, 1916.

World History Project, "Islam from the Beginning to 1300", "The Church in the High Middle Ages", and "The Rise of Trade and Towns", available on the internet at history-world.org

Wright, Robert, *The Evolution of God*, London: Little, Brown and Company, 2009.

Wright, Ronald, *A Short History of Progress*, Toronto: House of Anansi Press, 2004.

Wye, Meam, "Public Libraries in the Medieval Islamic World", available on the internet at shininghistory.com.

Yarshater, Eshan, *The Cambridge History of Iran*, volume 2, 1983.

Yusofi, Golam-Hosayn, "Behafarid", *Encyclopedia Iranica*, 1989, available on the internet at iranicaonline.org/

Zapotoczny, Walter, "The Political and Social Consequences of the Black Death, 1348-1351", available on the internet at wzaponline.com/BlackDeath.pdf

Zweig, Paul, "The heresy of self-love: A study of subversive individualism", New York: Harper & Row, 1968, available on the internet at abebooks.com.

Printed in the United States
By Bookmasters